This DVD shows basic cooking techniques that are essential for the new or seasoned cook. The techniques are not directly attached to specific recipes in this cookbook, but will be useful with any cookbook in your library.

Tying an apron and towel
Sharpening a knife
Positioning and using a knife
Sautéing like a chef
Grinding and crushing peppercorns
Opening wine and champagne
Making butter roses
Cutting parchment paper

Vegetables

Peeling, crushing, and chopping garlic
Peeling carrots
Cutting, washing, and julienning leeks
Peeling and trimming asparagus
Shelling peas and fava beans
Trimming corn
Peeling broccoli
Cleaning spinach
Prepping and cooking artichokes
Peeling peppers
Peeling tomatoes & Making tomato roses and balls
Cutting potatoes

Fruit

Peeling, coring, and slicing apples
Removing the seeds from pomegranates
Peeling and julienning orange skin & Segmenting
   oranges
Cutting lemons

Eggs

Separating eggs
Making mayonnaise
Cooked eggs: Hard-cooked, mollet, and in a circulator
Cooking and unmolding an egg cocotte
Deep-frying eggs
A classic omelet

Fish & Shellfish

Shucking oysters and clams
Cleaning calamari

Peeling and eviscerating shrimp
Killing a live lobster & Removing the meat
   from a cooked lobster
Scaling fish
Boning, cutting, and serving salmon
Boning monkfish and black bass
Cleaning sole & Boning cooked sole

Poultry & Meat

Trussing chicken
Cutting whole chicken: for stew, boned wings, lollipops,
   boned legs
Cutting, boning, and preparing chicken for galantine
Carving roasted chicken
Cleaning and cutting beef filet
Cutting and grilling (quadrillage) New York strip steak
Preparing sausage and cooking in a circulator
Cleaning, boning, and dividing leg of lamb
Skinning and skewering lamb kidneys
Cleaning and cutting rabbit

Stocks & Consommé

Skimming chicken stock
Clarifying stock: consommé

Breads

Forming and marking breads: baguette, gros pain,
   and épi
Making melba toast

Desserts

Making crepes
Making, rolling, and forming pie dough
Making, rolling, and forming sweet dough
Making and working with puff pastry
Making and piping meringue
Cutting genoise
Chocolate-covered leaves
Chocolate balloons
Working with sugar: making caramel cages and angel
   hair

I truly believe that any person who knows these techniques will get much more pleasure and greater rewards from any cookbook.

ESSENTIAL PEPIN

More Than 700 All-Time Favorites
from My Life in Food

Jacques Pépin

HOUGHTON MIFFLIN HARCOURT

BOSTON NEW YORK

Library of Congress Cataloging-in-Publication Data
Pépin, Jacques.
Essential pepin : more than 700 all-time favorites
  from my life in food / Jacques Pépin.
    p. cm.
ISBN 978-0-547-23279-9 (hardback)
1. Cooking, French. 2. Cooking. 3. Cookbooks.
I. Title.
TX719.P4578 2011
641.5944—dc23   2011016057

Printed in China

SCP 10 9 8 7 6 5 4

To Gloria,
My friend, Soulmate, and love,
for all these meals together

Acknowledgments

The making of a book is a complicated project, with many people involved in writing, editing, and designing. This book of many books was particularly complicated and goes back many years. I have always counted on my wife, Gloria, for food advice and ideas. Norma Galehouse, my longtime assistant, has worked on this book in various ways for the last twenty-five years, and I continue to rely on her patience and talent to make something readable out of my handwriting and notes. Thank you to Doe Coover, my agent, who came up with the idea for the book, and to Rux Martin, my editor, for her confidence and enthusiasm for the project and her willingness to listen to my grumbling. Thank you, too, to the copy editor, Judith Sutton, for her faithful attention to details; to George Restrepo, for his splendid design; to Jacinta Monniere, for her accurate typing; and to Rebecca Springer, for overseeing the production of the book.

With the book comes a DVD of techniques filmed at the home of my friend Susie Heller. Her friendship, dedication, and knowledge made it possible. Thank you to my friend and talented director Bruce Franchini; to Paul Swensen, the DVD editor; and to Amy Vogler, David Shalleck, Jean-Claude Szurdak, and the whole technical crew. Your hard work and professionalism made me look good. *Merci!*

After nearly twenty-five years of working at KQED, I feel I am coming home when I get to Mariposa Street in San Francisco. Although it's not possible to thank everyone at the station who has worked on my shows, I want to thank John Boland, the president of KQED and my supporter and friend; Michael Isip, the director of KQED and executive producer, for his confidence, enthusiasm, and friendship; and Jacqueline Murray, for raising the money. More than anyone else, I want to thank Tina Salter, my series producer, for her professionalism, insight, patience, humor, and devotion. Thanks, too, to the genial Bruce Franchini, our director, whose keen eyes made the food look incredible; Christine Swett, the culinary producer, for her kindness and talent; Elizabeth Pepin, the competent associate producer, among many others. And thank you to the back kitchen: first, to my dearest friend, Jean-Claude Szurdak, who appeared on the show with me, and to David Shalleck and his crew, including Michael Pleiss, as always.

Thank you to my daughter, Claudine, and granddaughter, Shorey, for appearing on the series with me, as well as to Roland Passot, Loretta Keller, and Emily Luchetti. A big thank-you to the operations/technical crew for their efficient, skilled work on my behalf. Last, but importantly, thank you to Wendy Goodfriend, the website genius, whose work I know I do not appreciate enough, because of my limited knowledge of the Internet.

There is no greater love
than the love of cooking.
One always cooks
for another.

Contents

Introduction

In my sixty years as a cook — as a professional chef, a husband, a father, a grandfather, an author of many cookbooks, and a cooking teacher — I have created thousands of recipes, each memorable and worthy in its own way. Now, for the first time, I have taken stock, reflected back over my life in the kitchen, and assembled the best in one place: the recipes I love the most.

This is a new book — everything has been rethought and updated — but it is familiar as well: it's like meeting up with an old friend, because it goes back to the beginning of my culinary writing. It is "essentially" the way I have cooked as a young man, as a mature man, and, now, as an older man. It demonstrates the ways I have changed through my many books, my many moods, my many styles, from elaborate classic French cooking to fast food done my way. It shows how I have changed and learned. Like any working chef, I have always experimented with different foods and different methods. The recipes that I have created through these years are the diary of my life. I am, have been, and always will be a cook: my culinary identity defines me.

When I decided to put this book together, I believed it would be a cinch to do, an easy matter of assembling and reorganizing recipes. It turns out to have been a huge endeavor, bigger by far than writing a cookbook from scratch. Each period of my past exemplifies widely different styles and methods, from the cooking times for fish and vegetables to the amount and types of fat used, to the presentation, as well as procedures and techniques. As a result, I had a real conundrum: either leave the recipes as they were, to represent exactly a moment in time, or adjust, correct, and retest the recipes for a modern kitchen to make them usable, friendly, and current for today's cook while retaining the spirit and flavor of the originals. I chose the second option, with a few reservations. Through all the adjustments, I have tried to keep the intrinsic quality of the recipes as they were conceived. The appetites of a young, a middle-aged, and an older man are different, but a certain continuity remains. In that context, this book represents me more today than at any other time in my life.

The food of my youth in France, during and after World War II, left an enduring mark on my cooking. My mother and aunt's thriftiness and creativity with leftovers and incidental ingredients unconsciously became part of my own approach, which, I believe, is one of my greatest assets as a cook. Even during my restaurant apprenticeship in the late 1940s and early 1950s, we were still feeling, to some extent, the burden of privation, and that was reflected in a great respect for ingredients and how they were used.

The 1960s was a decade of change, transformation, and learning. Fresh from France, I was discovering America. For the entire decade, I worked for Howard Johnson's, a chain of more than one thousand hotels and restaurants across the country. With my friend and mentor, Pierre Franey, with whom I'd worked at Le Pavillon, America's signature French restaurant and my first job in this country, I was hired to develop new ideas and recipes. It was a new world of food, where I learned about mass production, the chemistry of food, new technologies, and the American palate. Clam chowder and fried chicken were replacing quiche and coq au vin in my repertoire. I was both expanding on and breaking free of my classical French training, learning that there was more than one way to slice a tomato and that a chicken could be sautéed with or without the bones, covered or uncovered, and seasoned before or after sautéing. At the same time, paradoxically, I was rediscovering France. I left school at the age of thirteen to go into a restaurant apprenticeship, and although I was an avid reader, I had to wait until my time at Columbia University to meet Molière, Rousseau, and Voltaire and to familiarize myself with the philosophies of Descartes, Sartre, and Camus.

My social life was changing as well. There were fewer class differences in America, more time, and more money. I started skiing on weekends, something I had never had the time or means to do in France. I became a part-time ski instructor and even met my wife on the slopes. More than anything else, though, it was through the many weekends I spent at Craig Claiborne's home in East Hampton that I learned about America. Cooking and eating my way through these weekends, I mingled with authors, artists, and doctors on an equal footing. It was an amazing time. I had been trained with the rigidity and discipline of the French kitchen, and now I was embracing American informality. I was exploding in many directions, and the '60s were really America as I had dreamed it.

In the 1970s, I opened La Potagerie, a soup restaurant on Fifth Avenue in New York City; finished my studies at Columbia; and started writing and "giving back" by teaching. My mother, who had always had a restaurant featuring the essence of simple French home cooking, came to visit for a few weeks each year. She loved America and marveled at the ingredients, especially the beef and lobster. But she would taste my dishes and exclaim, "This is really good, but it is not French." I had already changed, and I was continuing to change.

When I started cooking on TV in the early 1980s, I presented the simple food of my youth in the series *Everyday Cooking with Jacques Pépin*. In the PBS series *Today's Gourmet*, which aired in the 1990s, I tried to reflect the times with a cuisine that was plain but elegant, while putting some emphasis on nutrition and presentation. In *Cooking with Claudine* and *Encore with Claudine*, my daughter, Claudine — her English much better than mine — became the vox populi, asking me the questions other people might have if they'd had the chance.

Today the food world is fundamentally different than it was when I published my first book, *The Other Half of the Egg*, with Helen McCully, the food editor of *McCall's*, in the late 1960s. Cooking in America has undergone a radical transformation and rebirth. Interest in cooking, cookbooks, restaurants, markets, organic food, nutrition, and diets is at an all-time high. Artisan goods — from wines, cheeses, breads, and preserves to all types of heirloom products — are the rage. The work of the cook, once considered lowly and unimaginative, is now lauded as the achievement of an inspired artist, or, at least, a respectable craftsman. With the help of books, magazine articles, and especially TV, some chefs have achieved the status of movie stars, with salaries to match. Restaurants that used to be the place you went for dinner before the theater have become the theater, where people go to see and be seen.

Yet as I look back on my gustatory voyage, I find continuity in my cooking and recipes: a desire to simplify techniques and methods, a striving for simplicity, a search for the best ingredients, and an emphasis on taste rather than presentation or originality. My approach to cooking has always been unpretentious and pragmatic, but this doesn't exclude elegance and sophistication. I often unconsciously adapted and modified my cooking, eventually becoming an American cook. I still poach an egg in the classic way, but now, instead of serving it with hollandaise sauce, I might serve it with some diced vegetables and a sprinkling of olive oil. Regardless of fashion, though, I always strive for the "proof of the pudding": good food on the plate. Going through all these recipes spanning so many years is like seeing my whole life again, and old recipes — roast duck à l'orange, leek gratin, eggs in aspic, crepes Suzette — coming back into fashion.

But while trends change, basic techniques do not, whether it's boning a chicken, cooking an omelet, or making a chocolate goblet. Since visualizing the intricacies of some of these procedures is difficult, I taped a three-hour DVD to accompany this book, demonstrating all the techniques that are essential for the novice as well as the seasoned cook — techniques I acquired during my arduous years as an apprentice. They are meant to stimulate you and get you involved in the basics, and they will help you not only with this book, but with any cookbook you have in your home.

Because some cooks enjoy the challenge of prepping everything from scratch, while others prefer to take full advantage of boneless, skinless chicken breasts, oven-ready roasts, washed spinach and salad greens, trimmed carrots, and the like, I have offered a choice: buy the ingredient partially ready, or prepare it yourself.

As I read through these recipes, they bring back vivid and sweet memories. I taste, smell, and feel the ingredients, and I see friends and family members. I recapture many joyful moments through all these many years, and I know that these food memories will stay with me for the rest of my life. One thing that will never change: the greatest meals are the ones shared and enjoyed with loved ones.

NOTE In the recipe listings at the beginning of each chapter, I've indicated which dishes work particularly well as hors d'oeuvres (marked with an ●) or first courses (with an ✕).

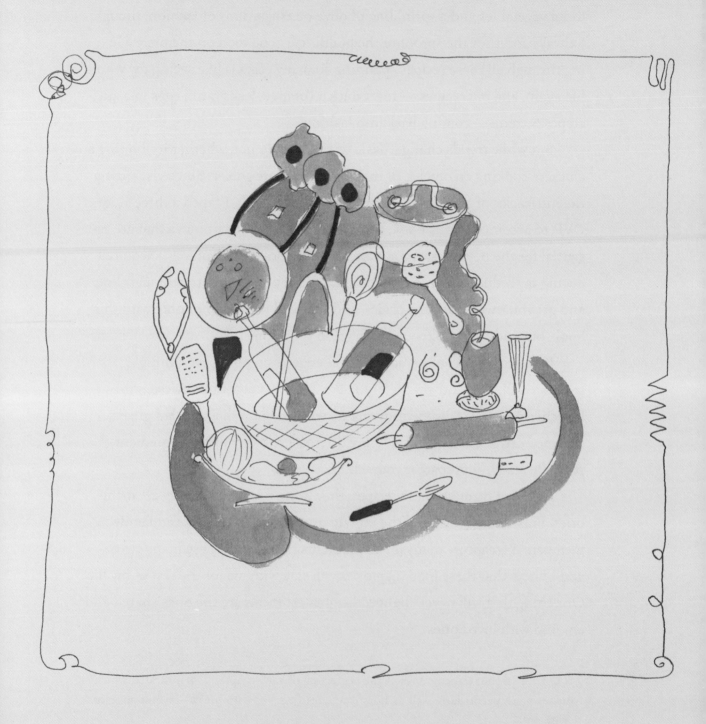

Soups

Soups

Cold Cream of Pea Soup with Mint

Serves 4

❧ **This soup is bright** green when freshly made. If you are preparing it more than a few hours ahead, don't add the yogurt until just before serving, or the acid in it will tend to discolor the puree, making the soup a darker, less appealing shade. For a smooth result, use thin-skinned fresh peas or frozen baby peas.

1 tablespoon olive oil
1 medium onion, thinly sliced (1¼ cups)
3 cups homemade chicken stock (page 612) or low-salt canned chicken broth
¾ teaspoon salt, or to taste
1 cup loosely packed fresh mint leaves
1 10-ounce package frozen baby peas, not thawed, or 2 cups fresh peas
1½ cups plain yogurt (regular or nonfat)
1 tablespoon unsalted butter
1 teaspoon sugar
¼ teaspoon Tabasco sauce

Heat the oil in a large stainless steel saucepan until hot. Add the onion and sauté for 2 minutes. Stir in the stock and salt and bring to a boil over high heat.

Reserve a few of the mint leaves to decorate the finished soup. Add the remainder of the mint, along with the peas, to the boiling stock. Bring the mixture back to a boil (this will take 3 or 4 minutes) and boil vigorously over high heat for 3 minutes.

Immediately transfer the pea mixture to a food processor and process it until very smooth. (You can process this in one or two batches, depending on the size of your food processor.) Add 1 cup of the yogurt and the butter. Strain the puree through a fine strainer for a smooth soup. (If not strained, the soup will have a slightly granular texture.) Mix in the sugar and Tabasco, cover with plastic wrap, and refrigerate until chilled.

At serving time, process the remaining ½ cup yogurt for a few seconds, until it is liquefied (it should have the consistency of a salad dressing). Divide the soup among four bowls and swirl 1 or 2 tablespoons of the yogurt over each serving. Decorate with the reserved mint leaves and serve.

Cold Sorrel Soup (Germiny)

Serves 8

❧ *Potage Germiny,* **the classic** sorrel soup served in elegant French restaurants, is usually presented cold, with fresh chervil sprinkled on top. The sorrel, which is high in oxalic acid, goes well with the luxurious soup base, which is enriched with egg yolks.

Other more ordinary sorrel soups are made with sorrel, leeks, and potatoes, which are cooked with stock or water, then pushed through a food mill and finished with cream. *Germiny,* however, is made like a custard: the egg yolks are cooked in the hot broth. Straining the hot soup into the cold cream, as I do here, helps ensure that the eggs do not overcook and scramble.

The soup should be generously seasoned with salt and pepper, since seasonings tend to lessen in intensity when chilled. Potato starch can be found in the kosher or baking section of many supermarkets.

4 cups cold homemade chicken stock (page 612) or low-salt canned chicken broth
1 tablespoon potato starch (see page 318)
4 large egg yolks
¾ cup heavy cream
1 bunch sorrel (about 3 ounces)
2 tablespoons water
Salt and freshly ground black pepper

GARNISH

Fresh chervil leaves (or another herb of your choice)

Mix ½ cup of the cold chicken stock with the potato starch in a small bowl; set aside. Mix another ½ cup of the stock with the egg yolks in a large bowl; set aside. Pour the cream into a large bowl, place a fine sieve on top, and set aside.

Bring the remaining 3 cups chicken stock to a boil in a medium saucepan. Stir in the dissolved potato starch and bring back to a boil (to ensure that the potato starch is cooked).

Add the boiling stock to the cold stock–egg yolk mixture and mix well with a whisk. Return to the saucepan and cook over medium heat, stirring with a wooden spatula, until the temperature reaches 180 degrees, 1 to 2 minutes; be careful not to overcook. As soon as the soup reaches 180 degrees and thickens, pour it through the fine sieve into the cold cream. Stir to mix well.

Pull off any fibrous ribs from the more mature sorrel leaves. Pile the leaves up, a few at a time, roll them into a bundle, and cut crosswise into ⅛-inch-wide strips (the shreds are known as *chiffonade*).

Put the chiffonade and water in a small stainless steel saucepan and bring to a boil (the sorrel will melt and turn a khaki color). Cook for 1 minute, then stir the sorrel into the soup. The sorrel may seem very mushy, but when it is mixed into the soup the strands will separate again and spread through the soup, giving it that wonderful, slightly acidic taste of sorrel. Season with salt and pepper and refrigerate until chilled.

Serve cold, sprinkled with herb leaves.

Watercress Soup
Serves 4

❧ **Sometimes tough and strong-flavored,** watercress stems are ideal for soup. I often have them left over when I make salads or garnish fish or meat with the leaves. Of course, you can use an entire bunch of watercress, both stems and leaves, for this soup. Since the soup will be pureed, the vegetables need only be coarsely cut before they are added to the pot. The soup can be transferred to a food processor or food mill for pureeing, but, to save time and labor, a hand blender immersed directly into the cooking pot works well.

This soup freezes well and can be served cold or hot. With the addition of cream or milk, the cold soup can be transformed into a variation of vichyssoise.

1 tablespoon canola oil
4 ounces watercress stems (about 3 cups), washed and dried
1 celery stalk (2 ounces), coarsely chopped (about 1 cup)
1 onion (6 ounces), coarsely chopped (about 1½ cups)
2 garlic cloves

2½ cups homemade chicken stock
(page 612), beef stock (page 612),
or a mixture of chicken, beef,
and/or veal stock, or low-salt
canned broth
¾ teaspoon salt, or to taste
12 ounces potatoes, peeled and cut into
2-inch pieces
Croutons, for garnish (optional)

Heat the oil in a large saucepan. When it is hot, add the watercress stems, celery, onion, and garlic and cook for 2 minutes. Add the stock, salt, and potatoes and bring the mixture to a boil. Cover, reduce the heat, and boil gently for 30 minutes.

Puree the soup with a hand blender, in the pan, or with a food mill or a food processor.

Serve the soup hot, garnished, if desired, with croutons.

Cold Cucumber, Yogurt, and Mint Soup
Serves 4

✂ **This refreshing summer soup** is made from peeled and seeded cucumbers that I puree in a food processor with some garlic and mint — an herb that grows profusely in my garden. Even "seedless" cucumbers have some seeds, and I like to remove them. Yogurt, olive oil, cider vinegar, and Tabasco sauce round out the flavors.

2 large seedless cucumbers (2 pounds
total), peeled, halved lengthwise,
seeded, and thickly sliced
¾ cup loosely packed fresh mint leaves
2 small garlic cloves
1¼ cups cold water
1½ cups plain yogurt (regular or low-fat)
2 tablespoons extra-virgin olive oil

2 tablespoons cider vinegar
1½ teaspoons salt
10 drops Tabasco sauce

Put the cucumber slices in a blender, along with the mint, garlic, and ½ cup of the cold water. Process until pureed.

Transfer the puree to a bowl and mix in the yogurt, olive oil, vinegar, salt, Tabasco, and remaining ¾ cup water. Chill.

Stir before serving.

I use chicken stock in many recipes — soups, stews, sauces, and others — throughout this book.

HOMEMADE STOCK is always my first choice, and I have an easy recipe for it on page 612. Little work is involved in this process; it's mostly just a matter of staying home for the 2 to 3 hours it takes the stock to cook. You end up with 3 flavorful quarts of nearly fat-free and salt-free stock that can be frozen in small quantities for future use.

LOW-SODIUM OR REGULAR CHICKEN BROTH, sold in cans or cartons, can be used in recipes calling for chicken stock. Since both of these products contain salt, cut back accordingly on any additional salt called for in the recipes.

While they are the least desirable alternative and I don't list them as an option in my recipes, you can use CHICKEN BOUILLON CUBES (dehydrated chicken broth) in recipes calling for chicken stock. These are so high in salt, however, that they must be thoroughly dissolved in liquid and added sparingly (1 cube to 2 cups liquid).

Pea Pod Soup
Serves 4

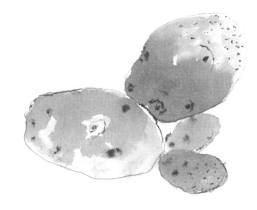

❧ **When I use fresh** peas for dishes like Stew of Peas and Ham (page 449), I always save the pods. Be sure to sort through the pods and discard any that are damaged.

It is essential that you strain the soup through a food mill before serving it. Pea pods are, of course, largely fiber, but they also contain some soft flesh, which is captured when the pods are pushed through the food mill. The puree you get from the insides of the pods is, if anything, sweeter and more flavorful than the puree from the peas. Using a food processor and pressing the mixture through a conventional strainer will not give the same results.

For a richer soup, add some light or heavy cream to the finished soup.

1½	teaspoons corn oil
1	onion (about 4 ounces), cut into 1-inch pieces
1	leek (about 5 ounces), trimmed (leaving some green), split, washed, and cut into 1-inch pieces
3	cups water
¾	teaspoon salt
12	ounces potatoes, peeled and cut into 2-inch pieces
	About 10 ounces fresh pea pods (reserved from peas shelled for any recipe using fresh peas)
1	tablespoon unsalted butter
	Croutons, for garnish (optional)

Heat the oil in a large saucepan. Add the onion and leek and cook over medium-high heat for 2 to 3 minutes. Add the water, salt, and potatoes and bring to a boil.

Meanwhile, wash the pea pods and discard any damaged ones. Add the pods to the saucepan, bring the mixture to a boil again, and boil, covered, for 30 minutes.

Push the soup through a food mill. (You should have about 5½ cups.) Add the butter and stir until it has melted.

Serve the soup with croutons, if desired.

ABOUT THE FOOD MILL

An invaluable (and modestly priced) kitchen utensil, the food mill is essentially a mechanized sieve. Turning the handle propels the paddle-blades set over a strainer plate in the base of the device. As the blades rotate, they push the food through the strainer, leaving behind skin, seeds, and — in the case of pea pods, for example — fiber. Most food mills come with three interchangeable straining screens, from coarse to fine.

Raw Tomato Soup
Serves 6 to 8

❧ **I make a variety** of hot and cold tomato soups when tomatoes are plentiful in my garden. This one is a quick recipe, consisting primarily of fresh ripe tomatoes and garlic that are first processed together until pureed, then seasoned, chilled, and served with a sprinkling of shredded basil.

Although you can simply process all the ingredients in a blender and serve the soup as such, the result is smoother and more appealing if you take the time to push the pureed garlic and tomatoes through a strainer or a food mill set with the finest screen to remove any skins and seeds before adding the remaining ingredients.

  4 garlic cloves
2½ pounds very ripe tomatoes, cut into
     1-inch pieces (about 6 cups)
  1 teaspoon salt
  ½ teaspoon freshly ground black pepper
  ½ teaspoon Tabasco sauce
  ⅓ cup peanut oil
  1 tablespoon white wine vinegar
  1 cup water
  ½ cup shredded fresh basil leaves

Process the garlic in a food processor for a few seconds. Add the tomatoes and process for 30 to 45 seconds, until pureed. For a smooth soup, push the pureed tomatoes and garlic through a food mill, or press through a strainer, rubbing as many of the solids as possible through the strainer by pressing on them with the back of a spoon.

Add the salt, pepper, Tabasco, oil, vinegar, and water to the pureed mixture and stir to mix well. Refrigerate until chilled.

Ladle the soup into bowls and serve with the basil sprinkled on top.

Cold Tomato Bisque
Serves 6

✼ **To give this soup** a creamier texture, I add a potato and then process the soup in a blender, rather than a food processor. Notice that the soup is first strained through a food mill to remove the skins and seeds of the tomatoes; if you prefer a soup with a coarser texture, skip the blending and simply strain it. I garnish the soup with dill, but you can substitute basil, chervil, or parsley for a different flavor. This soup is also good hot.

  1 tablespoon olive oil
  1 potato (5 ounces), peeled and cut into
     1-inch pieces (¾ cup)
  1 large onion, cut into 1-inch pieces
     (1½ cups)
  2 garlic cloves
  1 teaspoon fresh thyme leaves
2½ pounds ripe tomatoes, cut into 1-inch
     pieces (5½ cups)
1¼ teaspoons salt
  ¾ teaspoon freshly ground black pepper
  ¾ cup water
  2 tablespoons unsalted butter
  ½ cup fresh dill leaves

Heat the olive oil in a large, deep stainless steel saucepan. Add the potato and onion and cook over medium-high heat for 2 to 3 minutes. Add all the remaining ingredients except the butter and dill, bring the mixture to a boil, and stir it well, then reduce the heat to low, cover, and cook for 20 minutes.

Push the mixture through a food mill to remove the tomato seeds and skin. Then emulsify the mixture in a blender, in 2 batches, to make it very smooth; add the butter to one of the batches in the blender, then combine the entire mixture in a bowl. (Alternatively, use a hand blender.) Cool the bisque, cover, and refrigerate until chilled.

At serving time, divide the soup among six bowls and serve it cool (not ice cold), garnished with the dill.

Cream of Tomato Soup with Basil Oil
Serves 4

❧ **To deepen the color** of this soup and intensify the flavor of the fresh tomatoes, I add a little tomato paste and some sugar. Any leftover soup can be used as a sauce for pasta; in fact, the entire recipe (minus the basil oil) can be transformed into a tomato sauce by reducing the water to ½ cup.

1	tablespoon olive oil
1	medium onion, coarsely chopped (1 cup)
2	large garlic cloves
2	fresh thyme sprigs
1	fresh oregano sprig
2	pounds ripe tomatoes, cut into 2-inch pieces
2½	tablespoons tomato paste
2	teaspoons sugar
1½	teaspoons salt
½	teaspoon freshly ground black pepper
1¼	cups water
2	tablespoons unsalted butter
	About ¼ cup Basil Oil (page 619)

Heat the olive oil in a large stainless steel saucepan. Add the onion, garlic, thyme, and oregano and cook over medium heat for 5 minutes. Add the tomato pieces, tomato paste, sugar, salt,

pepper, and water, mix well, and bring to a boil, then cover, reduce the heat to low, and boil gently for 15 minutes.

Push the tomato mixture through a food mill fitted with a fine screen. (*The soup can be made to this point up to 1 day ahead and refrigerated.*)

At serving time, reheat the soup if necessary, and add the butter a little at a time, stirring it in gently until incorporated. For a smoother, creamier soup, emulsify the mixture with a hand blender for 15 to 20 seconds.

Divide the soup among four soup plates and drizzle about 1 tablespoon of basil oil over the top of each serving (do not stir it in) to decorate as well as flavor the soup.

Tomato Chowder with Mollet Eggs and Croutons
Serves 4

❧ **A French favorite,** *mollet* (moll-*ay*) eggs are similar to poached eggs in texture, with runny yolks and soft whites. Large eggs are cooked in their shells in barely boiling water for about 6 minutes, then thoroughly cooled and carefully shelled. This basic tomato soup, topped with the eggs and large croutons made from country-style bread, can be made vegetarian by replacing the chicken stock with vegetable stock or water.

2 tablespoons olive oil

1 medium onion, coarsely chopped (1¼ cups)

6 scallions, trimmed (leaving some green) and chopped (¾ cup)

1 carrot, peeled and coarsely chopped (½ cup)

3 garlic cloves, crushed and chopped

2 tablespoons all-purpose flour

3 cups homemade chicken stock (page 612) or low-salt canned chicken broth

1 28-ounce can plum tomatoes

12 ounces cherry tomatoes

1 teaspoon salt, or to taste

½ teaspoon freshly ground black pepper

1 teaspoon dried thyme

¼ teaspoon dried sage

GARNISHES

4 slices country-style bread, slightly stale

2 teaspoons olive oil

1 small garlic clove

4 large eggs

½ cup grated Gruyère or Emmenthaler cheese

Heat the olive oil in a large stainless steel saucepan. When the oil is hot but not smoking, add the onion, scallions, carrot, and garlic and cook over high heat, stirring constantly, for 4 to 5 minutes. Sprinkle the flour on top of the mixture, stir thoroughly, and cook for 1 minute longer, stirring. Mix in the stock.

Add the canned tomatoes, cherry tomatoes, salt, pepper, thyme, and sage to the soup. Bring to a boil, stirring occasionally, then cover, reduce the heat to low, and cook for 20 minutes.

Using a hand blender, blend the soup for 15 to 20 seconds (or process in a food processor and return to the pan).

MEANWHILE, PREPARE THE GARNISHES: Preheat the oven to 400 degrees.

Brush the bread slices with the olive oil and arrange them in a single layer on a cookie sheet. Bake for 10 to 12 minutes, or until nicely browned. Rub one side of the croutons with the garlic clove and set them aside.

Using a thumbtack or pushpin, make a hole in the rounded end of each egg. Gently lower the eggs into a pan containing enough boiling water to cover them and cook for about 6 minutes in barely boiling water. Drain the hot water from the pan and shake the pan to crack the shells of the eggs on all sides. Fill the pan with ice and water and set the eggs aside to cool completely.

When the eggs are cool, peel them carefully (so as not to damage the yolks, which are still runny) under cool running water. Keep the eggs in cold water until just before serving. (*The eggs can be cooked up to a few hours ahead and refrigerated in the cold water.*)

At serving time, drain the cold water from the eggs and replace it with hot tap water. Let stand for 5 minutes, so the eggs are lukewarm inside.

Bring the soup to a strong boil and ladle it into four bowls. Place an egg in the center of each bowl and wait for a couple of minutes for the eggs to warm in the center. Place a crouton in each bowl and serve, sprinkled with the cheese.

Gazpacho with Black Olives
Serves 4

✄ **Low in calories, this** classic Spanish soup is like a raw vegetable salad and ideal for summer. The idea is to create a smooth liquid with the vegetables, which is why I push the mixture through a food mill after it is processed. If you don't object to small pieces of vegetables or tomato skin in your soup, you can serve it unstrained. A little of each vegetable is reserved and diced for a colorful garnish, along with chopped olives and toasted bread cubes.

  3   ripe tomatoes (about 1 pound)
  3   cucumbers (about 1¾ pounds)
  1   large red bell pepper
  1   medium red onion
  3   garlic cloves, crushed
  1½   cups cold water
  1½   teaspoons salt
  1   teaspoon paprika
  ⅛   teaspoon cayenne pepper
  3   tablespoons extra-virgin olive oil
  2   tablespoons red wine vinegar
  3   ounces bread, preferably from a dense
       sourdough loaf, cut into ½-inch cubes
       (1¾ cups)
12–15   oil-cured black olives, pitted and cut
       into ¼-inch pieces

Preheat the oven to 400 degrees.

Cut one of the tomatoes in half and squeeze the halves over the bowl of a food processor to catch the seeds and juice. Cut the flesh into ½-inch pieces and set aside for use as a garnish. Cut the 2 remaining tomatoes into 1-inch pieces and add them, seeds and all, to the processor bowl.

Peel the cucumbers. Halve 1 of them lengthwise and scrape it with a spoon to remove the seeds. Cut the flesh of the seeded cucumber into ½-inch pieces and set aside for garnish. Cut the 2 remaining cucumbers into 1-inch pieces and add them to the processor bowl, seeds and all.

Using a vegetable peeler, peel the skin from about half of the red pepper, then cut the pepper so that you have 1 peeled half and 1 unpeeled half. Core and seed the pepper, and cut the peeled half into ¼-inch pieces; set these aside for garnish. Cut the remainder of the pepper into 1-inch pieces and add them to the processor bowl.

Cut the onion in half and finely mince half of it. Place the minced onion in a small strainer and rinse it thoroughly under cold water. Drain well and set aside for garnish. Coarsely chop the remainder of the onion and add it to the processor bowl.

Add the garlic cloves to the processor bowl. (You should have about 6 cups vegetable pieces.) Add the water, salt, paprika, and cayenne and process until pureed. (If you have a small food processor, do this in 2 batches.) Push the mixture through a food mill fitted with a fine screen. Mix in 2 tablespoons of the olive oil and the vinegar. (You should have 5 cups gazpacho.) Refrigerate the gazpacho until cold.

Meanwhile, put the bread cubes in a small bowl and mix them with the remaining 1 tablespoon olive oil. Spread the cubes on a cookie sheet and bake for 8 to 10 minutes, until nicely browned. Remove from the oven and set aside for garnish.

At serving time, ladle the gazpacho into four soup bowls and let guests sprinkle spoonfuls of the chopped olives and other garnishes on top.

Cold Corn Vichyssoise
Serves 4

꙰ **Onion, corn kernels, and** potatoes — which act as a thickening agent — are cooked together in water, then pureed in a food processor and finished with half-and-half and chopped chives. This soup can be served hot as well as cold. It can also be made well ahead; it will keep, refrigerated, for 4 or 5 days (in that case, however, I would not add the half-and-half or herbs until just before serving it).

1 tablespoon unsalted butter

1 tablespoon corn oil

1 medium onion, sliced (about 1¾ cups)

8 ounces potatoes, peeled and cut into
   1-inch chunks

4 large ears corn, husked and kernels
   cut off (3½ cups)

1 teaspoon salt

2½ cups water

1½ cups half-and-half

2 tablespoons chopped fresh chives
   or tarragon

Heat the butter and oil in a large saucepan. Add the onion and sauté for 2 minutes. Mix in the potatoes, corn kernels, salt, and water and bring to a boil, then cover, reduce the heat to low, and boil gently for 20 minutes.

Using a hand blender, puree the soup in the saucepan; alternatively, transfer the soup to a food processor and process until pureed. For a soup with a smoother, finer texture, push it through a fine sieve set over a bowl. Stir in the half-and-half and chives or tarragon. Refrigerate until chilled before serving.

Corn Chowder
Serves 6

✎ **We are great corn** aficionados in our family and are always looking for new ways to take advantage of the late-summer crop. This simple soup is a variation on one my mother and aunts used to make when I was a child, called *soupe au lait*, or "milk soup." They sautéed diced scallions and onions, parsley, and a bit of garlic in butter, then added milk. After it simmered, they poured this infusion into a soup tureen over toasted slices of bread sprinkled with grated Swiss cheese. The corn is added at the end, because it cooks in just a few seconds.

TOASTS (optional)

18 slices baguette, ¼ inch thick

CHOWDER

2 tablespoons unsalted butter

½ cup grated onion

½ cup sliced scallions, including some
   green

4 cups milk

1 teaspoon salt

½ teaspoon freshly ground black
   pepper

3 cups corn kernels (from about 5 ears)

FOR THE OPTIONAL TOASTS: Preheat the oven to 400 degrees.

Arrange the bread slices in a single layer on a cookie sheet. Bake for 8 to 10 minutes, until browned on both sides (they brown without turning). Set aside.

FOR THE CHOWDER: Melt the butter in a large saucepan. Add the onion and scallions and sauté over medium heat for about 2 minutes, until soft and sizzling. Add the milk, salt, and pepper and bring to a boil. Add the corn and stir. As soon as the soup boils again, remove it from the heat.

Serve with (or without) the toasts, either on the side or in the soup.

VARIATION

OYSTER CORN CHOWDER

Corn chowder is exquisite combined with freshly shucked oysters — a truly delicate and elegant soup. Prepare the soup as directed, adding a dozen and a half shucked oysters, with their juice, after you have stirred in the corn. Sprinkle with chopped fresh herbs and serve.

Hot or Cold Leek Soup
Serves 6

❧ **The creamy hot version** of this quintessential French leek and potato soup is called *Parmentier.* Served cold, with the addition of cream, the soup is vichyssoise. If the vegetables are cut into 1-inch pieces and the soup is served hot, it is a *potage Parisienne.*

Be sure to use the green as well as the white part of the leeks, after trimming them to eliminate any damaged or wilted sections. The green leaves lend color as well as taste and texture to the soup. Chervil is the classic herb of choice for garnishing the hot soup. If it's unavailable, use another fresh herb of your choice.

  2 tablespoons olive oil
  1 large or 2 medium leeks (about 10 ounces), trimmed (leaving most of the green), split, washed, and cut into 1-inch pieces
  1 medium onion, sliced
  6 cups homemade chicken stock (page 612) or low-salt canned chicken broth
  1½ pounds potatoes, peeled and cut into 2-inch pieces

  1 teaspoon salt, or to taste
  ½ teaspoon freshly ground black pepper

FOR HOT SOUP

  3 tablespoons unsalted butter
     Croutons, for garnish
  ¼ cup fresh chervil leaves

FOR COLD SOUP

  1 cup light cream
  3 tablespoons chopped fresh chives

Heat the oil in a medium pot. When it is hot, add the leek and onion and cook over medium heat for about 5 minutes, until they soften and begin to brown lightly. Add the stock, potatoes, salt, and pepper and bring to a boil. Boil for 30 minutes, or until the potatoes are tender.

FOR HOT SOUP: Add the butter to the soup. Puree the soup with a hand blender or process it in a food processor. (You should have about 7 cups.) Serve immediately, garnished with croutons and a sprinkling of chervil leaves.

FOR COLD SOUP: After the soup is pureed, cool it, then stir in the cream and chives and refrigerate until chilled.

Oatmeal Leek Soup
Serves 4

❧ **I opened La Potagerie**, a soup restaurant, at 44th Street and 5th Avenue in New York City in 1970. We featured thick, hearty, flavorful soups with various breads and offered cheese and fruit for dessert. At the beginning, we also served breakfast, and I created this soup with oatmeal, bacon, and milk. It was a big hit. My wife still makes it regularly, although usually now for lunch or a light dinner, and my friends always come back for more. Made with quick-cooking oats, it is prepared in a few minutes. You can substitute scallions for the leek. Crumble the bacon on top at serving time.

4 slices bacon
1 leek, trimmed (leaving some green), split, washed, and thinly sliced (about 1½ cups)
3½ cups milk, plus more if needed
½ teaspoon salt
¼ teaspoon freshly ground black pepper
1 cup quick-cooking oats

Cook the bacon on a rimmed plate in a microwave oven, covered with a paper towel to prevent splattering, for 5 to 6 minutes, until crisp. Transfer to paper towels to drain, leaving the fat behind, then crumble the bacon into ½-inch pieces and set it aside for garnish.

Transfer the accumulated bacon fat to a saucepan, add the leek, and sauté for 2 minutes. Add the milk, salt, and pepper and bring to a boil. Reduce the heat and simmer for 2 minutes, then stir in the oats. Cook for about 2 minutes, until thickened.

Serve immediately, with the bacon pieces sprinkled on top, or keep warm, covered, in a double boiler over warm water until ready to serve. (If the soup thickens, thin it to the desired consistency with milk or water.)

Onion Soup Lyonnaise-Style
Serves 6 to 8

From the Lyon region of France, this onion soup is much thicker than the usual kind. It's often served as a late-night dish. When I was a young man, I often made it with my friends at 2 or 3 A.M. after returning home from a night of dancing. The soup is strained through a food mill (although this is not essential) and put in a large

tureen or casserole that goes into the oven. Once it is baked, egg yolks and some port are mixed together in front of the guests and poured into a hole made in the center of the cheese crust. Then the whole soup is mixed together — both the crust and the softer insides — and served in hot bowls. It looks thick and messy, but it is delicious.

15–20 slices baguette, ¼ inch thick
3 tablespoons unsalted butter
3 medium onions, thinly sliced (about 4 cups)
8 cups homemade chicken stock (page 612) or low-salt canned chicken broth
½ teaspoon salt, or to taste
½ teaspoon freshly ground black pepper
2 cups grated Gruyère or Emmenthaler cheese
2 large egg yolks
½ cup sweet port

Preheat the oven to 400 degrees.

Arrange the bread slices on a cookie sheet and bake for 8 to 10 minutes, until browned. Remove from the oven and set aside. (Leave the oven on.)

Melt the butter in a large saucepan. Add the onions and sauté for 15 minutes, or until dark brown.

Add the stock, salt, and pepper. Bring to a boil and cook for 20 minutes. Push the soup through a food mill, if desired.

Arrange one third of the toasted bread in the bottom of an ovenproof soup tureen or large casserole. Sprinkle with some of the cheese, then add the remaining bread and more cheese, saving enough to sprinkle over the top of the soup. Fill the tureen with the hot soup, sprinkle the reserved cheese on top, and place on a cookie sheet. Bake for 35 minutes, or until a golden crust forms on top.

Combine the yolks with the port in a deep

soup plate and whip with a fork. With a ladle, make a hole in the top of the *gratinée,* pour in the port mixture, and fold into the soup with the ladle. Stir everything together, bring the soup to the table, and serve.

Bread and Onion Soup
Serves 4

When I have no vegetables on hand, I make this soup, which requires only onions and leftover bread. Grated Gruyère, one of my mother's favorite additions to the soup, is a great flavor enhancer.

4–5	slices leftover bread, cut into ½-inch cubes (2–2½ cups)
1½	tablespoons peanut oil
2	medium onions, thinly sliced (about 3 cups)
5	cups homemade chicken stock (page 612) or low-salt canned chicken broth
¼	teaspoon salt, or to taste
½	teaspoon freshly ground black pepper
1	cup grated Gruyère or Emmenthaler cheese
1	tablespoon minced fresh chives

Preheat the oven to 400 degrees.

Spread the bread cubes on a cookie sheet and bake for 10 to 12 minutes, until golden brown. Set aside.

Heat the oil in a large saucepan until hot. Add the onions and cook over high heat for 8 to 10 minutes, until nicely browned.

Add the stock, salt, and pepper and bring to a strong boil.

Meanwhile, drop the baked bread cubes into a large soup tureen and sprinkle the cheese on top.

Pour the boiling stock and onion mixture into the soup tureen and mix well. Ladle into soup plates, sprinkle the chives on top, and serve immediately.

Garlic Soup
Serves 6 to 8

There are almost endless possibilities for variation here. Potatoes are my favorite thickening agent for garlic soup, but it can also be thickened with a roux of flour and butter or with bread, the traditional choice in the South of France, where this dish is a specialty. Onions or scallions can be used instead of leeks, although the soup won't have the same subtle taste. If you use the leeks, include most of the green leaves.

Poultry or meat stock gives the soup more body and flavor, although it's also good made with water. I have purposely kept the soup simple, but for a party, you could enrich it by adding a cup of light cream at the last minute.

¼	cup olive oil
2	cups sliced leeks, including some green
12–15	garlic cloves
7	cups homemade chicken stock (page 612) or low-salt canned chicken broth
2	pounds potatoes, peeled and cut into 1-inch cubes (about 4 cups)
1	teaspoon salt, or to taste
2	cups cubed (½-inch) firm white bread
2	tablespoons unsalted butter

Heat 2 tablespoons of the oil in a heavy pot. When it is hot, add the leeks and garlic and cook over medium heat for about 2 minutes, until the vegetables begin to soften. Add the stock, potatoes, and salt and bring to a boil. Cover, reduce the heat, and boil gently for 30 minutes.

Meanwhile, heat the remaining 2 tablespoons oil in a large skillet. When it is hot, add the bread cubes and sauté, stirring almost continuously, until they are evenly browned on all sides. Remove with a slotted spoon and set aside.

When the soup is cooked, use a hand blender to puree it, or push it through a food mill. Stir the butter into the hot soup and serve with the croutons.

Celery Soup
Serves 6 to 8

❦ **Vermicelli, or thin egg** noodles, give creaminess and body to this soup; the taste reminds me of my grandmother's vegetable pasta. The soup is perfect when I have a cold.

Many similar versions can be prepared in the same manner. You can use leftover vegetables, such as a rib of celery, a bit of lettuce, an onion, and a carrot. I puree the soup to make it creamy, but for a different texture, you can grate the vegetables on a box grater instead of slicing them and skip the pureeing. When the vegetables are cut thin, the soup takes less than 15 minutes to cook.

If you use large ribs of celery, peel them first, because they are likely to be fibrous. To check, scratch the top of the ribs with your thumbnail to see if there are a lot of strings. Save the peelings; they can be used in stock. Use the leafy parts of the celery too; they will add flavor to the soup.

1 tablespoon unsalted butter, plus more for optional garnish
1 tablespoon olive oil
3 cups sliced celery (peeled if necessary; see the headnote), including some leaves
1 cup sliced onion
½ cup sliced scallions, including some green
6 cups water
1 teaspoon salt
⅛ teaspoon freshly ground black pepper
½ teaspoon dried thyme
1½ cups very thin egg noodles (sometimes called vermicelli)
1 cup milk

Melt the butter in a pot. Add the oil, celery, onion, and scallions and sauté gently over medium heat for about 2 minutes, just to soften the vegetables slightly. Add the water, salt, pepper, and thyme and bring to a boil. Reduce the heat, cover, and simmer for 8 to 10 minutes, until the vegetables are soft.

Use a hand blender to liquefy the soup in the pot, or pour the soup into a food processor and liquefy; the consistency will be thin. Return the soup to the pot if necessary and add the noodles. Bring to a boil and simmer for 3 to 4 minutes, until the noodles are cooked.

Add the milk and stir to heat through. Serve in individual soup bowls. To make the soup a bit richer, first put a dab of butter in each bowl and then pour the soup on top.

Cauliflower Soup
Serves 6

❦ **I am crazy about** the taste of cauliflower, and I use it in gratins, sautés, purees, and soups. This creamy, smooth soup is much less caloric than one made with potatoes, and for an even leaner version you can omit the cream. A perfect start to dinner, the soup can be made ahead and frozen or refrigerated for a few days and reheated as needed.

2 tablespoons peanut or canola oil
2 cups sliced onions
2 tablespoons all-purpose flour
1 teaspoon curry powder
2 cups homemade chicken stock (page
     612) or low-salt canned chicken broth
2 cups water
1 teaspoon salt, or to taste
½ teaspoon freshly ground black pepper
1 large or 2 small heads cauliflower (about
     1¾ pounds total), cored, separated into
     florets, and trimmed
2 tablespoons unsalted butter
½ cup heavy cream
2 tablespoons chopped fresh parsley

Heat the oil in a large saucepan. When it is hot, add the onions and sauté for 2 to 3 minutes, until they start browning. Sprinkle the flour and curry powder over the onions and mix well. Stir in the chicken stock, water, salt, and pepper, mix well, and bring to a boil, stirring occasionally. Add the cauliflower and return to a boil, then cover, reduce the heat to very low, and boil gently for 30 minutes.

Pour the soup into a food processor, in batches if necessary, and puree, with the butter. Return to the saucepan and stir in the cream. You should have about 7 cups soup; if you have less, add enough water to bring it to this level.

Reheat the soup, then divide it among six soup dishes, sprinkle with the parsley, and serve.

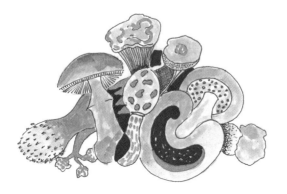

Dried and Fresh Mushroom Soup
Serves 4

❧ **Dried mushrooms** are responsible for the intensity of flavor in this soup, but fresh mushrooms — primarily stem pieces — help create the base for it, and their caps are used as a garnish. The soup can be enriched with cream at the end, and it can be served cold as well as hot. Cèpes are called porcini in Italy and king boletes in the U.S.

½ ounce (½ cup) dried cèpes (porcini)
1 cup milk
4–6 large mushrooms, cleaned
1½ teaspoons olive oil
¾ cup cubed (½-inch) onion
1 small leek, trimmed (leaving some
     green), split, washed, and thinly sliced
     (1 cup)
1 medium to large potato (about 6 ounces),
     peeled and cut into ½-inch cubes
1 teaspoon salt
2½ cups water

Soak the dried cèpes in the milk for at least 1 hour. Lift out the mushrooms, strain the milk, and reserve, leaving the sandy residue behind.

Cut enough of the fresh mushroom caps into matchsticks to measure ¾ cup. Reserve for garnish. Coarsely chop the remaining mushrooms.

Heat the oil in a large saucepan. When it is hot, add the onion and leek and sauté for 2 minutes over low heat. Add the cèpes, potato, chopped fresh mushrooms, salt, and water and bring to a boil. Cover, reduce the heat to low, and simmer gently for 25 minutes.

Puree the soup in the saucepan using a hand blender, or puree it in a food processor and return it to the pan. Add the julienned mushroom caps and bring to a boil. Stir in the reserved milk and bring to a boil. Serve immediately.

Farmer's-Style Soup
Serves 6

✀ **This soup is called** "farmer's-style," or *cultivateur* in France, because it is made with vegetables and a piece of slab bacon or pancetta, which the farmer would have had on hand. Although it can be made with stock, the flavor is purer and more authentic with just water. Serve it with croutons, if you like. Leftover soup can be pureed in a food processor, giving it another look, texture, and taste.

6	ounces slab bacon or pancetta
1	tablespoon olive oil
2	leeks, trimmed (leaving some green), split, washed, and sliced (3 cups)
3	carrots, peeled and cut into ½-inch dice (1 cup)
1	celery stalk, peeled and cut into ½-inch dice (¾ cup)
7	cups water
	Salt
1	medium to large turnip, peeled and cut into ½-inch dice (1 cup)
2	large potatoes (12 ounces), peeled and cut into ½-inch dice
1	garlic clove
4–5	fresh parsley sprigs, leaves only (for 1 tablespoon chopped)
6–8	fresh basil leaves (for 3 tablespoons chopped)

Cut the bacon or pancetta into short ¼-inch-thick strips.

Blanch the bacon in a Dutch oven or other large heavy pot: put the bacon pieces in the pot, add enough cold water to cover, bring to a boil, and boil for about 1 minute; drain in a sieve and rinse under cold water.

Rinse and dry the pot and add the oil and bacon to it. Sauté over medium-high heat for 3 to 5 minutes, until the bacon pieces are well fried and have rendered most of their fat. Add the leeks, carrots, and celery and sauté gently over medium heat for 1 to 2 minutes.

Add the water and salt to taste, bring to a boil, and boil for about 10 minutes. Add the turnip and potatoes and return to a boil, then cover and boil gently for about 20 minutes. Taste for salt and add a little if necessary, depending on the saltiness of the bacon.

At serving time, chop the garlic, parsley, and basil together. Add to the boiling soup and serve immediately.

Collard Greens and Grits Soup
Serves 4

✀ **Bright green collard greens** give a slightly bitter, nutty taste to this soup. You can also use turnip greens. For the deepest taste, use stone-ground grits, which need to cook for 25 to 30 minutes. (If you have instant grits, add them for the last 5 minutes of cooking.) Instead of the grits, you can use couscous or farina to thicken the soup. If you make it ahead and find that it is too thick when reheated, add water to bring it to the desired consistency.

2	tablespoons olive oil
12	ounces collard greens, leaves cut into 1-inch pieces, stems into ½-inch pieces (7 cups loosely packed)
2	carrots, peeled and cut into ½-inch pieces (1 cup)
7	cups homemade chicken stock (page 612), beef stock (page 612), or low-salt canned chicken or beef broth
1	teaspoon salt, or to taste
⅓	cup white or yellow grits, preferably stone-ground

Heat the oil in a pot. When it is hot, add the collard greens and sauté over high heat for 4 to 5 minutes, stirring occasionally, until wilted.

Add all the remaining ingredients and bring to a boil. Reduce the heat to low, cover, and boil gently for 25 to 30 minutes, stirring occasionally so the grits don't stick to the bottom of the pot. Serve.

Vegetable Soup with Pistou and Cornmeal Dumplings
Serves 8 to 10

✃ **Almost a stew, this** sturdy vegetable soup is a particularly good one-dish meal in summer and early fall, when fresh vegetables are plentiful. You can use almost any vegetable, but it's best to balance strong ones, such as turnips or cabbage, with those that have a less pronounced flavor, such as potatoes or carrots. You can also make do with leftovers from the refrigerator — some wilted lettuce, scallions, pieces of celery or carrots. The stronger

and tighter the vegetable — green pepper, butternut squash, and carrots, for example — the smaller the pieces should be (about ½-inch dice). Softer vegetables, such as eggplant and zucchini, should be cut into 1-inch dice. Lettuce or spinach leaves can be left whole or cut in half.

A mixture of basil, garlic, cheese, and olive oil or salt pork (or bacon), called *pistou*, is added at the end, and the soup itself is often called *pistou* or *soupe au pistou*. Similar to pesto, *pistou* is a specialty of the South of France.

Here the corn dumplings are not poached in the soup, which is the conventional method, but baked in the oven so that they become golden and crusty on top. Added to the soup just before serving, they absorb some of the liquid and get a bit soft but still hold their shape well. This soup can be made ahead and reheated, or even frozen.

- 4 ounces salt pork, bacon, or pancetta or ⅓ cup vegetable oil
- 1½ cups diced (½-inch) onions
- 1½ cups diced (½-inch) celery
- 2 cups loosely packed mixed sliced scallions and leeks, including some green
- 1 medium green bell pepper, cored, seeded, and diced (½-inch)
- 9 cups water
- 1 tablespoon salt
- 1½ cups diced (½-inch) carrots
- 1½ cups diced (1-inch) unpeeled eggplant
- 1½ cups diced (½-inch) peeled butternut squash
- 1 cup diced (½-inch) peeled kohlrabi or white turnips
- 1½ cups diced (½-inch) peeled potatoes
- 1½ cups diced (1-inch) zucchini
- 1 cup sliced string beans
- 1 cup lettuce leaves
- 2 cups spinach leaves, washed

PISTOU

2 cups tightly packed fresh basil leaves,
    blanched in boiling water for
    10 seconds
4 garlic cloves
¼ cup freshly grated Parmesan cheese
¼ cup olive oil
¼ cup liquid from the soup

BAKED CORNMEAL DUMPLINGS

½ cup cornmeal
1 cup all-purpose flour
1 teaspoon baking powder
1 teaspoon salt
2 large eggs
½ cup milk
¼ cup peanut oil

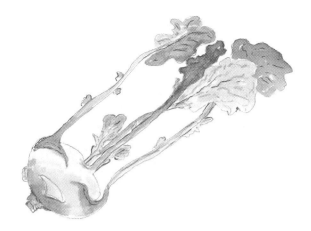

Bake for 13 to 15 minutes, until golden brown.

Just before serving, stir the *pistou* into the soup and bring to a boil. Drop the dumplings into the soup 1 or 2 minutes before serving so that they absorb some of the liquid and get soft, or pass them separately.

If using salt pork, bacon, or pancetta, cut it into ½-inch pieces. Fry in a large pot until they sizzle, then cook over medium heat for 5 to 6 minutes, until the pieces are nicely crisp and brown. Or, if using the oil, heat it in the pot over medium heat.

Add the onions, celery, scallions and leeks, and green pepper and sauté for 2 to 3 minutes. Add the water, salt, and the remaining vegetables except the lettuce and spinach and bring to a boil. Reduce the heat, cover, and simmer for 30 minutes.

Add the lettuce and spinach and cook for another 15 minutes.

MEANWHILE, PREPARE THE PISTOU AND DUMPLINGS: Preheat the oven to 375 degrees.

FOR THE PISTOU: Puree all the ingredients in a blender until smooth.

FOR THE CORNMEAL DUMPLINGS: Combine all the ingredients except the oil in a bowl and mix well. Oil one or two large cookie sheets and spoon large tablespoons of the batter onto them. (You should have approximately 16 dumplings.) Sprinkle the tops with the remaining oil.

MAKING PISTOU

In the summer, when you have fresh basil, prepare large batches of *pistou* in a food processor, divide among ½- or 1-cup containers, and freeze. Add a frozen ½-cup block to the soup 10 to 15 minutes before serving, bring to a boil, and let it melt. *Pistou* can be used to enhance other types of soups, and it is also very good tossed with steamed vegetables, sautéed potatoes, or pasta.

Pumpkin and Pastina Soup
Serves 6

❧ **The beautiful color of** the creamy pumpkin against the green leeks and pasta bits makes this delicately flavored but hearty soup as visually appealing as it is delicious. Instead of the small pasta called pastina, you can use another member of the pasta family, from tiny noodles to small elbows to broken pieces of spaghetti.

1 large leek (about 8 ounces), trimmed (leaving some green), quartered lengthwise, washed, and sliced (2 cups)
1 tablespoon unsalted butter
1 tablespoon corn oil
1 piece (about 2¼ pounds) pumpkin
2 cups homemade chicken stock (page 612) or low-salt canned chicken broth
4 cups water
½ teaspoon salt, or to taste
½ cup pastina (any tiny pasta in alphabet, star, or square shapes)

Place the leek in a large pot with the butter and oil and sauté over high heat for 2 to 3 minutes, until it begins to sizzle lightly.

Meanwhile, with a sharp knife, carefully peel the tough outer skin from the pumpkin. (You should have about 1½ pounds pumpkin flesh.) Remove the seeds (which can be roasted as a snack) and cut the flesh into ½-inch pieces. (You should have about 5½ cups.)

Add the cubed pumpkin, chicken stock, water, and salt to the leek and bring to a boil. Cover, reduce the heat, and cook at a gentle boil for 30 minutes.

Add the pastina and cook for 10 minutes longer. Stir, and serve immediately.

Black Bean Soup with Bananas
Serves 8 to 10

✄ **I have created several** versions of black bean soup through the years, but this one, flavored with pancetta and finished with bananas, ranks at the top of my list of favorites.

1 pound dried black or turtle beans
4 quarts water
½ cup brown rice
8 ounces pancetta or very lean unsmoked or lightly smoked bacon
2 medium onions (12 ounces), cut into 1-inch pieces
8 large garlic cloves, coarsely chopped (¼ cup)
1 tablespoon herbes de Provence
1 tablespoon chili powder
1 14½-ounce can diced tomatoes
1 tablespoon salt (less if the pancetta or bacon is salty)
2 tablespoons olive oil
2 tablespoons red wine vinegar
1½ teaspoons Tabasco sauce

GARNISHES
2 bananas
1 tablespoon fresh lemon juice
¼ teaspoon freshly ground black pepper
¼ cup coarsely chopped fresh cilantro

Remove and discard any damaged beans or debris and wash the remaining beans well in cool water. Drain the beans, place them in a bowl, cover with cold water, and soak for 3 hours.

Drain the beans, put them in a stainless steel pot with the 4 quarts water, and add the rice. Cut the pancetta or bacon into ¼-inch cubes and add them to the pot. Bring to a boil over high heat, uncovered (this will take about 20 minutes), stirring occasionally. Skim off and discard any foam that rises to the top. Reduce the heat to very low, cover, and cook for 1 hour.

Add the onions, garlic, herbes de Provence, chili powder, tomatoes, and salt to the pot, stir well, and bring to a boil. Reduce the heat to very low, cover, and cook for 1½ hours.

Using a hand blender, emulsify the mixture in the pot for 5 to 10 seconds. (Alternatively, remove 2 cups of the mixture, puree it in a food processor, and return it to the pot.) You want to thicken the mixture slightly while still maintaining its overall chunkiness.

Mix together the oil, vinegar, and Tabasco in a small bowl and add to the soup.

JUST BEFORE SERVING, PREPARE THE GARNISHES: Peel the bananas and cut them into ¼-inch-thick slices. Toss them in a small bowl with the lemon juice and pepper.

Divide the hot soup among individual bowls. Top with the banana slices, sprinkle on the cilantro, and serve.

Split Pea Soup with Cracklings
Serves 6

✄ **Served with crusty bread** and a simple first-course salad, this makes a great winter meal. The soup can be frozen, although it may require additional water when reheated, since it tends to thicken when refrigerated or frozen.

    6   ounces chicken skin, cut into 1-inch
           pieces
    2   medium onions, cut into 1-inch pieces
           (about 2 cups)
  2–3   garlic cloves, crushed and coarsely
           chopped (about 1 tablespoon)
    8   cups water
    2   teaspoons herbes de Provence
    2   teaspoons salt
    ½   teaspoon freshly ground black pepper
    ¼   teaspoon Tabasco sauce, plus more for
           serving
    1   pound dried split peas, picked over and
           rinsed

Put the chicken skin in a large skillet and sauté over high heat for 8 to 10 minutes, until the fat is rendered and the skin is crisp. Transfer the cracklings and fat to a large saucepan.

Add the onions to the saucepan and sauté for 5 minutes. Add the garlic and mix well, then stir in the water, herbes de Provence, salt, pepper, Tabasco sauce, and split peas. Bring to a boil, cover, reduce the heat, and boil gently for 1 hour.

Stir the soup well. It should be fairly thick, but if you prefer to thin it a little, add some water. Divide the soup among six bowls and offer extra Tabasco sauce for serving.

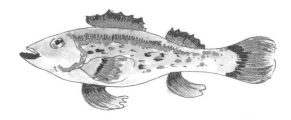

Fish Soup with Rouille and Garlic Croutons
Serves 8

✄ **The bones and heads** — the parts of the fish that are free — give fish stocks, soups, and stews their flavor. The best bones are from flatfish such as sole, dab, flounder, or halibut, but you can use almost any nonoily fish. Collarbones from cod also are very good, as they yield a great deal of flesh.

When I can't get free bones and heads, I buy whole fish and have the fishmonger gut and fillet them, reserving the heads and bones for the soup and the fillets for another dish. (Alternatively, if I buy a whole fish and fillet it for dinner, I'll freeze the head and bones for later use.)

Fresh is best, but you can still get good results with frozen bones, provided they were very fresh, clean, and properly packed when frozen. If the bones have been frozen, defrost slowly in the refrigerator, then wash well under cold water.

This soup is enriched with a *rouille*, which is a type of mayonnaise. *Rouille* means "rust," and that is the color it imparts to the soup. I mix some of the *rouille* into the soup and serve the rest on the side, with garlic-flavored croutons.

3 pounds fish bones and heads
3 tablespoons olive oil
10 cups water
1 cup sliced onion
1 cup diced celery
1 cup sliced scallions, including some green
½ cup loosely packed fresh parsley leaves
2½ cups diced tomatoes
½ teaspoon anise seeds
1 teaspoon turmeric
1 teaspoon herbes de Provence
2½ teaspoons salt
½ teaspoon freshly ground black pepper

ROUILLE

4–5 garlic cloves
¼ cup of the soup
1 large egg
⅛ teaspoon cayenne pepper
½ cup olive oil

CROUTONS

3 tablespoons olive oil
30 slices stale baguettes, no more than ¼ inch thick
2 large garlic cloves

Wash the fish bones and heads under cold water; be sure to remove any gills.

Heat the oil in a large stainless steel pot. Add the bones and heads and sauté over high heat, stirring, for about 5 minutes; they will break into pieces. Add the water, bring to a boil, and boil for 15 minutes. If any scum comes to the top, skim it off and discard it.

Strain the fish stock and pour it back into the pot. Pick the meat off the bones and set it aside; discard the bones.

Add the rest of the soup ingredients to the stock and bring to a boil, then reduce the heat, cover, and boil gently for 35 to 40 minutes.

MEANWHILE, MAKE THE ROUILLE AND CROUTONS: Preheat the oven to 375 degrees.

FOR THE ROUILLE: Process the garlic, soup, egg, and cayenne in a blender. With the motor running, slowly add the oil to make a light mayonnaise.

FOR THE CROUTONS: Spread the oil on a large cookie sheet. Dip the slices of bread in the oil and turn them over; they will pick up a bit of oil on both sides. (This technique is easier than brushing each one with oil.) Bake for 8 to 10 minutes, or until the bread is brown and crisp. (Bread browns more uniformly in the oven than under the broiler.)

When the bread is cool, rub it lightly with the garlic on both sides, so it absorbs some of it.

TO FINISH THE SOUP: Use a hand blender or a food processor to liquefy the soup. You should have about 8 cups soup. If you have more, reduce it; if you don't have enough, add water to bring it to 8 cups. Add the reserved pieces of fish and bring the mixture back to a boil.

Mix some of the *rouille* into the soup and pass the rest at the table. Serve the soup in large bowls, with the garlic croutons in it or on the side.

Seafood Gumbo
Serves 6

❧ **I first tasted gumbo** in New Orleans a few years after I came to the U.S., and I loved it. The dark roux gives it both flavor and color and the sassafras powder, or filé, contributes a certain thickness, although it is not essential. This is a great one-dish meal in the style of paella or cassoulet.

There are more ingredients here than I generally use, but you can make substitutions in the fish, shellfish, and vegetables based on market availability. Tasso ham can be added instead of or with the andouille, a spicy Louisiana sausage popular in New Orleans.

8 cups water
12 ounces fish fillets (pollack, cod, or other white-fleshed fish), cut into 1-inch pieces
8 ounces peeled fresh or frozen small shrimp (50–55 to the pound)
¼ cup canola oil
⅓ cup all-purpose flour
4 ounces hot Italian sausage or andouille, removed from casings if necessary and separated into pieces the size of olives
2 onions (about 10 ounces), sliced (about 2½ cups)
½ cup long-grain white rice
12 scallions, trimmed (leaving some green) and cut into ½-inch pieces (about 1½ cups)
5 garlic cloves, crushed and chopped (1 tablespoon)
2 large tomatoes, cut into 1-inch pieces (about 2½ cups)
1 cup sliced celery
1 large green bell pepper, cored, seeded, and cut into ½-inch pieces (about 1½ cups)
8 ounces okra, ends trimmed and cut into ½-inch-thick rounds
2 teaspoons salt
1 teaspoon dried thyme
1 jalapeño pepper, seeded and finely chopped
¼ teaspoon cayenne pepper
1 tablespoon filé (gumbo) powder

Bring the water to a boil in a large pot. Add the fish and shrimp, stir, and cook over high heat for 2 to 3 minutes. (The water will not have returned to a boil.) With a slotted spoon, transfer the seafood to a bowl, cover, and set aside. Reserve the poaching liquid in the pot.

Meanwhile, mix the oil and flour together in a small skillet and cook over high heat for about 1 minute, until the mixture sizzles. Reduce the heat to low and cook for about 15 minutes, stirring every minute or two, until the roux is a deep mahogany color. Add the sausage and onions and cook for another minute.

Whisk the onion mixture into the poaching liquid and bring to a boil, stirring constantly. Add the rice and stir well to incorporate it. Add the remainder of the ingredients except the reserved seafood and the filé powder, stir, and bring to a boil. Reduce the heat to low, cover, and boil gently for 20 minutes.

Stir the gumbo, sprinkle the filé powder on top, mix well, and cook for another 5 minutes.

To serve immediately, add the fish and shrimp, return to a boil, and serve. To serve a bit later, set aside to cool, then reheat at serving time, adding the fish and shrimp at the last minute to warm them through.

Lobster Broth with Pastina
Serves 4

✂ **Good cooks are thrifty,** using all the ingredients at their disposal. Their creativity is shown more by how they economize than by how lavishly they decorate their food. This recipe is an example of how ingredients can be extended. Reduced, the stock left over from steaming or poaching lobster makes a simple and delicious soup with the addition of pastina or, if you prefer, angel hair pasta or rice, and shredded lettuce. I like to use the large green outer leaves, which tend to be too tough for serving in salads, or any wilted lettuce I have on hand. Roll up the leaves together and shred them for a delicate addition.

For a more complex lobster soup, look at Cream of Lobster Soup (opposite).

- 1 tablespoon olive oil
- 2 cups shredded lettuce
- 6 cups lobster broth (see the sidebar)
- ½ cup pastina (any tiny pasta in alphabet, star, or square shapes)
  Salt to taste
- ½ teaspoon freshly ground black pepper
- 2 tablespoons chopped fresh chives

Heat the oil in a stainless steel saucepan. Add the lettuce and cook for about 1 minute, then add the lobster broth and bring to a boil. Add the pastina and stir well. Bring the broth back to a boil, cover, and boil gently for about 10 minutes, until the pastina is tender. Add the salt and pepper.

Ladle the soup into four soup bowls and sprinkle with the chives. Serve immediately.

Cream of Lobster Soup
Serves 10 to 12

❧ If the lobsters you use are female, you can dry the roe in the oven and use it as a decorative garnish for this rich soup.

Reserved roe from 1 lobster (optional)

STOCK

- 1 tablespoon unsalted butter
- 1 onion, coarsely chopped
- 1 leek, trimmed (leaving some green), split, washed, and coarsely chopped (1¼ cups)
  About 1½ cups lobster-steaming liquid
  Shells and bodies from 2 lobsters (about 1½ pounds each)
- 2 tomatoes (about 1 pound), coarsely chopped
- 1 cup dry white wine
- 1 teaspoon dried thyme
- 2 teaspoons paprika
- 3 bay leaves, crumbled
- 4 garlic cloves, crushed but not peeled
- 1 teaspoon salt
- 4 quarts water

TO FINISH

- 3 tablespoons unsalted butter, softened
- ¼ cup all-purpose flour
- ⅛ teaspoon cayenne pepper
- ½ teaspoon salt, or to taste
- 1½ cups heavy cream
- 1 tablespoon cognac

If you have the lobster roe, preheat the oven to 375 degrees. Spread the roe on a small cookie sheet and bake for 12 to 15 minutes, until dry and red. Crumble in a spice grinder or with a mortar and pestle. Set aside for garnish.

FOR THE LOBSTER STOCK: Heat the butter in a large stainless steel pot. When it is hot, add the onion and leek and sauté for 2 to 3 minutes, until they begin to brown. Add the lobster-steaming liquid and stir to loosen all the particles on the bottom of the pot. Add the lobster shells and bodies, tomatoes, white wine, thyme, paprika, bay leaves, garlic, salt, and water. Bring to a boil, reduce the heat, and cook gently for 1½ hours.

Strain the stock through a fine strainer into a saucepan, pressing down with a spoon to force through as much of the solids as possible. Boil to reduce the stock to 8 cups.

TO FINISH THE SOUP: Mix the butter and flour together with a whisk in a bowl. Gather this kneaded butter — a *beurre manié* — on the whisk and add it to the stock, whisking so it dissolves well. (You should not have any lumps.) Bring to a boil, then add the cayenne and salt and simmer for 3 to 4 minutes. If there are any lumps, strain and return to the pot. Add the cream and cognac and heat briefly (it doesn't need to come back to a boil).

Serve the soup in hot bowls, sprinkled with the lobster roe, if you have it.

Chicken and Spinach Velouté
Serves 4

Velouté means "velvety" in English, and any cream soup that is particularly smooth and unctuous can be called a velouté. This soup can be made in 10 minutes. Its quality depends on the quality of the chicken stock, which should be homemade, completely defatted, and highly concentrated. I thicken the velouté with Cream of Wheat, which cooks quickly, but cornmeal, tapioca, and semolina work equally well.

4	cups homemade chicken stock (page 612)
1	cup water
¾	teaspoon salt
¼	teaspoon freshly ground black pepper
6	tablespoons instant Cream of Wheat
6	ounces spinach, tough stems removed
⅓	cup heavy cream

Bring the stock, water, salt, and pepper to a boil in a stainless steel saucepan. Add the Cream of Wheat and mix well. Bring back to a boil, reduce the heat to low, and cook gently for 3 minutes.

Meanwhile, wash the spinach and very coarsely chop it.

Add the spinach to the pan, bring back to a boil, and boil for 2 minutes. Stir in the cream and serve immediately.

Petite Marmite
Serves 6

A pot-au-feu is the archetype of the earthy one-dish family meal. Meat and vegetables are cooked together with water in a large stockpot. The meat is then served with the vegetables, with the broth on the side, accompanied by bread and, sometimes, cheese. *Petite marmite* is the classic, more elegant form of pot-au-feu. The rich broth is served with the vegetables and meat still in it and a garnish of croutons and grated cheese on the side.

In my version, the bones and meat are first cooked to produce a rich, lean stock, then the sliced vegetables are put in, along with the (optional) chicken "balloons." The vegetables are arranged directly on top of the sliced meat in a colorful pattern, the stock is added, and the vegetables are cooked without being mixed into the liquid, thus keeping their shape and arrangement. Since they're cooked for only 30 minutes, they retain their taste, texture, and color.

STOCK

4 pounds beef bones (shin, neck, ribs, or leg bones)
2 pounds chicken bones
4 quarts cold water
2 pounds boneless beef (chuck, shank, or short ribs)
4 bay leaves
1 teaspoon dried thyme
Salt

CHICKEN "BALLOONS" (optional)

12 chicken wings
5 ounces chicken meat (from 1 single breast or leg)
2 ounces chicken fat
¼ cup loosely packed fresh parsley leaves
Small pinch of freshly grated nutmeg
¼ teaspoon salt

VEGETABLES

5–6 dried shiitake mushrooms, soaked in 1½ cups tepid water for 30 minutes
3 carrots, peeled and cut into 3- to 4-inch ½-inch-thick strips

2 medium leeks, trimmed (leaving some green), split, washed, and cut into 3- to 4-inch ½-inch-wide strips
¼ white cabbage (about 10 ounces), cut into wedges (reserve 1 large cabbage leaf for garnish)
1 large white turnip (about 8 ounces), peeled and cut into wedges
1 teaspoon salt

FOR SERVING

18 slices baguette, ¼ inch thick
Freshly grated Parmesan cheese

FOR THE STOCK: Put the beef and chicken bones in a large pot, cover with the water, and bring to a boil. Reduce the heat and cook at a very gentle simmer for 2½ hours, removing the scum as it comes to the surface.

Add the beef, bay leaves, and thyme and cook for 2 hours longer. Add extra water if it reduces too much.

Strain the stock, reserving the beef, and refrigerate until thoroughly chilled, or overnight. Trim the cooked beef of any fat and cut into ½-inch-thick slices. Refrigerate. Remove any fat that has solidified on top of the stock. (You should have 8 cups stock.)

FOR THE OPTIONAL CHICKEN "BALLOONS": Cut the wing tip, including the joint, away from each chicken wing, then cut away the bone and the joint at the other end, keeping only the middle part. (The object is to loosen the bones in the center section so they can be pulled out and stuffing put inside.) Using a towel for a better grip, pull out the bones; they should come out easily. Put the chicken meat, fat, parsley, nutmeg, and salt in a food processor and process for 25 to 40 seconds, until well blended.

Spoon the mixture into a pastry bag fitted with a ½-inch plain tip and pipe into the wings until they take on a roundish balloon shape. Don't worry if the stuffing is still visible.

Put the "balloons" in a saucepan, cover with cold water, and bring to a boil. Boil gently for 1 minute, then drain and rinse under cold water. Set aside until ready to finish the dish.

FOR THE PETITE MARMITE: Lift the shiitake mushrooms from the soaking liquid and remove the stems (the stems are tough, but they can be used to flavor stock); strain the soaking liquid and reserve.

Arrange the meat slices in a large casserole or Dutch oven nice enough to be brought to the table. Arrange the carrots, leeks, cabbage, and turnip on top of the meat in the pot. Arrange the chicken "balloons," if using, around the dish, on top of the vegetables, and the mushroom caps in the center. Pour the mushroom liquid on top and add the salt and 4 cups of the stock; reserve the remaining 4 cups. Bring the *petite marmite* to a boil, cover, and cook at a gentle simmer for 30 minutes.

Meanwhile, preheat the oven to 400 degrees.

Arrange the baguette slices on a cookie sheet and bake for 10 to 12 minutes, until nicely browned. Set aside.

Just before serving, reheat the remaining 4 cups stock and season with salt. Put the grated Parmesan cheese in the center of the reserved cabbage leaf and place on a serving plate, with the croutons around it.

For each serving, scoop a few pieces of meat, some vegetables, a couple of chicken "balloons," if you have them, and some stock into a soup plate. Serve immediately, while very hot, with the extra stock, croutons, and cheese.

Chicken Hearts and Gizzards Soup
Serves 6

❧ **Cooked chicken gizzards** are tender and moist, with a flavorful, meaty taste. At my market they are sometimes mixed with chicken hearts — so much the better. They are very inexpensive and truly delicious in soup or cooked into a stew with rice or beans.

Because the gizzards are difficult to cut raw (they are rubbery and tough and tend to slip under the knife), here they are first cooked for 45 minutes before being sliced into pieces.

Cornmeal is the thickening agent in the soup, but farina (Cream of Wheat) or couscous can be substituted.

2 pounds chicken gizzards and hearts (or gizzards only)

6 cups water

2–4 celery stalks, cut into ½-inch pieces (about 2 cups)

4 medium carrots, peeled and cut into ½-inch pieces (about 2 cups)

1½ teaspoons salt

⅓ cup yellow cornmeal

8 scallions, trimmed (leaving some green) and coarsely chopped (1¼ cups)

½ teaspoon dried dill

GARNISH

½ cup sour cream

¼ cup chopped fresh dill

Wash the gizzards and hearts under cool running water. Put them in a large saucepan with the 6 cups water and bring to a boil over high heat. Boil for 1 to 2 minutes, then skim off and discard any fat and impurities that have risen to the surface. Cover, reduce the heat to low, and boil gently for 45 minutes.

With a slotted spoon, remove the gizzards and hearts and place them on a chopping board; set the saucepan aside.

When they are cool enough to handle, cut the gizzards and hearts into ¼-inch pieces, or coarsely chop them in a food processor. Return them to the cooking liquid, along with the celery, carrots, and salt, and bring to a boil over high heat, then cover, reduce the heat to low, and boil gently for 45 minutes.

Stir in the cornmeal, scallions, and dried dill and cook for 10 minutes longer, stirring occasionally.

Ladle the soup into bowls. Garnish each with a generous tablespoon of the sour cream and a sprinkling of the dill.

Cooked Turkey Carcass Soup
Serves 4 to 6

⅙ **This soup can be** made with uncooked turkey bones, which are available at most markets, but my family prefers it with the bones from a roast turkey. Any leftover solidified juices or vegetables from the turkey — a clove of garlic, perhaps, or pieces of onion — can be added as flavor enhancers.

> About 2 pounds bones from a cooked turkey, plus any leftover juices and/or cooked garnishes (such as pieces of carrot, onion, or garlic)
> 4 quarts water

> 2 carrots, peeled and cut into ½-inch pieces (1 cup)
> 1 medium leek, trimmed (leaving some green), split, washed, and cut into 1-inch pieces (2 cups)
> 1 cup diced (½-inch) celery
> 3 cups coarsely chopped outer lettuce leaves or leftover salad greens
> ½ cup fine egg noodles (vermicelli)

Put the turkey bones, juices, and cooked garnishes, if you have them, in a large stainless steel stockpot. Add the water and bring to a strong boil, skimming off and discarding the fat and scum from the surface as it appears. Reduce the heat and boil gently, uncovered, for 1½ hours.

Strain the stock. You should have 8 cups. If you have more, return the stock to the rinsed-out pot and boil until it is reduced to 8 cups; if you have less, add water to bring it up to 8 cups and return to the rinsed-out pot. Pick the meat from the bones and add it to the stock.

Add all the remaining ingredients except the egg noodles to the pot and bring to a boil, then reduce the heat to low, cover, and boil gently for 10 minutes.

Add the egg noodles and continue to boil gently, covered, for another 10 minutes. Serve.

Poultry Soup
with Shredded Lettuce
Serves 6

✎ **I keep the bones** from roasted chicken, goose, and, especially, turkey to make soup. This soup, made with turkey bones, includes vegetables and a garnish of chiffonade (shredded) lettuce, which makes the soup more special. It's a great way of repurposing leftover or wilted lettuce. The carcass of any cooked bird can be used here.

STOCK

> 3   pounds bones from a cooked
>   turkey or chicken, including back
>   and neck (approximate yield from a
>   15-pound turkey)
> 10 cups water
> 1   teaspoon dried thyme
> 2   bay leaves
> ½   teaspoon crushed black peppercorns
>
> 3   tablespoons unsalted butter
> 1   cup coarsely chopped onion
> 1   cup coarsely chopped leeks, including
>   some green
> 1   pound potatoes, peeled and cut into
>   1-inch cubes
> 1   teaspoon salt

GARNISH

> 1   medium head Boston lettuce
> 2   tablespoons unsalted butter

FOR THE STOCK: Put the bones in a large stockpot, cover with the water, and bring to a boil, skimming off and discarding the foam that rises to the surface. Add the thyme, bay leaves, and peppercorns, reduce the heat, and boil gently for 1½ hours.

Strain the stock. You should have about 8 cups. If you have more, boil the stock to reduce it to 8 cups; if you have less, add enough water to make 8 cups.

Rinse and dry the stockpot and melt the butter in it. Add the onion and leeks and sauté over medium heat for 2 minutes. Add the stock, potatoes, and salt, bring to a boil, and boil gently, partially covered, for 45 minutes.

Using a hand blender, liquefy the soup until it has a fine, creamy texture. Or puree in a food processor, in batches if necessary.

MEANWHILE, FOR THE GARNISH: Separate the lettuce into leaves and wash them thoroughly; drain. Pile the leaves together and cut them crosswise into thin strips (chiffonade).

Melt the butter in a saucepan. Add the lettuce and cook for 1 to 2 minutes, until wilted.

At serving time, top the soup with the lettuce and serve.

Consommé
Serves 8

✎ **When perfectly made, beef** or chicken consommé is a beautifully clear, sparkling broth that can be served with many different garnishes, such as *célestine* (shredded crepes) or *royale* (cubed custard). With all of the protein of meat, it has none of the fat. It is also the base for aspic.

Clarification is the process that gives the consommé its crystal-clear appearance. Egg whites mixed with ground beef form a crust, or "raft," on top of the liquid, and the lightly boiling liquid filters gently through the crust until it is clear. The ground beef enriches the final stock, but if the basic stock is strong, the beef can be omitted. In that case, the consommé will need to cook for only 15 minutes after it comes to a boil. Be sure to use a fat-free stock and immaculately clean equipment.

8 cups homemade beef stock (page 612) or chicken stock (page 612), or a mixture
1 pound very lean ground beef
⅓ cup coarsely chopped celery leaves
½ cup coarsely chopped fresh parsley
1 cup coarsely chopped leek greens
¾ cup coarsely chopped carrots
1 tablespoon black peppercorns
½ teaspoon dried thyme
4 large egg whites
1 cup water
½ teaspoon salt, or to taste

Bring the stock to a boil.

Meanwhile, combine the remaining ingredients in a large heavy pot, preferably stainless steel. Mix by hand until homogeneous. Add the hot stock and stir it in well. Bring to a boil over high heat, stirring constantly with a large spoon to prevent scorching. The stock will become very cloudy and a white foam will form on top: the albumin in the egg whites and the meat is solidifying, and this is the process that will clarify the stock. When the mixture comes to a rolling boil, immediately stop stirring and reduce the heat to a simmer. As the mixture simmers, you will notice that the ingredients form a crust on the surface of the liquid with one or two holes, through which the liquid boils gently. Allow the consommé to simmer very gently for 1 hour without disturbing the little "geysers" in any way.

Place a sieve lined with wet paper towels over a saucepan. Strain the consommé, using a ladle to scoop the liquid out, taking care not to disturb the crust. Let the consommé rest for 1 hour.

Check to see if there is any fat on the surface of the consommé. If so, remove it by blotting the top with paper towels. Reheat the consommé before serving, as is or with the garnish of your choice.

Hanoi Soup

Serves 4 to 6

❧ **Here is my wife's** rendition of a classic Vietnamese soup. One of my favorites, it is a meal in itself, satisfying for dinner. The base of the soup is a very good stock made with oxtail, beef shank, and beef bones. It is flavored with star anise and with ginger and shallots that have been held over a gas flame or hot electric burner until well charred on all sides. In addition to giving the stock a rich color, the burned shallots impart a very specific taste.

The more esoteric ingredients — star anise, rice sticks, and nuoc mam — are available in Asian markets and can be found in the Asian section of many supermarkets.

Nuoc mam is the Vietnamese name for the thin, salty, brownish fermented fish sauce that is as popular throughout Southeast Asia as soy sauce is in China and Japan. Some cooks consider *nam pla*, the Thai version, to be the finest. Related to the magnolia family, star anise is an eight-pointed, star-shaped cluster of brown pods, each containing a pea-sized seed that has a flavor similar — though more bitter — to regular anise seeds. Two or three points of this aromatic spice are usually sufficient to add fragrance and subtle spiciness to dishes like this one.

This colorful soup should be served in large bowls (2- to 3-cup capacity) to accommodate all the garnishes.

1½ pounds oxtails, cut into 2- to 3-inch pieces (have the butcher cut up the oxtails and beef)
1½ pounds beef shank (about 2 slices, each 1 inch thick, with bones)
1 pound beef bones, cut into 3-inch pieces
6 quarts cold water
3 large shallots

1 2-inch piece ginger, not peeled

3 star anise points

1 thin cinnamon stick (about 3 inches long)

1 teaspoon salt

GARNISHES

1½ cups (6 ounces) bean sprouts

5 ounces rice sticks (rice vermicelli)

1½ cups shredded napa cabbage
Asian fish sauce, preferably nuoc mam

1 cup loosely packed fresh cilantro leaves

1 cup very thinly sliced red onion

2 tablespoons seeded and sliced hot chile pepper

4 scallions, trimmed (leaving some green) and minced

1 lime, cut into 4–6 wedges

Combine the oxtails, shank, beef bones, and cold water in a stainless steel stockpot and bring to a boil over high heat. (This will take 25 to 30 minutes.) Skim off and discard any impurities that have risen to the surface and continue to cook at a fairly high boil for 5 minutes, removing surface scum as it collects. Reduce the heat to low.

Meanwhile, impale the shallots and ginger on a skewer and hold them over the flame of a gas stove or a hot electric burner, turning them often, until they are charred on all sides.

Add the shallots, ginger, star anise, and cinnamon to the stock and boil gently for 4 hours.

Transfer the bones and meat to a bowl. Strain the stock twice through a paper towel–lined strainer to eliminate the fat. (You should have 8 to 9 cups stock.)

Wash the stockpot, return the stock to it, and add the salt. Pick the meat from the bones, avoiding any fat and sinew, and break it into pieces. (You should have about 3 cups.) Set aside.

FOR THE GARNISHES: Bring 3 cups water to a boil in a saucepan. Add the bean sprouts and cook for 3½ to 4 minutes, until the water comes back to a strong boil. Drain.

Bring 6 cups water to a boil in a medium saucepan. Add the rice sticks, bring back to a boil, and boil for about 2½ minutes, until tender. Drain in a colander and run briefly under cold water to cool.

At serving time, bring the stock to a boil. Heat the meat in a microwave oven or in a saucepan on top of the stove with a little stock.

Divide the rice sticks, shredded cabbage, bean sprouts, and meat among four to six large bowls and fill the bowls with the boiling stock. Bring to the table and pass the fish sauce, cilantro, red onion, hot pepper, and scallions; each diner can add as much of these ingredients as desired. Squeeze the juice of a lime wedge over each bowl and eat the soup immediately.

Lamb Barley Soup
Serves 6

✄ **Lamb and barley soup** with mushrooms is a classic Scottish dish that I often make with leftovers from a roast leg of lamb. The bones and any trimmings yield a very flavorful stock that is ideal with barley. Served with crusty bread and a salad, this robust soup makes a meal.

2	pounds bones, meat trimmings, and juices from a roast leg of lamb (see Roast Leg of Lamb, page 351)
3	quarts water
1	cup pearl barley
2	cups diced mushrooms (about 6 ounces)
1½	cups diced celery
1½	cups peeled and diced carrots
1	cup diced onion
3	cups diced leeks (about 2 medium leeks, including some green)
1	tablespoon salt
1	teaspoon freshly ground black pepper
3	tablespoons chopped fresh parsley Worcestershire sauce, preferably Lea & Perrins (optional)

Combine the lamb bones, trimmings, and juices in a large pot, add the water and barley, and bring to a boil. Reduce the heat to low, cover, and boil gently for 1½ hours.

Remove the bones from the pot with a skimmer or tongs and set them aside. Add the mushrooms, celery, carrots, onion, leeks, salt, and pepper to the pot, bring to a boil, cover, and cook gently for 45 minutes.

Meanwhile, pick the meat off the bones and shred it into ½-inch pieces. Add to the soup as it cooks.

Add the parsley to the soup, and serve. Pass Worcestershire sauce at the table, if desired.

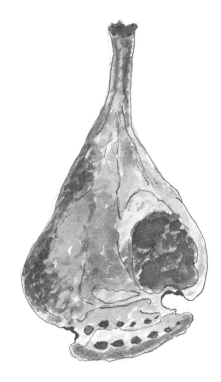

Sausage, Potato, and Cabbage Soup
Serves 8

✄ **It's worthwhile to make** a large batch of this soup and freeze the leftovers for another meal. Followed by a salad, it is a perfect lunch for a cold winter day. Leftovers can be reheated, and they taste better every time.

8	ounces mild Italian sausage meat
2	small onions, cut into 1-inch-thick slices (1½ cups)
6	scallions, trimmed (leaving some green) and cut into ½-inch pieces (1¼ cups)
6	cups water
1	pound potatoes, peeled and cut into ½-inch-thick slices
8	ounces savoy cabbage, cut into 1½-inch pieces (4 cups)
1¼	teaspoons salt Crusty French bread

Break the sausage meat into 1-inch pieces and place it in a saucepan over high heat. Sauté, stirring and scraping the bottom of the pan with a wooden spoon to keep the meat from sticking, for 10 minutes, or until the sausage is well browned.

Add the onions and scallions and cook for 1 minute. Stir in the water, potatoes, cabbage, and salt and bring to a boil. Cover, reduce the heat to low, and cook for 45 minutes.

Serve the soup in bowls with chunks of crusty French bread.

Lentil and Barley Soup
Serves 8

✖ **Like beans and rice**, lentils and barley are one of those magical combinations. Nourishing, delicious, and inexpensive, this substantial winter soup is a meal in itself when served with bread and a piece of cheese. You can freeze the leftovers. (The soup thickens as it cools; thin it by adding a little water.)

- 1 pound lentils, picked over and rinsed
- ½ cup pearl barley
- 4 quarts light homemade chicken stock (page 612), beef stock (page 612), or low-salt canned chicken or beef broth (use 2 parts stock to 1 part water)
- 2 hot Italian sausages (about 5 ounces total), casings removed and broken into ½-inch pieces
- 1 tablespoon herbes de Provence
- 1 tablespoon salt
- 2 medium leeks, trimmed (leaving some green), split, washed, and cut into ½-inch pieces (about 3 cups)
- 1 large onion, cut into ½-inch pieces (about 2 cups)

- 2 carrots, peeled and cut into ½-inch pieces (about ¾ cup)
- 5 large garlic cloves, crushed and coarsely chopped
- ½ teaspoon Tabasco sauce
- ½ cup grated Monterey Jack or mozzarella cheese (optional)

Combine all the ingredients except the Tabasco and optional cheese in a large pot and bring to a boil. Reduce the heat to very low, cover, and cook gently for 1½ hours.

Emulsify the cooked soup with a hand blender for 8 to 10 seconds to make it somewhat creamy but still a little chunky. Alternatively, puree 2 cups of the soup in a food processor for 20 seconds and combine the puree with the remaining soup.

Add the Tabasco to the soup. Serve in bowls, garnished, if desired, with the cheese.

Garbure
Serves 8

✖ *Garbure* is a soup from the Southwest of France. Traditionally very rich, it often includes goose or duck confit (pieces of duck or goose poached in their own fat), a variety of sausages, pork shoulder, and other types of meat, such as pig's feet.

I love *garbure* prepared in the classical style, but I also like this lighter version, with pork shoulder as the only meat. I trim the shoulder first, removing the "skin" and surrounding fat, then cook it with a selection of vegetables. Served in the traditional manner with a layer of bread and crispy cheese on top, it makes a delicious one-dish meal.

1 fully cooked boneless smoked pork shoulder (about 2 pounds), trimmed of "skin" and surrounding fat

8 ounces (about 1¼ cups) dried cannellini (white kidney) beans, picked over and rinsed

3 quarts water

2 potatoes, peeled and cut into 1-inch pieces (1¾ cups)

1 large leek, trimmed (leaving some green), split, washed, and cut into 1-inch pieces (2 cups)

1 large celery stalk, cut into ½-inch pieces (1 cup)

3 small carrots, peeled and cut into ½-inch pieces (1 cup)

3 parsnips, peeled and cut into ½-inch pieces (1 cup)

1 8-ounce piece savoy cabbage, cut into 2-inch pieces (4 cups)

½ teaspoon salt, or to taste

6–8 thin (¼-inch-thick) slices country bread

2 cups loosely packed grated Gruyère or Comté cheese (6 ounces)

Put the pork in a large pot and add the beans and water. Bring to a boil over high heat, cover, reduce the heat to low, and boil gently for 1 hour.

Add the potatoes, leek, celery, carrots, parsnips, cabbage, and salt and bring back to a boil. Cover, reduce the heat to low, and boil gently for 1 hour longer. By this time the meat will have separated into pieces. You should have 4 quarts of soup. If you have less, add water to make 4 quarts.

At serving time, preheat the broiler. Bring the soup back to a full boil and pour it into a 4- to 5-quart casserole dish or enameled cast-iron pot. (The pot should be nearly full.)

Arrange the bread slices on top in one layer to cover the soup and push them gently into the liquid until they are moist. Sprinkle the cheese on top and place the casserole under the hot broiler, about 4 inches from the heat. Broil for about 10 minutes, until the cheese on top is bubbly and brown. Carry the casserole to the table and serve the *garbure* in bowls or soup plates.

Salads

Salads

Boston Lettuce Salad
with Cream Dressing
Serves 6

🐝 **This dressing, a specialty** of my mother's and her own invention, is particularly good with tender salad greens such as Bibb, oak leaf, and Boston lettuce. The dressing can be prepared ahead, but it should not be tossed with the salad until serving time, or the greens will wilt. Take care when washing and drying the salad greens so as not to bruise the leaves.

½   teaspoon salt
½   teaspoon freshly ground white
       pepper
4   teaspoons red wine vinegar
6   tablespoons heavy cream
2   tablespoons canola oil
2   heads Boston lettuce, leaves gently torn
       into bite-sized pieces (8–10 cups),
       washed, and dried

Combine the salt, white pepper, vinegar, and cream in a large bowl. Beat with a whisk for about 20 seconds. The mixture should be foamy and creamy in consistency; it will thicken as you beat it. Add the oil and mix with a spoon to blend it.

At serving time, toss the lettuce gently in the dressing.

Spinach Salad
with Lemon Dressing
Serves 4

🐝 **A plain spinach salad** with lemon-garlic dressing is a satisfying accompaniment for any roast poultry. Use baby spinach if possible, and wait until serving time to toss it with the dressing.

12   ounces spinach, preferably baby
        spinach

DRESSING
1   teaspoon crushed and finely chopped
       garlic
1   tablespoon fresh lemon juice
⅛   teaspoon salt
¼   teaspoon freshly ground black pepper
2   tablespoons peanut oil

Remove and discard any tough stems and damaged or wilted areas from the spinach leaves; break them into 2-inch pieces if the leaves are large. (You should have about 8 loose cups.) Wash the spinach in a basin of cool water, then lift it from the water, drain, and dry thoroughly in a salad spinner, so no water remains to dilute the dressing.

FOR THE DRESSING: Combine all the ingredients in a bowl large enough to hold the spinach, whisking briefly to mix but not emulsify.

Add the spinach and toss well. Serve immediately, since the spinach will wilt quickly once it is mixed with the dressing.

Spinach and Mozzarella Salad with Croutons
Serves 4

✁ **Spinach tends to bruise** easily, so handle the leaves gently, without pressing or squeezing them, when washing them. Dry them thoroughly, so as not to dilute the dressing. I serve the salad topped with croutons made from a day-old baguette and thin slices of mozzarella cheese.

DRESSING

- 1 tablespoon Dijon mustard
- 1 tablespoon red wine vinegar
- 1 tablespoon light soy sauce
- 2 tablespoons extra-virgin olive oil
- ½ teaspoon freshly ground black pepper

- 1 5-ounce piece day-old baguette, cut into 16 thin (¼-inch-thick) slices
- 10 ounces small, tender spinach leaves
- 6 ounces mozzarella cheese, cut into ½-inch-thick slices (3–4 slices per person)

Preheat the oven to 400 degrees.

FOR THE DRESSING: Combine all the ingredients in a bowl large enough to hold the spinach. Set aside.

Arrange the baguette slices in a single layer on a cookie sheet and bake for 10 minutes, or until nicely browned.

Meanwhile, trim the spinach of any tough stems or damaged leaves. Wash the spinach in a basin of cool water, then lift it gently from the water, drain, and dry it thoroughly in a salad spinner.

At serving time, toss the spinach with the dressing in the bowl. Divide the salad among four plates, top with the croutons and mozzarella, and serve immediately.

Endive, Radicchio, Carrot, and Walnut Salad
Serves 4

✁ **Made with two bitter** greens, endive and radicchio, this salad awakens the taste buds. Carrots and walnuts provide a nice contrast in both taste and texture, and the mustard-flavored vinaigrette complements them.

- 2 Belgian endives, washed
- 1 small head radicchio, washed
- 2 carrots, peeled and shredded on the large holes of a box grater or in a food processor (1½ cups)
- ½ cup walnut pieces

DRESSING

- 1 tablespoon Dijon mustard
- ½ teaspoon salt
- ½ teaspoon freshly ground black pepper
- 1½ tablespoons red wine vinegar
- 3 tablespoons extra-virgin olive oil

Cut 1½ inches from the root end of the endives and the radicchio head and cut these pieces into ½-inch chunks. (You should have about 3 cups.) Reserve the endive and radicchio leaves. Combine the root-end chunks with the shredded carrots and nuts in a bowl.

FOR THE DRESSING: Combine all the dressing ingredients in a small bowl. Add the dressing to the endive and radicchio pieces, carrots, and nuts. Toss well.

Arrange the reserved radicchio leaves attractively on four plates and spoon the dressed mixture into the center of the leaves. Arrange the endive leaf tips so they stand, pointed tips up, next to one another all around the dressed salads. Serve immediately.

Frisée with Croutons and Spicy Olives
Serves 4

❧ **Frisée, also called curly** endive, is cultivated so that its leaves are pale (nearly white), mild, and tender. It can be costly, so feel free to substitute other greens. Spicy olives and sun-dried tomatoes in oil can be found at most supermarkets.

About 1½ cups 1-inch pieces bread, preferably from a French country loaf
1 tablespoon olive, canola, or peanut oil

DRESSING

1 tablespoon spicy mustard
1 teaspoon crushed and finely chopped garlic
¼ teaspoon salt
¼ teaspoon freshly ground black pepper
2 teaspoons red wine vinegar
3 tablespoons extra-virgin olive oil

1 large or 2 small heads frisée, any damaged leaves removed, the remainder cut into 2-inch pieces (5–6 cups)
¼ cup pitted spicy green olives
¼ cup sun-dried tomatoes in oil

Drop the bread cubes into a skillet and sprinkle the oil over them. Toss gently to coat the bread lightly with the oil and cook over high heat, tossing occasionally, until the cubes are browned on all sides. Remove from the skillet and set aside.

FOR THE DRESSING: Mix the mustard, garlic, salt, pepper, and vinegar together in a serving bowl large enough to hold the greens. Stir in the oil.

At serving time, add the frisée, olives, and sun-dried tomatoes to the dressing and toss thoroughly. Divide the salad among four salad plates, sprinkle the croutons on top, and serve immediately.

Black Truffle Salad
Serves 6

❧ **Serve this extravagant salad** for a very special dinner. Its mild dressing highlights the taste of the truffles.

2 cups thin zucchini slices (from small zucchini)
Salt
2 medium black truffles (about 3 ounces)

DRESSING

2 tablespoons peanut oil
1 tablespoon walnut or hazelnut oil
1 tablespoon red wine vinegar
½ teaspoon salt
¼ teaspoon freshly ground black pepper

3 cups loosely packed mâche, washed and dried
3 cups loosely packed torn Bibb lettuce
1 cup julienned mushrooms
Truffle or peanut oil, for sprinkling
Freshly ground black pepper

Preheat the oven to 400 degrees.

Arrange the sliced zucchini on a cookie sheet and sprinkle lightly with salt. Bake for 3 to 4 minutes, until slightly softened and wilted.

Meanwhile, clean and peel the truffles. (The skin can be chopped and stored in cognac for use in sauces.) Thinly slice the truffles with a truffle slicer or vegetable peeler.

FOR THE DRESSING: Combine the oils, vinegar, salt, and pepper in a bowl.

Just before serving, toss the greens and mush-

rooms in the dressing and arrange on six plates. Arrange a ring of zucchini around each salad and arrange the sliced truffles on top. Sprinkle or brush the truffles lightly with truffle or peanut oil, sprinkle with pepper, and serve.

Garlicky Romaine with Croutons
Serves 6

❧ **I make this salad** with romaine lettuce because it holds up well to the garlicky mustard dressing. The chewy croutons made with stale bread complement the salad perfectly.

CROUTONS

3	tablespoons peanut or corn oil
2½	cups 1-inch pieces stale country bread

DRESSING

1	tablespoon crushed and finely chopped garlic
½	teaspoon salt
½	teaspoon freshly ground black pepper
1	tablespoon grainy mustard, such as Meaux
2	tablespoons red wine vinegar
⅓	cup peanut or corn oil

1	large head romaine lettuce, damaged leaves removed, the remainder cut into 1½-inch pieces, washed, and dried (about 10 cups lightly packed)

FOR THE CROUTONS: Heat the oil in a large skillet. When it is hot, add the bread and sauté for about 4 minutes, until nicely browned on all sides. Remove from the skillet and set aside.

FOR THE DRESSING: Combine the garlic, salt, pepper, mustard, vinegar, and oil in a bowl suitable for serving the salad.

When ready to serve, add the lettuce to the bowl and toss with the dressing. Sprinkle with the croutons and serve immediately.

Romaine with Creamy Yogurt Dressing
Serves 4

❧ **This light dressing substitutes** yogurt for most of the oil. Cool and tangy, the yogurt gives the dressing a creamy consistency and a refreshingly tart taste.

DRESSING

1	tablespoon white wine vinegar
¼	teaspoon salt
¼	teaspoon freshly ground black pepper
3	tablespoons plain yogurt
1	tablespoon extra-virgin olive oil

8–10	ounces romaine lettuce, leaves cut lengthwise in half, torn into 1½- to 2-inch pieces, washed, and dried (about 6 cups)
1	tablespoon chopped fresh herbs (tarragon, chives, and/or parsley)

FOR THE DRESSING: Whisk together the vinegar, salt, pepper, and yogurt in a bowl large enough to hold the lettuce. Whisk in the oil.

Add the lettuce to the dressing and toss until coated. Sprinkle on the fresh herbs and serve immediately.

"Caesar" Salad with Blue Cheese
Serves 1

✄ **Here's a salad** I suggest when people ask me what they can prepare when dining alone. The ingredient amounts can be increased, of course, to accommodate any number of guests. Not a true Caesar salad, because it doesn't contain raw egg, this one includes blue cheese in place of the standard Parmesan, or, if you like, some Camembert or goat cheese.

In keeping with traditional Caesar salad recipes, lemon juice replaces vinegar in the dressing, which also includes garlic and anchovy.

CROUTONS

  1   slice stale bread (about ¾ ounce)
  1½ teaspoons canola or peanut oil

DRESSING

  ½   garlic clove
  1   anchovy fillet, coarsely chopped
  2   teaspoons fresh lemon juice
  1   tablespoon olive or peanut oil
      Pinch of salt
      Pinch of freshly ground black pepper

  2   cups loosely packed 2-inch pieces romaine lettuce
  2   tablespoons crumbled blue cheese, or a combination of blue and Camembert or goat cheese

Preheat the oven to 400 degrees.

FOR THE CROUTONS: Brush both sides of the bread with the oil and place it on a small cookie sheet. Bake for 10 minutes, or until nicely browned on both sides. Break or cut the toasted bread into 1-inch pieces.

FOR THE DRESSING: Mash the garlic with the tines of a fork into a coarse puree. Combine it in a medium bowl with the anchovy, lemon juice, oil, salt, and pepper.

No more than 30 minutes before serving time, add the romaine to the dressing and toss well. Sprinkle with the croutons and cheese and serve.

Watercress Salad
Serves 4

✄ **When I roast a** duck or a chicken, I like to serve it with this salad, which is tossed with a dressing flavored with the fat of the roasted bird. It's a harmonious combination. The salad also goes with roast pork, veal, or beef. The slightly pungent watercress is set off well by the light dressing. Make sure that you toss your salad at the last moment, because watercress wilts quickly once it is dressed.

DRESSING

  1   tablespoon red wine vinegar
  ¼   teaspoon salt
  ½   teaspoon freshly ground black pepper
  2   tablespoons peanut or canola oil
  1   tablespoon rendered duck or chicken fat

  2   large or 3 small bunches watercress

FOR THE DRESSING: Mix all the ingredients together in a large bowl.

Cut the lower 1½ to 2 inches off the watercress

stems (these can be reserved for soup). Wash the watercress tops and dry thoroughly. (You should have about 5 cups.)

At serving time, toss the watercress with the dressing. Divide the salad among four plates and serve immediately.

Arugula and Olive Salad
Serves 4

✶ **Arugula, called *roquette*** in France and sometimes rocket in the United States, is a spicy salad green that goes particularly well with lemon dressing. Serve the salad garnished with olives and croutons.

About 12 ounces arugula

CROUTONS

   2 thick slices firm white bread
       (2 ounces)
1½ teaspoons olive oil

DRESSING

1½ tablespoons fresh lemon juice
   2 tablespoons extra-virgin olive oil
  ¼ teaspoon salt
  ⅛ teaspoon freshly ground black pepper

 20 oil-cured black olives, pitted and cut into
      ½-inch pieces

Preheat the oven to 400 degrees.

Remove and discard the tough stems from the arugula. Wash and dry it thoroughly, taking care not to bruise the leaves. (You should have 8 lightly packed cups.)

FOR THE CROUTONS: Trim the crusts from the bread and cut the bread into ½-inch cubes. (You should have 1¼ cups.) Place the bread cubes

in a bowl, add the olive oil, and rub the oil gently into the cubes to coat them well. Arrange the cubes on a cookie sheet and bake for 8 minutes, or until they are well browned. Set aside.

FOR THE DRESSING: Mix all the ingredients together in a bowl large enough to hold the arugula.

At serving time, add the arugula to the dressing and toss well to combine. Divide the arugula among four plates, sprinkle the olives and croutons over and around the greens, and serve.

Mesclun, Avocado, and Tomato Salad
Serves 4

✶ **Cubes of ripe avocado,** tossed with a little lemon juice and olive oil, are piled on top of thick tomato slices and presented on a bed of mesclun greens with a lemon dressing. If you can't find mesclun, a mixture of young greens and herbs, substitute Boston lettuce or other greens.

 1 large ripe avocado
 2 teaspoons fresh lemon juice
 1 tablespoon extra-virgin olive oil
¼ teaspoon salt
¼ teaspoon freshly ground black pepper
 1 large ripe tomato (at least 12 ounces)

DRESSING

1½ tablespoons fresh lemon juice
 3 tablespoons extra-virgin olive oil
 ¼ teaspoon salt
 ¼ teaspoon freshly ground black pepper

 4 cups loosely packed mesclun (a mixture
    of young, tender greens and herbs),
    washed and dried
 ¼ cup coarsely chopped fresh cilantro

No more than 2 hours before serving, cut the avocado in half, remove the pit, and cut the flesh into ½-inch pieces. Toss the avocado pieces with the lemon juice, olive oil, and ⅛ teaspoon each of the salt and pepper in a small bowl. Set aside.

At serving time, cut the tomato into 4 thick slices and sprinkle with the remaining ⅛ teaspoon each salt and pepper.

FOR THE DRESSING: Combine all the ingredients in a bowl large enough to hold the salad greens.

Add the mesclun to the dressing and toss thoroughly. Divide the greens among four salad plates. Place a slice of tomato in the center of each plate and top with one quarter of the avocado. Sprinkle with the cilantro and serve immediately.

Curried Coleslaw
Serves 4

A dash of curry gives this coleslaw an interesting tang. An invigorating accompaniment, it's perfect with fish. It can be made ahead; the slaw will keep, refrigerated, for a couple of days.

1 small head cabbage or ½ larger head
(1¼ pounds)

DRESSING

⅓ cup mayonnaise
3 tablespoons cider vinegar
1 tablespoon sugar
1 teaspoon salt
2 teaspoons poppy seeds
¼ teaspoon Tabasco sauce
1 teaspoon curry powder

1 large carrot, peeled and shredded on the large holes of a box grater or in a food processor (1 lightly packed cup)

Trim the cabbage, removing and discarding any damaged parts. Shred it on a vegetable slicer or cut it into thin strips with a sharp knife. (You should have 5 to 6 lightly packed cups.)

FOR THE DRESSING: Mix together all the ingredients in a bowl large enough to hold the finished coleslaw.

Add the cabbage and carrot to the dressing and mix well. Serve immediately, or cover and refrigerate to serve later.

Napa Cabbage Salad
Serves 6

Napa cabbage resembles a pale, compact head of romaine lettuce. Delicately flavored, it makes a deliciously crunchy coleslaw. Wash the cabbage and prepare the dressing hours ahead if you like, then mix them together shortly before serving so the dressing softens the cabbage a little.

DRESSING

2 teaspoons crushed and finely chopped garlic
½ teaspoon salt
½ teaspoon freshly ground black pepper
2 teaspoons Dijon mustard
1 tablespoon red wine vinegar
1 tablespoon light soy sauce
3 tablespoons canola oil
1 tablespoon toasted sesame oil

1 firm head napa cabbage (about 1 pound)
3 tablespoons chopped walnuts

FOR THE DRESSING: Combine all the ingredients in a large salad bowl and mix well.

Trim the cabbage, removing and discarding any damaged or wilted leaves, and cut it crosswise into 1-inch-wide strips. (You should have about

8 cups.) Wash well and spin dry in a salad spinner (any moisture will dilute the dressing).

About 10 to 15 minutes before serving, add the cabbage and walnuts to the dressing and toss well. Let stand so the dressing can penetrate the cabbage and soften it slightly, then serve.

Coleslaw with Anchovies
Serves 6

✀ **This highly flavored coleslaw** can be made with white or red cabbage or with both. The dressing is an *anchoïade*, a pungent, glossy garlic and anchovy sauce.

The salad can also be made with iceberg lettuce or any other crunchy, slightly tough salad green, such as escarole, chicory, or frisée. Cabbage does not wilt as fast as lettuce, so the slaw can be prepared an hour or so ahead.

DRESSING

4–5	garlic cloves
1	2-ounce tin anchovy fillets in oil
1	tablespoon red wine vinegar
⅓	cup olive or vegetable oil
½	teaspoon salt
½	teaspoon freshly ground black pepper

8	cups shredded red or white cabbage, or half red and half white
	Fresh parsley sprigs, for garnish

FOR THE DRESSING: Crush and chop the garlic with the anchovy fillets to form a puree. Stir the puree into the vinegar, oil, salt, and pepper in a large bowl. (Do not make the sauce in a food processor, or it will thicken too much, like a mayonnaise; you want a transparent dressing the consistency of a broken vinaigrette.)

Mix the cabbage with the dressing: If you are using both red and white cabbage, mix them with the dressing in separate bowls, then transfer the red cabbage to a pretty glass or crystal bowl, make a well in the center to form a nest, and mound the white cabbage in the center. Or, if you are using only one type of cabbage, mix it with all the dressing and transfer to a serving bowl. Decorate with little sprigs of parsley.

Asian Savoy Salad
Serves 4

✀ **With its pale and** darker green colors, savoy cabbage is attractive, and its crinkly leaves hold a dressing well. The savory mixture of oyster sauce and garlic goes nicely with the cabbage. This salad is great as a side dish for roast or grilled poultry, meat, or fish, and it also makes a good first course.

DRESSING

2	tablespoons rice vinegar
1½	tablespoons dark soy sauce
1	tablespoon oyster sauce
½	teaspoon Tabasco sauce
1	teaspoon sugar
3	garlic cloves, crushed and finely chopped (2 teaspoons)
2	tablespoons toasted sesame oil

8	ounces tender savoy cabbage leaves, tough lower part of central ribs removed and discarded, leaves finely shredded (about 6 cups loosely packed)
½	cup julienned carrots (2-inch-long matchsticks)

FOR THE DRESSING: Combine all the ingredients in a plastic bag large enough to hold the cabbage.

Add the cabbage and toss it with the dressing. Allow the mixture to macerate for at least 2 hours in the refrigerator.

Transfer the salad and dressing to a serving bowl, sprinkle with the carrots, and serve.

JULIENNED CARROTS

To make julienned carrot strips, cut a peeled and trimmed carrot into very thin lengthwise slices, using a vegetable slicer, a sharp knife, or even a vegetable peeler. Stack the slices and cut them first lengthwise, then crosswise, to create matchsticks about 2 inches long.

Composed Salad of Greens, Goat Cheese, and Caramelized Pecans
Serves 4

✄ **A composed salad consists** of greens and any of an almost endless variety of other ingredients, from cooked vegetables to fruits, nuts, poultry, lamb, beef, fish, or shellfish, arranged on a plate or platter, rather than tossed. In this one, I add cheese, apple, and caramelized pecans to tender greens. The combination makes an ideal summer supper or lunch main course or elegant dinner first course.

CARAMELIZED PECANS

¼ cup pecan halves
½ teaspoon canola oil
1 tablespoon sugar
   Pinch of salt
   Pinch of cayenne pepper

1 medium apple, preferably russet or Golden Delicious
1½ teaspoons fresh lemon juice

DRESSING

1½ tablespoons oil, preferably a mixture of walnut, hazelnut, and/or canola
1½ teaspoons sherry vinegar
⅛ teaspoon salt
¼ teaspoon freshly ground black pepper

4 cups salad greens, preferably mesclun (a mixture of young, tender greens and herbs), washed and dried
1 ounce semi-dry or hard goat cheese, crumbled into ½-inch pieces

FOR THE PECANS: Put the pecans in a skillet and cover (barely) with water. Bring to a simmer over high heat and immediately drain.

Return the pecans to the pan and add the oil, sugar, salt, and cayenne. Cook over medium-high heat, stirring, until the nuts brown and the sugar mixture caramelizes. Transfer to a plate to cool.

Halve the apple and remove the core. Cut it into ½-inch-thick slices. Stack the slices and cut them into ½-inch-wide strips. Mix the apple strips with the lemon juice and set aside.

FOR THE DRESSING: Mix all the ingredients together in a large bowl.

At serving time, toss the greens with the dressing and arrange on individual plates. Sprinkle with the apple strips, crumbled cheese, and pecans. Serve immediately.

Mâche with Pecans, Pears, and Goat Cheese

Serves 6

❧ **I originally created this** flavorful combination of mâche or field salad, pecans, goat cheese, pears, and walnut oil dressing for Sally Darr at her restaurant La Tulipe in New York City. Mâche, or corn salad, also called lamb's lettuce, is planted around the end of August and gets large enough to be ready for picking at the end of November. After the first frost, it becomes sweeter and more tender.

The pears must be ripe — Bartlett, Comice, or Anjou are best here. A semi-hard goat cheese, preferably a small round variety, is best, and the pecan halves should be freshly toasted.

36	small bunches mâche
1	tablespoon unsalted butter
36–40	pecan halves
	Pinch of salt
3	ripe Bartlett, Comice, or Anjou pears
1	tablespoon fresh lemon juice
12	ounces semi-hard goat cheese, preferably a small round cheese

DRESSING

1	tablespoon sherry vinegar
2	tablespoons walnut or hazelnut oil
1	tablespoon peanut or safflower oil
¼	teaspoon salt
¼	teaspoon coarsely ground black pepper

Carefully wash the mâche in cold water. Drain and dry in a salad spinner.

Heat the butter in a medium skillet. When it is hot, add the pecans and salt and toss, cooking for a couple of minutes until lightly browned. Set aside to cool.

Halve the pears lengthwise. Core and peel them and cut each half lengthwise into quarters. Sprinkle with the lemon juice to prevent discoloration.

Cut the goat cheese into small wedges.

FOR THE DRESSING: Combine all the ingredients in a small bowl and mix well.

At serving time, arrange 4 slices of pear around the edge of each plate, with the cheese and pecans in between them. Mound 6 bunches mâche in the center of each plate. Sprinkle the mâche with the dressing and serve immediately.

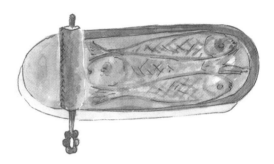

Arugula and Sardine Salad

Serves 4

❧ **I love canned sardines,** preferring the plump ones in olive oil from Portugal, Spain, or the Southwest of France. The peppery taste of arugula balances perfectly with the mild, fatty taste of the fish. This salad makes a great first course.

½	cup chopped onion
3	plum tomatoes, cut into 1-inch dice (1½ cups)
2½	tablespoons extra-virgin olive oil
1½	tablespoons red wine vinegar
¼	teaspoon salt
¼	teaspoon freshly ground black pepper
4	cups arugula, washed and dried
⅓	cup pitted green olives, cut into ½-inch pieces
1	4-ounce can sardines in olive oil

Mix all the ingredients except the sardines in a bowl.

Divide the salad among four plates. Arrange the sardines on top, sprinkle on some of the oil from the can, and serve.

Bressane Frisée Salad with Chicken Livers and Hearts
Serves 6

❦ **I named this flavorful,** inexpensive salad after the place where I was born, Bourg-en-Bresse, the area of France best known for its excellent chickens. In this recipe, the skin of a chicken is used (the meat is reserved for another meal), along with gizzards, hearts, and livers. Small boiling potatoes and an earthy garlic dressing complete this country salad. The frisée can also be served by itself with the same dressing.

Choose frisée that is white inside to ensure that it will be tender with a nutty taste; the outer leaves are bitter and tougher. If frisée is not available, substitute escarole or a mixture of romaine and iceberg lettuce.

CRACKLINGS

    Skin from 1 chicken or equivalent from chicken parts
¼ teaspoon salt

INNARDS

6 chicken gizzards
4 chicken livers
12 chicken hearts

2 heads frisée
6 small boiling potatoes (12 ounces)

DRESSING

2 teaspoons finely chopped garlic

2 tablespoons Dijon mustard
1 tablespoon cider vinegar
¼ teaspoon salt
¼ teaspoon freshly ground black pepper
2 tablespoons olive oil
2 tablespoons canola oil

3 tablespoons unsalted butter
¼ teaspoon salt
¼ teaspoon freshly ground black pepper
⅓ cup Basic Brown Sauce (page 613)

Preheat the oven to 400 degrees.

FOR THE CRACKLINGS: Spread the chicken skin on a baking sheet, with the side of the skin that touched the meat down. Sprinkle with the salt and bake for 20 minutes, or until very crisp. Remove the crisp skin to a plate and set aside. (The rendered chicken fat can be used to sauté potatoes or for a stew.)

MEANWHILE, FOR THE INNARDS: To remove the fleshy part of the gizzards, cut down along the lump of meat, sliding your knife around it, and remove it from the skin in one piece. Cut each piece into 2 or 3 slivers; set aside.

Cut away and discard any green areas on the livers and remove any sinews. Cut the livers into slivers about ½ inch wide; set aside.

Cut the hearts lengthwise into quarters or thirds; set aside.

FOR THE SALAD GREENS AND POTATOES: Trim off any dark green areas from the frisée and cut the remainder into 1½-inch pieces. (You should have about 8 cups loosely packed.) Wash in a bowl of cold water, then lift the greens from the water and dry thoroughly in a salad spinner.

Cover the potatoes with water in a saucepan, bring to a boil, and boil gently for about 30 minutes, until tender. Drain. The potatoes should be served lukewarm. Cut them (with or without the skin, as you prefer) into ½-inch-thick slices.

MEANWHILE, FOR THE DRESSING: Combine the garlic, mustard, vinegar, salt, and pepper in a small bowl, mixing well. Slowly add the olive and canola oils in a stream, whisking constantly. Set aside.

AT SERVING TIME, COOK THE INNARDS: Melt the butter in a skillet large enough to hold all the chicken pieces in one layer. When it is hot, add the chicken gizzards and sauté for 30 seconds over high heat. Add the heart pieces and sauté for another 15 seconds. Finally, add the livers, salt, and pepper and sauté for about 1½ minutes longer. Add the brown sauce and bring just to a boil. Set aside.

Combine the greens with the dressing in a large bowl, tossing well to mix. Add the potatoes, tossing gently to avoid breaking them. Arrange on six plates.

Spoon 1 to 2 tablespoons of the chicken innards on top of each salad, along with 1 to 2 tablespoons of the juices in the skillet. Break the chicken skin into pieces, sprinkle the cracklings on top of the salad, and serve immediately.

Dandelion Salad with Bacon and Croutons
Serves 6

☙ **Served on cold plates** and accompanied by red wine, this salad breaks traditional rules. Customarily, when a salad is made with a vinegar dressing, wine is avoided, because it conflicts with the vinegar. This version, originally from the Lyonnaise region, is an exception. It goes especially well with a cool light Beaujolais.

¼ cup peanut oil
15–20 ½-inch-thick slices French bread
(if the loaf is large, cut 10 slices and cut them in half)

1 large garlic clove, plus 2 teaspoons chopped garlic
1 4-ounce piece pancetta
6 anchovy fillets, chopped
¼ cup extra-virgin olive oil
Salt and freshly ground black pepper
1 pound dandelion greens, preferably wild, washed and dried
2 tablespoons red wine vinegar
3 hard-cooked eggs (see page 66), quartered

Heat 3 tablespoons of the peanut oil in a large skillet. Add the bread and brown on both sides. Let cool enough to handle, then rub each piece with the garlic clove.

Cut the pancetta into ½-inch-thick strips and then into ½-inch pieces.

Drop the pieces into a saucepan, cover with cold water, and bring to a boil. Let simmer for 3 to 4 minutes. Drain in a sieve and cool under cold water.

Cook the pancetta pieces in a skillet with the remaining 1 tablespoon peanut oil over medium heat, stirring occasionally, until crisp and brown, about 8 minutes.

Meanwhile, mix the anchovies, chopped gar-

LARDONS

Lardons are small pieces of pork used to season salads or savory dishes. They are made from salt-cured pork (pancetta) or smoked salt-cured pork (bacon). When preparing lardons, I usually purchase a slab or block of the cured meat, which I cut into slices and then into little cubes, each about ½ inch square. You can, of course, buy presliced versions of pancetta or bacon and then cut them into small pieces.

lic, and olive oil with some salt and pepper in a large salad bowl.

Add the dandelion greens to the salad bowl. Pour the pancetta and any fat on top of the salad. Immediately pour the vinegar into the hot skillet and shake the pan back and forth. Pour over the salad and toss, then add the egg quarters and croutons and serve immediately.

Beets with Mâche
Serves 6 to 8

One of my favorites for the holidays, this classic winter salad features mâche, also called field salad, corn salad, or lamb's lettuce. The vinaigrette is enriched with an egg yolk, which makes the mixture emulsify, creating a dressing with the consistency of a light mayonnaise.

4 medium beets (about 1¼ pounds)
Salt

DRESSING
1 large egg yolk
1 tablespoon tarragon vinegar
1½ teaspoons Dijon mustard
1 tablespoon chopped shallots
(1–2 shallots) or scallion whites
¼ teaspoon salt
¼ teaspoon freshly ground white pepper
⅓ cup vegetable oil (or a mixture of olive and peanut oil)

6 cups mâche, washed and dried

Cut the tops off the beets, leaving about ½ inch. Put the beets in a saucepan, cover with tepid water, add a dash of salt, and bring to a boil. Cover, reduce the heat to low, and cook for 1 to 1¼ hours, or until the beets are very tender when pierced with the point of a sharp knife.

MEANWHILE, FOR THE DRESSING: Combine the egg yolk, vinegar, mustard, shallots or scallions, salt, and white pepper in a bowl and whip together with a whisk for about 10 seconds. Add the oil very slowly, whisking constantly.

When the beets are tender, drain and cool them. When they are cool enough to handle, peel and cut into ½-inch-thick slices. (If you are concerned about staining, wear plastic gloves and cover your cutting board with plastic wrap.) Stack the slices together and cut them into ½-inch-wide julienne strips.

Mix the beets with the vinaigrette.

At serving time, add the mâche to the beets and toss together well.

COOKING BEETS THE QUICK WAY

If you have a microwave oven, by all means cook your beets in it; they will take less than half the time. Otherwise, cook them in the conventional manner, on top of the stove. Be sure to protect your work surface with newspaper when peeling them and wash your hands directly afterward, since beets stain whatever they touch.

Beet Salad
in Sour Cream Dressing
Serves 6

✎ **Try to get organic** beets for this recipe. Seasoned with sour cream, cider vinegar, a dash of sugar, and lots of sliced onion, they make a delightful first course or accompaniment to a roast.

3–4 large beets (about 1¾ pounds)
  1 cup halved and very thinly sliced
      onion
  ½ cup sour cream
 1½ tablespoons cider vinegar
  1 teaspoon salt
  ½ teaspoon freshly ground black pepper
 1½ teaspoons sugar

Cut the tops off the beets, leaving about ½ inch. Put the beets in a large saucepan, cover with salted tepid water, and bring to a boil over high heat. Reduce the heat to low, cover, and cook gently for 1¼ to 1½ hours, until tender. Drain and cool to lukewarm.

Peel the beets and cut them into ¼-inch-thick slices. (If you are concerned about staining, wear plastic gloves and cover your cutting board with plastic wrap.) Put the slices in a bowl and stir in the remaining ingredients. Serve at room temperature, not cold.

Carrot and Celery Root Salad
in Mustard Dressing
Serves 6

✎ **A mixture of celery** root and carrots with a mustard-mayonnaise dressing, this salad is always welcome at a buffet. It is particularly good served with Eggs in Aspic (page 73). The dressing

is also good with poached fish or used for a beef salad made from leftover boiled beef.

If you are in a hurry, you can replace the mustard dressing with about 1 cup regular mayonnaise mixed with ¼ cup Dijon mustard.

  1 large celery root (celeriac, about 1 pound)
  2 carrots

DRESSING
  3 large egg yolks
  ¼ cup Dijon mustard
  ½ teaspoon salt
  ½ teaspoon freshly ground black pepper
  ½ cup olive oil
  ½ cup peanut oil

Fresh parsley sprigs, for garnish

Peel the celery root to remove all the skin, and cut it in half. Sometimes the center of celery root gets slightly soft; if that is the case, remove any soft areas. Cut each half into thin slices (no more than ¼ inch thick). Stack the slices and cut into fine julienne strips. (You should have about 4 cups.)

Peel the carrots and cut them lengthwise into thin slices (⅛ inch thick), using a vegetable slicer or a sharp knife. Stack the slices and cut them a few at a time into very fine julienne strips. (You should have about 1½ cups.)

FOR THE DRESSING: Put the egg yolks, mustard, salt, and pepper in a bowl large enough to hold the salad and whisk until well blended.

Slowly add the oils in a stream, whisking constantly. The dressing will be quite thick.

Combine the celery root and carrots with the dressing and toss to mix well. Garnish with the parsley and serve.

Carrot and Parsley Salad
Serves 4

✂ **Lots of parsley and** garlic flavor this salad, which is seasoned with a simple oil and vinegar dressing. The salad is even better prepared an hour ahead, to allow the dressing to soften the carrots and parsley. It is great in sandwiches.

4–5 carrots, peeled and shredded on the large holes of a box grater or in a food processor (2½ cups)
1¼ cups fresh flat-leaf parsley leaves
2 large garlic cloves, crushed and finely chopped (1½ teaspoons)
½ teaspoon salt
¼ teaspoon freshly ground black pepper
1 tablespoon red wine vinegar or cider vinegar
3 tablespoons peanut or safflower oil

Put the carrots, parsley leaves, and garlic in a bowl. Stir in the remaining ingredients and mix well. Serve.

Carrot and Scallion Salad
Serves 6

✂ **The heat of the** Tabasco sauce and the spiciness of the curry powder in this dressing are accented by the pungency of the cilantro — flavors that combine well with the crunchy carrots. The salad can be prepared ahead and refrigerated un-

til serving time. Any leftover salad is excellent in sandwiches with cold cuts or tuna.

DRESSING
1 teaspoon salt
1 teaspoon freshly ground black pepper
¼ teaspoon Tabasco sauce
2 tablespoons rice vinegar
½ teaspoon curry powder
⅓ cup safflower or canola oil

1 pound carrots, peeled and shredded on the large holes of a box grater or in a food processor (about 4 cups)
2 bunches (about 12) scallions, trimmed (leaving some green) and cut into ¼-inch-thick slices (2 cups)
2 garlic cloves, crushed and very finely chopped (about 1 teaspoon)
½ cup coarsely chopped fresh cilantro
8–10 lettuce leaves, for garnish
Crusty French bread

FOR THE DRESSING: Combine all the ingredients in a large bowl.

Add the carrots, scallions, and garlic to the dressing and mix well. Stir in the cilantro.

Wash the lettuce leaves, removing the center rib from each if it is thick and tough. Dry the leaves and arrange on individual serving plates. Arrange spoonfuls of the carrot mixture on top of the lettuce and serve with crusty bread.

Carrot and Sunflower Seed Salad on Red Leaf Lettuce
Serves 6

✂ **The dressing for this** salad is best prepared with a nut oil, which complements the nutty flavor of the crunchy, highly nutritious sunflower seeds. The salad can be served as a side or a first course, and it is also good as a sandwich filling, either on its own or with cold cuts.

6 medium carrots (about 12 ounces), peeled and shredded on the large holes of a box grater or in a food processor (about 3 cups)
½ cup sunflower seeds
2 teaspoons crushed and chopped garlic
½ cup chopped mild onion, such as Vidalia or Walla Walla
½ teaspoon salt
1 teaspoon freshly ground black pepper
2 tablespoons sherry vinegar
5 tablespoons peanut, almond, walnut, or hazelnut oil
6 red lettuce leaves, for garnish

Combine the carrots, sunflower seeds, garlic, onion, salt, pepper, vinegar, and oil in a bowl. Mix well and serve on the lettuce leaves.

Warm Cauliflower and Carrot Salad
Serves 6

✶ **This salad makes a** great main course for a vegetarian lunch. If you prepare it ahead, warm it for a few seconds in a microwave oven or heat in a conventional oven to take the chill off before serving. The dressing can be doubled and the leftovers stored in a small jar in the refrigerator for up to a few weeks. It's excellent on any green salad.

4 medium carrots (about 8 ounces)
4 celery stalks, preferably tender inner stalks
5–6 scallions

1 small head cauliflower (about 1 pound), cored and separated into 1½-inch florets
6 large radishes, cut into ¼-inch-thick slices
2 cups diced (1-inch) mushrooms

DRESSING

3 tablespoons hot or Dijon mustard
⅓ cup peanut oil
2 tablespoons cider vinegar
½ teaspoon salt
½ teaspoon freshly ground black pepper

Bring 4 cups water to a boil in a medium saucepan. Meanwhile, peel the carrots and celery and cut into julienne strips, 2 inches by ½ inch. Trim the scallions, quarter them lengthwise, and cut them into 2-inch-long strips.

Add the carrots, celery, and cauliflower to the boiling water and cook for 2 minutes. Stir in the scallions and radishes and cook for 10 seconds; drain (reserve the vegetable stock for soup).

FOR THE DRESSING: Mix all the ingredients together in a serving bowl.

Add the hot vegetables and the mushrooms and toss to coat with the dressing. Serve lukewarm or at room temperature.

Celery and Apple Salad
Serves 6

✶ **The sweetness of the** apples is offset nicely by the mildly acidic combination of sour cream and lemon juice. Don't peel the apples; along with the celery, the skin lends texture to the dish.

6 celery stalks (about 8 ounces), preferably tender inner stalks
2 medium Red Delicious apples (12 ounces)

- 1½ tablespoons fresh lemon juice
- ⅓ cup heavy cream
- ½ teaspoon salt
- ¾ teaspoon freshly ground black pepper
- 1 teaspoon sugar
- 6 romaine lettuce leaves, for garnish

Remove any leaves from the celery stalks (reserve the trimmings for stock), and if the outer surface is tough or fibrous, peel the stalks with a vegetable peeler. Cut the stalks into 2-inch-long pieces, then press the pieces flat on a cutting board and cut them lengthwise into thin strips. (You should have about 2½ cups.) Put them in a bowl.

Wash the apples thoroughly in warm water, scraping them lightly with a sharp knife if necessary to remove any surface wax. Stand each apple upright on the cutting board and cut vertically into ½-inch-thick slices — stop when you reach the core, pivot the apple, and cut again, until only the core remains. Then stack the apple slices together, a few at a time, and cut them into ½-inch-wide strips. Add the strips to the celery, along with all the remaining ingredients except the lettuce leaves, and mix well.

To serve, arrange the lettuce leaves on six individual plates and spoon the salad onto the leaves.

Cucumber, Dill, and Mint Summer Salad

Serves 6

This salad of onion, cucumber, dill, and mint makes a refreshing addition to most any summer menu. It's best if it's refrigerated for at least 2 to 3 hours before serving.

- 2 large cucumbers, peeled, halved lengthwise, seeded, and thinly sliced (about 4 cups)
- 1 large mild onion, such as Vidalia, thinly sliced (about 2 cups)
- ⅓ cup shredded fresh dill leaves
- ⅓ cup shredded fresh mint leaves
- 1 teaspoon salt
- 3 tablespoons cider vinegar
- 1 tablespoon canola oil
- 2 teaspoons sugar
- ½ teaspoon Tabasco sauce

Combine all the ingredients in a large bowl. Mix well and refrigerate for at least 30 minutes, and as long as 8 hours.

Serve cold.

Grilled Eggplant on Greens

Serves 4

My family loves the unique taste that grilling gives eggplant, and this simple recipe makes an ideal first course. I like to serve the eggplant on young homegrown greens such as radicchio and arugula. Their slightly bitter flavor offsets the eggplant's natural sweetness. Sweet rice vinegar and salty soy sauce combine with the olive oil to make a light but tasty dressing.

- 2 small firm eggplants, preferably the long narrow Japanese variety (about 1 pound total)
- 1 tablespoon canola oil
- ½ teaspoon salt
- 2 tablespoons olive oil
- 1 tablespoon dark soy sauce
- 1 tablespoon rice vinegar
- 3 cups loosely packed mixed salad greens (see the headnote), washed and dried

Cut off and discard the ends of the eggplants, and cut them lengthwise into ½-inch-thick slices.

(You should have about 8 slices.) Rub the slices on both sides with the canola oil and sprinkle with the salt.

Heat a grill until very hot. Place the eggplant slices on the grill and cook them for about 3 minutes on each side, until softened.

Meanwhile, combine the olive oil, soy sauce, and vinegar in a small bowl.

Arrange the salad greens on a platter and top with the grilled eggplant. Pour the dressing over both and serve immediately.

Braised Shiitake Mushrooms on Bitter Greens
Serves 4

❧ **I prefer dried shiitake** mushrooms to fresh, because they have more flavor. (If you use fresh shiitakes, discard the stems.) The quality of dried mushrooms in Asian markets varies widely. I tend to buy the costlier winter specimens; usually the caps are cracked with white lines and they are thicker, meatier, and more flavorful than other dried shiitakes.

Bitter-tasting radicchio and Belgian endive give distinction to this first course.

16 dried shiitake mushrooms,
      preferably winter specimens
      (see the headnote)
 3 cups hot water
 1 small head radicchio
 1 large Belgian endive
 ¼ teaspoon salt
 ¼ teaspoon freshly ground black pepper
1½ tablespoons olive oil

DRESSING
1–2 garlic cloves, crushed and finely chopped
      (1 teaspoon)
 ¼ teaspoon salt
 ¼ teaspoon freshly ground black pepper
 4 teaspoons white wine vinegar
 3 tablespoons extra-virgin olive oil

12 fresh basil leaves, coarsely shredded

Put the mushrooms in a bowl and cover them with the hot water. Let soak for 1 to 2 hours, stirring them occasionally.

Lift out the mushrooms and strain the liquid if necessary, reserving 1½ cups for cooking the mushrooms (reserve the remainder for soup or stock). Remove the stems (reserve for stock).

No more than 1 hour before serving, rinse and dry the radicchio and endive. Cut the radicchio lengthwise in half and then into 1-inch pieces; transfer to a bowl. Cut the endive lengthwise in half and then lengthwise into ¼-inch-wide strips; put in another bowl.

Arrange the shiitake caps in one layer in a large skillet, add the reserved 1½ cups mushroom-soaking liquid, the salt, pepper, and olive oil, and bring to a boil. Reduce the heat to medium, cover, and boil gently for about 12 minutes, removing the lid occasionally to check on the mushrooms, until the caps are cooked and most of the liquid has evaporated. Uncover and continue cooking until all the liquid is gone, then cook for 3 to 4 minutes longer, turning the caps occasionally, until they are lightly browned on both sides.

MEANWHILE, FOR THE DRESSING: Combine all the ingredients in a bowl.

At serving time, divide the dressing between the radicchio and endive and toss well. Make a border of endive around the edges of four plates and pile the radicchio in the center. Sprinkle the shredded basil over the endive and radicchio, and arrange the mushroom caps on top of the radicchio, with half cap side up and half gill side up. Serve immediately.

When you reconstitute dried mushrooms in water, save the flavorful soaking liquid. I cook the mushrooms in some of that liquid in Braised Shiitake Mushrooms on Bitter Greens (opposite), and then reserve the remainder (covered and refrigerated or frozen) for later use in soups, stocks, or sauces. You can save the mushroom stems as well; although they are too fibrous and tough for this dish, they lend flavor to stocks and, finely chopped, are good in stuffings.

Tomato Salad

Serves 6

❧ **I serve tomato salad** several times a week during the summer, especially when my garden is producing fresh tomatoes daily.

1½ pounds ripe tomatoes (about 5 medium)
1 teaspoon salt, preferably fleur de sel
½ teaspoon freshly ground white pepper
1½ tablespoons red wine vinegar
⅓ cup oil (preferably half olive oil, half peanut oil)
1½ teaspoons minced fresh basil (if fresh basil is unavailable, use fresh tarragon, chervil, or parsley; do not use dried herbs)

Core the tomatoes and cut them into thin slices, arranging them attractively on a platter as you go. Sprinkle with the salt and white pepper, and then with the vinegar and oil. Sprinkle with the herbs and serve.

Tomatoes and Shallots with Parsley Vinaigrette

Serves 4

❧ **This salad is best** when tomatoes — preferably organically grown — are at their peak. The seasoning is simple: vinegar, oil, salt, and pepper. You can replace the parsley with basil, tarragon, or another herb to your liking.

2 large ripe tomatoes (about 1 pound)
2 medium shallots
¼ teaspoon salt
¼ teaspoon freshly ground black pepper
1 tablespoon rice vinegar
3 tablespoons olive oil
2 tablespoons coarsely chopped fresh parsley

Core the tomatoes, cut into ¼-inch-thick slices, and arrange on a platter. Cut the shallots into very thin slices and arrange the slices on top of the tomatoes. Sprinkle with the salt, pepper, vinegar, and oil, and then the parsley, and serve.

Tomato Salad with Red Onion and Basil

Serves 6

❧ **Using ingredients directly from** the garden rather than the supermarket makes an extraordinary difference in the taste of this simple dish. The leftover salad can be enjoyed on its own or in sandwiches containing meat or poultry. I always plant small-leaf bush basil, which is very pungent. If it is unavailable, use regular basil. If you don't have a red onion, you can use a mild Texas or Vidalia onion instead.

This salad goes well with crusty French bread.

4 large ripe tomatoes (1½–2 pounds)
1 large red onion
1 teaspoon salt
¾ teaspoon freshly ground black pepper
2 tablespoons red wine vinegar
5 tablespoons extra-virgin olive oil (or a
mixture of olive and hazelnut oil)
¼ cup shredded fresh basil leaves,
preferably small-leaf bush basil

Core the tomatoes and cut into ¼-inch-thick slices. Arrange the slices, overlapping them slightly, in a large oval or round gratin dish.

Cut the onion into ⅛-inch-thick slices. Separate the slices into rings and arrange them over the tomatoes. Sprinkle with the salt, pepper, vinegar, and oil, coating the vegetables as evenly as possible. Sprinkle the shredded basil on top and serve.

Diced Tomato Salad
with Chervil
Serves 4

❦ **Tomatoes should be ripe** but not cold for salads. Here the tomatoes are peeled, which makes the salad a bit more elegant. The flavorful dressing is made with nut oil. Chervil gives the salad a special dimension, but you can substitute tarragon.

3–4 large ripe tomatoes (about 1½ pounds)
¾ teaspoon salt
½ teaspoon freshly ground black pepper
1 tablespoon white wine or tarragon
vinegar
2 tablespoons peanut oil
1 tablespoon walnut or hazelnut oil
⅓ cup fresh chervil leaves

To peel the tomatoes, impale each one on a fork and roast it over a gas flame or a hot electric burner for 10 to 15 seconds. Using a paring knife, pull off the skin — it will release easily. Alternatively, drop the tomatoes into a pot of boiling water for a few seconds, then remove them from the hot water, let cool for a few minutes, and peel off the skin. (The latter method is particularly efficient when you have a large number of tomatoes to peel, which makes boiling a large pot of water worthwhile.)

Cut the tomatoes crosswise in half and squeeze out the seeds. (Keep the skin and liquid for stock, if you like.) Cut the tomatoes into ½-inch cubes and combine them with the salt, pepper, vinegar, and oils in a serving bowl.

Mix in the chervil and serve.

Tomato, Red Onion,
and Orange Salad
Serves 4

❦ **This colorful salad is** a standard at our house. I like it with a Torpedo onion, a long, narrow red variety. Although I use regular seedless oranges here to lend acidity to the dish, if you live in an area where blood oranges are available, substitute them for their vivid color and taste.

1 red onion, preferably a large Torpedo
onion (about 6 ounces)
2 navel oranges
6 ripe plum tomatoes
½ cup loosely packed fresh parsley
leaves

2 tablespoons sherry vinegar

¼ cup extra-virgin olive oil

1 teaspoon Worcestershire sauce

½ teaspoon salt

½ teaspoon freshly ground black pepper

Cut the onion into ⅛-inch-thick slices. Separate the slices into rings and put them in a serving bowl large enough to hold the finished salad.

Using a sharp knife, peel the oranges, removing all the white pith. Cut the oranges into ¼-inch-thick slices and add them to the onion rings.

Cut the tomatoes crosswise in half and squeeze them gently to remove the seeds (which can be reserved for stock). Cut the tomatoes into 1-inch pieces and add them to the oranges and onion. Add the parsley leaves.

FOR THE DRESSING: Mix all the ingredients together in a small bowl.

Add the dressing to the onion, oranges, and tomatoes, toss the salad, and serve.

Tomato, Mozzarella, and Cucumber Salad
Serves 6 to 8

❧ You can make this salad ahead and let it macerate in the refrigerator until serving time. It will keep for a couple of days, but be sure to let it come back to room temperature before serving. Serve with country bread.

Leftovers can be used as a terrific vegetarian sandwich filling or as a zesty addition to sandwiches containing meat.

1½ pounds ripe plum tomatoes

About 1½ cups diced (½-inch) onions

About 1½ cups peeled, seeded, and diced (½-inch) cucumber

8 ounces mozzarella cheese, cut into sticks about ½ inch thick by 1½ inches long

½ cup shredded fresh basil leaves

¼ cup chopped fresh chives or parsley

1 teaspoon salt

1 teaspoon freshly ground black pepper

About 1 teaspoon seeded and finely chopped jalapeño pepper (optional)

3 tablespoons red wine vinegar

½ cup extra-virgin olive oil

Cut the tomatoes crosswise in half and then into 1-inch pieces.

Put the onions in a sieve and rinse under cold water to remove some of the strong-smelling sulfurous compounds. Drain thoroughly.

Combine all the ingredients in a bowl, stirring well. Serve right away, or cover and refrigerate. Bring to room temperature before serving.

Zucchini and Olive Salad
Serves 6

❧ For this salad, the zucchini is cut into thin slices, arranged on a cookie sheet in a single layer, salted, and placed in a hot oven for a few minutes to draw out some of its moisture. The slices soften slightly but stay a bit crunchy. The salad is seasoned simply with pepper, vinegar, and oil and garnished with black olives and chives.

2 zucchini (about 1½ pounds)

½ teaspoon salt

½ teaspoon freshly ground black pepper

2 tablespoons white wine vinegar

¼ cup corn or safflower oil

¼ cup pitted oil-cured black olives

2 tablespoons chopped fresh chives

Preheat the oven to 400 degrees.

Wash the zucchini, trim off the ends, and cut into ¼-inch-thick rounds. Arrange the rounds in one layer on a large cookie sheet and sprinkle with the salt. Bake for 5 to 7 minutes, until the zucchini renders some of its moisture and softens slightly.

Transfer the zucchini rounds to a bowl and toss them gently with the pepper, vinegar, and oil. Serve immediately, garnished with the black olives and chives.

Mixed Vegetable Salad with Croutons
Serves 4

✺ **String beans, peas, tomatoes,** and romaine lettuce are tossed in a garlicky dressing and garnished with large croutons made from leftover bread. I prefer earthy country-style bread, which I cut into chunks and brown in the oven. Added to the salad a few minutes before it is served, the croutons absorb a little of the dressing and soften slightly while still retaining their crunch.

- 8 ounces haricots verts or very thin string beans, tips removed
- 1 cup fresh peas or frozen baby peas
- 3 ounces bread, preferably a country-style French loaf, cut into 1- to 1½-inch cubes
- 2 regular tomatoes or 5–6 plum tomatoes, cut into 1-inch pieces (about 2½ cups)
- ½ head romaine lettuce, cut into 2-inch pieces, washed, and dried (5 cups)

DRESSING

- 2 garlic cloves, crushed and finely chopped
- 1 tablespoon balsamic vinegar
- 1 tablespoon white wine vinegar

- ¼ cup extra-virgin olive oil
- ½ teaspoon salt
- ½ teaspoon freshly ground black pepper

Preheat the oven to 400 degrees.

Bring 1 cup water to a boil in a skillet. Add the beans and cook over medium-high heat, covered, until tender but still firm, about 6 minutes. Drain and transfer to a large serving bowl.

If using frozen peas, put them in a colander and run them under hot water to defrost them. Add the fresh or frozen peas to the beans.

Arrange the bread cubes in one layer on a cookie sheet and bake until brown, about 8 minutes. Remove from the oven.

Add the tomato pieces and lettuce to the beans and peas. Add the croutons and dressing ingredients and mix well. Let stand for a few minutes, so the croutons soften just slightly, and serve.

Potato and Watercress Salad
Serves 4

✺ **Potato and watercress are** a terrific salad combination. This one is made with the leaves and some of the stems of the greens. I like to use unpeeled small red potatoes, cooking them whole, then cutting them into ½-inch slices. Because watercress tends to wilt quickly, I don't mix the greens in until just before serving. I buy red pimientos at my supermarket deli counter, and they are also available in small jars.

- 1 pound small red potatoes
- 2 bunches watercress

DRESSING

- 1 tablespoon hot mustard
- ¼ cup peanut oil

2 teaspoons light soy sauce
1½ tablespoons red wine vinegar
¼ teaspoon salt
½ teaspoon freshly ground black pepper

⅓ cup diced (½-inch) pimientos

Remove and discard the eyes and any damaged parts of the potatoes, but do not peel them. Rinse the potatoes well under cold water, place in a saucepan, and cover with cold water. Bring to a boil over high heat, then reduce the heat to medium and boil gently until the potatoes are tender, about 30 minutes.

Drain the potatoes and spread them out in a large gratin dish to cool slightly. When they are cool enough to handle, cut the potatoes into ½-inch-thick slices, and spread the slices out in a single layer (so they are less likely to break).

Trim the watercress, removing about 2 inches from the stem ends (if desired, set these ends aside for soup). Wash the watercress and dry it thoroughly. (You should have about 3 cups.)

FOR THE DRESSING: Mix all the ingredients together in a bowl large enough to hold the finished salad. (Do not worry if the ingredients separate; the mixture should not be emulsified.)

At serving time, add the potatoes and watercress to the dressing and toss lightly but thoroughly. Serve garnished with the pimientos.

Bulgur and Mint Salad
Serves 4

❧ **I like Tabasco sauce** and use it liberally here: its heat contrasts nicely with the coolness and pungency of the mint and other herbs. Light and delightful, this summer salad can be served as a first course or as an accompaniment to almost any meat or fish main course. It will keep, refrigerated,

for 4 or 5 days; bring to room temperature before serving.

Bulgur is steamed cracked wheat, needing only to be reconstituted in water.

1 cup bulgur wheat
1 cup lightly packed fresh mint leaves
1 cup lightly packed fresh cilantro leaves
1 large carrot, peeled and shredded on the large holes of a box grater or in a food processor (about ½ cup)
4 scallions, trimmed (leaving some green) and minced (about ⅓ cup)
2 teaspoons crushed and finely chopped garlic
1 teaspoon salt
¾ teaspoon Tabasco sauce (less if you prefer milder seasoning)
¼ cup fresh lemon juice
¼ cup corn oil
¼ cup golden raisins

Put the bulgur in a bowl and add 4 cups cool water. Soak for at least 2 to 3 hours, or as long as overnight.

Drain the bulgur in a sieve for 10 to 20 minutes.

Meanwhile, coarsely chop the mint and cilantro together.

Put the bulgur in a bowl and add the remaining ingredients, including the herbs and scallions. Mix well and serve.

Lentil and Potato Salad
Serves 4

❧ *Lentilles du Puy* are tiny green lentils, named after their place of origin in the center of France. Available at specialty food stores and some supermarkets, they hold their shape well as they cook.

If you can't find them, substitute another dried lentil. Lentils come in various sizes, with colors ranging from black to brown to red. Some take longer to cook than others, so adjust the cooking times accordingly if using another variety. This sturdy salad is a great accompaniment to roasts and grilled meats.

¾ cup dried *lentilles du Puy* (French
        green lentils)
1 teaspoon salt
4 small to medium potatoes (12 ounces),
        washed
¾ cup finely chopped onion
3 garlic cloves, crushed and finely chopped
        (1½ teaspoons)
¼ cup chopped fresh herbs, such as parsley,
        basil, savory, and tarragon
3–4 scallions, trimmed (leaving some green)
        and finely minced (3 tablespoons)
¼ cup extra-virgin olive oil
2 tablespoons red wine vinegar
½ teaspoon freshly ground black pepper

Combine the lentils and ¼ teaspoon of the salt in a large saucepan, add 2¾ cups cold water, and bring to a boil. Cover, reduce the heat, and boil gently for 30 to 45 minutes, until the lentils are tender. Remove the pan from the heat and let the lentils cool for 15 minutes. (Most of the liquid will have evaporated or been absorbed by the lentils.)

Meanwhile, put the potatoes in a saucepan with enough cold water to cover them and bring to a boil over high heat. Reduce the heat to low and cook gently, uncovered, for about 35 minutes (replacing the water as needed to keep the potatoes covered), until tender when pierced with the point of a knife. Drain and let the potatoes cool to lukewarm.

When the potatoes are cool enough to han-dle, peel them, cut them into ⅜-inch-thick slices, and put the slices in a bowl. Add the lentils and combine gently with the potatoes. Add the onion, garlic, herbs, scallions, olive oil, vinegar, pepper, and the remaining ¾ teaspoon salt and mix just to combine well.

Transfer the salad to a large platter and serve lukewarm.

Cranberry Bean and Tuna Salad
Serves 4

✖ **I especially like to** prepare this recipe when fresh cranberry beans are in season, but you can use canned beans with good results. The beans are combined with tuna seasoned with garlic, parsley, pepper, oil, and mustard, and everything is served on salad greens.

2 pounds fresh cranberry beans, shelled
        (about 1 pound shelled, or 2½ cups),
        or 2 cans (about 1 pound each)
        cranberry beans, drained and rinsed
1 bay leaf
1 medium onion, cut into 1-inch pieces
        (1 cup)
1 teaspoon salt
1 teaspoon herbes de Provence
2 6-ounce cans tuna, preferably in
        olive oil
2 large garlic cloves, crushed and finely
        chopped (1½ teaspoons)
¼ cup minced fresh parsley
¾ teaspoon freshly ground black pepper
2 tablespoons extra-virgin olive oil
1 tablespoon Dijon mustard
8–10 lettuce leaves, preferably Boston lettuce

Combine the beans, bay leaf, onion, salt, herbes de Provence, and 1½ cups water in a saucepan and bring to a boil. Cover, reduce the heat to very low, and cook gently for 35 to 40 minutes (slightly less if using canned beans), until the beans are tender. Remove from the heat and let cool to lukewarm. (Most of the liquid will have been absorbed by the beans.)

Put the tuna, including its oil, in a salad bowl. Add the garlic, parsley, pepper, oil, and mustard and mix well, breaking the tuna into small pieces. Add the beans, discarding some of the liquid if there is too much, and toss gently to mix all the ingredients together (the mixture should be moist but not liquid).

Divide the lettuce leaves among four plates and spoon the bean mixture onto the leaves. Serve at room temperature.

Warm Bean and Bacon Salad
Serves 6

✂ **This recipe calls for** small white navy beans, but you can substitute any other variety, from kidney to Great Northern to pea beans. I buy lean slab bacon or pancetta in thick slices and then cut it into little cubes. Regular sliced bacon can be used as well.

10	ounces (about 2 cups) dried navy or other small white beans
1½	teaspoons salt
8	ounces slab bacon (lardons) or pancetta, cut into ½-inch pieces
1	medium onion, chopped (about 1 cup)
6	garlic cloves, crushed and chopped (1½ tablespoons)
½	cup chopped fresh parsley
1½	tablespoons red wine vinegar
1½	tablespoons balsamic vinegar
3	tablespoons olive oil
1	teaspoon freshly ground black pepper

Wash the beans and remove and discard any damaged ones and any foreign material. Put the beans in a pot with 6 cups cold water and 1 teaspoon of the salt and bring to a boil, then cover, reduce the heat to low, and cook until tender, 1½ to 2 hours. (There should be only a little water remaining in the pot.) Let cool to lukewarm.

Place the bacon in a saucepan and sauté over low heat, covered, for about 8 minutes, until it has rendered much of its fat. Add the onion and garlic and cook, stirring, for about 5 seconds. Add the contents of the saucepan, fat and all, to the beans, then add the remaining ½ teaspoon salt and the remaining ingredients and mix well. Serve warm or at room temperature.

COOKING DRIED BEANS

The dried beans in supermarkets are usually from this year's crop, so it is not necessary to soak them. In fact, if the beans are soaked overnight in water, as many recipes suggest, bubbles often form on the surface of the water, indicating that the beans are fermenting — making them a less than desirable component of any recipe. I prefer to wash the beans, cover them with cold water containing a pinch of salt, and cook them immediately.

Salad of Fresh Foie Gras
Serves 6

❧ **Fresh foie gras is** expensive, but, as it is quite rich, a sliver weighing about 2 ounces is enough for each person. Served lukewarm, foie gras can be combined with an almost endless variety of greens and vegetables.

> About 12 ounces Grade A fresh duck foie gras
> ¼ teaspoon salt
> ¼ teaspoon freshly ground black pepper
> ½ large celery root (celeriac), peeled and cut into julienne strips about ⅛ inch thick and 2 inches long (2½ cups)
> 6 oyster mushrooms, cleaned and sliced
> 1 large head (or several small) curly endive, very white, cut into 2-inch pieces, washed, and dried (about 6 cups)
> 1½ tablespoons sherry vinegar
> 6 tablespoons Basic Brown Sauce (page 613) or juices from roasted chicken, veal, or beef, warmed (optional)

Cut the foie gras into slivers, allowing approximately 2 ounces per person (1 or 2 slivers). Refrigerate until ready to serve.

At serving time, sprinkle ⅛ teaspoon each of the salt and pepper on the pieces of foie gras. Heat a large heavy aluminum or stainless steel skillet (or two smaller skillets) until hot. Add the foie gras slices and sauté over high heat for about 45 seconds on each side. Remove the foie gras to a plate.

You will notice that some of the foie gras has melted. Add the celery root to the foie gras fat in the pan and sauté over high heat for about 1 minute. Add the mushrooms and sauté for another 2 minutes. Sprinkle with the remaining ⅛ teaspoon each salt and pepper and add any drippings that have accumulated around the slices of foie gras on the plate. Finally, add the curly endive and vinegar and toss very briefly, just enough to coat the salad.

Divide the salad among six serving plates. Place the slices of foie gras on top, sprinkle each serving with 1 tablespoon of the Brown Sauce or juices, if using, and serve.

Eggs and Cheese

Eggs and Cheese

General Information About Eggs

The entries in this glossary are listed "chrono-logically," from the selection and buying of eggs through storing, cooking, and serving them. Most supermarkets now offer organic eggs, and these are certainly my first choice. Most of my recipes are made with large eggs; if a recipe calls for a jumbo egg, you can usually substitute 2 small ones.

Sizes

Eggs are generally available in the following sizes: jumbo, extra-large, large, medium, and small. One dozen extra-large eggs weigh 27 ounces; 12 large eggs, 24 ounces; 12 medium eggs, 21 ounces; and 12 small eggs, 18 ounces.

Shell Color

Shell color varies from white to deep brown because of pigment produced by the hen. Color does not affect the flavor, nutritive value, or cooking performance of eggs, nor is it a dependable guide to yolk color. Although there is no advantage to paying more for brown or white eggs of the same quality and size, I tend to like brown eggs better — possibly because these are the eggs I ate as a child.

Yolk Color

I buy organic eggs at a farm, and the yolks are deep yellow-orange and thick when they are cooked, showing that they are high in lecithin.

Calorie Count

One large egg (2 ounces) has 77 calories.

Volume Equivalents

About 7 large egg whites, about 12 large egg yolks, or 4 to 6 whole raw eggs will fill 1 standard measuring cup.

Storing Whole Eggs

Eggs should always be stored in the refrigerator. Keep them in the carton and do not place them near any strong-flavored food, since the shells are porous. They will keep for several weeks.

Storing Egg Whites

Egg whites freeze perfectly. Since 1 large egg white fits neatly into an individual plastic ice-cube mold, this is the ideal way to freeze them. It also makes it easy to tell at a glance how many whites you have on hand. Once the egg white cubes are frozen, transfer them to a plastic freezer bag. Thaw and use exactly as you would fresh egg whites; allow about 30 minutes to thaw a single frozen egg white cube.

Storing Egg Yolks

Unlike egg whites, yolks do not freeze well — they will develop bacteria unless they are frozen commercially at very, very low temperatures. Raw egg yolks can be stored for a couple of days in the refrigerator if placed intact in a container and covered with cold water.

Room Temperature

Most authorities assert that egg whites should be brought to room temperature before beating them because they will beat up faster and to a greater volume. The air bubbles created are larger if the egg whites are not too cold. But I find that the texture is tighter, smoother, and better if the egg whites are cold, even though the volume after beating is slightly less.

Aluminum and Eggs

Whites and whole eggs will discolor when mixed or cooked in aluminum pans, bowls, or molds because of the sulfur content of eggs. Use heavy-bottomed enameled or stainless steel pans and stainless steel, Pyrex, or porcelain bowls or molds.

Boiled Eggs

Cooking eggs in boiling water over high heat leads to rubbery whites and cracked and leaking shells. To avoid cracked shells when cooking the eggs, make a hole with a pushpin or thumbtack in the rounder end of each egg, where there is an air chamber. Then, when the egg is lowered into the water, the pressure is relieved as tiny air bubbles escape through the hole. The eggs should be cooked in barely boiling water so the whites don't get rubbery.

Soft-Cooked Eggs

When the egg is perfectly cooked, the white is tender but solidified and the hot yolk is liquid to semiliquid. Use a pushpin or thumbtack to make a hole in the rounder end of each egg. Plunge the eggs into boiling water, reduce the heat, and cook for 2½ to 3 minutes at a very low boil. Remove from the heat.

Mollet Eggs

Eggs *mollet* are a stage between soft- and hard-boiled; the yolks are still runny. In professional kitchens, these eggs are often cooked in a circulator, a vessel that moves or circulates the cooking water so as to maintain an even temperature (the same principle is used in sous-vide cooking), but they are just as easily made in a saucepan. Use a pushpin or thumbtack to make a hole in the rounder end of the eggs, lower the eggs into barely boiling water, and cook for 6 minutes. Pour out the hot water and shake the pan to crack the eggshells, then plunge the eggs into ice water to stop the cooking and cool slightly. Peel the eggs carefully under cold running water. Before serving, replace the cold water with hot tap water, so the eggs are lukewarm.

Hard-Cooked Eggs

The cold-water method: Put the egg, or eggs, straight from the refrigerator, in a saucepan large enough to accommodate them without crowding. Add enough warm tap water to cover the eggs by at least a generous inch and set the pan, uncovered, over high heat. Once the water begins to show signs of reaching a rolling boil (212 degrees on a thermometer), keep it at close to this temperature for 8 minutes. Then plunge the eggs into cold water at once to stop the cooking.

Another way: When the water reaches a rolling boil, remove the pan from the heat, cover, and allow the eggs to stand for 15 minutes, then cool immediately as above.

The boiling-water method: Use a pushpin or thumbtack to make a hole in the rounder end of each egg. Plunge the eggs into boiling water, reduce the heat, and cook at a very low boil for 10 minutes. When an egg is lowered into boiling water, the sulfur in the white moves toward the center of the egg to escape the intense heat. The iron in the yolk then reacts with the sulfur and can turn the outside of the yolk green and sulfur-smelling. To prevent this, do not overcook the eggs, and as soon as they are ready, pour out the hot water and shake the pan to crack the eggshells, which makes the eggs easier to peel. Add cold water and ice to the pan and keep the eggs in the ice water until thoroughly chilled.

Shelling Cooked Eggs

It is said that the reason eggs are sometimes hard to shell is that they are very fresh. Two days in the refrigerator changes the acid-alkaline balance, so the shell will be more willing to leave the cooked egg. However, I have had very fresh eggs that peel quite well and older eggs that are impossible to peel. To shell either soft- or hard-cooked eggs, hot or cold, crack each shell gently all over on a flat surface, taking care not to break the egg itself. Holding an egg in the palm of one hand under cold running water, ease the shell and membrane off the egg. Shelled hard-cooked eggs can be refrigerated for a couple of days. Shelled soft-cooked eggs can be stored in the refrigerator in cold water, which helps to keep their shape, for the same length of time. They can be reheated as you would reheat *mollet* eggs (see page 66).

Eggs in Ramekins
Serves 4

❧ **These eggs are cooked** in cocottes, little ramekins or molds. I use small soufflé dishes, but you can use any ovenproof dishes that hold about ½ cup. The eggs are placed in the buttered dishes and cooked in a pan of gently boiling water, a process that gives them a soft, creamy texture. I've given several variations, and the only limit to concocting others is your imagination. Mushrooms, shellfish, fish, meat, and vegetables are all possibilities. These make excellent appetizers.

2½	teaspoons unsalted butter
⅛	teaspoon salt
⅛	teaspoon freshly ground black pepper
¼	cup peas, cooked, ¼ cup heavy cream, or ¼ cup chopped cooked ham
4	large eggs, preferably organic
4	slices firm white bread

Butter the insides of four ½-cup soufflé dishes or ramekins with half of the butter and sprinkle lightly with the salt and pepper, dividing it evenly among the dishes. If using peas, spoon 1 tablespoon peas into each dish. Break 1 egg into each dish.

Bring ½ inch of water to a boil in a large saucepan or high-sided skillet. Place the dishes in the water, cover the pan, and boil gently for about 4 minutes, until the whites are set but the yolks are still soft inside; if using the cream, after the eggs have cooked for about 2 minutes, pour 1 tablespoon of the cream around each yolk, then cover and cook for another 2 minutes.

Meanwhile, toast the bread and spread one side of each slice with some of the remaining butter. Trim off the crusts and cut each slice into 4 thin strips.

If using ham, sprinkle 1 tablespoon of the chopped ham around the yolk of each cooked egg.

Serve the eggs with the toasted bread strips.

EGGS WITH HERBS

Here the eggs are unmolded and served, covered with herbs, on croutons.

Substitute 2 tablespoons plus 2 teaspoons minced fresh herbs, such as tarragon, chives, or chervil, for the peas (or ham or cream). Omit the toasted bread strips. Make sure the soufflé dishes or ramekins are very cold, and butter them heavily with 2½ teaspoons butter. Prepare 4 round croutons, by cutting a large disk from each of 4 thin slices of firm white bread and lightly toasting the rounds in a toaster.

Press 2 teaspoons herbs over the bottom and around the sides of each buttered dish. Break an egg into each dish, and cook as indicated above. To serve, run the blade of a sharp knife around each egg and unmold onto a round crouton.

Skillet Eggs with Brown Butter
Serves 4

❧ **One of the fastest** and tastiest methods of cooking eggs is to drop them into a skillet and fry them. But when they are seared in butter that is too hot, the edges of the whites crisp, curl, and toughen. Here the eggs are gently fried and then topped with croutons, sautéed asparagus, and mushrooms. The garnishes can be changed at will to include different kinds of diced vegetables.

2 tablespoons peanut oil

2 slices firm white bread, cut into ½-inch cubes

4 asparagus spears, trimmed, peeled, and cut into ¼-inch dice (1¼ cups)

4 mushrooms, cleaned and cut into ¼-inch dice (1¼ cups)

¼ teaspoon salt

4 tablespoons (½ stick) unsalted butter

8 large eggs, preferably organic
About 1 tablespoon sherry vinegar

2 tablespoons chopped fresh parsley
Freshly ground black pepper

FOR THE GARNISHES: Heat the oil in a large skillet. When it is hot, sauté the bread cubes for a couple of minutes, until they are nicely browned all over. Add the asparagus and mushrooms and sauté for another 45 seconds to 1 minute, until they begin to soften and are heated through. Add the salt and set aside.

Heat 1 teaspoon of the butter in another large skillet, preferably nonstick. When it is foaming at the edges, break 2 of the eggs into the pan and cook over medium-low heat (the edges should not brown) for about 30 seconds. Cover the pan with a lid and continue to cook for another minute, or until the egg whites are set and the egg yolks are just shiny. Slide the eggs onto a warm plate and keep warm in a 150-degree oven while you cook the remaining eggs in batches, adding an additional teaspoon of butter if needed for each batch.

When all the eggs are cooked, divide the garnishes among the plates, spooning them over the eggs. Add the remaining butter to the skillet and cook until it becomes a hazelnut color. Pour the brown butter around the eggs and sprinkle each serving with a few drops of the vinegar.

Sprinkle some chopped parsley on top of each, add a few grindings of pepper, and serve immediately.

Fines Herbes Omelet
Serves 4

✶ A *fines herbes* omelet reminds me somehow of spring, when fresh herbs begin to appear. This mixture is the classic combination, but you can replace some or all of these with other fresh herbs. I often serve this omelet with a salad and sautéed potatoes for dinner.

10 large eggs, preferably organic

¼ teaspoon salt

½ teaspoon freshly ground black pepper

½ cup loosely packed chopped fresh herbs (¼ cup chopped parsley plus ¼ cup combined tarragon, chives, and chervil)

1 tablespoon canola oil

2 tablespoons unsalted butter

Using a fork, beat the eggs, salt, and pepper in a bowl until thoroughly mixed. Stir in the herbs.

Heat half of the oil and butter in a 10-inch nonstick skillet over high heat. When the oil and butter are hot, add half of the egg mixture. Stir continuously with a fork, shaking the pan, for about 2 minutes to create the smallest-possible curds. When most of the mixture is solid, cook it without stirring for 10 seconds to create a thin "skin" on the underside of the omelet, binding it together.

Roll the omelet by folding over one side and then the opposite side, and invert it onto a plate. Repeat the process, using the remainder of the ingredients, to make a second omelet. Cut each omelet in half and serve immediately, half an omelet per person.

Potato Omelet
Serves 4

In this omelet, which is flat, not rolled, the eggs serve as a binder for thinly sliced potatoes and onions, which are first sautéed, then covered with thin slices of tomato. At my house we usually serve the omelet hot, often with a salad. It is also delicious served at room temperature in the Spanish style.

- 1½ tablespoons olive oil
- 1 tablespoon unsalted butter
- 1½ cups sliced onions
- 2 medium baking (Idaho) potatoes, peeled and thinly sliced (about 2½ cups)
- 1 large tomato (about 8 ounces), cut into thin slices
- 6 large eggs, preferably organic
- ⅓ cup coarsely chopped fresh chives
- ½ teaspoon salt
- ¼ teaspoon freshly ground black pepper

Heat the oil and butter in an 8- to 10-inch nonstick skillet until hot but not smoking. Add the onions and potatoes and cook, covered, for about 10 minutes, stirring occasionally to brown on all sides.

Add the tomato slices to the skillet, arranging them so they cover most of the potato and onion mixture. Cover and cook for 1 minute.

Meanwhile, break the eggs into a bowl. Add the chives, salt, and pepper and mix with a fork.

Preheat the broiler. Add the egg mixture to the skillet and stir gently with a fork for about 1 minute so the eggs flow between the potatoes and tomatoes. Slide the skillet under the broiler, 3 to 4 inches from the heat, and cook for about 3 minutes, until the eggs are set.

Slide onto a platter, cut into wedges, and serve.

Stuffed Omelet Hunter-Style
Serves 1

The classic mixture of mushrooms, chicken livers, tomatoes, and herbs produces a filling omelet that is ideal for lunch, brunch, or a light dinner served with a salad.

- 2 tablespoons unsalted butter
- 1 medium mushroom, cleaned and diced
- 1 chicken liver, trimmed of any sinew and cut into ¼-inch dice
  Salt and freshly ground black pepper
- 2 tablespoons tomato sauce or juice
- 4 teaspoons chopped fresh chives
- 3 large eggs, preferably organic

Heat 1 tablespoon of the butter in a small skillet. When it is hot, sauté the mushroom for about 30 seconds. Add the chicken liver and a pinch each of salt and pepper. Sauté for another 30 seconds, then add the tomato sauce or juice and 1 teaspoon of the chives. Set aside.

Break the eggs into a bowl. Add a pinch each of salt and pepper and mix with a fork. Heat the remaining 1 tablespoon butter in an 8-inch nonstick skillet. When it is hot, add the eggs and stir with a fork, shaking the pan with your other hand. Cook over high heat, stirring, until the eggs are uniformly coagulated but still moist in the center.

Fold the "lip" of the side of the omelet nearest you over. Arrange the solids from the liver-mushroom mixture down the center of the omelet, pushing down lightly with the fork to hold them in place.

Gently tap the end of the skillet handle to nudge the far lip up, rolling it over the stuffing, making sure that the ends of the omelet are pointed. Bang the end of the skillet gently so the omelet sits at the far edge of the pan. Invert onto a serving plate. Spoon the sauce from the mushrooms around the omelet, sprinkle with the remaining tablespoon of chives, and serve immediately.

Scrambled Eggs in Bread Cases with Caramelized Mushrooms
Serves 6

🍳 **Whisking scrambled eggs almost** continuously as they begin to set allows only the smallest-possible curds to form, producing the creamiest mixture. To prevent the eggs from overcooking once they have reached the proper consistency, a portion of reserved uncooked eggs is stirred in with cream at the end.

Crisp bread cases make an ideal receptacle, but they should be filled only at the last moment so they don't get soggy. The mushrooms that are served alongside are cooked in a skillet until they are dry and brown, concentrating their taste. A brown sauce, shallots, and white wine are added, and the sauce becomes rich and meaty, balancing the mild eggs. If you don't have brown sauce on hand, good-quality demi-glace is available in specialty stores and high-end supermarkets.

The sautéed mushrooms here can be used as a garnish for most meats and roasts.

Scrambled eggs prepared this way can be kept warm after cooking in a double boiler over 150-degree water for at least 30 minutes.

BREAD CASES

- 6 1-inch-thick slices Pullman (firm white) bread, from a 1- to 2-day-old loaf (not dry or soft)
- 2 tablespoons unsalted butter, softened

MUSHROOMS

- 4 ounces oyster or shiitake mushrooms (about 18–20), cleaned
- 2 tablespoons unsalted butter
- ¼ teaspoon salt
- 1 tablespoon chopped shallots
- 2 tablespoons dry white wine
- ½ cup Basic Brown Sauce (page 613) or good-quality store-bought demi-glace

EGGS

- 12 large eggs, preferably organic
- ½ teaspoon salt
- ¼ teaspoon freshly ground black pepper
- 2 tablespoons unsalted butter
- 3 tablespoons heavy cream

Preheat the oven to 400 degrees.

FOR THE BREAD CASES: Trim off the crust of each bread slice to form a square. Then, ⅜ inch in from the edge, cut a square in each slice, cutting at least ½ inch into the bread, to create a border. Remove the bread in the center by cutting slices of it out on the bias, then cutting and scraping out the inside to create a receptacle with walls approximately ⅜ inch thick and a bottom of the same thickness (save the trimmings for bread crumbs). Butter the bread cases inside and out with the soft butter (using about 1 teaspoon of butter for each one). Arrange the cases on a cookie sheet and bake for about 7 minutes, until nicely browned all over. Set aside.

FOR THE MUSHROOMS: Remove the stems if using shiitake mushrooms (although tough and fibrous, they can be used for stock).

Melt the butter in a large skillet. When it is hot, add the mushrooms and cook over medium-high heat until most of the moisture comes out of them and evaporates. As this occurs, the mushrooms will start sizzling in the butter. Continue cooking for a few minutes longer (a total of 7 to 8 minutes), until the mushrooms are brown and look almost candied. Add the salt and shallots and sauté for about 1 minute, then add the wine.

Toss and keep cooking until most of the wine has evaporated and the mushrooms are just barely moist. Add the brown sauce, bring to a boil, and simmer for 1 to 2 minutes, until it reduces and coats the mushrooms. Set aside.

FOR THE EGGS: Break the eggs into a bowl, add the salt and pepper, and beat with a whisk to mix well. Set ⅓ cup of the raw eggs aside.

Melt the butter in a large heavy saucepan. When it is foaming, pour in the eggs and cook over medium-low heat, stirring gently with the whisk; be sure to get around the bottom edges of the pan with your whisk, since the eggs have a tendency to set and harden there first. Keep cooking and whisking gently until the mixture gets very creamy; the eggs should have the smallest-possible curds. Continue cooking just until you can see the bottom of the pan as the whisk is drawn through the eggs.

Remove the pan from the heat (the eggs will continue cooking, especially around the edges of the pan). Add the reserved raw eggs and the cream and keep whisking; the uncooked eggs and cream will absorb the heat still generated by the pan.

Place a bread case in the center of each serving plate. Distribute some of the coated mushrooms around it and fill the cases with the scrambled eggs. Serve immediately.

Mollet Eggs Florentine
Serves 8

❧ *Mollet,* which means "soft" in French, refers to eggs that are cooked in water in the shells for a longer period of time than soft-cooked eggs, but not as long as hard-cooked eggs — about 6 minutes total. The yolks are creamy and the whites less watery than in soft-cooked eggs. Then the eggs are shelled, leaving their shape intact.

8 large eggs, preferably organic

SPINACH

2 pounds spinach
3 tablespoons unsalted butter
2 teaspoons salt
½ teaspoon freshly ground black pepper
¼ teaspoon freshly grated nutmeg
3 tablespoons grated Gruyère
    or Emmenthaler cheese

MORNAY SAUCE

1 tablespoon unsalted butter
1 tablespoon all-purpose flour
1 cup half-and-half
½ teaspoon salt
¼ teaspoon freshly ground white pepper
1 large egg yolk
1½ tablespoons freshly grated Parmesan
    cheese

Bring 4 to 6 cups water to a boil in a shallow saucepan (about 8 inches wide and 3 inches deep). With a pushpin or thumbtack, prick a small hole in the rounder end of each egg (this will help prevent the shells from cracking during cooking). Using a small sieve, lower the eggs into the boiling water and let it come back to a simmer. Cook for about 6 minutes. Pour the water out and shake the pan to crack the eggshells. Cool thoroughly.

Gently shell the eggs (to avoid breaking them) under cold running water. Set aside.

FOR THE SPINACH: Remove and discard the spinach stems. Wash the spinach well. Heat a large pot until hot. Add the spinach, cover, and cook for about 1 minute, until wilted. Drain the spinach in a colander, pressing on it to extract as much water as possible.

Put the spinach on a chopping block and coarsely chop.

Melt the butter in a skillet over high heat and

cook until it turns brown. Add the spinach, salt, pepper, and nutmeg, mix well with a fork, and cook for 2 minutes.

Arrange the spinach in the bottom of an ovenproof dish large enough to accommodate the eggs. Embed the cold eggs in the spinach, with a little space between them, and sprinkle the cheese on top.

FOR THE SAUCE: Melt the butter in a heavy saucepan. Stir in the flour until smooth and cook, stirring constantly, for about 1 minute, until the mixture froths, without browning. Add the half-and-half, whipping constantly with a whisk, and bring to a boil, whisking constantly. Stir in the seasonings and continue cooking over low heat for 1 minute, stirring constantly with the whisk. Remove from the heat.

Preheat the broiler. Whisk the egg yolk into the sauce.

Coat the eggs with the sauce and sprinkle with the Parmesan cheese. Place under the hot broiler (not too close, so the eggs have a chance to get hot inside) for 5 minutes, or until the sauce is nicely browned. Serve immediately.

Hard-Cooked Eggs in Mustard Sauce
Serves 4

❧ **The sauce for this** dish is a vinaigrette containing lots of mustard, a perfect combination with the eggs. The sauce can also dress up a salad made with sturdy greens, like escarole or frisée, and it is good as well on a chicken or beef salad.

SAUCE

2	large garlic cloves, crushed and chopped (about 1½ teaspoons)
1	tablespoon hot or Dijon mustard
⅛	teaspoon salt
⅛	teaspoon freshly ground black pepper
2	teaspoons white wine vinegar
3	tablespoons olive or safflower oil

4	large hard-cooked eggs (see page 66), preferably organic, peeled
8	Boston lettuce leaves, rinsed and dried
1	tablespoon chopped fresh chives

FOR THE SAUCE: Combine the garlic, mustard, salt, pepper, and vinegar in a bowl. Add the oil slowly, mixing it in with a whisk or spoon. Set aside at room temperature until ready to use; do not worry if the sauce separates.

Cut the eggs lengthwise in half. Divide the lettuce among four plates and place 2 egg halves, cut side up, on top. Coat the eggs with the mustard sauce, sprinkle with the chives, and serve.

Eggs in Aspic
Serves 8

❧ **My wife, Gloria, loves** this appealing summer-party first course of poached eggs glistening in a beautiful dark, rich aspic. As a base for the aspic,

I sometimes use the stock she makes for Hanoi Soup (page 30), flavored with blackened shallots, pieces of ginger, and star anise. The eggs are garnished with fresh mushrooms, red pepper, and cooked ham, but the garnish can be varied almost infinitely, with pieces of chicken, fresh herbs, vegetables, fish, or shellfish. You can prepare the eggs in individual ramekins and unmold them, or serve them directly from one large dish.

Get large eggs that are as fresh as possible — they will hold their shape better than older eggs as they poach. A little white vinegar added to the water tightens the albumen and gives the egg whites a rounder shape. After the eggs are poached, they are plunged into ice water, which stops the cooking and removes any vinegar taste.

Make the stock before poaching the eggs. You can also use it in soups, sauces, or stews.

STOCK

- 4 pounds chicken bones, chopped into 3-inch pieces
- 5 quarts water
- 3 star anise points
- 3 large shallots
- 1 1½- to 2-inch piece ginger, cut in half

- 2 tablespoons white vinegar
- 8 large eggs, preferably organic, as fresh as possible

ASPIC

- 1 cup coarsely chopped leek greens
- 1 cup coarsely chopped fresh parsley
- 1 cup coarsely chopped celery leaves
- 4 envelopes unflavored gelatin (about 3 tablespoons)
- 3 large egg whites
- 2 teaspoons salt
- ½ teaspoon freshly ground black pepper

GARNISHES

- ½ red bell pepper
- 3 large mushrooms (about 3 ounces)
- 1 cup strips cooked ham

FOR THE STOCK: Heat the oven to 400 degrees.

Spread out the chicken bones in a roasting pan and roast them for 1 hour and 15 minutes, turning them once or twice so they brown nicely on all sides. With a slotted spoon, transfer the bones to a large pot and add the water and 2 pieces of the star anise.

Discard the fat that accumulated in the roasting pan and add 2 cups of water from the pot. Bring to a boil, scraping the bottom of the pan with a wooden spatula to dislodge the solidified fat and browned bits. Add this mixture to the pot and bring to a boil. Reduce the heat and boil gently, uncovered, for 2 hours.

Meanwhile, impale the shallots and ginger on a skewer and char them over a gas flame or a hot electric burner. After 3 or 4 minutes of turning them over the heat, they should be nicely browned and slightly blackened on all sides. Set aside.

Add the remaining piece of star anise and the blackened shallots and ginger to the stock and boil gently for 1 hour more. As the stock boils, skim off the fat that accumulates on the surface.

Strain the stock through a very fine strainer into a saucepan and let it cool. When it is cold, spoon off any fat that has risen to the surface. You should have about 6 cups stock. If you have less, add enough water to bring it to this amount; if you have more, boil gently to reduce it. Set aside.

MEANWHILE, POACH THE EGGS: Combine 3 quarts water and the vinegar in a shallow nonstick saucepan about 10 inches wide; the depth of the water should be 1½ to 2 inches. Bring the water to a boil; as soon as the first egg is added, the water temperature will go down and the boiling will cease, which is what you want, since boiling toughens egg whites.

One at a time, crack each egg on a flat surface (breaking eggs on the edge of a pan or table can push the shell inside and break the yolks), insert your thumb in the little opening created, and break the shell directly above the water, close enough so the water doesn't splash as the egg drops into it. Work as fast as you can, adding the eggs one after the other. You will see that threads of the egg whites rise to the surface and float a little in the water. Drag the back of a skimmer or slotted spoon across the surface of the water to catch these threads and to move the eggs enough that they don't stick to the bottom of the pan. After the eggs have been moved once, they won't stick again. Let the water return almost to a boil (about 200 degrees). When the water begins to simmer, reduce the heat and continue poaching the eggs for approximately 4 minutes. Lift one of the eggs out of the water with a slotted spoon and press on it gently to determine the degree of doneness; the yolk should be soft to the touch, indicating it is soft and runny inside. Transfer the cooked eggs to a bowl of ice water to cool completely, 10 to 15 minutes.

Lift the eggs out of the ice water and trim off any hanging pieces of white to create nice oval shapes; return them to the water. (*The trimmed eggs can be kept in a bowl of water in the refrigerator for up to 24 hours.*)

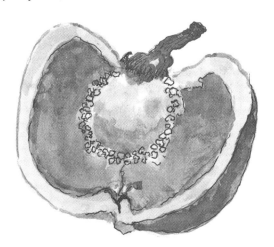

FOR THE ASPIC: Combine the leeks, parsley, celery, and gelatin in a large stainless steel stockpot. (Four envelopes of gelatin are used because the strength of the gelatin will lessen as the stock boils.) Add the egg whites, salt, and pepper and mix well.

Bring the stock to a boil and add to the clarification mixture, mixing carefully. Cook over high heat, stirring constantly, until the mixture comes to a strong boil. Reduce the heat and simmer very gently for 3 to 4 minutes, without disturbing the mixture. Set the aspic aside to rest for 15 minutes.

Strain the aspic through a strainer lined with wet paper towels. You should have about 5 cups of aspic.

FOR THE GARNISHES: With a vegetable peeler, remove as much skin from the red pepper as possible. Cut the pepper into sections at the pleats and peel off any remaining skin, which will now be accessible. Remove and discard the ribs and seeds and cut the flesh into julienne strips about ¼ inch wide. Put the strips into a saucepan, add 3 cups water, bring to a boil, and cook for about 10 seconds. Drain.

Remove and discard the mushroom stems, and cut the caps into ⅛- to ¼-inch-thick slices. Stack the slices together a few at a time and cut them into julienne strips. (You should have about ¾ cup.)

Put the mushrooms in a saucepan and add ½ cup of the aspic, or enough to cover. Bring to a boil and cook for about 1 minute. Remove the pan from the heat and stir in the pepper strips.

TO SERVE THE EGGS IN INDIVIDUAL DISHES: Pour about 1 cup of the aspic into a small stainless steel bowl, set it over ice, and stir until it starts to get syrupy. Spoon about 2 tablespoons of the cold aspic into the bottom of each of eight individual soufflé dishes or ramekins (about 3½ inches across and 2 inches deep). Refrigerate until the aspic is set.

When the aspic is set, drain the eggs on paper towels and dry them thoroughly. Arrange 3 or 4 ham strips in each dish and then add a few strips of red pepper and mushrooms. Place the poached eggs on top of the aspic and garnishes, then top with the remaining garnishes. Cool additional aspic over ice until it gets syrupy, then pour it over the eggs and garnishes, filling up the dishes. (The aspic is cooled over ice before using because the finished dish will be shinier and more beautiful this way than if the aspic were poured directly over the eggs while lukewarm or just cool.) Refrigerate until set.

To serve the eggs, gently run the blade of a small sharp knife around the edge of each dish, holding the knife tightly against the side of the dish so you don't cut into the egg. Invert onto a plate and shake to unmold.

TO SERVE THE EGGS IN ONE LARGE DISH: Sprinkle some of the garnishes over the bottom of a 6- to 8-cup gratin dish and arrange the drained and dried eggs on top. Sprinkle the remaining garnishes over and around the eggs. Put 4 cups of the aspic in a bowl over ice and stir until it is syrupy. With a large spoon, nap the eggs with enough aspic until they are completely covered and the aspic is almost set. Refrigerate until set hard before serving from the dish.

Eggs with Rich Vinaigrette and Anchovies
Serves 4

❧ This recipe makes a great first course for a summer menu. To serve it as a main course, double the ingredients. The rich vinaigrette is also great with poached fish.

6 large hard-cooked eggs (see page 66), preferably organic, peeled

VINAIGRETTE

1 large egg yolk
1 tablespoon Dijon mustard
1 tablespoon sherry vinegar
1 tablespoon water
¼ teaspoon salt
¼ teaspoon freshly ground black pepper
⅓ cup extra-virgin olive oil

1 2-ounce can anchovy fillets in oil
2 tablespoons chopped fresh chives

Halve the hard-cooked eggs lengthwise and arrange them on a serving platter.

FOR THE VINAIGRETTE: Put all the ingredients except the oil in a bowl and mix well. Whisking constantly, slowly add the oil to create a rich vinaigrette with the consistency of a very light mayonnaise.

Spoon the sauce over and around the eggs and arrange 2 anchovy fillets over each egg half. Sprinkle with the chives and serve.

Stuffed Eggs with Mushrooms and Tomato Coulis
Serves 3 or 4

❧ Easy and inexpensive, this unusual first course is a winner with guests. Since I always have eggs in the house, it's a great recipe to prepare when friends drop by unexpectedly.

6 large hard-cooked eggs (see page 66), preferably organic, peeled
2 tablespoons unsalted butter, softened
1 tablespoon olive oil
2 tablespoons minced onion
1½ cups coarsely chopped mushrooms
1 tomato, coarsely chopped (about ¾ cup)

3 tablespoons chopped fresh parsley
½ teaspoon salt
¼ teaspoon freshly ground black pepper

Cut the hard-cooked eggs lengthwise in half. Lift the yolks out carefully, so as not to break the whites, and transfer to a small bowl. Mash the yolks with 1 tablespoon of the butter until smooth.

Melt the remaining tablespoon butter in a large skillet. Add the oil and sauté the onion over medium heat until limp but not brown. Stir in the mushrooms, increase the heat slightly, and cook for 2 to 3 minutes. Add the tomato, 1 tablespoon of the parsley, the salt, and the pepper. Remove from the heat and mix in the mashed yolks.

Fill the whites with some of the mushroom mixture and arrange on a platter with the extra mushroom mixture spooned over and around the eggs. Sprinkle with the remaining 2 tablespoons parsley and serve.

Eggs Jeannette
Serves 6

❧ My mother used to make this dish regularly when I was a child. It is usually served lukewarm or at room temperature as a first course for dinner, but it is equally good as a brunch, lunch, buffet, or picnic dish.

Many variations can be made on the same principle. Here the yolks are seasoned with garlic and parsley, but bits of leftovers such as shellfish, meat, fish, or vegetables like spinach or mushrooms can be mixed with the yolks for different flavors.

6 large hard-cooked eggs (see page 66), preferably organic, peeled
2 tablespoons milk

2 garlic cloves, finely chopped (1 tablespoon)
2 tablespoons chopped fresh parsley
¼ teaspoon salt
¼ teaspoon freshly ground black pepper

1½ tablespoons peanut oil

DRESSING
About 2 tablespoons reserved egg yolk mixture (from above)
2 teaspoons Dijon mustard
2 teaspoons red wine vinegar
1 tablespoon water
Pinch of salt
Pinch of freshly ground black pepper
¼ cup olive oil

Cut the eggs crosswise in half at the widest point. Remove the yolks and push them through a food mill fitted with a fine screen into a bowl. (If you do not have a food mill, mash the yolks with a fork.) Mix the egg yolks with the milk, garlic, parsley, salt, and pepper; the mixture should be moist and hold together. Stuff the whites with the yolk mixture, reserving approximately 2 tablespoons for the dressing. (The egg yolk mixture adds texture to the dressing.)

Heat the oil in a large skillet, preferably nonstick. When the oil is hot, add the egg halves, stuffed side down, and fry over medium heat for about 2 minutes; they will brown beautifully. (Do not cook the white side.) Remove the eggs from the skillet and arrange them on a platter or in a gratin dish.

FOR THE DRESSING: Put all the ingredients except the oil in a food processor. With the motor running, slowly add the oil.

Pour the dressing on top of and around the eggs and serve.

Egg and Onion Gratin

Serves 6

✎ **The ingredients for this** gratin are almost always at hand, so it is a real savior when unexpected guests arrive for dinner. The onion-flavored white sauce can be used to make gratins from all kinds of cooked vegetables, such as cauliflower, zucchini, or carrots.

7 large hard-cooked eggs (see page 66), preferably organic, peeled
2 tablespoons unsalted butter
1½ cups sliced onions
1 tablespoon all-purpose flour
1½ cups milk
½ teaspoon salt
¼ teaspoon freshly ground black pepper
½ cup grated Gruyère or Emmenthaler cheese

Slice the eggs crosswise with an egg slicer or a knife and arrange them in a 4- to 6-cup gratin dish.

Preheat the oven to 400 degrees.

Melt the butter in a medium saucepan. When it is hot, add the onions and cook over medium-high heat, stirring once in a while, for 2½ to 3 minutes, until they sizzle and have just started to brown. Add the flour, mix well with a wooden spatula, and cook for about 30 seconds. Add the milk, salt, and pepper, stirring constantly to prevent lumps, and bring to a boil, stirring constantly. Reduce the heat and let the sauce simmer gently for about a minute.

Pour the sauce over the eggs and mix the sauce and eggs gently. Sprinkle with the grated cheese and bake for 10 to 12 minutes.

Turn the oven to broil. Place the eggs under the hot broiler for 4 to 5 minutes to make a nice brown crust. Serve immediately.

Egg and Spinach Gratin

Serves 6

✎ **You can assemble this** gratin ahead of time, but reheat it in a 425-degree oven for 7 or 8 minutes to ensure that it is hot throughout before sliding it under the broiler. If you're serving it immediately after assembling it, while the spinach and cream sauce are still warm, simply broil it for a few minutes.

1½ tablespoons olive oil
1 pound spinach, tough stems removed and washed (about 16 loosely packed cups)
¼ teaspoon salt
¼ teaspoon freshly ground black pepper
6 large hard-cooked eggs (see page 66), preferably organic, peeled

CREAM SAUCE
1½ tablespoons unsalted butter
1½ tablespoons all-purpose flour
1½ cups half-and-half
¼ teaspoon salt
¼ teaspoon freshly ground black pepper

1½ tablespoons freshly grated Parmesan cheese

Heat the olive oil in a large deep skillet. When it is hot, add the spinach, still wet from washing, and press it into the skillet. Add the salt and pepper and cook until the spinach is soft and wilted, about 3 minutes.

Spread the spinach evenly in a 6-cup gratin dish. Slice the eggs crosswise with an egg slicer or a knife, or cut into wedges, and arrange them in one layer on top of the spinach.

FOR THE SAUCE: Melt the butter in a small saucepan. Add the flour and mix it in with a whisk. Add the half-and-half and bring to a boil, stirring constantly (especially in the corners, where the mixture tends to stick and burn). Stir in the salt and pepper and boil for about 10 seconds.

Pour the sauce over the eggs and sprinkle on the cheese.

Preheat the broiler. Place the gratin under the broiler for about 5 minutes, until the surface is nicely browned. Serve immediately.

Flan of Green Herbs with Raw Tomato Sauce
Serves 6

❧ In home cooking, a flan — be it sweet or savory — is a custard. The choice of herbs and greens used to season this savory flan can be altered based on your garden or market; bear in mind, though, that certain herbs — tarragon, basil, and cilantro, for example — have a stronger flavor and so should be used in smaller quantities than milder herbs like parsley or chervil. This makes a terrific first course.

FLAN

- 6 cups loosely packed mixed fresh herbs and greens, such as sorrel, cilantro, parsley, chervil, chives, basil, tarragon, and arugula
- 4 cups loosely packed baby spinach leaves
- 1 tablespoon unsalted butter
- 2 tablespoons olive oil
- ¼ cup pine nuts
- 6 large eggs
- ½ cup light cream
- ½ teaspoon salt
- ¼ teaspoon freshly ground black pepper
- 2 tablespoons freshly grated Parmesan cheese

SAUCE

- 2 pounds ripe tomatoes (about 4 large), coarsely chopped
- 1 tablespoon finely chopped jalapeño pepper (optional)
- 1 teaspoon salt
- ½ teaspoon freshly ground black pepper
- 1½ tablespoons white wine vinegar
- ¼ cup extra-virgin olive oil

Preheat the oven to 375 degrees.

FOR THE FLAN: Wash the herbs, greens, and spinach and drain well. Coarsely chop.

Melt the butter with the olive oil in an 8- to 10-inch ovenproof nonstick saucepan. Add the nuts and sauté for 1 to 2 minutes, until lightly browned. Stir in the herbs and spinach and cook for 3 minutes, or until soft and tender.

Break the eggs into a bowl and whisk with the cream until blended. Add the mixture to the saucepan, along with the salt and pepper, and cook, stirring, for about 15 seconds, until semiset. Sprinkle the cheese on top.

Transfer the flan to the oven and bake for 10 minutes, or until set and lightly browned.

MEANWHILE, FOR THE TOMATO SAUCE: Put the tomatoes in a food processor with the jalapeño, if using, and process until smooth. Add the salt, pepper, vinegar, and olive oil and process for a few seconds. Transfer to a serving bowl and set aside.

Spoon the hot flan onto plates and serve with the sauce.

Quiche with Bacon
Serves 6 to 8

❧ The dough for this quiche is made with butter and lard (or vegetable shortening). The result is very flaky, with the taste of the lard complimenting the bacon in the filling. The dough is not precooked but is prepared in the home style, by baking it filled, as my mother and aunt used to do. The quiche may not be as elegant as one made in a precooked shell, as chefs do in fancy restaurants, but it's faster and easier to make it this way — and it's very good too.

DOUGH

- 1½ cups all-purpose flour
- ¼ teaspoon salt
- 4 tablespoons (½ stick) unsalted butter
- 3 tablespoons lard or vegetable shortening
- ¼ cup ice-cold water

FILLING

- 4 large eggs
- 1½ cups milk
- ½ cup heavy cream
- 1 teaspoon salt
- ¼ teaspoon freshly ground white pepper
- 5 slices bacon, cooked in a microwave oven or skillet until crisp and broken into pieces
- 1½ cups diced (½-inch) Gruyère or Emmenthaler cheese (5 ounces)

Preheat the oven to 400 degrees.

FOR THE DOUGH: Combine the flour, salt, butter, and lard or shortening together in a food processor and process until you have a coarse mixture, about 10 seconds. Add the water and process for 5 seconds. Turn the dough out and gather together into a ball.

Roll the dough out with a rolling pin into an 11- or 12-inch circle and use it to line a 9- to 10-inch tart pan with a removable bottom or a pie pan. Refrigerate until you are ready to fill the quiche shell.

FOR THE FILLING: Beat the eggs in a bowl only until well mixed. Stir in the milk, cream, salt, and white pepper.

Scatter the bacon and cheese over the dough. Place the pan on a cookie sheet and pour in the egg mixture. Bake for 1 hour, or until the filling is set and browned on top. Remove from the oven and let cool slightly; the quiche is best after it has rested for at least 15 to 20 minutes.

Cut into slices and serve lukewarm.

Leek and Gruyère Quiche
Serves 6 to 8

The filling possibilities are endless — from bacon to mushrooms to spinach to truffles. So that the filling will not be overcooked, the dough is partially prebaked since the filling needs only 20 to 25 minutes, which is not enough time to cook the dough completely.

The quiche can be baked ahead and reheated, uncovered, in a 375-degree oven until warmed through.

DOUGH

- 1 cup all-purpose flour
- 6 tablespoons (¾ stick) cold unsalted butter, cut into ½-inch pieces
- ⅛ teaspoon salt
- ¼ teaspoon sugar
  About 3 tablespoons ice-cold water

FILLING

- 1 large or 2 small leeks, trimmed (leaving most of the green), split, washed, and thinly sliced (2 cups)
- 4 large eggs
- ½ teaspoon salt
- ½ teaspoon freshly ground black pepper
- 1½ cups grated Gruyère or Emmenthaler cheese (5 ounces)

1¼ cups milk
¼ cup heavy cream

Preheat the oven to 400 degrees.

FOR THE DOUGH: Put the flour, butter, salt, and sugar in a food processor and pulse the mixture for 5 to 10 seconds, just until the butter is broken into small but still visible pieces. Add 3 tablespoons ice water (you may have to add a little less or a little more, depending on the dryness of the flour) and process for 10 to 15 seconds; the dough may not have formed into a ball at this point. Transfer it to a bowl and press it gently together into a ball.

Place the ball of dough in the center of a sheet of plastic wrap about 12 inches square and lay another piece of plastic wrap the same size on top. Roll the dough between the plastic wrap to form a circle about 12 inches in diameter. Remove the plastic wrap from the top of the dough and invert the dough into a 9- to 10-inch tart pan with a removable bottom. Use the remaining sheet of plastic wrap to press the dough into place in the pan, then peel off the plastic wrap. The dough should extend about ½ inch above the edge of the pan; roll or press this overhang back over the dough at the edges to make it thicker.

Line the shell with a double layer of aluminum foil, pressing the foil gently into place; the foil should be rigid enough to hold the dough in place as it cooks. Place the pan on a cookie sheet and bake the dough for 20 minutes. Then carefully remove the aluminum foil and bake the dough for another 20 to 25 minutes, until it is lightly browned inside.

MEANWHILE, FOR THE FILLING: Put the leeks and ¾ cup water in a saucepan and bring to a boil over high heat. Boil, uncovered, for about 5 minutes, until the water has evaporated and the leeks are soft. Remove from the heat.

Beat the eggs in a bowl until smooth. Stir in

the salt, pepper, cheese, milk, and cream. Mix in the leeks.

Reduce the oven temperature to 375 degrees. Pour the filling into the precooked shell while the pan is still on the cookie sheet in the oven. (The filling will come to the rim of the shell, and there is less likelihood of its spilling if the pan is not removed from the oven.) Bake for 20 to 25 minutes, until the filling is completely set and beautifully browned on top.

Let the quiche rest for 10 to 15 minutes before cutting it into wedges and serving.

Grits and Cheese Soufflé
Serves 6

The slightly grainy yet creamy texture of grits is tasty with cheddar cheese. The soufflé can be baked in a soufflé dish, but if cooked in a gratin dish it is crustier, beautiful to look at, and easy to serve. It can also be reheated and served as a savory pudding.

6 scallions, trimmed (leaving some green)
and cut into ¼-inch-thick slices
(½ cup)
2½ cups milk
½ teaspoon salt
¼ teaspoon freshly ground black pepper
⅓ cup white grits
4 ounces cheddar cheese, 1 slice reserved
for garnish and the remainder grated
(1¼ cups)
5 large eggs, separated

Preheat the oven to 350 degrees. Butter a 6-cup gratin dish and set it aside.

Combine the scallions, milk, salt, and pepper in a saucepan and bring to a boil over medium-high heat. Stir in the grits and return the mixture to a boil, then reduce the heat and boil gently for 12 to 15 minutes, stirring occasionally, until the grits are thickened and cooked.

Stir in the grated cheese, then immediately mix in the egg yolks and remove the pan from the heat. (*The recipe can be prepared to this point several hours ahead. However, be sure to thin the mixture with a little water before completing the recipe, as grits tend to thicken as they cool.*)

Beat the egg whites in a large bowl until firm. Fold them into the warm grits mixture with a rubber spatula. Pour the mixture into the buttered gratin dish. Cut the reserved slice of cheese into strips and place them decoratively over the soufflé.

Bake the soufflé in the center of the oven for about 20 minutes, until it is just set and puffy. The soufflé will deflate quickly, so serve it as soon as it emerges from the oven. Or serve it lukewarm — it will still be good.

GRITS BREAKFAST SOUP

For a hearty breakfast soup, cook the grits in the milk with the scallions, salt, and pepper, as directed in the recipe. Dilute with another cup of milk and serve hot.

Herb and Goat Cheese Soufflé
Serves 4

❧ **There is just one** secret to preparing a soufflé: timing. When I make this herb soufflé for a family dinner, I prepare the mixture at my leisure in the afternoon, transfer it to the soufflé dish, and refrigerate it. Then, as I begin to serve apéritifs and set the table, I bake the soufflé in a preheated oven. Usually we are ready to sit down to eat just when it is ready for us.

2½ tablespoons unsalted butter
3 tablespoons freshly grated Parmesan cheese
1 tablespoon olive oil
¼ cup all-purpose flour
1½ cups milk
½ teaspoon salt
⅛ teaspoon freshly ground black pepper
2 ounces soft goat cheese
2 cups loosely packed fresh herbs (a mixture of parsley, basil, and tarragon leaves and chives)
1 large egg
5 large eggs, separated

Preheat the oven to 375 degrees.

Using ½ tablespoon of the butter, butter a 6-cup soufflé dish. Add 2 tablespoons of the grated Parmesan and shake the dish to coat the bottom and sides with the cheese. Refrigerate until needed.

Heat the remaining 2 tablespoons butter and the oil in a large heavy saucepan over medium heat. Add the flour and mix it in well with a whisk. Add the milk, salt, and pepper and bring to a boil over medium-high heat, stirring constantly. Boil for 10 seconds, then add the goat cheese and mix until smooth. Set aside.

Coarsely chop the herbs, then put them in a blender or mini-chop with the whole egg and the egg yolks. (Don't use a food processor — the mixture will not puree as it will in a blender.) Process until you get a smooth green puree. Add this to the mixture in the saucepan and mix well.

Beat the egg whites in a bowl until they are firm and fold them into the mixture in the saucepan until well blended. Transfer to the prepared dish and sprinkle with the remaining tablespoon of Parmesan. (*You can refrigerate the soufflé for 2 to 3 hours before baking.*)

Place the soufflé dish on a cookie sheet and

bake in the center of the oven for 30 minutes, or until the soufflé is puffy but still a little runny inside. Spoon onto plates and serve.

Tomato, Basil, and Cheese Soufflés
Serves 4

✀ **For this summery delight,** which makes a good first course, individual soufflés are baked in hollowed-out tomatoes. The tomato tops and insides are processed into a puree and mixed into a sauce of egg yolks, cheese, and basil, then lightened with egg whites, spooned into the tomatoes, and baked. The tomato juices give the soufflés somewhat soft centers.

        4 large firm but ripe tomatoes (about
           2½ pounds)
        ¾ teaspoon salt
        3 large eggs
        2 tablespoons olive oil
        1 tablespoon unsalted butter
        ¼ cup all-purpose flour
        ¼ teaspoon freshly ground black pepper
        3 tablespoons slivered fresh basil leaves
           (chiffonade)
        ¼ cup grated Gruyère or Emmenthaler
           cheese
        1 tablespoon freshly grated Parmesan
           cheese

Preheat the oven to 375 degrees.

Using a sharp knife, remove the top ½ inch from the smooth end of each tomato; reserve these "caps." Scoop out the insides of each tomato, including the ribs, with a measuring spoon, leaving tomato shells that are about ½ inch thick, and reserve the insides in a bowl.

Sprinkle the shells with ¼ teaspoon of the salt

and place them hollow side down in a gratin dish nice enough to bring to the table. Bake the shells for 8 to 10 minutes to soften them.

Meanwhile, process the reserved tomato caps and tomato insides in a food processor for 15 seconds. (You should have about 2 cups.)

Separate the eggs, placing the yolks in a small bowl and the whites in a larger bowl.

Heat the oil and butter in a medium saucepan. Add the flour, mixing it in with a whisk, and cook over medium-high heat, stirring with the whisk, for 30 seconds. Add the processed tomato insides, the remaining ½ teaspoon salt, and the pepper, bring to a boil, stirring constantly, and boil for about 30 seconds. Remove from the heat and whisk in the yolks, basil, and Gruyère or Emmenthaler.

Beat the egg whites until they form soft peaks (they should not be too firm), then combine them well with the tomato mixture.

Turn the tomato shells over in the gratin dish and fill with the tomato mixture. Spoon any remaining soufflé mixture around the tomatoes and sprinkle them with the Parmesan cheese. Bake the tomatoes in the center of the oven for 25 minutes, or until the soufflé mixture puffs up and browns nicely on top.

Serve 1 tomato per person, with some of the extra soufflé mixture, if there was any, alongside.

Broccoli Rabe, Ham, and Parmesan Soufflé
Serves 6 to 8 as a first course

✎ **The Parmesan cheese and** bread crumb crust and topping of this soufflé will be browner and crunchier when it is prepared in a gratin dish, making it easier to serve at the table. It can also be made in a conventional soufflé dish.

Leftover soufflé will reinflate when reheated in a 350-degree oven.

10	ounces broccoli rabe, trimmed
1	slice firm white bread, processed to crumbs in a food processor (½ cup)
½	cup freshly grated Parmesan cheese
4	tablespoons (½ stick) unsalted butter
3	tablespoons all-purpose flour
1½	cups milk
¼	teaspoon salt
¼	teaspoon freshly ground black pepper
3	large eggs, separated
2	large egg whites
4	ounces lean ham, cut into julienne strips (1 cup)

Preheat the oven to 375 degrees.

Wash the broccoli rabe and transfer it, still wet, to a skillet. Cook over medium-high heat for 2 minutes, or until wilted. Remove from the heat, drain well, and cool.

Coarsely chop the broccoli rabe; set aside.

Mix the bread crumbs and 3 tablespoons of the Parmesan cheese together in a small bowl.

Using 1 teaspoon of the butter, grease the sides and bottom of a 6-cup gratin dish. Add half of the bread crumb mixture and shake the dish until the crumbs coat the sides and bottom. Set aside.

Melt the remaining 3 tablespoons plus 2 teaspoons butter in a saucepan. Add the flour, mixing with a whisk, and cook over medium-high heat for about 30 seconds. Whisk in the milk, salt, and pepper, bring to a boil, whisking constantly, and cook, whisking, until the mixture thickens. Remove from the heat and whisk in the egg yolks. Add the reserved broccoli rabe and the ham and mix well.

Beat the 5 egg whites in a large bowl until firm but still soft. Fold them into the broccoli rabe mixture, along with the remaining tablespoon of cheese.

Pour the soufflé mixture into the prepared gratin dish and sprinkle the remaining bread crumb mixture on top.

Place the dish on a cookie sheet and bake in the center of the oven for about 30 minutes, until the soufflé is set and the top is puffy and brown.

Spoon the soufflé directly from the gratin dish onto plates and serve immediately. (The soufflé can be unmolded from the dish by inverting it onto a plate, if you would prefer to present it in this way.)

Fresh White Cheese with Cream
Serves 4

❧ This is an interpretation of a classic cheese dish I ate growing up. Sieved cottage cheese and cream cheese are mixed with herbs and whipped cream and the mixture is drained in cheesecloth to create a soft cheese. At serving time, the cheese is turned upside down onto a serving plate, covered with thick cream, and brought to the table. It is very easy to make, and it can be prepared a couple of days ahead. Cheese similar to this is sold ready-made in all the little shops around Lyon and Bourg-en-Bresse, where I was born, but often the housewife makes it herself with unpasteurized fresh milk and rennet. A few drops of rennet are added to a quart of milk and left to stand in a lukewarm place for a couple of hours. When the milk has curdled, it is ready to be poured into small tins pierced with holes (called *faisselles*) and allowed to drain.

People sometimes sprinkle the cheese with sugar and mix it with fresh berries, such as raspberries or wild strawberries, which is excellent, but in Lyon, we mix it with garlic, chives, and parsley — all chopped fine — then sprinkle it with salt and pepper, and enjoy it as a last course, in place of dessert.

You'll need to start this dish the night before so the cheese has time to drain.

- 2 cups large-curd cottage cheese
- 8 ounces cream cheese
- 1 teaspoon salt
- 1 teaspoon freshly ground black pepper
- 2 tablespoons chopped fresh chives
- 2 tablespoons chopped fresh parsley
- 1 teaspoon finely chopped garlic
- 1½ cups heavy cream

SAUCE

- 1 cup sour cream
- ¼ cup heavy cream

Push the cottage cheese and cream cheese through a food mill into a bowl. Add the salt, pepper, chives, parsley, and garlic and mix well.

Whip the heavy cream until it holds soft peaks. Mix it into the cottage cheese mixture: the texture of the cheese is too firm to fold the cream in; it has to be incorporated with a whisk. Mix just enough to blend all the ingredients; if you mix it too long, it will turn into butter.

Pour the mixture onto a square of cheesecloth and tie the four corners together. Push a spoon handle or a chopstick through the opening in the knot and suspend over a deep pot, so that the cheese has space to drain. Refrigerate overnight.

FOR THE SAUCE: Combine the sour cream and heavy cream.

At serving time, turn the cheese upside down onto a serving platter and lift off the cheesecloth. Serve with the sauce.

Fromage Fort
Makes 2 cups (enough for about 50 toasts)

❧ A specialty of my father, *fromage fort* ("strong cheese") is made of leftover pieces of cheese — any kind — that are pureed in a food processor and seasoned with garlic and white wine. It's best on bread or toast. As a child, I would spread the cheese mixture on a thick slab of country bread, impale the bread on a fork, and then hold it in the fireplace, with the cheese side as close as possible to the fire. When the cheese bubbled and a nice glaze formed, I would rub the crusty cheese with a piece of butter and eat it piping hot. Although I have a strong attachment to that early memory, I find that the toasts glaze just as well when placed under the broiler for a few minutes. Refrigerated, this original and economical cheese combination will keep for a week or two.

If you use only unsalted cheeses, or a large amount of unsalted farmer's cheese, for example, you may want to add a little salt. Usually, however, the cheese itself is salty enough so that additional salt is not needed.

3–4 garlic cloves
1 pound leftover cheeses— a combination of as many hard and soft varieties as you like (such as Brie, cheddar, Swiss, blue, mozzarella, and/or goat), pieces trimmed if necessary to remove dried-out places and mold
½ cup dry white wine, leek broth, or vegetable broth, or a mixture of these
  Salt, if needed (see the headnote)
1 teaspoon freshly ground black pepper
  Bread or toast, for serving

With the motor running, drop the garlic into a food processor and process for a few seconds, until coarsely chopped. Add the cheeses, white wine and/or broth, salt (if needed), and pepper, and process for 30 to 45 seconds, until the mixture is soft and creamy. Transfer to a crock, cover with plastic wrap, and refrigerate until ready to use.

To serve, spread generously on slices of bread or toast and eat cold; or arrange on a tray and broil for a few minutes to melt the cheese before serving.

Cheese Fritters
Serves 6 to 8

❧ **I often serve this** last-minute hors d'oeuvre with drinks when unexpected guests show up. It is a cinch to make fresh bread crumbs in the food processor: just tear the slices into pieces and process for a few seconds.

2 large egg whites
  Pinch of salt
1 cup grated Gruyère or Emmenthaler cheese
1 cup fresh bread crumbs
2 cups vegetable oil, for deep-frying

Beat the egg whites with the salt in a medium bowl with an electric mixer or with a whisk until they stand in peaks when you lift up the beater. Add the cheese and beat for a few seconds. Fold in the bread crumbs. Form the mixture into balls about the size of marbles.

Heat the oil to 350 degrees in a small deep saucepan. Drop the little balls into the hot oil in batches (don't crowd the pan) and cook for about 2 minutes, or until golden brown. Lift out of the oil with a slotted spoon and drain on paper towels.

Serve warm, in a napkin-lined dish.

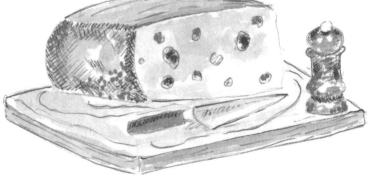

Pasta, Rice, Grains, and Potatoes

Pasta, Rice, Grains, and Potatoes

Pasta, Noodles, and Gnocchi

Red Pepper Linguine with Walnuts

Serves 4

❧ **With its brilliant red** color, this red pepper sauce has eye appeal as well as great taste. The pasta is seasoned with chopped onion, olive oil, Romano cheese, and parsley. It's an ideal meatless main dish for a summer dinner.

It's important to use a food mill for the red pepper sauce. If the peppers are pureed in a food processor, the puree must be strained afterward to remove the skin. The food mill does the pureeing and straining in one easy step.

SAUCE

2–3 large red bell peppers (1½ pounds), cored, seeded, and cut into 1-inch pieces
½ cup water
¾ teaspoon salt
¼ teaspoon freshly ground black pepper
3 tablespoons extra-virgin olive oil

12 ounces linguine
1 tablespoon olive oil
1 medium onion, chopped (1 cup)
½ cup walnut pieces
5 garlic cloves, crushed and finely chopped (1½ tablespoons)
½ teaspoon salt
¼ teaspoon freshly ground black pepper
2 tablespoons coarsely chopped fresh parsley
2–3 tablespoons freshly grated Pecorino Romano cheese

Bring 4 quarts of salted water to a boil in a large pot.

MEANWHILE, FOR THE SAUCE: Drop the red pepper pieces into a saucepan with the ½ cup water. Bring to a boil, cover, and boil gently for 10 minutes.

Push the peppers and their cooking liquid through a food mill and return to the saucepan. (You should have 1¾ cups.) Add the salt, pepper, and oil and stir well with a whisk. Set aside in the saucepan.

Add the linguine to the boiling water, stir well, and cook for about 8 minutes, until tender but still slightly al dente.

While the linguine is cooking, heat the tablespoon of oil in a skillet. When it is hot, add the onion, walnut pieces, and garlic and sauté over medium heat for about 2 minutes, until the onion begins to brown. Transfer the mixture to the bowl in which you will serve the linguine and stir in the salt, pepper, and parsley.

Scoop out ½ cup of the pasta cooking liquid and add it to the bowl, then drain the linguine. Add the linguine to the bowl and mix well.

Bring the red pepper sauce to a boil and divide it among four large plates. Mound the linguine in the center of each plate, sprinkle with the cheese, and serve immediately.

Spaghetti with Fresh Vegetable Sauce

Serves 4

❧ **Bringing the water to** a boil is the most time-consuming part of this preparation. It takes only about 7 minutes to make the sauce and 8 minutes to cook the pasta. The sauce is a kind of ratatouille made with summer vegetables. Zucchini and bell peppers can be added or substituted for one or more of the vegetables.

To prevent the finished pasta from sticking together or being too dense, I reserve a little of the cooking water and add it to the vegetables before tossing them with the spaghetti.

12 ounces spaghetti
¼ cup olive oil
1 large red onion, thinly sliced (1½ cups)
1 small eggplant (6 ounces), cut into ½-inch pieces
3–4 garlic cloves, crushed and finely chopped (about 2 teaspoons)
2 ripe tomatoes (12 ounces), halved, seeded, and cut into ½-inch pieces (about 2 cups)
1 teaspoon salt
½ teaspoon freshly ground black pepper
2 tablespoons coarsely chopped fresh parsley
About ⅓ cup grated mozzarella cheese

Bring 4 quarts of salted water to a boil in a large pot. Add the pasta, stir well, and cook for about 8 minutes, until tender but still slightly al dente.

Meanwhile, heat the oil in a large saucepan.

Add the onion and eggplant and sauté until soft and lightly browned, 6 to 7 minutes. Remove the pan from the heat and mix in the garlic. Add the tomatoes, salt, and pepper and mix thoroughly to warm the tomatoes.

Scoop out ½ cup of the pasta cooking liquid and add it to the eggplant mixture. Drain the pasta, add it to the saucepan, and toss to coat it with the vegetables.

Divide the pasta and vegetables among four plates, sprinkle with the parsley and grated mozzarella cheese, and serve immediately.

Fettuccine with Summer Vegetables
Serves 4

❧ **The fettuccine is tossed** with a puree of garlic, basil, tarragon, and a portion of the pasta cooking water and served with a large assortment of chopped vegetables. Beautiful and fresh-tasting, it makes a wonderful light main course.

¼ cup olive oil
1 tablespoon unsalted butter
½ cup water
About 6 ounces broccoli, stems peeled, stems and florets cut into 1-inch pieces (2 cups)
6 scallions, trimmed (leaving some green) and cut into ½-inch pieces (1¼ cups)
4 large mushrooms, cleaned and cut into ½-inch pieces (1¾ cups)
1 small zucchini, trimmed and cut into ½-inch pieces (1 cup)
1 ear corn, husked and kernels cut off (¾ cup)
2 plum tomatoes, cut into ½-inch pieces (1 cup)
1¼ teaspoons salt

½ teaspoon freshly ground black pepper

5 garlic cloves

1 cup loosely packed fresh basil leaves

2 tablespoons loosely packed fresh tarragon leaves

12 ounces fettuccine

Freshly grated Parmesan cheese, for serving (optional)

Combine 1 tablespoon of the olive oil, the butter, and water in a large skillet and bring to a boil over high heat. Add the broccoli and scallions, bring back to a boil, and cook over high heat for 3 minutes. Add the mushrooms and zucchini and cook for another 2 minutes. Add the corn, tomatoes, ¾ teaspoon of the salt, and ¼ teaspoon of the pepper and toss the mixture for about 30 seconds. Set aside.

Crush the garlic with the remaining ½ teaspoon salt in a mortar with the pestle until partially pureed. (Alternatively, you can use a food processor.) Add the basil and tarragon leaves and continue pounding with the pestle (or pulsing) until you have a coarse puree. Add the remaining 3 tablespoons oil and ¼ teaspoon pepper and continue stirring and pounding the mixture with the pestle (or pulsing) until it is smooth.

Bring 4 quarts of salted water to a boil in a large pot. Add the fettuccine, stir well, and cook for 10 to 12 minutes, or until tender but still slightly al dente.

Meanwhile, combine the herb puree with 1 cup of the pasta cooking liquid in a large bowl.

Drain the pasta, add it to the bowl, and toss well. Reheat the reserved vegetables if necessary and spoon 2 tablespoons of the vegetable mixture into the center of each of four dinner plates. Divide the pasta among the plates, arranging it on top of the vegetables, and sprinkle the remainder of the vegetables on top. Serve immediately, passing grated cheese, if desired.

Tagliatelle and Peas
Serves 4

I often make this quick dish when I'm pressed for time. The pasta is tossed with baby peas, Parmesan cheese, salt, pepper, and some of the pasta cooking water.

12 ounces tagliatelle

1 cup frozen baby peas

3 tablespoons freshly grated Parmesan cheese, plus more for serving

2½ tablespoons extra-virgin olive oil

½ teaspoon salt

½ teaspoon freshly ground black pepper

Bring 4 quarts of salted water to a boil in a large pot. Add the pasta, stir well, and cook until tender but still slightly al dente, about 10 to 12 minutes.

Meanwhile, put the frozen peas in a strainer and run them under hot tap water until they are defrosted. Drain and combine the peas with the cheese, oil, salt, and pepper in a large serving bowl.

When the pasta is cooked, scoop out ⅔ cup of the cooking water and add it to the bowl with the peas. Drain the pasta, add it to the bowl, and toss well. Serve immediately, with extra cheese.

Spaghettini with Spicy Basil Pesto
Serves 4

Conventionally pesto is made with pine nuts, but here I use pecans, along with a jalapeño, for a distinctive effect. You may want to double or triple the recipe for the pesto. It is very good on grilled fish or meat, as a delicious flavoring for baked potatoes, or as a topping for other pastas. It will keep for up to a week in the refrigerator. Be sure to cover it with a piece of plastic wrap, pressing it down so it touches the surface of the pesto. "Blanching" the basil and parsley in a microwave helps prevent them from discoloring when the pesto is held for a few hours.

PESTO

2	cups packed fresh basil leaves
1	cup tightly packed fresh parsley leaves
¼	cup freshly grated Parmesan cheese
¼	cup pecans
5	garlic cloves, peeled and crushed
1	small jalapeño pepper, cut in half and seeded
½	cup extra-virgin olive oil

1	pound spaghettini
½	teaspoon salt
	Freshly ground black pepper
	Hot pepper flakes (optional)
½	cup freshly grated Parmesan cheese

Bring 4 quarts of salted water to a boil in a large pot.

MEANWHILE, FOR THE PESTO: Put the basil and parsley in a plastic bag and microwave on high for 1 minute. Transfer, while still hot, to a blender and add the Parmesan cheese, nuts, garlic, and jalapeño pepper. Process for about 30 seconds, until the mixture is finely pureed. Add the oil and process for a few more seconds. (You should have about 1½ cups.) Transfer to a large bowl and set aside.

Add the spaghettini to the boiling water, stir well, and cook for 8 to 9 minutes, until tender but still slightly al dente.

Scoop out 1 cup of the pasta cooking liquid and mix it with the pesto. Drain the pasta well and add it to the sauce, along with the salt, and black pepper to taste. Toss and serve immediately, with hot pepper flakes, if desired, and the grated Parmesan cheese.

Fusilli with Escarole, Eggplant, and Olive Sauce
Serves 4

Pasta is one of the most versatile ingredients available to the cook. Here I combine it with a sauce made of olives, escarole, eggplant, pine nuts, garlic, and peas. On another day, depending on the contents of my refrigerator, red onion, zucchini, green pepper, tomato, and broccoli can find their way into the sauce, along with capers or anchovy fillets. When I was a kid, we used grated Gruyère cheese rather than Parmesan on pasta. I still love that taste of my youth.

SAUCE

1	eggplant (about 1 pound)
½	teaspoon salt
1	tablespoon canola oil
¼	cup extra-virgin olive oil
2½	tablespoons pine nuts
3	large garlic cloves, thinly sliced (2 tablespoons)
10	ounces escarole (about ½ head), cut into 2-inch pieces, washed, and drained (about 6 cups loosely packed)
½	cup baby peas (fresh or defrosted frozen)
24	kalamata olives, pitted
¼	teaspoon freshly ground black pepper

12 ounces (3 cups) fusilli

½ teaspoon salt

½ teaspoon freshly ground black pepper

½ cup grated Gruyère or Emmenthaler
   cheese

FOR THE SAUCE: Preheat the oven to 400 degrees.

Trim off and discard the ends of the eggplant and cut it lengthwise into 5 slices of about equal thickness. Sprinkle the slices with ¼ teaspoon of the salt. Line a baking sheet with a nonstick baking mat or parchment paper and coat the mat (or paper) with the canola oil.

Press the slices of eggplant into the oil on the baking sheet, then turn them over, so they are lightly oiled on both sides, and arrange them in a single layer. Bake for 30 minutes, or until the slices are very tender and slightly browned.

When the eggplant slices are cool enough to handle, cut them into 1½-inch pieces. (You should have about 1½ cups.)

Heat the olive oil in a large skillet. Add the pine nuts and garlic and sauté for about 20 seconds. Add the escarole, still wet from washing, cover, and cook over medium-high heat for 3 to 4 minutes, until the escarole is wilted and starting to brown. Add the peas, olives, eggplant, the remaining ¼ teaspoon salt, and the pepper. Mix well and set aside. (*The sauce can be made up to a few hours ahead.*)

At serving time, bring 4 quarts of salted water to a boil in a large pot. Add the pasta, stir well, and cook for 10 to 12 minutes, until tender but still slightly al dente.

Scoop out ½ cup of the pasta cooking liquid and add it to the sauce. Drain the pasta and combine it with the sauce, adding the salt and pepper. Mix well.

Divide among four plates, sprinkle with the grated cheese, and serve immediately.

Linguine with Clam Sauce and Vegetables

Serves 4 as a main course, 8 as a first course

❧ **Clams are a favorite** at our house, and I make this recipe at least once a week in the summer. I like cherrystones, which are larger than littlenecks and meatier. Bring them just to a simmer.

1 pound linguine

SAUCE

2 tablespoons olive oil

1 tablespoon unsalted butter

2 medium onions, coarsely chopped (1 cup)

1 teaspoon fresh oregano leaves

4–6 large garlic cloves, sliced (¼ cup)

2 dozen cherrystone clams, shucked (see page 154), cut in half with scissors, and kept in their juices

½ cup dry white wine

½ teaspoon freshly ground black pepper

VEGETABLES

1 tablespoon peanut oil

1 tablespoon unsalted butter

8–10 asparagus spears, trimmed, peeled, and cut into 1-inch pieces (1 cup)

1¼ cups chopped mushrooms (4 ounces)

2 medium zucchini, trimmed and cut into ½-inch dice (1½ cups)

¼ teaspoon salt

1/8 teaspoon freshly ground black pepper

1¼ cups seeded and diced (½-inch) tomatoes

Freshly grated Parmesan cheese, for serving (optional)

Bring 4 quarts of salted water to a boil in a large pot. Add the pasta, stir well, and cook until tender but still slightly al dente.

MEANWHILE, FOR THE SAUCE: Heat the olive oil and butter in a large skillet until hot. Add the onions and sauté for about 2 minutes. Add the oregano and garlic and cook for about 30 seconds. Add the juices from the clams and the wine, and boil gently for 7 to 8 minutes. Add the clams and pepper and bring to a simmer. Set aside.

FOR THE VEGETABLES: When the pasta is cooked, drain it in a colander. Add the peanut oil and butter to the pot and heat until hot. Add the asparagus, mushrooms, and zucchini, season with the salt and pepper, and sauté for about 2 minutes. Toss in the tomatoes and heat briefly to warm them.

Divide the pasta among individual plates or transfer to a large serving platter. Spoon the hot clam sauce on top and arrange the vegetables on top of the pasta. Serve immediately, with Parmesan cheese, if desired.

Ziti with Sausage and Vegetables
Serves 4

Take **advantage of the** market when preparing this dish: If cauliflower is less expensive than broccoli rabe, use it instead. Likewise, omit the tomatoes if they are too costly. As for the sausage, look for the best price — sometimes links are less expensive, sometimes patties are cheaper, and often it is more economical to buy sausage in bulk.

- 8 ounces hot Italian sausage, casings removed if necessary
- 2½ tablespoons olive oil
- 12 ounces ziti
- 1 pound broccoli rabe
- 1 tablespoon finely chopped garlic
- 2 large ears corn, husked and kernels cut from the cob (about 2 cups)
- 12 ounces cherry tomatoes, halved if large
- ¾ teaspoon salt
- ¼ cup freshly grated Pecorino Romano cheese

Break the sausage into ½-inch pieces and place it in a saucepan with ½ tablespoon of the oil. Cook over medium heat for about 10 minutes, until most of the fat has been released from the sausage and the pieces are nicely browned.

Meanwhile, bring 4 quarts of salted water to a boil in a large pot. Add the pasta, stir well, and cook for about 10 minutes, until tender but still slightly al dente.

While the pasta is cooking, separate the leafy tops of the broccoli rabe from the stalks and cut the florets into 1-inch pieces. Peel the fibrous skin from the stalks and cut them into 1-inch pieces.

When the sausage has cooked for 10 minutes, add the broccoli rabe to the saucepan and mix well. Stir in the garlic, cover, and cook over medium heat for about 5 minutes.

When the pasta is cooked, scoop out ½ cup of the cooking liquid, then drain the pasta. Add the reserved cooking liquid to the sausage and broccoli mixture, along with the corn, tomatoes, the remaining 2 tablespoons oil, and the salt. Cover, bring to a boil, and boil for 1 minute.

Combine the pasta with the sausage and vegetables in a large serving bowl, tossing the mixture well. Serve immediately, with the grated cheese.

Orzo with Arugula Sauce
Serves 4

Since **each kernel of** orzo releases starch as it cooks, it should be boiled in a lot of water — otherwise, it tends to stick together or doesn't cook throughout. Although I like most pasta slightly al dente, I prefer orzo cooked for at least 8 minutes.

2 tablespoons olive oil

½ cup pine nuts

1 small onion, finely chopped (½ cup)

5–6 scallions, trimmed (leaving some green) and coarsely minced (1 cup)

1 2-ounce can anchovy fillets in oil, drained (reserve the oil) and cut into ½-inch pieces

8 cups loosely packed arugula (8–10 ounces), washed, dried, and cut into 2-inch pieces

½ teaspoon salt

½ teaspoon freshly ground black pepper

2 large tomatoes, peeled, halved, seeded, and cut into 1-inch pieces (about 2 cups)

12 ounces orzo

¼ cup shaved or freshly grated Parmesan or Pecorino Romano cheese

Heat the olive oil in a saucepan. When it is hot, add the pine nuts and onion and cook over medium heat for 5 minutes, or until the nuts are nicely browned and the onion is soft.

Add the scallions, anchovies, along with their oil, and the arugula, mix well, and cook for 5 minutes, or until the arugula is wilted and soft. Add the salt, pepper, and tomatoes and cook for 1 minute. Set aside. (*The sauce can be made up to 1 hour ahead.*)

Bring 8 cups salted water to a boil in a saucepan. Add the orzo, stir well, and cook, stirring occasionally, for 7 to 8 minutes, or until cooked to your liking.

Meanwhile, reheat the sauce if necessary.

Drain the orzo, add to the sauce, and mix well. Divide among four plates and sprinkle each serving with 1 tablespoon of the Parmesan or Romano. Serve immediately.

Macaroni Beaucaire
Serves 6

From the small town of Beaucaire in Provence, this is actually two dishes incorporated into one. The elbow macaroni, which is tossed with olive oil, Parmesan cheese, seasonings, and chives, can be served as is. But I've expanded on it by layering thin slices of sautéed eggplant and tomato underneath and on top of the pasta, then finishing the dish with shredded cheddar cheese.

8 ounces elbow macaroni

¼ cup olive oil

2 tablespoons freshly grated Parmesan cheese or Gruyère or Emmenthaler

1 teaspoon salt

½ teaspoon freshly ground black pepper

¼ cup minced fresh chives

VEGETABLES

About ½ cup canola oil

2 eggplants (about 1½ pounds total), trimmed and each cut lengthwise into 6 slices about ½ inch thick

About ½ teaspoon salt

3 ripe tomatoes (about 1 pound), cut into ½-inch-thick slices

1 cup shredded cheddar cheese (about 4 ounces)

Bring 4 quarts of salted water to a boil in a large pot. Add the macaroni and stir frequently until the water returns to a boil, so the elbows don't stick to the bottom of the pot. Cook the macaroni for about 15 minutes, until just tender but still slightly al dente.

Scoop out about ¾ cup of the cooking liquid and place it in a bowl large enough to hold the macaroni, then drain the elbows. Add the olive oil,

Parmesan, salt, and pepper to the cooking liquid in the bowl and mix well, then add the macaroni and chives and mix well again. Set aside.

FOR THE VEGETABLES: Heat 2 tablespoons of the canola oil in a large skillet. When it is hot, add a few of the eggplant slices in one layer, sprinkle them with a little salt, and cook for 2½ to 3 minutes on each side, until soft and nicely browned. Remove with a slotted spoon and put on a plate. Repeat with the remaining eggplant, adding more oil to the pan as necessary.

Preheat the oven to 400 degrees.

Reserve the 6 nicest slices of eggplant and half of the tomato slices (the prettiest ones) and arrange the remainder of the vegetables in a 14-by-10-inch gratin dish so they completely cover the bottom. Distribute the macaroni evenly on top and arrange the reserved eggplant and tomato slices in an alternating pattern over the macaroni. Sprinkle with the shredded cheese. (*The dish can be prepared a few hours ahead to this point and refrigerated.*)

Bake the gratin for 20 minutes (25 to 30 if the dish has been refrigerated), or until the cheese has melted and the macaroni is heated through. Serve immediately.

Pasta Shells with Ricotta Filling
Serves 6

✄ **Count on 5 or 6** stuffed shells per person. A few of the shells usually break in the cooking process; any broken pieces can be cut into smaller pieces and sprinkled around the stuffed shells in the gratin dish or used as a garnish for soup.

    12 ounces (about 3 dozen) large
            pasta shells
     2 slices firm white bread (2 ounces)

FILLING

    1½ pounds ricotta cheese
     3 large eggs
     ½ cup shredded fresh basil or parsley
            leaves, or a mixture
     ⅓ cup freshly grated Parmesan cheese
     ¾ teaspoon salt
     1 teaspoon freshly ground black pepper

SAUCE

     ¼ cup olive oil
     2 cups coarsely chopped onions
     5 garlic cloves, thinly sliced (about
            2 tablespoons)
     ½ teaspoon chopped fresh thyme
            or ¼ teaspoon dried thyme
    4–5 medium very ripe tomatoes, cut into
            1-inch pieces (about 4 cups), or 3 cups
            canned tomatoes, preferably imported,
            with their juice
    1½ cups water
     1 teaspoon salt
     ½ teaspoon freshly ground black pepper

     ¼ cup shredded fresh basil leaves

Bring 4 quarts of salted water to a boil in a large pot. Add the shells, stir well, and cook for about 15 minutes, until tender but still slightly al dente. Drain in a colander and rinse briefly under cold water to stop the cooking. Set aside.

Tear the bread into pieces and drop them into a food processor. Process briefly, until crumbled. (You should have 1 cup bread crumbs.)

FOR THE FILLING: Combine the ricotta cheese, eggs, basil and/or parsley, Parmesan cheese, bread crumbs, salt, and pepper in a bowl and mix well. Using a spoon, fill the pasta shells. (If some of the pasta shells broke into pieces during the cooking process, cut them into small pieces and set aside.)

Arrange the filled shells in one or two large gratin dishes so that they touch one another but are not overlapping or crowded. Sprinkle any broken pieces of pasta around them. (*The dish can be prepared a few hours ahead to this point and refrigerated.*)

Preheat the oven to 400 degrees.

FOR THE SAUCE: Heat the oil in a saucepan. When it is hot, add the onions, garlic, and thyme and cook for about 2 minutes. Add the tomatoes, water, salt, and pepper, bring to a boil, and boil for 3 to 4 minutes.

Spoon the sauce on top of and around the filled shells and cover with aluminum foil. Bake for about 20 minutes, until heated through. (If the assembled dish was refrigerated, add 10 to 12 minutes to the baking time.)

Sprinkle with the shredded basil and serve.

Penne au Gratin
Serves 4

✻ **Tomatoes add another dimension** to this variation of the old favorite, macaroni and cheese. I use only milk in this recipe, as my mother used to do, but the result is still velvety and rich.

- 6 ounces (2¼ cups) penne
- 1½ teaspoons unsalted butter
- 1 tablespoon olive oil
- 2 tablespoons all-purpose flour
- 2½ cups milk
- 4½ ounces cheddar cheese, cut into ½-inch dice (1 cup)
- ¾ teaspoon salt
- ¾ teaspoon freshly ground black pepper
- 1 large tomato, halved, seeded, and cut into ½-inch dice (1¼ cups)
- 1½ tablespoons freshly grated Parmesan cheese
- ½ teaspoon paprika

Bring 4 quarts of salted water to a boil in a large pot. Add the penne, stir well, and cook for about 8 minutes, until tender but still slightly al dente. Drain the penne in a colander, rinse it for a couple of minutes under cold water to stop the cooking, and set it aside.

Heat the butter and oil in a saucepan until hot. Add the flour and cook, stirring, over medium heat for about 10 seconds, then add the milk, stirring it in quickly with a whisk so the mixture doesn't scorch. Bring to a boil and boil for 10 seconds. Add the cheddar cheese, salt, and pepper, mix well, and cook over low heat, stirring, for 3 to 4 minutes or until smooth.

Mix the pasta with the cheese sauce and transfer the mixture to a 6-cup gratin dish. Scatter the tomato on top of the pasta. Combine the Parmesan and paprika in a small bowl and sprinkle the mixture on the pasta. (*The dish can be assembled a few hours ahead and refrigerated.*)

When ready to bake the gratin, preheat the oven to 400 degrees. Or, if you did not assemble the gratin ahead and the sauce and pasta are both still hot, preheat the broiler.

Bake for 30 minutes, or until the gratin is bubbly and nicely browned on top. Or, if you assembled the gratin at the last moment and the ingredients are still hot, broil for 3 to 4 minutes, until golden brown on top. Serve immediately.

Ratatouille Ravioli
Serves 6 as a main course, 12 as a first course, side dish, or soup garnish

✻ **The filling for these** ravioli is spicy and flavorful. The vegetables must be chopped fine enough so they can be pushed through a pastry bag and the ratatouille should be well cooked to remove most of its moisture. Although the dough is rolled with a pasta machine here, it can be rolled by hand.

If served as a meal in itself, double the quantity. Uncooked ravioli can be frozen for a few days and then cooked (directly from the freezer) in boiling water for about 5 minutes.

FILLING

- 3 tablespoons olive oil
- 1 large onion, finely chopped (1¼ cups)
- 2 small eggplants, not peeled, finely chopped (3½ cups)
- 2 medium green bell peppers (8 ounces), cored, seeded, and finely chopped (1¼ cups)
- 2 small zucchini (12 ounces), trimmed and finely chopped (3 cups)
- 2 medium to large tomatoes, halved, seeded, and finely chopped (2 cups)
- 3 garlic cloves, crushed and chopped (2 teaspoons)
- 1 teaspoon salt
  Pinch of cayenne pepper

DOUGH

- 2 cups all-purpose flour
- ¼ teaspoon salt
- ½ cup loosely packed fresh parsley leaves
- 2 large egg yolks
- ⅓ cup water
- 1 tablespoon olive oil

- 8 tablespoons (1 stick) unsalted butter, melted
- ½ teaspoon salt
- ½ teaspoon freshly ground black pepper
- 1 cup freshly grated Parmesan cheese

FOR THE FILLING: Heat the olive oil in a large saucepan. When it is hot, add the onion and sauté for 2 minutes over medium heat. Add the eggplant and green peppers and cook for about 5 minutes, stirring occasionally, until beginning to brown. Add the zucchini, tomatoes, garlic, and salt, mix well, cover, and cook over very low heat for about 20 minutes.

Remove the cover and cook over medium heat for 12 to 15 minutes, stirring occasionally, until most of the liquid has evaporated. Add the cayenne, remove to a bowl, and refrigerate.

FOR THE DOUGH: Process the flour, salt, and parsley in a food processor for about 30 seconds to mix. Add the egg yolks, water, and oil and process until the mixture begins to pull away from the sides of the bowl and form a ball. Press the dough together, wrap in plastic wrap, and refrigerate for at least 1 hour.

When ready to roll, divide the dough into 4 pieces. Run each segment through a pasta machine on the widest setting. Continue to run the dough through the machine several times, changing the setting until you reach the level (usually #7) where the dough becomes extremely thin (about 1/16 inch thick). Each quarter of the dough will give you a rectangle about 24 inches long by 5 inches wide. Cut each rectangle in half, for 2 rectangles 12 inches long by 5 inches wide.

Place one of the dough rectangles on a piece of waxed paper and brush it with water. Fill a pastry bag fitted with a ½-inch plain tip with the cold ratatouille. Pipe neat mounds (about 1 tablespoon each) of the ratatouille mixture approximately 1 inch apart in 2 rows down the length of the dough. Place a second rectangle of dough on top, pressing with your fingers between the stuffing so the top layer of dough sticks to the bottom layer. Using an inverted shot glass or the dull side of a cookie cutter about the size of the mounds, press around each mound to compact the stuffing into a uniform round.

Using a large round cutter, cut the ravioli into neat rounds. Or, to make square ravioli, use the same techniques, pressing around the mounds of filling with the inverted shot glass or cookie cutter so the stuffing is defined neatly inside. Then cut between the mounds to make square ravioli. Lift up and remove the trimmings of the dough from the waxed paper. (The trimmings can be rerolled for immediate use or cut into pieces and used as a garnish in soup.) Repeat with the remaining dough and filling. If you are not going to cook the ravioli right away, since they are all arranged on the waxed paper, it is easy to place them still on the paper on a tray; refrigerate or freeze.

When ready to cook the ravioli, bring 4 quarts of salted water to a boil in a large pot. Reduce the heat to a gentle boil, slide the ravioli into the water, and cook gently for 4 to 5 minutes (the green dough will become paler). Lift from the water with a skimmer, draining well, transfer to a serving dish, and toss with the melted butter, salt, pepper, and Parmesan cheese. Serve immediately.

Mushroom-Stuffed Wontons in Red Wine Sauce

Serves 4 as a light main course, 6 as a first course

These easy mushroom ravioli use square wonton wrappers, which are available in most supermarkets. I serve the ravioli in a red wine sauce flavored with onion, garlic, tomato juice, and thyme, but you can substitute another sauce or serve them with a little melted butter or olive oil.

- 1 tablespoon peanut oil
- 1 tablespoon unsalted butter
- ¼ cup chopped shallots (about 3 large)
- ⅓ cup chopped leek (half white and half green; about ½ small leek)
- 8 ounces mushrooms, all cultivated or a mixture of cultivated and wild, trimmed, cleaned, and coarsely chopped (about 3 cups)

- ½ teaspoon salt
- ¼ teaspoon freshly ground black pepper
- 24 wonton wrappers (3 inches square; 6 ounces total)

SAUCE

- 1 tablespoon peanut oil
- 1 medium onion, chopped (1 cup)
- 3 garlic cloves, crushed and finely chopped (2 teaspoons)
- ½ teaspoon fresh thyme leaves or ¼ teaspoon dried thyme
- 1 cup robust fruity red wine (anything from a Rhône to a Cabernet)
- ½ cup tomato juice
- 1 tablespoon dark soy sauce

- 1 tablespoon chopped fresh chives

Heat the peanut oil and butter in a large saucepan until hot. Add the shallots and leek and sauté over medium-high heat for 2 minutes. Add the mushrooms, salt, and pepper and cook, uncovered, over high heat for about 7 minutes, until the liquid that emerges from the mushrooms evaporates and the mushrooms begin to brown. Transfer to a dish and let cool.

Lay 12 of the wonton wrappers out on a work surface and brush the edges lightly with water. Divide the mushroom mixture among the wrappers, mounding approximately 1½ tablespoons in the center of each. Cover with the remaining wrappers and press gently around the edges with the bottom of a glass or cup to seal well. Trim the edges, if desired, to make round ravioli. Arrange the wontons in one layer on a tray, with no overlap. Set aside, uncovered, while you make the sauce. (*The ravioli can be assembled up to 12 hours before cooking and refrigerated, uncovered, to prevent them from becoming wet and sticky.*)

FOR THE SAUCE: Heat the peanut oil in

a skillet until hot. Add the onion and sauté over medium-high heat for about 2 minutes. Add the garlic and thyme and sauté for 30 seconds. Stir in the wine, bring to a boil, and boil until it is reduced by half.

Add the tomato juice and soy sauce, bring the mixture back to a boil, and boil vigorously over high heat for 30 seconds. Using a blender, food processor, or hand blender, puree the sauce until fairly smooth. (You should have 1⅓ cups.) Set aside in the skillet.

When ready to cook the wontons, bring 4 quarts of salted water to a boil in a large pot. Drop the wontons into the boiling water, bring the water back to a boil, and boil very gently for 2 to 3 minutes, or until the wonton wrappers are al dente and the filling hot.

Meanwhile, rewarm the sauce.

Using a skimmer, remove the wontons from the water, draining as much water from them as possible, and arrange them on a serving platter. Top with the sauce, garnish with the chives, and serve immediately.

Rice Noodles with Dried Mushrooms

Serves 4 as a first course or side dish, 2 as a main course

❧ **Dried shiitake mushrooms go** well with rice stick noodles, which are first soaked in warm water to soften them, then finished on the stove with all the seasonings. An excellent first course, this makes a great vegetarian main course or side dish.

4 ounces mixed dried shiitake and tree ear mushrooms

4 cups hot water

5 ounces medium rice stick noodles

2 tablespoons peanut oil

1 small onion, chopped (about ½ cup)

3 garlic cloves, crushed and finely chopped (2 teaspoons)

1 teaspoon peeled and finely chopped ginger

½ teaspoon seeded and chopped jalapeño pepper

2 tablespoons rice wine or dry white wine

4 teaspoons dark soy sauce

1 tablespoon oyster sauce

Soak the dried mushrooms in the hot water for 45 minutes.

Meanwhile, put the noodles in a large bowl and cover them with hot water. Soak for 20 minutes, then drain. If you prefer shorter noodles, cut them into pieces with scissors.

Lift out the mushrooms, leaving any grit behind; reserve ½ cup of the soaking liquid. (If you like, freeze the remainder for use in soup or stock.) Cut off and discard the stems of the shiitake mushrooms. Cut the caps into ½-inch-thick slices. Remove any roots or dirt from the tree ear mushrooms and cut them into ½-inch-wide strips. (You should have about 2 cups mushrooms.)

Heat the oil in a large saucepan. Add the onion and cook for 1 minute over high heat. Add the garlic, ginger, jalapeño pepper, wine, soy sauce, oyster sauce, and the reserved ½ cup mushroom soaking liquid, then add the mushrooms and mix well. Bring the mixture to a boil over high heat, then reduce the heat to medium, cover, and cook for 12 minutes. Most of the liquid will have evaporated but there still will be some moisture in the pan.

Add the noodles to the mushroom mixture, mix well, and cook for 1 to 2 minutes, stirring constantly, until the noodles soften and become transparent. Divide among plates and serve immediately.

Gnocchi Maison
Serves 4

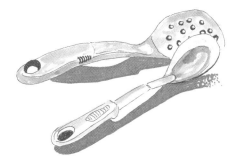

There are four different types of gnocchi: Roman-style, which are made with semolina that is cooked into a mush and then cooled, molded, and cut into shapes; potato gnocchi, which are made with mashed potatoes; Parisian gnocchi, made with *pâte à choux* (cream puff dough); and ricotta gnocchi.

For this recipe, I add mashed potatoes to the dough for Parisian gnocchi to create an appealing hybrid that I particularly like. The mixture can be prepared and even poached ahead, either by dropping spoonfuls of it into boiling water or piping it, as I do here, from a pastry bag held directly over the pot. As the mixture emerges from the bag, I cut it into 1½-inch lengths, letting them drop into the pot. This technique is faster and produces gnocchi of a more uniform size and shape than the spoon method. Gnocchi make an excellent side dish for poultry, fish, or meat.

The gnocchi can be made up to a day ahead and refrigerated, then heated in the oven just before serving.

1	medium baking (Idaho) potato (about 5 ounces)
½	cup water
2	tablespoons olive oil
¼	teaspoon salt
⅛	teaspoon freshly ground black pepper
½	cup all-purpose flour
2	tablespoons freshly grated Pecorino Romano cheese
2	large eggs
2	tablespoons chopped fresh parsley

Put the potato in a small saucepan, cover it with water, and bring to a boil. Cover, reduce the heat to low, and boil gently for about 40 minutes, or until the potato is tender. Drain and let cool. When the potato is cool enough to handle, peel it; set aside.

Combine the water, 1 tablespoon of the oil, the salt, and pepper in a saucepan and bring to a boil. Remove from the heat, add the flour all at once, and mix well with a wooden spoon until the mixture forms a ball, then place the pan back over the heat for 15 to 20 seconds to dry out the dough a little. Set aside.

Preheat the oven to 400 degrees.

Bring 5 cups of water to a boil in a wide saucepan. Meanwhile, transfer the ball of dough to a food processor. Add the potato in pieces and process for about 10 seconds. Add 1 tablespoon of the cheese and the eggs and process for 5 to 10 seconds, until smooth. Transfer the mixture to a pastry bag fitted with a ¾-inch plain round tip (or use a spoon to drop spoonfuls of the mixture into the water).

Pipe the mixture from the pastry bag into the boiling water, cutting it off with a knife into 1½-inch pieces as it emerges from the tip and letting the pieces drop into the water. (You should have 35 to 40 pieces.) Bring the water back to a light boil, then reduce the heat and boil very gently, uncovered, for 5 minutes. The gnocchi will rise to the surface as they cook. With a slotted spoon, transfer the gnocchi to a bowl of ice water.

When the gnocchi are cold, drain them and place them in a 3- to 4-cup gratin dish. Add the remaining tablespoon each oil and cheese, along with the parsley, and mix well.

At serving time, heat the gnocchi in the oven for 12 to 15 minutes. Serve immediately.

Ricotta Dumplings
with Red Pepper Sauce
Serves 4

Creamy white, these dumplings are made of ricotta, Gruyère, eggs, and flour pureed in a food processor until smooth and seasoned with chives. Dropped by spoonfuls into hot water, they cook in about 10 minutes. With the red sauce spooned over them, they look beautiful, and the flavors of the sauce and dumplings are wonderfully compatible.

To prepare the dumplings ahead, cook the red pepper sauce and refrigerate it. Cook the dumplings as indicated, then transfer them to a bowl of ice water. When they are thoroughly cool, drain, arrange in one layer in one large or four individual gratin dishes, cover, and refrigerate until 30 minutes before serving time. To serve, spoon some sauce over the dumplings, sprinkle on about 2 tablespoons of grated Parmesan, and bake in a preheated 400-degree oven for 25 minutes, or until hot and bubbly. Serve with additional warm sauce and grated cheese.

SAUCE

1 small red bell pepper (6 ounces), cored, seeded, and cut into 1-inch pieces
1 medium tomato (6 ounces), cut into 1-inch chunks
1 cup water
½ teaspoon salt
¼ teaspoon freshly ground black pepper
1 tablespoon potato starch (see page 318), dissolved in 1 tablespoon water
1½ tablespoons unsalted butter
1 tablespoon extra-virgin olive oil

DUMPLINGS

8 ounces (about 1 cup) ricotta cheese
½ teaspoon salt
¼ teaspoon freshly ground black pepper
1 large egg
⅓ cup grated Gruyère or Emmenthaler cheese
½ cup all-purpose flour
2 tablespoons minced fresh chives

¼ cup freshly grated Parmesan cheese

FOR THE SAUCE: Put the red pepper and tomato in a saucepan with the water and bring to a boil over high heat, then reduce the heat to low, cover, and boil gently for 8 minutes. Put the mixture through a food mill or sieve to remove the skin and tomato seeds. (You should have 1¾ cups.)

Return the pureed mixture to the saucepan and stir in the salt, pepper, and dissolved potato starch. Bring to a boil, add the butter and oil, and emulsify with a hand blender (or use a food processor) for about 10 seconds. Set aside.

FOR THE DUMPLINGS: Bring 4 quarts of water to a simmer in a large pot. Preheat the oven to 160 degrees.

Meanwhile, put the ricotta, salt, pepper, egg, cheese, and flour in a food processor and process for 10 seconds. Transfer the dumpling batter to a bowl and mix in the chives.

Make the dumplings in 2 batches, dropping the batter about 1 tablespoon at a time, as quickly as possible, into the simmering water. Let the dumplings cook at a low simmer for 10 minutes; they will rise to the top of the water and float as they cook. Lift the dumplings from the water with a slotted spoon or skimmer, drain well, and arrange on a platter. Keep warm in the oven while you make the remainder of the dumplings.

Meanwhile, reheat the sauce.

When the second batch of dumplings is cooked, add to the platter with the first batch, or divide all the dumplings among individual plates. Spoon on the warm red pepper sauce and serve sprinkled with the Parmesan.

Rice

Jasmine Rice
Serves 4

✂ **Jasmine rice, a fragrant** rice from Thailand, is similar to India's basmati, which is available in most supermarkets. While jasmine rice used to be imported, it is now grown in California and Texas. It has a wonderful aroma and a nutty taste that complements poultry, meat, and fish. It also makes excellent rice pudding.

    1   cup jasmine or basmati rice
    ¾   teaspoon salt
    2   cups water

Combine all the ingredients in a saucepan and bring to a boil over high heat. Cover, reduce the heat to low, and boil the rice gently for 16 to 18 minutes, or until it is tender but not mushy. Serve.

Yellow Rice with Orange Rind
Serves 4

✂ **Virtually tasteless, annatto seeds,** available in specialty markets and in some supermarkets, lend bright color to the rice. For a more conventional white rice, omit the annatto seeds and orange rind.

    1   tablespoon canola oil
    1   tablespoon unsalted butter
    1   medium onion, chopped (1 cup)
    1   teaspoon annatto (achiote) seeds
    ¼   teaspoon hot pepper flakes
    1   cup long-grain white rice
    2   cups water
    ½   teaspoon salt
    1½ teaspoons grated orange rind

Heat the oil and butter in a medium saucepan. When they are hot, add the onion, annatto seeds, and hot pepper flakes and cook over medium heat for 3 to 4 minutes. Mix in the rice, then add the water, salt, and orange rind. Bring to a boil, cover, reduce the heat to low, and cook gently for 20 minutes, or until the rice is tender and the liquid is absorbed. Fluff the rice and serve.

Rice with Onions
Serves 6

✂ **Chances are you have** all the ingredients on hand for this classic dish, which is good with most poultry, meat, or fish. Quick and easy, it rounds out a menu.

    1   tablespoon unsalted butter
    1   tablespoon canola oil
    2½   cups chopped onions
    ½   teaspoon dried thyme
    2   bay leaves
    2   cups long-grain white rice
    4   cups homemade chicken stock (page
         612) or low-salt canned chicken broth
         Salt
    ½   teaspoon freshly ground black pepper

Heat the butter and oil in a medium saucepan. When they are hot, add the onions and sauté over medium-high heat for 3 to 4 minutes. Stir in the thyme, bay leaves, and rice, mixing until the rice is coated with the butter and oil. Add the chicken stock, salt to taste, and the pepper and bring to a strong boil, stirring occasionally, over high heat. Reduce the heat to very low, cover with a tight-fitting lid, and cook for about 20 minutes, until the rice is tender and the liquid is absorbed.

Fluff the rice with a fork and serve.

Brown Rice and Onion Pilaf
Serves 6

❧ **While some brands of** brown rice cook in as little as 25 to 30 minutes, others require as long as 1¼ hours and absorb substantially more liquid than is needed for white rice. For consistent results, find a brand that you like and stick with it.

2	tablespoons olive oil
1	tablespoon unsalted butter
12	ounces onions (3–4), cut into ½-inch cubes (about 2½ cups)
1	tablespoon chopped garlic
1	teaspoon herbes de Provence or Italian seasoning
1	teaspoon chili powder
2	cups (about 1 pound) brown rice
5	cups water
2	teaspoons salt
½	teaspoon freshly ground black pepper

Heat the oil and butter in a large saucepan. When they are hot, add the onions and garlic and sauté over medium-high heat for 2 to 3 minutes.

Add the herbes de Provence or Italian seasoning, chili powder, and rice and mix well to combine. Add the water and salt and pepper and bring to a boil, stirring so the rice does not stick. Reduce the heat and cook, covered, over very low heat for about 45 minutes, until the rice is tender but still a little chewy and most of the moisture has been absorbed. Check the rice near the end of the cooking time; if it is not cooked through, cook it a little longer, adding water as needed.

Fluff the rice and serve.

Arborio Rice with Pecans
Serves 4

❧ **Usually reserved for risotto,** Arborio has a nutty taste and slightly firmer grains than long-grain rices. Although Arborio used to be grown exclusively in Italy, this grain with short, fat kernels is now being cultivated in California. This dish goes especially well with stews, braised meat, or fish.

1	tablespoon olive oil
⅓	cup chopped onion
⅓	cup chopped (½-inch pieces) pecans
1	cup Arborio rice
1¾	cups homemade chicken stock (page 612) or low-salt canned chicken broth
½	teaspoon salt
¼	teaspoon freshly ground black pepper

Heat the oil in a medium saucepan. Add the onion and pecans and cook over medium-high heat for 1 minute, stirring constantly. Add the rice and mix well. Stir in the stock, salt, and pepper and bring to a boil. Cover, reduce the heat to low, and cook for 18 to 20 minutes, until the rice is tender and the liquid is absorbed.

Fluff the rice with a fork and serve.

RICE PILAF PANCAKE

Make a rice pancake with leftover pilaf: Heat 2 tablespoons oil in a 7-inch nonstick skillet. When it is hot, add 1½ cups cooked brown rice and press lightly with a spatula to flatten. Cook over medium heat for 5 to 6 minutes, then invert onto a flat pan lid or plate, slide back into the skillet, and brown on the other side for 5 to 6 minutes.

Serve plain or topped with a fried egg as a light lunch, accompanied by a green salad.

Wehani Brown Rice

Serves 4

❧ **The extra-long reddish-brown kernels** of Wehani rice, from California, take a long time to cook, but they have a nutty, chewy texture that I love. Wehani rice is available in many health food stores and well worth the search.

2 tablespoons olive oil
1 medium onion, chopped (1 cup)
⅓ cup natural pumpkin seeds
1 cup Wehani rice
¾ teaspoon salt
2½ cups warm water

Heat the oil in a medium saucepan until it is hot but not smoking. Add the onion and sauté for 2 minutes. Add the pumpkin seeds and cook for 1 minute. Mix in the rice thoroughly, add the salt and water, and bring to a boil, stirring occasionally. Cover, reduce the heat to low, and boil gently for 1 hour, or until the rice is tender and the water has been absorbed.

Fluff the rice and serve.

Wild Rice
with Pine Nuts and Peas

Serves 4

❧ **Not really rice at** all, but a long-grain marsh grass, wild rice makes any meal a little more elegant. I flavor it with grated lemon rind and jalapeño pepper and garnish it with baby peas and pine nuts. When wild rice "blossoms," or breaks open, it is cooked.

¾ cup wild rice
3 cups water
1 tablespoon olive oil

1 tablespoon unsalted butter
½ cup chopped onion
¼ cup pine nuts
1 teaspoon grated lemon rind
1 teaspoon chopped jalapeño pepper
(or less if you prefer)
½ teaspoon salt
1¼ cups homemade chicken stock
(page 612) or low-salt canned
chicken broth
½ cup frozen baby peas

Combine the rice and water in a medium saucepan and bring to a boil. Cover, reduce the heat to low, and boil gently for 40 minutes, or until some of the rice has "blossomed" (burst open). Drain.

Heat the oil and butter in a large saucepan until hot. Add the onion and nuts and cook over medium-high heat for about 5 minutes, stirring occasionally, until the nuts are nicely browned.

Add the rice, lemon rind, jalapeño, salt, and chicken stock and cook, covered, over low heat for 20 to 30 minutes, until most of the chicken stock is absorbed and the rice is tender.

Add the peas and cook for 2 minutes longer. Serve.

Broccoli and Rice Stew

Serves 4

❧ **An excellent vegetarian** main dish, this brown rice stew also complements chicken. The rice is simmered slowly on top of the stove until soupy, then topped with broccoli and cooked until both are tender. The combination is delicious and involves only one pan. Other green vegetables, such as zucchini, asparagus, or green beans, can be substituted and cooked with the rice in the same manner.

2 tablespoons peanut oil

¾ cup chopped onion

1 cup brown rice

3 cups homemade chicken stock (page 612), homemade beef stock (page 612), or low-salt canned chicken or beef broth

½ teaspoon salt

Pinch of hot pepper flakes

3 broccoli stalks (about 12 ounces)

½ cup grated Monterey Jack cheese

Heat the oil in a medium saucepan. When it is hot, add the onion and cook over medium heat for about 2 minutes, stirring occasionally, until lightly browned. Add the rice and stir well, then add the stock, salt, and hot pepper flakes. Bring to a boil, cover, reduce the heat to very low, and cook for 30 minutes.

Meanwhile, peel the broccoli stalks to remove the fibrous skin. Cut the stems into 1-inch pieces and the florets into 1-inch pieces.

When the rice has cooked for 30 minutes (it will still be soupy), arrange the broccoli on top of the rice (don't stir it in). Cover and cook over low heat for 10 minutes, or until the rice and broccoli are tender. Add the grated cheese and serve.

Spicy Rice
Serves 6

The taste of the spicy pork mixture in this rice is similar to that of a pâté. Although it can be used right away, it develops more taste and color when left to cure in the refrigerator for at least 24 hours before being cooked and combined with the rice. A great side dish, this complements many different types of meat and poultry.

SPICY PORK

8 ounces boneless pork shoulder, coarsely ground

1½ teaspoons salt

¼ teaspoon freshly ground black pepper

1 small garlic clove, chopped

½ teaspoon paprika

⅛ teaspoon cayenne pepper

½ teaspoon fennel seeds

1 teaspoon dried oregano

½ cup diced (¼-inch) prosciutto

1½ cups chopped onions

½ cup sliced scallions (including some of the green)

2 teaspoons chopped jalapeño pepper

1 teaspoon chopped garlic (2–3 cloves)

1 cup basmati rice

½ cup tomato sauce

2 cups homemade chicken stock (page 612) or low-salt canned chicken broth

½ teaspoon salt

FOR THE PORK: Mix together all the ingredients in a bowl. Refrigerate, covered, for 28 to 48 hours to cure.

Break the pork mixture into 1-inch pieces. Sauté in a heavy saucepan over low heat for 12 to 15 minutes, until well browned.

Add the fennel seeds, oregano, prosciutto, onions, and scallions and cook for 3 to 4 minutes. Add the jalapeño pepper and cook for another minute. Add the garlic and rice and mix well. Add the tomato sauce, stock, and salt and bring to a boil, stirring occasionally, then cover and cook over very low heat for about 25 minutes, until the rice is fluffy but holds together. Serve.

Risotto with Vegetables
Serves 4

✂ **Traditionally risotto is flavored** with stock, butter, oil, and cheese. For color, texture, and flavor, I incorporate vegetables. The result is almost a complete meal in itself, perfect as a meatless luncheon or dinner main dish.

Canned chicken stock is often salty; if you use it instead of homemade, don't add as much salt as is called for here. I add more stock at the beginning of the cooking period because I know the rice will absorb at least this much liquid. Later I pour in the remaining stock in smaller increments, letting the rice absorb each addition before adding another and then stopping when the rice is tender.

2	tablespoons olive oil
¼	cup chopped onion
1	cup Arborio rice
3½	cups homemade chicken stock (page 612) or low-salt canned chicken broth
1	4-ounce piece fennel bulb, coarsely chopped (⅔ cup)
4	asparagus spears, trimmed, peeled, and cut into ½-inch pieces (about 1 cup)
1	cup frozen baby peas
1	small red bell pepper, peeled with a vegetable peeler, cored, seeded, and cut into ¼-inch pieces (about 1 cup)
3	large mushrooms, trimmed, cleaned, and cut into ¼-inch-thick julienne strips (about 1 cup)
¾	teaspoon salt (less if using canned broth)
¼	cup freshly grated Parmesan cheese
2	tablespoons unsalted butter

Heat the oil in a large skillet. When it is hot, add the onion and sauté for 1 minute. Add the rice and mix well, then stir in 2½ cups of the stock. Cook for 12 minutes, covered, over medium heat, removing the lid two or three times to stir the rice (which otherwise tends to stick to the pan). Then uncover the pan and continue cooking, stirring occasionally, until all the stock has been absorbed.

Add the fennel to the pan, along with another ½ cup of the stock, and cook, covered, for 5 minutes, removing the lid once or twice to stir the rice.

Add the remainder of the vegetables, the remaining ½ cup stock, and the salt and cook, uncovered, for another 5 minutes, stirring, or until the mixture is creamy and the rice is tender. Stir in the cheese and butter and serve immediately.

Rice Salad
Serves 6 to 8

✂ **Hearty enough to be** served as a luncheon main course, this rice salad is the type of dish that can be prepared at the last moment when you have nothing planned for lunch or dinner. I always have these ingredients in my pantry.

3	cups water
	Salt
1½	cups long-grain white rice
1	6-ounce jar artichoke hearts in olive oil
1	6-ounce can tuna in olive oil
2	tablespoons drained capers
	Juice of 1 lemon
½	teaspoon freshly ground black pepper
2	tablespoons chopped fresh parsley
2	hard-cooked eggs (see page 66), peeled and diced with an egg cutter or finely chopped
1	tablespoon chopped fresh basil

Bring the 3 cups water to a boil in a saucepan. Salt it, add the rice, and cook, covered, over low heat for 18 to 20 minutes, until the liquid has been absorbed and the rice is tender but firm.

Meanwhile, drain the artichoke hearts, reserving a little of the oil, and coarsely chop. Put in a large serving bowl with the reserved oil.

Add the rice, tuna with its oil, capers, lemon juice, ½ teaspoon salt, the pepper, and parsley to the artichokes and mix gently but thoroughly. Sprinkle the eggs and basil on top and serve.

Grains

Green Couscous
Serves 4

Couscous, a favorite in North African cuisine, is now available in supermarkets everywhere. With its green herb puree, this is ideal served with fish.

- 1 cup loosely packed fresh herb leaves (a mixture of chives, parsley, tarragon, and basil)
- 2 garlic cloves
- ¾ cup boiling water
- 1 tablespoon unsalted butter
- 1 cup instant couscous
- ½ teaspoon salt

Process the herbs, garlic, and ¼ cup of the boiling water in a blender or mini-chop for about 30 seconds, or until smooth.

Melt the butter in a saucepan. Add the couscous and salt and mix well to coat the couscous with the butter. Add the herb puree and the remaining ½ cup boiling water and mix well. Cover and let stand off the heat for 10 minutes.

Fluff the couscous with a fork and serve.

Curried Bulgur with Currants
Serves 4

Like its uncooked relative, cracked wheat, bulgur wheat — steamed, dried, and crushed wheat berries — is a staple of Middle Eastern cooking. Although bulgur is available now boxed in supermarkets, I prefer the coarser grinds sold in bulk in health food stores.

You can make a salad with bulgur by simply soaking it in water and tossing it with vinegar, lemon juice, and seasonings — anything from scallions to garlic. Here I cook the bulgur with onions, flavor it with curry, and mix in some currants. It goes particularly well with grilled lamb chops.

- 1 tablespoon olive oil
- 1 small onion, chopped
- 2 scallions, trimmed (leaving some green) and coarsely chopped
- 2 tablespoons dried currants
- 1 teaspoon curry powder
- 1 cup bulgur wheat
- 2 cups homemade chicken stock (page 612) or low-salt canned chicken broth
- ½ teaspoon salt, or to taste

Heat the oil in a medium saucepan. When it is hot, add the onion and scallions and sauté for 1 minute. Stir in the currants and curry powder, then add the bulgur, stock, and salt and mix well. Bring to a boil, cover, reduce the heat, and cook gently for 20 minutes.

Fluff with a fork and serve.

Polenta with Mushroom Ragout

**Serves 4 as a first course or side dish,
2 as a main course**

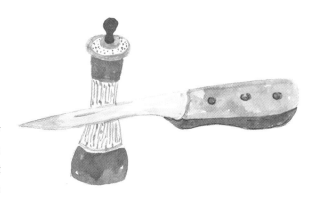

Polenta is cornmeal, and it comes in yellow and white as well as in instant form. Served on soup plates and eaten with a spoon, this soft polenta is topped with a mushroom stew that is particularly delicious when it incorporates some wild varieties. A satisfying side, the polenta can also be served in larger portions as a vegetarian main course.

POLENTA

2   cups water
½   cup yellow cornmeal
¼   teaspoon salt
¼   teaspoon freshly ground black pepper

MUSHROOM RAGOUT

1   tablespoon unsalted butter
1   tablespoon peanut oil
1   small onion, chopped (½ cup)
5   ounces mushrooms (cultivated, wild, or a combination), trimmed, cleaned, and cut into ½-inch pieces (2 cups)
3   garlic cloves, crushed and finely chopped (2 teaspoons)
4   plum tomatoes, halved, seeded, and cut into ½-inch pieces (1¼ cups)
2   small ears corn, husked and kernels cut off (1 cup)
½   cup homemade chicken stock (page 612) or low-salt canned chicken broth
¼   teaspoon salt, or to taste
⅛   teaspoon freshly ground black pepper
2   tablespoons chopped fresh chives

FOR THE POLENTA: Bring the water to a boil in a medium saucepan. Sprinkle the corn-meal on top while mixing it in with a whisk and stir in the salt and pepper. Bring the mixture to a boil, then reduce the heat to low, cover with a lid to prevent splattering, and cook gently for 6 to 8 minutes, stirring occasionally, until the polenta is cooked and has the consistency of a creamy puree. Set aside, covered.

FOR THE RAGOUT: Heat the butter and oil in a large saucepan. When they are hot, add the onion and sauté for 30 seconds. Add the mushrooms and sauté over high heat for about 2 minutes, until the liquid emerges from them and evaporates. Add the garlic, tomatoes, corn, chicken stock, salt, and pepper and bring to a strong boil. Reduce the heat to medium and cook for 2 to 3 minutes.

To serve, ladle the polenta into the center of soup plates and pour the mushroom ragout on top of and around it. Sprinkle with the chives and serve.

Polenta and Vegetable Gâteau
Serves 4

This *gâteau*, or molded "cake" of layered polenta and vegetables, makes an unusual and stunning side dish to a roast, or it can be served as the first course of a special meal. The water in which the vegetables are boiled is used to cook and flavor the polenta. Depending on the cornmeal you use, the cooking may take anywhere from 3 to 4 minutes, for regular cornmeal, and up to 25 to 30 minutes, for the coarse stone-ground kind. A tomato sauce, spooned over the *gâteau*, adds more color.

2	tablespoons olive oil
1½	teaspoons salt
2	ounces snow peas, ends trimmed and strings removed (⅔ cup)
1	large carrot, peeled and cut into strips with a vegetable peeler (1 cup)
4	ounces trimmed spinach, washed (about 2½ cups loosely packed)
½	cup chopped onion
2	tablespoons pine nuts
8	ounces cherry tomatoes, quartered (1½ cups)
¼	teaspoon freshly ground black pepper
¾	cup coarse stone-ground white cornmeal, preferably organic

Oil a 6-cup measuring cup or medium bowl with a little of the olive oil and set aside.

Bring 4 cups of water to a boil in a medium saucepan and add 1 teaspoon of the salt. Add the snow peas, bring the water back to a boil, and boil for 2½ minutes. Using a slotted spoon, remove the peas and drop them into a small bowl. Toss with ⅛ teaspoon of the salt and 1 teaspoon of the olive oil and set aside.

Add the carrot strips to the boiling water, bring the water back to a boil, and boil for 1 minute. Using a skimmer, remove the carrots from the water and place them in a small bowl. Toss the carrots with ⅛ teaspoon of the salt and 1 teaspoon of the olive oil and set aside.

Measure the vegetable cooking liquid and add enough water so that you have 3 cups; return it to the saucepan.

Heat 1 teaspoon of the olive oil in a medium skillet and add the spinach (still wet from washing) with ⅛ teaspoon of the salt. Cook over me-dium-high heat for about 1 minute, covered, until the spinach is wilted. Transfer the spinach to a bowl and set aside.

Pour the rest of the olive oil (about 1 table-spoon) into a skillet, add the onion and pine nuts, and sauté for 1 minute. Add the tomatoes, the remaining ⅛ teaspoon salt, and the pepper and cook for 2 to 3 minutes, until the tomatoes are wilted. Set aside.

To cook the polenta, add the cornmeal to the saucepan of reserved vegetable cooking liquid, mixing it well with a whisk as you do so to prevent caking and lumping. Bring to a boil, cover, reduce the heat to very low, and cook for 20 to 30 minutes, depending on the cornmeal, stirring occasionally with the whisk until the liquid is absorbed.

Spoon about one quarter of the polenta into the oiled cup or bowl and arrange the spinach on top to create a second layer. Add another layer of polenta, then spoon on the carrots. Add another layer of polenta and spoon the snow peas on top. Finish with the rest of the polenta. Cover with a plate and let stand for 10 to 15 minutes to set the polenta.

When the polenta is set, turn the *gâteau* upside down on a plate, leaving the cup or bowl in place over it. (*The* gâteau *can be kept warm in a 160-degree oven until ready to serve, up to 1 hour.*)

Unmold the *gâteau*, spoon the tomato mixture over it, and serve. Eat with a spoon.

Potatoes and Sweet Potatoes

Buttered Potatoes with Parsley
Serves 4

🐝 **Potatoes with butter and** parsley are always welcome at my table. Cut the potatoes into pieces of nearly equal size so they cook evenly. After you have boiled and drained them, return them to the stove briefly to eliminate any remaining moisture — a simple step that gives them a creamy, smooth interior. These potatoes are excellent with fish, shellfish, roasts, or poultry.

1½	pounds all-purpose potatoes, peeled
1½	tablespoons unsalted butter
¼	teaspoon salt
3	tablespoons chopped fresh parsley

Cut the potatoes into 2-inch pieces, then trim the pieces (reserve the trimmings for soup, if desired), rounding them off to make shapes of about the same size. Rinse the potatoes well, put them in a saucepan, and add enough cold water to cover. Bring to a boil, reduce the heat to low, and boil gently for 15 to 20 minutes, or until the potatoes are tender.

Drain off the water, return the saucepan with the potatoes to the stove, and heat over high heat for about 30 seconds to evaporate any remaining moisture from the potatoes. Add the butter, salt, and parsley, tossing gently (to avoid breaking the potatoes). Serve.

Sautéed Potatoes with Parsley and Garlic
Serves 4

🐝 **These are a standard** on bistro menus. Don't cook them ahead, or they will soften and lose the crisp exterior that contrasts so well with their soft insides. They can, however, be peeled and cut into cubes in advance and covered with water so they don't discolor. Just before cooking, drain and dry them with paper towels.

3	large Red Bliss potatoes (18 ounces), peeled
3	tablespoons canola oil
3	garlic cloves
¼	cup loosely packed fresh parsley leaves
½	teaspoon salt
½	teaspoon freshly ground black pepper

Cut the potatoes into ⅜-inch cubes. Put in a sieve and rinse well under cool water. Transfer to a bowl, add water to cover, and set aside until ready to cook.

Heat the oil in a large nonstick skillet. Drain the potatoes, pat dry with paper towels, and add to the hot oil. Sauté over high heat for 12 to 14 minutes, stirring occasionally, until the potatoes are browned on all sides.

Meanwhile, chop the garlic and parsley together until finely minced.

Add the salt, pepper, and parsley mixture to the potatoes in the skillet, tossing to combine. Serve.

Oven-Roasted Potatoes and Onions
Serves 4

✂ **Baked cut side down** in a minimum of oil (much of it remains in the pan afterward), these halved potatoes emerge brown and moist and have fewer calories than fried potatoes. They are great with grilled meat. To save on cleanup time, line the baking pan with foil.

> 4 baking (Idaho) or large all-purpose potatoes (about 8 ounces each), washed
> 4 medium mild onions, such as Vidalia or Maui (about 5 ounces each), not peeled
> 1½ tablespoons peanut or safflower oil
> ¼ teaspoon salt

Preheat the oven to 400 degrees, with a rack in the bottom third.

Split the potatoes lengthwise in half. Cut the onions crosswise in half.

Pour the oil onto a foil-lined baking sheet. Sprinkle the salt over the potatoes and onions and arrange them cut side down in one layer in the pan. Bake for 40 minutes, or until the potatoes and onions are tender when pierced with a fork, lightly browned on top, and dark brown on the underside. Let the potatoes and onions rest for 10 minutes; serve the onions in their skins.

Lift the potatoes and onions from the pan with a spatula and serve.

Potatoes Savonnettes
Serves 6

✂ **These thick potato slices** resemble oval soap bars, called *savonnettes* in French — hence their name. They were a specialty of the Plaza-Athénée, where I worked in Paris. The slabs stay moist inside because water is added to the skillet along with the butter and oil. Then, when the water evaporates, the potatoes brown in the butter and oil.

> 6 baking (Idaho) potatoes (about 8 ounces each), peeled
> ½ teaspoon salt
> ½ teaspoon freshly ground black pepper
> 4½ tablespoons unsalted butter
> 2 tablespoons canola oil

Preheat the oven to 425 degrees.

Cut the potatoes into thick slices, 1 to 1½ inches thick. Trim each slice into an oval so that all the slices have about the same shape and will lie flat in a big ovenproof nonstick skillet. Add the slices to the pan as you go. The slices must not overlap; use two skillets if necessary. (You should have about 20 to 25 slabs; save the trimmings to make soup or mashed potatoes.)

Sprinkle the potatoes with the salt and pepper. Add 4 tablespoons of the butter, the oil, and just enough water to barely cover the slices and bring to a rolling boil. Transfer to the oven and bake for 35 to 40 minutes, or until all the water has evaporated and the slices are sizzling in the oil-and-butter mixture. Check to see if the potatoes are nicely browned underneath. If not, place over direct heat on top of the stove for 2 to 3 minutes.

To serve, turn the slices upside down, so the brown side is showing, onto a serving platter. Melt the remaining ½ tablespoon butter and brush the potatoes to "shine" them. Serve.

Potato Slabs with Tapenade

Serves 4

These potato slabs sauced with tapenade need no salt, because the sauce is salty enough. They can be served without the tapenade with meat or poultry. If serving the potatoes on their own, however, add ½ teaspoon salt to the cooking water.

- 4 baking (Idaho) potatoes (about 8 ounces each), washed
- 2 tablespoons olive oil
- 1 tablespoon unsalted butter
- ¾ cup water

TAPENADE

- ⅔ cup kalamata olives (about 20), pitted
- 2 garlic cloves
- 3 tablespoons drained capers
- ½ (2-ounce) can anchovy fillets in oil
- 2 scallions, trimmed (leaving some green) and minced (¼ cup)
- ¼ teaspoon freshly ground black pepper

- 1 tablespoon minced fresh chives

Trim 2 opposite long sides of each potato and then cut each potato lengthwise in half, to create 2 slabs about 1 inch thick. Arrange the potatoes cut side down in one layer in a large nonstick skillet.

Add the oil, butter, and water to the skillet and bring to a boil over high heat. Cover, reduce the heat to medium, and cook for 15 minutes, or until the water evaporates. Keep cooking the potatoes, uncovered, for 1 or 2 minutes longer, until they are well browned on the underside. Turn the potatoes over and cook over low heat, covered, for 10 to 12 minutes longer to brown them on the other side.

MEANWHILE, FOR THE TAPENADE: Put all the ingredients in a food processor and pulse for about 20 seconds, until the mixture is well combined but still chunky. (You should have about 1 cup.)

When the potatoes are tender, moist, and nicely browned on both sides, transfer them to a large serving plate and spoon the tapenade on top. Sprinkle with the chives and serve.

Potato Slabs with Raclette Cheese

Serves 4

Raclette cheese comes from both Switzerland and France, and the word *raclette* comes from the French *racler*, meaning "to scrape." The name reflects the traditional practice of exposing a chunk of the cheese to heat — often an open fire — then scraping the cheese off as it melts and eating it on boiled potato slices. In my version of the dish, the cheese is sliced, melted under a broiler atop thick slices of boiled potatoes, and served, if you like, with cornichons.

- 2 large baking (Idaho) potatoes (about 10 ounces each), washed
- 1 8-ounce piece raclette cheese (or cheddar, Gruyère, or Fontina)
- ¼ teaspoon freshly ground black pepper
- ¼ teaspoon paprika
- Cornichons (tiny French gherkins; optional)

Put the potatoes in a saucepan and add enough water to cover them by about 1 inch. Bring to a boil, reduce the heat to low, and boil gently for 40 to 45 minutes, until the potatoes are tender but not mushy. Drain.

Preheat the broiler. When the potatoes are cool enough to handle, peel them and cut each one lengthwise into 3 slices. Arrange the slices on a cookie sheet.

Cut the cheese into 12 slices and cover each potato slab with 2 slices of cheese. Sprinkle with the pepper and paprika.

Cook the slabs under the preheated broiler for 4 to 6 minutes, watching them closely, until the cheese is nicely browned and bubbly. Serve with cornichons, if desired.

Glazed Potatoes

Serves 4

These classic potatoes, called *Parisienne* in France, are cooked in butter and oil, then finished with a reduction of stock, which glazes them and makes them very flavorful. They are conventionally cut with a melon baller into neat small balls.

- 4 large baking (Idaho) potatoes (about 10 ounces each), peeled
- 2 tablespoons canola oil
- 1 tablespoon unsalted butter
- 3 tablespoons Basic Brown Sauce (page 613)
- Salt

Press and twist a melon baller into one of the potatoes until it is practically embedded, using your thumb to push it firmly into the potato. Turn the melon baller around, to make an almost completely round potato ball, and scoop it out. Continue making balls with the potatoes. If the balls are not round, it's probably because you are not pressing the melon baller firmly enough into the potato before twisting it around. (The trimmings of the potatoes can be kept for soups, mashed potatoes, or croquettes.) As you go, drop the potato balls (and trimmings) into cold water to prevent discoloration. (*The potato balls can be prepared to this point a day ahead.*)

When you are ready to use them, drain the potatoes, put them in a saucepan, and cover with fresh cold water. Bring to a boil and boil for 2 minutes; drain. This blanching prevents the potatoes from discoloring once out of the water and allows them to cook faster when sautéed in the butter, and the additional moisture gives them a softer, nicer consistency.

Heat the oil and butter in a large skillet. When they are hot, add the potato balls in one layer and sauté for about 10 minutes over medium-high heat, shaking the skillet so the potatoes brown evenly on all sides. When the potatoes are browned and tender, drain the fat out of the skillet and add the brown sauce. Continue to cook the potatoes over high heat, shaking the pan occasionally, until the sauce reduces and forms a glaze that coats the potatoes. Salt lightly and serve.

Garlic Mashed Potatoes

Serves 6

My Aunt Aimée in Valence made the best garlic mashed potatoes, which inspired these. It is important to mash the potatoes while they are still hot, directly after draining. If left to cool, they tend to get stringy. If the potatoes are put through a food mill, as they are here, or a ricer, you don't need to peel the garlic. If, however, you plan to mash the potatoes by hand or with an electric mixer, peel the garlic cloves before adding them to the cooking water.

Leftover potatoes can be reheated in a microwave oven, fried as potato cakes in a skillet, or added to soup as a flavor enhancer and thickener.

- 2 pounds Yukon Gold potatoes
- 4 large garlic cloves (peeled or not; see the headnote)
- ¾ teaspoon salt
- 4 tablespoons (½ stick) unsalted butter

1 cup milk

⅛ teaspoon freshly ground black pepper

Peel the potatoes and cut into large chunks (2- to 2½-inch pieces). Drop the potatoes into a pot, cover with water, and add the garlic and ½ teaspoon of the salt. Bring to a boil, reduce the heat, and boil gently for 22 to 25 minutes, until the potatoes are tender.

Place a pot underneath a food mill to catch the cooking liquid (you can use it in stocks, soups, or bread) and drain the potatoes in the mill, then push them through the mill into a bowl. Add the butter and mix in thoroughly, then add the milk, mixing again until incorporated. Mix in the remaining ¼ teaspoon salt and the pepper and serve.

Turnips and Mashed Potatoes
Serves 4

🐾 **Potatoes make turnip puree** milder and give it a smoother, creamier texture. The potatoes and turnips are cooked in just enough water so that there is about ½ cup of liquid remaining in the pan when they are tender — enough to incorporate with them to create a nice puree.

3 large Red Bliss potatoes (18 ounces)

2 white or purple-top turnips (6 ounces total)

1 large garlic clove

½ teaspoon salt

1 cup water
  Chicken stock or broth (optional)

4 tablespoons (½ stick) unsalted butter

Peel the potatoes and turnips and cut them into 2-inch pieces.

Combine the pieces in a saucepan with the garlic, salt, and water and bring to a boil. Cover, reduce the heat, and boil gently for 20 minutes, or until the vegetables are tender. (About ½ cup of liquid should remain. If necessary, add a splash of water or stock; or, if too much liquid remains in the pan, remove the lid and quickly boil to reduce the liquid to ½ cup.)

Push the mixture through a food mill or ricer or use a hand blender or an electric mixer to puree it. Add the butter and mix or blend until smooth and creamy. Serve.

Potato and Spinach Galette
Serves 4

🐾 **The word** *galette* **denotes** a flattish disk-shaped pancake of fried sliced potatoes; this one is really a "sandwich" of panfried potatoes with a filling of garlic-flavored spinach. Use a nonstick skillet or omelet pan so it releases easily when inverted onto a plate. It's especially good in summer with a green salad. Serve as soon as possible after cooking, because the potatoes will soften quickly from the moisture in the spinach.

1 pound spinach
1½ pounds potatoes (3–4), preferably Yukon Gold
3 tablespoons olive oil
1 tablespoon unsalted butter
½ teaspoon salt
3–4 large garlic cloves, very thinly sliced (1½ tablespoons)
¼ teaspoon freshly ground black pepper

Preheat the oven to 400 degrees.

Remove and discard the tough stems and damaged leaves from the spinach and wash the remaining leaves. Set aside in a colander.

Peel the potatoes and cut them into very thin slices by hand, with a vegetable slicer, or in a food processor fitted with the slicing disk. Wash the slices, drain them, and pat them dry with paper towels.

Heat 1 tablespoon of the oil and the butter in a 10-inch nonstick ovenproof omelet pan or skillet until hot. Add the potato slices and season with ¼ teaspoon of the salt. Sauté over high heat for 2 to 3 minutes, gently stirring the potatoes, until all the slices are coated with oil and butter and are just starting to soften and become transparent. Transfer the potatoes to a plate and set aside.

Heat 1 tablespoon of the remaining oil in the same pan (unwashed) until it is hot. Add the garlic and sauté for 10 seconds. Add the spinach, the remaining ¼ teaspoon salt, and the pepper and sauté for about 2 minutes, until the spinach is wilted and most of its liquid has evaporated. Transfer the spinach to a plate and set aside.

Put the remaining tablespoon of oil in the skillet, off the heat, and arrange a layer of the potato slices in an attractive pattern to cover the bottom of the pan, extending about ¼ inch up the sides. Arrange another layer of potatoes on top, using half the potatoes for the 2 layers. Spread the spinach on top of the potatoes and cover it with the remaining potatoes. (*The recipe can be prepared to this point up to 6 hours ahead; set the galette aside at room temperature.*)

Bake the galette for 30 minutes or until the top is nicely browned.

Move the pan to the top of the stove and cook over medium-high heat for 2 to 3 minutes to brown the bottom, shaking the pan so the bottom of the galette doesn't stick to it. Invert the galette onto a large plate or platter, cut into wedges, and serve.

Potato Gâteau
Serves 8

✂ **A cake of hash-browned** potatoes is called *pommes macaire* in classic French cooking. In my version, the *gâteau* of coarsely chopped cooked potatoes is cooked in oil and butter in the oven, then further enriched with cream and cheese and glazed under the broiler.

2½ pounds large Yukon Gold potatoes, washed
1 tablespoon unsalted butter
3 tablespoons canola oil
¼ teaspoon freshly grated nutmeg
½ teaspoon salt
¼ teaspoon freshly ground black pepper
¼ cup heavy cream
3 tablespoons freshly grated Parmesan cheese

Dump the potatoes into a pot, cover with cold water, and bring to a boil. Reduce the heat and simmer for 30 to 35 minutes, until the potatoes are tender. Drain.

Preheat the oven to 450 degrees.

When the potatoes are cool enough to handle, scrape off the skin and coarsely chop the potatoes, as for hash browns.

Heat the butter and oil in a 10-inch oven-proof nonstick skillet until hot. Add the potatoes and stir in the nutmeg, salt, and pepper, mixing well so the potatoes are well coated. Sauté for 1 to 2 minutes, stirring occasionally so the potatoes absorb the seasonings. Using a spatula, press on the potatoes to compact them in the pan.

Bake the *gâteau* for 35 to 40 minutes, until nicely browned underneath and slightly brown on top.

Preheat the broiler. Place a flameproof round serving dish upside down on top of the skillet and invert the pan to unmold the potatoes into the dish. Pour the cream over the potatoes, sprinkle with the cheese, and broil about 4 inches from the heat for about 5 minutes, until nicely browned on top. Serve.

Paillasson Potatoes
Serves 4

✀ **Literally translated**, *paillasson* means "door-mat." Raw potatoes are shredded, pressed into a nonstick pan, and cooked to create a compact cake that is excellent with any kind of roast or on its own with a salad. The dish, also known as *pommes Darphin*, after the chef who created it, is similar to what the Swiss call *rösti* potatoes.

If you are reluctant to try flipping the compacted potato cake over in the skillet with a spatula, loosen it (it should be a solid mass) around the edges and underneath, cover the pan with a flat lid or plate, and, holding the lid in place, invert the pan. Then slide the potato cake, crusty side up, back into the skillet to cook on the other side.

3 baking (Idaho) potatoes (about
　　8 ounces each)
2 tablespoons corn oil

1 tablespoon unsalted butter
4 scallions, trimmed (leaving some green)
　　and minced (½ cup)
½ teaspoon salt
¼ teaspoon freshly ground black pepper

Peel the potatoes and, using the large holes of a box grater, shred them. (You should have about 4 cups.) Squeeze the potatoes gently with your hands to remove some of the liquid.

Heat the oil and butter in a 10- to 12-inch nonstick skillet until hot. Add the potatoes, scallions, salt, and pepper and sauté, stirring occasionally, for about 2 minutes, until the potatoes are well mixed with the seasonings. Press on the mixture with the back of a spoon to compact it, cover, reduce the heat, and cook gently for about 12 minutes.

Flip the potato mixture over and cook it for 10 minutes on the other side.

Invert it onto a serving plate, cut into wedges, and serve.

Potato Lace
Serves 6 to 8 (makes 12 to 14 pancakes)

✀ **This is an ideal** dish to serve when unexpected guests arrive or when you need to round out a family meal. It is best eaten immediately after it is cooked, when it is most savory and crisp. Leftovers can be crisped under the broiler, but they are never as good as when they have just come out of the skillet.

The potatoes are shredded into little strips, although they can also be finely grated like the onions to give a different texture and taste. If you make the batter ahead, refrigerate it, tightly covered with plastic wrap to lessen discoloration. The top of the batter will turn brown anyway, but it doesn't change the taste, and as you stir, the discoloration will disappear. Don't prepare the batter more than a few hours ahead, though, or it will become watery.

1 large or 2 medium onions (to make ½ cup grated)
1¾ pounds (3–4 large) baking (Idaho) potatoes, peeled
3 large eggs
2 tablespoons all-purpose flour
⅓ cup chopped fresh parsley
1 teaspoon salt
½ teaspoon freshly ground black pepper
About 1 cup peanut oil

Grate the onions with a box grater, using the side of the grater that looks as if it was perforated with nails — these tiny holes abrade in any direction and will liquefy the onions to a smooth puree.

Shred the potatoes on the large holes of the grater. (You should have about 3 cups.) Wrap the shredded potatoes in a towel, twist the towel with one hand, and press on it with the other to extrude most of the liquid.

Combine all the ingredients except the oil in a bowl, preferably stainless steel (to prevent discoloration), and mix thoroughly. The batter will be fairly loose.

Heat 2 to 3 tablespoons of the oil in an 8- to 10-inch nonstick skillet. Spoon about 3 tablespoonfuls of the mixture into the skillet for each pancake and immediately spread the mixture out with the back of a spoon so that the pancakes are thin, with little holes. Fry over medium-high heat, turning once, for 2 to 3 minutes on each side; use a large spatula to flip them over. The potatoes should be thin and crispy, with jagged edges. Remove with the spatula. Continue making pancakes, adding more oil as necessary.

Serve as soon as possible.

Mushroom-Stuffed Potato Pancakes
Serves 6 as a first course, 3 as a main course

❧ These pancakes consist of two layers of mashed potatoes with a layer of cooked mushrooms in the center. It's an unusual and delicate combination. Do not use a food processor to puree the potatoes, or they will be gluey; however, an electric mixer will work if you don't have a food mill or ricer. I like to serve these pancakes as a first course, but they make a delightful main too. The pancakes can be cooked about an hour or so ahead and reheated in the oven or under the broiler just before serving.

1½ pounds (4–5 large) Red Bliss potatoes, washed
¾ teaspoon salt
½ teaspoon freshly ground black pepper
5 tablespoons canola oil
4 shallots, thinly sliced (⅓ cup)
2 garlic cloves, crushed and finely chopped (1 teaspoon)
4 ounces mushrooms, cleaned and chopped (1 cup)
12 oil-cured black olives, pitted and cut into ½-inch dice

Put the potatoes in a saucepan, cover with cool water, and bring to a boil. Reduce the heat to low and boil gently for 30 minutes, or until the potatoes are tender. Drain the potatoes and let cool slightly.

Peel the potatoes and push them through a food mill or ricer into a bowl. Season with ½ teaspoon of the salt and ¼ teaspoon of the pepper. Cool to room temperature.

Meanwhile, heat 1 tablespoon of the oil in a large skillet or saucepan. Add the shallots and sauté for 1 minute. Add the garlic and mushrooms and cook for about 3 minutes, until the moisture is almost gone. Remove from the heat and add the olives and the remaining ¼ teaspoon each salt and pepper. Cool.

Shape the cooled potato puree into 24 balls of equal size. Working in batches, arrange the balls about 6 inches apart on a large sheet of plastic wrap. Cover with a second piece of plastic and press on each ball to create a pancake about 3 inches in diameter and ¼ inch thick. Spoon 1 tablespoon of the mushroom mixture onto each of 12 pancakes and cover with the remaining pancakes. Press the edges together to seal.

Heat 2 tablespoons of the remaining oil in each of two large nonstick skillets over medium-high heat. When it is hot, add 6 of the filled pancakes to each pan, in a single layer, and cook for about 3 minutes. Turn carefully with a large spatula and cook for about 3 minutes on the other side, until lightly browned and heated through. Remove to a serving platter and serve.

Baker's Wife Potatoes
Serves 8

❧ **"Baker's wife potatoes,"** or *pommes de terre à la boulangère,* is the classic side dish for Roast Leg of Lamb (page 351). Mine are made with chicken stock and flavored with lots of onion; I add wine for a dash of acidity. It is important to cook the potatoes long enough: they should be soft and moist, but most of the liquid surrounding them should be evaporated or absorbed.

The peeled potatoes can be set aside in water to cover, but don't slice them until just before

assembling the dish. Soaking the slices in water would extract their starch, which is needed as a thickening agent to give the dish the proper texture.

2	pounds Yukon Gold potatoes
1	tablespoon peanut oil
4	cups thinly sliced onions (about 14 ounces)
6	large garlic cloves, thinly sliced (3 tablespoons)
3	cups homemade chicken stock (page 612) or low-salt canned chicken broth
1	teaspoon salt, or to taste
½	teaspoon freshly ground black pepper
½	cup dry white wine
3	bay leaves
2	fresh thyme sprigs

Preheat the oven to 375 degrees.

Peel the potatoes and cut them into ⅛-inch-thick slices.

Heat the oil in a large saucepan. When it is hot, add the onions and sauté them for 3 to 4 minutes. Add the remaining ingredients, including the potatoes, mixing gently, and bring to a boil. Transfer the mixture to an 8-cup gratin dish.

Bake for 50 minutes to 1 hour, until most of the moisture is absorbed and the potatoes are tender when pierced with a fork. Serve.

Gratin Dauphinois
Serves 6 to 8

❧ **This dish is my** version of a classic from my youth. My mother always makes her gratin exclusively with milk and tops the potatoes with grated Gruyère cheese before baking. Sometimes I use grated cheese in this dish, but other times I don't, depending on my mood.

It is important not to rinse or soak the potatoes after slicing them. Rinsing would remove most of the starch, which is needed to thicken the mixture as it comes to a boil on top of the stove.

The gratin goes well with a salad of frisée or escarole dressed with a mustardy garlic dressing. One of the greatest treats of this dish is the leftovers, which can be enjoyed cool or at room temperature the next day.

1¾ pounds potatoes, preferably Yukon Gold
2½ cups milk
2–3 garlic cloves, crushed and finely chopped (1½ teaspoons)
¾ teaspoon salt
½ teaspoon freshly ground black pepper
1 cup heavy cream

Preheat the oven to 375 degrees.

Peel the potatoes and slice them ¼ inch thick, by hand, with a vegetable slicer, or with the slicing blade of a food processor. Do not rinse the slices.

Combine the potato slices, milk, garlic, salt, and pepper in a large saucepan and bring to a boil, stirring gently to separate the slices and prevent the mixture from scorching. It will thicken as it reaches a boil.

Pour the potato mixture into a 6-cup gratin dish and pour the cream on top. Place the dish on a baking sheet and bake for 1 hour, or until half of the liquid is absorbed and the potatoes are tender when pierced with a fork. Let the potatoes rest for 20 to 30 minutes before serving.

Potato Ragout
Serves 6

❧ **These stewed potatoes recall** summer for me, when our garden in Lyon gave forth the tiny fingerling potatoes that are particularly good in the dish. It is true family food and it remains a favorite in both my mother's home and mine.

The ragout reheats well and is excellent served with a tough, slightly bitter green, such as frisée or escarole, seasoned with a strong vinegary or garlicky dressing.

Potato ragout is usually made with lardons (strips of salt pork or pancetta), but it can also be made with leftover ham or sausage. Salt pork comes from the same part of the belly as bacon and is salted but not smoked, as is bacon. Get the leanest piece you can find. Many recipes direct you to blanch salt pork to make it less salty. Here you need only wash it well under cold water.

1 10-ounce slab salt pork or 10 ounces pancetta, as lean as possible
1 tablespoon peanut oil
3 large onions (1 pound), cut into 8 wedges each
2 tablespoons all-purpose flour
1 tablespoon crushed and coarsely chopped garlic
3 bay leaves
1 fresh thyme sprig or ½ teaspoon dried thyme
2½ cups water
2½ pounds fingerling or small Yukon Gold potatoes, peeled

Rinse the salt pork or pancetta under cold running water, then cut it into ½-inch-thick strips. (If using salt pork, don't remove the rind: it gives the sauce a slightly gelatinous texture.) Pile the strips together and cut into ¼- to ½-inch-wide strips.

Fry the strips of salt pork or pancetta in the oil in a large saucepan over medium-high heat for 10 to 12 minutes, stirring occasionally, until they are nicely browned and crisp and have rendered most of their fat. Add the onions and cook for 5 more minutes, or until lightly browned.

Add the flour and cook for a minute, stirring to brown the flour lightly, which will give the stew a nutty taste. Add the garlic, bay leaves, thyme, and water, stir, and bring to a boil.

Add the potatoes and return to a boil, then reduce the heat, cover, and simmer gently for about 1 hour, until the potatoes are well cooked. They should be soft and creamy. Serve.

Sautéed Potato Slices
Serves 4

✳ **Sautéed sliced potatoes should** have crisp exteriors and creamy interiors. To brown properly, the potatoes must be cooked at a fairly high temperature; I cook them in oil, because it can withstand higher temperatures than butter without burning. Then I add a little butter at the end of the cooking period for maximum flavor.

The potatoes are best served immediately after cooking, but they can be peeled and even sliced a couple hours ahead, as long as they are kept in water to cover and then carefully drained and patted dry just before sautéing.

4 baking (Idaho) potatoes (about 2 pounds)
3 tablespoons canola oil
1 tablespoon unsalted butter
¼ teaspoon salt

Peel the potatoes and cut them into ¼-inch-thick slices. Rinse them and set them aside in a bowl of cool water to cover. (*This can be done a couple of hours ahead.*)

About 20 minutes before serving, drain the potato slices and pat them dry with paper towels.

Heat the oil in a very large nonstick skillet.

When it is hot, add the potatoes and cook over medium-high heat, half covered (to prevent splattering), for about 15 minutes, tossing them every 2 minutes or so to prevent them from burning and to brown them on all sides. (Some of the slices will be browner than others, but this gives contrast of texture, color, and taste to the dish.)

When the potatoes are tender, toss them with the butter and salt and serve.

French Fries
Serves 4

✳ **Prepared in the manner** of professional kitchens, these fries are first blanched in oil that is not too hot, so they cook without taking on any color. This step can be done hours ahead. Just before serving, the fries are browned quickly in very hot oil. Some chefs blanch the cut potatoes in boiling water for 30 seconds or so before blanching them in oil the first time, which makes the fries extra-crisp.

3 large baking (Idaho) potatoes (2 pounds)
About 3 cups canola oil
Salt to taste

Peel the potatoes and cut them lengthwise into ½-inch-thick sticks. Wash in cold water, drain, and pat dry.

Heat about 1½ inches of oil to 325 degrees in a large deep skillet or saucepan. Add the potatoes and cook for 5 minutes, until they are tender but still whitish. Remove and set aside until serving time. Set the pan of oil aside. (*You can prepare the recipe up to this point a few hours ahead.*)

At serving time, reheat the oil to 400 degrees. Add half the potatoes and fry, shaking the pan occasionally to prevent them from sticking, for 4 to 5 minutes, until nicely browned and crisp. Remove the potatoes from the oil and set them on paper towels. Repeat with the second batch. Sprinkle with salt and serve immediately.

"Cream Puff" Potato Fritters
Serves 6 to 8
(makes 3 dozen potato puffs)

✂ **My mother always served** these potato puffs in her small restaurants. They are made with a combination of cream puff dough (the same as for profiteroles) and mashed potatoes. In fancy restaurants, chopped truffles are sometimes added.

The dough keeps for a couple of days, so a few fritters can be cooked to order as needed. They puff beautifully in the hot oil and should be served as soon as possible after frying.

2 medium Yukon Gold potatoes (about 6 ounces each), washed
   Salt
½ cup milk
⅛ teaspoon freshly ground black pepper
3 tablespoons unsalted butter, cut into pieces
½ cup all-purpose flour
2 large eggs
   About 3 cups canola oil, for deep-frying

Put the potatoes in a pot with cold water to cover, add ½ teaspoon salt, and bring to a boil. Boil gently for about 40 minutes, until very tender; be sure the potatoes are always covered with water during cooking. Drain the potatoes.

When they are cool enough to handle, peel the potatoes, cut into chunks, and push through a food mill or a ricer.

Combine the milk, ¼ teaspoon salt, the pepper, and butter in a heavy saucepan and bring to a boil. Remove from the heat and add the flour all at once, working the mixture with a wooden spoon until it forms a ball. Return to the stove and cook for 30 seconds over low heat, stirring the mixture, which will become a shiny, homogenous mass. Transfer to a bowl and let cool for 5 minutes.

Add the eggs to the dough one at a time, beating well with a whisk after each addition, then stir in the potatoes. Alternatively, transfer the dough to a food processor and, with the motor running, add the eggs. Process for 15 to 20 seconds, then combine in a bowl with the mashed potatoes.

Preheat the oven to 160 degrees.

Heat 1½ to 2 inches of oil to about 350 degrees in a deep 10- to 12-inch skillet. Spoon 1 tablespoon of the dough at a time into the oil, pushing it out of the spoon with your finger; cook 10 to 15 pieces at a time. Cook for 8 to 10 minutes, turning the fritters in the oil to brown them evenly on all sides. As soon as the first batch is done, remove with a slotted spoon and place on a tray lined with paper towels. Keep hot in the oven while you cook the remaining fritters. Sprinkle lightly with salt and serve. (If the fritters sit too long, they will lose their delicious crispness.)

Potato Croquettes
Serves 6

✂ **Golden and crispy on** the outside, these deep-fried nuggets have soft interiors. In my youth, when I worked in restaurants in Paris, they were the standard accompaniment to grilled meat. They are not made as often as they used to be, but they are well worth the effort. It is important to dry the potatoes in the oven after they are cooked. If they are too wet, the croquettes will tend to break up in the fryer.

3 large baking (Idaho) potatoes (about
　　8 ounces each)
1 tablespoon unsalted butter, softened
3 large egg yolks
½ teaspoon salt
⅛ teaspoon freshly grated nutmeg
1 large egg
　　About 3 cups canola oil, for
　　　deep-frying
2 tablespoons water
⅛ teaspoon freshly ground black
　　pepper
　　About 1 cup all-purpose flour
5 cups fresh bread crumbs (from about
　　10 slices firm white bread)

Preheat the oven to 400 degrees.

Peel the potatoes and cut into quarters. Cook in a pot of boiling salted water, covered, for about 30 minutes, until tender when pierced with the point of a small sharp knife. Drain and dry thoroughly in the oven for 5 or 6 minutes.

Put the potatoes through a food mill or ricer into a bowl; or mash them with a potato masher. Beat in the butter, egg yolks, ¼ teaspoon of the salt, and the nutmeg with a wooden spatula. The potatoes should be very smooth and without any lumps. Refrigerate until cold.

Beat together the egg, 1 tablespoon of the oil, the water, the remaining ¼ teaspoon salt, and the pepper in a shallow bowl. Place the flour in another small bowl. Flour your hands, then shape the potato mixture into cylinders about 3 inches long by 1½ inches thick and roll in the flour. Dip the potato cylinders into the egg mixture, then coat well with the bread crumbs. Refrigerate.

At serving time, heat the remaining oil to 375 degrees in a large deep saucepan; the oil should be at least 1½ inches deep. Deep-fry the croquettes for 3 to 4 minutes, or until golden. Drain on paper towels and serve as soon as possible.

Pommes Soufflés
Serves 6

✄ **According to** *Larousse Gastronomique*, this recipe was created in 1837 on the inauguration day of a railroad in a small town near Paris. A chef had prepared fried sliced potatoes for the official delegation, but the train was late, so he removed them from the frying pan half-cooked and set them aside. When the guests finally arrived, he dipped the potatoes back into the hot oil and, to his amazement, some of them puffed up.

Pommes soufflés are still made in French restaurants. It is a delicate operation: if the potatoes are new and have too much moisture, or if they are too old and soft, they will not puff. In any case, it is customary for 10 to 20 percent of the slices to stay flat, and they are fine to serve as well.

The slices are cooked three times, the first time to create a skin on the outside, which traps the moisture inside. Then the slices are cooked right away for a second time in the hotter oil, the steam from the inside inflates them. The slices deflate when the potatoes are removed from the oil, but the "good ones" will inflate again when refried at serving time.

3 large baking (Idaho) potatoes (about
　　8 ounces each)
3 quarts canola oil, for deep-frying
　　Salt

Trim each potato to create a long cylinder 2½ to 3 inches in diameter. With a vegetable slicer or by hand, slice the potatoes into ⅜-inch-thick slices. Rinse in cold water and dry well with paper towels.

Divide the canola oil between two large saucepans. Heat the oil in one to 300 degrees and the oil in the other pan to 375 degrees. Drop 15 to 20 potato slices into the 300-degree oil and fry, shaking the pan back and forth, for 6 to 7 minutes. The potatoes have to be agitated to puff up, but be careful not to splash your hand or the stove with the hot oil. After 4 to 5 minutes, some blisters should start to appear on the slices. Keep shaking the pan for another minute.

Lift up a few slices at a time with a skimmer and dip into the 375-degree oil. The slices should swell instantly. As they puff, transfer the slices to paper towels to drain. Then fry the remaining potatoes in batches. The potatoes will collapse as they cool; pick out the ones that puffed and arrange them on a tray before final cooking. The slices that did not puff can be served as fried potatoes. (*At this point, the potatoes can be kept, covered with a towel, for several hours.*)

At serving time, drop the prepuffed slices into 375-degree oil (they will puff again). Cook them for about 1 minute, moving them with a skimmer so they brown evenly. They should be crisp enough to stay puffed. Sprinkle with salt and serve immediately, on a folded napkin.

Skillet Sweet Potatoes
Serves 4

✴ **An easy dish, these** sliced sweet potatoes are cooked in butter, oil, and water until the water evaporates and they are nicely browned. They are good with almost any meat or fish main course.

- 1 large long sweet potato (about 1 pound), peeled and cut into 12 slices, about ½ inch thick
- 1 tablespoon unsalted butter
- 1 tablespoon corn oil
- ½ cup water
- ¼ teaspoon salt
- 1 tablespoon minced fresh chives

Arrange the sweet potato slices in a single layer in one very large or two slightly smaller nonstick skillets. Add the butter, oil, water, and salt. Bring to a boil, cover, and boil over high heat for about 5 minutes. Most of the water will have evaporated and the potatoes will be soft. Continue to cook, uncovered, over medium heat, turning, until the slices are nicely browned on both sides, about 2 additional minutes per side. Serve, sprinkled with the chives.

Crispy Baked Sweet Potatoes
Serves 6

✴ **A fall and winter** favorite, these sweet potatoes are baked until the skin is crisp. Baking them on a foil-lined cookie sheet will eliminate time-consuming cleanup, but don't wrap them in foil: they would lose their delicious crisp skin and become wet and soggy.

- 6 sweet potatoes (about 8 ounces each)
- 2 tablespoons unsalted butter, softened
- 2 teaspoons fleur de sel

Preheat the oven to 400 degrees.

Remove any dark spots or damaged areas from the sweet potatoes and wash them thoroughly under cool water. If you did not have to cut out any damaged areas from the potatoes, trim them at either end or prick them to allow steam to escape.

Arrange the potatoes on a foil-lined cookie sheet and bake for about 50 minutes, until soft and tender.

Arrange the potatoes on a plate and crack them by pressing on them with a fork or spatula. Brush with the butter, sprinkle with salt, and serve.

Breads, Sandwiches, and Pizzas

Breads, Sandwiches, and Pizzas

Breads

Brioche
Makes 12 small brioches or 1 large one

❧ Brioches are buttery, moist, light breads made with a yeast dough. The perfect accompaniment to a café au lait in the morning, brioche can be made as a large loaf or small individual ones. The dough is also ideal for encasing sausages or pâté. A food processor yields excellent results.

If possible, make the dough a few hours ahead or even the day before you plan to use it — it will be more malleable after it has rested overnight.

DOUGH

- 1 envelope (2¼ teaspoons) active dry yeast
- 3 tablespoons warm water
- 1 teaspoon sugar
- ¼ teaspoon salt
- 3 large eggs
- 2 cups all-purpose flour
- ½ pound (2 sticks) unsalted butter, softened
- 1 tablespoon unsalted butter to coat the mold(s)

- 1 large egg, beaten, for egg wash

FOR THE DOUGH: Combine the yeast, warm water, and sugar in a food processor. Let stand for 10 to 15 minutes, until bubbly.

Add the salt, eggs, and flour to the yeast mixture and process for about 30 seconds. With the machine running, add the butter in chunks and process for another 15 to 20 seconds. Transfer the dough to a bowl, cover with plastic wrap, and let rise in a warm, draft-free place (about 70 degrees) for 1½ to 2 hours, until it has doubled in bulk.

Flour your hands and push the dough down with your fingers. Cover and let rest for at least 4 hours, or up to 12 hours. Wrap the dough in foil or plastic wrap and refrigerate. (*The dough can be frozen, well wrapped, for up to 1 month, but not longer, because yeast is affected by extreme cold. If you freeze it, defrost it in the refrigerator before using it.*)

If making small brioches, butter twelve individual brioche molds; if making one large brioche, butter a 9-by-5-inch loaf pan or large brioche mold.

For little brioches, cut the dough into 12 pieces (about 2½ ounces per brioche) and roll into little balls. Place in the buttered brioche molds. Brush with the egg wash and let rise in a warm, draft-free place for 1¼ to 1½ hours, or until doubled. For a large brioche, put the dough in the buttered pan. Brush with the egg wash and let rise for about 3 hours, until almost doubled.

Preheat the oven to 375 degrees.

Bake individual brioches for about 25 minutes, the large brioche for about 45 minutes, until puffed and beautifully browned. Unmold and cool on a rack.

Croissants and Pains au Chocolat
Makes about 20 small croissants and 6 *pains au chocolat*

❧ Served with café au lait and jam, these flaky rolls are the quintessential French breakfast.

Croissant dough is a cross between puff pastry and brioche. It is a buttery dough that is rolled and folded like puff pastry, but it also contains yeast. Unlike classic puff pastry, which requires six turns, or folds, croissant dough is given only four turns. Because the yeast in it makes the dough rise and break through the layers you have created by folding, too many turns would blend the dough too much and cause it to lose its flakiness. The dough can be made ahead and frozen, but it should not be frozen for too long, as the yeast will eventually die in the freezer.

The croissants here are small (approximately 1½ ounces each), unlike those served with meals or with savory fillings, which are often as large as 3 ounces. It is important that the dough rise in a very moist environment; I use a plastic bag and a cut-out cardboard box to take the place of a professional proof box.

The *petit pains au chocolat* are made by rolling a chocolate stick up in a rectangle of croissant dough. This is a refined version of the *pain au chocolat* that I remember eating as a child, which was simply a piece of crusty bread and a bar of dark chocolate (see Bread with Chocolate and Hazelnuts, page 130).

DOUGH

¾ pound (3 sticks) unsalted butter
1 envelope (2¼ teaspoons) active
     dry yeast
1¼ cups warm milk (90–100 degrees)
2 teaspoons sugar
3 cups unbleached all-purpose flour
1 teaspoon salt

1 large egg

FOR THE PAINS AU CHOCOLAT

3–4 ounces bittersweet chocolate, cut into
       8 sticks (each about 3½ inches long;
       see the sidebar, page 130)

FOR THE DOUGH: Cut each stick of butter into 4 lengthwise slices. Place on a plate and refrigerate.

Combine the yeast with the milk and sugar in the bowl of a stand mixer or a food processor. Let stand for about 10 minutes, until bubbly. Add the flour and salt to the yeast mixture and mix with the flat beater for about 20 to 30 seconds, just until smooth; or process for 10 to 15 seconds, just until the dough comes together.

Place the dough on a board, preferably cold, and press down on it with your floured hands to extend it, using as little flour as possible. (The board can be set outside to cool in winter or in the refrigerator. A jelly-roll pan filled with ice can also be placed on the board to cool it.) It doesn't matter if the dough is crushed at this point, since there is no butter in it yet. Using a rolling pin, roll it out into a rectangle 18 to 20 inches long by 8 to 10 inches wide and about ¼ inch thick.

With a short end of the dough toward you, arrange the slices of butter side by side on the top two thirds of the dough, covering it to within ¾ to 1 inch from the edges. Lift up the bottom third of the dough and fold it over the butter-covered middle third of the dough. Press on the sides of the dough so the layers stick together. Then fold the dough over the butter-covered top third of dough. Press on the edges so the pastry layers hold together well.

The first turn can be completed now: Place the rectangle of dough in front of you so a short end faces you and roll it out, flouring the bottom and top of it as necessary, into a rectangle approximately 18 inches long by 9 inches wide and ⅜ inch thick. (Using a large rolling pin with ball bearings helps.) Brush off any excess flour from the top of the dough and fold the top and bottom of the dough over so the two ends meet in the center. Fold the dough again to create a 4-layered piece of dough. (This is called a double turn.) Place the dough in a plastic bag and refrigerate for at least 30 minutes, to allow the dough to relax.

Give the dough 1 double turn. Wrap the dough again and refrigerate for at least a couple hours.

FOR THE CROISSANTS AND PAINS AU CHOCOLAT: Roll out the dough on a floured board into a square about 20 inches by 20 inches and ⅛ inch thick. Be sure to roll in one direction and then in the other direction, extending the dough from the center forward and backward, then rolling from left and right. Avoid going back and forth on the dough, which tends to develop the gluten and give the dough too much elasticity. Let the dough rest for 8 to 10 minutes on the work surface (or in the refrigerator on a tray), to allow it to lose some of the elasticity developed from rolling it out.

Trim the edges and cut the dough into 3 strips, each about 6½ inches wide. Two of the strips will be used to make croissants and one to make *pains au chocolat*. Transfer 1 strip to a baking sheet and refrigerate until ready to make the *pains au chocolat*. You can shape all the croissants now and refrigerate half of them while the first batch rises and bakes, or freeze half of them for later; when ready to bake, let rise and bake as directed.

FOR THE CROISSANTS: Mark each strip into 5-inch segments and then cut into triangles. The 2 strips should yield about 20 croissants.

Roll each triangle of dough up from the base, first folding the bottom edge of the dough over itself and pressing so it sticks, then rolling with your fingers and the palms of your hands while pressing down and out on the dough to extend it; it should be pressed forward and rolled tightly. Wet the tip of the triangle, then press it into the croissant so it adheres to the dough. Place the shaped croissants tip side down on a cookie sheet lined with parchment or a nonstick baking mat and bend the ends forward to create the traditional crescent shape.

Brush the croissants with water to eliminate any patches of flour left on top and to prevent them from drying out. Insert the tray of croissants into a proof box (see the box) and tie the plastic bag closed; be sure the plastic doesn't touch the

MAKING A PROOF BOX

Choose a cardboard box large enough to hold the baking sheet and tall enough to allow the croissants to rise. Cut off the top and ends. Insert the box in a large plastic bag. The bag seals in moisture and the cardboard prevents the plastic bag from falling onto and sticking to the croissants. It is especially important to use a proof box in very dry climates; otherwise, instead of rising, the dough tends to form a crust on top that prevents it from rising well. After the croissants are formed, the dough should still be moist on top, so that the yeast can develop and expand the dough. If you don't have a proof box, you can use a large deep roasting pan, inverted over the croissants.

croissants. Let them rise in a warm, draft-free place (about 75 degrees) for 1¼ to 1½ hours, or until almost doubled in size.

Preheat the oven to 425 degrees. Whisk the egg yolk with half the white in a small bowl to make an egg wash.

Brush the croissants with the egg wash. Bake for 20 to 25 minutes, until nicely browned. Let cool and serve at room temperature.

FOR THE PAINS AU CHOCOLAT: Cut the remaining strip of dough crosswise into rectangles 3 inches wide and 5 inches long. Dampen them with water and place a piece of chocolate along one short edge of each rectangle. Roll up tightly and place seam side down on a cookie sheet lined with parchment paper or a baking mat. Let rise in the proof box for 1 to 1½ hours, until almost doubled in bulk.

Brush with the egg wash and bake in a 425-degree oven for 20 to 25 minutes, until golden brown. Let cool and serve at room temperature.

CHOCOLATE FOR PAINS AU CHOCOLAT

For the *pains au chocolat*, pieces of chocolate can be used. However, if you are making a great many, it is better to melt the chocolate and spread it on a piece of parchment or waxed paper into a strip approximately 3½ inches wide and ¼ inch thick. Refrigerate or cool until it begins to set, then cut into sticks approximately ¾ inch wide. Allow the chocolate to chill and harden further, and when it is completely cold, lift the strips of chocolate from the paper. If you are making only a few *pains au chocolat*, just break the chocolate into pieces and arrange on the dough.

Bread with Chocolate and Hazelnuts
Serves 4

❧ **Eating a piece of** crusty *ficelle* (from the French word "string") and a chunk of bittersweet chocolate together takes me back to my youth. My brother and I typically enjoyed this combination for our after-school snack. Even though I occasionally sample the updated, more refined version of *pain au chocolat* (see Pains au Chocolat, page 127) — I still prefer this treat. I serve it here with toasted hazelnuts and grapes. The combined flavors of these disparate ingredients are wonderful.

Toasting hazelnuts — or for that matter, any nuts — in their shells has its advantages. Protected by the shells, the nuts keep for weeks longer without getting rancid than when shelled before roasting. And even weeks later, if they are not cracked open, they retain their rich, roasted taste.

4 dozen unshelled hazelnuts (about 7 ounces)

1 large bunch seedless green grapes (about 1 pound)

1 *ficelle* (thin French bread), broken into 4 pieces

6 ounces bittersweet chocolate, broken into 4 pieces

Preheat the oven to 400 degrees.

Spread the unshelled hazelnuts on a baking sheet and bake for about 15 minutes to toast them lightly inside. Cool.

Wash the grapes (do not pull them from the stems) and separate them into 4 small bunches.

Arrange a bunch of grapes on each of four plates. Crack the shells of the hazelnuts and divide the nuts among the plates. Put a piece of *ficelle* and chocolate on each plate. Eat the crusty bread, chocolate, hazelnuts, and grapes together.

Gros Pain (Big Bread)
Makes 1 large loaf

❧ **Gros pain, or** "big bread," was the regular daily home bread of every French family when I was a kid. It is a bit coarser in texture than a baguette and less expensive, and it keeps longer.

4½ cups bread flour, preferably organic, plus 3 tablespoons for kneading and for sprinkling on the loaves

2½ teaspoons salt

1 envelope (2¼ teaspoons) active dry yeast

2 cups cool water (70 degrees)

1 tablespoon cornmeal or farina (Cream of Wheat)

Put the flour, salt, yeast, and water in the bowl of a stand mixer fitted with a dough hook or a large food processor. If using a mixer, beat on medium speed for 2 to 3 minutes, until a smooth, elastic dough forms. If using a food processor, process the mixture for about 45 seconds on low speed if your processor has variable speeds, or for about 30 seconds if your processor has only one speed. (The temperature of the dough should not exceed 75 degrees.)

Transfer the dough to a plastic bucket (preferable) or a large deep ceramic or stainless steel bowl. Cover tightly with a lid or plastic wrap and let rise in a warm, draft-free place (about 70 degrees) for about 3 hours, until doubled in bulk.

Break down the dough by bringing the outer edges into the center and pressing down to release the air inside. Lift the dough from the bucket with one hand and sprinkle 2 tablespoons of the remaining flour into the bucket with the other. Return the dough to the bucket and knead it until the flour is incorporated and the dough is elastic, about 1 minute. Form the dough into a ball, stretching and pinching it together underneath so it is nicely rounded and taut on top.

Line a large cookie sheet with parchment paper or a nonstick baking mat and sprinkle the cornmeal or farina on top. Place the dough seam side down on the sheet and cover it with the overturned bucket or bowl. Let rise for 2 hours, or until doubled. Alternatively, let it rise, covered, in the refrigerator overnight.

Preheat the oven to 425 degrees.

Sprinkle the top of the dough with the remaining tablespoon of flour. Cut several slits across the top of the loaf with a serrated knife. Place the loaf in the oven. Using a spray bottle filled with tap water, mist the interior of the oven a few times to create steam, then quickly close the door. After 5 minutes, mist again. Bake the loaf for 15 minutes longer, then reduce the oven temperature to 400 degrees and bake for 1 hour longer, or until brown.

Cool the bread on a rack for at least 3 hours before slicing.

Small Light Country Loaves
Makes 4 round loaves

❧ **Made with a very** soft dough, these loaves are airy, with large holes inside, and have a nutty taste, similar to Italian ciabatta. Because it is so soft, the dough is not worked by hand until after the second rise, when it is formed into a ball, divided into 4 pieces, placed on a lined cookie sheet, and allowed to rise again. Then the bread and liner are slid onto a pizza stone (if available) for baking. In full summer or in areas where there is great humidity, the 2¼ teaspoons of yeast in the recipe can be reduced to 1½ or even 1 teaspoon, as yeast develops more rapidly in these conditions.

    4   cups bread flour, preferably organic
    1   envelope (2¼ teaspoons) instant yeast
    2   teaspoons salt
    2   cups cool water (70 degrees)

Reserve 1 tablespoon of the flour for dusting the tops of the loaves. Put the remaining flour, the yeast, salt, and water in a large food processor and process for 15 seconds. The dough will be soft and sticky.

Transfer the dough to a bowl, cover it with plastic wrap, and let it rise in a warm, draft-free place (about 70 degrees) for about 3½ hours, until doubled in bulk.

Release the dough from the sides of the bowl with your fingers and press it firmly into the center of the bowl, then repeat this procedure until all the dough is deflated and in a ball again. Cover the dough again with plastic wrap and let it rise for 2 hours.

Deflate the dough and form it into a ball as

described above. Moisten your hands and divide the dough into 4 equal pieces. Arrange the pieces of dough evenly spaced on a cookie sheet lined with parchment paper or a nonstick baking mat. Moisten your hands again and press on the dough pieces to flatten them. Place an inverted roasting pan over the cookie sheet to simulate a proof box and prevent the dough from crusting on top as it rises. (See the box on page 129.) Let the dough rise for 45 minutes, or until almost doubled.

Meanwhile, put a pizza stone, if you have one, on the center oven rack, set the oven to 425 degrees, and preheat for at least 30 minutes. If you don't have a pizza stone, preheat a cookie sheet in the oven for 10 to 15 minutes.

Remove the roasting pan and dust the tops of the loaves with the reserved 1 tablespoon flour. Firmly holding the sides of the liner, slide it and the loaves carefully onto the hot stone or cookie sheet. Using a spray bottle filled with water, mist the interior of the oven a few times to create steam and quickly close the door. Repeat this misting process after 2 or 3 minutes, then bake the bread for a total of 35 to 40 minutes, until golden brown.

Slide the loaves and liner onto a rack. Let the loaves cool for 10 to 15 minutes, then remove the liner and cool the loaves completely on the rack.

VARIATION

Add ½ cup mixed grains (oats, millet, bulgur, and/ or other favorite grains) and 2 additional tablespoons water to the food processor with the other ingredients and proceed as instructed.

Baguettes
Makes 4 baguettes

✂ **The long rising time** in this recipe gives the baguettes a better texture and a more pronounced flavor.

To have fresh-baked bread whenever you want it, you can partially bake the baguettes, for about 25 minutes, until they have achieved maximum size but are not yet brown. Let the loaves cool until lukewarm, then wrap tightly and freeze. When needed, unwrap a frozen loaf, place directly on the center rack of a preheated 400-degree oven, and bake for about 20 minutes, until brown and crusty.

4½ cups bread flour, preferably organic, plus 2½ tablespoons for sprinkling
1 envelope (2¼ teaspoons) active dry yeast
2½ teaspoons salt
2 cups cool water (70 degrees)
2 tablespoons cornmeal

Put the 4½ cups flour, the yeast, salt, and water in the bowl of a stand mixer and mix with the dough hook on low speed for 2 to 3 minutes, or until a smooth, elastic dough forms. Alternatively, process the ingredients in a large food processor for 45 seconds.

Transfer the dough to a plastic bucket or a large deep ceramic or stainless steel bowl. Cover and let rise in a warm, draft-free place (about 70 degrees) for at least 4½ hours, or until doubled in bulk.

Break down the dough by bringing the outer edges into the center of the bowl and pressing down to release the air inside. Form the dough into a ball. Sprinkle the work surface with 2 tablespoons of the remaining flour, place the dough on top, and press down to form it into a rough rectangular shape. Cut the rectangle lengthwise into 4 equal strips. Roll each strip under your palms into an 18-inch length.

Line a large baking sheet with parchment paper or a nonstick baking mat and sprinkle with the cornmeal. Place the baguettes on the baking sheet. Let the baguettes rise, covered with an upside-down roasting pan, in a warm, draft-free place for 1 hour.

Preheat the oven to 425 degrees.

Sprinkle the tops of the risen loaves with the remaining ½ tablespoon flour. Cut 4 diagonal slits in the top surface of each loaf with a serrated knife or razor blade and place in the oven. Using a spray bottle filled with water, mist the inside of the oven to create steam and immediately close the door. Bake the baguettes for 35 minutes, or until brown and crusty.

Cool the baguettes on a rack for at least 45 minutes before slicing.

Whole-Grain Épi and Crown Bread
Makes 3 *épis* and 1 crown loaf

✼ *Épi,* bread shaped to look like a stalk of wheat, and crown bread, made to look like a wheel, were favorites at a small restaurant my wife and I had in Connecticut. We used to make thirty *épis* a day. Both are chewy, tough breads with a thick crust and a strong, nutty taste. These shapes are traditional in any bakery in France.

Any leftover bread should be stored in a plastic bag to prevent it from drying out. Just before eating, it can be dampened with water and placed back in the oven for a few minutes to re-crisp. Or, it can be sliced thin and baked to make delicious croutons, which go well with salad, pâtés, and other dishes.

2 cups warm water (95–100 degrees)
1 teaspoon sugar
2 envelopes (4½ teaspoons total) active dry yeast
1 tablespoon salt
8 cups bread flour, plus more as needed
1 cup wheat bran
1½ cups (7 ounces) cracked wheat
3 tablespoons semolina or farina (Cream of Wheat)

Combine the warm water, sugar, and yeast in the bowl of a stand mixer. Let stand for 10 minutes, or until bubbly.

Add the salt and 7 cups of the bread flour and, using the dough hook, mix the dough on medium speed for 5 minutes, or until it is tight, elastic, and smooth. Add the remaining cup of flour and mix on medium speed for 1 to 2 minutes longer, until thoroughly incorporated.

Turn the dough out onto a work surface; it will still be fairly soft. Add the bran and cracked wheat to the work surface and press and turn the dough into them until they are incorporated. Then knead the dough, pressing it, pushing it, and folding it over, rotating it each time, for 5 minutes. If the dough is still a bit sticky, knead in a few tablespoons more flour until it is strong and springy to the touch and doesn't stick to your fingers anymore.

Put the dough in a large bowl, cover, and let rise in a warm, draft-free place (about 70 degrees) for 3 hours, or until doubled in size.

Break down the dough by bringing the outer edges into the bowl, pressing down to release the air inside. Turn out onto a board. The dough will weigh about 5 pounds; you will use three 1-pound pieces for the *épis* and the remaining 2 pounds for the crown loaf. Refrigerate the dough for the crown until you have finished forming the *épis* and they are rising.

FOR THE ÉPIS: Cut the remaining dough into three 1-pound pieces. Roll 1 piece under your palms into an 18-inch length. Place on a cookie sheet coated with 1 tablespoon of the semolina or farina.

Using scissors, cut down into the dough from the top, keeping the scissors almost parallel to the work surface and cutting deeply enough so the "grain of wheat" is almost severed from the "stalk." As you cut, pick up the tip of the grain of wheat and move it to one side of the stalk. Make another cut 1½ inches down from the first cut in the same way and move the next grain of wheat to the other side of the stalk. Continue cutting at 1½-inch intervals down the length of the loaf, alternating the placement of the grains of wheat to create a whole head of wheat with about 8 points.

Repeat with the other 2 épis.

Place the loaves in a proof box (see the box on page 129) or invert a large deep roasting pan over them. Let rise in a warm, draft-free place (about 70 degrees) for 1½ hours, or until doubled in size.

Preheat the oven to 425 degrees.

Brush the loaves with water and sprinkle 1 tablespoon of the semolina or farina on top. Place them in the oven and, using a spray bottle filled with water, mist the inside several times to create steam and immediately close the door. Bake for 30 to 35 minutes, misting the oven 2 more times at 2- to 3-minute intervals during the first 10 minutes, until crusty and nicely browned. Cool on a rack.

FOR THE CROWN: Knead the remaining 2 pounds of dough into a smooth round. With your thumb, make a hole in the center of the ball of dough. Pressing both thumbs into the center, turn the dough around, stretching and squeezing at the same time, to extend and increase the size of the hole in the center, until you have created a ring about 2 inches wide and 9 inches across.

Sprinkle the remaining tablespoon of semolina or farina on a cookie sheet and place the crown loaf on top. Slide the loaf into the proof box, or invert the roasting pan over it, and let rise in a warm, draft-free place (about 70 degrees) for 2 hours, or until doubled in bulk. Brush the loaf with water and sprinkle with flour. Score with a razor blade or serrated knife, slashing the top of the ring in a crisscross pattern.

Put the loaf in the preheated oven, mist the oven to create steam, and immediately close the door. Bake for 1 hour, misting the floor of the oven again after 3 minutes, until very crusty and nicely browned. Cool on a rack.

Buttermilk Bread
Makes 1 round loaf

❧ Cut into very thin slices, this dense bread is ideal for breakfast or brunch with smoked trout, caviar, smoked salmon, or the like. The bread freezes well, and it will keep for a few days without freezing.

- 1 envelope (2¼ teaspoons) active dry yeast
- ½ cup warm tap water (about 100 degrees)
- 1 tablespoon sugar
- 4 tablespoons (½ stick) unsalted butter
- 2 cups whole wheat flour
- 2 cups bread flour
- 1 cup buttermilk, plus 1 tablespoon for brushing
- 1 teaspoon salt
- ½ teaspoon canola oil

Put the yeast, water, and sugar in a large food processor and let stand for 10 minutes, or until bubbly.

Add the butter, whole wheat flour, bread flour, buttermilk, and salt to the yeast mixture and process for 1 minute.

Use the oil to coat a large bowl and place the

dough in the bowl. Let rise, covered with a towel or plastic wrap, in a warm, draft-free place (about 70 degrees) for 2 hours, or until doubled in bulk.

Gently punch the dough down in the bowl and shape it into a ball about 6 inches in diameter. Place the ball of dough on a cookie sheet and cover with the overturned bowl. Allow to rise for 1 hour more, or until doubled.

Preheat the oven to 400 degrees.

Brush the dough with the remaining 1 tablespoon buttermilk. Using a razor blade or sharp serrated knife, make a crisscross slash in the top of the loaf. Bake for 45 to 50 minutes, until the bread sounds hollow when tapped on the bottom. Let cool on a rack before serving.

Soda Bread
Makes 1 round loaf

✴ **When you're pressed for** time, soda bread is the perfect solution, since this Irish classic requires only a few minutes of work. In fact, if you turn on your oven before starting to combine the ingredients, the bread will be ready to bake by the time the oven reaches the right temperature. No rising is necessary — the dough must be baked immediately in order for the baking powder to work effectively.

Soda bread is conventionally made with buttermilk, but for convenience, I achieve the same result with regular milk, using baking powder instead of the usual baking soda to compensate for the lack of acidity in the milk. If you want to make the classic version, substitute the same amounts of buttermilk and baking soda.

Covering the dough with an inverted stainless steel bowl during the first 30 minutes of baking creates a moist environment in which this heavy bread can rise. Then, after the bowl is removed, the crust of the bread hardens and browns.

3 cups all-purpose flour
1½ teaspoons salt
1½ teaspoons baking powder
1½ cups milk
½ teaspoon canola oil

Preheat the oven to 425 degrees.

Reserve 1 teaspoon of the flour and combine the remaining flour with the salt and baking powder in a large bowl. Add the milk and mix gently but quickly with a wooden spatula or spoon until the dough comes together.

Oil a nonstick cookie sheet with the canola oil (or line a regular cookie sheet with parchment paper and brush with the oil) and place the dough on the sheet. Using a piece of plastic wrap, press and mold the dough to create a round loaf about 7 inches in diameter and 1 inch high. Sprinkle the reserved teaspoon of flour on top of the loaf. Using a serrated knife, make 2 intersecting ¼-inch-deep cuts across the top of the loaf to create a cross.

Place a stainless steel bowl upside down over the bread and bake for 30 minutes. Remove the bowl and bake for another 30 minutes, or until golden brown.

Using a wide spatula, remove the bread to a rack. Let cool for at least 30 minutes before slicing.

Cranberry Bread
Makes 1 round bread

✴ **Because the acidity and** astringency of the berries cuts the richness of meat or cheese, this bread is best served with savories: it is excellent with game or a rich cheese, such as Gorgonzola or ripe Brie. Any leftover bread is great cut into thin slices and toasted.

Do not overmix the berries into the batter: fold them in just until they are suspended throughout.

Use fresh cranberries — frozen ones bleed more readily into the batter and the effect and taste is entirely different.

To give the bread a different look, I bake it in a springform pan and then cut it into wedges. It can also be baked in a loaf pan.

1⅓ cups milk
4 tablespoons (½ stick) unsalted butter
1½ cups cranberries (not frozen)
3 cups all-purpose flour
⅓ cup bran flakes
2 tablespoons sugar
1 teaspoon salt
1 teaspoon baking powder
1 teaspoon baking soda
2 large eggs
½ cup coarsely chopped walnuts

Preheat the oven to 350 degrees. Butter and flour an 8- or 9-inch springform pan.

Heat the milk until lukewarm, then cut the butter into it, stirring until the butter melts. Set aside.

Coarsely chop the cranberries with a knife or pulse them a few times in a food processor. They should be in good-sized pieces.

Combine the flour, bran flakes, sugar, salt, baking powder, and baking soda in a bowl. Add the milk mixture and eggs and mix until well combined. Add the cranberries and walnuts and stir just enough to incorporate them into the batter.

Gently press the batter into the buttered pan. Place the pan on a cookie sheet and bake for 55 minutes to 1 hour, or until the bread is nicely browned and baked through (a knife inserted in the center should come out clean). Set the bread on a rack and let stand for at least 1 to 2 hours to cool completely and firm up inside.

Remove the bread from the pan, cut into wedges, and serve.

Oatmeal Pan Bread
Serves 6

❧ **This versatile quick bread** can be served at breakfast, brunch, lunch, or dinner. It's an ideal accompaniment to dishes that are light and in need of some substance. It is good served with crudités as a first course and it is excellent with cheese. A mixture of chives, basil, tarragon, and other fresh herbs can be used in place of the parsley.

The bread is at its best when lukewarm. If you make it ahead, reheat it for a few minutes in the oven before serving.

1 cup quick-cooking oatmeal
1 teaspoon baking powder
1 cup grated onion (grated on the large holes of a box grater)
½ cup chopped fresh parsley
1 large egg
½ teaspoon salt
¼ teaspoon freshly ground black pepper
½ cup milk
3 tablespoons vegetable oil

Preheat the oven to 400 degrees.

Mix all the ingredients except the oil together in a bowl.

Heat 2 tablespoons of the oil in a 7- to 8-inch skillet. When it is hot, pour in the batter and spread the last tablespoon of oil on top of it. Wrap two layers of aluminum foil around the skillet handle if it's not ovenproof. Bake for 20 minutes, or until nicely browned on top.

Flip the bread over to brown the other side. The bread can be flipped like a crepe or inverted onto a flat plate or the back of a cake pan and then slid back into the skillet. Bake for another 5 to 8 minutes, or until browned. Slide onto a plate and let cool for 2 to 3 minutes.

Slice the bread into wedges and serve.

Corn and Scallion Spoon Bread
Serves 4

✂ **Prepared with yellow cornmeal** and scallions, this simple-to-make spoon bread emerges puffy and soufflé-like from the oven. It's best eaten immediately, but it remains moist and flavorful even after it cools and deflates a little.

2	teaspoons unsalted butter, for the baking dish
2¾	cups milk
¾	cup yellow cornmeal
6–8	scallions, trimmed (leaving some green) and minced (1 cup)
¼	teaspoon salt
¼	teaspoon freshly ground black pepper
⅛	teaspoon Tabasco sauce
3	large eggs

Preheat the oven to 400 degrees. Butter a 4- to 6-cup round or oval gratin dish or an oven-proof 9-inch nonstick skillet.

Bring the milk to a boil in a saucepan. Add the cornmeal and mix well with a whisk. Bring back to a boil, stirring, and cook, partially covered to prevent splattering, stirring occasionally, for 3 to 4 minutes. The mixture will be quite thick.

Transfer the cornmeal mixture to a bowl and mix in the scallions, salt, pepper, and Tabasco. Let cool for 10 to 15 minutes.

Beat the eggs in a bowl with a fork, then add them to the cornmeal mixture and mix in well with a whisk.

Pour the batter into the buttered dish. Place on a cookie sheet and bake for 30 minutes, or until firm, puffy, and brown. (If you prefer the spoon bread browner still, place it under a hot broiler for 1 to 2 minutes.)

Cut the spoon bread into wedges or squares and serve immediately.

Bread and Onion Pancakes
Makes 16 pancakes

✂ **An ideal way to** use up leftover bread, these pancakes are served with a spicy sauce of vinegar, soy sauce, ginger, Tabasco, and garlic. They are good without the sauce too. Either way, they make a very good accompaniment to a roast or a baked chicken. I like mine small, with crisp edges, but you can make yours larger if you prefer.

Although the pancakes are best eaten immediately after cooking, they can be cooked ahead and then reheated under a hot broiler just before serving.

BATTER

10	ounces day-old bread, preferably coarse-textured, cut into 1-inch cubes (8–10 cups)
2	cups homemade chicken stock (page 612) or canned low-salt chicken broth
1½	cups finely chopped onions
⅓	cup loosely packed minced fresh cilantro or parsley
½	teaspoon Tabasco sauce
4	large eggs
½	teaspoon salt

SAUCE

¼	cup red wine vinegar
¼	cup dark soy sauce
1	teaspoon sugar
½	teaspoon peeled minced ginger
½	teaspoon Tabasco sauce or hot chile oil
4	garlic cloves, crushed and chopped (about 2 teaspoons)
1	tablespoon corn oil
½	cup peanut or corn oil, for cooking the pancakes

FOR THE BATTER: Soak the bread cubes in the chicken stock in a bowl for a few minutes.

Add the remaining ingredients and mash with your hands, kneading the mixture until it is well blended but with pieces still visible.

FOR THE SAUCE: Mix all the ingredients together in a bowl. Set aside.

Preheat the oven to 150 degrees.

Heat 1½ tablespoons of the oil in a large non-stick skillet. When it is hot, add about ⅓ cup of the batter to the skillet, spreading it out with a spoon into a disk about 4 inches in diameter and ⅜ inch thick. Repeat, working quickly, to shape 2 or 3 more pancakes, depending on the size of your skillet, and cook over medium-high heat for about 4 minutes, until lightly browned underneath and bubbly on top. Turn the pancakes and cook for about 4 minutes on the other side, to cook through and brown the second side. Transfer the pancakes to an ovenproof plate and keep warm in the oven while you continue making pancakes with the remaining batter and oil.

Serve warm, with the sauce.

VARIATION

BREAD AND FRUIT PANCAKES

Soak the bread in milk instead of chicken stock. Omit the onion, cilantro, Tabasco, and salt from the batter and add 2 cups ½-inch cubes of peeled apple, pear, or banana, along with 2 tablespoons sugar. Cook the fruit pancakes the same way as in the recipe and serve them for breakfast with a little maple syrup or a dusting of sugar.

Potato Crepes with Red and Black Caviar
Serves 6 as a first course

✂ **Potatoes thicken the batter** of these crepes, giving them a smooth, soft, and creamy texture, which perfectly complements the caviar. The amount and type of caviar can be varied to suit your pocketbook. To make the dish superlative, I use a little of the expensive black caviar from sturgeon — beluga, osetra, or sevruga — as a garnish.

CREPES

1 large all-purpose potato (about 9 ounces)
2 tablespoons all-purpose flour
3 large eggs
⅓ cup milk
¼ teaspoon salt
⅛ teaspoon Tabasco sauce

¼ cup canola oil

GARNISHES

About 8 ounces (¾ cup) red salmon caviar
About 1 cup sour cream
1 tablespoon finely chopped fresh chives
About 2 ounces (3 tablespoons) beluga, osetra, or sevruga caviar (preferably *malossol*, or lightly salted)

FOR THE CREPES: Put the potato in a saucepan with water to cover and bring to a boil. Cover, reduce the heat, and boil gently for 45 minutes, or until the potato is tender.

Preheat the oven to 200 degrees.

When the potato is cooked, drain it, peel, and press through a food mill or a ricer into a bowl. Add the flour and eggs and mix well with a whisk. Mix in the milk, salt, and Tabasco.

Heat 2 teaspoons of the oil in a nonstick skillet. When it is hot, add about ¼ cup of the crepe batter, which should spread to create a circle 4½ to 5 inches in diameter. Cook over medium heat for about 3 minutes on each side. Transfer to a cookie sheet and keep warm in the oven while you make 5 more crepes with the remaining batter and oil.

To serve, arrange the warm crepes on individual serving plates. Spread the top surface of the crepes with red caviar (about 2 tablespoons on each), extending the caviar clear to the edges. Mound 2 rounded tablespoons sour cream in the center of each crepe. Sprinkle with the chives, spoon about 1½ teaspoons of the black caviar onto the center of each sour cream mound, and serve immediately.

Bread Galettes on Salad Greens
Serves 4

❧ To make these galettes, or pancakes, I moisten cubed stale bread with water, then mix it with eggs and a variety of vegetables and herbs, but you can use any vegetables you have on hand and herbs of your choice. The galettes go beautifully with salad greens. They make a great lunch main dish or first course for dinner.

GALETTES

- 2½ ounces stale bread, preferably French-type bread, cut into 1-inch pieces (2 cups)
- ½ cup lukewarm water
- 1 large mushroom, cleaned and coarsely chopped
- ½ cup diced (¼-inch) zucchini
- 2 tablespoons chopped onion
- 1½ tablespoons chopped fresh chives
- 1 garlic clove, crushed and chopped (½ teaspoon)
- ¼ teaspoon salt
- ¼ teaspoon freshly ground black pepper
- 2 large eggs

- 2 tablespoons peanut oil

SALAD

- 2 tablespoons extra-virgin olive oil
- 2 teaspoons fresh lemon juice
- ⅛ teaspoon salt
- ¼ teaspoon freshly ground black pepper
- 4 cups loosely packed mesclun (a mixture of young tender greens and herbs), washed and dried

FOR THE GALETTES: Put the bread in a bowl, add the water, and squeeze the bread lightly to saturate it with the water. After a couple minutes, squeeze the extra water out of the bread and drain it away. Add the mushroom, zucchini, onion, chives, garlic, salt, pepper, and eggs and mix until the ingredients are well combined but not a puree.

Heat the peanut oil in one large or two smaller skillets. Using about ½ cup of the bread mixture for each of 4 galettes, spoon it into the skillet(s) and spread it with a fork to make cakes that are about 5 inches in diameter and ½ inch thick. Cook the galettes for about 5 minutes over medium-high heat, then flip them over and cook for 5 minutes, or until cooked through and nicely browned on both sides. Transfer the galettes to a warm plate and set aside while you make the salad.

FOR THE SALAD: Mix together the olive oil, lemon juice, salt, and pepper in a bowl large enough to hold the salad greens. Add the mesclun and toss well to coat the leaves with the dressing.

Divide the salad among four plates and place a galette on top of or alongside the greens on each plate. Serve.

Sandwiches

Pan Bagna
Serves 4

✤ **A specialty of the** South of France, *pan bagna* literally means "bathed bread." Originally the dish was a vegetable salad mixed with pieces of leftover bread, so that the bread became soaked with vegetable juices. In the modern version, which is a great sandwich for a picnic, a split loaf is filled with salad ingredients and anchovies. The loaf is wrapped and weighted down so the juices from the filling flow through the bread, and the loaf becomes moist and compact enough that it can be cut into wedges.

½	cucumber (about 7 ounces)
1	round crusty loaf country-style bread (about 1 pound)
18	oil-cured black olives, pitted and coarsely chopped
3	garlic cloves, crushed and finely chopped (about 2 teaspoons)
10	small anchovy fillets, coarsely chopped, with their oil
2	tablespoons extra-virgin olive oil
4–5	thin slices red onion
⅓	green bell pepper, cored, seeded, and thinly sliced
1	ripe tomato, thinly sliced
¼	teaspoon salt
¼	teaspoon freshly ground black pepper
12	large fresh basil leaves

Peel the cucumber and slice it lengthwise with a vegetable peeler into long thin strips, avoiding the seedy center.

Cut the loaf of bread horizontally in half.

Mix together the olives, garlic, anchovies with their oil, and olive oil in a bowl. Spread the mixture on the cut surface of both bread halves. Arrange the slices of onion, green pepper, and tomato on the bottom half of the loaf, sprinkle with the salt and pepper, and arrange the basil leaves and then the cucumber slices on top.

Invert the top half of the bread to re-form the loaf and wrap tightly in plastic wrap. Refrigerate for 2 to 3 hours, with a 5-pound weight (such as canned goods or a carton of milk) on top.

At serving time, unwrap the loaf and cut it into wedges.

Pissaladière Baguettes
Serves 6 as a first course, 3 as a main course

✤ **In Provence, anchovies are** often salted to preserve them as soon as they are caught. Then, when needed, they are washed and the fillets separated from the central bone and combined with olive oil. When crushed to a puree, the mixture is called *pissalat*. I crush canned anchovies and their oil with some additional olive oil into a puree, then brush cut rolls or bread slices with the *pissalat*. Tomatoes, onion, garlic and grated Swiss or mozzarella cheese are layered on top and the *pissaladière* is cooked in the oven until the cheese melts. This is a good first course and it also makes a terrific lunch main course with a salad.

If you don't have a mild onion on hand, use a regular onion and rinse the slices in a sieve under running water before using.

3	French rolls (about 6½ inches long by 2½ inches wide and 2½ ounces each) or equivalent-sized pieces cut from a baguette
1	2-ounce can anchovy fillets in oil
3	tablespoons extra-virgin olive oil

6 medium garlic cloves, very thinly sliced

1½ cups thinly sliced mild onions, such
   as Vidalia or Walla Walla (see the
   headnote)

24 cherry tomatoes, halved

6 ounces Gruyère, Emmenthaler,
   or mozzarella cheese, grated (1½ cups)

1 teaspoon dried oregano

¼ teaspoon salt

¼ teaspoon freshly ground black pepper

Preheat the oven to 400 degrees.

Split the rolls open, as for sandwiches.

Put the anchovy fillets and their oil in a bowl and chop and crush them into a puree with a fork. Stir in the olive oil to create a *pissalat,* and brush this mixture on the cut sides of the rolls. Cover with the sliced garlic and then a layer of the sliced onion.

Arrange 8 cherry tomato halves on each of the roll halves. Sprinkle with the grated cheese and then with the oregano, salt, and pepper.

Arrange the rolls on a cookie sheet and bake for about 10 minutes, until the cheese is melted and the tomatoes are soft. Serve.

Croques-Monsieur

Serves 4

✺ **The** *croque-monsieur* **is a** classic toasted ham and cheese sandwich. I make it with Gruyère, which is traditional in France. Cut into little squares as it emerges from the oven, it makes a terrific hot hors d'oeuvre. For a *croque-madame,* replace the ham with a slice of cooked chicken breast.

3 tablespoons olive oil

8 slices white bread (8 ounces)

8 slices Gruyère or Emmenthaler cheese
   (about 4 ounces)

4 slices honey-cured ham (4 ounces)

Preheat the oven to 400 degrees. Spread the oil on a cookie sheet.

Arrange the bread slices on a work surface. Place a slice of cheese on top of each slice. Arrange a slice of ham on 4 of the bread slices, invert the remaining cheese-covered bread slices on top, and press together.

Dip both sides of the sandwiches in the oil on the cookie sheet and arrange the sandwiches on the sheet. Bake for 10 minutes, or until the cheese is melted.

Trim the crusts from the bread and cut the sandwiches diagonally into triangles. Serve warm.

Roasted Eggplant Sandwiches

Serves 4

✺ **Thin slices of sautéed** eggplant are layered with dried tomatoes, fresh basil, and cheddar cheese on crusty rolls.

You can reconstitute sun-dried tomatoes yourself quite inexpensively, as opposed to buying the commercially reconstituted tomatoes in oil. Soak the tomatoes in boiling water, transfer them to a jar, and mix in a little olive oil, plus whatever garnishes you like — from sliced garlic to sprigs of rosemary, pieces of walnuts or hazelnuts, or hot peppers. Use the mixture on pasta as well as on sandwiches.

1 cup (about 1½ ounces) sun-dried tomatoes (not tomatoes in oil)
1 tablespoon extra-virgin olive oil
¼ cup canola oil
1 eggplant (about 1 pound), peeled and cut crosswise into 16 slices, each about ⅜ inch thick
　Salt and freshly ground black pepper
4 crusty oval-shaped rolls or kaiser rolls
12 large fresh basil leaves
6 ounces cheddar cheese, thinly sliced or grated

Preheat the oven to 400 degrees.

Bring 1½ cups water to a boil in a saucepan. Add the tomatoes, remove from the heat, and soak for about 10 minutes.

Drain (reserving the liquid for stock, if desired) and mix the tomatoes with the olive oil. Set aside.

Heat 1 tablespoon of the canola oil in each of two nonstick skillets. When it is hot, place 4 slices of eggplant in each skillet, sprinkle with salt and pepper, and cook over medium heat for 5 minutes on each side. Remove to a dish and repeat with the remaining canola oil and eggplant.

Split the rolls in half and place them cut side up on a work surface. Place 2 slices of eggplant on the bottom half of each roll. Arrange the tomatoes on top of the eggplant and place 3 basil leaves on top of each. Cover with the sliced or grated cheese. Sprinkle, if desired, with a little salt and pepper and add the remaining eggplant slices, 2 per roll. Put the tops of the rolls in place and arrange the assembled sandwiches on a cookie sheet.

Bake for 10 to 12 minutes, until the cheese inside is completely melted. Cut into halves and serve.

James Beard's Onion Sandwiches
Serves 4

I first tasted this great combination when I visited James Beard in his home one Sunday morning in the midsixties. This is my recollection of the sandwiches he served, which have been a favorite at my house ever since. Rolled on their edges in mayonnaise and then in minced chives, the sandwiches are as attractive as they are delicious. Cut into smaller pieces, these make a great hors d'oeuvre.

8 thin slices firm white bread (6–8 ounces)
6 tablespoons mayonnaise
1 tablespoon Dijon mustard
4 ⅛-inch-thick slices mild onion, such as Vidalia or Walla Walla, about 3½ inches in diameter
¼ cup minced fresh chives

Arrange the bread slices next to one another on a work surface. Using a glass or a round cutter, cut circles as large as possible out of the slices.

Mix the mayonnaise and mustard together. Spread each bread circle with 2 teaspoons of the mixture. Place an onion slice on 4 of the bread rounds (it should cover them to the edges). Top with the remaining bread circles. Press slightly to make them adhere.

Holding each sandwich in your hand, spread some of the remaining mayonnaise-mustard on the outside edges, then roll the edges in the chives until coated. Press lightly to make the chives adhere and serve.

Sandwich Assortment

Each sandwich serves 1;
the assortment serves 4

✄ **Ideal for picnics, these** sandwiches are very good made a few hours ahead to allow the flavors to mingle, and they also keep well, refrigerated, overnight. Although each guest can be served a single sandwich, I recommend quartering the various sandwiches and serving each guest a section from each.

Tuna Sandwich

1 Small Light Country Loaf (page 131)
4 ounces canned tuna in oil, drained
¼ cup loosely packed fresh cilantro leaves
6 anchovy fillets
⅛ teaspoon freshly ground black pepper
1 large garlic clove, sliced with a vegetable peeler into 12 thin slices
1 hard-cooked egg (see page 66), sliced
3–4 lettuce leaves, washed and dried

Split the bread horizontally in half and place the 2 halves crust side down on the work surface. Spread the tuna on the bottom half and cover it with the cilantro. Arrange the anchovies on top and sprinkle on the pepper. Arrange the garlic slices on top, then add the egg slices and lettuce leaves. Cover with the top half and press on the sandwich to help combine the flavors of the various ingredients.

Serve within 2 hours, cut into 4 wedges.

Vegetable Sandwich

The sandwich will have more flavor if made at least an hour ahead.

1 Small Light Country Loaf (page 131)
1½ teaspoons extra-virgin olive oil
1½ teaspoons tarragon vinegar
1 cup loosely packed arugula leaves, washed and dried
5 ½-inch-thick tomato slices
⅛ teaspoon freshly ground black pepper
18 oil-cured olives, pitted and coarsely chopped (¼ cup)
4 very thin slices red onion (use a vegetable peeler to ensure thinness)

Split the bread horizontally in half and place the 2 halves crust side down on the work surface. Sprinkle both halves with the olive oil and vinegar. Arrange the arugula on the bottom half and add the tomato and pepper. Add the olives and, finally, the red onion slices. Cover with the top half and press on the sandwich to help combine the flavors of the various ingredients.

Cut the sandwich into 4 wedges and serve.

Cheese Sandwich

1 Small Light Country Loaf (page 131)
¼ cup tomato salsa
3 ounces Gorgonzola cheese, softened
1 cup loosely packed watercress leaves, washed and dried
½ cup pecan halves
8 very thin slices cucumber (use a vegetable peeler to ensure thinness)
3 slices Gruyère or Emmenthaler cheese
⅛ teaspoon freshly ground black pepper
1 mushroom, cleaned and thinly sliced

Split the bread horizontally in half and place the 2 halves crust side down on the work surface. Sprinkle 2 tablespoons of the salsa over the surface of each bread half. Spread the Gorgonzola on the bottom half and press the watercress into the cheese. Scatter the pecan halves over and arrange the cucumber slices and Gruyère or Emmenthaler cheese on top. Sprinkle with the pepper and add the mushroom slices. Cover with the top half and press on the sandwich to help combine the flavors of the various ingredients.

Serve within 1 to 2 hours, cut into 4 wedges.

Ham Sandwich

  1 Small Light Country Loaf (page 131)
1½ teaspoons Dijon mustard
1½ teaspoons mayonnaise
  3 radishes, thinly sliced
  8 fresh basil leaves
  4 ounces sliced ham, preferably honey-baked
  ⅛ teaspoon freshly ground black pepper
1½ cups loosely packed mesclun (a mixture of young tender greens and herbs), washed and dried

Split the bread horizontally in half and place the 2 halves crust side down on the work surface. Spread one of the bread halves with the mustard and the other with the mayonnaise. Cover the bottom half with the radish slices and arrange the basil leaves on top. Layer on the ham and sprinkle with the pepper. Finish with the mesclun. Cover with the top half and press on the sandwich to help combine the flavors of the various ingredients.

Serve within 2 hours, cut into 4 wedges.

Open-Faced Sandwiches
Each recipe makes 4 sandwiches

✂ **These open-faced sandwiches**—each consisting of several colorful and complementary tidbits of food layered on a single thin slice of toasted bread or a cracker—can be prepared ahead. Arranged on a large platter, they are pretty and varied. They are ideal for a large cocktail party, birthday, or graduation celebration. Feel free to select toppings from what you have on hand.

Salami Toasts

  4 ½-inch-thick slices baguette, lightly toasted
  1 teaspoon unsalted butter, softened
  4 slices dry-cured salami
  4 slices dill pickle
     Freshly ground black pepper

Spread the baguette slices lightly with the butter. Arrange 1 salami slice on each slice, then top with a pickle slice and a sprinkling of pepper. Arrange on a serving plate.

Mozzarella Toasts

  4 small slices mozzarella cheese
  4 melba toast rounds
  4 strips pimiento
  1 garlic clove, thinly sliced
     Freshly ground black pepper

Arrange a piece of mozzarella on each melba toast round. Place a piece of pimiento on top and finish each with a slice or two of garlic and a sprinkling of pepper. Arrange on a serving plate.

Blue Cheese Toasts

  ¾ ounce blue cheese, preferably Stilton, softened
  4 bagel chips

1 tablespoon finely diced pimiento

1 tablespoon minced scallion

Spread the blue cheese on the bagel chips and top with the pimiento and scallions. Arrange on a serving plate.

Scrambled Egg Toasts with Ham

2 large eggs
  Pinch of salt
  Pinch of freshly ground black pepper
2 teaspoons unsalted butter
1 tablespoon sour cream
4 slices pumpernickel cocktail bread
    (2½ inches square)
1 slice boiled ham (¾ ounce), cut into
    julienne strips
2 teaspoons chopped fresh chives

Break the eggs into a bowl, add the salt and pepper, and beat with a fork.

Heat the butter in a small saucepan. Add the eggs and cook over medium heat, stirring constantly with a whisk, until creamy and lightly set but not dry. Transfer to a bowl and mix in the sour cream (which will stop the cooking).

Divide the scrambled eggs among the bread slices. Sprinkle the ham and chives on top. Arrange on a serving plate.

Herring Toasts

2 Boston lettuce leaves, washed and
    dried
4 water or rice crackers (about 2½ inches
    in diameter)
1 tablespoon sour cream
3 ounces herring in wine sauce (available
    in jars in specialty food stores and
    some supermarkets)
2 tablespoons thinly sliced red onion
1 tablespoon chopped fresh chives

Break each lettuce leaf into 2 pieces and arrange 1 piece on each cracker. Top each leaf with ¾ teaspoon of the sour cream and 1 or 2 pieces of the herring. Top with the red onion and chives. Arrange on a serving plate.

Tuna Toasts

2 teaspoons mayonnaise
1 teaspoon Dijon mustard
4 water or rice crackers (about
    2½ inches in diameter)
1 tablespoon minced scallion
2 ounces canned tuna in water, drained
    and broken into 4 pieces
4 oil-cured black olives, pitted

Mix the mayonnaise and mustard together in a small bowl. Spread lightly on the crackers, then sprinkle the scallion on top. Arrange 1 piece of tuna on each cracker and garnish with an olive. Arrange on a serving plate.

Ham Toasts

4 ½-inch-thick slices baguette
1 teaspoon extra-virgin olive oil
1 teaspoon Dijon mustard
2 slices boiled ham (1½ ounces total),
    each rolled up from a narrow end
    and cut in half
4 oil-cured black olives, pitted

Preheat the oven to 400 degrees.

Brush the baguette slices lightly on both sides with the oil. Arrange them in one layer on a cookie sheet and bake for about 10 minutes, or until nicely browned.

Spread the mustard on the toasted bread rounds and arrange a piece of rolled ham on top of each. Garnish each with a black olive. Arrange on a serving plate.

Smoked Mussel Toasts

- 2 radicchio leaves, washed and dried
- 4 melba toast rounds or bagel chips
- 4 teaspoons sour cream
- 8 smoked mussels (available in cans in specialty food stores and some supermarkets)
- 1 radish, thinly sliced
  Freshly ground black pepper

Break each radicchio leaf into 2 pieces and arrange 1 piece on each melba toast round or bagel chip. Spoon 1 teaspoon of sour cream on each leaf and arrange 2 mussels on top. Place a slice or two of radish on top of the mussels on each round and sprinkle with pepper. Arrange on a serving plate.

Anchovy Toasts

- 2 Boston lettuce leaves, washed and dried
- 4 slices pumpernickel cocktail bread (2½ inches square)
- 4 teaspoons mayonnaise
- 1 hard-cooked egg (see page 66), sliced
- 4 anchovy fillets

Break each lettuce leaf into 2 pieces and arrange 1 piece on each bread square. Spoon 1 teaspoon of the mayonnaise on top of each leaf and add 1 or 2 slices of egg. Garnish each with an anchovy fillet. Arrange on a serving plate.

Smoked Salmon Toasts

- 1½ teaspoons unsalted butter, softened
- 4 slices pumpernickel cocktail bread (2½ inches square)
- 8 thin slices unpeeled cucumber
- 4 small slices smoked salmon (about 1½ ounces)
- 1 tablespoon chopped red onion
- 2 teaspoons drained capers
  Freshly ground black pepper

Butter the bread slices and arrange 2 slices of cucumber on each. Top each with a salmon slice and sprinkle with the onion, capers, and pepper. Arrange on a serving plate.

Sardine Toasts

- 2 spinach leaves, washed and dried
- 4 slices rye cocktail bread (2½ inches square)
- 4 ounces sardines in tomato sauce (available in cans in specialty food stores and some supermarkets)
  Salt
- 2 tablespoons thinly sliced red onion
- 1½ teaspoons red wine vinegar

Break each spinach leaf into 2 pieces and arrange 1 piece on each bread square. Arrange the sardines, with some of their sauce, on top of the spinach. Salt lightly, top with the onion slices, and sprinkle with the vinegar. Arrange on a serving plate.

Brie Toasts

- 2 Boston lettuce leaves, washed and dried
- 4 slices rye cocktail bread (2½ inches square)
- 1 small tomato (4 ounces), cut into 4 slices
  Salt
- 1 tablespoon thinly sliced onion
- 2 ounces Brie (or other soft, creamy cheese), cut into 4 slices
  Freshly ground black pepper

Break each lettuce leaf into 2 pieces and arrange 1 piece on each bread square. Place a slice of tomato on top of each leaf and sprinkle lightly with salt. Top with the onion slices, Brie, and a sprinkling of pepper. Arrange on a serving plate.

Pizzas

Pita Pizzas
Serves 4 to 6

✀ **Many people are put** off by the difficulty of making pizza dough — obviously the hardest part of the process. Here, instead of conventional pizza dough, I use pita bread rounds, splitting them in half to have 6 very thin "crusts." Fun, colorful, and delicious, these pizzas couldn't be easier.

3 large pita breads (7–8 inches in diameter), each cut open along the seam and separated into halves

FOR THE PITA BREADS: Preheat the oven to 400 degrees. Arrange all the pita bread halves crust side down in one layer on a large cookie sheet.

Yellow Pepper, Gruyère, and Pine Nut Pizza

3 tablespoons diced (½-inch) yellow bell pepper
1 pita bread half (see above)
2 tablespoons pine nuts
10 oil-cured black olives, pitted and coarsely chopped
2 scallions, trimmed (leaving some green) and coarsely chopped
1 tablespoon extra-virgin olive oil
Pinch of freshly ground black pepper
½ cup grated Gruyère or Emmenthaler cheese

Arrange the diced yellow pepper on the pita bread half and add the nuts. Sprinkle the olives and scallions over the yellow pepper and top with the oil, pepper, and cheese. To bake, see the box, page 148.

Shrimp-Cilantro Pizza

¾ cup small shelled raw shrimp
2 tablespoons fresh cilantro leaves
1 pita bread half (see opposite)
¼ cup coarsely chopped mushrooms
1½ teaspoons toasted sesame oil
1½ teaspoons canola oil
1 teaspoon dark soy sauce
12 drops Tabasco sauce
1 tablespoon freshly grated Parmesan cheese

Arrange the shrimp and cilantro leaves on the pita bread half. Sprinkle on the mushrooms, oils, soy sauce, Tabasco, and cheese. To bake, see the box, page 148.

Tomato and Herbes de Provence Pizza

2 thin slices red onion
1 pita bread half (see opposite)
1 plum tomato (4 ounces), cut into 6 slices
½ teaspoon herbes de Provence
Pinch of salt
Pinch of freshly ground black pepper
1 tablespoon minced fresh chives
⅓ cup grated Jarlsberg and/or Gruyère cheese
1 tablespoon extra-virgin olive oil

Arrange the onion slices on the pita bread half and cover them with the tomato slices. Top with the herbes de Provence, salt, pepper, chives, and cheese. Sprinkle on the oil. To bake, see the box, page 148.

Green Pizza

- 1 cup loosely packed mesclun (a mixture of young tender greens and herbs), washed and dried
- 1 pita bread half (see page 147)
- ⅓ cup diced (½-inch) tomato
- 2 tablespoons coarsely chopped mild onion, such as Vidalia or Walla Walla

  Pinch of salt

  Pinch of freshly ground black pepper
- 1 tablespoon extra-virgin olive oil
- 1½ tablespoons freshly grated Parmesan cheese

Spread the salad greens on the pita bread half and arrange the tomatoes on top. Top with the onion, salt, pepper, oil, and cheese. To bake, see the box.

Chicken Pizza

- 1 boneless, skinless chicken breast, cooked and thinly sliced
- 1 pita bread half (see page 147)
- ⅓ cup thinly sliced mushrooms
- ¾ cup julienne strips zucchini
- 1 garlic clove, thinly sliced (1 teaspoon)
- 2 tablespoons soft goat cheese
- 1 tablespoon extra-virgin olive oil

  Pinch of salt

  Pinch of freshly ground black pepper

Arrange the sliced chicken on top of the pita bread half and cover it with the mushrooms and zucchini. Top with the garlic, goat cheese, oil, salt, and pepper. To bake, see the box.

Anchovy Pizza

- 2 scallions, trimmed (leaving some green) and thinly sliced
- 1 large garlic clove, thinly sliced (1 teaspoon)
- 1 pita bread half (see page 147)
- 12 kalamata olives, pitted and cut into ½-inch pieces (¼ cup)
- 4 anchovy fillets, halved
- 1 teaspoon extra-virgin olive oil
- ¼ cup shredded mozzarella cheese

Arrange the scallions and garlic on the pita bread half. Top with the olives, anchovy fillets, oil, and mozzarella. To bake, see the box.

TO BAKE THE PIZZAS

Place the cookie sheet containing the pizzas in the oven and bake for 13 to 15 minutes, until the pizzas are bubbly, browned, and cooked through.

Transfer the pizzas to a cutting board, cut each of them into 4 wedges, and arrange on a platter. Serve.

Shellfish and fish

Shellfish and Fish

Shellfish

Warm Oysters with Spinach, Garlic, and Ginger
Serves 8 as a first course, 4 as a main course

❧ **We used to serve** this simple oyster dish at Gloria's French Café, the restaurant my wife ran in the early 1980s in Madison, Connecticut.

4	dozen oysters, such as Apalachicola, Blue Point, or Belon, shucked (see page 153) and kept in their juices, bottom shells reserved
½	cup dry white wine
6	tablespoons (¾ stick) unsalted butter Salt and freshly ground black pepper
3	tablespoons olive oil
2	tablespoons finely chopped garlic (5–6 cloves)
2	tablespoons finely chopped ginger
1½	pounds spinach, preferably baby spinach, trimmed and washed

Preheat the oven to 180 degrees.

Pour about ¾ cup of the liquid from the oysters into a stainless steel saucepan and add the wine. Bring to a boil and reduce to about ⅓ cup. Add the butter piece by piece, whisking constantly over low heat until all the butter has been added. Taste and season the sauce with salt if needed and with pepper. Set aside.

Heat 1½ tablespoons of the oil in each of two large skillets. Add half the garlic and ginger to each pan and sauté for 10 to 20 seconds, then add the spinach. (If the spinach is wet from washing, no extra liquid is necessary; if the spinach is dry, add about ¼ cup water to each skillet.) Cover and steam the spinach, stirring occasionally to make sure the garlic and ginger don't burn, for 2 to 3 minutes, until the spinach is wilted and soft. Season with ½ teaspoon each salt and pepper and set aside.

Warm the reserved oyster shells in the oven. Meanwhile, cook the oysters in the remaining juices in a saucepan over high heat just until they curl, or "frill," at the edges; the liquid should not be heated above about 170 degrees.

Arrange 6 oyster shells on each plate and arrange the spinach in the warm shells. Place 1 oyster in the center of each shell, top with the sauce, and serve.

Poached Oysters with Mushrooms and Red Pepper
Serves 8 as a first course, 4 as a main course

❧ **Although I prefer raw** oysters on the half-shell, I do enjoy cooked oysters in chowder or in dishes like this one. Be careful not to overcook the oysters, or they will be rubbery. The red and green garnish makes this ideal for the Christmas holidays. If you are not proficient at shucking oysters, the fishmonger can usually do it for you.

4	dozen oysters, such as Wellfleet, Cotuit, or Blue Point, shucked (see the sidebar, page 153) and kept in their juices
½	cup dry white wine
8	tablespoons (1 stick) unsalted butter Salt and freshly ground black pepper
1	large red bell pepper
12	ounces firm white mushrooms, cleaned and thinly sliced
3	cups loosely packed fresh parsley leaves, very finely chopped or pureed in a mini-chop or spice grinder

You should have a good cup of juice with the shelled oysters. Pour ¾ cup of the juice into a stainless steel saucepan and add the wine. Bring to a boil and reduce to ½ cup. Add 6 tablespoons of the butter piece by piece, whisking constantly over low heat. Season with salt if necessary and with pepper. Set the butter sauce aside.

Meanwhile, core and seed the pepper. Cut eight ⅛-inch-wide rings from the pepper; reserve the rest for another dish.

Pour 3 tablespoons water into a saucepan. Add the pepper rings and a pinch of salt, bring just to a very gentle boil, and simmer gently for 1 minute at the most, just long enough to wilt and warm the pepper. Set aside.

Melt the remaining 2 tablespoons butter in a large skillet. Add the mushrooms and sauté until most of the liquid the mushrooms release has evaporated and the mushrooms are beginning to sizzle again, 4 to 5 minutes. Set aside.

Meanwhile, put the oysters in a saucepan in their remaining juices and heat over high heat to about 170 degrees: the frill on the oysters should just begin to curl. Using a fine skimmer, remove and discard any foam or curdled juices from the top. Remove from the heat.

Arrange the mushrooms on eight plates. Place a red pepper ring in the center of each plate and arrange 6 drained oysters within the ring. Add the parsley to the butter sauce and coat the oysters on each plate with 2 to 3 tablespoons of the sauce. (If the parsley is added to the butter sauce too early, the green color will darken.) Serve.

Breaded Oyster Gratin
Serves 4 as a first course

✳ This recipe is best with freshly shucked oysters. Either shuck them yourself or ask your fishmonger to shuck them at the time of purchase and save the juices for you. After the oysters are poached, they are flavored with Chinese oyster sauce and

SHUCKING OYSTERS

Wash the oysters under cold water. Placing the oysters in the freezer for 10 minutes will make them easier to open. Protecting your hand with a towel or oven mitt, grasp each oyster firmly, with the flat bottom shell down. Pry and push the tip of a sturdy oyster knife into the hinge where the shells connect, exerting a fair amount of pressure. Press down to pop open the shell, then move your knife back and forth against the top shell to sever the muscle that holds the meat to the shell. Discard the top shell. Slide your knife under the oyster to sever the muscle and release the oyster. If serving on the half-shell, leave the oyster in the bottom shell with the juices. Otherwise, transfer the oyster and juices to a container.

chile paste, arranged in individual gratin dishes, topped with seasoned bread crumbs, and placed under the broiler until golden brown.

Chile paste and oyster sauce are available in Asian markets and the ethnic food sections of many supermarkets.

2 dozen oysters, such as Blue Point, Chincoteague, or Malpeque, shucked (see above) and kept in their juices
1 slice firm white bread (1 ounce)
1 tablespoon chopped fresh chives
1½ teaspoons chopped fresh tarragon
2 teaspoons extra-virgin olive oil
½ teaspoon freshly ground black pepper
1 teaspoon Chinese oyster sauce
½ teaspoon Chinese chile paste with garlic

Lift the shucked oysters from their juices and put them in a stainless steel saucepan. Allow the juices to sit for a few minutes, then carefully pour

Using a towel to protect your hand, hold each cleaned clam in the palm of your hand with the hinge toward you. Place the tip of the blade of a small paring knife or clam knife at the junction of the two shells. Press the blade forward, so it slides between the shells of the clam. Keep cutting to sever the muscles on each side and the clam will open. Run your knife along the shells on either side to separate the meat from the shells. If serving the clam on the half-shell, keep it in one of the shells. Otherwise, transfer the clam and juices to a container.

them into the pan with the oysters, leaving behind any sandy residue. Bring to just under a boil, until you see the surrounding frill on the oysters beginning to curl. Remove from the heat and set aside.

Break the bread into a food processor and process it into crumbs. (You should have ½ cup.) Toss the crumbs lightly with the chives, tarragon, oil, and pepper; the mixture should be fluffy, not gooey or pasty.

Drain the oysters (freeze the juice for use in a soup or sauce, if you like). Combine the oysters with the oyster sauce and chile paste in a bowl.

Preheat the broiler. Divide the oyster mixture among four small gratin dishes and sprinkle the crumbs evenly on top. Arrange the dishes on a cookie sheet, place about 6 inches from the heat, and cook for about 4 minutes, until the crumbs are well browned and the oysters are hot. Serve.

Clams on the Half-Shell with Cold Horseradish-Vinegar Sauce

Serves 6 to 8 as a first course

Littlenecks are the smallest of the quahog clams, ideal for serving on the half-shell cold and always welcome for a first course, aperitif, or snack. The clams can be enjoyed "au naturel" or with my refreshingly sharp sauce. I always shuck clams over a bowl and keep the juices to use in pasta or soup.

If you've dug the clams yourself, be sure to clean them under cold running water to remove the mud from the shells and make them disgorge any sand and dirt. Keep the clams in the refrigerator — they open more readily and taste better when very cold. Sometimes I put them in the freezer for 10 minutes to help them open.

I like to present the clams on seaweed to keep them cool and steady, although they can be served on ice.

SAUCE

- 2 tablespoons coarsely chopped scallions
- ¼ cup chopped shallots
- ¼ cup grated fresh horseradish
- 1 teaspoon freshly ground black pepper
- ¾ cup red wine vinegar
- 1 tablespoon olive oil
  Pinch of salt

- 6 dozen littleneck clams, shucked (see the sidebar)
  Buttered black bread, for serving

FOR THE SAUCE: Mix together all the ingredients in a bowl.

Arrange the clams on a bed of seaweed or crushed ice.

Serve the clams immediately, with the sauce and buttered black bread.

Clam and Fish Ceviche
Serves 10 to 12 as a first course

✳ **The combination of raw** fish and citrus juice called ceviche is common in Latin American cooking, from Peru to Mexico, and can be flavored with many different seasonings. In this summer ceviche, which makes a great buffet centerpiece, clams and their salty juices are added to a mixture of raw fish and shrimp. The acidity of vinegar and lemon as well as the salt cure the seafood, and the vegetables — cucumbers, tomatoes, jalapeño pepper, red onion, and scallions — give wonderful taste, varied texture, and beautiful color to the dish.

The ceviche should macerate for at least 2 hours before being served and it will keep, refrigerated, for up to 1 day. Don't add the avocado too far ahead, however, as it tends to disintegrate and will muddy the dish.

Vary the selection of fish and shellfish to take advantage of the freshest ingredients available.

1½   dozen cherrystone clams, shucked (see opposite) and kept in their juices
8   ounces shelled shrimp, cut into about 24 pieces
12   ounces skinless sea bass fillets
12   ounces skinless fish fillets with a different texture from the sea bass, such as cod, sole, or bluefish
   About 10 strips lemon rind, removed with a vegetable peeler
4   garlic cloves, finely chopped (1 tablespoon)
1   large cucumber, peeled, halved lengthwise, seeded, and cut into ¼-inch dice (about 2 cups)
1   cup fresh cilantro leaves, coarsely chopped
1   teaspoon seeded and chopped jalapeño pepper

1   large red onion, coarsely chopped (1¼ cups)
4   scallions, trimmed (leaving some green) and cut into ½-inch pieces (½ cup)
2   tomatoes, cut into ¾-inch pieces (2 cups)
1   medium ripe avocado, peeled, pitted, and cut into ½-inch pieces
2   tablespoons peanut oil
2   teaspoons salt
½   teaspoon freshly ground black pepper
2   tablespoons white wine vinegar
3   tablespoons fresh lemon juice
½   teaspoon Tabasco sauce
   Small fresh basil or mint sprigs, for garnish

Lift the clams from their juices, pour the juices into a bowl, and let stand briefly to allow the sediment to settle. Shake each clam in the bowl of clam juice to wash off any sand that may be clinging to it, and lift out. Cut any large clams into pieces. (This is easiest with scissors.) Put the clams in a large bowl. Set the juice aside to rest until the sediment has fallen to the bottom again. Mix the shrimp in with the clams.

After making sure that all sinews and any bones are removed, cut the fish fillets into ½-inch pieces. Add them to the clams and shrimp.

Cut the lemon rind into julienne strips (you should have about 1 tablespoon) and add them to the seafood. Add the garlic, cucumber, cilantro, jalapeño pepper, red onion, scallions, tomatoes, and avocado. Slowly pour the clam juice into the bowl, so as not to disturb the sediment settled on the bottom. Add the oil, salt, pepper, vinegar, lemon juice, and Tabasco and mix well. Taste to make sure that the dish is highly seasoned. Cover tightly with plastic wrap and let macerate in the refrigerator for at least 2 hours.

At serving time, fill martini glasses or small serving dishes with the ceviche and arrange each one in the center of an individual serving plate. Decorate each one with a little sprig of basil or mint and serve.

Clam Fritters

Serves 4 as an hors d'oeuvre
(makes about 16 fritters)

The little touch of tarragon gives these fritters a delicious, different taste. The fritters are drained on a wire rack rather than on paper towels, the conventional procedure, because they tend to become soft on the bottom when placed on towels.

- 1 cup shelled clams, preferably large quahog or chowder clams (about 12), plus 3 tablespoons reserved clam juice
- ⅔ cup all-purpose flour
- ⅓ cup yellow cornmeal
- 1½ teaspoons baking powder
- 1 large egg
- 1 large garlic clove, crushed and chopped (1½ teaspoons)
- 4–5 scallions, trimmed (leaving some green) and minced (½ cup)
- 1 tablespoon chopped fresh tarragon
- Salt
- ¼ teaspoon freshly ground black pepper
- About 3 cups safflower oil, for deep-frying

Using a knife or food processor, chop the clams coarsely.

Combine the flour, cornmeal, baking powder, egg, and half the clam juice in a bowl, mixing until you have a smooth batter. Add the clams, the remaining clam juice, the garlic, scallions, tarragon, ¼ teaspoon salt, and the pepper and mix well.

Pour enough oil into a saucepan so that it is about 2 inches deep and heat the oil to 375 degrees. Drop about 1½ tablespoons of the batter into the hot oil for each fritter (cook about 8 fritters at a time) and cook for 4 to 6 minutes, moving the fritters occasionally, until they are browned well on all sides. Lift the fritters from the oil with a slotted spoon and drain on a rack.

Sprinkle with salt, if desired, and serve immediately.

Mussels Marinière

Serves 4

Mussels in white wine is a classic bistro dish. The mussels are traditionally cooked with onion, garlic, herbs, and white wine. My version also includes fennel, which lends a mild anise flavor that complements the other ingredients.

Choose small or medium mussels that are heavy, indicating plumpness and freshness. Since they are usually grown on lines or nets now, mussels are fairly clean, although you should still rub them against one another under cool water to remove any dirt or sand.

- 4 pounds small to medium mussels, cleaned and debearded
- 1 cup ½-inch pieces fennel bulb (about 4 ounces)
- About 6 scallions, trimmed (leaving some green) and cut into ½-inch pieces (1 cup)
- 1 medium onion, coarsely chopped (1 cup)
- 5–6 large garlic cloves, thinly sliced (3 tablespoons)
- 1 cup fruity dry white wine (such as Sauvignon Blanc)
- ½ teaspoon freshly ground black pepper

Combine the mussels, fennel, scallions, onion, garlic, wine, and pepper in a large stainless steel saucepan, cover the pan, and begin timing the cooking as you bring the mixture to a boil over high heat. Cook the mussels, shaking the pan occasionally to mix the ingredients, for 7 to 8 minutes from start to finish, until they have opened. Discard any that have not opened after 8 minutes.

Divide the mussels, vegetables, and juices among four soup plates and serve. Or, for a fancier presentation, remove and discard the empty top shells and serve the mussels on the half-shell in soup plates, with the vegetables and cooking juices.

Mussels with Saffron Tomato Sauce
Serves 6

❦ Flavored with wine, tomato, garlic, and saffron, this mussel stew evokes the tastes and smells of the South of France. Real saffron, the stigmas of crocus flowers, is essential. It's expensive but has a unique taste.

3	tablespoons unsalted butter
2	tablespoons olive oil
¾	cup chopped onion
1	small green bell pepper, cored, seeded, and finely chopped (½ cup)
2	teaspoons chopped garlic
3	tomatoes, peeled, halved, seeded, and coarsely chopped (1½ cups)
1	teaspoon freshly ground black pepper, or to taste
1	cup dry white wine
5	pounds mussels, cleaned and debearded
½	teaspoon saffron threads
	Salt
¼	cup chopped fresh parsley

Heat the butter and oil in a large stainless steel pot until hot. Add the onion, green pepper,

MUSSELS

Available nationwide year-round, mussels are one of the most flavorful and least expensive of shellfish. Generally speaking, avoid very large mussels, as invariably you'll just be paying for shell, since the mussel itself will be no larger than normal. Large mussels are also likely to be tough. Buy heavy medium-sized mussels, approximately 15 to 18 per pound.

If you bring mussels home from the store in a plastic bag, remove them from the bag, but do not put them in water. They need to breathe and are best stored in the refrigerator, either in a bowl loosely covered with plastic wrap or in a brown paper bag.

The best mussels are the freshest. After they are cleaned, they can be kept for 3 or 4 days refrigerated.

It used to be that mussels were covered with barnacles, had beards that had to be removed, and were sandy or muddy. Nowadays most mussels bought in markets have been raised on lines and are clean and usually beardless.

Contrary to what many people think, an opened mussel is not necessarily bad. If it closes when tickled inside with the point of a knife, it is still alive and good. More than anything else, rely on your nose: if an open mussel has an unpleasant odor, discard it.

and garlic and sauté for 1 minute. Add the tomatoes, pepper, wine, and mussels, cover, and bring to a boil. Cook, shaking the pot occasionally to redistribute the mussels, for 3 to 4 minutes, or until they have opened. Lift the mussels from the broth with a slotted spoon (discard any that have not opened). Pull the shells apart, keeping only the shells containing mussels, and arrange in one layer, so they will be covered with the broth when served, in a deep earthenware casserole or tureen. Cover to keep warm.

Add the saffron to the broth, bring to a boil, and reduce the broth by half (you should have about 2 cups). Add salt and/or pepper if necessary.

Pour the broth over the mussels, sprinkle with the parsley, and serve.

Mussels in Cream Sauce
Serves 8

❧ **This dish was on** the menu of my aunt's restaurant when I was a kid. Rich and flavorful, it was always a winner with her patrons.

5	pounds mussels, cleaned and debearded
1½	cups coarsely chopped onions
2	teaspoons chopped garlic
¼	cup small fresh parsley sprigs, chopped
2	fresh thyme sprigs
1	bay leaf
1	teaspoon freshly ground black pepper
1½	cups dry white wine (such as Chablis)
2	tablespoons unsalted butter, softened
2	tablespoons all-purpose flour
⅓	cup heavy cream

Combine the mussels, onions, garlic, half the parsley, the thyme, bay leaf, pepper, and wine in a large stainless steel pot, cover tightly, and cook over high heat, tossing occasionally, for 7 to 8 minutes, or until the mussels have opened; discard any that do not open.

Lift the mussels from the broth. Pull the shells apart, keeping only the shells containing mussels, and put them in a deep earthenware casserole or

THICKENING A SAUCE WITH A BEURRE MANIÉ

When a sauce has to be thickened, a kneaded butter, *beurre manié*, a mixture of butter and flour in equal quantities, may be used. With a whisk, mix the soft butter with the flour in a small bowl until it combines into a paste. When you lift up the whisk, the *beurre manié* will be attached to the end of it. Put it directly into the hot sauce or other liquid to thicken it, mixing it in rapidly with the whisk. This is the reverse of a roux. For a white roux, you melt butter in a saucepan, mix in the flour, and cook it for about 30 seconds, then add the liquid. Many white sauces are made with a *beurre manié*.

tureen. Keep warm on the side of the stove or in a 140-degree oven.

Strain the broth into a clean stainless steel saucepan, leaving any sand behind. Work the butter into the flour to make a *beurre manié* and add to the broth, whipping constantly with a whisk until smooth. Bring to a boil, whisking, then reduce the heat and cook for 1 minute. Add the cream and bring to a boil.

Pour the cream sauce over the warm mussels, sprinkle with the remaining parsley, and serve.

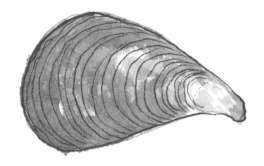

Mussels Gratiné

Serves 4 as a first course

❧ **A topping of bread**, garlic, parsley, and olive oil creates a crust that flavors the mussels and makes the dish look as appetizing as it is delicious. The mussels can be opened up to a day ahead and refrigerated, with the seasonings arranged on top, until you are ready to run the dish under the broiler.

2	pounds mussels (24–26), cleaned and debearded
3	garlic cloves
½	cup loosely packed fresh parsley leaves
1½	slices firm white bread (1½ ounces)
⅛	teaspoon salt
¼	teaspoon freshly ground black pepper
¼	cup extra-virgin olive oil
	A few drops of Tabasco sauce

To open the mussels, drop them into a dry pot and cook over high heat, covered, stirring the pot every 2 minutes, for 6 to 8 minutes, just until they have opened and released their juices. (Do not overcook — they will be reheated under the broiler at serving time.)

Pull off the empty top shell of each mussel and arrange the mussels on the half-shell on a cookie sheet (discard any mussels that have not opened).

Put the garlic and parsley in a food processor and process until coarsely chopped. Add the bread and process until the bread is finely chopped and the mixture is fluffy. Transfer to a bowl and add the salt, pepper, oil, and, if desired, Tabasco. Mix the ingredients with your fingers or a fork, tossing them gently so they are moistened with the oil but still fluffy. Sprinkle the mixture over the mussels. (*The mussels can be covered and refrigerated for up to 24 hours.*)

You will notice that the cooking times often vary in mussel recipes. A recipe is a reflection of the moment, and its outcome depends on many things, including your mood and the quality of the ingredients. One day the mussels will cook more quickly than on another, possibly because of their freshness or the size of the pot used, or because they have more juices surrounding them. The goal is to cook them just until they open, and there will always be variations in the time required to do this.

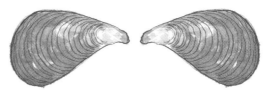

At serving time, preheat the broiler. Broil the mussels for 2 to 3 minutes, until nicely browned on top and warm inside. Serve.

Lima Bean and Mussel Stew with Spinach

Serves 4

❧ **Mussels are first cooked** in a little wine and then removed from their shells, and some of the cooking liquid is used in the stew. I also add dried lima beans, which cook faster than most other dried beans. As they cook, the skins separate from some of the beans and rise to the surface; remove and discard the floating skins, but don't attempt to remove the skins from beans that don't shed them on their own. The stew is served with sautéed spinach.

For a bonus recipe, the remainder of the juice from cooking the mussels can be thickened lightly with the starchy reserved liquid from cooking the beans, a little sour cream, and chives (see the sidebar). The result is a flavorful soup similar to the traditional cream of mussel soup, billi-bi.

8 ounces (about 1⅓ cups) large dried lima beans, picked over and rinsed
4 cups cold water
1½ teaspoons salt
3 pounds mussels, cleaned and debearded
1 cup fruity dry white wine (such as a Sauvignon Blanc)
4½ tablespoons olive oil
12 scallions, trimmed (leaving some green) and coarsely chopped (1¼ cups)
5–6 garlic cloves, crushed and chopped (1 tablespoon)
1 pound spinach, tough stems removed and washed
½ teaspoon freshly ground black pepper

Put the lima beans in a saucepan, add the cold water and 1 teaspoon of the salt, and bring to a boil. Cover, reduce the heat, and boil gently for 30 to 40 minutes, until the beans are tender. (Remove and discard any skins that float to the surface.) Drain the beans, reserving the cooking liquid, if you like, for Cold Mussel and Bean Soup (you should have about 2 cups of liquid; if you have less, add water).

Put the mussels and wine in a large stainless steel saucepan, cover, and cook over high heat until the mussels have opened, 7 to 8 minutes from start to finish. Drain, reserving the cooking liquid. You should have 3 cups of liquid; if you have less, add water. Reserve 1 cup of the liquid for use in this recipe and keep the remaining 2 cups for use in the soup, or freeze for another dish.

Remove the mussels from their shells and set aside; if desired, keep a few of the shells for decoration.

At serving time, heat 3 tablespoons of the olive oil in a medium saucepan. When it is hot but not smoking, add the scallions and sauté over medium heat for 1 minute. Add the reserved cup of mussel liquid, the drained beans, and mussels and mix well. Set aside.

Heat the remaining 1½ tablespoons oil in a large saucepan. Add the garlic and sauté for 30 seconds. Mix in the spinach, cover, and cook for 3 to 4 minutes, until wilted and tender. Add the remaining ½ teaspoon salt and the pepper and mix well. Transfer any juices that emerged from the spinach to the mussel and bean mixture.

Divide the spinach among four soup plates, arranging it around the periphery to create an attractive border. Heat the mussel mixture until warmed through and spoon into the center of

COLD MUSSEL AND BEAN SOUP Serves 4

When you cook mussels for gratins, pilafs, or soups or stews, you'll generally have extra broth left over. Be sure to keep it to make a flavorful soup, like this vichyssoise that is a great starter for a chic little dinner party.

2 cups reserved liquid from cooking the beans, cooled
2 cups reserved liquid from cooking the mussels, cooled
½ cup sour cream
3 tablespoons chopped fresh chives
¼ teaspoon Tabasco sauce

Put all the ingredients in a large bowl and whisk together. Refrigerate until cool.

At serving time, spoon the chilled soup into soup bowls and serve.

the plates. Decorate, if desired, with the reserved mussel shells. Serve.

Mussel Pilaf
Serves 6 as a first course

✳ **This molded pilaf of** mussels and rice is very good and looks stately on the plate. The shellfish and rice are cooked separately, then layered in small custard cups and moistened with a sauce made from the mussel-cooking liquid, scallions, and garlic. Your guests see only the rice when the dishes are presented. The inside — filled with mussels — is a delectable surprise.

PILAF

1	tablespoon unsalted butter
1	cup chopped onion
½	teaspoon dried thyme
1½	cups long-grain white rice
3	cups water
½	teaspoon salt

MUSSELS

4	pounds mussels, cleaned and debearded
½	cup dry white wine
½	cup chopped onion
⅓	cup chopped celery
¼	cup chopped scallions
3	garlic cloves, crushed and chopped (2 teaspoons)
1	tablespoon unsalted butter, softened
1	tablespoon all-purpose flour
½	cup chopped fresh parsley
½	teaspoon freshly ground black pepper
	Salt, if needed

FOR THE PILAF: Melt the butter in a small saucepan. Add the onion and thyme and sauté for about 1 minute. Add the rice and stir to coat it with butter. Add the water and salt and stir until the mixture comes to a boil. Reduce the heat to very low, cover, and cook for 20 minutes, or until the rice is tender and most of the liquid is absorbed. Remove from the heat and fluff the rice.

MEANWHILE, FOR THE MUSSELS: Combine the mussels and wine in a large stainless steel saucepan, cover, and bring to a boil, tossing occasionally. After 6 to 8 minutes, all the mussels should be open; remove from the heat and discard any mussels that haven't opened. Lift the mussels from the liquid and slowly pour the liquid into a clean saucepan, leaving any sand behind.

Remove the mussels from the shells. (At this stage of cooking, the mussels could be served plain with their natural juices.)

Add the onion, celery, scallions, and garlic to the mussel liquid, bring to a boil, and boil gently for 5 minutes.

Meanwhile, knead together the butter and flour with a whisk. Using the whisk, stir the kneaded butter (*beurre manié*) into the broth. Add 6 tablespoons of the parsley, mix well, and bring to a boil, whisking to prevent lumps, then reduce the heat and simmer for 1 minute. Add the pepper and taste for seasoning; usually no salt is necessary because the juice of the mussels is salty enough. Remove from the heat.

Generously butter six ¾- to 1-cup custard cups. Spoon ¼ cup of the cooked rice into one custard cup and press it against the bottom and sides of the cup with a spoon to make a nest in the center. Put 6 to 8 mussels in the nest and cover with 2 tablespoons sauce. Spoon another 3 tablespoons of rice on top of the mussels and press down with the back of the spoon, then invert the cup onto a serving plate. The pilaf should slide out easily. Repeat for the other servings.

Reheat the sauce if necessary and pour 3 to 4 tablespoons of sauce around the rice on each plate. Sprinkle the 2 tablespoons of remaining parsley on top and serve.

Mussel
and Potato Salad
Serves 4

❧ **This salad of cooked** potatoes and mussels flavored with a mustard dressing is inspired. It is infinitely better served lukewarm or at room temperature, rather than chilled.

1 pound Yukon Gold potatoes (about 6), washed
3 pounds mussels, cleaned and debearded
½ cup dry white wine
½ cup water
⅓ cup chopped shallots
2 garlic cloves, crushed and finely chopped (1 teaspoon)

DRESSING

½ teaspoon salt
1 teaspoon freshly ground black pepper
1 tablespoon hot or Dijon mustard
1 tablespoon balsamic vinegar
¼ cup extra-virgin olive oil
1 tablespoon Tabasco sauce
2 tablespoons chopped fresh parsley

Put the potatoes in a large saucepan, add enough cold water to cover them, and bring to a boil over high heat. Reduce the heat to low and boil the potatoes gently, uncovered, until tender, 30 to 40 minutes, depending on their size.

Meanwhile, put the mussels in a large stainless steel pot, add the wine and water, cover, and bring to a boil over high heat. Cook, tossing the mussels occasionally, for 3 to 4 minutes longer, until they open. If a few of the mussels still have not opened, lift out those that are open with a slotted spoon and put them in a bowl. Continue to boil any unopened mussels for 1 to 2 minutes longer to give them another chance to open. Discard any mussels that have not opened at this point.

Let the cooking liquid settle in the pot for a few minutes, then pour it slowly into a bowl, leaving behind any sediment. You will have about 3 cups of stock; reserve it for use in a soup or other dish.

When the mussels are cool enough to handle, remove them from their shells and put them in a bowl large enough to hold the finished salad.

When the potatoes are done, drain them and set them aside just until they are cool enough to handle.

Peel the warm potatoes and cut them into ½-inch-thick slices. Add them to the mussels, along with the shallots and garlic.

FOR THE DRESSING: Mix all the ingredients together in a small bowl. Add the dressing to the potatoes and mussels and toss gently to mix.

Arrange the salad on four individual plates and sprinkle with the parsley. Serve warm or at room temperature.

Stuffed New Zealand
Green Mussels
Serves 4

❧ **Beautiful large green-lipped mussels** from New Zealand are available year-round in most fish stores, but if you can't find them in your area, substitute other large mussels. My inspiration for this recipe was a similar dish I enjoyed in the South

of France featuring mussels stuffed with sausage, bread, onion, and garlic and cooked in a light tomato sauce.

2 pounds large New Zealand mussels (about 16), cleaned and debearded

8 ounces sweet Italian sausage meat

2 slices bread (2 ounces), preferably a country-style variety, processed to coarse crumbs in a food processor (¾ cup)

1 large egg

⅓ cup chopped onion

2 small garlic cloves, crushed and finely chopped (1 teaspoon)

½ teaspoon freshly ground black pepper

½ cup coarsely minced fresh chives

SAUCE

2 tomatoes (12 ounces), quartered

3 garlic cloves, crushed

¼ cup dry white wine

¼ teaspoon salt

½ teaspoon herbes de Provence

Using a clam knife, paring knife, or very thin-bladed knife, cut between the mussel shells to sever the hinge, or adductor muscle, and pull the shells open. Set the mussels, in their open shells, aside.

Mix together the sausage, bread crumbs, egg, onion, garlic, chives, and pepper in a bowl. Divide the mixture into 16 or so equal portions, and ar-range a portion on top of each mussel half. Cover with the other mussel half or close the mussel shells over the stuffing (they may not close completely) and arrange the mussels in one layer in a large stainless steel saucepan.

FOR THE SAUCE: Put the tomatoes, garlic, wine, salt, and herbes de Provence in a food processor and process for 10 to 15 seconds, until the mixture is partially liquefied. Pour the sauce on top of the stuffed mussels.

Bring the sauce to a rolling boil, uncovered; cover the pan, reduce the heat to low, and cook the mussels gently for 18 to 20 minutes. Using a slotted spoon, transfer the mussels to a platter. Boil the sauce for 3 to 4 minutes, until it is reduced to 1 cup.

Pour the sauce over the mussels and serve.

Sautéed Soft-Shell Crabs with Spinach, Asparagus, and Mushrooms
Serves 8 as a first course, 4 as a main course

❧ Once a year, blue crabs shed their hard shells as they grow. This is the time when one can enjoy one a great delicacy: soft-shell crabs. Fishermen who gather hard-shell crabs have told me that the tip of one of the small legs turns red, indicating that the crab will shed within forty-eight hours. The best crabs are those that have shed only the day before; they haven't yet formed any hard cover, and their shells are completely edible. Within a few days, the shells begin to harden, so crabs that have shed four or five days before will have tough, leathery outsides.

The soft-shells here are served on a bed of sautéed spinach and garnished with mushrooms and asparagus. If desired, you can pour melted butter on top just before serving to enrich the dish.

SPINACH

- 2 tablespoons unsalted butter
- ½ teaspoon chopped garlic
- 1½ pounds spinach, washed and tough stems removed
- ¼ teaspoon salt
- ¼ teaspoon freshly ground black pepper

CRABS

- ½ cup all-purpose flour
- ½ teaspoon salt
- ¼ teaspoon freshly ground black pepper
- 8 soft-shell crabs (3–4 ounces each), cleaned (see the sidebar, page 165)
- 4 tablespoons (½ stick) unsalted butter
- 1 tablespoon fresh lemon juice

GARNISHES

- 1 tablespoon unsalted butter
- 2 cups shiitake mushrooms, caps cut into ¼-inch-wide strips (5–6 mushrooms; the tough stems can be reserved to flavor stock)
- 6 asparagus spears, trimmed, peeled, cut into 2-inch segments, and each segment quartered lengthwise
  Pinch of salt
  Melted butter, for serving (optional)

FOR THE SPINACH: Heat the butter in a large stainless steel saucepan. When it is hot, add the garlic and sauté for 4 to 5 seconds. Add the spinach, which should still be wet from washing (that will provide enough moisture for cooking), then add the salt and pepper, cover, and cook over high heat for 3 to 4 minutes, until the spinach is thoroughly wilted and just tender. Set aside, covered, to keep warm.

FOR THE CRABS: Mix the flour, salt, and pepper together. Dust the crabs lightly on both sides with the flour.

The crabs should be cooked in two large skil-lets — if they are crowded, they won't cook properly. Melt 2 tablespoons of the butter in each skillet. Dust the crabs with flour again, shaking off the excess. When the butter is hot and foamy, put the crabs top side down in the skillets and sauté over medium-high heat for about 1½ minutes. Turn, cover the pans, and cook over medium-low heat for about 2 minutes longer, until nicely browned. Sprinkle the crabs with the lemon juice. Remove from the heat.

FOR THE GARNISHES: Melt the butter in a large skillet. When it is hot, add the mushrooms and sauté over high heat for about 1 minute. Add the asparagus and salt and continue sautéing for about 1 minute, until the vegetables are just tender but still firm.

Arrange the spinach on individual plates and place the crabs on top. Arrange the asparagus and mushrooms on top of the crabs and serve with melted butter poured on top, if desired.

Sautéed Soft-Shell Crabs on Asparagus
Serves 4 as a first course

✻ I particularly like serving soft-shell crabs to European visitors, who appreciate the introduction to an American treat. Be sure to buy your crabs from a reliable fishmonger.

Lightly sautéed, these crabs are served with sautéed asparagus, tomato, fresh tarragon, and red onion.

- 2 tablespoons unsalted butter
- ¾ cup chopped red onion
- 8 asparagus spears (about 6 ounces), peeled, trimmed, and sliced into ½-inch pieces
- ½ teaspoon salt
- ½ teaspoon freshly ground black pepper
- 2 tablespoons water

2 tablespoons peanut oil
1 large ripe tomato, peeled with a sharp vegetable peeler, halved, seeded, and cut into ½-inch pieces (1½ cups)
1 teaspoon finely chopped garlic
1 teaspoon chopped fresh tarragon
4 large soft-shell crabs (about 4 ounces each), cleaned (see the sidebar)

Heat 1 tablespoon of the butter in a large skillet until hot. Add the onion and sauté for 1 minute over high heat. Add the asparagus, ¼ teaspoon of the salt, ¼ teaspoon of the pepper, and the water, bring to a strong boil, and cook, covered, for 1 minute. (Most of the water will have evaporated at this point.) Transfer to a bowl and set aside.

Heat 1 tablespoon of the oil in the unwashed skillet. When it is hot, add the tomato pieces, the remaining ¼ teaspoon salt, the remaining ¼ teaspoon pepper, the garlic, and tarragon and sauté over high heat for about 45 seconds, just long enough to warm and slightly soften the tomato. Transfer to a bowl and set aside.

Pat the crabs dry.

Heat the remaining tablespoon each of butter and oil in a large skillet. When they are hot, add the crabs in one layer and cook over high heat for about 2 minutes on each side.

To serve, divide the asparagus among four plates and arrange the crabs on top of the as-

paragus. Spoon the tomatoes over and around the crabs, pour any juices that accumulated in the skillet on top of the crabs, and serve.

Crab Cakes with Avocado Salsa
Serves 4 as a first course

Delicate to handle, elegant, and refined in taste, these crab cakes have just enough bread in them to hold together, with some mayonnaise added for moisture and flavor. Although nothing can replace real crabmeat, you can substitute surimi, the imitation crabmeat made of fish such as pollack and cod. Surimi is widely available in markets.

CRAB CAKES

8 ounces crabmeat
¼ teaspoon salt
¼ teaspoon freshly ground black pepper
¼ teaspoon dried thyme
1 tablespoon chopped fresh chives
⅛ teaspoon Tabasco sauce
3 tablespoons mayonnaise
1½ slices firm white bread (1½ ounces), processed to crumbs in a food processor (¾ cup)
2 tablespoons peanut oil

SALSA

1 small ripe avocado
1 ripe tomato (5 ounces), peeled with a sharp vegetable peeler, halved, seeded, and coarsely chopped
1 tablespoon red wine vinegar
2 tablespoons peanut oil
¼ teaspoon salt
¼ teaspoon freshly ground black pepper
3 tablespoons water

1 tablespoon chopped fresh chives

CLEANING SOFT-SHELL CRABS

To prepare soft-shell crabs, lift up the skirt, or apron, on the bottom of each crab and twist or cut it off. Using scissors, cut off a strip from the front part of each shell that includes the eyes and antennae; discard. Lift up the top shell to expose the spongelike lungs on either side, pull them off, and discard.

FOR THE CRAB CAKES: Pick the crabmeat over for shells and cartilage. Cut it into ¼-inch pieces. (You should have 1½ loosely packed cups.)

Gently mix the crabmeat with the salt, pepper, thyme, chives, Tabasco, and mayonnaise in a bowl. Add the bread crumbs and toss them lightly into the mixture.

Divide the mixture into 4 portions and form it into patties about 1 inch thick. Handle the mixture gently; the cakes are fragile.

Heat the oil in a large skillet. When it is hot, carefully place the patties in the skillet and cook over medium heat for 3 to 4 minutes on each side, until nicely browned.

MEANWHILE, FOR THE SALSA: While the crab cakes are cooking, peel and pit the avocado and coarsely chop it. Combine the avocado and tomato in a bowl. Add the vinegar, oil, salt, pepper, and water, tossing gently to mix.

To serve, spoon the avocado salsa onto four individual plates and sprinkle with the chives. Place the crab cakes on top and serve.

Grilled Squid on Watercress

Serves 6 to 8 as a first course, 4 as a main course

I like the chewy texture of squid. To firm it, I blanch it briefly in boiling water, so it can easily be impaled on skewers, then I season it lightly with olive oil and Italian seasoning. It is imperative that the grill be very hot and the rack clean so the squid will be nicely marked but not stick. Be careful not to overcook or undercook it. Squid is available almost everywhere and usually comes cleaned, which makes it very convenient.

Make certain that the watercress is well washed and thoroughly dried so there is no water to dilute the dressing. Toss the salad just before serving, since watercress wilts quickly.

- 1½ pounds cleaned medium squid (about 16 bodies, plus tentacles)
- ¼ teaspoon salt, plus a pinch
- ¼ teaspoon freshly ground black pepper
- 2 tablespoons extra-virgin olive oil
- 1 teaspoon dried Italian seasoning
- 1 large bunch watercress (about 8 ounces), about 2 inches of the stems removed, the leaves washed and dried
- 1 tablespoon peanut oil
- 1 teaspoon sherry vinegar

Bring 6 cups water to a boil in a large saucepan. Drop the squid and tentacles into the boiling water and cook for 1 minute. (The water will not even return to a boil.) Drain the squid in a colander; its residual heat will help it dry.

Arrange the squid in a dish and sprinkle with the ¼ teaspoon salt, the pepper, olive oil, and Italian seasoning. (*This can be done a few hours ahead and the squid refrigerated.*)

Just before serving time, heat a grill until very hot.

Skewer the squid and tentacles, dividing them among three or four skewers. Grill them for 1½ minutes on each side.

Most fish markets now sell cleaned squid, but if you need to clean it, here is how to do it.

Wash the squid well. Pull off the head and tentacles; these will come away from the body in one piece. Pull the pen, or central cartilage, which looks like a long piece of plastic, out of the body. Remove the flap on each side of the body and pull off the dark skin.

Cut off the tentacles at the head and eyes. Pull off and discard the black skin from the flaps also, and set aside. Press on the round part where the tentacles come together, and a knotty beak will come out of the center. Discard it. Put the tentacles in cold water and rinse carefully. Lift them out of the water and use as directed.

At the last moment, toss the watercress with the peanut oil, sherry vinegar, and the pinch of salt. Arrange the salad on plates.

Remove the squid and tentacles from the skewers. Arrange on top of the watercress and serve.

Squid with Garlic and Scallions

Serves 6 as a first course

✂ **For tender squid, you** must cook them briefly on very high heat. But when sautéed raw, the squid are often crowded, release their juices, and take too long to brown: the result is rubbery. To avoid this problem, I first blanch them in boiling water to cook them partially and shrink them. Then, just before serving, I sauté them over high heat with oil, butter, and seasonings.

2	pounds cleaned squid
3	tablespoons olive oil
1½	tablespoons unsalted butter
14–15	scallions, trimmed (leaving some green) and cut into 1-inch pieces (about 2¼ cups)
¾	teaspoon salt
¾	teaspoon freshly ground black pepper
3–4	garlic cloves, chopped (1½ teaspoons)
3	tablespoons chopped fresh parsley

Bring 4 cups water to a boil in a saucepan. Meanwhile, cut the bodies of the squid into ½-inch-wide strips and the tentacles into pieces. When the water is boiling, drop in the squid and cook for 30 seconds (the water will not return to a boil). Drain in a colander and set aside.

At serving time, divide the oil and butter between two skillets and heat over high heat until very hot. Add the scallions and sauté for about 10 seconds. Add the squid, season with the salt and pepper, and sauté for 2 to 3 minutes. Mix in the garlic and parsley and cook for another 10 to 15 seconds.

Divide among six plates and serve.

Mushroom-Stuffed Squid

Serves 4

✂ **A mushroom-bread stuffing, seasoned** with garlic, onion, celery, and thyme, is the filling for these squid. Don't overstuff them: 2 to 3 tablespoons is sufficient; the bodies will look about half full initially, but they shrink as they cook and the filling expands.

Saffron is costly but has a unique flavor; however, the dish will still be excellent without it. Serve with couscous, rice, potatoes, or noodles.

1½ tablespoons olive oil

1 large onion, coarsely chopped
(1¼ cups)

1 celery stalk, coarsely chopped (¼ cup)

6 ounces mushrooms, cleaned and
coarsely chopped (2 cups)

3 large garlic cloves, thinly sliced
(1 tablespoon)

1½ teaspoons chopped fresh thyme
or ½ teaspoon dried thyme

½ teaspoon salt

½ teaspoon freshly ground black pepper

1 piece slightly stale bread (1½ ounces),
coarsely chopped (¾ cup)

1¼ pounds cleaned medium to large squid
(about 8 bodies, plus tentacles),
tentacles cut into small pieces

2 tomatoes (about 1 pound), cut into
large chunks

2 tablespoons tomato paste

1½ teaspoons chopped fresh oregano
or ½ teaspoon dried oregano

1 teaspoon saffron threads, crumbled
(optional)

Heat the oil in a large saucepan. When it is hot, add the onion and celery and sauté for 2 minutes. Add the mushrooms, garlic, and thyme, reduce the heat to low, cover, and cook for 8 minutes. Remove the lid and add half the salt and pepper. If necessary, cook for another 2 to 3 minutes, until most of the moisture has evaporated. Gently stir in the bread and set aside until cool enough to handle.

Rinse the squid bodies inside and out and pat dry. Stuff the cooled mushroom mixture loosely into the squid bodies, taking care to fill them only partially (see the headnote). Secure the open ends of the squid with wooden toothpicks and arrange them in one layer in a large skillet. Arrange the tentacles around the squid bodies.

Drop the tomato chunks into a food processor, add the tomato paste and the remaining salt and pepper, and process for a few seconds to create a sauce.

Pour the sauce over the squid and sprinkle on the oregano and saffron, if using. Bring the mixture to a boil over high heat, then reduce the heat to low, cover, and cook for 15 to 20 minutes at a very gentle boil to cook the squid and heat the stuffing. Serve.

Stuffed Squid with Cream Sauce
Serves 12 as a first course, 6 as a main course

❧ **The bodies of these** squid are stuffed with a shrimp and vegetable mixture and the sauce is thickened with a butter-flour mixture, a *beurre manié*. Serve the squid with rice or couscous.

STUFFING

1 tablespoon unsalted butter

1 cup loosely packed coarsely chopped
leeks (including some green parts)

½ cup coarsely chopped carrots

1 teaspoon finely chopped garlic
(2 cloves)

Reserved chopped squid tentacles
(from below)

¼ teaspoon salt

⅛ teaspoon freshly ground black pepper

8 ounces shrimp, peeled

1 large egg

About 2 pounds cleaned medium to
large squid (12 bodies), tentacles
cut into small pieces and reserved
for stuffing

2 tablespoons unsalted butter

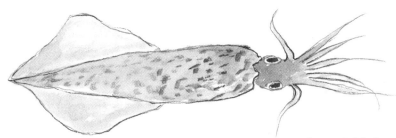

¾ cup diced (½-inch) onion

1 cup dry white wine

1 teaspoon salt

1 teaspoon freshly ground black pepper

TO FINISH THE SAUCE

1 tablespoon unsalted butter, softened

1 tablespoon all-purpose flour

½ teaspoon finely chopped garlic

½ cup heavy cream

2 tablespoons chopped fresh chives

FOR THE STUFFING: Melt the butter in a large saucepan. When it is hot, add the leeks and carrots and sauté over high heat for 1 minute. Add the garlic, chopped squid tentacles, salt, and pepper and cook for about 1 minute. With a slotted spoon, lift out the squid mixture and transfer to a bowl, reserving any remaining juices in the saucepan; set the pan aside. Refrigerate the squid mixture until cold.

Put the shrimp in a food processor and process for about 10 seconds. Add the egg and process until the mixture is smooth. Combine the shrimp paste with the cooled tentacle mixture.

Transfer the stuffing to a pastry bag without a tip (or use a small spoon to stuff the squid). Rinse the bodies of the squid inside and out under cold water and dry briefly with paper towels. Insert the end of the pastry bag into the body of each squid and stuff the cavity. Press gently with your hand to distribute the stuffing evenly. The squid should be stuffed only about half full, because the bodies will shrink considerably during cooking and the stuffing will expand.

Melt the butter in the saucepan you used for the stuffing. When it is hot, add the onion, then arrange the stuffed squid on top in one layer. Add the white wine and season with the salt and pepper. Cover with a buttered round of parchment paper cut to fit the saucepan and bring to a boil over high heat. Turn the heat down to very low, cover the saucepan with a lid, and simmer the mixture very gently for 15 to 20 minutes.

Transfer the squid to a tray or cookie sheet, lay the round of parchment on top, and keep warm in a 150-degree oven or on the side of the stove.

FOR THE SAUCE: Boil the juice in the saucepan to reduce the liquid to 1½ cups.

Meanwhile, mix the butter and flour together with a whisk in a small bowl to make a *beurre manié*. Using the whisk, stir it into the reduced juice and bring to a boil, stirring constantly. Add the garlic and cream and return the mixture to a boil. Add the chives.

Place the squid on a platter, pour the sauce over it, and serve.

Octopus Catalan-Style
Serves 8 as a first course

☙ **Octopus is delectable when** properly cooked. Dipped in boiling water for about half a minute to firm it and then served raw, still in its purple skin and sliced very thin, for sashimi or sushi, it will be tender. Brought to a gentle boil from a cold-water start and cooked gently for 30 to 45 minutes, it will also be tender. (As it simmers, the red-purplish skin tends to become gummy, but it is easily removed after this first cooking.) When cooked for either too long or too little, or at too high a boil, though, octopus can be tough. Some recipes advise cooking it with a couple of wine corks to tenderize the meat, but I have tried it and haven't found much difference. Beating the octopus before cooking with a rolling pin or a meat pounder, as many recipes specify, doesn't seem to tenderize the meat either. Still, in the Mediterranean countries, freshly caught octopus is often pounded on rocks and hung for a few hours in the sun to develop a better taste and texture.

This octopus is simmered, then sautéed in oil with celery and onion. It is spooned into tomato halves and served with a sharp dressing of vinegar, lemon juice, and oil — just as it is served in Southwest France and in the north of Spain.

1	large octopus (fresh or frozen; about 3¼ pounds dressed)
2	tablespoons corn or safflower oil
1	cup diced (¼-inch) celery
¾	cup chopped onion
½	teaspoon Tabasco sauce
½	cup dry white wine
¾	teaspoon salt
4	tomatoes (about 1½ pounds)

DRESSING

¼	cup extra-virgin olive oil
1	tablespoon fresh lemon juice
1	tablespoon red wine vinegar
¼	teaspoon salt

Fresh parsley leaves, for garnish

Octopus coming from the market is usually dressed, and the big sac of the head has already been turned inside out and the ink sac removed. If not, it should be removed and the head just below the eyes and the beak cut off, as for squid (see page 167).

Wash the octopus carefully under cold running water. Put it in a large pot, add 5 to 6 quarts of cold salted water, and bring just to a boil. Re-

duce the heat to maintain a gentle simmer and cook for 30 to 40 minutes, until the octopus is tender but still firm.

Lift the octopus out of the water into a pan of cold water. Remove the reddish-purplish skin: just rub and push it off under cold water. Most of it, except on the suction cups, will come off easily. Drain the octopus and cut the meat into ½-inch pieces. (You should have about 4 cups.) Pat dry.

Heat the oil in a large saucepan. When it is hot, add the celery and onion and sauté over medium heat for 1 minute. Add the octopus, Tabasco, wine, and salt, cover, and cook just long enough to heat the mixture through, 3 to 4 minutes.

Meanwhile, dip the tomatoes into a large saucepan of boiling water for 30 seconds, then remove the skins. Cut the tomatoes in half, press out the seeds, and remove some of the ribs with a spoon (reserve the juices, ribs, and seeds for stock, if desired).

FOR THE DRESSING: Mix the olive oil, lemon juice, vinegar, and salt together in a bowl.

Arrange the tomato halves on a platter and spoon some of the octopus mixture into and around each. Sprinkle the dressing on the octopus and garnish with parsley leaves.

VARIATION

As an alternative, cut the tomatoes into 1-inch pieces and mix with the cooked octopus, along with the olive oil, lemon juice, vinegar, and salt. Serve lukewarm in a salad bowl, garnished with the parsley leaves.

Lobster in
Artichoke Hearts
Serves 4 as a first course

🦞 **Lobster and artichokes are** two of my favorite foods, and I combine them in this elegant starter. Whole lobsters are messy to eat and much of the meat is wasted because many people don't know how to remove it from the shells, so I cook the lobsters and extract the meat. Then I serve it in tender artichoke hearts with a light sauce made from the lobster stock.

8 cups water
2 lobsters (about 1½ pounds each), preferably female

ARTICHOKE HEARTS

4 medium to large artichokes (about 8 ounces each), trimmed to artichoke hearts (see page 404)
1 tablespoon olive oil
1½ teaspoons fresh lemon juice
¼ teaspoon salt

2 tablespoons unsalted butter
2 tablespoons minced fresh chives
Salt and freshly ground black pepper

Bring the 8 cups water to a boil in a large pot. Add the lobsters and bring the water back to a boil, then cover, reduce the heat, and simmer the lobsters gently for 5 minutes. Leave them in the cooking liquid for 30 minutes off the heat, then lift them from the liquid and set them aside until cool enough to handle; set the pot aside.

Crack the shells and remove the meat, and any red coral, from the shells. Reserve the shells. Cut the meat of each tail lengthwise in half and remove and discard any remaining intestinal tract. If you have it, set the coral aside.

Put the shells back in the pot with the cooking liquid, bring to a boil, and boil, covered, for 30 minutes. Strain the stock. (You should have about 7 cups.) Set 1 cup of stock aside in a small saucepan for the sauce and freeze the remainder for use in a bisque or a soup (see below).

FOR THE ARTICHOKE HEARTS: Preheat the oven to 200 degrees.

Put the artichoke hearts in a saucepan, add 1 cup water, the oil, lemon juice, and salt, and bring to a boil. Cover, reduce the heat, and boil the artichokes gently for about 20 minutes, until they are tender and most of the cooking liquid has evaporated. Let cool.

When the artichokes are cool enough to handle, remove and discard the chokes.

At serving time, reheat the artichoke hearts for about 1 minute in a microwave oven or for 10 minutes in the oven; set aside in a warm spot.

Put the red coral, if you have it, in an ovenproof dish and heat it for 5 minutes in the oven to dry it. Coarsely chop the coral.

Just before serving, reheat the lobster meat for 20 to 30 seconds in the microwave oven (or for 8 to 10 minutes in the oven).

Meanwhile, bring the cup of reserved stock to a boil and boil until it is reduced to ½ cup. Add the butter, chives, and salt and pepper to taste and bring to a strong boil.

Place an artichoke heart on each of four plates and arrange the meat of half a lobster tail in the cavity of each, with a piece of claw meat alongside. Spoon the sauce on top, sprinkle with the coral, and serve.

Leftover lobster stock is good as the base for a bisque, or you can add pasta and seasonings to it for a simple and delicious soup (see Lobster Broth with Pastina, page 23).

Lobster Soufflé Plaza-Athénée

Serves 8 as a first course

❧ **This luxurious soufflé was** and still is a specialty of the Plaza Athénée hotel in Paris, where I worked in the 1950s. The lobster is cooked lightly, so it doesn't toughen, and a rich sauce for it is made with the lobster shells, vegetables, herbs, and wine and finished with cream and cognac. The cheese soufflé is served right out of the oven, puffy and golden, with the lobster and sauce alongside.

At the hotel, we placed a spiral of sliced lobster tail meat and black truffle on top of the soufflé just before serving, but I have omitted that expensive garnish.

LOBSTERS AND SAUCE

- 2 lobsters (about 2 pounds each)
- 3 tablespoons all-purpose flour
- ¾ cup dry white wine
- 2 tablespoons olive oil
- 4 tablespoons (½ stick) unsalted butter
- 3 tablespoons cognac
- 1 tomato, coarsely chopped (about 1 cup)
- 3 tablespoons tomato paste
- ¼ cup chopped carrot
- ½ cup chopped onion
- ¼ cup minced celery
- 1 garlic clove, crushed
- ½ teaspoon minced fresh tarragon or a pinch of dried tarragon
- 2 bay leaves
- ½ teaspoon dried thyme
  Salt and freshly ground black pepper to taste
- ½ cup heavy cream

SOUFFLÉ

- 3½ tablespoons unsalted butter
- 3 tablespoons all-purpose flour
- ¾ cup milk
  Salt and freshly ground black pepper
- 4 large eggs, separated
- 1 large egg white
- ½ cup grated Gruyère or Emmenthaler cheese

FOR THE LOBSTERS AND SAUCE: Push the point of a sharp heavy knife into the center of each lobster's head between the eyes and cut down through it. This will split the head in half, severing the spinal cord and killing the lobster instantly. Separate the lobster tails from the bodies and cut each tail into 3 pieces. Break off the claws and crack them with a hammer.

Cut the lobster bodies into pieces. Discard the stomach (the small sac behind the eyes) and the intestinal tract.

Combine the coral, if any, the tomalley (green liver), and any juices in a bowl with the flour and ¼ cup of the wine and mix thoroughly. Set aside.

Heat the oil and half the butter in a large heavy saucepan until very hot. Add the lobster pieces and sauté for 2 minutes. Add the remaining ½ cup of the wine and half of the cognac and carefully ignite with a long match. When the flames die out, add all the remaining ingredients (including the rest of the cognac) except the cream and the wine-flour mixture. Bring to a boil, then reduce the heat and simmer for 1 to 2 minutes, covered. Lift the lobster pieces to a tray to cool slightly; set the saucepan aside.

When the lobster pieces are cool enough to handle, remove the meat from the shells (the meat should be practically raw). Cut the meat into 1½-inch pieces and set aside; put the shells back in the saucepan along with the lobster bodies.

Add the wine-flour mixture to the sauce and mix well with a wire whisk. Bring to a boil, then reduce the heat and simmer for 25 minutes. Strain the sauce into another saucepan, pushing hard with a metal spoon to extract all the liquid. Add the cream and bring to a boil. Add the remaining cognac and butter, mix well and set aside.

FOR THE SOUFFLÉ: Preheat the oven to 400 degrees. Butter a 6-cup gratin dish with 1 tablespoon of the butter and set aside.

Melt the remaining 2½ tablespoons butter in a heavy saucepan. Whisk in the flour until smooth and cook, whisking constantly, over medium heat for about 30 seconds (do not allow the flour to brown). Add the milk and salt and pepper to taste and cook, whipping constantly, until the sauce comes to a boil. Boil for 1 minute, then take off the heat and beat in the egg yolks.

Beat the 5 egg whites in a large bowl with an electric mixer or by hand until they hold firm, shiny peaks. Whip about one third of the whites thoroughly into the yolk mixture with the whisk. Fold in the remainder with a rubber spatula, along with the cheese. Go as fast as you can when adding the whites, or they will be grainy. Transfer to the buttered gratin dish.

Put the soufflé on a cookie sheet and bake for 20 to 25 minutes, until puffed and golden.

Meanwhile, add the lobster to the sauce and heat gently for a few minutes to reheat the sauce and finish cooking the lobster.

As soon as the soufflé comes out of the oven, divide the lobster and sauce among eight warm plates. Spoon some of the soufflé into the center of the lobster on each plate and serve immediately.

Broiled Lobster with Bread Stuffing
Serves 4

✳ I am very fond of both broiled and grilled lobster and prepare it at least a few times every summer. I blanch the lobsters in boiling water for a few minutes before broiling or grilling them; as a result, their meat retains its moisture and is more tender. Dropping lobsters into boiling water is one of the fastest and easiest ways to kill them.

4	lobsters (about 1½ pounds each), preferably female
4	slices bread (8 ounces) from a large country loaf, cut into 1-inch pieces
2	tablespoons unsalted butter
2	tablespoons olive oil
4	large shallots, finely minced (1 cup)
8	scallions, trimmed (leaving some green) and finely minced (1 cup)
¼	teaspoon freshly ground black pepper Tabasco sauce to taste
½	cup fruity dry white wine

Preheat the oven to 400 degrees.

Bring 4 quarts water to a boil in a large pot. Drop in the lobsters, cover the pot, and cook for about 5 minutes, just until the water barely returns to a boil. Remove the lobsters from the water and set them aside to cool slightly.

Meanwhile, toast the bread on a baking sheet in the oven for about 10 minutes. Let cool, then place in a food processor and process into coarse crumbs. (You should have 2 cups.)

Melt the butter in a medium saucepan. Add the oil, shallots, and scallions, then add the bread crumbs, pepper, and Tabasco and toss lightly. Remove from the heat.

When the lobsters are cool enough to handle, remove the claws from each and put them in a plastic bag (to prevent splattering). Pound the claws with a meat pounder to crack the shells, then either arrange them as they are on a large baking sheet lined with foil or remove the claw meat intact from the shells and place it on the foil-lined pan.

Split each lobster lengthwise in half. Remove and discard the stomach (the small sac behind the eyes) and intestinal tract from each. Combine the juices emerging from the lobsters with the wine in a bowl.

Preheat the broiler. Arrange the lobster body halves side by side, flesh side up, next to the claws. Fill the body cavities with the stuffing mixture and sprinkle enough stuffing on the flesh of the tails to protect the meat while it is broiling. Pour the wine mixture around the lobsters.

Put the pan under the hot broiler, 10 to 11 inches from the heat, and cook for about 8 minutes, until the stuffing is nicely browned and the lobsters are cooked through and hot.

Arrange 2 stuffed lobster body halves on each of four plates and place 2 lobster claws or the meat from 2 claws alongside. Spoon some of the pan juices over the lobsters and serve.

Lobster Couscous with Chive Sauce

Serves 4

❧ **Lobster meat is combined** with flavorful couscous and accompanied with a fresh chive sauce. For an impressive presentation, the couscous and lobster are served in the shells.

Initially the lobster is cooked for just 5 minutes, only enough so that the meat can be removed from the shells. Just before serving, the lobster meat is reheated in the stock, then set aside for a few minutes to finish cooking in the residual heat of the hot poaching liquid. Avoid boiling the liquid — doing so will toughen the lobster meat.

2	lobsters (about 2 pounds each), preferably female

COUSCOUS

1½	cups water
2	tablespoons olive oil
1	medium onion, chopped (1 cup) Tomalley and coral from the lobster (optional)
1½	cups (about 10 ounces) couscous
½	teaspoon salt
¼	teaspoon freshly ground black pepper

SAUCE

½	cup reserved lobster stock
¼	cup olive oil
¼	cup finely minced fresh chives
⅛	teaspoon salt
⅛	teaspoon freshly ground black pepper

Bring 3 quarts water to a boil in a large stockpot. Add the lobsters, cover, and bring the water back to a boil. Reduce the heat to low and boil gently for 5 minutes. Leave the lobsters in the hot liquid off the heat for 20 minutes, then remove them from the pot and set aside.

To concentrate the taste of the lobster stock, reduce it to 4 cups. You will need 1 cup to reheat the lobster meat and ½ cup for the sauce; freeze the remainder for use in another dish.

When the lobsters are cool enough to handle, remove the claws and the meat; set aside (discard the claw shells). Cut the lobster bodies, including the tails, lengthwise in half and remove the tomalley (green liver) and red coral, if any; set aside. Remove the meat from the tails and set aside. Reserve the lobster shells.

FOR THE COUSCOUS: Bring the water to a boil in a small saucepan.

Meanwhile, heat the oil in a medium saucepan. Add the onion and sauté over medium heat for about 2 minutes. Add the tomalley and the coral, if you have it, and mix well, crushing the coral with a fork. Stir in the couscous, then add the boiling water, salt, and pepper, mixing well. Remove from the heat, cover, and let stand for 10 minutes.

Combine the lobster meat with 1 cup of the reduced stock in a saucepan, slowly heat the stock just until hot (about 160 degrees), and keep it at this temperature for 3 to 4 minutes. Do not boil, or the meat will toughen.

FOR THE SAUCE: Combine the ½ cup reserved stock with the remaining ingredients in a saucepan and bring to a strong boil.

Fluff the couscous and mound some couscous on each of four plates. Place the lobster half-shells on top. Fill the shells with the remaining couscous, arrange the warm lobster on top, and spoon on the sauce. Serve.

Scallop Ceviche
Serves 4 as a first course

✂ **This interpretation of a** South American dish is very flavorful and, since I prepare it without oil, it's also lean. The mixture of hot pepper, cilantro, and mint gives the ceviche a piquant fresh taste, making it a perfect first course for a muggy summer day. The heat can be increased or decreased depending on your tolerance for chile peppers.

1 pound sea scallops, washed, tough muscles removed, and cut into ½-inch pieces or slices

1 small red onion, cut into ¼-inch pieces (1 cup)
1 large ripe tomato, halved, seeded, and cut into ½-inch pieces (1½ cups)
3 tablespoons coarsely chopped fresh cilantro
2 tablespoons coarsely chopped fresh mint
1 tablespoon finely julienned lime rind
¼ cup fresh lime juice
1 jalapeño pepper, seeded and finely minced (about 1 tablespoon), or to taste
1 teaspoon salt
½ teaspoon freshly ground black pepper
2 teaspoons sugar
2 tablespoons rice vinegar
1 small cucumber (8 ounces)

Place all the ingredients except the cucumber in a plastic bag, seal it, and refrigerate for 3 to 4 hours, turning the bag occasionally so the mixture is well combined.

Meanwhile, peel the cucumber, cut it lengthwise in half, and scrape out the seeds with a sharp spoon. Cut each cucumber half lengthwise into 12 strips.

At serving time, make a decorative arrangement of 6 cucumber strips on each of four plates. Drain the ceviche, spoon it on top of the cucumber strips, and serve.

Steamed Scallops on Spinach with Walnut Sauce

Serves 4 as a first course

❧ **The beautiful simplicity of** this recipe is reflected in its pure, straightforward taste. Boiling the walnuts beforehand softens them and makes them taste like fresh green walnuts, which are more delicate and fruity than the mature nuts we commonly find in our markets. Make sure your ingredients are of the utmost freshness and quality.

SAUCE

 8 walnut halves, cut into ½-inch pieces
 1 teaspoon grated lemon rind
 2 tablespoons fresh lemon juice
 ¼ cup extra-virgin olive oil
 ½ teaspoon salt
 ½ teaspoon freshly ground black pepper

 1 pound spinach, washed and tough stems removed
 12 ounces sea scallops (16–20), washed and tough muscles removed

FOR THE SAUCE: Bring 2 cups water to a boil in a small saucepan. Add the walnuts, bring the water back to a boil, and boil for 30 seconds; drain. Combine the walnuts, lemon rind, lemon juice, olive oil, salt, and pepper in a bowl and mix well. Set aside.

Put the spinach leaves, still damp from washing, in a large saucepan and cook over high heat for about 2 minutes, until they start to steam and wilt. Arrange the scallops on top of the spinach, cover, and cook for about 3 minutes: the scallops should be just firm and cooked and the spinach wilted. Remove the scallops and put them on a plate.

If there is still water remaining in the pan, cook the spinach over high heat, uncovered, for about 1 minute longer, until most of the moisture is gone.

Divide the spinach among four plates and arrange the scallops on top. Coat with the sauce and serve.

Scallops in Scallion Nests

Serves 4 as a first course

❧ **Seared in a very** hot skillet, the scallops form a sweet brown crust on both sides. This recipe is often made with leeks, but scallions work well, are less expensive, and can be found all year round. The scallions, which are cooked briefly in boiling water and served with a mustard sauce, are also good on their own as a first course or salad.

I like this dish made with large scallops, sometimes called "diver scallops." If you have smaller ones, reduce the cooking time a little. They should not be cooked until dry, but they shouldn't be flabby and soft inside either.

 4 bunches small scallions (6–8 scallions per bunch)
 1 cup water

SAUCE

 1 tablespoon Dijon mustard
 1 tablespoon red wine vinegar
 ¼ cup extra-virgin olive oil
 ¼ teaspoon salt
 2 teaspoons reserved scallion cooking juices (from above)

 12 very large scallops (about 1 pound), washed, tough muscles removed, and patted dry
 2 teaspoons olive oil
 ⅛ teaspoon paprika

FOR THE SCALLIONS: Cut off and discard the root ends of the scallions and about 2 inches of the green ends, as well as any damaged leaves. Wash the scallions thoroughly.

Bring the water to a boil in a large stainless steel saucepan. Add the scallions, cover, and boil over high heat for 3 to 4 minutes, until tender. Remove the scallions with a slotted spoon and place them on a tray to cool. Reserve 2 teaspoons of the cooking juices for the mustard sauce.

When the scallions are cool, cover them with plastic wrap and refrigerate until serving time.

FOR THE SAUCE: Combine all the ingredients in a small bowl and mix with a spoon. (Do not worry if the ingredients separate.)

Put the scallops in a bowl and mix in the olive oil.

Heat a large heavy skillet, preferably cast iron or aluminum, until very hot, at least 5 to 6 minutes. Add the scallops and brown for about 1 minute on each side. Set them aside to continue cooking in their own residual heat while you prepare the plates.

Reheat the scallions in a microwave oven for 20 to 30 seconds (or reheat in a pan of boiling water), just long enough to take the chill off. Arrange them on four plates, twisting them to form a circle or "nest." Place 3 scallops in the center of each nest and coat with the mustard sauce. Sprinkle the paprika on top and serve.

Instant-Smoked Scallops with Orange and Onion Sauce
Serves 4 as a first course

This recipe illustrates an easy technique for smoking scallops and the same process can be used for fish and other shellfish. When a stovetop smoker is placed on a hot burner of an electric or gas stove, the chips or sawdust in the bottom emit enough smoke and generate enough heat to flavor and cook the seafood in a few minutes. Since the amount of wood and the length of cooking time determine the amount of smoke created, you can make adjustments as necessary. Here the scallops are smoked lightly, as I prefer them, but you can smoke them longer for a heavier taste, if that is more to your liking.

SAUCE

- 1 seedless orange
- 1 tomato (about 5 ounces), peeled, halved, seeded, and cut into ½-inch pieces (½ cup)
- 2 tablespoons chopped red onion
- 2 tablespoons chopped fresh cilantro
- 1½ teaspoons red wine vinegar
- 1½ tablespoons olive oil
- ½ teaspoon salt
- ¼ teaspoon freshly ground black pepper

- 12 large sea scallops (about 1 pound), washed, tough muscles removed, and patted dry
- 1 teaspoon corn oil

- ⅓ cup hickory, cherry, or maple wood chips or sawdust

FOR THE SAUCE: Using a paring knife, peel the orange down to the flesh. Cut enough of the flesh into ½-inch pieces to make ½ cup. Squeeze enough juice from the remaining flesh to measure 2 tablespoons. Put the orange flesh and juice in a small bowl, add the remaining sauce ingredients, and mix well. Set aside.

Put the scallops in a bowl and toss with the corn oil.

Arrange the wood chips or sawdust in the bottom of a stovetop smoker and place the screen 1 inch above the chips. Arrange the scallops in one layer on the screen. Cover the smoker and cook the scallops over high heat for about 1 minute, then reduce the heat to low and cook for 4 minutes longer. Set the smoker off the heat and let the scallops cool, still covered, for 5 minutes.

Remove the scallops from the smoker. (They will be lightly cooked and have a golden yellow exterior.)

Divide the sauce among four plates. Cut the scallops horizontally in half and arrange 6 halves on top of the sauce in the center of each plate. Serve.

IMPROVISING YOUR OWN SMOKER

If you don't own a smoker, you can make one from an old pot or roasting pan. Put a layer of wood chips or sawdust in the bottom of the pot and arrange a piece of mesh screening or a rack so it sits about 1 inch above the wood (small balls of aluminum foil can be used to elevate and support the screening). Arrange the seafood on top of the screen, cover the pot with a lid or piece of aluminum foil, and cook as indicated in the recipe.

Minute-Smoked Seafood
Serves 8 as a first course

❧ **Fish and shellfish cook** quickly and absorb seasonings well, making them ideal for smoking. Here the seafood is partially cured in advance with a dash of salt and pepper and the smoking and cooking take just a few minutes. Different herbs can be added to the cure or to the sawdust, although the smoky flavor tends to dominate.

Fish that are more porous and have a softer texture, such as salmon, will cook and smoke faster than firmer fish like monkfish. Firmer-fleshed sea-

food (in this case, the shrimp) will take longer to cook and, in this recipe, they are cut in half so that the pieces will be ready in the same amount of time as the salmon and swordfish, which are left in larger pieces. The fish should be barely cooked, the inside moist with a center that looks a little transparent. Serve the seafood lukewarm or at room temperature, coated with the dressing.

Because the seafood is only lightly smoked and cured, it cannot be kept as long as commercially smoked fish. It should be consumed within a day.

8   ounces skinless swordfish fillet
8   ounces skinless salmon fillet
8   large shrimp (about 12 ounces), shelled
      and cut in half
1   teaspoon salt
¼   teaspoon freshly ground black pepper

About ⅔ cup hardwood sawdust

DRESSING
⅓   cup chopped onion, rinsed in a sieve
      and drained
½   cup diced (½-inch) tomato
⅔   cup olive oil
3   tablespoons sherry vinegar
¾   teaspoon salt
¾   teaspoon freshly ground black pepper

Fresh basil leaves, for garnish

Cut the swordfish and salmon into 8 strips each. Put the fish and shrimp in a bowl and sprinkle with the salt and pepper. Cover and refrigerate for 1 to 2 hours.

If the wires of the smoker rack are too far apart, the fish will tend to fall through the openings; to prevent this, place a piece of metal screen over the rack and then arrange the fish and shrimp on it. The fish, which is softer and will cook faster, should be packed a little closer to each other and the firmer shrimp arranged more loosely.

Sprinkle the sawdust in the bottom of the smoker and place it over fairly high heat for about 1 minute, or until it starts smoking. Set the rack with the fish on top of the sawdust, cover tightly with the lid, and cook over medium-low heat for 3 minutes. Remove from the heat and set aside, with the lid still in place, for a few minutes so the fish and shrimp continue cooking gently in their own residual heat. They should be golden but still juicy.

MEANWHILE, FOR THE DRESSING: Combine the onion, tomato, olive oil, vinegar, salt, and pepper in a bowl.

Arrange the seafood on a platter or individual plates and spoon the dressing on top. Decorate with basil leaves and serve.

Seared Shrimp on Mesclun
Serves 4 as a first course

✶ **Often when I make** this dish at home, I leave the shrimp in the shells and my family peels them right at the table. The shells add extra taste. For guests, though, you might want to use shelled shrimp.

16	large shrimp (about 1 pound), shelled
½	teaspoon dried thyme
½	teaspoon dried oregano
1	teaspoon dried tarragon
¼	teaspoon ground coriander
¼	teaspoon freshly ground black pepper
⅛	teaspoon cayenne pepper
2	tablespoons olive oil

GREENS

2	tablespoons olive oil
10	ounces mesclun (a mixture of young,

tender greens and herbs), washed and drained (10–12 cups)

¼	teaspoon salt
¼	teaspoon freshly ground black pepper
2	tablespoons water

Sprinkle the shrimp with the thyme, oregano, tarragon, coriander, and both peppers. Arrange in a single layer in a dish and sprinkle with the oil.

Heat a heavy aluminum or cast-iron skillet until very, very hot (do not use a nonstick skillet). Arrange the shrimp in one layer in the skillet and cook over high heat for 1 minute. Turn and cook for about 1½ minutes on the other side.

FOR THE GREENS: Heat the oil in a large saucepan. When it is hot, add the greens and sauté for 2 minutes. Add the salt and pepper and mix well. Divide among four plates.

Arrange 4 shrimp on top of the greens on each plate. Add the water to the juices in the pan and stir to deglaze. Pour the juices over the shrimp and serve.

Shrimp and Spinach Timbales

Serves 4 as a first course

❧ **Although this easy dish** takes only minutes to prepare, it makes an impressive dinner party starter. For a fancy presentation, I layer the sautéed shrimp and spinach in small cups and then unmold the timbales onto plates. If you prefer, you can just arrange the spinach on individual plates and spoon the shrimp on top. Tomato strips make an attractive garnish.

2½ tablespoons peanut oil
3 garlic cloves, crushed and chopped (2 teaspoons)
12 ounces spinach, tough stems removed, washed, and dried
½ teaspoon salt
½ teaspoon freshly ground black pepper
10 extra-large shrimp (about 14 ounces), shelled and cut into 3 pieces each
2 plum tomatoes (about 8 ounces total), peeled, halved, seeded, and cut into thin julienne strips

Heat 1½ tablespoons of the oil in a large skillet. When it is hot, add the garlic and sauté for 10 seconds. Add the spinach, stir well, and add ¼ teaspoon each of the salt and pepper. Cook over high heat, stirring occasionally, for about 2 minutes, until the spinach is wilted. Transfer to a bowl.

Heat the remaining tablespoon of oil in the skillet. When it is hot, add the shrimp and the remaining ¼ teaspoon each salt and pepper and cook over high heat, shaking the pan occasionally, for about 1 minute, just until the shrimp become firm. Transfer the shrimp to a bowl. Put the tomato strips in the skillet. Sauté for about 10 seconds, just long enough to soften them slightly. Set aside.

Line the bottom and sides of four round-bottomed coffee cups or small custard cups with about half of the spinach, pressing it into place. Divide the shrimp among the cups and arrange the remaining spinach on top, so that the shrimp are completely covered.

To serve, unmold the timbales onto individual plates and garnish with the tomato strips.

Sautéed Shrimp, Potato, and Escarole Salad

Serves 4 as a first course

❧ **Potatoes, escarole, and sautéed** shrimp combine in a garlicky dressing. The salad is best eaten at room temperature.

12 ounces small Yukon Gold potatoes, washed
1 teaspoon finely chopped garlic (about 2 cloves)
2 teaspoons Dijon mustard
   Salt and freshly ground black pepper
1½ tablespoons sherry vinegar
¼ cup extra-virgin olive oil
1 tablespoon unsalted butter
1 pound large shrimp (16–20), shelled and halved crosswise
1½ teaspoons chopped fresh tarragon
1½ teaspoons chopped fresh parsley

1 head escarole (8–10 ounces), as white
   as possible inside, trimmed, cut into
   1½-inch pieces, washed, and dried
   (about 4 cups)

Put the potatoes in a saucepan with enough water to cover them by 1 inch and bring to a boil over high heat. Reduce the heat to low and boil the potatoes gently for 25 to 35 minutes, until they are tender when pierced with the point of a sharp knife. Drain and cool slightly.

When the potatoes are lukewarm, peel them and cut them into 1-inch cubes. Put them in a bowl, add the garlic, mustard, ½ teaspoon each salt and pepper, the vinegar, and olive oil, and toss well. Set the potatoes aside to cool to room temperature.

At serving time, heat the butter in a large skillet. When it is hot but not smoking, add the shrimp and ⅛ teaspoon each salt and pepper and sauté the shrimp for 1½ to 2 minutes. Stir in the tarragon and parsley.

Add the escarole to the potato salad and mix well. Divide the mixture among four salad plates, sprinkle the shrimp on top, and serve.

Shrimp shells can be frozen for later use in soup or stock. My wife makes a delightful Thai soup with a stock made from shrimp shells and flavored with lime juice and lemongrass.

Shrimp Pané on Watercress
Serves 4

✺ **For each serving of** this dish, four shrimp are coated with a shrimp mousse made from the tails. The resulting "patties" are breaded (*pané* means "breaded"), sautéed in oil with a dash of butter, and served on a watercress salad.

20 extra-large shrimp (16–20 per pound),
   shelled and deveined
 1 large egg
 1 small garlic clove
 ¼ teaspoon salt
 ¼ teaspoon freshly ground black pepper
 1 tablespoon fresh parsley leaves
 3 slices firm white bread (3 ounces),
   processed to crumbs in a food
   processor (1½ cups)
 2 tablespoons canola oil
 1 tablespoon unsalted butter

SALAD

 1 bunch watercress (8 ounces)
 1 tablespoon sherry vinegar
 3 tablespoons walnut oil
 ¼ teaspoon salt
 ¼ teaspoon freshly ground black pepper

Cut off about 1 inch from the lower tail segment of each shrimp and put these tail pieces, along with the 4 smallest shrimp (total weight about 6 ounces) in a food processor. Add the egg, garlic, salt, and pepper and process for about 20 seconds. Scrape down the sides of the bowl, add the parsley, and process for another 15 to 20 seconds, until the mixture is smooth. Transfer to a bowl. (You should have about 1 cup.)

Divide the remaining 16 shrimp into 4 portions. Arrange them on a tray so that each group of 4 shrimp is clustered together to form a flat patty. Coat the top surface of each patty with about 1½ tablespoons of the shrimp mousse. Sprinkle half the bread crumbs over the mousse on the patties and press the crumbs gently into the mousse. Using a spatula, gently turn the patties over. Spread the remaining mousse over the patties and coat as before with the remaining bread crumbs. Cover and refrigerate until ready to cook.

At serving time, heat the canola oil and butter in a large skillet until hot. Carefully transfer the patties to the skillet and cook them gently for 3 minutes, or until golden brown. Turn carefully (they are delicate) and cook for 3 minutes on the other side. Cover and set aside.

FOR THE SALAD: Cut off the bottom 2½ inches from the watercress stems (reserve, if you desire, in the refrigerator or freezer for use in soup). Wash the watercress well and dry it in a salad spinner.

Combine the sherry vinegar, walnut oil, salt, and pepper in the bowl in which you will toss the salad.

Just before serving, add the watercress to the bowl and toss to coat with the dressing. Divide the salad among four plates, place a shrimp patty on top of each, and serve.

Crawfish with Scallop Mousse
Serves 6

Crawfish, or crayfish, is a freshwater crustacean that looks like a tiny lobster; it can be found under rocks in small streams and lakes, as well as in the mud of swamps. Crawfish come primarily from Louisiana and California, although several other states, from Texas to Washington, are now farming them. They are available fresh in good fish markets at certain times of the year.

At crawfish festivals, whole crawfish are boiled in a spicy broth. You chew the body and claws and then suck out the meat. In restaurants, usually only the meat of the tail is served and the remainder of the bodies used in chowder or in a sauce, as in this recipe. (There is so little meat in the claws that it isn't worth picking it out.)

The scallop mousseline is made with a puree of scallops and whipped cream. It can be served by itself, with a butter and lemon sauce, or it can be used to stuff fillets of fish. I originally modeled this dish after one made by my Aunt Hélène, a great cook who used to make a wonderful crawfish gratin.

2 dozen crawfish
1 tablespoon unsalted butter

STOCK

2 tablespoons unsalted butter
1 tablespoon olive oil
   Reserved crawfish bodies and claws (from above)
1 cup coarsely chopped onion
½ cup coarsely chopped carrot
½ cup coarsely chopped celery
¼ teaspoon dried thyme
¼ teaspoon dried oregano
½ teaspoon salt
½ teaspoon freshly ground black pepper
2 fresh tarragon sprigs
1 cup dry white wine
2 tablespoons cognac
1 cup homemade chicken stock (page 612) or low-salt canned chicken broth
2 cups water
2 cups diced tomatoes (2 large or 3 smaller tomatoes)

MOUSSELINE

2 teaspoons unsalted butter, for buttering the molds
8 ounces scallops, washed, tough muscles removed, and refrigerated
⅛ teaspoon curry powder
1 cup very cold heavy cream
½ teaspoon salt
⅛ teaspoon freshly ground black pepper

TO FINISH

½ teaspoon arrowroot, dissolved in 1 tablespoon water
   Pinch of cayenne pepper

4 tablespoons (½ stick) unsalted butter
 Salt and freshly ground black pepper if
 needed

Crawfish are very vivacious, so wearing a glove or using a towel may prevent getting your fingers pinched. Hold the crawfish by the tops of their bodies and break off the claws. Break off the tails and set aside.

Using a meat pounder, crush the claws to expose the meat inside. With a large sturdy knife, coarsely chop the bodies; reserve for the sauce.

It is best to remove the intestinal tract from each crawfish tail, as it tends to be bitter (especially in a sauce, as here). Take hold of the central flap of the tail, twist it to the left and then to the right, and pull: the intestinal tract will come out attached to the flap.

Heat the butter in a large skillet. When it is hot, sauté the tails for 3 to 4 minutes, until they turn red. Remove to a plate.

When they are cool enough to handle, shell the tails; reserve the shells.

FOR THE STOCK: Heat the butter and olive oil in a large skillet until hot. Add the crushed claws, chopped bodies, and tail shells and sauté for 4 to 5 minutes over high heat. Add the onion, carrot, celery, thyme, oregano, salt, and pepper and cook for 3 to 4 minutes. Add the tarragon, white wine, cognac, chicken stock, water, and tomatoes and boil gently for 40 minutes.

Strain the stock through a colander, pressing on the shells to extract as much liquid as possible.

Strain the stock through a fine strainer into a saucepan. You should have about 1¼ cups. If not, reduce it by boiling it rapidly, or add water to obtain this amount. Set aside.

FOR THE MOUSSELINE: Preheat the oven to 350 degrees. Butter six ½-cup molds and refrigerate. Chill a medium bowl.

Put the scallops and curry powder into a food processor and process for 10 to 15 seconds, until smooth. With the motor running, slowly add ¼ cup of the cream and process just enough to incorporate. Transfer the mixture to a bowl.

Pour the remaining ¾ cup cream into the chilled bowl and whip just until it holds a soft peak. Add the scallop mixture to the whipped cream and combine, using a spatula or whisk. Add the salt and pepper.

Fill the molds with the mousseline. Place in a baking pan or a saucepan and surround with lukewarm water, to create a water bath. Butter a piece of parchment paper and place it buttered side down on the mousselines.

Bake for approximately 20 minutes, until cooked and firm throughout; during cooking, the water should not go above 170 to 180 degrees, or the mousselines will tend to expand and get rubbery. Remove from the oven. (*The mousselines can be kept warm in the hot water bath in a warm spot for 30 minutes or reheated gently in a saucepan of hot water without affecting their quality.*)

TO FINISH THE DISH: Add the dissolved arrowroot to the crawfish stock, along with the cayenne pepper, and bring to a boil. Add the butter in pieces, whisking well after each addition until it is thoroughly incorporated before adding the next. When all the butter has been added, taste for salt and pepper and add if needed.

Meanwhile, warm the crawfish tails in a 250-degree oven for a few minutes.

Unmold the mousselines onto a platter or individual plates and partially coat with the sauce. Pour the rest of the sauce around them. Arrange the crawfish tails around the dish and serve.

SHOPPING ONLINE

You can find crawfish at any time of the year online.

Whelk Salad
with Mustard Vinaigrette
Serves 6 as a first course

❧ **I find whelk, also** called scungilli, in Italian or Vietnamese markets. A relative of the tiny periwinkle and the conch, it is firm, a bit chewy, and tender at the same time — somewhat like the texture of snail (escargot). It makes a great salad or unusual first course and is often quite inexpensive.

Serve the salad with crusty French bread and a dry white wine.

1½ pounds whelk meat, or 10 whelks (about
    5 pounds), cleaned (see the sidebar)
Salt

VINAIGRETTE

1 tablespoon Dijon mustard
½ teaspoon salt
¼ teaspoon freshly ground black pepper
1 tablespoon red wine vinegar
⅓ cup oil, preferably a mix of walnut
    and peanut oil

2 tablespoons chopped onion
1½ teaspoons chopped garlic (about
    3 cloves)
1 tablespoon chopped fresh chives
1 cup peeled and diced (½-inch) tomatoes
    (1–2 tomatoes)
4 large radishes, stems removed, root ends
    left intact, and halved lengthwise, for
    garnish

Put the whelk in a large saucepan, cover with 8 cups cold water, and add a pinch of salt. Bring to a boil, reduce the heat, and simmer gently for about 1 hour and 15 minutes. When pierced with a fork, the whelk should be tender but still firm.

CLEANING WHELK

Whelk can be found already cleaned at ethnic markets and some fish markets. If you get whole whelk, you will need to clean and parboil it.

Pour boiling water over the whelk and let stand for 5 minutes. Then, using a fork, pry each whelk out of its shell. Pull off the operculum (the leathery piece on the meaty end) and the coil, or twisted part of the intestine, on the other side and discard them. Brush the meat all over with a nail brush to remove any dirt.

Drain and cut into ¼-inch-thick slices. Discard any guts as you are slicing.

FOR THE VINAIGRETTE: Combine the mustard, salt, pepper, and vinegar in a bowl. Slowly add the oil, stirring constantly with a whisk.

Add the whelk, onion, and garlic to the vinaigrette and toss. Sprinkle with the chives and tomatoes and toss gently to mix.

Arrange the salad in a shallow bowl and decorate with the radish halves. Serve.

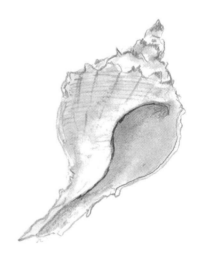

Mushrooms Stuffed with Escargots
Serves 8 as a first course

🐌 **This recipe was a** specialty of the Plaza Athénée in Paris, where I worked in the early 1950s. We used fresh Burgundy snails, but canned snails can be substituted. Instead of shells, mushroom caps are used to hold the snails, and they are served with garlic butter. Shrimp or scallops can be prepared in the same way.

MUSHROOMS

4	dozen white mushroom caps, about 1½ inches in diameter (reserve the stems for vegetable stock or mushroom soup)
½	teaspoon salt
3	tablespoons vegetable oil

SNAILS

4	dozen very large canned snails (two 4.4-ounce cans)
1½	tablespoons unsalted butter
¼	teaspoon freshly ground white pepper

SNAIL BUTTER

½	cup fresh parsley leaves
1	tablespoon sliced shallot
3	tablespoons whole almonds
5	garlic cloves, sliced
1¼	teaspoons salt
1	teaspoon freshly ground black pepper
1	slice firm white bread (1 ounce), cubed
¾	pound (3 sticks) unsalted butter, softened
2	tablespoons dry white wine
1	tablespoon Ricard or Pernod (optional)

Crusty bread, for serving

FOR THE MUSHROOMS: Preheat the oven to 400 degrees.

Lay the caps hollow side up on a cookie sheet and sprinkle with the salt and oil. Bake for about 8 minutes; there should be some liquid accumulated in the caps. Turn the caps upside down and let cool. (Leave the oven on.)

FOR THE SNAILS: Drain the snails in a colander and rinse thoroughly under cold water.

Melt the butter in a large skillet. Add the snails and white pepper and toss gently for a few seconds. Set aside.

FOR THE BUTTER: Put all the ingredients except the butter, wine, and Ricard or Pernod, if using, in a food processor and process until finely chopped. Add the remaining ingredients and process until smooth.

Spoon ½ teaspoon snail butter into each mushroom cap. Push 1 snail into each buttered cap and top with another teaspoon of the butter, or enough to cover the snail. (*Any extra snail butter can be frozen for future use. The snails and mushrooms can be prepared ahead and refrigerated for a few hours.*)

At serving time, place 6 filled mushroom caps in each of eight small gratin dishes. Arrange the dishes on a cookie sheet and bake for 12 to 14 minutes, until hot and bubbly. Serve with bread to soak up the butter.

Fish

Fried Roe with Garlic and Parsley
Serves 6 as a first course

❧ **Fresh shad roe** is an eagerly awaited harbinger of spring. But don't limit yourself to the roe of this fish. Ask your fishmonger for the long, tapered roe of flatfish such as sole, flounder, fluke, or brill, as well as eggs from other fish; these are usually discarded, so you'll need to request them ahead of time. The milt (the male sperm repository, as opposed to the eggs of the female) of most fish is also highly prized, especially herring and salmon. (The milt should be cooked for less time than the roe.) Fish livers, like cod livers, are good too. Soft in texture, fish livers are moist and tender when properly cooked. Like chicken livers, they become dry when overcooked.

1 pound fish roe and/or liver (see the headnote)
½ teaspoon salt
2 tablespoons all-purpose flour
2 tablespoons vegetable oil
3 tablespoons unsalted butter
1 garlic clove, crushed and very finely chopped (½ teaspoon)
⅓ cup chopped fresh parsley
½ teaspoon fresh lemon juice or vinegar

Clean the roe and/or liver of any black filaments or sinews, which are bitter. As with any other liver, make sure to remove any yellowish-green bits on top of the liver, which indicate that the gallbladder (a little sac filled with bitter liquid and attached to the liver) broke. Pat the roe and liver dry. Sprinkle with the salt and flour.

Heat the oil and 1 tablespoon of the butter in a large skillet until hot. Lay the roe in the pan and cook over medium-high heat for about 3 minutes, until lightly browned. Be careful, as it tends to splatter. Turn the roe with a spatula, add the liver (which does not have to cook as long as the roe), cover, reduce the heat to medium, and cook for another 2 to 3 minutes.

Arrange the roe and liver on a serving platter or individual plates. Melt the remaining 2 tablespoons butter in the skillet. Add the garlic and parsley and cook for a few seconds, until the mixture foams; do not let the garlic burn.

Spoon the garlic butter on top of the roe and liver, sprinkle with the lemon juice or vinegar, and serve.

SUBSTITUTIONS

When cooking fish, you can usually substitute one type for another. Think in terms of texture and ask your fishmonger for advice. A white flaky fish like striped bass can be replaced by black sea bass or even cod. A fatty fish like salmon can be replaced by Arctic char or trout. The most important factor is freshness.

Fish Friture with Fried Celery Leaves
Serves 6 as a first course

❧ A *friture* is a dish of deep-fried tiny fish: whitebait or other fish found in rivers or ponds are coated with flour and fried until crisp, like French fries. Small freshwater minnows, roach, gudgeon, and even very small sunfish are delectable prepared this way. *Friture* is commonly served in small cafés along the little lakes and rivers in France, often with aperitifs before a meal.

Although some cooks fry the fish without gutting them, they tend to taste bitter, and the final result is well worth the work required to clean them.

Deep-fried celery leaves have an assertive taste. They are prepared like fried parsley and are good with different types of fried foods.

1 pound small minnows, whitebait, smelt, small sunfish, or other tiny fish
  About 6 cups corn oil, for deep-frying
4 cups loosely packed celery leaves, washed and thoroughly dried
  Salt
¼ teaspoon freshly ground black pepper
1 cup all-purpose flour
  Lemon wedges, for garnish (optional)

Freshly caught fish will live for a while in a pail of water. To prepare them, using your thumb and index finger, press and push down on the belly of each one, starting at the head and pushing toward the tail so the guts come out. Wash the fish in cold water, changing the water several times. Drain on paper towels.

Heat the oil to 275 to 300 degrees in a large pot; the oil should be at least 1 inch deep. Drop the celery leaves into the hot oil, averting your face because the oil will splatter momentarily, stir with a skimmer, and cook for about 1 minute, moving the celery leaves in the oil, until crisp. Drain on paper towels and sprinkle with salt.

Heat the oil to about 400 degrees. Meanwhile, put the fish in a plastic bag with ¼ teaspoon salt, the pepper, and flour. Shake so the fish are well coated with the mixture. (Be sure to do this at the last moment; you cannot keep the fish floured too long, or the moisture in them will come out and make their outsides gummy.) Shake the fish in a colander to remove excess flour. Cook in batches, dropping the fish into the hot oil and cooking for 3 to 5 minutes, until crisp and brown. Lift out of the oil, drain on paper towels, and sprinkle with salt.

Arrange the fish on a platter with the fried celery leaves in the center and serve, if desired, with wedges of lemon. Eat piping hot with your fingers.

Pike Quenelles and Chicken Liver Timbale with Tomato Sauce
Serves 8 to 10; Makes about 16 quenelles

✂ **These quenelles, or dumplings,** are a specialty of the Lyon area. They are usually prepared with freshwater fish, often pike, but sometimes with a combination of carp and pike, both firm-fleshed and high in albumin. There is less fish in these quenelles than in their classic counterparts made of fish, egg whites, and cream (see page 190), and they are denser because they are made with cream puff dough (called a *panade*) and butter. They are sold, cooked, with different sauces, in specialty stores throughout France.

This combination of quenelles with a chicken liver timbale and a fresh tomato sauce made with wild mushrooms is a specialty of my cousin Merret and a great favorite at our table. The timbale can be served on its own, as can the quenelles.

It is important to poach the quenelles gently, just until they are cooked through, during the first cooking. If covered and allowed to boil, they will expand, then deflate and become mushy on the second cooking. Although I reheat the quenelles in water, they can also be rewarmed on top of the stove in the sauce, covered, and served that way or reheated in the oven in a gratin dish with the sauce.

1 pound skinless yellow or walleye pike
   fillets

8 tablespoons (1 stick) unsalted butter,
   softened

PANADE

1¼ cups milk

1¼ teaspoons salt

3 tablespoons unsalted butter

1¼ cups all-purpose flour

4 large eggs

½ teaspoon freshly ground black pepper

⅛ teaspoon freshly grated nutmeg

TIMBALE

3 ounces chicken livers (about 3),
   preferably pale in color (these are
   milder and more flavorful), trimmed
   of any sinew

3 garlic cloves, crushed

2 teaspoons unsalted butter

5 large eggs

1 teaspoon potato starch (see page 318)

1 cup milk

½ teaspoon salt

¼ teaspoon freshly ground black pepper

1½ cups heavy cream

1 tablespoon chopped fresh parsley

2 fresh thyme sprigs, chopped

TOMATO SAUCE

2 tablespoons olive oil

1 tablespoon unsalted butter

1½ cups coarsely chopped onions

½ cup coarsely chopped carrot

4 garlic cloves, not peeled, crushed
   Leaves from 1 fresh thyme sprig
   Leaves from 1 fresh oregano sprig

2 pounds ripe tomatoes, quartered

3 tablespoons tomato paste

½ teaspoon salt

¼ teaspoon freshly ground black pepper

½ cup water

12 ounces cremini mushrooms, cleaned
   and cut into 1-inch pieces

½ cup pitted green olives

1 teaspoon chopped fresh chives

Put the fish in a food processor and process until smooth. Add the butter and process until smooth. Set aside.

FOR THE PANADE: Heat the milk in a saucepan. Add ¼ teaspoon of the salt and the butter and bring to a boil. Immediately remove from the heat and add the flour all at once, stirring with a wooden spoon. As the ingredients come together, the mixture will separate from the sides of the pan. Place it back over low heat and cook for about 1 minute, stirring, to dry out the mixture further. Transfer to a plate, cover with plastic wrap, and press to flatten. Refrigerate to cool.

When the panade mixture is cool, put it in the food processor. With the motor running, add the eggs one at a time, then add the remaining 1 teaspoon salt, the pepper, nutmeg, and the fish mixture and process until the mixture is smooth. Transfer to a bowl, cover with plastic wrap, and chill in the refrigerator for a few hours, until set.

Place about half of the quenelle mixture on a well-floured board and roll the dough gently under your hands, extending it to a cylinder about 1½ inches thick. With a knife dipped in flour to prevent sticking, cut the cylinder on the bias into 8 pieces about 3 to 4 inches long. Repeat with the remaining mixture. (You can also simply scoop the mixture up with two large spoons and then drop it into the hot water.) Cupping your hand, roll the pieces back and forth on the board to round them on the ends, creating an elongated football shape. The dumplings are delicate; roll them gently onto a cookie sheet.

Bring 3 inches of water to a boil in a large saucepan. Add half the quenelles. The temperature of the water will drop when they are added; let it return to just about 170 to 180 degrees (under a boil) and cook the quenelles for 12 to 15 minutes, until they float to the surface. Transfer the quenelles to a bowl of ice water and cook the remaining quenelles in the same manner. When the quenelles are cold, drain on paper towels, then cover and refrigerate. (*The quenelles can be refrigerated for 2 to 3 days.*)

FOR THE TIMBALE: Preheat the oven to 375 degrees. Butter a 5- to 6-cup mold, such as a soufflé dish.

Drop the chicken livers and garlic cloves into a food processor and process until smooth.

Heat the butter in a large skillet. When it is hot, add the liver mixture and sauté for 1 to 2 minutes, until the liver turns brownish and sets. (If left raw, the liver would sink to the bottom of the dish later.)

Place the liver back in the food processor and process until very smooth. Add the eggs and potato starch and process to incorporate. Add the milk, salt, and pepper and process until smooth. Add the cream, parsley, and thyme and blend.

Pour the mixture into the buttered dish and set the dish in a roasting pan. Add enough lukewarm water to come at least halfway up the dish, place in the center of the oven, and cook for 1 hour, or until the timbale is set in the center. Remove from the oven.

MEANWHILE, FOR THE SAUCE: Heat the oil and butter in a large skillet until hot. Add the onions and carrot and sauté for 2 to 3 minutes. Add the garlic, thyme, and oregano and sauté for a few seconds. Add the tomatoes, tomato paste, salt, and pepper and cook over high heat for 1 minute. Cover, reduce the heat to low, and cook for about 15 minutes, until thickened. Pour into a food mill set over a bowl. Rinse the skillet with

the ½ cup water, pour over the coulis, and push through.

Pour the tomato mixture back into the skillet and bring to a boil. Add the mushrooms, bring back to a boil, and cook, covered, for 1 to 2 minutes. Set aside.

At serving time, bring about 3 inches of water to a boil in a large saucepan. Slip in the quenelles, cover, reduce the heat to low, and poach them gently for about 10 minutes. (They should cook at just under a boil so they do not expand too much.)

Add the olives to the sauce and bring to a boil.

Unmold the chicken liver timbale onto the center of a large platter. Arrange the hot quenelles, drained and patted dry with a paper towel, around the timbale. Cover with some of the tomato sauce and sprinkle with the chopped chives. Use a spoon to scoop out the timbale and serve 1 or 2 quenelles per person, with the extra sauce.

Escoffier Quenelles with Mushroom Sauce

Serves 8 as a first course, 4 as a main course

✂ **A quenelle is an** oval-shaped dumpling that can be made with fish, meat, liver, or poultry. Firm and airy — moist, dense, and light at the same time — these quenelles are made with white fish, heavy cream, and egg white. They are perfect as the main course at a special dinner.

Since it's the albumin in the fish that holds the quenelle mixture together, you need a species that is high in albumin and as fresh as possible. Albumin contracts when cold and, for that reason, all the ingredients should be cold so the mixture stays firm and tight. Whiting has tender, soft flesh, while lemon sole contains plenty of albumin, so the two fish work well together. Any fresh white-fleshed fish can be used in combination, according to availability and one's taste.

The sauce is made with a puree of mushrooms, but other garnishes, like sliced mushrooms, tomatoes, and herbs can be substituted. The quenelles can be served individually or home-style in a gratin dish.

QUENELLES

- 8 ounces skinless lemon sole fillets
- 8 ounces skinless whiting fillets
- 1 large egg white
- 1¼ cups very cold heavy cream
- ½ teaspoon salt
- ½ teaspoon freshly ground white pepper

STOCK

- 1 pound fish bones, rinsed (available at fish markets)
- ½ cup sliced onion
- ½ cup sliced leek (including some green)
- ½ cup sliced celery
- 1 bay leaf
- 1 fresh thyme sprig
- ½ teaspoon freshly ground black pepper
- ½ cup dry white wine
- 3 cups water

SAUCE

- 5 ounces mushrooms, cleaned
- 1½ cups reduced fish stock (from above)
- ½ cup heavy cream
- ½ teaspoon salt
- ⅛ teaspoon freshly ground black pepper
- 1 teaspoon arrowroot or potato starch (see page 318), dissolved in 1 tablespoon water

FOR THE QUENELLES: Chill the bowl of a food processor. Make sure the fish are very cold.

Process the fish and egg white in the food processor until pureed. With the machine on, slowly add the cream in a thin stream, mixing until incorporated. Add the salt and pepper and process for 20 seconds to tighten the mixture.

Transfer to a bowl and chill, covered, in the refrigerator for at least 1 hour.

Bring a large saucepan of water to a boil, then reduce to just a simmer (the water should be at least 2 inches deep). Using a large serving spoon, scoop up some of the quenelle mixture, pressing it against the side of the bowl to smooth the top. (Each quenelle should weigh about 2 ounces, and you should have at least 8.) Place a second serving spoon against the side of the mounded mixture and slide it underneath to lift up the quenelle and shape it further. Scoop up the quenelle with the other spoon again and let it drop into the hot water. Repeat the process to make more quenelles.

The water should remain at about 180 degrees. (If the water boils, the quenelles will cook too fast and expand, which they should not do during this first cooking.) Poach for about 12 minutes, turning them over after 5 to 6 minutes.

When they are cooked, remove the quenelles with a slotted spoon and transfer to a bowl of ice-cold water. When they are cold, after about 30 minutes, drain the quenelles, arrange them on a tray, cover, and refrigerate.

MEANWHILE, FOR THE STOCK: Combine the fish bones, onion, leek, celery, bay leaf, thyme, pepper, white wine, and water in a stainless steel saucepan and bring to a boil, then reduce the heat and boil gently for 20 minutes. Strain the stock through a fine strainer into another saucepan. (You should have approximately 1½ cups.)

Preheat the oven to 350 degrees.

FOR THE SAUCE: Process the mushrooms in the food processor until finely chopped. Add to the fish stock, along with the cream, salt, and pepper, and bring to a boil, then reduce the heat and simmer for 4 to 5 minutes.

Add the dissolved arrowroot or potato starch to the sauce, stir, and bring to a boil again to thicken it.

Arrange the quenelles in a gratin dish and coat with the warm sauce. Bake for 25 to 30 minutes, until puffy and hot; shake the dish after 10 minutes to be sure the quenelles are not sticking to the bottom. Serve immediately.

Smoked Whitefish Molds
Serves 4 as a first course

✻ **This is an ideal** party dish because it can and should be made several hours ahead. The savory mixture of smoked fish and cream cheese is nicely balanced by the crunchiness of the radishes.

In place of the radishes, you can layer cucumbers or other vegetables in the molds; caviar, arranged between the layers of cream cheese, is also a possibility.

Any good market — especially Jewish markets — sells nice, plump whitefish. Be careful when you bone the fish, since it has many small bones. Smoked salmon or another type of smoked fish can be substituted.

4 teaspoons chopped fresh chives
About 6 tablespoons whipped cream cheese
8–10 ounces smoked whitefish or sable
4 large radishes, thinly sliced
⅛ teaspoon freshly ground black pepper
4 slices firm white bread (4 ounces), toasted and cut into triangles

Line four ½-cup molds or custard cups with plastic wrap. Sprinkle 1 teaspoon of the chives over the bottom of each mold and spoon in 2 teaspoons of the cream cheese, pressing on the cheese to embed the chives.

Remove the skin and bones from the fish and divide the flesh into 8 pieces.

Arrange about 3 slices of radish on top of the cheese in each mold and press down again to make the mixture more compact. Place 1 piece of fish on top of each, add another 2 teaspoons cream cheese, and press down. Sprinkle with the pepper and add another layer of fish and a layer of the remaining radishes. Cover with plastic wrap and press on the mixture in each mold to make it more compact. Refrigerate until chilled, or for up to 6 hours.

Unmold onto individual plates, remove the plastic wrap, and serve with the toast triangles.

Steamed Salmon in Nori
Serves 4 to 6 as an hors d'oeuvre

✻ **The dried seaweed sheets** called *nori* inspired this simple dish. I dampen both sides of the nori with water before arranging the pieces of salmon on top. The sheets soften immediately, the salmon is rolled up in them, and the rolls are cut into pieces and steamed.

Dark green or purplish, nori sheets measure about 7 by 8 inches and come in plastic packages. They are available at some supermarkets and health food stores and at most Asian markets.

1 salmon fillet (about 1 pound), skin removed and reserved
  Pinch of salt
3 dried nori sheets

SAUCE

2 tablespoons canola oil
1 teaspoon julienned lemon rind
1½ teaspoons fresh lemon juice
1½ teaspoons balsamic vinegar
¼ teaspoon salt
¼ teaspoon freshly ground black pepper

Preheat the oven to 375 degrees.

Lay the salmon skin on a cookie sheet, flesh side down, salt it lightly, and bake for 30 minutes, or until crisp. Let cool, then break into 1-inch pieces.

Meanwhile, cut the salmon lengthwise into 3 pieces, each about 1¼ inches wide and 7 inches long.

Wet the nori sheets on both sides with water and place them on a work surface. Place a strip of salmon at one end of each sheet and roll it up tightly, enclosing the salmon. Cut each roll in half, then cut each half into thirds. You will have 18 slices in all, enough for 4 slices per person with a couple left over to pass around.

Arrange the pieces on a heatproof plate that fits into a steamer and steam, covered, over boiling water for about 5 minutes, until the salmon is barely cooked; it should still be slightly rare in the center.

MEANWHILE, FOR THE SAUCE: Combine all the ingredients in a small bowl.

Arrange the salmon on a serving plate. Spoon the sauce over the salmon and sprinkle the salmon skin cracklings on top. Serve.

MAKING GOOD CHOICES

It is important to choose fish and shellfish that are not endangered by overfishing. This can be difficult, since the list of good and bad choices changes often and is different from the West to the East Coasts and from the North to the South. Ask your fishmonger for options and consult Internet sites, like the Monterey Bay Aquarium (www.monterey bayaquarium.org) for the latest information on sustainable seafood choices available in different regions.

Cured Salmon on Fennel and Mustard Seed Salad
Serves 4 as a first course

Slices of salmon are quickly cured in a mixture of salt, pepper, and sugar, then served on wafer-thin slices of fennel seasoned with black or yellow mustard seeds. The seeds are available in Asian markets and can be ordered on the Internet.

SALMON

1 center-cut salmon fillet (about 1 pound), skin removed
¾ teaspoon salt
½ teaspoon coarsely ground black pepper
½ teaspoon sugar

SALAD

½ fennel bulb (about 6 ounces), stalks removed, ½ cup of the fuzzy leaves reserved for garnish
1 tablespoon cider vinegar
2 teaspoons peanut oil

1 teaspoon toasted sesame oil

½ teaspoon salt

½ teaspoon mustard seeds (see the
    headnote)

1 tablespoon drained capers

1 tablespoon olive oil (optional)

FOR THE SALMON: Cut the salmon fillet into 12 slices, each about ½ inch thick.

Mix the salt, pepper, and sugar in a small bowl. Lay a sheet of plastic wrap large enough to hold the salmon slices in a single layer on a tray and sprinkle half the seasoning mixture on the plastic. Arrange the slices flat and close together on top of the seasonings and sprinkle the remaining seasoning mixture on top. Cover with another sheet of plastic wrap, enclose the salmon completely in the wrap, and cure in the refrigerator for 1 hour.

MEANWHILE, FOR THE SALAD: Cut the fennel bulb into very thin slices, preferably using either a food processor fitted with the 1-millimeter slicing blade or a vegetable slicer. Put the fennel slices in a bowl, add the vinegar, peanut and sesame oils, salt, and mustard seeds, and mix well. Cover and refrigerate.

At serving time, arrange the salad in a thin layer on a long oval platter or divide it among four plates. Place the cured salmon slices on top and garnish with the capers, reserved fennel leaves, and, if desired, a drizzle of olive oil.

Molasses-Cured Salmon
Serves 8 as a first course

🖈 **Sweet molasses in combination** with dark soy sauce not only gives this cured salmon an intense flavor but also colors the flesh of the fish, turning it almost black on the outside. When you slice it, the inside is a beautifully transparent gold and pink and contrasts dramatically with the exterior.

This recipe is easy to do, but it takes time — the salmon is cured in the sugar, salt, spices, molasses, and soy for 24 hours and set aside to dry for another 24 hours before it is sliced and served. Because so much time is involved, it makes sense to cure a large fillet, so this is a great dish for entertaining. Any leftover salmon will keep for a week under refrigeration. It's nice on salad greens.

1 center-cut salmon fillet (about
    1½ pounds), of even thickness
    throughout, skin removed

¼ cup kosher salt

1 tablespoon sugar

1 teaspoon ground cumin

½ teaspoon ground allspice

½ teaspoon paprika

¼ teaspoon freshly grated nutmeg

¼ teaspoon cayenne pepper

¼ cup dark molasses

2 tablespoons dark soy sauce

Buttered black bread, for serving

GARNISH (optional)

Chopped onion
Drained capers
Extra-virgin olive oil

Place the salmon in the center of a large piece of plastic wrap. Mix the salt, sugar, cumin, allspice, paprika, nutmeg, and cayenne together in a small bowl. Spread the mixture evenly on both sides of the salmon.

Mix the molasses and soy sauce together in a small bowl. Pour half of the molasses mixture over the top of the salmon and spread it evenly over the surface. Turn the salmon over and coat the other side with the remainder of the molasses mixture. Wrap the salmon tightly in the plastic wrap. Put it on a tray and refrigerate for 24 hours.

Unwrap the salmon (it will have absorbed most of the marinade) and discard any remaining marinade. Pat the fish lightly with paper towels and arrange it on a wire rack set over a tray. Refrigerate it for another 24 hours to dry.

At serving time, thinly slice the salmon on a diagonal. Serve 2 or 3 slices per person, with buttered bread. Garnish the salmon, if desired, with chopped onion, capers, and a drizzle of olive oil.

Salmon Fillets in Basil Sauce
Serves 4

❧ **This is one of** those fast, easy, delicious recipes that please even the most discriminating guests. The freshness of the broiled, rich fish marries well with the slight acidity of the warm tomatoes.

- 4 salmon fillets (about 4 ounces each and ½ inch thick), skin removed
- 1 tablespoon olive oil
- ½ teaspoon salt
- 3 tablespoons unsalted butter
- 3 tomatoes, peeled, halved, seeded, and cut into ½-inch dice (2 cups)
- ¼ teaspoon freshly ground black pepper
- 24 medium fresh basil leaves

Preheat the broiler. Brush the fillets on both sides with the olive oil. Sprinkle with ¼ teaspoon of the salt. Arrange on a cookie sheet, ready to go under the broiler.

Melt the butter in a large skillet. When it is hot, add the tomatoes and sauté over medium-high heat for about 1 minute to warm them. Add the remaining ¼ teaspoon salt, the pepper, and basil, and set aside.

Meanwhile, place the fillets under the broiler about 2 inches from the heat source and cook for 1½ minutes: they should still be rare in the center. (There is no need to turn the salmon.)

Arrange some of the tomato-basil mixture on four plates and place the fillets on top. Spoon the remaining tomato-basil mixture on top of the fish and serve.

Crusty Salmon on the Skin
Serves 4

❧ **Seared in a skillet** on the skin side only — first uncovered, then covered — salmon fillets cook all the way through, with the flesh remaining slightly rare. The fat that melts out in the cooking process is discarded and a little butter is browned in the skillet, then a little vinegar is added. This flavorful blend is poured over the fillets, which are served with a garnish of croutons, caper berries, and chives. Caper berries come in brine, like capers, and are available in many supermarkets.

- 1½ tablespoons canola oil
- 2 slices firm white bread, cut into ½-inch croutons (1 cup)
- 4 skin-on salmon fillets (6–7 ounces each)
- ½ teaspoon salt
- ¼ teaspoon freshly ground black pepper
- ¼ cup diced (½-inch) tomato
- 8 caper berries
- 2 teaspoons minced fresh chives
- 2 tablespoons unsalted butter
- 1 tablespoon red wine vinegar

Heat the oil in a large nonstick skillet until it is hot but not smoking. Add the croutons and cook for about 2 minutes, stirring occasionally, until nicely browned on all sides. Transfer to a bowl and set aside.

Sprinkle the salmon on both sides with the salt and pepper and place skin side down in the hot skillet. (No additional fat is required.) Cook, uncovered, for 2 minutes over medium-high heat, then cover and cook for another 2 minutes. (Because the fish is covered, it will create enough steam to cook the fish on top.) Place the fillets skin side up on a warm platter and sprinkle them with the croutons, tomato pieces, caper berries, and chives.

With a paper towel, wipe out any fat that accumulated in the skillet. Add the butter to the pan and cook over medium heat until it is lightly browned. Add the vinegar and shake the pan to mix it in, then pour the mixture over the fish. Serve.

Baked Salmon in Green Herb Sauce
Serves 4

❧ **The sauce for this** dish is best made at the last moment. Before the spinach and herbs are pureed in a blender, they are blanched in the salmon cooking liquid, which contains wine. When fresh from the blender, the sauce is a beautiful dark green, but the color begins to fade after an hour or so (the taste is not affected), because of the acidity in the wine. The salmon is best served lukewarm or at room temperature.

3 shallots, chopped (⅓ cup)
1 cup fruity dry white wine
¾ teaspoon salt
½ teaspoon freshly ground black pepper
1 skinless center-cut salmon fillet (about 1¼ pounds)
1½ cups loosely packed spinach leaves (about 3 ounces), washed and dried

1¼ cups loosely packed fresh herbs (a mixture of chopped chives and parsley and tarragon leaves)
2 tablespoons mayonnaise
Pinch of cayenne pepper
1 tablespoon white wine vinegar
⅓ cup extra-virgin olive oil

Preheat the oven to 350 degrees.

Combine the shallots, wine, half the salt, and the pepper in an ovenproof stainless steel or other nonreactive skillet. Arrange the salmon on top of the shallots and bring the mixture to a boil over high heat.

Place the skillet in the oven and bake the salmon, uncovered, for about 12 minutes, or until it is medium-rare. Remove the salmon from the skillet and place it on a plate.

Add the spinach and herbs to the liquid in the skillet and cook over high heat for about 2 minutes, until the herbs are wilted and soft.

Transfer the mixture to a blender and blend into a smooth puree. Add the mayonnaise, cayenne, vinegar, and the remaining salt and blend for a few seconds. Add the oil and continue processing for about 10 seconds.

Spoon the sauce onto a large platter, arrange the salmon on top, and serve.

Steamed Salmon Patties with Cucumber and Red Pepper Salsa
Serves 4

❧ **Made with chopped salmon**, bread, egg, and mushrooms for moisture and flavor, these steamed patties are exquisitely tender. The cucumber and red pepper salsa balances their mild taste. The patties can also be sautéed in oil in a skillet, but the result is drier and more caloric.

SALSA

½ cucumber
⅓ red bell pepper
2 scallions, trimmed (leaving some green) and minced
1 garlic clove, crushed and finely chopped
⅓ cup water
2 tablespoons rice vinegar
1 teaspoon sugar
½ teaspoon salt
⅛ teaspoon freshly ground black pepper
¼ teaspoon Tabasco sauce

SALMON PATTIES

1 cup chopped onion
3 tablespoons water
1 tablespoon canola oil
1 cup chopped mushrooms
2 slices firm white bread (2 ounces)
1 skinless salmon fillet (about 1 pound)
2 tablespoons coarsely chopped fresh parsley
2 tablespoons chopped fresh chives
½ teaspoon salt
¼ teaspoon freshly ground black pepper

FOR THE SALSA: Peel the cucumber, halve lengthwise, and remove the seeds. Finely chop. (You should have about ½ cup.) Put in a small bowl.

Using a vegetable peeler, remove the skin from the bell pepper. Finely dice the flesh. (You should have ¼ cup.) Add to the cucumbers. Add the scallions, garlic, water, vinegar, sugar, salt, pepper, and Tabasco. Set aside.

FOR THE SALMON PATTIES: Combine the onion, water, and oil in a skillet and bring to a boil. Cook, covered, for 1 minute. Add the mushrooms and cook, uncovered, until most of the moisture has evaporated, about 3 minutes. Let cool.

Put the bread in a food processor and process to make crumbs. (You should have 1 cup.)

Chop the salmon into ¼-inch pieces. Put it in a bowl and add the cooked onion and mushrooms, parsley, chives, salt, and pepper. Mix until well combined. Add the bread crumbs and mix just enough to incorporate. Divide the mixture into 4 equal parts (each about 6 ounces) and form into round or oval patties. (The mixture will be soft; dampen your hands to help in the molding process.) Arrange the patties on a heatproof plate that fits into a steamer.

Steam, covered, over boiling water for 6 to 7 minutes; the patties should still be moist in the center. Serve with the salsa.

Poached Salmon in Ravigote Sauce

Serves 4

Salmon fillets are poached briefly, then served with a *ravigote* sauce. *Ravigoter* means "to invigorate" in French, and this sauce, containing tomatoes, scallions, garlic, parsley, lemon juice, and olive oil, awakens the taste buds and complements the salmon. The pickled capers lend wonderful piquancy to the sauce.

SAUCE

2 plum tomatoes (5 ounces total), halved, seeded, and cut into ¼-inch pieces (¾ cup)
1 tablespoon drained capers
2–3 scallions, trimmed (leaving some green) and chopped (⅓ cup)
⅓ cup chopped onion, rinsed in a sieve and drained

2 garlic cloves, crushed and chopped
   (1 teaspoon)
⅓ cup coarsely chopped fresh parsley
½ teaspoon salt
¼ teaspoon freshly ground black pepper
¼ cup extra-virgin olive oil
1 teaspoon grated lemon rind
2 tablespoons fresh lemon juice

4 skinless salmon fillets (about
   5 ounces each and 1½ inches thick)

FOR THE SAUCE: Mix all the ingredients together in a small bowl. Set aside.

Bring 3 cups of salted water to a boil in a large stainless steel saucepan. Add the salmon to the pan and bring the water back to a boil over high heat (this will take about 2 minutes). Immediately turn off the heat, or slide the pan off the heat if using an electric stove, and let the salmon steep in the hot liquid for 5 minutes. (The salmon will be slightly underdone in the center at this point; adjust the cooking time to accommodate thicker or thinner fillets and to satisfy your personal taste preference.)

Remove the fillets from the liquid with a large spatula or skimmer, drain them well, and place on four warm plates. Sponge up any liquid that collects around the fillets with paper towels, then spoon the sauce over and around the fillets and serve.

Arctic Char in Savory Broth
Serves 4

✁ Arctic char fillets are poached in a flavorful broth containing fennel, leek, carrot, mushrooms, wine, lemon juice, and lemon rind. The broth is enriched at the end with a little butter and oil and the fish is topped with the resulting sauce and gar-nished with a sprinkling of chives. From the cold water of Alaska and similar to salmon but milder, char is buttery and moist. You can substitute it for salmon in most recipes.

Use a vegetable peeler to peel the lemon, taking care to remove only the yellow outer surface of the skin, which contains the essential oils. Then pile the strips of peel together and cut or shred them finely into thin strips to create a julienne. Follow the same stacking and cutting procedures when preparing the leek, carrot, and mushrooms, all of which are julienned, cutting them first into thin strips.

1½ teaspoons julienned lemon rind
1½ tablespoons fresh lemon juice
   About 3 ounces fennel bulb, preferably
      from the tender center, cut into ¼-inch
      pieces (¾ cup)
   About 2 ounces leek (with some
      green), split, washed, and cut
      into julienne strips (1 cup loosely
      packed)
1 small carrot, peeled and cut into julienne
   strips (1 cup loosely packed)
2 large mushrooms (2 ounces), cleaned
   and cut into julienne strips (1 cup
   loosely packed)
½ cup dry white wine
½ cup water
¾ teaspoon salt
¼ teaspoon freshly ground black pepper
4 skinless Arctic char fillets (about 6
   ounces each)
1 tablespoon unsalted butter
2 tablespoons olive oil
1 tablespoon minced fresh chives

Put the lemon rind, lemon juice, fennel, leek, carrot, mushrooms, wine, water, salt, and pepper in a large stainless steel saucepan and bring to a boil over medium-high heat, then cover and cook for 3 minutes.

Add the char fillets to the saucepan in one layer and cook, covered, over medium heat for 3 minutes, or until cooked but still very rare in the center.

Lift the fillets one at a time from the saucepan and arrange on four plates. Using a slotted spoon, lift out the vegetables and divide them among the plates, arranging them on top of and around the char.

Add the butter and oil to the juices remaining in the saucepan and bring to a strong boil. Boil for about 10 seconds. Pour the sauce over the fish, sprinkle the chives on top, and serve.

Grilled Salmon
Serves 4

✍ **Grilling is one of** the best ways to cook salmon. The success of this dish depends on using fillets with the skin left on. The fillets are grilled only on the skin side, which makes the skin appealingly crisp; the skin, in turn, protects the flesh, keeping it moist. I cook the salmon for only a few minutes, until slightly rare.

Ask your fish market to scale the skin if necessary, or do it yourself.

You can also cook the salmon in a skillet: Heat a sturdy cast-iron or other heavy skillet over high heat for 2 to 3 minutes. Add the salmon fil-

lets skin side down and cook, covered, for about 3 minutes (slightly longer or less, as you prefer, depending on the thickness of your fillets). Let stand, covered, for 2 to 3 minutes and serve when the salmon is still slightly pink inside.

4 skin-on salmon fillets (6–7 ounces each and about 1 inch thick)
¼ teaspoon salt
1 teaspoon corn or canola oil
1 4- to 6-inch piece daikon radish

Heat a grill until very hot. Preheat the oven to 180 degrees.

Sprinkle the flesh side of the salmon fillets with the salt and rub the skin side with the oil.

Place the salmon skin side down on the clean hot grill rack, cover with the lid, and cook for about 2 minutes for slightly rare. (Decrease or increase the cooking time based on the thickness of your fillets and your taste preferences.)

Arrange the salmon skin side up on an oven-proof platter and place in the oven for a few minutes, while you prepare the daikon. The salmon will continue to cook in its own residual heat.

With a vegetable peeler, peel the daikon radish. Cut it into strips, stack the strips, and cut them into fine julienne strips.

Serve the salmon on the platter or arrange skin side up on individual plates. Sprinkle the julienne of radish on top and serve.

Tuna Tartare on Marinated Cucumbers
Serves 4 as a first course

✍ **Delicious and attractive, this** simple but sophisticated dish makes a great first course. The tartare is served on fresh-tasting mixture of strips of cucumber, vinegar, sugar, peanut oil, and salt.

The tuna is better chopped by hand rather than in a food processor.

> About 1 pound tuna steaks, preferably
>   center-cut bluefin tuna
> Salt
> 1 large shallot, finely chopped
>   (2 tablespoons)
> 2 garlic cloves, crushed and finely chopped
>   (1 teaspoon)
> ½ teaspoon freshly ground black pepper
> 2 tablespoons olive oil
> 1½ teaspoons white vinegar
> ¼ teaspoon Tabasco sauce

CUCUMBERS

> 1 cucumber (about 12 ounces)
> 1 teaspoon red wine vinegar
> ½ teaspoon sugar
> 1 teaspoon peanut oil
> ¼ teaspoon salt
>
> 3 tablespoons minced fresh chives
> 1½ teaspoons drained capers
>   About 2 tablespoons extra-virgin
>   olive oil

Cut 4 small slices (1 ounce each) from the tuna and reserve. Cut the remainder into ¼-inch dice.

Place 1 tuna slice between two sheets of plastic wrap and pound it into a thin slice about 4 inches in diameter. Repeat with the other 3 slices. Remove the top sheets of plastic wrap from the slices and season them lightly on both sides with salt. Set aside.

Mix the chopped tuna, shallot, garlic, 1 teaspoon salt, the pepper, oil, vinegar, and Tabasco in a bowl. (Mixed with vinegar, the chopped tuna will whiten somewhat, becoming opaque. This is because the acetic acid in the vinegar coagulates, thus "cooking" the protein in the tuna.)

FOR THE CUCUMBERS: Peel the cucumber.

With a vegetable peeler, cut long, thin strips from it on all sides until you come to the seeds. Discard the seedy center and mix the strips with the vinegar, sugar, oil, and salt.

To serve, divide the cucumbers among four plates. Form the tuna tartare into 4 balls and place 1 on top of the cucumbers on each plate. Wrap a slice of tuna around each tuna ball, sprinkle with the chives and capers, and drizzle with the olive oil.

Tuna Steaks with Peppercorns
Serves 4

Thick tuna steaks, served rare, remain wonderfully moist in this takeoff on steak au poivre. The amount of pepper can be adjusted to accommodate your taste preferences, although the cracked pepper here is milder than you might imagine.

I use a mixture of four different peppercorns: mild brown-speckled Szechuan peppercorns; black peppercorns; white peppercorns, which are the same berry as black but with the skin removed; and Jamaican peppercorns — better known as allspice. One or another of these varieties can be omitted if not available.

> 1 teaspoon Szechuan peppercorns
> ½ teaspoon white peppercorns
> ½ teaspoon black peppercorns
> 1 teaspoon allspice berries
> 4 bluefin or yellowfin tuna steaks (about
>   6 ounces each and 1 inch thick)
> 1 tablespoon corn oil
> ½ teaspoon salt
> 3 tablespoons unsalted butter, softened

Crush the peppercorns and allspice with a meat pounder or the bottom of a saucepan. Brush both sides of the steaks with the oil and sprinkle both sides with the salt and crushed pepper.

Heat a large cast-iron skillet for 3 to 4 minutes, until very hot. Place the steaks in the pan and cook over very high heat for about 1½ minutes on each side. Cover the pan, remove from the heat, and let stand for 3 to 5 minutes before serving. The steaks will continue to cook in their own residual heat but should remain pink inside.

Serve with the softened butter on top and any juices that have come out of the tuna.

Tuna Steaks
with Tapenade Coating
Serves 4

✻ **Small but fairly thick** tuna steaks are covered with tapenade, made from a mixture of different types of olives, capers, anchovy fillets, and garlic. For maximum flavor transfer, I cook the steaks tapenade side down over high heat to start. This recipe is excellent prepared with tuna, but it's good, too, with other fish that will hold their shape when sautéed, such as black sea bass or salmon.

TAPENADE

¼	cup pitted kalamata olives
¼	cup oil-cured black olives
2	tablespoons drained capers
3	anchovy fillets
1	large garlic clove
1	tablespoon olive oil

4	center-cut yellowfin tuna steaks (about 4 ounces each and 1 inch thick), trimmed of all sinew
1	tablespoon olive oil
½	teaspoon salt
	Freshly ground black pepper
1	cup arugula leaves, washed and dried

FOR THE TAPENADE: Put all the ingredients in a small food processor and process until finely chopped but not pureed.

Cover the top of each tuna steak with 2 tablespoons of the tapenade mixture, patting it firmly over the surface of the steak.

Preheat the oven to 160 degrees.

Heat the oil in a large skillet until hot. Place the steaks tapenade side down in the hot skillet and sprinkle them with the salt and pepper to taste. Cover and cook over high heat for about 1½ minutes. Turn the steaks over, cover, and cook for another 1½ minutes over medium-high heat.

Transfer the steaks to an ovenproof platter and let them finish cooking in the oven for 5 to 10 minutes. (*The steaks can be left in the oven for up to 30 minutes.*)

Serve the steaks whole or sliced, surrounded by the arugula leaves.

Grilled Tuna with Sage Butter
Serves 4

✻ **Briefly grilled, tuna picks** up a roasted taste from the hot grill. Then it finishes cooking in its own juices in a low oven so it does not become dry.

The sage butter is a good complement, and the sea beans, available in specialty stores or along the shore in some parts of the country, are a nice addition. If they are not available, serve the tuna with haricots verts or thin string beans.

Also called glasswort or saltwort, sea beans grow in abundance along the coast of New England. Only young, very tender shoots should be picked. They can be eaten in salads, steamed, boiled, or sautéed. Sometimes sea beans have a central stalk that is fibrous and leathery. Young sprouts, which do not have this stalk, are tender. They do tend to be salty, however, and I soak them in water for a few hours before cooking them in a large quantity of unsalted water.

4 tuna steaks (5–6 ounces each and about 1 inch thick)
¼ teaspoon salt
⅛ teaspoon freshly ground black pepper
1 tablespoon olive oil

SEA BEANS (see the headnote)

3–4 cups young sea beans, soaked in cool water for 2 hours to remove some of the natural salt
1½ cups peeled, seeded, and diced cucumber
2 tablespoons unsalted butter
Pinch of freshly ground black pepper

SAGE BUTTER

6 large fresh sage leaves
⅓ stick (2⅔ tablespoons) unsalted butter, softened
1 teaspoon fresh lemon juice
⅛ teaspoon salt
⅛ teaspoon freshly ground black pepper

Heat a grill until very hot. Make sure the grill grate is very clean.

Preheat the oven to 160 degrees.

Sprinkle the tuna steaks with the salt, pepper, and olive oil. When the grill is red hot, arrange the fish steaks in the center and close the grill. Grill the tuna for 1½ minutes on the first side, then turn and cook for 1½ minutes on the other side. The steaks won't be quite cooked. Transfer the tuna steaks to a warm platter, cover, and set in the oven to continue to cook in their own heat and juice for 5 to 10 minutes.

MEANWHILE, FOR THE SEA BEANS: Bring 3 quarts of water to a strong boil in a large saucepan. Add the sea beans, bring back to a boil, and boil, uncovered, for 1 to 2 minutes. Drain the beans and immediately transfer to ice water to cool and stop the cooking.

Bring 2 cups water to a boil in a small saucepan and add the cucumber. Return the water to a boil and immediately drain the cucumber. Return the cucumber to the pan, add the butter, sea beans, and pepper, and warm on top of the stove just enough to heat through.

FOR THE SAGE BUTTER: Chop the sage leaves very fine and combine with the soft butter, lemon juice, salt, and pepper, mixing well.

At serving time, divide the sea bean–cucumber mixture among four plates. Slice the tuna steaks and arrange a sliced steak, with its juices, in the center of each plate. Top with approximately 2 teaspoons of sage butter and serve.

Roast Monkfish in Ratatouille
Serves 6

✃ **Monkfish is available in** most markets. The enormous head of the fish is about three times the weight of its body, and the edible part is the tail, consisting of two fillets alongside the central backbone. The white, very firm flesh can be broiled, stewed, or baked, or the whole tail can be roasted, as in this recipe. The flesh is studded with slivers of garlic, like a leg of lamb, and roasted in the same manner. Ratatouille is a great accompaniment.

RATATOUILLE

- 2 tablespoons olive oil
- 2 cups diced (½-inch) onions
- 3 cups diced (1-inch) zucchini (1 pound)
- 3 cups diced (1-inch) eggplant (skin on)
- 1 large green bell pepper, cored, seeded, and cut into ½-inch dice (about 1 cup)
- 3 cups quartered plum tomatoes
- 1 teaspoon fresh oregano leaves
- 1 tablespoon finely chopped garlic (6–7 cloves)
- 1 teaspoon salt
- ½ teaspoon freshly ground black pepper
- 1 teaspoon grated lemon rind
- 1 teaspoon grated orange rind

- 1 cleaned whole monkfish tail (skin and yellow fat removed; about 3 pounds)
- 3 garlic cloves, each cut into 3 slivers
- ¼ teaspoon salt
- ¼ teaspoon freshly ground black pepper
- 2 tablespoons unsalted butter

- ¼ cup chopped fresh parsley

Preheat the oven to 400 degrees.

FOR THE RATATOUILLE: Heat the oil in a large Dutch oven. When it is hot, add the onions and sauté for 2 minutes. Add all the remaining ingredients except the lemon and orange rind and bring to a boil. Cover and cook for 15 minutes. Uncover and cook for another 10 minutes to evaporate most of the liquid.

Meanwhile, cut 9 randomly spaced incisions in the fish. Stud it with the garlic slivers and sprinkle with the salt and pepper.

Heat the butter in a large gratin dish or ovenproof skillet. When it is hot, add the fish and brown it all over on medium heat, turning occasionally, 2 to 4 minutes.

Transfer to the oven and roast for 20 minutes, basting the fish with the pan juices after 10 minutes.

When the ratatouille is cooked, add the lemon and orange rind and spoon the mixture around the fish. Sprinkle with the parsley. Cut the fish into ½-inch-thick slices and serve with the ratatouille.

Monkfish à l'Américaine
Serves 4

✎ **This is a classic** way to cook monkfish, and the one that I remember from childhood. Because the fish absorbs flavors well and withstands long cooking, it is excellent simmered in this stew, which is flavored with cognac, herbes de Provence, cayenne, fennel seeds, and tarragon. The stew can be made ahead and reheated. Serve it with rice.

- About 2 pounds cleaned monkfish, preferably large fillets
- 2 tablespoons olive oil
- 1 onion, cut into ½-inch pieces (1 cup)
- 1 carrot, peeled and cut into ½-inch pieces (½ cup)
- 1 small leek, trimmed (leaving some green), split, washed, and cut into ½-inch pieces (1 cup)
- 1 celery stalk (2 ounces), cut into ½-inch pieces (⅓ cup)
- 1 large tomato, cut into ½-inch pieces (1¼ cups)
- 2 tablespoons tomato paste
- 3 garlic cloves
- 1 teaspoon herbes de Provence
- 1½ teaspoons salt
- ⅛ teaspoon cayenne pepper
- ½ teaspoon fennel seeds

½ cup fruity dry white wine

1 tablespoon cognac or Armagnac

1 cup water

1 tablespoon unsalted butter

1 tablespoon chopped fresh tarragon

Cut the monkfish into 12 large pieces.

Heat the oil in a large heavy saucepan until hot but not smoking. Add the onion, carrot, leek, and celery and cook over medium-low heat for 5 minutes. Add the tomato, tomato paste, garlic, herbes de Provence, salt, cayenne, fennel seeds, wine, cognac or Armagnac, and water, bring to a boil, and cook over medium heat for 5 minutes.

Add the fish, cover, and simmer gently over low heat for 15 minutes.

Remove the pieces of fish from the saucepan and set aside on a platter. Add the butter to the mixture in the pan and, using a hand blender, emulsify the vegetables into a fine puree. (Alternatively, transfer the mixture to a conventional blender and process, then return to the pan.) You can also leave the sauce chunky.

Add the fish to the sauce, sprinkle with the tarragon, and bring to a boil. Serve.

Monkfish Roulade with Broccoli Rabe Stuffing and Tarragon Tomato Sauce

Serves 4

✄ **A large monkfish fillet** is butterflied, rolled up around a stuffing of broccoli rabe that has been sautéed with mushrooms and garlic, and cooked on top of the stove. The roulade is served with a tarragon and tomato sauce.

STUFFING

10 ounces broccoli rabe

1½ teaspoons olive oil

2 garlic cloves, crushed and finely chopped (1½ teaspoons)

4 ounces mushrooms, cleaned and finely chopped by hand or in a food processor (1½ cups)

¼ teaspoon salt

¼ teaspoon freshly ground black pepper

1 cleaned large monkfish fillet (about 1 pound, 2 ounces)

1 tablespoon olive oil

1 tablespoon unsalted butter

¼ teaspoon salt

SAUCE

3 tablespoons dry white wine

1–2 ripe tomatoes (7 ounces), peeled, halved, seeded, and cut into ½-inch pieces (1 cup)

¼ teaspoon salt

¼ teaspoon freshly ground black pepper

1 tablespoon chopped fresh tarragon

FOR THE STUFFING: Peel the fibrous outer layer of skin from the stems of the broccoli rabe; cut off and discard the bottoms of the stems if they are tough. Wash the broccoli rabe well and cut into ½-inch pieces.

Heat the oil in a large heavy skillet. When it is hot, add the garlic and sauté for 5 seconds, then add the broccoli, still wet from washing, along with the mushrooms, salt, and pepper. Mix well, cover, and cook over medium heat for 5 minutes. The broccoli should be tender and the moisture gone from the pan. If any liquid remains, cook, uncovered, until the liquid has evaporated. Let cool to room temperature.

Place the monkfish fillet on a work surface and, using a long, thin, sharp knife held horizontally to the fish, starting from a long side, cut through it, stopping about 1 inch from the opposite side, so

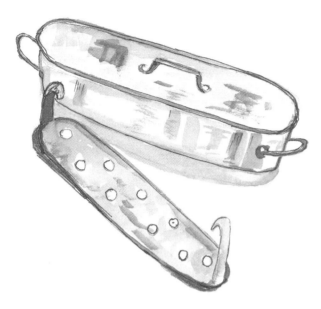

Poached Swordfish with Lemon-Parsley Sauce

Serves 4 as a first course

✳ **Because I like swordfish** slightly undercooked so it stays moist, I poach it only briefly, then serve it in a refreshing lemon-parsley sauce. If you want to serve the swordfish as a main course for 4, double the sauce ingredients and use four 7- to 8-ounce steaks.

SAUCE

- 1½ tablespoons fresh lemon juice
- 3 tablespoons extra-virgin olive oil
- 1½ tablespoons hot water
- ⅓ teaspoon salt
- ¼ teaspoon freshly ground black pepper
- ¼ cup chopped fresh parsley

- 4 swordfish steaks (about 4 ounces each and 1¼ inches thick), preferably center-cut

it can be opened like a book. Butterflying will create a ½-inch-thick rectangle about 7 inches by 9 inches. One side of the fillet will be whiter than the other; place it white side down on a work surface. Spread the cooled stuffing mixture on top. Starting from a long side, roll up the monkfish to encase the filling and tie it securely with kitchen twine. The finished roulade should be about 2½ inches in diameter. (*The roulade can be prepared up to 24 hours ahead, covered, and refrigerated.*)

Heat the oil and butter in a deep skillet. Sprinkle the roulade with the salt and brown it on the smooth (unseamed) side over high heat for about 1 minute. Turn the roulade over, cover, reduce the heat to medium, and cook for about 15 minutes, or until the fish is tender when pierced with a fork. Transfer the roulade to a platter.

FOR THE SAUCE: Add the wine to the drippings in the skillet and boil for 1 minute. Add the tomatoes, salt, and pepper and boil for another minute. Stir in the tarragon.

To serve, remove the twine from the monkfish and cut the roulade into 8 slices, each about ¾ inch thick. Divide the sauce among four plates, arrange 2 slices of the roulade on top, and serve immediately.

FOR THE SAUCE: Mix all the ingredients together thoroughly in a small bowl. (*The sauce can be made up to 30 minutes ahead and set aside; if preparing the sauce further ahead, wait to add the parsley until just before serving, or the lemon juice will tend to yellow it.*)

At serving time, bring 6 cups water to a boil in a large saucepan. Holding the fish steaks with a slotted spoon or skimmer, lower them individually into the pan. Bring the water back to a boil, then reduce the heat to very low and poach the fish at a very light boil for about 3 minutes, until barely cooked through.

Using the slotted spoon or skimmer, lift the fish from the water, drain thoroughly, and arrange on four plates. Spoon the sauce over the fish and serve.

Grilled Swordfish with Spicy Yogurt Sauce
Serves 4

✺ **Before grilling the swordfish** steaks, I rub them lightly with oil and coat them with herbes de Provence. The steaks are served with a piquant yogurt sauce that can also accompany other grilled or poached fish, as well as grilled poultry.

Grilling the steaks for 4 to 5 minutes gives them the distinctive surface markings and taste of grilled meat without drying them out. Finished in a warm oven, they emerge tender, juicy, and flavorful.

4 swordfish steaks (5–6 ounces each and about 1 inch thick), preferably center-cut
½ teaspoon canola oil
1 teaspoon herbes de Provence
½ teaspoon salt

SAUCE

⅓ cup loosely packed fresh cilantro leaves
¼ cup loosely packed fresh mint leaves
2 small garlic cloves
1 piece ginger (about the size of the 2 garlic cloves), peeled
1 small jalapeño pepper
½ teaspoon salt
1 cup plain Greek-style yogurt

Rub the steaks on both sides with the oil and sprinkle with the herbes de Provence and salt. Arrange the steaks on a plate, cover them with plastic wrap, and refrigerate until ready to cook.

FOR THE SAUCE: Put all the ingredients except the yogurt in a blender or mini-chop and process until finely chopped. Add the yogurt and process until smooth. Set aside, covered.

Heat a grill until very hot. Preheat the oven to 180 degrees.

Place the steaks on the clean hot grill rack and cook for about 2 minutes on each side, until lightly browned. Transfer the steaks to a tray and place them in the oven for 10 minutes to finish cooking.

Spoon enough sauce onto four plates to coat the bottom of each, place a steak in the center of each plate, and serve, passing the extra sauce on the side.

Catfish Goujonnettes
Serves 6 as a first course, 3 to 4 as a main course

✺ **With its firm white** flesh, catfish lends itself to a variety of preparations, from broiling and poaching to grilling. This fish is ideal for *goujonnettes*, since it holds its shape well, and the taste is nutty and flavorful. *Goujonnettes*, from the French word for "gudgeon," a little freshwater fish usually fried whole, can be prepared with any type of fish fillets by cutting them into little strips and sautéing the strips briefly to make them crisp. In this recipe, the *goujonnettes* are tossed with sautéed potato sticks and artichoke hearts — a delightful combination. Farmed catfish is widely available in markets.

1 pound baking (Idaho) potatoes (2)
4 medium artichokes (about 1½ pounds), trimmed to artichoke hearts (see page 404)
1 tablespoon fresh lemon juice
About 1½ pounds catfish fillets, skin and excess underlying white fatty tissue removed if necessary
¼ cup peanut oil
2 tablespoons unsalted butter

(see page 404)

FISH SEASONINGS

¼ teaspoon salt
¼ teaspoon freshly ground black pepper
⅛ teaspoon cayenne pepper
1 teaspoon paprika
¼ teaspoon dried thyme
½ cup all-purpose flour

TO FINISH

1 large garlic clove, finely chopped (½ teaspoon)
2 tablespoons unsalted butter
Salt (optional)
6–8 fresh sage leaves, stacked together and cut crosswise into ¾-inch-wide strips
1 teaspoon fresh lemon juice

Peel the potatoes and cut them into 1½- to 2-inch long sticks about ½ inch thick. Set aside in water to cover.

Use a teaspoon to scrape out the choke from the artichoke hearts and cut the hearts into slices about ⅜ inch thick. Drop the sliced artichokes into a bowl of water with the lemon juice to prevent discoloration.

Cut the fish into strips about ½ inch wide and 2½ inches long.

Heat 2 tablespoons of the oil and 1 tablespoon of the butter in a large skillet until hot.

Add the potatoes and sauté for about 5 minutes over high heat, until they start browning. Drain the artichoke slices and pat dry, then add to the pan and cook for another 8 minutes.

MEANWHILE, TO SEASON THE FISH: Combine all the seasonings in a plastic bag. Add the fish and shake to coat all the pieces with the mixture, then dump into a colander and shake to remove the excess flour.

Heat the remaining 2 tablespoons oil and tablespoon of butter in a very large skillet, preferably nonstick, until hot. Add the pieces of fish in one layer and sauté for about 5 minutes over very high heat, turning occasionally, until nicely browned all around.

TO FINISH THE DISH: Add the fish to the potato-artichoke mixture, then add the garlic, butter, and salt if needed and toss together.

Arrange on a large platter, sprinkle with the sage and lemon juice, and serve.

Catfish with Croutons and Nuts
Serves 6

✖ **Croutons and nuts add** texture and taste to these sautéed catfish fillets. A few drops of vinegar added at serving time cut the richness. The skin will usually have been removed from the fillets, but if any fatty tissue remains, cut away as much of it as possible, holding your knife almost horizontal to the fish. Particularly evident on larger catfish, the fat tends to have a strong flavor.

3 tablespoons canola or sunflower oil
About 2 ounces baguette, cut into ½-inch cubes (about 1½ cups)
½ cup walnut pieces (or other nuts, such as pecans)

2 tablespoons unsalted butter

2 tablespoons olive oil

6 catfish fillets (6–8 ounces each), skin and excess underlying fatty tissue removed if necessary

½ teaspoon salt

½ teaspoon freshly ground black pepper

4 garlic cloves, crushed and finely chopped (about 1 tablespoon)

¼ cup chopped fresh chives or parsley

¼ cup water

Red wine vinegar (optional)

Heat the canola or sunflower oil in a large skillet. When it is hot, add the bread cubes and nuts and sauté for about 4 minutes, until nicely browned on all sides. Transfer to a plate.

Heat the butter and olive oil in the same skillet until hot. Sprinkle the fish fillets on both sides with the salt and pepper, arrange them in one layer in the skillet, and cook for 1½ minutes on each side, or until just cooked in the center.

Arrange the catfish on a platter or on individual plates. Add the garlic and chives or parsley to the drippings in the skillet and cook for about 15 seconds. Add the water and stir to dissolve all the solidified bits in the bottom of the pan.

Pour the pan sauce over the fish, spoon on the croutons and nuts, and serve, sprinkling the fish, if desired, with a few drops of red wine vinegar.

Halibut Antibes-Style
Serves 4

✒ **Served with a fresh** olive and tomato sauce, this halibut is prepared in the style of Antibes on the French Riviera. The sauce can be made ahead. If you can't get halibut, substitute cod or striped bass.

2 tablespoons olive oil

½ cup chopped onion

1 teaspoon chopped fresh thyme

2 tomatoes (12 ounces), peeled, halved, seeded, and cut into ½-inch pieces (1½ cups)

¼ cup water

½ teaspoon salt

¼ teaspoon freshly ground black pepper

24 kalamata olives, pitted and cut into ½-inch pieces (½ cup)

2 tablespoons shredded fresh basil leaves

4 halibut steaks (about 7 ounces), cleaned of sinew

½ teaspoon salt

1 teaspoon olive oil

FOR THE SAUCE: Heat the olive oil in a medium skillet until hot. Add the onion and thyme and cook over medium heat for 1½ minutes. Add the tomatoes, water, salt, and pepper and cook for 1 minute longer, then set the pan aside.

Preheat the broiler. Sprinkle both sides of the halibut steaks with the salt and brush them with the olive oil. Arrange the steaks on a cookie sheet (lined, if desired, with aluminum foil), set under the hot broiler so the steaks are about 4 inches from the heat, and cook for 2 minutes on each side.

Arrange a steak on each of four dinner plates. Add the olives and basil to the sauce and bring to a boil. Pour the sauce over the steaks and serve.

Halibut Steaks Grenoble-Style
Serves 4

✄ **Sautéed halibut sprinkled with** a garnish of croutons, lemon, and capers and some brown butter is simple and tasty. The garnish is also excellent with other fish, from trout and sole to cod and catfish.

¼ cup olive oil
2 slices firm white bread, crusts trimmed and cut into ¾-inch cubes (about 1 cup)
1 large lemon
1 teaspoon salt
½ teaspoon freshly ground black pepper
4 halibut steaks (about 6 ounces each and ¾–1 inch thick)
¼ cup all-purpose flour
8 tablespoons (1 stick) unsalted butter
3 tablespoons drained capers
2 tablespoons chopped fresh parsley

Heat 2 tablespoons of the oil in a large skillet until hot. Add the bread cubes and cook, turning them with a spoon, until uniformly browned on all sides. Drain in a sieve and set aside.

Using a sharp knife, remove the rind and white pith from the lemon. Cut the flesh into ½-inch cubes, removing the seeds as you go. (You should have about ⅓ cup.)

Sprinkle the salt and pepper on both sides of the fish and dip the steaks in the flour to coat on all sides; shake off any excess flour.

Heat 3 tablespoons of the butter and the remaining 2 tablespoons oil in a large heavy skillet. When the mixture is foaming, add the fish and cook over medium heat for about 3 minutes. With a wide spatula, turn the fish and cook for another 3 minutes, or until browned and crusty on both sides.

Arrange the fish on a serving platter with the nicest side showing. Sprinkle the croutons, lemon, and capers on top and set in a warm place (such as a 150-degree oven).

Melt the remaining 5 tablespoons butter in a skillet and cook until it takes on a hazelnut color. Pour the hot butter on top of the fish, sprinkle with the parsley, and serve.

Black Sea Bass Gravlax
Serves 12 as a first course

✄ **Made with salmon, a** fatty fish, gravlax is moist and rich, but it can also be made with very firm, thinner, white-fleshed fish such as black sea bass. I sometimes catch sea bass in summer in Long Island Sound and my fishmonger carries it regularly too. It is a great favorite in Chinese restaurants and its white, firm flesh is one of the best. Black cod, also called sablefish, is a good substitute.

It is imperative to use the freshest possible fish for gravlax.

1½ tablespoons sugar
2½ tablespoons kosher salt
4 skinless black sea bass fillets (5–6 ounces each)

FLAVORING

1 tablespoon gin
½ teaspoon freshly ground black pepper
2 teaspoons grated lime rind
3 tablespoons chopped fresh parsley
1 tablespoon chopped fresh dill
2 teaspoons chopped fresh mint

GARNISH

2 cucumbers, peeled, halved lengthwise, seeded, and cut into ¼-inch dice
4 hard-cooked eggs (see page 66), coarsely chopped

1   8-ounce container sour cream

¼   teaspoon salt

¼   teaspoon freshly ground black pepper

12   large slices rye or other bread, crusts
       removed and cut into ovals

Fresh parsley, mint, or dill sprigs,
   for garnish

Mix the sugar and salt together. Lay the fillets on a piece of plastic wrap placed on top of a piece of aluminum foil. Sprinkle the salt and sugar mixture over both sides of the fillets and pat it all over them. Wrap in the plastic wrap and aluminum foil and refrigerate on a tray for 5 to 6 hours to cure. When cured, the fillets will have absorbed most of the sugar-salt mixture and be firm.

FOR THE FLAVORING: Pat the fish dry with a paper towel. Rub the fillets with the gin. Mix the pepper, lime rind, parsley, dill, and mint together and pat this over the fillets. Wrap again and refrigerate, with a 3- or 4-pound weight on top to press the fish down and make the flesh more compact, for at least 3 hours, or for as long as overnight.

At serving time, remove the wrappings and place the fillets on a cutting board. Using a long thin knife, cut the fillets on the bias into thin slices 2 to 3 inches long. Each of the slices should be bordered with a thin layer of the green flavoring.

FOR THE GARNISH: Mix together the cucumbers, hard-cooked eggs, sour cream, salt, and pepper.

Toast the 12 bread ovals until nicely browned. Cover each slice with approximately ⅓ cup of the cucumber-egg mixture and top with 3 or 4 slices of cured fish. The fillets should be arranged on the bread so the green border on the fish remains on the outside, forming a design.

Arrange the toasts on a platter. Place a sprig of parsley, mint, or dill in the center of each and serve.

Broiled Striped Bass with Broccoli Rabe and Anchovies
Serves 4

Striped bass is one of the best fish found on the East Coast and is widely available wild (better) or farmed. Here it is served on a bed of broccoli rabe that has been sautéed with sliced garlic and potatoes. The saltiness and intense flavor of the anchovies accentuate the richness.

8   ounces small Yukon Gold or red
       potatoes, washed

10   ounces broccoli rabe

1   2-ounce can anchovy fillets in oil

4   black olives

4   small cherry tomatoes

4   skin-on striped bass fillets (about
       7 ounces each and ¾ inch thick)

1   teaspoon salt

2   tablespoons olive oil

2   tablespoons sliced garlic (about 5 large
       cloves)

½   teaspoon freshly ground black pepper

Put the potatoes in a medium saucepan, add water to cover, and bring to a boil. Reduce the heat to low, cover, and boil gently for 25 to 30 minutes, until the potatoes are tender. Drain.

When the potatoes are cool enough to handle, peel them and cut into ½-inch-thick slices. Set aside in a bowl.

Cut off the stems of the broccoli rabe and, using a small sharp knife, peel them to remove their fibrous outer skin. Cut the stems into 2-inch pieces and cut the leaves into 1-inch pieces. Wash the leaves in cold water and drain in a colander.

Combine the leaves and stems in a bowl and set aside.

Pour the oil from the anchovies into a small bowl and reserve it. Wrap an anchovy fillet around each of the black olives and cherry tomatoes. Set aside for use as garnish.

Score the striped bass fillets by cutting 4 diagonal slits, about ¼ inch deep, through the skin on each fillet. Using about ¼ teaspoon of the salt, sprinkle the fillets on both sides. Then coat them, again on both sides, with the reserved anchovy oil. Arrange the fillets skin side up on a cookie sheet lined with aluminum foil. (*The fish can be prepared to this point a few hours ahead and refrigerated.*)

Preheat the broiler. Heat the olive oil in a large heavy skillet. When it is hot, sauté the garlic for about 1 minute, until it is blond in color. Add the broccoli rabe stems and leaves, ⅓ cup water, the remaining ¾ teaspoon salt, and the pepper. Mix thoroughly, cover, and cook over high heat for 3 to 5 minutes, until the broccoli rabe is tender and the water has evaporated. Add the cooked potato slices, cover, and set the pan aside while you cook the fish. (The heat in the pan will warm the potatoes.)

Place the cookie sheet of fish fillets under the broiler so the fish are about 4 inches from the heat and broil for about 5 minutes. The heat will penetrate and cook the fish through the slits in the skin, and the skin will get brown and crunchy.

Divide the broccoli rabe and potatoes among four plates and place a fillet of fish on top of the

vegetables on each plate. Arrange an anchovy-wrapped olive and tomato on top of each fillet and serve.

Cold Striped Bass with Mixed Vegetable Salad
Serves 8 to 10

❧ **A fresh vegetable salad** is bound with mayonnaise and enveloped in poached fish fillets, then the whole dish is covered with more mayonnaise and decorated with basil. This is an ideal dish for a large party and it makes a nice presentation for a buffet.

4 skinless striped bass fillets (10–12 ounces each)
1 teaspoon salt
1 teaspoon freshly ground black pepper
2 tablespoons unsalted butter
1 cup finely chopped onion
1 cup dry white wine

MAYONNAISE

3 large egg yolks
1 teaspoon salt
¼ teaspoon freshly ground black pepper
3 tablespoons Dijon or Düsseldorf mustard
2 cups oil, preferably a mix of peanut and olive oil

SALAD

1 pound small red potatoes, washed
1½ cups diced (½-inch) celery
2 cups frozen baby peas
1½ cups diced (½-inch) carrots
1½ cups diced (½-inch) small white turnips
¾ cup finely chopped onion
¼ cup finely chopped fresh parsley
Salt

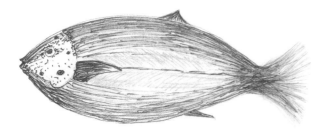

Freshly ground black pepper

2 tablespoons finely chopped fresh basil

Preheat the oven to 400 degrees.

Sprinkle the fillets with the salt and pepper. Butter the bottom of a large flameproof baking dish with the 2 tablespoons butter. Scatter the onion over the bottom of the dish. Arrange the fish fillets on top and sprinkle with the wine. Cut a piece of parchment or waxed paper to fit the dish, butter it, and cover the fish with it.

Put the dish over high heat and bring to a boil, then set on a cookie sheet and bake for 10 minutes. Transfer the fish to a plate and refrigerate. Strain the cooking liquid into a saucepan and boil to reduce to about 3 tablespoons. Let cool.

FOR THE MAYONNAISE: Put the yolks in a bowl and add the salt, pepper, mustard, and reduced cooking liquid. Gradually add the oil, beating with a wire whisk or an electric mixer until thickened. Refrigerate.

FOR THE SALAD: Boil the potatoes in salted water until tender, about 30 minutes. Drain and let cool.

Meanwhile, cover the celery, peas, carrots, and turnips with water in a saucepan, bring to a boil, and boil for 5 minutes; drain.

Peel the potatoes and cut them into ½-inch cubes. (You should have about 3 cups.)

Combine the potatoes, cooked vegetables, onion, and parsley in a large bowl. Add half the mayonnaise, the salt, and pepper to taste. Blend well.

Put 1 fillet on a serving platter. Spoon half of the vegetable salad on top and cover with another fillet. Spoon a few tablespoons of mayonnaise on top of the fillet and smooth it over, using enough additional mayonnaise to coat the fillets nicely. Repeat with the other 2 fillets and the remaining vegetable salad and mayonnaise. Chill well.

To serve, sprinkle the basil on top of the fish and cut into pieces.

Poached Striped Bass in Flavored Broth
Serves 4

✂ **If you can't find** striped bass, replace it with fillets of approximately the same size and texture — anything from red snapper to porgy to black sea bass.

4 strips lemon rind, removed with a
      vegetable peeler
1 leek (about 5 ounces), trimmed
      (leaving some green), split, washed,
      and cut into julienne strips (about
      2 cups)
1 large carrot, peeled and cut into julienne
      strips (about 1 cup)
½ cup coarsely chopped celery
1 small red onion, thinly sliced (1 cup)
5 garlic cloves, thinly sliced
      (1½ tablespoons)
¾ cup water
¾ cup dry white wine
2 tablespoons olive oil
2 tablespoons unsalted butter
1 teaspoon salt
4 skin-on striped bass fillets (about
      6 ounces each)
¼ teaspoon freshly ground black
      pepper

Stack the strips of lemon rind and cut into fine julienne strips. (You should have about 1½ tablespoons.)

Combine the rind, leek, carrot, celery, red onion, garlic, water, wine, olive oil, butter, and salt in a large stainless steel saucepan and bring to a boil over high heat. Cover, reduce the heat to medium, and boil gently for 4 minutes.

Add the fish and return to a boil, then cover, reduce the heat to low, and simmer for 1 minute.

Set the fish aside, covered, in the broth for 5 minutes to rest and finish cooking.

To serve, carefully remove the fillets from the broth with a slotted spoon and transfer to four individual serving plates. (Serve the fillets with or without the skin, as desired.)

Add the pepper to the broth and return to a boil. Spoon the broth and vegetables over the fish and serve.

Whole Striped Bass in Salt Crust
Serves 6 to 8

One of the simplest and most elegant ways of serving a whole fish is to bake it in a salt crust. The salt adds only a mildly salty taste to the striped bass, while keeping it moist. For best results, it is imperative that the fish be superfresh.

I bake it on a large stainless steel fish platter that can go from the oven to the table, but you can use a baking sheet. The fish is cooked at a high temperature, and it is best to let it rest and continue cooking in its hot crust for 10 minutes after removing it from the oven. Served at the table, it makes a dramatic presentation.

A sauce made of a simple emulsion of the best possible olive oil and lemon juice complements the fish, as does one of melted butter, lemon juice, and herbs; the choice is yours. Any leftover fish can be served cold with tartar sauce.

SALT CRUST

6 cups kosher salt
5 large egg whites
1½ cups all-purpose flour
   About 1 cup water

1 striped bass (3½–4 pounds),
   gutted and scaled, fins trimmed

LEMON SAUCE

1 tablespoon fresh lemon juice
⅓ cup extra-virgin olive oil
¼ teaspoon salt
¼ teaspoon freshly ground black pepper

OR

HERB SAUCE

1 tablespoon fresh lemon juice
6 tablespoons (¾ stick) unsalted
   butter, melted
¼ teaspoon salt
¼ teaspoon freshly ground black pepper
2 tablespoons finely chopped fresh
   herbs, such as basil, tarragon,
   or chives, or a mixture of
   these or other herbs of your
   choosing

Preheat the oven to 425 degrees.

FOR THE SALT CRUST: Mix all the ingredients together in a bowl to form a pasty mixture that holds together.

Place the fish on a stainless steel platter or a baking sheet and, using your hands, pack the crust mixture on top of and around the body of the fish (do not cover the head or the underside of the fish). Bake for about 30 minutes, or until the internal temperature of the fish is 125 to 130 degrees, no more. Remove from the oven and let the fish rest for about 10 minutes before serving. (The internal temperature will go up a few degrees.)

FOR THE SAUCE: Whisk together all the ingredients for either sauce in a bowl.

To serve, crack the salt crust with the back of a heavy knife and lift it off. Scrape off the skin of the bass, lift up pieces of the fish from the bone, and transfer them to plates; remove the backbone and lift up the remaining fish. Pass the sauce at the table.

Haddock Steaks in Rice Paper with Shallot and Soy Sauce

Serves 4

❧ **Available at most Asian** markets, Vietnamese rice paper disks soften when dampened with cold water and make ideal edible wrappers. I fold them around haddock steaks that have been seasoned with tarragon, sauté the packets, and serve the fish in the lightly browned wrappers.

- 4   Vietnamese rice paper disks (8½ inches in diameter)
- ½   teaspoon salt
- ½   teaspoon freshly ground black pepper
- 1   tablespoon finely chopped fresh tarragon
- 4   haddock fillets (5–6 ounces each, 3 to 4 inches across and 1 inch thick)

SAUCE

- 2   large shallots, finely chopped (3 tablespoons)
- 2   tablespoons chopped fresh chives
- 1   large garlic clove, crushed and finely chopped (1 teaspoon)
- 3   tablespoons rice vinegar
- ¼   cup dark soy sauce
- 1   teaspoon sugar
- ¼   teaspoon Tabasco sauce

- 1   tablespoon canola or corn oil

Brush the rice paper disks generously on both sides with water and set them aside to soften for about 3 minutes.

Mix the salt, pepper, and tarragon in a small bowl and sprinkle on both sides of the haddock fillets. Place each fillet in the center of a softened rice paper disk, then fold the paper around the fish to enclose it securely. Arrange the fish packages seam side down on a plate, cover, and refrigerate

until cooking time. (*The packages can be assembled a few hours ahead.*)

FOR THE SAUCE: Mix all the ingredients in a small bowl. Cover and set aside.

At serving time, heat the oil in a large non-stick skillet. When it is hot, place the haddock packages seam side down in the skillet and cook, uncovered, over medium heat for about 2 minutes. Turn, cover, and cook for an additional 2 minutes. Remove the skillet from the heat and set aside, covered, for 3 to 4 minutes to allow the haddock to finish cooking in its own residual heat.

Arrange the packages on individual serving plates, drizzle the sauce over and around them, and serve.

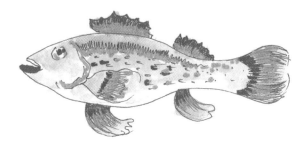

Blackfish in Shredded Potato Crust

Serves 4

❧ **Blackfish, also called tautog,** is readily available on the East Coast during summer. White-fleshed, firm, and juicy, this is one of the best fish around. You can substitute halibut, swordfish, or even Arctic char. These fillets are cooked in a shredded potato crust. The crisp crust keeps the fish juicy and provides a nice balance to the tender flesh. Use large baking potatoes. Peel them (although they can be left unpeeled, if you prefer) and wash them, then shred them on a box grater. At this point, the potatoes can be used immediately or kept in water to cover until ready to cook.

2 large baking (Idaho) potatoes (1 pound)
½ medium leek, trimmed (leaving some green), split, washed, and finely chopped (½ cup)
1 tablespoon safflower or peanut oil
1 tablespoon unsalted butter
½ teaspoon salt
4 skinless blackfish fillets (about 6 ounces each)

Peel the potatoes (or leave them unpeeled, if desired) and wash them. Shred the potatoes on the large holes of a box grater. (You should have about 2½ cups.) Drain well in a colander, then combine in a bowl with the leek and mix well.

Heat the oil and butter in a large skillet, preferably nonstick. Meanwhile, sprinkle half the salt on the fillets. When the oil and butter are hot, spoon 4 small, evenly spaced mounds of the shredded potatoes and leek (each about ⅓ cup) into the skillet. Press a portion of fish into each mound and cover the fish with the remaining potatoes. Sprinkle with the remaining salt. Cook the potato packages over medium-high heat for 6 to 7 minutes. Turn them carefully with a large spatula and cook them for 6 to 7 minutes on the other side. The potatoes should be nicely crusted on both sides and the fish just cooked. Serve.

Cod in Olive and Horseradish Sauce
Serves 4

✳ **The pungent flavors of** horseradish, capers, cilantro, and black olives contrast with the mild cod.

My wife and I like our fish barely cooked in the center; she prefers hers very rare, even more undercooked than mine. So when we do a recipe like this, I choose the thinnest fillet for myself and a little thicker one for her and cook them the same length of time. If you like your fish cooked more or less, adjust accordingly.

If cod is not available, use fillets from another fleshy white fish, such as haddock or sole.

4 cod fillets (5–6 ounces each and about 1½ inches thick)
½ cup chopped onion
1 cup fruity dry white wine (an Alsatian Gewürztraminer would be good)
½ teaspoon salt
½ teaspoon freshly ground black pepper
About 12 oil-cured black olives, pitted
2 tablespoons drained small capers
2 tablespoons grated fresh or bottled horseradish
½ cup sour cream
¼ cup coarsely chopped fresh cilantro

Combine the cod, onion, wine, salt, and pepper in a stainless steel saucepan and bring to a boil over high heat, then cover, reduce the heat, and boil gently for 2 minutes. (The cod will be undercooked at this point.) With a slotted spoon, carefully transfer the cod to a platter, cover it, and set it aside to continue cooking in its own residual heat.

Add the olives, capers, horseradish, and sour cream to the saucepan, bring to a boil, and boil over high heat for 1 minute.

Arrange a cod fillet on each of four plates and top with the sauce. Sprinkle with the cilantro and serve.

Sole Claudine
Serves 8

✳ **Named after my daughter,** Claudine, this dish was a specialty at our restaurant, Gloria's French

Café, in the early 1980s. Rolled-up sole fillets and chopped mushrooms are wrapped in lettuce leaves, then poached and finished with a cream sauce. Iceberg lettuce is best here, as it stays slightly crunchy after cooking.

- 1 large head iceberg lettuce
- 8 gray or lemon sole or flounder fillets (about 4 ounces each)
- 1 teaspoon salt, or more to taste
- ½ teaspoon freshly ground white pepper, or more to taste
- 5 tablespoons unsalted butter
- 2½ cups cleaned and coarsely chopped mushrooms
- 3 shallots, finely chopped (⅓ cup)
- 1 large or 2 smaller carrots, peeled and cut into fine julienne strips (2 cups)
- 1 cup dry white wine
- ½ cup dry vermouth
- 2 tablespoons all-purpose flour
- ½ cup heavy cream

Remove 8 of the larger outside leaves from the lettuce and wash carefully; save the heart for salad or another use. Plunge the leaves into a pot of boiling water, bring back to a boil, and boil for 1 minute. Cool immediately under cold water and dry on paper towels.

Cut each fillet lengthwise in half, discarding the strip of little bones that separates the 2 halves. Sprinkle the fillets with ½ teaspoon of the salt and ¼ teaspoon of the white pepper. Set aside.

Melt 3 tablespoons of the butter in a saucepan. (Set the remaining 2 tablespoons butter aside to soften for the *beurre manié*.) Add the mushrooms and the remaining ½ teaspoon salt and ¼ teaspoon pepper and cook until all the liquid rendered by the mushrooms has evaporated. Set aside to cool slightly.

Preheat the oven to 400 degrees. Butter a large shallow flameproof gratin dish with 1 tablespoon of the butter and sprinkle with the shallots and carrots.

Spread the lettuce leaves out on a work surface and spoon a generous tablespoon of the mushrooms into the center of each leaf. Roll up 2 fish fillets and place side by side on top of the mushrooms on 1 leaf (be sure that the whitest part of the flesh is on the outside). Fold the lettuce leaf over the fillets and place seam side down in the gratin dish. Repeat the process until you have 8 neat little packages; they should fit tightly, one against the other, in the dish, without overlapping.

Add the wine and vermouth to the gratin dish and bring to a boil on top of the stove. As soon as the liquid boils, cover and bake for 8 to 10 minutes, or until tender to the point of a knife.

Remove the fish from the oven and lift the packages onto a serving platter. Keep warm in a 150-degree oven or at the back of the stove.

Mix the flour and the remaining tablespoon of butter together to make a *beurre manié*. Add to the broth, mixing fast with a whisk to prevent lumps. Bring to a boil and simmer for 2 minutes. (At this point, you may pour in any liquid that accumulated on the platter around the fillets.) Add the cream and bring to a boil, then simmer gently for another 2 minutes. Check the seasonings, as more salt and white pepper may be needed.

Spoon the sauce over the fish, coating the packets, and serve.

Clam-Stuffed Sole with Cucumbers
Serves 6

✁ **Flatfish fillets are pounded** and used as wrappers to enclose the stuffing, re-formed into an elongated oval to approximate the shape of a

fish. The stuffing is made with bread, leek, garlic, mushrooms, and razor clams, but other types of clams or oysters can be used. Razor clams do not get as rubbery as regular clams do if they are slightly overcooked.

For the large fillets required, large lemon sole or the petrale sole of the Pacific Coast (when very large), as well as the gray sole of the East Coast, can be used. Fillets from a small halibut are also good here. Brill, a fish resembling a small halibut, is excellent but rarely available. While all of these flatfish are related, some have firmer and moister flesh than others.

> 4 gray, petrale, or lemon sole fillets (about 8 ounces each)

STUFFING

> 1½ pounds razor clams or soft-shell clams
> ¼ cup corn or safflower oil
> 2 tablespoons unsalted butter
> 4 ounces whole wheat or other whole-grain bread (about 4 slices), cut into ½-inch cubes
> 1¼ cups finely chopped onions
> 1 leek, trimmed (leaving some green), split, washed, and thinly sliced (1 cup)
> ½ teaspoon chopped garlic
> 2 teaspoons fresh thyme leaves, coarsely chopped
> 4 mushrooms, cleaned and cut into ¼-inch dice (1 cup)
> 1 large egg

> ½ teaspoon salt
> ¼ teaspoon freshly ground black pepper

CUCUMBER GARNISH

> 2 large cucumbers (about 1¼ pounds)
> 1 tablespoon unsalted butter
> Pinch of salt

> ½ cup dry white wine

SAUCE

> Reserved fish cooking juices (from above)
> 1 tablespoon unsalted butter, softened
> 2 teaspoons all-purpose flour
> ½ cup heavy cream
> 2 tablespoons chopped fresh chives
> Salt and freshly ground black pepper

Arrange 1 fillet between two sheets of plastic wrap and, using a meat pounder, gently pound it to extend it and equalize its thickness. Do the same with the remaining fillets, pounding them to a thickness of about ½ inch. Set aside.

FOR THE STUFFING: Wash the clams in several changes of cold water, lifting them up from the water after you finish washing so any sand remains in the bottom of the bowl. (If they are very sandy, toss a handful of salt into a bowl of cold water and let the clams soak in the salted water; it helps them disgorge some of the sand. Then lift them out of the water and rinse again under fresh water.)

Put the clams in a stainless steel saucepan, cover, and cook over medium-high heat for 4 to 5 minutes, just until all the clams open. Discard any that do not open.

Open up the clams completely. Strain the juices through a sieve lined with a paper towel to remove all the sand. You should have 1 cup of juices; if necessary, add water. Set aside.

Remove the clams from the shells. Using a knife or scissors, cut the clams into 1-inch pieces.

Heat the oil and 1 tablespoon of the butter in a large skillet until hot. Add the bread cubes and sauté until nicely browned on all sides. Set aside to cool.

Heat the remaining tablespoon of butter in another large skillet. When it is hot, add the onions and leek and sauté for 3 to 4 minutes. Add the garlic and remove from the heat.

Drop the bread into a food processor and process until it is completely crumbled. (You should have about 1½ cups.) Combine the crumbs, thyme, mushrooms, and onion-leek mixture in a bowl. Add the clams, along with the egg, and mix well. Add the salt and pepper and mix well.

Butter a large deep stainless steel platter or roasting pan and place 2 pounded fillets side by side in the bottom. Arrange the stuffing on top, spreading it to within ½ inch of the sides, and lift up the sides of the fillets to enclose the stuffing. Place the remaining 2 fillets on top, with the whitest side showing, so the stuffing is completely encased.

Preheat the oven to 375 degrees.

FOR THE CUCUMBERS: Peel the cucumbers and cut each into 3 or 4 segments about 1½ inches long. Cut each segment lengthwise in half and then into 3 or 4 wedges, depending on the size of the cucumber. Using a sharp paring knife, trim the pieces, especially on the sides containing the seeds, until the sides are smooth and the pieces look like small elongated footballs.

Bring 4 quarts of water to a boil in a small saucepan. Drop the cucumbers into it and bring back to a boil. As soon as the water boils, drain the cucumbers in a colander. Set the pan aside.

Pour the reserved cup of clam juice and the white wine around the fish. Butter a piece of parchment paper and lay it over the fish, tucking it in so it fits all around the fish to prevent it from drying out in the oven. Place the pan on top of the stove and bring to a boil, then bake for about 10 minutes. There is only a thin layer of fish around the stuffing, so it will be cooked in this length of time, but the stuffing, although cooked, will not be hot enough. Drain off the cooking juices and strain into a saucepan. (You should have about 1 cup.) Place the fish (still covered with the paper) in a low oven (about 180 degrees) to warm the stuffing while you prepare the sauce. (If you have only one oven, turn down the heat and open the door briefly to cool it down.)

FOR THE SAUCE: Bring the strained juices to a boil. Meanwhile, in a bowl, mix the softened butter and flour with a whisk to make a *beurre manié*. Lift up the mixture on the end of the whisk and place in the hot juices, mixing very quickly to prevent lumping. Bring to a boil, stirring gently with the whisk, then reduce the heat and boil gently for about 1 minute. (If it is lumpy, strain the sauce and return to the pan.) Add the cream, chives, and salt and pepper to taste and bring just to a boil; set aside.

Return the cucumbers to their saucepan, add the butter and salt, and toss briefly over medium heat.

With two large spatulas, transfer the fish to a serving platter. Surround it with the cucumbers. Spoon the sauce over the fish.

Cut the fish into 1-inch-thick slices and serve with the cucumbers and sauce.

Sole Paupiettes with Lobster Mousse
Serves 6

✽ **The word** *paupiette* **refers** to a piece of meat or fish that is stuffed and rolled before cooking. The stuffing can be herbs, ground meat, vegetables, or a mousse. In this recipe, I use lobster mousse.

The body and shells of the lobster are used to make the sauce. If the lobster is a female, the roe, dried in the oven, flavors the sauce and makes a beautiful decoration. Pieces of zucchini and carrot are colorful garnishes.

2 pounds lemon sole fillets, cleaned of sinew (about 6) and cut in half lengthwise

MOUSSE

1 lobster (about 1½ pounds), preferably female
4 ounces shrimp, shelled
¼ cup heavy cream
¼ teaspoon salt
⅛ teaspoon freshly ground black pepper
1 tablespoon chopped mixed fresh herbs, such as chives, tarragon, chervil, and/or parsley

½ teaspoon salt
1 tablespoon unsalted butter
5–6 shallots, sliced (⅓ cup)
1 cup dry white vermouth

STOCK

1 tablespoon unsalted butter
1 tablespoon olive oil
1 tablespoon paprika
2 teaspoons chopped garlic
3 cups water

GARNISHES

3 large carrots, peeled and cut into 3-inch by ½-inch-thick sticks
2 small to medium zucchini, quartered lengthwise, seeds removed, and cut into 3-inch pieces
2 teaspoons potato starch (see page 318), dissolved in 2 tablespoons water

⅓ cup heavy cream
1 tablespoon unsalted butter
Pinch of salt

Arrange the fillets in one layer between sheets of plastic wrap on the work surface. Using a meat pounder, pound them gently until they are of approximately equal thickness throughout. Refrigerate.

FOR THE LOBSTER MOUSSE: Kill the lobster by plunging a sharp heavy knife between the eyes. Steam it in a steamer over boiling water, covered, for 2 minutes, just enough for the flesh to firm up slightly so the meat can be extracted from the shells easily.

Crack the claws and the tail and remove the meat. Refrigerate to cool thoroughly. If the lobster is a female, remove the dark green roe, put it in a small baking pan, and cook in a 400-degree oven for a few minutes, until it turns red and firm. Set aside for decoration. Reserve the shells and insides of the lobster for the sauce.

Cut the lobster meat and shrimp into pieces and puree in a food processor. With the motor running, slowly add the cream in a stream. Add the salt and pepper and process until smooth. Transfer to a bowl, mix in the herbs, and refrigerate until cold.

There are visible lines, which are fibers, on one side of each sole fillet; they indicate that this side of the fillet was next to the skin of the sole. The meat is whiter and fleshier on the other side of the fillet; this side was touching the bones. During cooking, the fish will contract in the direction of the fibers. Therefore, the fillets should be rolled so the fibers are inside; as they contract, the roll will tighten. The other side, fleshy and more attractive, should be on the outside.

Arrange the fillets of sole on the work surface so the side with the fibers is visible. Transfer the mousse to a pastry bag fitted with a plain tip.

Sprinkle the fillets with ¼ teaspoon of the salt and pipe the cold mousse the length of the fillets. Alternatively, use a spoon to coat the fillets with the mousse. Spread the mousse evenly with a spatula, and roll up the fillets, starting at the thickest end.

Coat the bottom of a large ovenproof saucepan with the 1 tablespoon butter. Sprinkle the shallots over the bottom of the pan. Stand the fillets on top of the shallots, sprinkle with the remaining ¼ teaspoon salt, and add the vermouth. Cut a piece of parchment paper to fit into the pan, butter it, and lay it, buttered side down, on top of the fillets. Refrigerate until ready to cook.

FOR THE STOCK: Coarsely chop the lobster shells. Heat the butter and olive oil in a saucepan until hot. Add the shells, with their juices and the lobster insides and sauté for 2 to 3 minutes. Add the paprika, garlic, and water and bring to a boil, then cover and boil for 20 minutes. Strain through a colander into a saucepan.

Preheat the oven to 400 degrees.

FOR THE GARNISHES: Bring about 2 cups water to a boil in a small saucepan. Add the carrots and boil for about 5 minutes, until tender but still firm. Add the zucchini and boil for another minute. Remove with a slotted spoon.

Bring the paupiettes to a boil on top of the stove. Place in the oven and cook for 10 to 12 minutes, until tender.

When the fillets are cooked, add the juice that has accumulated in the pan to the lobster stock. (You should have approximately 3 cups of liquid.) Put the paper back on top of the paupiettes and keep warm in a low oven or on top of the stove.

FOR THE SAUCE: Bring the lobster stock mixture to a boil and reduce to approximately 1¼ cups. Using a whisk, add the dissolved potato starch to the liquid. Mix well and bring back to a boil. Add the cream and return to a boil, then strain through a very fine strainer. Set aside.

At serving time, toss the carrots and zucchini in a skillet with the 1 tablespoon butter just to heat through; add the salt. Reheat the sauce if necessary.

Arrange the paupiettes on a large platter and coat well with the sauce. Arrange the carrots and zucchini around the paupiettes. Crumble the roe, if you have it, and sprinkle around the platter and on top of the paupiettes. Serve.

This mousse can also be used as a garnish for soup or served on its own.

Sole with Tomatoes
Serves 6

❧ **This fast, elegant dish** has a classic garnish of tomatoes and shallots. Any flat fillets from the sole family — fluke, gray sole, or petrale sole — can be used.

4	tablespoons (½ stick) unsalted butter
1	teaspoon salt, or more to taste
½	teaspoon freshly ground black pepper, or more to taste
½	cup chopped shallots
6	lemon sole fillets (about 2 pounds)
2	large ripe tomatoes, peeled, halved, seeded, and chopped (2 cups)
3	tablespoons chopped fresh parsley
1½	cups dry white vermouth
2	tablespoons all-purpose flour
½	cup heavy cream
2	tablespoons cognac

Preheat the oven to 400 degrees.

Butter a heavy shallow baking pan or large ovenproof skillet with 2 tablespoons of the butter (set the remaining butter aside to soften). Sprinkle with half the salt and pepper and scatter half the shallots over the bottom of the pan. Fold the fillets in thirds and line them up in the pan. (Be sure that the outside of the roll is the whitest side, or the fillets will unroll during cooking.) Scatter the remaining shallots over the fish and sprinkle with the remaining salt and pepper. Scatter the tomatoes and 2 tablespoons of the parsley over and around the fish and add the vermouth.

Bring the liquid to a boil over high heat. Cover with a lid or foil, transfer to the oven, and cook for 10 minutes, or until a fork pierces the flesh of the fish easily.

Arrange the fillets on a platter and keep warm in a 150-degree oven (see the sidebar).

Bring the broth in the pan to a boil and reduce to about 1¾ cups. Meanwhile, mix the remaining 2 tablespoons butter with the flour to make a *beurre manié*. Add to the broth, whisking, bring to a boil, and cook, stirring, for about 2 minutes. Add the cream and bring to a boil.

Take the sauce off the heat, add the cognac, and check for seasoning; add salt and pepper if needed. Pour the sauce over the fillets, sprinkle with the remaining tablespoon of parsley, and serve.

OVENS

I have several ovens, so I can cook meat, fish, poultry and other foods at one temperature and then transfer them to another oven set at a lower temperature to keep warm, and in some cases to finish cooking, until serving time. If you have only one oven, after you remove your fish or roast, turn off the oven, open the oven door, and let the oven cool down for a few minutes. Then return your food to this cooler — but still warm — oven to keep it warm until ready to serve.

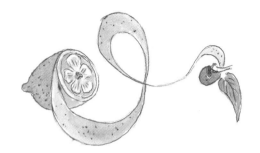

Grilled Dover Sole with Herb Butter
Serves 4 as a first course

Authentic Dover sole, from the English Channel, has very firm, white delicate flesh, which makes it particularly good to grill or poach. It is available, usually frozen, from good fishmongers. An average Dover sole weighs about 1 pound and yields about 6 ounces of pure flesh. Expensive but very special, it is well worth obtaining.

The gray, lemon, petrale, or rex sole or flounder or fluke from our domestic waters can be prepared in the same manner, but these should be handled with extra care, especially when grilled, as their softer meat tends to break and crumble more easily than that of Dover sole.

So that it does not overcook, the sole is grilled only on one side. The white skin protects the fish during cooking and the charcoal taste permeates the flesh. Then the fish finishes cooking in the oven.

Be sure the grill is immaculately clean and extremely hot, so the fish won't stick to it. The fire is better made with wood or hardwood charcoal than briquettes, which contain fossil fuel derivatives.

HERB BUTTER

- 2 tablespoons unsalted butter, softened
- 1 tablespoon chopped fresh herbs, such as tarragon, chives, basil, dill, and/or parsley
- 1 teaspoon fresh lemon juice

Salt and freshly ground black pepper
    to taste
2 Dover sole (about 1 pound each)
1 teaspoon peanut oil

FOR THE HERB BUTTER: Mix all the ingredients together well. Refrigerate until serving time.

Preheat the oven to 400 degrees. Heat a grill until very hot; be sure the grill is extremely clean, so the fish won't stick to it.

Cut the head off each sole on the bias. Grasp the black skin at the head and pull it off. (If using other sole, flounder, or fluke, be sure to pull the skin slowly and carefully to avoid pulling the flesh off with it.) Scrape the skin on the white side with a knife to remove the scales. (Since the white skin is tender and browns beautifully, it is generally left on, especially when the fish is to be grilled.) Wash thoroughly under cold water.

With sharp scissors, cut off the fins and the thin strip of bones on each side of the fish. Dry thoroughly with paper towels. Sprinkle the fish with salt and rub with the peanut oil on both sides.

Lay skin side down on the hot grill and cook for about 1½ minutes. Then lift each sole and turn it 90 degrees on the grill, to form a crisscross pattern on the white skin, and cook for another 1½ minutes.

Place the sole unmarked side down in a buttered dish and put in the oven for 4 to 5 minutes to finish the cooking.

Using a knife and fork, separate the top fillet of each fish along the central bone and push both halves off the bone — they should slide easily if the sole is cooked, although it may still be slightly pink at the bones. Remove the central bone, reform the sole in its original shape by pushing the fillets back together, and arrange on a platter.

Top each sole with 1 tablespoon of the herb butter and serve.

Broiled Breaded Red Snapper
Serves 4

It's important to make fresh bread crumbs for this recipe, with bread that is 1 or 2 days old yet still somewhat moist. Any white fish fillets of the same thickness can be used instead of snapper.

2 garlic cloves
3 slices firm white bread (3 ounces), cut into pieces
4–5 scallions, trimmed (leaving some green) and finely minced (⅓ cup)
¾ teaspoon salt
½ teaspoon freshly ground black pepper
2 tablespoons extra-virgin olive oil
4 skinless red snapper fillets (about 6 ounces each and ¾ inch thick)
1 lemon, cut into 4 wedges

Preheat the broiler. Drop the garlic cloves into a food processor and process until finely chopped. Add the bread and process to crumbs. (You should have about 1½ cups.) Transfer the bread crumbs to a bowl and mix in the scallions, salt, and pepper. Add the oil and rub the mixture gently between your hands to moisten the bread crumbs. The mixture should be loose, not pasty.

Arrange the fillets side by side on a nonstick baking sheet. Cover them with the crumbs, patting the crumbs lightly over the surface. Broil the fillets about 5 inches from the heat for 3 to 4 minutes, until the crumbs are nicely browned and the fish is just cooked through. The cooking time will vary depending on the thickness of the fillets, so check to see if they are done by cutting into one; if more cooking is needed, turn off the broiler and let the fish remain in the hot oven for 3 to 4 minutes.

Serve with the lemon wedges.

Red Snapper with Leeks, Mushrooms, and Shallots
Serves 4

✄ **This quick, easy recipe** can be prepared with fillets from any fresh, firm-fleshed fish. First, all the ingredients except the snapper are boiled in wine. Then the fish is added and cooked for a couple of minutes, and it is served with the pan sauce, enriched with butter.

1 small leek, trimmed (leaving some green), split, washed, and thinly sliced (1½ cups)

3 ounces mushrooms, cleaned and cut into julienne strips (1½ cups)

¼ cup chopped shallots

⅓ cup peeled and diced (¼-inch) red bell pepper

1 cup dry white wine (such as Chablis)

2 tablespoons olive oil

½ teaspoon salt

¼ teaspoon freshly ground black pepper

4 skin-on red snapper fillets (about 5 ounces each and ¾ inch thick)

1 tablespoon unsalted butter

Put all the ingredients except the fish and butter in a large stainless steel saucepan, cover, and bring to a boil, then reduce the heat to low and boil gently for 3 minutes.

Add the fish, cover, and cook for 2½ to 3 minutes, or until just cooked through.

Arrange a fillet on each of four plates. Add the butter to the liquid in the saucepan and bring to a strong boil. Divide the mixture among the plates, spooning both sauce and vegetables on top of the fish, and serve.

Red Snapper Fillets in Potato Jackets
Serves 4

✄ **Cooked between layers of** sliced potato, these moist fish fillets make an impressive dish. Serve the fish just as it emerges from the skillet, while the potatoes are still crisp. The zucchini garnish makes a good first course on its own.

The most important consideration when selecting the fish is freshness. Any variety of thick fillets will work. If you can't get an ocean fish like snapper or blackfish, use trout, perch, or catfish fillets instead, adjusting the cooking time to accommodate variations in thickness.

To slice the potatoes, I use a mandoline, a professional slicer. Any slicer will work well, including the 1-millimeter blade of a food processor.

2 large baking (Idaho) potatoes (about 1 pound)

4 skinless red snapper fillets (about 5 ounces each and 1 inch thick)

¼ teaspoon salt

⅛ teaspoon freshly ground black pepper

GARNISH

1 medium zucchini (about 8 ounces)

1 tablespoon peanut oil

1 tablespoon dark soy sauce

2 tablespoons olive oil

2 tablespoons peanut oil

2 tablespoons chopped fresh parsley

Preheat the oven to 400 degrees.

Peel the potatoes and thinly slice them lengthwise with a vegetable slicer; or use the slicing blade of a food processor. (You should have about 50 slices.) Wash the potatoes, drain, and pat the slices dry with paper towels.

Place four pieces of plastic wrap (about 7 inches square) on a work surface. Arrange 6 overlapping slices of potato in the center of each square, duplicating the general shape of a fish fillet, and place a fillet on top. Sprinkle with the salt and pepper. Arrange another 6 slices of potato, also overlapping, on top of each fillet and fold the plastic around them so they are completely wrapped. Refrigerate while you prepare the garnish.

FOR THE GARNISH: Cut the zucchini into 2-inch chunks, then cut lengthwise into ⅛-inch-thick slices and finally into julienne strips. Spread the zucchini out on a cookie sheet and bake for 5 to 6 minutes to soften.

Transfer the zucchini to a bowl and toss with the peanut oil and soy sauce.

Divide the olive and peanut oils between two large nonstick skillets and place over medium heat. Carefully unwrap the potato-fish packages and, with a large spatula, transfer them to the skillets. Sauté for 5 minutes, then carefully turn (so the arrangement is not disturbed) and sauté for 5 more minutes, or until the potatoes are nicely browned.

To serve, arrange the zucchini in a circle on four plates and place the fish in the center. Sprinkle with the parsley and serve.

Skate Meunière with Mushrooms

Serves 4

✻ **Skate, or ray,** is a mild fish that is soft-fleshed, tender, and moist. It is excellent poached, sautéed, or grilled. Although the central bony part of the body is good for soup, only the wings are available in fish markets. If the skate wing is large, as here, it is cut into pieces.

Meunière refers to fish that are dredged in flour and sautéed in oil and butter. Most any fish can be prepared this way.

1 large skinned skate wing (about 2 pounds)
  Salt and freshly ground black pepper
  About ⅓ cup all-purpose flour, for dredging
4 tablespoons (½ stick) unsalted butter
2 tablespoons corn oil
2 cups sliced mushrooms (about 4 ounces)
1 tablespoon fresh lemon juice
1 tablespoon chopped fresh parsley

Cut the skate wing into 4 slabs. Sprinkle the pieces of skate with ¼ teaspoon salt and ⅛ teaspoon pepper and dredge in the flour, shaking off any excess.

Heat 2 tablespoons of the butter and the oil in a large heavy skillet until hot. Add the skate and cook over medium-high heat for 5 minutes on the first side. Turn and cook for 5 minutes longer on the other side, or just until the skate is cooked through; the meat should separate from the bone when pulled but still be slightly moist and pink in the center. Arrange the skate on a serving platter.

Add the sliced mushrooms to the drippings in the pan and cook for just 1 minute; they should still be firm. Season with a pinch each of salt and pepper, then scatter the mushrooms on top of the skate.

Heat the remaining 2 tablespoons butter in a small skillet until it is foamy and brown. Sprinkle the lemon juice on the skate, pour the hot butter on top, garnish with the parsley, and serve.

Skate with Beets and Flavored Oil
Serves 4

✤ **Skate is often poached,** as here, in vinegar and water. I coat it with a sauce featuring capers and garnish it with a julienne of beets seasoned with a fairly acidic dressing. For flavor and eye appeal, I surround the fish on each plate with some brilliant red beet cooking liquid that I sprinkle with a little bright yellow curry oil and vivid green cilantro oil.

2 beets (about 10 ounces)
¼ cup red wine vinegar
¾ teaspoon salt
¼ teaspoon freshly ground black pepper
½ teaspoon sugar
1 large skinned skate wing (about 1½ pounds), cut into 4 pieces

SAUCE

3 tablespoons chopped red onion
2 tablespoons coarsely chopped scallions
1 tablespoon capers, drained
2 tablespoons Curry Oil (page 620)
1 tablespoon red wine vinegar
¼ teaspoon salt
¼ teaspoon freshly ground black pepper

4 teaspoons Curry Oil (page 620)
4 teaspoons Cilantro Oil (page 620)

Put the beets in a saucepan, cover them with cold water, and bring to a boil. Reduce the heat to low and boil gently, covered, for about 1 hour, until tender. Drain, reserving ⅓ cup of the cooking liquid. (Alternatively, put the beets in a bowl with 2 tablespoons water, cover with a glass lid, and cook in a microwave oven until tender, about 30 minutes; there will be enough juice remaining from the beets for use around the fish.)

When the beets are cool enough to handle, peel them and cut them into ¼-inch-thick julienne strips. Put the strips in the reserved cooking liquid and set aside. (*The beets can be prepared up to 1 hour ahead.*)

At serving time, drain the beets, reserving the liquid, and put in a bowl. Add 1 tablespoon of the vinegar, ¼ teaspoon of the salt, the pepper, and sugar and mix well.

Bring 6 cups water to a boil in a large saucepan. Stir in the remaining 3 tablespoons vinegar and ½ teaspoon salt. Add the skate and bring back to a boil, then cover, reduce the heat to low, and boil gently for 12 minutes.

MEANWHILE, FOR THE SAUCE: Combine all the ingredients in a bowl. Mix well.

To serve, arrange the beets on four plates. Remove the fish from the water and drain on a paper towel. Separate the flesh from the bones — it will lift off easily — and arrange on top of the beets. Cover with the caper sauce. Spoon about 1½ tablespoons of the reserved beet juice around the fish on each plate and sprinkle 1 teaspoon curry oil and then 1 teaspoon cilantro oil on top of the beet juice. The blending of these liquids will create a beautiful design. Serve.

Flaked Cod with Zucchini, Tomatoes, and Black Olives
Serves 4

✤ **I like scrod, haddock,** and pollack, but my first preference in this family of fish is cod. Cod fillets tend to separate into beautiful flakes as they cook, and here those chunks are combined with sautéed onion, zucchini, tomatoes, and black olives, all scented with tarragon.

2 tablespoons peanut oil

1 tablespoon unsalted butter

1 medium onion, finely chopped (1 cup)

1 large or 2 medium cod fillets (1½ pounds total, about 1¼ inches thick)

2 small zucchini, trimmed and cut into ½-inch dice (2 cups)

1 teaspoon salt

½ teaspoon freshly ground black pepper

⅔ cup fruity dry white wine (such as Sémillon or Sauvignon Blanc)

6 plum tomatoes (about 12 ounces), halved, seeded, and cut into ½-inch dice (2 cups)

¼ cup diced (½-inch) pitted oil-cured black olives

2 teaspoons chopped fresh tarragon

Heat the oil and butter in a large saucepan until hot. Add the onion and sauté for 1 minute. Add the cod, zucchini, salt, pepper, and wine and bring to a boil, then cover, reduce the heat, and cook for about 3 minutes, until the fish flakes but is still slightly underdone in the center. Transfer the fish to a platter and cover it with a pan lid so it continues to cook in its own residual heat.

Add the tomatoes and olives to the pan and sauté them for 1 minute. Add the tarragon and mix it in.

To serve, flake the cod into pieces and divide the pieces among four dinner plates. Divide the vegetable mixture, juices and all, among the plates and mix it gently into the fish flakes. Serve.

Cod à l'Espagnole
Serves 4

❧ I use cod in this recipe, but any fish with firm-textured flesh that separates into large flakes when cooked, like haddock or pollack, can be substituted. Smothered with vegetables ranging from green peppers to zucchini and tomatoes, the fish stays moist and flavorful.

¼ cup olive oil

6 scallions, trimmed (most of the green left on) and minced (¾ cup)

4 large garlic cloves, thinly sliced (2 tablespoons)

1 green bell pepper, cored, seeded, and cut into ½-inch pieces (1¼ cups)

1 zucchini (6 ounces), trimmed and cut into ½-inch pieces (1¼ cups)

1 teaspoon salt

½ teaspoon freshly ground black pepper

4 plum tomatoes (10 ounces), halved, seeded, and cut into ½-inch pieces (1½ cups)

1 teaspoon saffron threads

4 cod fillets (about 6 ounces each and 1½ inches thick)

Heat the oil in a large skillet until it is hot but not smoking. Add the scallions and garlic and sauté for 1 minute. Add the bell pepper and zucchini and sauté for 1 minute.

Add the salt, pepper, tomatoes, and saffron to the skillet and mix well. Push the pieces of fish into the mixture, completely embedding them in the vegetables. Cover, reduce the heat to low, and cook for about 10 minutes, or until the cod is just cooked through.

Serve.

This is a delicious and economical way of using leftovers from a whole fish or fillets of any fish from salmon to catfish. I often prepare this meal — or a variation on it — when I have leftover cooked fish or shellfish, layering it on top of cooked spinach and farfalle in a casserole. A light béchamel sauce and a sprinkling of Parmesan cheese complete the dish, which is then gratinéed in a hot oven.

- 2 tablespoons olive oil
- 12 ounces spinach, washed and tough stems removed
- ¾ teaspoon salt
- ½ teaspoon freshly ground black pepper
- 6 ounces farfalle (bow-tie pasta)
- 8–10 ounces leftover cooked fish
- 1 tablespoon unsalted butter
- 2 tablespoons all-purpose flour
- 2 cups milk
- 3 tablespoons freshly grated Parmesan cheese

Preheat the oven to 400 degrees.

Heat 1 tablespoon of the oil in a large skillet until it is hot but not smoking. Add the spinach, still wet from washing, and cook, covered, over medium-high heat for about 4 minutes, until wilted and soft. Add ¼ teaspoon each of the salt and pepper and mix well. Spoon the spinach into a 6-cup gratin dish.

Bring 4 quarts of salted water to a boil in a large pot. Add the farfalle, stir, and cook for about 10 minutes, until tender but still slightly al dente. Drain the pasta in a colander, then cool it by running cold water over it for 30 seconds; drain well.

Toss the pasta with the fish, breaking up the fish if necessary, and spread it on top of the spinach in the gratin dish.

Heat the remaining tablespoon of oil and the butter in a large saucepan. Add the flour and mix well. Cook for 30 seconds, whisking, then add the milk and bring to a boil, stirring with the whisk. Add the remaining ½ teaspoon salt and ¼ teaspoon pepper and mix well. Pour the sauce over the fish and pasta mixture and sprinkle the Parmesan cheese on top.

Bake the gratin for 25 to 30 minutes, until hot throughout and browned on top. Serve.

Steamed Cod on Tapenade
Serves 4

⚘ The word *tapenade* comes from *tapeno*, which means "caper" in Provence, the region where it originated. I add a little coarsely chopped fig to my version, which gives it a slight sweetness. The steamed cod is served on the strong-flavored tapenade.

TAPENADE

- ⅔ cup oil-cured black olives, pitted and finely chopped
- 8 anchovy fillets, finely chopped
- 2 tablespoons capers, rinsed and finely chopped
- 2 small dried black figs, finely chopped (3 tablespoons)

¼ cup extra-virgin olive oil

¼ teaspoon freshly ground black pepper

2 tablespoons water

4 cod fillets (about 5 ounces each and
 1½ inches thick)

6 fresh basil leaves

1 tomato slice, cut into strips

FOR THE TAPENADE: Mix together the olives, anchovies, capers, figs, oil, pepper, and water in a bowl. Alternatively, pulse all the ingredients together in a food processor a few times, until coarsely chopped. Set aside.

Pour about 1 inch of water into a steamer and bring it to a strong boil. Arrange the fish in a single layer on a heatproof plate, place the plate in the steamer, and steam, covered, for 4 to 5 minutes, until just cooked through.

Meanwhile, spoon the tapenade onto four individual plates.

Put one fillet in the center of each plate. Thinly slice the basil leaves, to make a chiffonade, and sprinkle over the cod. Arrange the tomato strips on top and serve.

Salt Cod
with Potatoes and Olives
Serves 4

When buying salt cod, buy the thickest fillets you can get. The salted codfish at my supermarket comes from Canada in little wooden boxes, each holding a pound. If you are fortunate enough to be in an area where there are Italian, Spanish, or, especially, Portuguese markets, you may find large fillets of salted dried codfish hanging in the markets. Sold this way, the cod — *bacalao* in

Spanish — is usually thicker and of better quality.

If you leave the olives unpitted, you may want to warn your guests about the pits.

1 pound salt cod

2–3 medium red potatoes (1 pound total)

3 tablespoons olive oil

1 large green bell pepper, cored, seeded,
 and cut into 1-inch pieces (2 cups)

6 scallions, trimmed (leaving some green)
 and minced (about ¾ cup)

1 small onion, chopped (about ½ cup)

5 garlic cloves, thinly sliced
 (2 tablespoons)

½ cup dry sherry or dry Madeira

½ teaspoon freshly ground black pepper

1 cup mixed olives (kalamata, green, oil-
 cured, etc.), rinsed in cold water,
 pitted if desired

2 tablespoons chopped fresh parsley

Pour 3 quarts of cold water into a large bowl, add the salt cod, and soak it for 4 hours. Drain off the water, add fresh water to the bowl, and soak the cod for 4 hours longer, or overnight. Drain.

Bring 6 cups of water to a boil in a medium saucepan. Add the fish and bring back to a boil. Boil very gently, uncovered, for about 6 minutes. Drain and cool the fish in a bowl of cold water.

Using your fingers, separate the fish into flakes, removing and discarding any bones and skin. (You should have 2 cups.) Set aside.

Put the potatoes in a medium saucepan, cover them with cold water, and bring to a boil, then reduce the heat and boil the potatoes gently until tender, about 30 minutes. Drain.

When they are cool enough to handle, peel the potatoes and cut them into ¾-inch-thick slices. Set aside.

Heat the olive oil in a large heavy saucepan

until hot. Add the green pepper, scallions, onion, and garlic and cook over low heat for 5 minutes. Add the flaked fish, potato slices, sherry or Madeira, and pepper. Cover and cook over low heat for 10 minutes. (*The recipe can be made to this point up to 2 hours ahead and set aside at room temperature; reheat before proceeding.*)

Add the olives and mix them in gently.

Arrange a couple of potato slices on each of four dinner plates and ladle the fish mixture on top. Sprinkle with the chopped parsley and serve.

Brandade au Gratin
Serves 8 to 10 as an hors d'oeuvre

✎ *Brandade* **is a puree** of salt cod, garlic, and potato emulsified with olive oil. You can prepare the brandade ahead and reheat it in a gratin dish at serving time until hot, bubbly, and brown on top. Then let your guests either dip the toasts in the brandade or spread some of the mixture on them.

- 1 pound salt cod
- 2 large red potatoes (about 12 ounces)
- 1½ cups milk, heated until hot
- 8 garlic cloves, peeled
- 1 teaspoon grated lemon rind
- 2 tablespoons fresh lemon juice
- ½ teaspoon freshly ground black pepper
- ⅛ teaspoon cayenne pepper
- ½ cup olive oil
- 2 tablespoons freshly grated Parmesan cheese
- 2 baguettes, cut into about 50 rounds, ½ inch thick

Rinse the cod under cold running water and put it in a large bowl containing about 5 quarts cold water. Let soak for at least 4 hours, changing the water after 2 hours.

Meanwhile, put the potatoes in a saucepan, cover them with cold water, and bring to a boil, then reduce the heat and boil the potatoes gently for about 40 minutes, until tender. Drain and set aside.

Drain the cod. Put it in a saucepan with 8 cups cold water, bring just to a gentle boil, and drain immediately.

When the cod is cool enough to handle, remove any bones with your fingers and discard, breaking the flesh into pieces. Return the cod to the pan, add the milk and garlic, and bring to a boil, then cover, reduce the heat to low, and cook gently for 12 minutes.

Peel the potatoes and cut them into 2-inch pieces.

Preheat the oven to 400 degrees.

Put the cod, with the milk and garlic, in a food processor. Add the lemon rind and potatoes and process for about 1 minute, until smooth. Add the lemon juice, black pepper, and cayenne pepper and process briefly to incorporate. With the motor running, slowly add the oil and continue processing until the mixture is very smooth.

Lightly oil an 8-cup gratin dish and transfer

the brandade to the dish, spreading it out evenly. (*The brandade can be made several hours ahead. Cover with plastic wrap and refrigerate.*)

Sprinkle the brandade with the cheese and bake for 10 to 15 minutes, until the top is lightly browned and it is hot throughout. (If the brandade has been refrigerated, increase the baking time by about 10 minutes.)

Meanwhile, arrange the rounds of bread in a single layer on a cookie sheet. Bake for about 10 minutes, or until nicely browned.

Serve the brandade with the toasts for dipping or spreading.

Grand Aïoli
Serves 6 to 8 as a first course

✂ *Aïoli* is the name given to a mayonnaise that is loaded with garlic. *Le grand aïoli* refers to a whole meal of salted codfish, many vegetables, shellfish, hard-cooked eggs, and, in the original recipe, snails, all of which are served with the garlic mayonnaise.

This is a classic dish from Provence, great for a large party, where the guests can help themselves. It should be served lukewarm or at room temperature. It is important that you use good-quality extra-virgin olive oil, and that it be at room temperature; cold oil would cause the mixture to separate.

Try to get thick fillets of salt cod. Portuguese, Italian, and Spanish markets have the best ones. Wash the cod well under cool water and blanch it before cooking it in a lot of unsalted boiling water. Taste the fish after blanching it, though; if it is still salty, blanch it a second time.

All of the vegetables for the grand aioli can be cooked ahead and reheated at serving time in a microwave oven or on top of the stove. If using the stovetop method, add a few tablespoons of water to provide some additional moisture. The eggs can be hard-cooked ahead too. The broccoli and zucchini should be cooked at the last minute while you are finishing the cod.

AÏOLI

1½	slices firm white bread (about 1½ ounces)
6–8	garlic cloves
2	tablespoons Dijon mustard
3	large egg yolks
1	tablespoon fresh lemon juice
½	teaspoon salt
½	teaspoon freshly ground black pepper
⅛	teaspoon cayenne pepper
1½	cups extra-virgin olive oil, at room temperature

GRAND AÏOLI

2	pounds thickest-possible salt cod fillets
16	small potatoes (about 2 pounds), washed
8	carrots (about 1¼ pounds), peeled and halved
1¾	pounds broccoli, separated into florets, stems cut off and peeled, florets cut lengthwise in half
3	zucchini (about 1½ pounds), trimmed and cut lengthwise into quarters
½	teaspoon salt
1½–1¾	pounds cleaned small squid (18–20 bodies, plus tentacles)
6	large hard-cooked eggs (see page 66), peeled

Crusty French bread, for serving

FOR THE AÏOLI: Process the bread and garlic in a food processor for 10 to 15 seconds, until the garlic is finely chopped. Add the mustard, egg yolks, lemon juice, salt, black pepper, and cayenne and process for a few seconds to mix. With the motor running, slowly add the oil in a steady stream and process until the mixture is homogenized and thick. Transfer to a bowl, cover, and set aside at room temperature.

FOR THE GRAND AÏOLI: Rinse the cod thoroughly under cold water, then put it in a large saucepan and cover with 6 quarts cold water. Bring to a strong boil and boil for 5 minutes; drain. Rinse the fish thoroughly under cold water again.

Using your fingers, separate the fish into flakes, discarding any bones and skin. Place in a bowl with 4 quarts cold water and set aside.

Put the potatoes in a saucepan, cover with cold water, and bring to a boil. Cover, reduce the heat, and cook until tender, about 20 minutes. Drain and set aside in the pan to dry.

Meanwhile, place the carrots in a large saucepan with cold water to cover, bring to a boil, and boil for 8 to 12 minutes, or until tender. Lift the carrots from the water with a slotted spoon and set aside. Add the broccoli to the water, return it to a boil, and cook for 3 minutes. Remove the broccoli with a skimmer and set aside. Drop the zucchini into the water, return to a boil, and cook for 30 seconds. Drain and set aside.

At serving time, bring 2 cups of water to a boil in a saucepan. Add the salt and squid and bring back to a boil, then reduce the heat and simmer for about 2 minutes. Drain.

Bring 8 cups of water to a boil in a saucepan. Drain the cod, add it to the water, and return to a boil. Simmer for 2 minutes. Remove from the heat and let the cod stand in the water for 5 to 10 minutes.

Just before serving, reheat the hard-cooked eggs and the potatoes by placing them momentarily in the hot water with the salt cod.

Drain the cod and arrange it on a platter. Surround it with the squid, vegetables, and hard-cooked eggs. Serve with the aïoli and crusty French bread.

Fried Whiting with Compound Butter
Serves 6

Whiting is an inexpensive, underestimated fish with tender, white, soft-textured flesh. It is ideal for mousses and quenelles and it is also good broiled, as well as poached or fried. The large whiting known as hake is great poached and served whole, like salmon, with mayonnaise or hollandaise sauce.

Here whitings are prepared in a classic way, dipped in beer and seasoned flour and deep-fried. They are served with a compound butter seasoned with tarragon and lime juice and served on the side in a mushroom cap. The compound butter, as well as the parsley, can be served with other fried fish or even sautéed meat.

At the Asian market where I sometimes shop, the fish are not gutted, but my fishmonger guts them for me and removes the backbones.

6   whiting (about 11 ounces each)

GARNISH

6   large white mushroom caps
    Fresh lemon juice

COMPOUND BUTTER

8   tablespoons (1 stick) unsalted
      butter, softened
1   tablespoon fresh tarragon leaves
2   teaspoons fresh lime juice
¼   teaspoon salt
1   tablespoon reduced Basic Brown
      Sauce (page 613; optional)
2   tablespoons dry white wine

    Corn or vegetable oil, for deep-frying
1   cup Wondra (instant) flour
½   teaspoon salt

1 teaspoon freshly ground black
  pepper
1 teaspoon paprika
1 teaspoon herbes de Provence,
  finely crushed, or a mixture
  of dried oregano, thyme, and
  rosemary
1 12-ounce can beer

FRIED PARSLEY (Optional)

6 cups small curly parsley sprigs,
  any tough stems removed,
  washed, and thoroughly dried
  Salt

Lemon wedges, for garnish

TO PREPARE THE FISH: If the fish has not been cleaned, remove the gills from each fish and open the bellies; gut the fish, making sure to remove the thin black skin inside the cavities, which tends to be quite bitter. Trim off the fins on the top and the bottom of each fish. To remove the backbone, run your knife down each side of the cavity and, with your fingers, pry out the bone: break the bone at the base of the neck and the tail end of the cavity and pull it out. The only bone left in the fish will be the bone from the end of the cavity to the tail.

Wash and dry the fish inside and out. Bend each of them and insert the tail inside the mouth, pressing the teeth into the tail to make it secure. It is easier to fry them in this round shape. (A fish served this way is often called *merlan en colère,* or "angry whiting," in France.)

FOR THE GARNISH: Brush the mushroom caps with lemon juice to prevent discoloration. Set aside.

FOR THE BUTTER: Combine all the ingredients in a food processor and process until smooth.

Heat 3 inches of oil to 350 degrees in a deep fryer or deep pot. Meanwhile, combine the flour, salt, pepper, paprika, and herbs. Dip the fish into the beer, coating it all over, and then into the flour, covering it thickly. Fry the fish in batches for about 10 minutes, until crisp and brown; the fish should be completely submerged when frying. Drain on a wire rack.

If you're making the fried parsley, reduce the heat slightly and let the oil cool somewhat before frying the parsley; the oil should be approximately 275 degrees. Fry the parsley in the oil, in 2 batches, being very careful to avert your face, because the moisture in the parsley will cause the oil to splatter. Cook, moving the parsley around with a slotted spoon or skimmer, for about 1 minute. Drain on paper towels and sprinkle lightly with salt.

Arrange a fried fish on each serving plate and place a mushroom cap in the center of each fish. Fill the mushroom caps with the butter. Arrange the fried parsley (if using) and lemon wedges around the plates and serve.

Sautéed Trout with Tomato and Olives
Serves 4

Farm-raised trout are now available all over the country. Delicately flavored, they can often be purchased live from a tank at the local supermarket, so their freshness is guaranteed. I like to serve them whole, with the bone in. To create a sauce, I add mushrooms, tomato, olive pieces, and capers to the pan drippings.

¼ cup canola oil

4 trout (about 12 ounces each),
  gutted but heads left on

½ teaspoon salt

½ teaspoon freshly ground black pepper

2 tablespoons unsalted butter

3–4 large mushrooms, cleaned and
  cut into ½-inch dice (1½ cups)

½ cup peeled, seeded, and diced
  (¾-inch) tomato

24 oil-cured olives, pitted and cut into
  ⅜-inch pieces

2 tablespoons drained capers

2 tablespoons chopped fresh chives

Heat the oil in one very large or two medium nonstick skillets. Pat the trout dry and sprinkle with the salt and pepper. Add to the hot oil and cook over medium-high heat, covered, for 4 minutes. Turn and cook on the other side, covered, for 4 minutes. Transfer the trout to a platter and set aside in a warm place.

Add the butter and mushrooms to the drippings in the pan and sauté the mushrooms for 1 minute. Add the tomato and sauté for 1 minute. Add the olives and capers and toss well.

Spoon the sauce over the trout, garnish with the chives, and serve.

Vermouth-Poached Trout with Yellow Pepper Sauce and Corn
Serves 4

❧ **Cooking trout whole produces** a particularly moist and flavorful result, but trout fillets can be substituted. After the whole fish is poached, the skin pulls off easily and the flesh slides off the bone, yielding completely boneless fillets. A delicate yellow pepper sauce with corn gives a summery feel to this dish.

4 trout (about 12 ounces each),
  gutted and heads removed

1 cup dry white vermouth

1 large yellow bell pepper, cored, seeded,
  and cut into ½-inch pieces (2 cups)

½ cup sliced onion

1½ tablespoons olive oil

1 teaspoon salt

1 teaspoon freshly ground black pepper

2 tablespoons unsalted butter

2 ears corn, husked and kernels cut off
  (1½ cups)

2 tablespoons minced fresh chives

Arrange the trout in one layer in a large stainless steel saucepan. Add the vermouth, yellow pepper, onion, oil, salt, and pepper and bring to a boil, then reduce the heat to low, cover, and boil gently for 5 minutes. Remove from the heat.

Transfer 1 trout to a cutting board and pull off and discard the skin. Slide the 2 fillets off the central bone, then reassemble the fillets to simulate the look of a whole trout. Repeat with the remaining trout, then place on individual plates and set aside in a warm place.

Transfer the cooking juices and yellow pepper pieces to a blender, add the butter, and process until smooth and creamy. Pour the mixture into a saucepan and add the corn kernels. Bring to a boil and boil for 30 seconds to 1 minute.

Stir well, then pour the sauce over the trout. Sprinkle with the chives and serve.

Poached Trout in Vegetable Broth
Serves 2

✎ **Trout are poached with** onion, carrot, scallion, and herbs. Their skin is then removed, the meat slid off the bone, and the fillets finished with a sauce made from the broth, a little butter, and oil. This fish can be served whole if guests don't mind removing the skin and bones themselves.

2 Yukon Gold potatoes (about 8 ounces total)
½ cup sliced onion
1 carrot (2 ounces), peeled and thinly sliced (⅓ cup)
1 scallion, trimmed (leaving some green) and cut into 1-inch pieces (2 tablespoons)
1 bay leaf
1 fresh thyme sprig
2 strips lime rind, removed with a vegetable peeler
¼ teaspoon salt
½ teaspoon coarsely ground black pepper
¾ cup water
⅓ cup fruity dry white wine
2 trout (about 12 ounces each), gutted and heads removed
1½ tablespoons unsalted butter
1½ tablespoons olive oil

Put the potatoes in a saucepan, cover them with cold water, and bring to a boil over high heat. Reduce the heat to low and boil the potatoes, un-covered, for 30 minutes, or until they are tender. Drain off the water and set the potatoes aside until they are cool enough to handle.

Preheat the oven to 160 degrees.

Peel the potatoes and cut them into 1-inch cubes. Put the cubes in a baking dish and keep warm in the oven.

Combine the onion, carrot, scallion, bay leaf, thyme, lime rind, salt, pepper, water, and wine in a large stainless steel saucepan. Bring to a boil, then reduce the heat to low, cover, and boil gently for 1 minute.

Add the trout and return to a boil, then reduce the heat to low, cover, and cook for 5 minutes.

Using a slotted spoon, lift the trout from the broth and place on a plate. Remove and discard the skin, then remove the 2 fillets from the central bone of each fish (discard the bones); the meat will slide off the bone easily if the trout are cooked. Arrange the fillets in a baking dish and keep them warm in the oven while you make the sauce.

Add the butter and oil to the broth and bring to a strong boil.

Arrange a few cubes of potato in the bottom of each soup plate and place a trout fillet on top. Spoon the broth and vegetables on top and serve.

Mousse-Stuffed Trout with Sweet White Vermouth Sauce
Serves 4

✎ **In the traditional rendition** of this dish, boned whole trout is stuffed with a fish mousse and mushroom puree, poached in vermouth, and finished with cream. I use trout fillets, covering one fillet with the mousse and covering the mousse with a second fillet to simulate a whole trout minus the head and tail.

8 ounces sole fillets, cut into 1-inch pieces
1 large egg white
½ cup heavy cream
½ teaspoon salt
⅜ teaspoon freshly ground black pepper
1 tablespoon unsalted butter
1 tablespoon chopped shallot
2 cups sliced mushrooms

8 skinless trout fillets (about 3 ounces each)
⅓ cup chopped shallots
½ teaspoon salt, or more to taste
¼ teaspoon freshly ground black pepper, or more to taste
¾ cup dry white vermouth
1½ teaspoons unsalted butter, softened
½ cup heavy cream

FOR THE MOUSSE: Process the sole and egg white in a food processor for a few seconds. With the motor running, add the cream in a slow, steady stream. Add ¼ teaspoon of the salt and ⅛ teaspoon of the pepper and process for another 20 seconds to tighten the mixture.

Melt the butter in a saucepan. Add the shallot and sauté for 1 minute. Add the mushrooms and cook until the liquid from the mushrooms has evaporated. Add the remaining ¼ teaspoon salt and ¼ teaspoon pepper, then remove from the heat and let cool.

Preheat the oven to 400 degrees.

Mix the mushrooms with the mousse. Spoon the mixture into a pastry bag with a large plain tip. Pipe over 4 of the fillets. (Alternatively, spoon the mousse on the fillets.) Cover with the other 4 fillets.

Sprinkle the shallots into a flameproof baking dish or a large ovenproof saucepan and add the salt and pepper. Arrange the trout on top so they touch one another. Add the vermouth. Butter a piece of parchment paper with the 1½ teaspoons butter and cover the fish with the buttered paper.

Bring to a boil on top of the stove, then bake for 12 to 15 minutes. Pour the cooking juices into a stainless steel saucepan. Cover the fish with the buttered paper again and set aside in a warm place.

Bring the cooking juices to a rolling boil and boil for 1 minute to reduce. Add the cream and boil for 3 to 4 minutes, until the sauce thickens lightly. Add additional salt and pepper to taste if necessary.

Remove the buttered paper from the fish, pour the sauce over it, and serve.

Porgy Fillets Niçoise
Serves 8

Porgies are plentiful in the Long Island Sound, and in the summer, I occasionally go fishing for them — and fisherman friends are always willing to supply me with them.

This simple, light dish is made with tomatoes and wine, both of which complement the mildness and softness of the fish.

¾ cup very finely chopped onion
8 skinless porgy fillets (4½ ounces each)
½ cup peeled, seeded, and diced tomato
1½ teaspoons salt
¾ cup dry white wine
4 tablespoons (½ stick) unsalted butter

Preheat the oven to 400 degrees.

Wash the onion in a sieve under cold water. Press on it with your hand to release most of the water. (The washing prevents the onion from turning dark and makes it less bitter and strong-tasting.)

Arrange the fillets skin side up in a large gratin dish and sprinkle with the onion. Scatter the tomato over them and add the salt and wine.

Lay a piece of buttered parchment paper on top and bake for about 10 minutes, until the fillets are cooked through. Transfer the fillets to a serving platter; or, if you plan to serve them in the gratin dish, hold the fillets in place with a plate or a small lid and pour the juices into a skillet.

Bring the juices to a boil and reduce to about ⅔ cup. Add the butter piece by piece, beating with a whisk to incorporate it, then bring the sauce to a boil. As it comes to a strong boil, it will rise like milk ready to boil over — this is when the sauce will emulsify.

Pour the sauce over the fillets and serve.

Broiled Bluefish with Lemon Leeks and Garlicky Beans
Serves 4

🍶 **Fresh out of the** water, bluefish is excellent grilled, broiled, or cut into tartare, and it is superb smoked. But, like tuna and other dark fatty fish, it has a strong taste when older. Since it is fatty, it is best served plain rather than with a heavy sauce. Here lemony leeks and garlicky beans balance the fish's richness.

2 skin-on bluefish fillets (10 ounces each)
¼ teaspoon salt
⅛ teaspoon freshly ground black pepper
1 tablespoon canola oil

LEEKS
1 medium leek, trimmed (leaving some green), quartered lengthwise, washed, and sliced (1½ cups)
1 cup water
¼ teaspoon salt
¼ teaspoon freshly ground black pepper
⅓ stick (2⅔ tablespoons) unsalted butter
1 tablespoon fresh lemon juice

8 ounces wax beans, trimmed
1 tablespoon unsalted butter
½ teaspoon chopped garlic (1–2 cloves)
Salt and freshly ground black pepper

Make 3 or 4 diagonal slits in each fillet, cutting through the skin and approximately ½ inch into the flesh. This will help in the cooking and the seasoning will penetrate the fish. Sprinkle with the salt, pepper, and oil. Set aside.

FOR THE LEEKS: Put the leek and water in a saucepan, preferably stainless steel, bring to a boil over high heat, and boil for 4 to 5 minutes. The pieces should be firm but tender and only about ¼ cup water should remain. If not, boil a bit longer to reduce the water. Add the salt, pepper, butter, and lemon juice and bring to a boil. Set aside, covered, to keep warm.

Meanwhile, drop the beans into a saucepan of boiling salted water. Return to a boil and cook, uncovered, at a strong boil for 8 to 10 minutes, until tender but still firm. Drain.

Preheat the broiler. Arrange the bluefish fillets skin side up on a tray, slide under the broiler, no more than 2 inches from the heat, and broil for 5 to

6 minutes. The skin should start to blister, brown, and crack. (Do not turn the fillets over; because of the slits in the skin, they will cook through.)

Arrange the leeks in the center of a platter and place the fillets on top.

Melt the butter in a skillet. Add the garlic, then add the beans and a pinch each of salt and pepper and sauté just enough to heat through. Arrange around the fish and serve.

Mackerel with Potatoes, Onions, and Tomatoes
Serves 4

Fresh mackerel is nutty, fleshy, and moist — but it has to be fresh to be good. It's excellent broiled to release its fat. In this recipe, sliced potatoes, onions, and tomatoes are layered in a gratin dish and baked until tender, then the fish is arranged on top and finished under the broiler.

1 pound Red Bliss or Yukon Gold potatoes, peeled and thinly sliced (about 3 cups)
2 medium onions, thinly sliced (2 cups)
1 tablespoon chopped fresh savory or thyme
1½ tablespoons olive oil
¾ teaspoon salt
¼ teaspoon freshly ground black pepper
⅓ cup homemade chicken stock (page 612) or low-salt canned chicken broth
2 large ripe tomatoes (1 pound), cut into ½-inch-thick slices
½ cup dry white wine (such as Chablis)
4 large mackerel (12–14 ounces each), gutted and heads and tails removed

½ teaspoon herbes de Provence
2 tablespoons chopped fresh parsley

Preheat the oven to 400 degrees.

Rinse the potato slices well in cool water, then drain them thoroughly in a colander. Put the potato slices in a gratin dish, add the onions, savory or thyme, oil, ½ teaspoon of the salt, and the pepper, and mix well. Add the stock and arrange the sliced tomatoes over the top.

Bake for 1 to 1¼ hours, until the potatoes are tender. Remove from the oven and add the wine. (*The gratin mixture can be prepared to this point up to 1 hour ahead and set aside.*)

Preheat the broiler. Make 3 horizontal slits, each about ¼ inch deep, through the skin on both sides of each mackerel. Sprinkle the fish with the remaining ¼ teaspoon salt and the herbes de Provence and arrange them in one layer on top of the gratin, pushing them partially into the gratin.

Place the dish under the broiler so it is about 8 inches from the heat and broil for 10 minutes. Sprinkle with the parsley and serve.

Mackerel in Vinaigrette
Serves 6 as a first course

Because mackerel's dark, oily flesh is quite rich, it is best served with something acidic, such as tomato, white wine, or vinegar. This is a handy recipe for a first course, picnic, late supper, or a cold buffet because it can be made ahead and refrigerated for several days.

You can serve the vinaigrette with other poached fatty fish, such as herring, salmon, or bluefish, or with meats, particularly rich ones like roast pork. Or use it as a dressing for salads, like coleslaw, or vegetables, such as boiled potatoes in the skin.

3 large mackerel (12–14 ounces each),
   gutted and heads removed
⅓ cup white vinegar
1 teaspoon salt

1 large egg
3 tablespoons red wine vinegar
2 teaspoons Dijon mustard
1 teaspoon salt
1 teaspoon freshly ground black pepper
½ cup peanut oil

3 tablespoons chopped fresh chives or
   parsley

Cut each of the fish through the bones into 3 chunks and drop into a saucepan. Add 3 cups cold water, the vinegar, and salt, bring to a boil, and boil gently for 10 minutes.

MEANWHILE, FOR THE VINAIGRETTE: Process the egg, vinegar, mustard, salt, and pepper briefly in a blender, just to mix. With the machine running, slowly add the oil and process until it is incorporated. The sauce should be light — rather like light cream, not like a mayonnaise. If it is too thick, dilute it with 1 to 2 tablespoons water.

Lift the fish from the water, remove the meat from the bones, and arrange on a serving platter. Pour the vinaigrette over the fish. Serve, garnished with the chopped chives or parsley, at room temperature or chilled.

Sardines on Parsley Salad
Serves 10 to 12 as a first course

✿ Ideal eaten on thick, crusty bread or buttered black bread and served with a dry white wine, these sardines are cured in salt, boned, and covered with olive oil. Make sure they are very fresh:

the best will be still in rigor mortis. After curing, they are easy to bone, and they can remain in the oil for several days to develop flavor. They are accompanied by roasted yellow and red peppers and a garlicky parsley-carrot salad.

3 pounds very fresh sardines (about 24,
   about 2 ounces each)
¼ cup kosher salt
2 tablespoons brown sugar
2–3 tablespoons fresh thyme leaves
   About ½ cup olive oil

PEPPERS

3 red bell peppers
3 yellow bell peppers

PARSLEY-CARROT SALAD

6 cups fresh parsley leaves
2 cups grated carrots
2 tablespoons chopped onion
2 tablespoons chopped garlic (6–8 cloves)
½ teaspoon salt
½ teaspoon freshly ground black pepper
1 tablespoon red wine vinegar
¼ cup olive oil

Cracked black pepper (optional)

Gently scale the sardines with the back of a knife or by rubbing them under cold water (the scales will slide off). Cut off the heads and a strip of the belly so the insides can be cleaned out, and then gut them. Wash under cold running water and pat dry. Put in a shallow baking dish.

Mix the salt with the brown sugar and sprinkle all over the sardines. Cover with plastic wrap and refrigerate to cure for at least 3 hours, or overnight.

Rinse the sardines briefly under cold water and pat dry. To butterfly the sardines, open each one out by running your thumbnail inside along the central bone on each side. The flesh will be quite soft and will separate from the bone easily. Pull out the central bone. It will come out without any meat with it. Cut off the tail and remove any black skin or visible bones.

Pat the sardines dry with paper towels and arrange them in a baking dish. Sprinkle the thyme leaves on top and sprinkle with the olive oil. Cover with plastic wrap and refrigerate for at least 3 hours. (*The sardines can be refrigerated in the oil for up to 3 days.*)

FOR THE PEPPERS: Preheat the broiler. Arrange the peppers on a cookie sheet and broil about 1 inch from the heat, turning occasionally, for 12 to 15 minutes, until the skin is well browned all around. Seal the hot peppers in a plastic bag and let steam for 10 minutes to soften the skin, making it easy to remove.

Pull the skin off the peppers. Remove the cores, open the peppers, and remove the seeds (this can also be done under running water; pat the peppers dry). Flatten the peppers and cut into 6 to 8 pieces each.

FOR THE SALAD: Wash the parsley leaves carefully and dry. Combine the leaves with the car-

ROASTED RED PEPPERS

Roasted this way, peppers can be sliced into strips and packed in a jar with olive oil, a pinch of salt, a lot of freshly ground black pepper and chopped garlic. They will keep for a couple of weeks in the refrigerator and can be used in sandwiches or for seasoning pasta or other dishes.

---

rots, onion, garlic, salt, pepper, vinegar, and olive oil in a bowl, mixing well.

Arrange the parsley salad on a serving platter with the red and yellow peppers around it. Place the sardines on top. Sprinkle lightly with the oil from the sardines, then sprinkle with cracked pepper, if desired, and serve.

Saffron-Seasoned Fish and Shellfish Stew with Couscous
Serves 6

Although it is a complex dish with a lot of ingredients, this seafood stew of fish, shellfish, vegetables, saffron, wine, and fish stock doesn't take long to cook. You can ask your fish market for fish bones to make the fish stock, or you can substitute chicken stock or a mixture of chicken stock and water for the fish stock. This dish is best eaten with a fish spoon or a sauce spoon.

STOCK

1¼ pounds fish bones
     Reserved shells from 6 shrimp (from below)
4 cups water
1 teaspoon herbes de Provence
     Reserved tomato liquid and skin (see opposite page)

- 2 tablespoons olive oil
- 2 shallots, coarsely chopped (about ⅓ cup)
- 1 small leek, trimmed (leaving some green), split, washed, and cut into ½-inch pieces (about 1 cup)
- 2 tablespoons thinly sliced garlic
- 1 cup mushrooms, cut into 1-inch pieces
- ⅓ cup diced carrot
- 2 medium tomatoes (12 ounces), peeled, halved, and seeded, liquid and skin reserved for fish stock, flesh cut into 1-inch pieces (1½ cups)
- 1 tablespoon tomato paste
- ½ cup dry white wine (such as Chablis)
- 1 teaspoon fresh thyme leaves
- 2 teaspoons saffron threads
- 1½ teaspoons salt
- 1 teaspoon freshly ground black pepper
- 1½ cups couscous
- 1 cup 1½-inch pieces zucchini
- 1 ear corn, husked and kernels cut off
- 1 pound thick cod fillets, cut into 2-inch pieces
- 5 ounces cleaned squid, bodies cut into 2-inch pieces, tentacles left whole
- 6 sea scallops (about 4 ounces total), washed and tough muscles removed
- 6 large shrimp (about 5 ounces total), shelled, shells reserved for fish stock (see opposite page)
- 2 teaspoons chopped fresh tarragon

FOR THE STOCK: Combine all the ingredients in a stainless steel pot, bring to a boil, and boil, uncovered, for 30 minutes.

Strain the stock; you should have 3½ cups. If you have more, boil until reduced to 3½ cups; if less, add water. Reserve 1¼ cups for the couscous.

FOR THE COUSCOUS AND SEAFOOD: Heat 1½ tablespoons of the oil in a large stainless steel pot. Add the shallots, leek, and garlic and sauté for 2 minutes. Add the mushrooms, carrot, tomatoes, tomato paste, the 2¼ cups fish stock, the wine, thyme, saffron, salt, and pepper and bring to a boil. (*The recipe can be made to this point a few hours ahead and set off the heat; when ready to finish the dish, return the mixture to a boil.*)

Meanwhile, combine the couscous with the remaining 1½ teaspoons oil and the reserved 1¼ cups stock in a medium saucepan. Bring to a boil, remove from the heat, mix well, cover tightly, and set aside for 10 minutes.

Add the zucchini, corn, cod, squid, scallops, and shrimp to the vegetable mixture and bring to a strong boil. By the time the mixture comes to a strong boil (which will take about 10 minutes, so it is done when the couscous is ready), the vegetables, fish, and shellfish will be cooked. Stir in the tarragon.

At serving time, rake the couscous with the tines of a fork to separate it and make it fluffy. Ladle some couscous into the middle of each of six dinner plates. Then, using the bowl of the ladle, spread the couscous into a ring around the edges of each plate. Ladle the fish stew, including a fair amount of the liquid, into the centers of the plates. Serve.

Shoreline Seafood Combo
Serves 4

This is one of those excellent seafood stews that includes a colorful assortment of vegetables — mushrooms, tomato, broccoli, and zucchini — along with the shellfish and fish: in this instance, scallops, shrimp, and monkfish. Another firm-textured fish can be substituted if monkfish is not available. It takes a while to cut up all the vegetables and fish, but the dish takes only 5 to 6 minutes to cook.

½ cup fruity dry white wine (such as Sémillon)

1½ tablespoons olive oil

1½ tablespoons unsalted butter

1 teaspoon salt

1 teaspoon freshly ground black pepper

2 cups sliced mushrooms

1 large tomato, halved, seeded, and cut into 1-inch pieces (about 1 cup)

1 small broccoli stalk, stem peeled, cut into 1½-inch pieces (about 1½ cups)

1 zucchini (6 ounces), trimmed and cut into 2-inch-by-½-inch-thick sticks (about 1 cup)

¼ cup chopped onion

2 teaspoons finely chopped garlic

10 ounces sea scallops, washed, tough muscles removed, and cut in half

8 ounces medium shrimp, shelled and cut into 3 pieces each

1 cleaned monkfish fillet (about 9 ounces), cut into 1-inch pieces

Combine the wine, oil, butter, salt, pepper, mushrooms, tomato, broccoli, zucchini, onion, and garlic in a stainless steel saucepan, bring to a strong boil, and cook for 2 minutes. Add the scallops, shrimp, and monkfish, cover, and cook over high heat for 3 to 4 minutes, stirring once or twice. Set the pan aside, covered, off the heat for 5 minutes to finish cooking.

Ladle the stew into soup plates and serve.

Seafood Medley with Toasted Bread Crumbs
Serves 4

✄ **Fast and easy to** prepare, this fresh, light dish is perfect for special guests. The scallops, shrimp, and salmon are divided between two very hot skillets and sautéed quickly. (It's important to use two skillets here; the seafood won't cook properly if crowded into one pan.) Corn kernels and garlic are added and everything is topped with a wonderfully crunchy mixture of toasted bread crumbs, lemon rind, and parsley.

2 slices firm white bread (about 2 ounces), processed into coarse (¼-inch) crumbs in a food processor (1½ cups)

3 tablespoons olive oil

2 tablespoons unsalted butter

8 ounces sea scallops, washed and tough muscles removed

8 ounces medium shrimp (12–15), shelled

8 ounces salmon fillet, skin removed and cut into 1-inch pieces

⅓ cup chopped shallots

¾ teaspoon salt

½ teaspoon freshly ground black pepper

3 garlic cloves, crushed and finely chopped (2 teaspoons)

1 ear corn, husked and kernels cut off (1 cup)

1 tablespoon grated lemon rind

2 tablespoons chopped fresh parsley

Preheat the oven to 400 degrees.

Combine the bread crumbs with 1 tablespoon of the olive oil in a small bowl, rubbing the crumbs gently between your fingers to moisten them lightly with the oil. Spread the crumbs on a cookie sheet and bake for 7 to 8 minutes, stirring them occasionally, until browned on all sides. Set aside.

Divide the butter and the remaining 2 tablespoons olive oil between two large skillets and heat until very hot. Add half the scallops, shrimp, and salmon to each skillet, along with the shallots, sprinkle with the salt and pepper, and sauté over high heat for about 1 minute. Add the garlic and corn kernels, cover, and cook for another 2 minutes.

Meanwhile, combine the toasted crumbs with the lemon rind and parsley.

Divide the seafood among four plates, top with the bread crumb mixture, and serve.

Seafood with "Pocket Squares"
Serves 4

✍ **This recipe looks more** complicated than it is. Egg roll wrappers, available packaged at most supermarkets, are pliable enough to be rolled out easily. Watercress leaves, sandwiched between pairs of the wrappers, show through the almost transparent surface. Served on top of the poached seafood, the packets make a beautiful presentation.

While I use oysters, scallops, and salmon in this recipe, the oysters or the scallops can be replaced by other shellfish, such as shrimp, and another fish could be substituted for the salmon. If you omit the oysters, replace their juice with ¼ cup each water and dry white wine.

Canola oil, for coating the pocket squares
8   egg roll wrappers (6 inches square)
16 watercress leaves
12 oysters, shucked (see page 153), juices reserved in a small bowl
½   cup dry white vermouth
½   cup water
1   yellow bell pepper (8 ounces), peeled, cored, seeded, and cut into julienne strips (about 1 cup)
2   tablespoons chopped scallions
2   tablespoons olive oil
1   tablespoon unsalted butter
½   teaspoon salt
¼   teaspoon freshly ground black pepper

8   ounces bay scallops
8   ounces skinless salmon fillet, cut into 1-inch pieces

Bring about 6 cups of salted water to a boil in a medium saucepan. Meanwhile, lightly oil a nonporous work surface (such as marble or Formica). Place an egg roll wrapper on it and arrange 4 watercress leaves randomly on top. Lightly dampen a second wrapper on one side with water and press it, dampened side down, on top of the first wrapper, creating a "sandwich" with the watercress inside. Lightly oil the top and bottom of the sandwich and roll it out with a rolling pin to create an 8-inch square. Make 3 more pocket squares with the remaining wrappers and watercress leaves.

Poach the pocket squares one at a time, dropping them into the boiling water and cooking them for 1½ minutes each. Remove with a skimmer and transfer to a bowl of cold water. Be careful, as they are delicate. Set aside. (*These can be poached up to an hour before serving.*)

Allow the oyster juices to sit undisturbed for a few minutes, then carefully pour them into a large stainless steel saucepan, leaving behind any sandy residue. Add the vermouth, water, yellow pepper, scallions, olive oil, butter, salt, and pepper, bring to a boil, and boil for 1 minute. Add the scallops and salmon and return to a boil. Stir, add the oysters, stir again, and immediately remove from the heat.

Meanwhile, bring a pot of water to a boil. Lift the pocket squares from the cold water and plunge them into the boiling water for about 10 seconds to reheat them. (Alternatively, lift the squares from the cold water and place 1 on a plate, using a little oil between them so they don't stick together. Cover with a paper towel and reheat in a microwave oven for about 1 minute.)

Divide the seafood mixture among four plates and arrange a hot pocket square decoratively on top of each serving. Serve.

Eel with Potato Miettes
Serves 6

✂ **Eel used to be** a great favorite, almost up to the twentieth century. It is not, however, very common on today's tables. Most of the eels caught in this country are sent to Germany, Holland, and Belgium, the great eel-loving countries. Now usually found only at ethnic markets, eel is excellent served, as it is here, with very small diced potatoes, often called *miettes* ("crumbs") because of their size. The acidity of the sorrel goes well with the richness of the eel, but if sorrel is unavailable, substitute another herb of your choice.

2　live eels (1¼ pounds each) or 2 skinned eels (about 1 pound each)

Salt
All-purpose flour, for sprinkling
3　tablespoons peanut oil
2　tablespoons unsalted butter

POTATOES
2　pounds baking (Idaho) potatoes (4–5)
1　tablespoon unsalted butter
1　tablespoon corn oil
5　scallions, trimmed (leaving some green) and coarsely chopped (1 cup)
　　Salt and freshly ground black pepper

3　tablespoons unsalted butter
1　teaspoon chopped garlic (2–3 cloves)
1　tablespoon red wine vinegar
½　cup shredded sorrel (see the headnote)

If your eels are alive, kill them by covering them with salt. They will die within a few minutes. One at a time, hold each eel with a towel, cut open the belly, and pull the guts out. With your knife, cut an incision in the skin all around the head. Hold the head with one hand and pull the skin off with the other hand. (You may need pliers, as the skin is sometimes hard to pull off.) Cut off the head and, with scissors, cut off the fin on each side.

Cut each eel crosswise, bones and all, into 6 pieces.

Bring a saucepan of water to a boil. Drop in the eel pieces, bring back to a boil, and boil for 2 to 3 minutes. Drain the eel in a colander and rinse under cold water until cold. Peel or scrape off all the black surface, which is mostly fat, until the eel is practically clean of all that second skin and fat.

Dry the eel pieces with paper towels and sprinkle them with flour, coating well. Divide the oil and butter between two large skillets and heat until hot. Add the eel, sprinkle lightly with salt,

European and American eels are born in the Sargasso Sea and eventually migrate to different parts of the world, going up estuaries and rivers to end up in ponds, all the time getting larger and changing color. A beige color in the sea, they become dark brown in the rivers and ponds. Very tiny eels, which are spaghetti-like and transparent, called *civelles* in France and *anguilas* in Spain, are quite common in the French Basque country and Spain. They are sautéed in oil with garlic and served almost like spaghetti. These so-called elvers are rarely found in U.S. markets.

If you catch your own eels or buy them in a Chinatown, you have to kill them yourself. You can cut off their heads or cover them with table salt, which is easier: they will suffocate and die rapidly.

When sautéed or stewed, eel must be skinned. Underneath the skin is a fatty layer, and removing it greatly improves the taste. After the eel is skinned, it is blanched, which sets the fatty layer, which can then be scraped off or removed with a knife.

Eel is one of the best fish to smoke, since it is very fatty and retains the smoke well, and its meat stays moist and tender. If eel is smoked, it is not skinned.

and brown over medium-low heat for 7 to 8 minutes, turning the pieces after 3 to 4 minutes so they brown evenly. Cover the skillets and set the eel aside to continue cooking and softening in its residual heat for another 3 to 4 minutes.

MEANWHILE, FOR THE POTATOES: Peel the potatoes. Cut into ¼-inch-thick slices and then into ¼-inch dice. Rinse in cold water and drain well.

Heat the butter and oil in a large skillet, preferably nonstick. When it is hot, add the potatoes and sauté over high heat for 12 to 15 minutes, stirring occasionally, until nicely browned and cooked through.

Add the scallions, sprinkle with a pinch each of salt and pepper, and continue cooking for 2 to 3 minutes longer. Remove from the heat.

At serving time, arrange the potatoes and scallions on individual plates. Arrange the cooked eel on top.

Melt the butter in a small skillet. When it is foaming but not too hot, add the garlic and cook for a few seconds, then add the red wine vinegar and bring to a boil. Spoon the sauce over the eel, sprinkle with the sorrel, and serve.

Frogs' Legs in Tarragon Sauce
Serves 6

Frog was a delicacy when I was growing up in lower Burgundy. My brothers and I would hunt for them in local ponds, and we'd also search for snails and wild mushrooms after summer rains. Some of the frogs I've caught and used for this recipe are the larger bullfrogs, mostly brown, and a smaller variety, the leopard frog, striated with yellow and green. In New York City's Chinatown, one can buy fresh, live frogs even larger, weighing close to one pound each.

The most common way of cooking frogs' legs is to dredge them in flour and sauté them in butter and oil, then finish them with parsley and garlic. This recipe with cream and tarragon was made at the Hôtel de l'Europe, where I apprenticed in the early fifties. It's a casual dish: you can eat it with your fingers and enjoy the frogs' legs to their fullest.

- 2 pounds frogs' legs
- 1 cup chopped onion
- ½ teaspoon- chopped garlic (1–2 cloves)
- ¾ cup dry white wine (such as Chablis)
- ½ teaspoon salt, plus a pinch
- ¼ teaspoon freshly ground black pepper
- 2 pounds small new white or fingerling potatoes, peeled

SAUCE

- 1 tablespoon unsalted butter, softened
- 1 tablespoon all-purpose flour
- 1 cup reserved frog cooking juices (from above)
- ½ cup heavy cream
  Salt and freshly ground black pepper
- 1 tablespoon chopped fresh tarragon

- 1 fresh tarragon sprig, for garnish

Put the frogs' legs in a stainless steel saucepan with the onion, garlic, wine, ½ teaspoon salt, and the pepper and bring to a boil, then cover, reduce the heat, and simmer gently for 5 to 6 minutes, until the meat separates partially from the bones and is just tender but still firm and slightly chewy.

(If the frogs' legs are very large, increase the cooking time by 2 to 3 minutes; if they are very small, reduce the cooking time to 4 minutes.)

Remove the frogs' legs and set aside. Strain the cooking juices into a saucepan. Boil over high heat to reduce to 1 cup. Set aside.

Meanwhile, drop the potatoes into a saucepan, cover with cold water, and add the pinch of salt. Bring to a boil, reduce the heat, and boil gently just until the potatoes are tender, about 35 minutes. Drain off the water and set aside.

FOR THE SAUCE: Using a whisk, combine the butter and flour in a small bowl to make a *beurre manié*. Whisk into the reduced cooking juices, mixing well, and bring to a boil. Stir in the cream and salt and pepper to taste. Add the frogs' legs and chopped tarragon and bring to a boil.

Arrange the frogs' legs in a serving dish with the potatoes around them or on the side and a sprig of tarragon in the center. Serve.

Poultry and Game

Roast Chicken
Serves 4

❧ **The classic way to** cook chicken is still the simplest and best. Roasting the bird at a high temperature crisps the skin as it protects the flesh, keeping it moist. And roasting the chicken on its side helps the legs, which usually take longer than the breast, cook faster and also keeps the breast moist. Do not cover the bird with foil after it is roasted, or it will steam and taste reheated. For maximum flavor, the chicken should be served no more than 45 minutes after roasting.

1	chicken (about 3½ pounds)
½	teaspoon salt
½	teaspoon freshly ground black pepper
1	tablespoon olive oil
2–3	tablespoons water
1	bunch watercress, trimmed, washed, and dried

Preheat the oven to 425 degrees.

Sprinkle the chicken inside and out with the salt and pepper.

Heat the oil in a large ovenproof nonstick skillet until it is hot but not smoking. Place the chicken on its side in the skillet and brown it over medium-high heat for about 2½ minutes. Turn the chicken over and brown it on the other side for 2½ minutes.

Place the skillet, with the chicken still on its side, in the oven and roast, uncovered, for 20 minutes. Turn the chicken onto its other side and roast for another 20 minutes. Finally, turn the chicken onto its back, baste it with the fat that has emerged during cooking, and roast for 20 minutes.

Remove the chicken from the oven and place it, breast side down to keep the breast meat moist, on a platter. Pour the drippings from the skillet into a bowl and set aside.

Deglaze the skillet by adding the water and stirring to loosen and melt the solidified juices. Add to the drippings in the bowl and let stand briefly, then skim off and discard most of the fat, leaving the natural pan juices.

To serve, carve the chicken, separating the drumsticks from the thighs and cutting each breast in half. Arrange a piece of dark meat and a piece of white meat on each of four plates. Garnish each serving with a few sprigs of watercress and serve with the pan juices.

THERMOMETERS AND COOKING TIMES

Some recipes recommend using an instant-read thermometer to check the doneness of a whole chicken. Insert the thermometer in the thickest part of the joint connecting the thigh and drumstick; this part of the bird takes the longest to cook, and the temperature there should be between 150 and 160 degrees. After you cook a chicken a few times, however, you will come to recognize how it looks when done. If the juice coming out of the chicken is clear, it indicates that there is no blood left in the bird and it is ready.

Chicken with Cognac Sauce
Serves 6 to 8

❧ **This dish was the** specialty of the Pavillon restaurant, where I worked when I first came to New York City in 1959. In the old style, the chicken was carved in the dining room by the maître d'. Even for a single portion, a whole glorious chicken in a copper saucepan was brought to the guest's table. A rich sauce of chicken stock, cream, and cognac, enhanced by the glaze from the chicken juices, was served with it.

- 1 chicken (about 3½ pounds)
- ½ teaspoon salt
- ½ teaspoon freshly ground black pepper
- 1 tablespoon unsalted butter, softened
- 1 cup water

SAUCE

- 2 cups homemade chicken stock (page 612) or low-salt canned chicken broth
- ¾ cup dry white wine
- ½ cup chopped onion
- ½ teaspoon black peppercorns
- 1 tablespoon all-purpose flour
- 1 tablespoon unsalted butter, softened
- ½ cup heavy cream
  About 1½ teaspoons salt
  About ½ teaspoon freshly ground white pepper
- 2 tablespoons cognac

Preheat the oven to 425 degrees.

Sprinkle the chicken inside and out with the salt and pepper and rub all over with the butter. Place it on its side in a roasting pan and roast for 20 minutes. Turn onto the other side and roast for another 20 minutes. Turn the chicken breast side up and roast for 20 minutes. Transfer to a warm platter and set aside in a warm spot.

Discard all the fat that has accumulated in the pan. Deglaze the pan with the water, stirring to melt all the solidified juices, and pour the liquid through a fine strainer into a saucepan. Bring to a boil and reduce until thick as syrup. (This is a poultry glaze; you should have about 1 tablespoon.) Transfer to a double boiler and keep warm.

FOR THE SAUCE: Combine the stock, wine, onion, and peppercorns in a medium heavy saucepan, bring to a boil, and boil to reduce by half.

Work the flour into the butter to make a *beurre manié*. Add it to the sauce, mixing constantly with a whisk, and simmer slowly for 3 minutes. Stir in the cream and reduce again for 1 minute, or until the sauce reaches a nice smooth consistency and coats the spoon. Taste for seasoning and add salt and white pepper as needed (the amounts will depend on the seasoning of the chicken stock). Strain the sauce and stir in the cognac.

To serve, coat the chicken with the sauce, "sprinkle" the poultry glaze over the top, and serve. Alternatively, cut the bird into pieces and arrange on individual serving plates. Coat with the sauce, sprinkle with the poultry glaze, and serve.

BASTING

Recipes often instruct the cook to baste a chicken, turkey, or meat roast. Be aware that you should do this as quickly as possible: if the door is left open for more than a minute, the temperature of a 400-degree oven can drop to about 350 degrees. Allow the oven temperature to recover before basting again.

Baked Chicken with Herb Crumbs
Serves 4

❧ **Use fresh bread crumbs** if possible for this dish. If you use dried crumbs, you'll need only half the amount called for.

The chicken can be prepared in advance to the point where it is marinated in the olive oil, Tabasco, and salt. The herb coating can also be prepared ahead, but don't put it on the bird until you are ready to cook it.

While the chicken is baking, sauté the liver briefly to serve with aperitifs, or enjoy it yourself while you are cooking.

1 chicken (about 3½ pounds)
1 tablespoon olive oil
½ teaspoon Tabasco sauce
¼ teaspoon salt

HERB CRUMBS

2 fresh thyme sprigs or ½ teaspoon dried thyme
2 fresh oregano sprigs or ½ teaspoon dried oregano
3 slices firm white bread (3 ounces), processed to crumbs in a food processor (about 1½ cups)
¼ cup chopped fresh chives or parsley
½ teaspoon freshly ground black pepper
1 tablespoon olive oil

Preheat the oven to 425 degrees.

Cut the wing tips off the chicken. (The wing tips, neck, and gizzard can be frozen for use in stock or soup.) Butterfly the chicken (see the sidebar). Pull off the skin; it should come off easily except, perhaps, around the wings. Remove as much as you can (to use the skin, see the sidebar).

Place the chicken flesh side up on a large bak-

HOW TO BUTTERFLY A WHOLE CHICKEN (AND OTHER BIRDS)

Use a sturdy knife or poultry shears to butterfly a chicken (or other bird). Holding the chicken on its side, cut down along one side of the backbone. The backbone can be left on, but if you want to remove it, cut down along the other side of the bone to separate it. (Backbone pieces are, of course, good for stock.) Spread the chicken open, lay it bone side down on the cutting board, and press it against the board with your hands to flatten it.

ing sheet and rub with the oil and Tabasco. Sprinkle with the salt.

FOR THE HERB CRUMBS: If using fresh thyme and oregano, chop the leaves in a food processor or mini-chop or with a sharp knife. Combine the bread crumbs, thyme, oregano, chives or parsley, pepper, and oil in a bowl and toss gently to coat the bread crumbs lightly with the oil.

Pat the herb coating lightly over the surface of the chicken. Bake for 35 to 40 minutes, until the chicken is cooked through and the crumbs are nicely browned. Remove and let rest for 10 minutes.

Cut the chicken into pieces and serve. Discard the melted fat or use it to sauté potatoes.

CHICKEN OR DUCK CRACKLINGS

Chicken or duck skin can be used to make cracklings to crumble on an accompanying salad. Spread out the skin, outer side up, on a cookie sheet and sprinkle it with salt. Roast in a 400-degree oven for 20 to 25 minutes, until crisp. Break into pieces and serve.

Peking-Style Chicken
Serves 4

❧ **Prepared in the style** of Peking duck, the chicken is first blanched in boiling water to eliminate some of the fat and tighten the skin. This step helps the skin crisp as it cooks, so the bird becomes beautifully brown when it is roasted with a simple glaze of soy, honey, Tabasco, and vinegar.

1 chicken (about 4 pounds)
1½ teaspoons honey
2 tablespoons dark soy sauce
1 teaspoon Tabasco sauce
2 tablespoons balsamic vinegar
12 ounces small button mushrooms, cleaned
½ cup water

Preheat the oven to 375 degrees. Bring 10 cups water to a boil in a large pot.

Meanwhile, remove the wishbone from the chicken. Fold the wings of the chicken under its back and truss it with kitchen twine to help maintain the bird's compact shape.

Lower the chicken breast side down into the boiling water. Return the water to a boil over high heat (this will take about 3 minutes). As soon as the water is boiling, reduce the heat to low and simmer the chicken gently for 2 minutes. Drain and place the chicken breast side up on a rack in a roasting pan.

Mix the honey, soy sauce, Tabasco, and vinegar together in a small bowl. Brush the chicken on all sides with some of the mixture. Roast breast side up for about 30 minutes.

HOW TO REMOVE THE WISHBONE FROM CHICKEN AND OTHER BIRDS

The wishbone is often removed from chicken, duck, and other birds to make carving easier. To remove the wishbone, place the bird on its back and lift the skin at the neck to expose the flesh. Slide the point of a paring knife along either side of the wishbone, cutting into the flesh (about ½ inch deep for a chicken). Then insert your thumb and index finger on either side of the wishbone and pry it out.

Brush the breast side of the chicken again with the honey mixture, then roast for another 30 minutes.

Arrange the mushrooms in one layer under the rack in the pan and add the water. Brush the chicken with the remaining honey mixture and roast for 15 minutes longer.

Transfer the chicken to a platter. Pour the accumulated juices and the mushrooms into a saucepan. Let stand for 2 to 3 minutes, then spoon off as much fat from the surface as possible, and reheat if necessary.

Cut the chicken into pieces and serve with the juices and mushrooms.

HOW TO TRUSS A CHICKEN

Trussing a stuffed bird helps keep the stuffing in. Trussing also helps a bird hold its shape, whether it is stuffed or not, so it cooks evenly and looks better on the serving platter. Nevertheless, trussing is usually optional.

To truss a chicken (or other bird), use fairly thick cotton kitchen twine, so it doesn't cut your fingers. Slide a length of twine under the tail and around the tips of the drumsticks, then cross the twine above the chicken and slide both ends of the twine under the tips of the drumsticks to create a figure 8. Hold the ends of the twine together, which will close the tail opening. Pull the ends of twine around the sides of the bird until they join at the neck end, next to the wings, and tighten the twine, securing it behind the wings or behind the stump of the neck; tie a double knot so the twine doesn't slide off. Remove the twine before serving.

Poule-au-Pot Stew

Serves 4 to 6

❧ *Poule* is the French name for "hen." This famous "chicken in a pot" originated in the sixteenth century under the rule of Henry IV. It is an ideal winter family dish, a complete meal with the chicken, vegetables, and broth. Conventionally it is not as refined as I make it, by removing the meat from the bones and the fat from the stock.

1	chicken (about 3½ pounds), preferably with giblets
4	quarts water
1	teaspoon dried thyme
1	teaspoon dried rosemary
3	bay leaves
12	whole cloves
2	teaspoons salt
1	teaspoon black peppercorns
2	large leeks (about 12 ounces), trimmed (leaving some green), split, and washed
4	medium onions (about 12 ounces)
6	carrots (about 1 pound), peeled
1	small butternut squash (1 pound), peeled, halved, seeded, and halved again
1	small savoy cabbage (about 1 pound), quartered
4	large mushrooms (about 4 ounces), cleaned

ACCOMPANIMENTS

16	baguette slices, toasted
½	cup grated Gruyère or Jarlsberg cheese
	Cornichons (tiny French gherkins) or sour gherkins
	Fleur de sel
	Hot mustard

Place the chicken breast side down in a narrow stainless steel stockpot and add the neck, heart, and gizzard, if available. (Reserve the liver to sauté, or freeze for future use.) Add the water and bring to a boil over high heat. Reduce the heat and boil very gently for 10 minutes. Skim off the fat and impurities that come to the surface.

Add the thyme, rosemary, bay leaves, cloves, salt, and peppercorns, cover, and cook at a very gentle boil for another 15 minutes. Let the chicken sit in the hot broth for 30 minutes. Remove the chicken from the pot; set the stock aside.

When the chicken is cool enough to handle, pull off and discard the skin. Pull the meat from the bones, keeping it in the largest possible pieces. Put the meat in a saucepan, add about ½ cup of the stock, cover, and set aside.

Put the bones back in the remaining stock and boil very gently for another hour. If time permits, chill the stock until any remaining fat solidifies on top; after it hardens, you can easily remove and discard it. Otherwise, skim off the fat.

Strain the stock through a fine strainer. Rinse out the pot and return the stock to the pot. You should have 8 to 9 cups; if necessary, add water.

Add the leeks, onions, carrots, squash, cabbage, and mushrooms to the stock and bring to a boil. Boil gently, covered, for 20 minutes.

Just before serving, reheat the chicken in its liquid.

To serve, arrange the chicken in the center of a large platter. Remove the vegetables from the stock with a slotted spoon, cut them into serving pieces, and arrange around the chicken. Ladle

some of the stock into four to six bowls and serve the chicken and vegetables with the baguette slices and cheese. Pass the cornichons, fleur de sel, and hot mustard at the table.

Chicken Mayonnaise
Serves 6

✎ **This is a great** dish to serve on a hot summer day for a lunch or to feature on a buffet. The chicken can be cooked up to a day ahead and refrigerated. Then bring the beautifully assembled dish to the table or buffet to serve.

 1   chicken (3½–4 pounds)
 1   medium carrot, peeled
 1   medium onion
 4   whole cloves
 1   teaspoon salt
 ½   teaspoon freshly ground black pepper
 8   cups water
 1   large head Boston lettuce
 1   cup mayonnaise, homemade (page 614) or store-bought
 1   tablespoon Dijon mustard
 2   hard-cooked eggs (see page 66), quartered
 2   ripe tomatoes, cut into 4 wedges each
 1   2-ounce can anchovy fillets in oil
 2   tablespoons well-drained capers
 5–6   fresh parsley sprigs, leaves removed and chopped

Put the chicken in a stockpot and add the carrot, onion, cloves, salt, pepper, and water. Bring to a simmer and simmer for 30 minutes.

Cool the chicken in the broth for at least 30 minutes. (*The chicken can be cooked up to a day ahead; transfer to a platter and refrigerate. If desired, strain the stock and reserve for another use.*)

Pull off the outer leaves from the head of lettuce, leaving the center heart (about 2 inches long) intact. Wash and dry the lettuce leaves and cut crosswise into ½-inch-wide strips.

Skin the chicken and pull the meat off the bones in large pieces, then cut into thin slices.

Mix the mayonnaise with the mustard.

Put the shredded lettuce in a large glass bowl. Arrange the sliced chicken on top of the lettuce and coat with the mayonnaise, spreading it with a spatula so that all the chicken is coated. Stand the lettuce heart in the center of the mayonnaise (you may have to push the pieces of chicken aside to make a hole so that the heart can stand up) and arrange the quartered eggs, tomatoes, anchovy fillets, and capers in an attractive pattern on top. Sprinkle with the chopped parsley and serve.

Chicken Ballottine Stuffed with Red Rice or Spinach, Cheese, and Bread
Serves 4

✎ **A ballottine is a** whole chicken that has been boned and stuffed. Showy enough for company, it can be prepared up to a day ahead. (Freeze the bones and the neck, gizzard, and heart for later use in soup or stock.) This bird is best cooked in a sturdy, preferably aluminum, roasting pan, to ensure a good condensation of the cooking juices, which will be used to create the sauce.

Long-grain Wehani rice has a chewy texture that I love. I cook it with mushrooms in stock and then flavor it with leeks and onions for the stuffing. As an alternative, you can stuff the ballottine with a combination of spinach, cheese, and cubed bread or any other stuffing. The ballottine is served with a rich wine sauce made with the defatted chicken drippings and a mixture of finely diced vegetables called a *brunoise*.

1   chicken (about 3¾ pounds), boned
    (see the sidebar, opposite)
¼   teaspoon salt
¼   teaspoon freshly ground black pepper
    Red Rice Stuffing or Spinach, Cheese,
    and Bread Stuffing (recipes follow)

SAUCE

⅓   cup water
½   cup dry red wine
1   celery stalk (2 ounces), peeled and cut
    into ¼-inch dice (½ cup)
1   small onion, chopped (½ cup)
1   carrot (2 ounces), peeled and cut into
    ¼-inch dice (⅓ cup)
½   teaspoon potato starch (see page 318),
    dissolved in 1 tablespoon water
1   tablespoon dark soy sauce

1   tablespoon chopped fresh parsley

Preheat the oven to 400 degrees.

Lay the chicken skin side down on the work surface and sprinkle with the salt and pepper. Spread the cool rice or spinach mixture evenly over the chicken. If using the spinach stuffing, sprinkle the cheese and bread cubes on top of the spinach. Roll the chicken up, tie with kitchen twine (see page 256), and place in a roasting pan.

Roast the ballottine for 1 hour. Lift it from the pan and place it on a platter.

FOR THE SAUCE: Skim off and discard most of the fat from the drippings in the pan. Add the water and wine to the drippings to deglaze the pan and heat over medium heat, stirring to loosen and melt the solidified juices.

Strain the juices into a saucepan. Add the celery, onion, and carrot and bring to a boil over high heat. Cover, reduce the heat to low, and boil gently for 5 minutes. Stir in the dissolved potato starch and soy sauce and bring the mixture back

to a boil, stirring, to thicken it. Remove from the heat.

Transfer the ballottine to a cutting board and remove the twine. Cut half of it into 4 or 5 slices, each about 1 inch thick. Return the uncut half of the ballottine to the serving platter and arrange the cut slices in front of it. Pour the sauce over and around the ballottine, garnish with the parsley, and serve. Cut additional slices of ballottine as needed at the table.

Red Rice Stuffing
½   cup Wehani rice
1¼ cups homemade chicken stock (page
    612) or low-salt canned chicken broth
¼   teaspoon salt
½   ounce (about ½ cup) dried mushrooms,
    such as cèpes (porcini), rinsed and
    broken into pieces
½   leek, trimmed (leaving some green), split,
    washed, and sliced (1 cup)
1   onion (4 ounces), chopped (¾ cup)
1   tablespoon olive oil
¼   cup water

Combine the rice, stock, salt, and dried mushrooms in a large saucepan and bring to a boil, then cover, reduce the heat to low, and cook for 1 hour, or until the rice is tender. Set the rice aside in the pan, uncovered.

Meanwhile, combine the leek, onion, oil, and water in a saucepan and bring to a boil, then cover, reduce the heat, and cook at a gentle boil for 5 minutes. Remove the lid and continue to cook until all the water is gone. Add to the rice, mix well, and let cool to room temperature.

Spinach, Cheese, and Bread Stuffing
1   tablespoon olive oil
1   teaspoon finely chopped garlic
5   ounces baby spinach leaves

¼ teaspoon salt

¼ teaspoon freshly ground black
  pepper

1 cup grated Gruyère or mozzarella
  cheese (about 4 ounces)

1½ cups cubed (½-inch) bread

Heat the oil in a large saucepan or skillet. Add the garlic, spinach, salt, and pepper and cook for 1 minute to soften the garlic and wilt the spinach. Transfer to a bowl and let cool to room temperature. Reserve the cheese and bread and continue with the recipe on page 254.

HOW TO BONE A CHICKEN

Cut off the tips and second joint of each chicken wing, leaving only the first joint at the shoulder. (Keep the trimmings for stock.) Lift up the skin at the neck, slide a small sharp paring knife along each side of the wishbone, and, using your thumb and forefinger, remove the bone, prying it out at the point where it is attached to the breastbone.

Place the chicken on its side and make an incision through the skin of the back from the neck to the tail. With the chicken still on its side, lift up the skin at the shoulder joint. When you move the wing and skin, you will see the joint there. Place your knife at the joint and cut through it, wiggling the knife so it goes through it. Repeat on the other side of the chicken. Hold the chicken securely at the shoulder with the thumb and forefinger of one hand, grasp the wing at the joint with your other hand, and pull off the bones of the whole side of the carcass at the back. Repeat on the other side.

Then, to release the meat attached to the breastbone, place two fingers on each side of the sternum (breastbone) and pull down. The meat is now completely freed from the top and held only at the leg joints.

With the chicken on its side, cut through the little "oyster" of meat next to the joint of the hip on either side of the backbone. Open out one leg and crack it at the hip joint, then cut through the joint, severing the large sinew, and pull the leg free from the carcass. Repeat on the other side. Finally, pull the whole carcass away from the meat.

The only things left attached to the carcass will be the fillets, or tenders, on each side of the breastbone. Slide your thumb or finger underneath and pull each one off. Holding 1 fillet flat on the table, use a knife to scrape the meat free from the sinew that runs through it, pushing the meat off so the sinew comes out in one piece. Repeat with the other fillet. (Reserve for the recipe, if directed, or for another use.)

To remove the leg bones, cut the meat away from the tip of each thighbone so you can hold the bone. Then, holding the blade of the knife perpendicular to the bone, scrape the meat down off the bone until you get down to the joint. Cut around the joint with the knife and scrape the meat from the drumstick down to its tip. Break the bone at the end from the inside so the skin is not torn and the knuckle at the end of the drumstick is left intact. (This knuckle can be trimmed off after cooking; the skin would shrink if it were cut before cooking.) To remove the wing bones, cut around the joint and pull out each bone.

HOW TO TIE A STUFFED BONELESS CHICKEN OR A BONELESS ROAST

Wind a length of kitchen twine around one end of the chicken or roast and tie it with a double knot. Make a loop of twine at the other end (a half-hitch), then slide it back underneath to within 1 inch of the first knot. Repeat the looping down the entire length of the chicken or roast, making half-hitch ties. Turn the chicken or roast over, slide the twine around, and secure it to each back loop until you reach the end. Tie the end to the first loop to finish the process. Alternatively, simply tie the chicken or roast with several pieces of twine.

Spicy Chicken Breasts

Serves 4

✳ **This is a good** make-ahead dish that is easy to prepare and very tasty. The spices for this rub are readily available in your supermarket spice rack, and the mix can be changed based on your taste preferences. Toasting the spices intensifies their flavor.

> ½ teaspoon juniper berries
> ½ teaspoon coriander seeds
> ½ teaspoon mustard seeds
> ½ teaspoon salt
> 4 boneless, skinless chicken breasts (about 6 ounces each)
> 1½ tablespoons olive oil

Combine the juniper berries, coriander seeds, and mustard seeds in a small skillet and cook over medium-high heat for 2 minutes, or until lightly toasted. Transfer the toasted spices to a spice grinder or coffee grinder, add the salt, and process for 20 to 30 seconds, until finely ground.

Sprinkle both sides of the chicken breasts with the spice mixture and rub it gently into the meat. Brush the breasts on both sides with the olive oil. (*The recipe can be prepared to this point up to 12 hours ahead. Wrap the chicken in plastic wrap and refrigerate until ready to cook.*)

Preheat the oven to 180 degrees.

Heat a very large nonstick skillet until it is hot. Add the chicken breasts and cook over medium-high heat for 3 minutes. Turn the breasts over and cook for 3 minutes on the other side.

Arrange the breasts on an ovenproof platter and place them in the oven for at least 10 minutes to finish cooking. (*The chicken can be kept warm in the oven for up to 45 minutes.*)

Arrange a chicken breast on each of four dinner plates and serve.

Chicken Suprêmes Kiev-Style

Serves 4

✳ **In true chicken Kiev**, boneless chicken breasts, which are usually left unskinned, are stuffed with butter, dipped in eggs and bread crumbs, and deep-fried. I use skinless chicken breasts, stuff them with an herbed mushroom mixture, and roll them in bread crumbs that are seasoned with herbs and barely moistened with oil, then bake them. Much lower in calories than the traditional version, my chicken Kiev is intensely flavored, juicy, and delicious.

> 4 boneless, skinless chicken breasts (about 7 ounces each)

FILLING

> 2 tablespoons unsalted butter
> 1½ cups chopped onions

8 ounces white mushrooms, cleaned and chopped (3 cups)

4–5 garlic cloves, crushed and chopped (1 tablespoon)

½ teaspoon salt

¼ teaspoon freshly ground black pepper

2 tablespoons coarsely chopped fresh cilantro

COATING

4 slices firm white or whole wheat bread (4 ounces), processed to crumbs in a food processor (2 cups)

2 tablespoons olive oil

2 tablespoons chopped fresh cilantro

½ teaspoon salt

½ teaspoon freshly ground black pepper

1 large egg, lightly beaten

Preheat the oven to 400 degrees.

To butterfly the chicken breasts, holding your knife so the blade is parallel to the cutting surface, slice almost all the way through the thickness of each breast, stopping when you can open up the breast as you would a book. Open up each breast and, using a meat pounder, pound the breasts lightly to flatten them. (To help prevent the meat from tearing, you can pound the breasts between sheets of plastic wrap.)

FOR THE FILLING: Heat the butter in a large skillet. When it is hot, add the onions and sauté over medium-high heat for 2 minutes. Stir in the mushrooms, garlic, salt, and pepper and cook, covered, for 3 minutes. Remove the lid and continue cooking until there is no liquid remaining in the skillet. Add the cilantro and transfer the mixture to a plate to cool.

When the filling is cool, divide it into 4 equal portions. Mound 1 portion in the center of each butterflied chicken breast, then fold the edges of the breast over the filling to enclose it completely, making a roughly square packet.

FOR THE COATING: Combine the bread crumbs, oil, cilantro, salt, and pepper in a bowl. Dip the stuffed chicken breasts in the beaten egg, then roll them in the seasoned crumbs.

Arrange the chicken breasts in a roasting pan or on a baking sheet and bake for 20 to 25 minutes, until cooked through but still moist.

Arrange the chicken on four dinner plates and serve.

Chicken Breasts with Chervil Mousse
Serves 6

❧ The mousse for this special dish can be flavored with other types of herbs, mushrooms, or different spices. Instead of the cognac sauce, the stuffed chicken breasts can be served with the pan drippings only.

You may have to order the skin-on boneless breasts ahead.

MOUSSE

    1   pound boneless, skinless chicken thighs,
        cut into chunks
    ¼   cup chopped ice
    1   cup loosely packed fresh chervil or
        tarragon leaves
    1   cup very cold heavy cream
    1   teaspoon salt
    ¼   teaspoon freshly ground black pepper

    6   skin-on boneless chicken breasts
    ¼   teaspoon salt
    2   tablespoons unsalted butter
    ⅓   cup water

SAUCE

    1   cup homemade chicken stock (page 612)
        or low-salt canned chicken broth
    ½   cup dry white wine
    ½   cup heavy cream
    1   teaspoon potato starch (see page 318),
        dissolved in 1 tablespoon water
    1   tablespoon cognac
    ¼   teaspoon salt
    ¼   teaspoon freshly ground black pepper

FOR THE MOUSSE: Put the chicken, ice, and chervil or tarragon in a food processor and process for about 10 seconds. Scrape down the sides with a rubber spatula and process for 10 seconds more. Clean the sides of the bowl again and process for another 10 seconds. With the motor running, add the cream in a slow stream, then add the salt and pepper and process briefly to mix. Transfer to a bowl. (*The mousse can be made several hours ahead and refrigerated until ready to use.*)

TO STUFF THE CHICKEN BREASTS: Remove the fillet (tender) from each breast and remove and discard the sinew from each one. Set aside the fillets.

Place the chicken breasts skin side up on the work surface. Pull back the skin and spoon about ½ cup of the mousse on top of the meat. Arrange a fillet on one side of each breast, pressing it into the mousse, then bring the skin back over the mousse so it covers the whole surface.

Hold a stuffed breast skin side down in the palm of one hand and bring the edges of the skin around to the underside of the breast; the skin will not come all around the breast. Repeat with the remaining breasts. (*The breasts can be stuffed several hours ahead; arrange skin side down on a tray and refrigerate, covered.*)

At serving time, sprinkle the chicken breasts with the salt. Heat 1 tablespoon of the butter in each of two skillets, preferably nonstick. When it is hot, add the chicken skin side down and sauté over high heat for about 4 minutes. Cover, reduce the heat, and cook gently for 10 minutes. (The chicken is cooked only on the skin side so the meat won't toughen.)

Remove the lid and continue cooking until the juices are reduced and the chicken is sizzling in the fat and nicely browned. Remove to a serving platter and set aside in a warm place.

There will be a lot of fat in the pan drippings because of the skin. Boil down the drippings until the juices caramelize into a glaze on the bottom of the skillet and the clear fat is on top. Let sit for 1 to 2 minutes, then pour off most of the fat and discard. Add the water to the skillet and bring to a boil, then strain through a sieve into a small saucepan. Reduce again until you have about 3 tablespoons concentrated juices, or glaze.

MEANWHILE, FOR THE SAUCE: Bring the chicken stock and wine to a boil in a medium saucepan and boil to reduce to 1 cup. Add the cream and bring to a boil again, then add the dissolved potato starch. Add the cognac, salt, and pepper and strain through a fine sieve.

Pour the sauce over the chicken breasts, sprinkle with the chicken glaze, and serve.

Chicken Diable

Serves 4

For a special family meal, serve this chicken and a simple salad with a vinegar-and-oil dressing. For a slightly less pungent sauce for the bird, substitute white wine for half the vinegar.

- 1 chicken (3½–4 pounds) or 2 whole chicken legs, drumsticks and thighs separated, plus 2 boneless, skinless breasts
- ¾ teaspoon salt
- ¾ teaspoon coarsely ground black pepper
- 1 tablespoon olive oil
- 1 tablespoon unsalted butter
- 4 garlic cloves, crushed and finely chopped (about 1 tablespoon)
- ¼ cup red wine vinegar
- ¼ cup water
- ¾ cup tomato puree or sauce
- 1 teaspoon Tabasco sauce
- 1 tablespoon chopped fresh tarragon or 2 tablespoons coarsely minced fresh parsley

If using a whole chicken, cut off the chicken legs at the joint. If desired, chop off the tips of the drumsticks (reserve for stock). Separate the drumsticks from the thighs. Cut off the wings, leaving the first joints attached to the breasts. (Reserve the wings for stock.) Remove the wishbone by cutting along each side of it and pulling it out. Remove the 2 breasts, cutting them off at the shoulder and down each side of the breastbone; the breasts will be boneless except for the first joint of the wings. Pull off all the chicken skin and set it aside for cracklings (see page 250) or discard it.

If using chicken parts, pull the skin off the drumsticks and thighs (and reserve for cracklings or discard).

Sprinkle the chicken with ½ teaspoon each of the salt and pepper.

Heat the oil and butter in a large heavy skillet until hot. Add the drumsticks and thighs, cover, and sauté over medium-high heat for 5 minutes. Turn the pieces over and cook, covered, for 3 more minutes. Add the breasts skinned side down, cover, and cook for about 8 more minutes, until nicely browned. Transfer the chicken pieces to a serving platter and set aside in a warm place.

Add the garlic to the drippings in the pan and cook, stirring, for 20 to 30 seconds, without browning it. Deglaze the pan with the vinegar, stirring to melt all the solidified juices, and cook for 1 to 2 minutes; most of the vinegar should have evaporated. Add the water and tomato puree or sauce, bring to a boil, cover, and boil over high heat for 1 minute. Stir in the remaining ¼ teaspoon each salt and pepper and the Tabasco.

Spoon the sauce over the chicken, garnish with the tarragon or parsley, and serve.

Chicken with Red Wine

Serves 4

Chicken with red wine is called *coq au vin*, although historically the *coq*, "cock" — an older chicken — was so tough that it had to be cooked for a long time. Now the dish can be made quickly with tender parts from a young chicken. I divide the chicken into pieces, remove the skin, brown it, and cook it in the red wine, adding the breasts at the end so they don't get overdone. (You can instead buy chicken parts at the market.) The onions are glazed separately in a little olive oil and sugar, with the mushrooms stirred in near the end. Finally, everything is combined and served with large heart-shaped croutons.

1 chicken (3½–4 pounds) or 2 boneless, skinless breasts plus 2 whole chicken legs

12 small pearl onions (6 ounces)

2 tablespoons olive oil

½ teaspoon sugar

½ cup water

4 large mushrooms (4 ounces), cleaned and quartered

⅓ cup finely chopped onion

3 garlic cloves, crushed and finely chopped (2 teaspoons)

1½ cups fruity, dry, robust red wine (such as Syrah or Grenache)

1 fresh thyme sprig or ½ teaspoon dried thyme

2 bay leaves

¾ teaspoon salt

¾ teaspoon freshly ground black pepper

1 teaspoon potato starch (see page 318), dissolved in 2 tablespoons red wine

CROUTONS

4 slices firm white bread (4 ounces)

2 teaspoons canola oil

2 tablespoons finely chopped fresh parsley

If using a whole chicken, cut off the wings and cut them at the joints into 3 pieces each. Cut the chicken into 4 pieces: 2 breasts and 2 legs. Skin and bone the breasts. Set the breasts aside with the 4 meatier wing pieces. (Freeze the bones and wing tips for future use, if desired.)

To bone the chicken legs, first pull off the skin and cut the tips off the drumsticks. Then cut down each side of the thighbone and slide your knife under the bone to separate the meat from it. Holding the thighbone, cut all around the joint at the knee to loosen the meat. Scrape down the drumstick bone and pull out the bones. Set the legs aside with the breasts and wing pieces.

Put the pearl onions, 1 tablespoon of the oil, the sugar, and water in a large saucepan, bring to a boil over high heat, and boil until the water has evaporated and the onions start frying. Continue to cook, stirring or shaking the pan occasionally, until the onions are glazed on all sides. Add the mushrooms and sauté for 1 minute. Set aside, covered.

Preheat the oven to 400 degrees.

Heat the remaining 1 tablespoon oil in a large skillet. When it is hot, add the chicken wing pieces, if you have them, and sauté for 2 to 3 minutes, until lightly browned on all sides. Add the legs and brown for 2 to 3 minutes on each side. Add the breasts and brown for 2 minutes on each side. Remove all the chicken pieces to a plate.

Add the chopped onion to the drippings in the skillet and sauté for 1 minute. Add the garlic and cook for about 10 seconds. Add the wine, thyme, bay leaves, salt, and pepper and bring to a boil. Return the legs and the wings to the pan, cover, and boil very gently for 5 minutes. Add the chicken breasts and boil gently for another 6 minutes.

Add the dissolved potato starch to the chicken and stir until the pan juices are thickened. Add the pearl onions and mushrooms, with their juices. Keep warm.

MEANWHILE, FOR THE CROUTONS: Trim the crusts from the bread and cut each slice diagonally in half to form 2 triangles. Trim each triangle into a heart-shaped crouton.

Spread the oil on a cookie sheet and press the croutons into the oil so they are moistened on both sides. Bake for 8 to 10 minutes, until nicely browned.

At serving time, dip the tip of each crouton into the sauce to moisten it and then into the chopped parsley. Cut the chicken breast pieces and legs in half. Serve 1 breast piece, 1 drumstick or thigh, and, if you have them, 1 piece of wing per person, with 2 croutons, along with some of the sauce and vegetables. Sprinkle the remaining chopped parsley over the chicken.

Chicken in Vinegar
Serves 4

✂ Chicken in vinegar is a bistro specialty in Lyon. The spicy, piquant sauce of vinegar, garlic, and tomatoes has an assertive flavor that complements the bird well.

This is good served hot as well as warm on a buffet.

- 1 chicken (about 3½ pounds), cut into 8 pieces (2 legs, 2 thighs, and 2 breasts, halved)
- 1 teaspoon salt
- 1 teaspoon freshly ground black pepper, or to taste
- 2 tablespoons unsalted butter
- 3 garlic cloves, crushed and finely chopped (1 tablespoon)
- ½ cup red wine vinegar
- ⅓ cup water
- 1½ cups peeled, seeded, and chopped tomatoes
- 1 tablespoon chopped fresh parsley
- 2 teaspoons chopped fresh tarragon or basil

Sprinkle the chicken pieces with half the salt and pepper.

Melt the butter in a large heavy skillet. When the butter is hot, add the chicken leg pieces skin side down and brown for about 3 minutes over medium heat. Turn the pieces and brown for another 3 minutes on the other side. Add the breasts, skin side down, cover tightly, and cook over medium-low heat for about 20 minutes. Remove the chicken to a serving platter and keep warm at the back of the stove or in a 160-degree oven. (As soon as the chicken cools somewhat, you can remove the bones from the breasts — they will pull off easily — and the pieces of backbone, if you left it on. It is a little more elegant to remove the bones, but the chicken can certainly be served with them.)

Add the garlic to the skillet and sauté for 1 minute, without browning it. Add the wine vinegar and water and bring to a boil, stirring to melt all the solidified juices. Boil for 1 minute. Add the

---

HOW TO CUT A CHICKEN INTO 4, 8, OR 10 PIECES

You can buy your chicken already cut up at the market, but it is more expensive. Here is how to cut up your own.

Remove the tips of both wings (set these little pieces aside for use in stocks and stews). Then remove the other 2 sections of wing. To split the chicken in half, cut down through the center of the breastbone with a knife or poultry shears, then cut down along one side of the backbone. (You can remove the backbone from the half it is attached to and use it in stock or stew, or you can leave it on.)

To separate the legs from the breasts, cut right through the joint with a large knife. You now have 4 chicken quarters.

To separate the thighs from the drumsticks, cut through them at the joint. Cut the breasts, with the bone, in half as well. Your chicken is now in 8 pieces, with the 2 pieces of wing bringing the total to 10 pieces.

tomatoes and the remaining salt and pepper (the sauce should be peppery). Simmer for 4 to 5 minutes to thicken the sauce. (If the sauce separates, emulsify it by whisking in 2 tablespoons warm water.)

Pour the sauce over the chicken, sprinkle with the herbs, and serve.

Chicken in Tarragon Sauce
Serves 4

❧ **If you buy skinless,** boneless chicken breasts, you can make this dish quickly and easily. I enrich the chicken juices with cream at the end of cooking and garnish the dish with fresh tarragon.

- 4 boneless, skinless chicken breasts (about 7 ounces each)
- 1 medium onion, chopped (¾ cup)
- ¾ cup homemade chicken stock (page 612) or low-salt canned chicken broth
- ½ cup dry white vermouth
- 2 bay leaves
- 1 fresh thyme sprig
- ½ teaspoon salt
- ¼ teaspoon freshly ground black pepper
- 1 teaspoon potato starch (see page 318), dissolved in 2 tablespoons vermouth
- ¼ cup heavy cream
- 1 teaspoon chopped fresh tarragon

Combine the chicken breasts, onion, stock, vermouth, bay leaves, thyme sprig, salt, and pepper in a large stainless steel saucepan and bring to a boil. Reduce the heat, cover, and boil gently for about 10 minutes, or until the chicken is cooked through.

Transfer the chicken to a dish and set aside in a warm place.

Measure the cooking liquid: there should be

about 1 cup. Return it to the saucepan and, if necessary, boil to reduce it to 1 cup. Stir in the dissolved potato starch and bring to a boil. Add the cream and return to a boil. Return the chicken pieces to the pan and heat through.

Transfer to a platter, sprinkle with the tarragon, and serve.

Chicken African-Style with Couscous
Serves 4 to 6

❧ **I learned this recipe** from my brother, who lived in Senegal for several years. There it is usually served with "broken rice," which are grains of rice broken into bits; when cooked, they look a bit like the couscous that I use here. Marinating the chicken in lime juice, ginger, garlic, and hot pepper flakes gives it a robust and distinctive taste.

MARINADE

- 2 onions, very thinly sliced (2 cups)
- 4–6 garlic cloves, crushed and finely chopped (1½ tablespoons)
- ½ teaspoon hot pepper flakes
- 1½ teaspoons grated ginger
- 1 teaspoon salt
- ¼ teaspoon freshly ground black pepper
- ¼ cup fresh lime juice

- 1 chicken (3½–4 pounds), cut into 8 pieces (2 legs, 2 thighs, and 2 breasts, halved)

COUSCOUS

- 2 tablespoons unsalted butter
- 2 cups instant couscous
- 1¾ cups boiling water
- ¼ teaspoon salt

FOR THE MARINADE: Mix all the ingredients together in a large bowl.

Add the chicken to the marinade, turning to coat. Cover and refrigerate for 4 to 5 hours, or as long as overnight.

Cut off the little bits of fat clinging to the chicken thighs and cut the fat into small pieces.

Melt the fat in a large saucepan. Add the chicken pieces (set the marinade aside) and brown them in the fat, about 10 minutes. Transfer the chicken to a medium stainless steel pot.

Deglaze the saucepan with the marinade, stirring to melt the solidified juices, and add to the chicken. Bring to a boil, cover, reduce the heat, and simmer slowly for 25 minutes. Remove the cover and boil over high heat for 5 minutes to reduce the sauce.

MEANWHILE, FOR THE COUSCOUS: Melt the butter in a saucepan. Add the couscous and mix carefully so that all the grains are coated with butter. Pour the boiling water over the grains, add the salt, cover, and let stand for 10 minutes, off the heat. Stir with a fork to separate the grains.

Mound the couscous on a serving platter, arrange the chicken around it, and serve.

Normandy Chicken Fricassee
Serves 4

❧ **Chicken in cream and** wine sauce with a vegetable garnish is often featured in the restaurants of Normandy. It is always flavored with Calvados (apple brandy).

1 chicken (about 3½ pounds), cut into 8 pieces (2 legs, 2 thighs, and 2 breasts, halved), skin removed
½ teaspoon salt, or to taste
½ teaspoon freshly ground black pepper, or to taste

3 tablespoons unsalted butter
1 cup diced (½-inch) carrots
2 medium onions, cut into 1-inch dice (1½ cups)
½ cup diced (½-inch) celery
2 garlic cloves, coarsely chopped (1 teaspoon)
2 tablespoons chopped fresh parsley
¼ teaspoon dried thyme
1 bay leaf
1 cup dry white wine (such as Chardonnay)
½ cup water
1 tablespoon all-purpose flour
½ cup heavy cream
½ cup frozen baby peas
2 tablespoons Calvados or applejack

Sprinkle the chicken pieces with the salt and pepper.

Heat 2 tablespoons of the butter in a large heavy nonstick skillet. When it is hot, add the chicken pieces, reduce the heat to medium, and cook for 5 minutes, turning the pieces once or twice.

Add the carrots, onions, celery, garlic, parsley, thyme, and bay leaf, cover, and cook for 5 minutes. Add the wine and water, bring to a simmer, cover, and simmer for about 20 minutes, or until the chicken is tender when pierced with a fork.

Meanwhile, blend the remaining 1 tablespoon butter with the flour to make a *beurre manié*.

Lift the cooked chicken from the pan and arrange on a serving platter; set aside in a warm place.

Add the *beurre manié* to the sauce, whisking steadily. Add the cream and peas and bring to a boil, then reduce the heat and simmer for 1 minute. Take off the heat, stir in the Calvados or applejack, and taste for seasoning; add salt and pepper if needed.

Pour the sauce over the chicken and serve.

Chicken Chasseur

Serves 4

✍ *Chasseur* means "hunter" in French, and the term refers to a poultry or meat dish with mushrooms, tomato, and garlic; it is similar to an Italian cacciatore. My update of the classic French stew uses skinless chicken thighs in place of chicken pieces with skin. After sautéing the thighs in a little olive oil, I finish them in a sauce containing onion and leek, flavoring it in the traditional manner.

The dish can be prepared up to a day ahead. At serving time, reheat it gently.

2	tablespoons olive oil
8	chicken thighs (about 3 pounds), skin removed
1	small leek, trimmed (leaving some green), split, washed, and coarsely chopped (1¾ cups)
1	medium onion, chopped (1 cup)
1½	tablespoons all-purpose flour
1	cup dry white wine
1	15-ounce can whole tomatoes in juice
5–6	garlic cloves, crushed and finely chopped (1½ tablespoons)
20	medium mushrooms (about 12 ounces), cleaned
1	teaspoon chopped fresh thyme
1	teaspoon chopped fresh rosemary
¾	teaspoon salt
½	teaspoon freshly ground black pepper
1	tablespoon dark soy sauce
1	tablespoon chopped fresh chervil or tarragon

Heat the olive oil in a large deep nonstick skillet until hot. Add the chicken thighs in one layer and cook over medium-high heat for 3 minutes on each side, until lightly browned. Transfer to a plate.

Add the leek and onion to the drippings in the skillet and sauté for 30 seconds. Add the flour, mix it in well, and cook for about 30 seconds. Mix in the wine and tomatoes and bring to a boil over medium heat.

Add the chicken pieces, garlic, mushrooms, thyme, rosemary, salt, pepper, and soy sauce and bring to a boil over high heat, stirring occasionally to prevent scorching. Cover the pan, reduce the heat to low, and cook for about 20 minutes. Sprinkle on the chervil or tarragon and mix it in.

Serve 2 thighs per person, with some of the vegetables and sauce.

Sweet-and-Spicy Curried Chicken

Serves 6

✍ **The spiciness of this** curry is balanced by the sweetness of apple and banana, which lend smoothness and texture to the sauce. You can adjust the heat to your palate by increasing or decreasing the amount of cayenne and black pepper. Mint lends a refreshing quality. Although fresh mint is usually available at the supermarket, you can substitute dried if necessary. Serve with Brown Rice and Onion Pilaf (page 104). This dish is even better the next day.

1	tablespoon unsalted butter
1	tablespoon canola oil
6	whole chicken legs (about 3½ pounds), skin removed, drumsticks and thighs separated
12	ounces onions (3–4), diced (about 2½ cups)
1	tablespoon all-purpose flour
2	tablespoons curry powder
1	teaspoon ground cumin
1½	teaspoons salt

1½ teaspoons freshly ground black pepper

¼ teaspoon cayenne pepper

5 garlic cloves, crushed and coarsely chopped (about 1½ tablespoons)

1 cup water

1 Granny Smith apple (8 ounces), unpeeled, halved, cored, and cut into 1-inch dice (about 1½ cups)

1 large firm but ripe banana, cut into ½-inch-thick slices

1 large tomato, cut into 1-inch cubes (about 1 cup)

2 tablespoons shredded fresh mint leaves or 1 teaspoon dried mint

Heat the butter and oil in a large skillet until hot. Add the chicken, in batches if necessary to prevent crowding, and sauté over medium-high heat, turning occasionally, until lightly browned on all sides, a total of about 7 minutes. Transfer the chicken to a large flameproof casserole.

Add the onions to the hot fat in the skillet and sauté over medium heat, stirring, for 2 to 3 minutes. Add the flour, curry powder, cumin, salt, black pepper, cayenne, and garlic and mix well. Add the water, stir, and bring to a boil. Pour the mixture over the chicken.

Add the apple, banana, and tomato to the chicken and bring to a boil over medium-high heat. Cover, reduce the heat, and simmer gently for 30 to 40 minutes. If using dried mint, crumble it over the chicken a few minutes before it is done.

If using fresh mint, sprinkle it on top of the chicken. Serve.

My Mother's Chicken Ragout
Serves 4

✶ **The taste of certain** dishes you had as a child stays in your memory forever. This is one of those dishes for me.

In France, salt pork is called *lard* — hence the name *lardons,* for the small pieces that we add to stews and other dishes. Look for a salt pork slab with as much meat on it as possible, or use pancetta. The stew tastes even better when made ahead and reheated at serving time.

1 tablespoon canola or safflower oil

4 whole chicken legs (about 2½ pounds), skin removed

4 ounces salt pork, as lean as possible, or pancetta, cut into ½-inch pieces

6 scallions, trimmed (leaving some green) and cut into ½-inch pieces (⅔ cup)

1 large onion, coarsely chopped (1¼ cups)

2 teaspoons all-purpose flour

1¼ cups water

½ cup fruity dry white wine (such as Sémillon or Sauvignon Blanc)

2 large garlic cloves, crushed and coarsely chopped (1 teaspoon)

½ teaspoon dried thyme

2 bay leaves

½ teaspoon salt

1 pound small Red Bliss potatoes (8–10), peeled

¼ teaspoon Tabasco sauce (optional)

2 tablespoons coarsely chopped fresh parsley

Heat the oil in a large heavy stainless steel saucepan until hot. Add the chicken legs and sauté over medium heat for 6 to 8 minutes, turning occasionally, until lightly browned on all sides.

Meanwhile, place the salt pork or pancetta in a saucepan with 2 cups water, bring to a boil, and boil for 1 minute. Drain in a sieve and rinse under cold water.

When the chicken is browned, transfer it to a plate. Add the salt pork or pancetta to the drippings in the pan and sauté, partially covered (to prevent splattering), over medium heat for 5 minutes, or until browned. Add the scallions and onion, mix well, and cook for 1 minute, stirring occasionally. Add the flour, mix well, and brown the mixture for about 1 minute, stirring.

Add the water and wine and mix well. Stir in the garlic, thyme, bay leaves, and salt and bring to a boil, stirring occasionally. Add the potatoes and chicken legs, bring back to a boil, and boil very gently, covered, over low heat for 30 minutes.

Add the Tabasco, if desired, stir, sprinkle with the parsley, and serve.

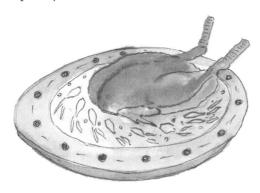

Chicken with Saffron Rice
Serves 4

My wife likes rice in any form and in any recipe, so this dinner is always welcome at our house. The dish is made with Arborio or other short-grain rice that I flavor with *alcaparrado*, a mixture of olives, capers, and red pepper that is available in jars in specialty food stores and some supermarkets. You can make your own by mixing together equal portions of diced green olives, capers, and pimientos. I use chicken legs, which stay moister

than breasts. I remove the skin before cooking them, since it tends to become gummy and adds a lot of fat without improving the taste.

1	tablespoon olive oil
4	whole chicken legs (about 3 pounds), skin removed, drumsticks and thighs separated
2	medium onions, thinly sliced (3 cups)
6	garlic cloves, coarsely chopped (2 tablespoons)
1½	cups Arborio or other short-grain rice
3	bay leaves
1	cup peeled, diced tomatoes
1½	cups *alcaparrado* (a mixture of green olives, capers, and pimientos; see the headnote)
1½	tablespoons chopped jalapeño pepper (or more or less, depending on your tolerance for hotness)
1¼	teaspoons salt
1	teaspoon saffron threads
2½	cups water
	Tabasco sauce (optional)

Heat the oil in a large skillet until hot. Add the chicken pieces in one layer and sauté over medium-high heat, turning occasionally, for 10 minutes, or until browned on all sides. Transfer the chicken to a plate and set aside.

Add the onions and garlic to the drippings in the skillet and cook for 2 minutes. Add the rice and mix well. Stir in the bay leaves, tomatoes, *alcaparrado*, jalapeño, salt, and saffron, add the water, and mix well.

Return the browned chicken pieces to the skillet, pushing them down into the liquid and rice until they are embedded in the mixture. Bring to a boil, reduce the heat to low, cover, and cook for 30 minutes, without stirring.

To serve, place a chicken thigh and drumstick, with some of the rice mixture, on each of four dinner plates. Sprinkle with Tabasco sauce, if desired, and serve.

Chicken Legs with Wine and Yams
Serves 4

❧ **This is one of** those casserole dishes that make a meal. The creaminess of the cooked yams and the seasonings of wine, onion, and mushrooms enhance the chicken. The legs used here stew better than breasts, which would get stringy.

2	tablespoons olive oil
4	whole chicken legs (about 3 pounds total), skin removed, drumsticks and thighs separated
¼	cup chopped onion
4	large shallots (about 6 ounces), sliced (about 1½ cups)
8	medium mushrooms (about 5 ounces), cleaned and halved
4	small yams or sweet potatoes (about 1 pound), peeled and halved lengthwise
1	cup dry white wine
8	large garlic cloves, crushed and chopped (2 tablespoons)
¾	teaspoon salt
½	teaspoon freshly ground black pepper
2	tablespoons chopped fresh parsley

Heat the oil in a large skillet. Add the chicken pieces in batches and sauté over medium-high heat until browned on all sides, about 10 minutes.

Add the onion and cook for 1 minute. Add the shallots, mushrooms, yams or sweet potatoes, wine, garlic, salt, and pepper. Bring to a boil, cover,

reduce the heat, and boil very gently for 20 minutes.

Garnish with the parsley and serve.

Spicy Ginger and Lemon Chicken
Serves 1

❧ **Intended for people who** dine alone, this dish is made with a single chicken leg that is skinned and then cooked with a sweet-and-spicy mixture that is especially complementary to the meat. It can be prepared ahead and reheated at serving time.

1	teaspoon olive oil
1	whole chicken leg (10–12 ounces), skin removed, tip of drumstick cut off
	Pinch of salt
⅛	teaspoon chili powder
⅛	teaspoon ground cumin
	Pinch of dried thyme
	Pinch of cayenne pepper
½	teaspoon all-purpose flour
½	teaspoon finely grated lemon rind
½	teaspoon finely grated orange rind
1	teaspoon chopped ginger
1	small garlic clove, crushed and chopped
¼	cup apple cider
¼	cup water

Heat the oil in a large stainless steel saucepan until it is hot but not smoking. Add the chicken leg and brown it over medium-high heat, turning occasionally, for 10 to 12 minutes.

Add the salt, chili powder, cumin, thyme, cayenne, flour, citrus rinds, ginger, garlic, cider, and water and bring to a boil. Reduce the heat to low, cover, and cook gently for 15 minutes.

Serve the chicken with the sauce.

Chicken and Seafood Paella
Serves 6 to 8

❧ **The name** *paella* **comes** from the Spanish word for the pan (usually a big cast-iron or steel skillet or pan) in which the classic concoction is cooked. Essentially it is a stew of rice cooked with poultry, meat, rabbit, and/or seafood — whatever one can afford — with some vegetables added near the end. In keeping with tradition, people in Spain often prepare the dish outdoors over a wood fire.

My paella contains pancetta and chorizo, the hot Spanish sausage; chicken legs; a seafood assortment of mussels, squid, and shrimp; and, finally, fresh vegetables. All of it is flavored with saffron; the best comes from Spain.

This one-pot meal requires attention to the timing. First the pork and sausage are browned, then the chicken is browned in their drippings. The rice is added next and simmered with the seasonings, and then the seafood is put in and, finally, the asparagus and peas. Staggered in this way, everything finishes cooking at the same time.

3 tablespoons olive oil
3 ounces pancetta or salt pork, cut into ¼-inch pieces (½ cup)
8 ounces Spanish chorizo, cut into 1-inch pieces
2 whole chicken legs (about 1½ pounds), skin removed, drumsticks and thighs separated
1 large onion, cut into ½-inch pieces (1¼ cups)
5–6 garlic cloves, crushed and finely chopped (1½ tablespoons)
2 cups Spanish short-grain or Carolina long-grain rice
½ cup (about ½ ounce) dried mushrooms, rinsed
1 teaspoon loosely packed saffron threads, crushed
1 teaspoon herbes de Provence
4 cups water
1 tomato (8 ounces), cut into ½-inch pieces (1⅓ cups)
1 red bell pepper (6 ounces), cored, seeded, and cut into ½-inch pieces
1 tablespoon chopped jalapeño pepper
1 teaspoon salt
½ teaspoon freshly ground black pepper
1 pound mussels (about 12), washed and debearded
8 ounces cleaned squid, bodies cut into 1½-inch pieces
12 shrimp (about 8 ounces), shelled
½ cup fresh peas or frozen baby peas
6 asparagus spears, trimmed and cut into 1-inch pieces (1 cup)
1 tablespoon chopped fresh chives
Tabasco sauce

Heat the olive oil in a large saucepan until hot. Add the pancetta or salt pork and chorizo and sauté over medium-high heat, partially covered to prevent splattering, for 5 minutes. Add the chicken and sauté over medium-low heat until browned on all sides, about 10 minutes.

Add the onion and garlic and cook for about 30 seconds. Add the rice and mix it in well. Stir

in the mushrooms, saffron, herbes de Provence, water, tomato, red pepper, jalapeño, salt, and pepper and mix well. Bring to a boil, cover, reduce the heat to low, and cook gently for 20 minutes.

Add the mussels, squid, and shrimp and cook for 8 minutes. Stir in the peas and asparagus and cook, covered, for another 5 minutes.

Sprinkle with the chives and serve with Tabasco sauce on the side.

Chicken Leg "Sausages" with Mushroom Sauce
Serves 4

✍ **Skinned and boned, these** chicken legs are stuffed with a mixture of portobello mushrooms, garlic, shallots, scallions, and cheese. Wrapped securely in aluminum foil, the resulting "sausages" are cooked in the oven long enough so they hold their shape. Then they are unwrapped and finished in a light sauce.

- 4 whole chicken legs (about 2½ pounds)
- 1½ tablespoons olive oil
- 2 large shallots, coarsely chopped (about ⅓ cup)
- 6 scallions, trimmed (leaving some green) and cut into ½-inch pieces (about ½ cup)
- 3 portobello mushroom caps, cleaned and cut into ½-inch pieces (3½ cups)
- 2 large garlic cloves, crushed and finely chopped (2 teaspoons)
- ½ teaspoon salt
- ¼ teaspoon freshly ground black pepper
- ¼ cup crumbled soft goat cheese (such as Montrachet)
- ½ cup dry white wine
- ¼ cup ketchup
- ¼ cup water
- 2 tablespoons chopped fresh parsley

Cut off the tip of each drumstick. Pull off the skin. To bone the legs, cut down each side of the thighbone and slide your knife under the bone to separate the meat from it. Holding the thighbone, cut all around the joint at the knee to loosen the meat. Scrape down the drumstick bone and pull out the bones. Remove any visible fat from each leg. (You should have about 1½ pounds skinless, boneless chicken; reserve the bones, if desired, for stock.)

Heat the oil in a large heavy saucepan until hot. Add the shallots and scallions and cook over medium heat for 1 minute. Add the mushrooms, garlic, salt, and pepper and cook for 5 minutes, or until the liquid the mushrooms release has evaporated and they are lightly browned. Remove from the heat.

Transfer ¾ cup of the mushroom mixture to a bowl. Add the cheese, mix well, and set aside to cool.

Add the wine, ketchup, and water to the remaining mushroom mixture in the pan and set aside.

Preheat the oven to 425 degrees.

Place each of the 4 boned chicken legs, boned side up, on a 10-by-12-inch piece of aluminum foil. Divide the cooled mushroom-cheese mixture among the legs. Then, using the foil to help you, roll each leg into a tight sausage about 5½ inches long and 1½ inches in diameter; pinch the ends of the foil to seal.

Arrange the foil-wrapped packages on a cookie sheet and bake for 20 minutes. Let cool for 5 minutes, while you bring the reserved sauce to a boil.

Carefully unwrap the chicken sausages and place them seam side down in the pan of sauce. Bring the sauce back to a boil, then reduce the heat to low, cover, and cook the sausages gently for 10 minutes.

Serve 1 chicken sausage per person, with some of the sauce and a sprinkling of the parsley on top.

Chicken and Bean Stew
Serves 6

❧ **Made with backs, necks,** wings, or other parts, left over or bought especially for this purpose, this chicken and bean stew is satisfying, hearty, and inexpensive — ideal for a family meal.

The small white beans — navy beans, pea beans, or Great Northern — found in the supermarket are usually not old enough to require soaking. If you decide to soak them, however, 1 or 2 hours is sufficient; overnight is often too long — bubbles may appear on top of the water, a sign of fermentation, which can cause digestive problems. Always start to cook beans in cold water. If started in hot water they will toughen and take much longer to cook.

Serve with Boston Lettuce Salad with Cream Dressing (page 37). For an alternate way of serving this dish, see the sidebar (opposite).

    4 pounds meaty chicken bones and parts
        (including backs and necks and, if
        available, gizzards and hearts)
    1 pound (about 2⅓ cups) navy beans,
        picked over and rinsed
    2 medium onions (about 12 ounces),
        each studded with 3 whole cloves
    3 medium to large carrots, peeled
    1 celery stalk
    2 teaspoons salt
    ½ teaspoon dried thyme
    4 bay leaves
    8 cups cold water

    1 cup canned diced tomatoes
    3 garlic cloves, crushed and chopped
        (2 teaspoons)
    ½ cup chopped fresh parsley

Put the bones in a large pot, add the beans, onions, carrots, celery, salt, thyme, bay leaves, and water, and bring to a boil; skim off the foam that rises to the surface. Cover, reduce the heat, and boil very gently for 1½ hours; stir every 15 or 20 minutes to prevent the beans from sticking to the bottom. Pour the mixture into a large roasting pan.

When the bean mixture is cool enough, remove the bones and vegetables from the beans and put the beans back into the pot.

When the bones are cool enough to handle, pick off the meat and discard any skin. (You should have at least 2 to 2½ cups of meat.) Remove the cloves from the onions and discard them. Coarsely chop the onions, carrots, celery, and gizzards and hearts, if you have them. Add to the pot, along with the meat, and mix with the beans.

Add the tomato, garlic, and parsley and bring back to a boil. Reduce the heat, simmer for 5 minutes, and serve.

Lentil and Chicken Fricassee
Serves 4 to 6

❧ **I make this fricassee** from bones and wings, which I always have in my freezer, so it costs only the price of the lentils and vegetables. It is excellent with a crunchy salad with garlic dressing and country bread. This is a meal to eat with family or close friends, because it is best enjoyed if you hold the bones in your fingers and bite off the meat.

    About 1½ pounds chicken wings (and/
        or meaty bones, neck, gizzard, and
        heart — fresh or frozen)

Here's an alternate way of serving the Chicken and Bean Stew (opposite). Adding sausage and bread crumbs to the leftover bean mixture makes it more like an authentic cassoulet and extends the dish further. You can also use chunks of ham or pork roast, as well as other types of sausages.

2 Italian sausage links, halved
  Approximately 4 cups leftover bean
    mixture
2 knockwurst, halved
½ cup fresh bread crumbs (from 1 slice
    firm white bread)
2 tablespoons olive oil

Preheat the oven to 400 degrees.

Sauté the sausage halves in a skillet for 4 to 5 minutes, until lightly browned. Remove from the heat.

Add enough water to the bean mixture to make it soupy (the bread crumbs and the oven heat will draw out moisture). Ladle the mixture into four individual ovenproof bowls and push in the sausages. Sprinkle about 2 tablespoons of bread crumbs on top of each bowl and moisten the crumbs with the olive oil.

Put the bowls on a cookie sheet and bake for about 20 minutes. Heat the broiler for a few minutes and broil for a few minutes to crust the top. Serve piping hot.

2 carrots, peeled and cut into ½-inch
    pieces (about 1 cup)
1 large onion, cut into ½-inch pieces
    (about 1 cup)
3 garlic cloves, crushed and coarsely
    chopped (about 2 teaspoons)
1 teaspoon dried oregano
2 bay leaves
1 pound dried lentils, picked over and
    rinsed
3 cups water
1¾ teaspoons salt
1 teaspoon freshly ground black pepper

Put the chicken wings (and/or other parts) in a large heavy pot. Cut the gizzards and hearts, if using, into ½-inch pieces and add to the pot. Cover and cook over medium-high heat for about 20 minutes, until the wings and/or bones are nicely browned. (During the first 5 to 10 minutes

of cooking, some liquid will come out of the bones and create steam, but eventually the bones will start to brown.)

Add the carrots, onion, garlic, oregano, and bay leaves, stir well, and cook for 1 minute. Add the lentils, water, and salt and bring to a strong boil, then reduce the heat and boil gently, covered, for about 45 minutes, until the lentils are very tender and most of the liquid has been absorbed.

Sprinkle with the pepper, stir to incorporate, and serve, bones and all.

Chicken Wing Stew
Serves 6 to 8

✒ **Rice and chicken casseroles** can be found in cuisines around the world. Although this recipe calls for wings, you can use other pieces. I make it with short-grain rice. Converted, or parboiled, rice (which has gone through a process to remove some of the starch) will be less sticky, but regular rice is also good, even if it becomes a bit mushy.

Olives and capers are optional additions to the peas, zucchini, and tomatoes. Adding saffron, shellfish, fish, and sliced sausages in the last 5 minutes of cooking would transform the dish into an excellent paella. If made ahead, the stew should be reheated slowly, preferably in an oven. Before reheating it, moisten it with some water if it is too thick.

If you have leftovers, prepare a rice pancake (see the sidebar) and serve it with fried eggs, if desired.

About 3½ pounds chicken wings (18–20)
1   tablespoon olive oil
3   cups water
1   cup chopped onion
¾   cup sliced scallions
1½ cups short-grain rice (see the headnote)
2   teaspoons salt
½   teaspoon freshly ground black pepper
½   teaspoon paprika
½   teaspoon turmeric
1   teaspoon dried oregano
3   garlic cloves, crushed and peeled

1   cup canned diced tomatoes
¾   cup diced (¼-inch) zucchini
¾   cup frozen baby peas
     Tabasco sauce (optional)

Twist the chicken wings and tuck the tip of each wing underneath itself to make the wings more compact, so they will take up less space and brown more evenly.

Heat the olive oil in a large skillet, preferably nonstick, until very hot. Add the chicken wings, flatter side down (don't crowd the pan; if the wings don't fit in one layer, use a second skillet), and cook, without disturbing, over medium-high heat until very crusty and brown, about 7 minutes. The wings will release some fat, which helps the browning. Flip the wings over and cook for another 7 minutes, until nicely browned on both sides.

If you used a second skillet, combine all the wings in one pan; they can overlap at this point. Pour ½ cup of the water into the extra skillet to melt the solidified juices in the bottom; set aside.

Add the onion and scallions to the chicken and cook for 1 minute. Add the rice and mix well so that it is coated with the fat. Add the water (including the water in the second skillet, if you used

---

RICE PANCAKE **Serves 2**

You can panfry any leftover rice to make a crusty rice cake. If it has bits of vegetables and meat in it, the pancake will be particularly good, and a fried egg on top is excellent.

2   tablespoons peanut oil
1½ cups leftover rice, with pieces of
        vegetables and meat if available
2   fried eggs (optional)

Heat the oil in a 7- to 8-inch nonstick skillet until hot. Add the rice and pack it down by pressing on it with the back of a spoon. Cook over medium heat for 10 minutes, or until nicely browned and crusty on the bottom.

Flip and cook for another 5 minutes on the other side. The pancake should be crunchy.

Slide onto a plate, cut in half, and serve with the fried eggs, if desired.

it), salt, pepper, paprika, turmeric, oregano, and garlic, stir, and bring to a boil, stirring once in a while. Cover, reduce the heat to very low, and simmer for 15 minutes.

Add the tomatoes, zucchini, and peas, cover, and cook for another 10 minutes.

Serve with Tabasco sauce on the side, if desired.

Chicken Livers Sautéed with Vinegar
Serves 6 as a first course

✻ **Bresse, the part of** France where I was born, is known as the home of the best chickens in France, and many good chicken-liver recipes come from that area. The method that follows is a bit different from the traditional method of sautéing livers. Although they are generally sautéed raw, here I blanch them first in boiling water for a few seconds to seal them.

Try to get pale yellowish livers, which are fatter, sweeter, and milder than the dark red ones.

1¼ pounds chicken livers (about 12), halved and trimmed of any sinew
3 tablespoons peanut oil
2 tablespoons unsalted butter
1 teaspoon salt, or to taste
½ teaspoon freshly ground black pepper, or to taste
⅔ cup finely chopped onion
⅓ cup cider vinegar
⅔ cup peeled, seeded, and chopped tomatoes
1 cup homemade chicken stock (page 612) or low-salt canned chicken broth
1 teaspoon unsalted butter, softened
1 teaspoon all-purpose flour

¼ cup finely chopped fresh parsley or a mixture of fresh herbs, such as chives and/or basil

Bring a large saucepan of water to a boil. Put the livers in a sieve, lower them into the boiling water, and stir them with a spoon for 20 to 30 seconds (the water will not have time to return to a boil). Lift the sieve and place it on a plate so the livers can drain.

Heat the oil and butter in a stainless steel skillet large enough to hold the livers in one layer (or use two smaller skillets). When the fat is foaming, add the livers, salt, and pepper, stir, and sauté over the highest heat for about 1 minute. With a slotted spoon, remove the livers to the sieve to drain again.

Add the onion to the drippings in the skillet and sauté over medium heat for 2 to 3 minutes, until lightly browned. Add the vinegar, bring to a boil, and boil until it is reduced to a glaze. Add the tomatoes and stock and bring to a boil.

Meanwhile, mix the 1 teaspoon butter and flour together with a whisk to make a *beurre manié*. Stir it into the sauce with the whisk, bring to a boil, still stirring, and boil gently for 1 minute. Taste for seasonings.

Add the livers and warm gently, without boiling. Sprinkle with the parsley or other herbs and serve.

Chicken Livers in Salad
Serves 6 as a first course

✻ **Easy to prepare and** refreshing, this salad should be made at the last minute and served while still warm. The iceberg lettuce adds crunchiness.

Prepared as they are here — cooked very fast in extremely hot fat so that the outside is sealed and the inside stays moist and a bit pink — the chicken livers also make a great hors d'oeuvre served on little slices of toasted bread.

12 chicken livers
1½ tablespoons unsalted butter
2 tablespoons corn oil
¾ teaspoon salt
¾ teaspoon freshly ground black pepper
1 tablespoon crushed, chopped garlic
3 tablespoons coarsely chopped fresh parsley
6 cups large dice (1-inch) iceberg lettuce
3 tablespoons balsamic vinegar

Separate the chicken livers into halves, cutting out and discarding the connecting sinews.

Heat the butter and 2 tablespoons of the oil in a very large saucepan or skillet (or two smaller pans) until very hot. Add the chicken livers in one layer, sprinkle them with half the salt and pepper, and sauté over high heat for 1 minute, partially covering the pan if they splatter. Turn and cook the livers on the other side for 1 minute, partially covering the pan again if necessary. The livers should be pink inside.

Add the garlic and parsley and mix well. Transfer the livers and any juices to a bowl, cover, and set aside; reserve the drippings in the pan(s).

Put the lettuce in a large serving bowl. Add the pan drippings and toss to mix well. Add the remaining salt and pepper and the vinegar and mix again.

Divide the salad among six individual plates, top with the livers (4 liver halves per person), and serve.

Grilled Chicken with Tarragon Butter
Serves 4

✻ **I prepare this dish** inside on my stovetop gas grill in winter and outdoors on my gas or charcoal grill in summer. Make sure your grill is very clean, or the chicken will stick. The bird is grilled long enough so that most of the fat in the skin drains away, and it is then transferred to a warm oven to finish cooking in its own juices.

A delicious tarragon butter, dotted on the chicken at serving time, replicates the flavor of a béarnaise sauce.

1 chicken (about 3 pounds), quartered, drumsticks and thighs separated
½ teaspoon salt
1 tablespoon olive oil

TARRAGON BUTTER

2 tablespoons unsalted butter, softened
1½ tablespoons olive oil
2 tablespoons chopped fresh tarragon
¼ teaspoon salt
2 teaspoons fresh lemon juice

Heat a grill until medium-hot. Preheat the oven to 160 degrees.

Sprinkle the chicken pieces with the salt and oil. Place the chicken skin side down on the clean hot grill. Grill the breasts for about 20 minutes and the leg pieces for about 30 minutes, turning occasionally, until nicely browned on all sides. As the chicken pieces are cooked, transfer them to a tray and put in the warm oven, uncovered, until ready to serve.

MEANWHILE, FOR THE TARRAGON BUTTER: Put all the ingredients in a blender or food processor and process until smooth.

Divide the chicken among four individual

plates, dot each serving with about 1 tablespoon of the tarragon butter, and serve.

Grilled Chicken with Cabbage Anchoïade
Serves 4

🦃 **Chicken breasts are marinated** in a finely chopped mixture of oregano, lemon rind, and black pepper and olive oil. Cooked on a hot grill, the breasts brown quickly but remain moist in the center. A mini-chop, smaller and faster than a food processor, is ideal for chopping the herbs and spices.

Anchoïade is a bold mixture of anchovy fillets, garlic, and olive oil that is combined here with cabbage and red bell pepper to serve as a bed for the chicken.

8	strips lemon rind, removed with a vegetable peeler, coarsely chopped
2	teaspoons black peppercorns
¼	cup loosely packed fresh oregano leaves
4	boneless, skinless chicken breasts (about 6 ounces each)
3	tablespoons olive oil

CABBAGE ANCHOÏADE

½	red bell pepper, peeled and cut into ¼-inch dice (½ cup)
4	garlic cloves, crushed and finely chopped (about 2 teaspoons)
6	anchovy fillets, finely chopped
½	teaspoon salt
½	teaspoon freshly ground black pepper
4	teaspoons red wine vinegar
¼	cup olive oil
8	cups shredded savoy cabbage
1	teaspoon salt

Combine the lemon rind, peppercorns, and oregano in a mini-chop and process to a coarse powder. (You should have about ¼ cup.)

Sprinkle the mixture over the chicken and arrange it in a dish. Drizzle with the oil. Cover and marinate in the refrigerator for at least 30 minutes. (*The chicken can marinate for as long as overnight.*)

FOR THE CABBAGE ANCHOÏADE: Reserve 1 tablespoon of the red bell pepper for garnish. Combine the rest of the red pepper, the garlic, anchovies, salt, pepper, vinegar, and oil in a large bowl. Add the cabbage and mix well. (*The cabbage can be prepared up to 1 hour ahead and refrigerated until serving time.*)

Heat a grill until hot.

Sprinkle the chicken with the salt and arrange it on the clean hot grill. Cook for about 4 minutes on each side. Transfer to a plate.

Arrange one quarter of the cabbage mixture in a mound in the center of each of four serving plates. Slice the chicken breasts lengthwise into halves and arrange on top of the cabbage. Sprinkle with the reserved red pepper and serve.

Grilled Chicken with Herb Sauce
Serves 6

An herb sauce adds flavor to the chicken and makes it look more luscious. It's always best to grill over hardwood charcoal or pieces of wood, not briquettes, but a gas grill will work almost as well.

1 chicken (3–3½ pounds), cut into
    8 pieces (2 legs, 2 thighs, and
    2 breasts, halved)
½ teaspoon salt
½ teaspoon freshly ground black pepper
1 tablespoon olive oil

SAUCE

2 tablespoons unsalted butter
2 garlic cloves, crushed and finely chopped
    (1 teaspoon)
⅓ cup chopped fresh herbs, such as thyme,
    rosemary, or savory
    Pinch of salt
    Pinch of freshly ground black pepper
⅓ cup Basic Brown Sauce (page 613)

Rub the chicken pieces with the salt, pepper, and olive oil and let marinate while you heat the grill.

Heat a grill until medium-hot.

Place the pieces of chicken skin side down on the hot grill and cook, turning the pieces every few minutes, for about 20 minutes for the wings and breasts, and up to 35 minutes for the legs and thighs. (If the heat is too great and the meat is cooking too fast, move the chicken to a cooler part of the grill or reduce the heat to low.)

MEANWHILE, FOR THE SAUCE: Melt the butter in a large skillet. Add the garlic and sauté for a few seconds. Add the herbs, salt, pepper, and brown sauce and bring to a boil, then reduce the heat to medium-low and cook for 1 minute.

As the pieces of chicken are cooked, coat each piece with the sauce and serve.

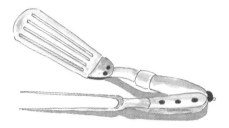

Roast Stuffed Cornish Hens
Serves 4

❧ **Nutty and wholesome, this** bulgur wheat and leek stuffing works well with the hens' juices. Cornish hens are more elegant and easier to eat when boned first, but you can skip the boning if you like. The birds are cooked at such a high temperature that most of the fat in the skin collects in the bottom of the roasting pan. The fat is discarded and combined with the remaining drippings and a little water to form a sauce that is delicious with the hens.

Try to buy your bulgur in a health food store, where it is usually of better quality than that sold in the supermarket. Be sure to buy bulgur, not cracked wheat. The latter is uncooked; the former is cracked wheat that has been steamed and dried, and it needs only to be reconstituted in water.

⅓ cup bulgur wheat
2 Cornish hens (about 1¼ pounds each)
2 tablespoons canola oil
1 leek (4 ounces), trimmed (leaving some
    green), split, washed, and chopped
    (1¼ cups)
1 onion (4 ounces), chopped (about ¾ cup)
3 garlic cloves, crushed and chopped
    (about 1½ teaspoons)
1 teaspoon chopped jalapeño pepper
    (or more or less, depending on your
    tolerance for hotness)
1 Granny Smith apple, cored and cut into
    ⅜-inch pieces (about 1¼ cups)
½ teaspoon salt
¼ teaspoon freshly ground black pepper
½ cup water

Bring 1 cup water to a boil in a small saucepan. Stir in the bulgur and set the pan aside for 1 hour. Drain.

Preheat the oven to 425 degrees.

Bone the Cornish hens from the neck opening, without tearing the skin (see page 302; reserve the bones to make stock or soup). Set aside.

Heat 1 tablespoon of the oil in a large skillet. When it is hot, add the leek and onion and sauté for 2 to 3 minutes. Add the garlic and jalapeño and mix well. Stir in the apple, ⅜ teaspoon of the salt, the pepper, and bulgur. Mix well and cook, uncovered, over medium heat for 2 to 3 minutes, until any moisture in the wheat is absorbed and it is fluffy. Let cool.

Stuff the boned hens with the cooled apple and wheat mixture and tie the hens with kitchen twine to keep the stuffing inside.

Place the hens in a roasting pan and spread the remaining 1 tablespoon oil on top. Sprinkle with the remaining ⅛ teaspoon salt. Roast for 40 minutes total, basting the hens with the juices and fat after 15 minutes and again after 30 minutes.

Remove the hens to a platter. Pour out and discard most of the fat that has accumulated in the roasting pan. Add the water to the pan and bring to a boil on the stovetop, stirring to melt the solidified juices in the bottom.

Cut the hens in half and remove the twine. Divide the juices among four plates, place half a hen on each plate, and serve.

Cornish Hens Tabaka
Serves 4

✂ **Cornish hens** *tabaka* is based on a Russian specialty featuring whole squab that are pressed before they are sautéed, which makes the skin crisp and the meat succulent. After the hens are flattened and cooked, they are cut in half for serving. To finish the dish, a sauce created from the cooking juices (minus most of the fat) is poured over them, followed by a sprinkling of lemon juice and fresh dill.

> 2 Cornish hens (1¼–1½ pounds each)
> ½ teaspoon salt
> ½ teaspoon freshly ground black pepper
> 2 teaspoons crushed dried savory
> ½ cup homemade chicken stock (page 612) or low-salt canned chicken broth
> 1 tablespoon fresh lemon juice
> ¼ cup coarsely chopped fresh dill

To butterfly the hens, using a heavy knife or poultry shears, cut down one side of the backbone of each hen. Cut away the backbone, if desired, and open up the hen. Place the hens bone side down on a work surface covered with plastic wrap and place another sheet of plastic wrap on top of them. Using a meat pounder or a heavy flat-bottomed pan, pound the birds until they are flattened to about equal thickness throughout.

Sprinkle the skin side of the hens with the salt, pepper, and savory.

Heat two large nonstick skillets until hot. Arrange the hens skin side up in the skillets, cover, and cook for 5 minutes over medium-high heat.

Meanwhile, wrap two clean bricks (each about 4 pounds) in aluminum foil (alternatively, use cans, heavy saucepans, or clean stones). Turn the birds over again so they are skin side down and place a brick on each bird. Cook, uncovered, over medium heat for 20 minutes, or until the skin is well browned and crisp.

Remove the bricks (be careful: they are hot) and then the birds from the skillets. Cut the hens in half and arrange on a platter.

Discard all but ½ tablespoon fat from each skillet, and stir ¼ cup of the stock into each. Bring to a boil and boil for 1 minute, then strain the pan sauce evenly over the hen pieces. Sprinkle on the lemon juice and dill and serve.

Roast Capon with Armagnac-Mushroom Sauce
Serves 10

⚜ **Vermouth and mushrooms combine** with the reduced juices of the chicken and Armagnac to make this dish rich and elegant.

Capons (neutered and fattened chickens) are available during the holiday season in many markets. They are moist, tender, and succulent and well worth their extra cost.

1	pound mushrooms (domestic, wild, or a mixture), cleaned and thinly sliced (about 7 cups)
1	cup dry white vermouth
1	cup homemade chicken stock (page 612) or low-salt canned chicken broth
1	capon (about 8 pounds)
1¼	teaspoons salt
1¼	teaspoons freshly ground black pepper
1	teaspoon herbes de Provence
1	cup heavy cream
2	tablespoons Armagnac
1	teaspoon potato starch (see page 318), dissolved in 1 tablespoon water
1	tablespoon chopped fresh tarragon

Preheat the oven to 400 degrees.

Put the mushrooms in a saucepan with the vermouth and stock and bring to a boil, then cover, reduce the heat to low, and boil gently for 5 minutes. Set aside.

Season the capon inside and out with 1 teaspoon each of the salt and pepper and the herbes de Provence. Place the bird breast side up in a roasting pan and roast it for 30 minutes. Turn it over and roast for 1 hour. Finally, turn the capon onto its back again and roast it for 20 more minutes. (An instant-read thermometer inserted into the joint connecting a thigh and drumstick should register about 160 degrees.) Transfer the capon to an ovenproof platter and keep it warm in a 160-degree oven. (If you only have one oven, turn off the oven and leave the door open for about 5 minutes to cool down, then return the capon to the oven to keep warm.)

Skim off as much fat as possible from the drippings in the roasting pan. Pour the juices from the mushrooms into the pan and heat over high heat for a few seconds, stirring to melt the solidified juices, then pour the resulting glaze through a strainer set over the mushrooms. Add the cream and Armagnac to the mushroom mixture, bring to a boil, and stir in the dissolved potato starch. Mix in the remaining ¼ teaspoon each salt and pepper and the tarragon.

Carve the capon and serve it with the sauce.

Sautéed Capon with Peaches and Basil
Serves 8

⚜ **Pieces of capon are** sautéed and served with a sweet-and-sour sauce made of the pan drippings, vinegar, and peach jam, flavored at the last moment with shredded fresh basil. It's important to let the pieces rest in a warm oven for at least 10 minutes before serving. Peach segments sautéed in butter and sugar accompany the capon.

You can sauté the liver and enjoy it sliced on toast with a glass of wine while you cook.

PEACHES

2½	pounds firm but ripe peaches (unpeeled)
2	tablespoons unsalted butter
2	tablespoons sugar
¼	teaspoon salt
1½	cups homemade chicken stock (page 612) or low-salt canned chicken broth

2 teaspoons canola oil

1 capon (about 8 pounds), cut into 6 pieces (2 breasts, 2 legs, and 2 wings, wing tips removed)

1 teaspoon salt, or to taste

½ teaspoon freshly ground black pepper, or to taste

½ cup fruity dry red wine (such as Zinfandel)

⅓ cup balsamic vinegar

2 tablespoons ketchup

2 tablespoons peach or apricot preserves

2 tablespoons shredded fresh basil leaves

FOR THE PEACHES: Cut the peaches into 1- to 1½-inch-thick slices. (You should have 6 to 8 slices per person.) Divide the butter between two nonstick skillets and melt it. Arrange the peach slices in one layer, cut side down, in the skillets and sprinkle the slices in each skillet with 1 tablespoon of the sugar and ⅛ teaspoon of the salt. Cook over medium-high heat for 2 to 3 minutes, then turn the slices over and cook on the other cut side for 2 to 3 minutes, or until nicely browned and caramelized on both sides. Arrange the cooked peach slices in a gratin dish (set the pans aside), cover, and keep warm in a 160-degree oven until ready to serve, or let cool and reheat at the last moment.

Divide the stock between the skillets and bring to a boil, stirring to melt all the caramelized bits in the skillets. Pour the stock into a bowl and set aside.

If necessary, preheat the oven to 160 degrees.

FOR THE CAPON: Heat the oil in one very large or two large heavy skillets. Sprinkle the capon legs and wings with ½ teaspoon of the salt and ¼ teaspoon of the pepper and place them skin side down in one layer in the skillet(s). Cook over high heat for 15 minutes. Turn and cook on the other side for another 5 minutes. Remove the wings and set them aside on an ovenproof platter.

Turn the legs over again and place the breasts skin side down next to them. Sprinkle the breasts with the remaining ½ teaspoon salt and ¼ teaspoon pepper, cover, and cook over medium-high heat for 10 to 12 minutes. Remove all the capon pieces and arrange them next to the wings on the platter. Place the capon in the oven for at least 10 minutes to finish the cooking and relax the meat. (*The capon can be kept warm in the oven for up to 45 minutes.*)

Pour off most of the fat rendered by the capon. Deglaze the skillet(s) by adding the wine and vinegar and cooking over high heat, stirring constantly, for 2 minutes, or until all the solidified juices have melted.

If you used two skillets, combine all the juices in one skillet. Add the reserved stock, the ketchup, and preserves and bring to a strong boil. Boil for a few minutes to reduce the sauce and concentrate its taste. Add any juices that have accumulated around the peaches to the skillet, then strain the sauce through a fine strainer. Add additional salt and pepper if needed.

To serve, slice the meat from the breasts and legs and arrange on individual plates, dividing the white and dark meat evenly. Cut each wing in half and serve to the guests who enjoy eating with their fingers. Divide the peach slices among the plates, arranging them around the meat. Stir the basil into the hot sauce, spoon the sauce over the capon and peaches, and serve.

Roast Turkey with Mushroom Stuffing
Serves 8 to 10

✦ **On holidays, I like** to serve a small roast turkey with a whole wheat–bread stuffing, which I make while the bird roasts. The stuffing is flavored with golden raisins and dried mushrooms and moistened with the mushroom-soaking liquid.

 1 turkey (about 12 pounds), preferably organic
 2 cups water
 1 teaspoon salt
 1 teaspoon freshly ground black pepper
 3 medium onions (about 12 ounces), cut into 1-inch dice
10 garlic cloves, unpeeled

STUFFING

 ¾ cup (about ¾ ounce) dried mushroom pieces, preferably chanterelles or morels
1½ cups warm water
 3 tablespoons unsalted butter
 2 tablespoons olive oil
 1 medium onion, finely chopped (1 cup)

1–2 pale inner celery stalks, chopped (½ cup)
 ½ teaspoon herbes de Provence
 3 garlic cloves, crushed and finely chopped (2 teaspoons)
 6 slices sprouted-wheat bread (whole wheat bread made with wheat kernels; about 7 ounces)
 ⅓ cup golden raisins
 ½ teaspoon salt
 ¼ teaspoon freshly ground black pepper

 1 teaspoon potato starch (see page 318), dissolved in 1 tablespoon water
 1 tablespoon dark soy sauce

FOR THE TURKEY: Place the turkey neck, gizzard, and heart in a saucepan with the water (reserve the liver for another use) and bring to a boil. Cover, reduce the heat to low, and cook for 1 hour.

Preheat the oven to 425 degrees.

Remove the turkey parts from the cooking liquid and reserve the liquid. (You should have about 1½ cups.) When it is cool enough, pull the meat from the neck bones. Cut the meat, gizzard, and heart into ¼-inch dice. Reserve.

Sprinkle the turkey inside and out with the salt and pepper. Place it breast side up in a large roasting pan and roast for 30 minutes.

Using pot holders, turn the turkey breast side down. Arrange the onions and garlic cloves around it. Reduce the oven temperature to 350 degrees, return the turkey to the oven, and cook for 1½ hours.

Add the reserved cooking liquid to the roasting pan, turn the turkey breast side up, and continue cooking for 30 minutes longer to brown the breast. Turn the oven off, transfer the turkey to an ovenproof platter, and return it to the warm oven to rest. Set the roasting pan aside.

Soak the mushrooms in the warm water in a bowl for at least 30 minutes, until softened.

Lift out the mushrooms, squeezing the excess liquid back into the bowl, and coarsely chop them. Set the mushrooms and soaking liquid aside separately.

Heat the butter and oil in a large skillet until hot. Add the onion and celery and sauté for 3 minutes. Add the herbes de Provence, garlic, and mushrooms, mix well, and remove from the heat.

Toast the bread slices well. Cut them into ⅜-inch croutons. (You should have 3 cups.)

Stir the croutons and raisins into the onion mixture.

Pour the reserved mushroom-soaking liquid into a measuring cup, leaving behind the sandy residue in the bottom of the bowl. (You should have about ¾ cup.) Add the soaking liquid, salt, and pepper to the onion mixture and toss gently to combine. Pack lightly into a loaf pan and cover with aluminum foil.

About 45 minutes before the turkey is done, put the loaf of stuffing in the oven and bake for 45 minutes. Then keep warm in a warm spot or in the turned-off oven.

WHILE THE TURKEY RESTS, MAKE THE GRAVY: Push the cooking juices and vegetables from the roasting pan through a sieve or a food mill into a saucepan. Let rest for 4 to 5 minutes, until most of the fat has risen to the top, then skim off as much of it as possible. (You should have approximately 2 cups cooking juices.)

Add the diced neck, gizzard, and heart to the cooking juices, bring to a simmer, and simmer for 5 minutes to reduce the liquid slightly. Stir in the dissolved potato starch and soy sauce until smooth. Pour into a sauceboat or serving bowl.

Carve the turkey and serve it with the gravy and stuffing.

Turkey Cutlets in Anchovy-Lemon Sauce
Serves 8

❧ **Pound for pound, unboned** turkey breast is about half the cost of ready-to-sauté cutlets, and if you bone it yourself, you get the benefit of the wings, bones, and skin for use in other dishes. Reserve the bones for soup or stew, and, if you like, spread the skin out on a cookie sheet and roast it in a 400-degree oven for 20 to 30 minutes, until brown and crisp, for use as cracklings to garnish soups and salads.

However, if you prefer, you can substitute 8 boneless turkey cutlets weighing 6 to 8 ounces each for the whole breast.

1	whole (double) turkey breast (about 5 pounds — see the headnote)
1	2-ounce can anchovy fillets in oil
1	tablespoon drained capers
2	tablespoons fresh lemon juice
1½	tablespoons unsalted butter
1	teaspoon salt
½	teaspoon freshly ground black pepper
	About ½ cup all-purpose flour
2	tablespoons chopped fresh parsley

TO BONE THE TURKEY BREAST: First remove the wings at the joints (reserve them to use in another recipe). Pull off the skin and discard it or use it for cracklings (see the headnote). Cut down along the breastbone and remove the meat from each side in 1 large piece. Holding the knife at an angle, cut each piece lengthwise into 4 large cutlets.

Using a meat pounder, pound the cutlets lightly between two sheets of plastic wrap to make them approximately equal in size and about ⅜ inch thick. Set aside.

Drain the anchovies, reserving the oil.

Coarsely chop the anchovies and put them in a bowl. Toss with the capers and lemon juice and set aside.

Divide the butter and anchovy oil between two large skillets and heat until hot. Sprinkle the cutlets with the salt and pepper and dredge in the flour, shaking the cutlets so they are lightly coated. Place in the pans and sauté for about 1½ minutes on each side. (They will still be slightly pink inside.)

Transfer the cutlets to a serving platter. Add the anchovy–lemon juice mixture to the juices in the skillets, stir to melt the solidified juices, and pour over the cutlets, and serve. (*The cutlets can be kept warm in a 160-degree oven until you are ready to serve.*)

Sprinkle the cutlets with the chopped parsley and serve.

Turkey Scaloppini
Serves 8

⅜ **Conventionally made with veal,** scaloppini are less expensive and just as good made with turkey cutlets. The longest part of this recipe is soaking the mushrooms, but it can be done ahead. This rich dish is excellent with rice or noodles.

16 dried shiitake mushrooms
 3 cups lukewarm water
 8 skinless turkey cutlets (about 6 ounces each)
 6 tablespoons (¾ stick) unsalted butter
1½ teaspoons salt, or to taste
 1 teaspoon freshly ground black pepper, or to taste
 6 scallions, trimmed (leaving some green) and chopped (about ½ cup)
 4 garlic cloves, crushed and chopped (about 1 tablespoon)

 2 tablespoons bourbon
 1 cup heavy cream
 1 teaspoon potato starch (see page 318), dissolved in 2 tablespoons water
 2 teaspoons fresh lemon juice
 1 tablespoon chopped fresh chives

Soak the shiitake mushrooms in the lukewarm water in a bowl for 1 hour.

Lift out the mushrooms, squeezing the excess liquid back into the bowl, and remove the stems, which are fibrous. Cut the mushroom caps into ½-inch-wide strips.

Strain the soaking liquid through a paper towel–lined sieve into a saucepan. Add the mushroom strips, bring to a boil over high heat, and cook gently for 10 minutes. Set aside.

Preheat the oven to 160 degrees.

Using a meat pounder, pound the turkey cutlets between two sheets of plastic wrap to about ⅜ inch thick.

Divide the butter between two large skillets and place the pans over medium heat. Sprinkle the turkey with the salt and pepper. When the butter is hot, add the turkey to the pans in one layer and cook over medium-high heat for approximately 1½ minutes on each side. Arrange in a baking dish and keep warm in the oven.

Add the scallions and garlic to the skillets and sauté for 30 seconds. Add the bourbon and carefully ignite it with a long match. Add the mushrooms and their juices and the cream and bring to a boil, stirring to dissolve any solidified pan juices. Add any juices that have collected around the turkey to the sauce and strain the sauce into a clean saucepan. Simmer for 1 to 2 minutes. Add the dissolved potato starch and more salt and pepper if needed and stir in the lemon juice.

Arrange the scaloppini on a platter and coat with the sauce. Sprinkle with the chives and serve.

Dark Turkey Fricassee
Serves 8

✂ **After Thanksgiving, turkey parts** are available for very little money at the supermarket. I particularly like the legs in this delicious and filling stew, which is perfect for cold weather.

  2 large turkey legs (about 5 pounds total), skin removed
  3 tablespoons peanut oil
  3 cups diced (1-inch) onions
  4 cups water
6–8 garlic cloves, crushed and chopped (about 2 tablespoons)
  2 tablespoons peeled, finely chopped ginger
  1 teaspoon ground cumin
 ½ teaspoon hot pepper flakes
  2 bay leaves
  2 teaspoons salt
  1 teaspoon freshly ground black pepper
1½ cups short-grain brown rice
  1 cup sun-dried tomatoes, cut into 1-inch pieces
  1 cup tiny fresh peas or frozen baby peas

Separate the drumsticks from the thighs. Cut each drumstick lengthwise into 2 pieces; one piece will have the bone. Cut each thigh into 3 pieces: cut a slice of meat away from each side of the center bone, leaving some meat on the bone, so you have 3 pieces with about the same amount of meat.

Heat the oil in a large Dutch oven or stockpot. Add half the pieces of turkey in one layer and brown over medium-high heat, turning occasionally, for about 20 minutes. Transfer to a tray. Add the remaining turkey pieces to the pot and brown them as before. Transfer the turkey to the tray.

Add the onions to the pot and sauté over medium heat for 10 minutes. Return the turkey to the pot, add the water, garlic, ginger, cumin, hot pepper flakes, bay leaves, salt, pepper, and rice, and stir well. Bring to a boil, stirring, then cover, reduce the heat to low, and cook gently for 1 hour and 10 minutes, or until all the liquid has been absorbed and the rice, sun-dried tomatoes, and meat are tender.

Mix in the peas and cook for a few minutes, until tender. Serve.

Grilled Turkey Wings
Serves 6

✂ **Boiling the wings briefly** before grilling keeps them moist — since they are large, they would tend to dry out and the sauce might burn if they were cooked entirely on the grill. This sauce can also be used with great success on other grilled meats or poultry.

  6 whole turkey wings, each with 3 sections (about 4 pounds total)

SAUCE

 ¼ cup cider vinegar
  2 tablespoons dark soy sauce
1½ tablespoons light brown sugar
 ¾ teaspoon dried thyme
  1 teaspoon crushed fennel seeds
  1 teaspoon Tabasco sauce
  3 garlic cloves, crushed and finely chopped (about 2 teaspoons)
  2 scallions, trimmed (leaving some green) and finely chopped (about 3 tablespoons)

Put the turkey wings in a pot, cover with 8 cups water, and bring to a boil. Cover and boil the

Roast Duck with Orange Sauce
Serves 8

⚓ **Many restaurants serve duck** breasts rare and the legs braised, but the classic way of preparing duck for the holidays is to roast it whole and serve it with orange sauce. It is excellent with wild rice.

- 2 ducks (about 5 pounds each)
- 1 teaspoon salt
- ½ teaspoon freshly ground black pepper
- 1 cup cold water

SAUCE AND GARNISH

- 1 tablespoon canola oil
- ¾ cup coarsely chopped leeks
- ¾ cup coarsely chopped carrots
- ½ cup coarsely chopped onion
- 1 cup coarsely chopped tomatoes
- ½ cup coarsely chopped celery
- 2 bay leaves
- 1 teaspoon dried thyme
- 2 garlic cloves, crushed but not peeled
- 2 tablespoons tomato paste
- 3 tablespoons all-purpose flour
- 4 cups homemade chicken stock (page 612) or low-salt canned chicken broth
- 1 cup dry white wine
- 5 navel oranges
- ⅓ cup sugar
- ⅓ cup cider vinegar
- 2 tablespoons currant jelly
  Salt and freshly ground black pepper
- 2 tablespoons Grand Marnier
- 2 tablespoons unsalted butter

Preheat the oven to 425 degrees.

Remove the neck, gizzard, liver, and heart from each duck and set aside (you can enjoy the sautéed livers on bread with a glass of wine while

wings gently for 20 minutes. Set them aside in the broth until ready to grill.

FOR THE SAUCE: Mix together all the ingredients in a stainless steel saucepan. Set aside.

Heat a grill until medium-hot to hot.

Remove the wings from the broth (freeze the broth for use in a soup or stew), place them flat side down on the grill, cover with the lid, and grill for about 12 minutes, until the underside is nicely browned.

Turn the wings over and brush them with the sauce. Grill, covered, for another 12 minutes. Turn again, brush with the sauce, and grill for another 5 minutes, or until the wings are well browned on all sides.

Arrange the wings on a serving platter. Bring the rest of the sauce to a boil and pour it over the wings. Serve, or let cool to lukewarm before serving.

VARIATION
GRILLED SPARERIBS
Substitute pork spareribs for the turkey wings. Prepare them as in the recipe, first boiling them gently for 30 minutes and then finishing them on the grill in the same manner and for the same length of time.

---

you are cooking, if you like). Cut the wings off each duck and reserve.

Season the ducks inside and out with the salt and pepper. Place breast side up in a large roasting pan and add the water. Roast for 1 hour.

Pour off all the fat that has accumulated in the pan, or remove it with a bulb baster. Continue roasting the ducks for another 45 minutes.

MEANWHILE, FOR THE SAUCE: Cut the duck necks, hearts, and gizzards into 2-inch pieces. Cut the wings apart at the joints.

Heat the oil in a heavy pot until hot. Add the duck parts and sauté, turning occasionally, for about 20 minutes, or until they are browned on all sides. Add the vegetables, herbs, and garlic and cook for 5 minutes.

Stir in the tomato paste and flour, mixing well. Add the stock and wine and bring to a boil, then reduce the heat and simmer slowly for 1 hour.

Strain the sauce. (You should have about 3 cups.) Set aside.

Remove the rind of one of the oranges in strips with a vegetable peeler, taking care not to pick up any of the white pith underneath the skin. Stack a few strips at a time and cut lengthwise into thin julienne strips. Blanch the strips in a saucepan of boiling water for 1 minute, then drain in a strainer and rinse under cold water. Set aside.

Squeeze the juice from the peeled orange and another of the oranges; you should have 1 cup juice. Using a paring knife, peel the 3 remaining oranges right down to the flesh. Separate the segments by cutting down along the membranes surrounding the segments, so that you have only pure flesh sections. Set aside.

When the ducks have roasted for 1 hour and 45 minutes, transfer them to an ovenproof platter; set the roasting pan aside. Keep the ducks warm in a 160-degree oven while you finish the sauce. (If you only have one oven, turn off the oven and leave the door open for about 5 minutes, then return the ducks to the oven to keep warm.)

Skim the fat from the duck cooking juices and add the sauce to the roasting pan. Bring to a boil, stirring to melt all the solidified juices, then strain again.

Combine the sugar and vinegar in a large heavy saucepan, bring to a boil, and boil for about 4 minutes, until the mixture turns a pale caramel color. Add the orange juice and currant jelly and bring to a boil, then add the strained sauce and simmer for about 8 minutes. Taste for seasoning, add salt and pepper if needed, and stir in the Grand Marnier. Finally, add the butter bit by bit, shaking the pan as you add it so it blends into the sauce.

Spoon some of the sauce over the ducks. Sprinkle the top with the julienned orange rind and surround with the orange sections as garnish. Carve at the table, or present the duck, then bring back into the kitchen to carve. Serve the extra sauce on the side.

Roast Duck with Caramelized Yellow Turnips, Onions, and Lima Beans
Serves 8

Yellow turnips, sometimes called rutabagas, have an assertive taste. Blanching them in boiling water for a few minutes makes them milder. If you

prefer, substitute an equal weight of white turnips for the yellow in this recipe.

The leftover carcasses, necks, and gizzards are excellent to gnaw on the following day and make a good lunch served with a salad. By all means, use your fingers when enjoying the meat on the bones. The carcasses can also be boiled for 2 hours in 2 quarts of water for a delicious stock or soup.

2 ducks (about 5 pounds each)
1 teaspoon salt
½ teaspoon freshly ground black pepper

VEGETABLES

1 large yellow turnip (rutabaga; about 1¾ pounds), peeled
1 pound pearl onions (25–30)
1½ tablespoons unsalted butter
1½ teaspoons peanut oil
1 tablespoon sugar
1 teaspoon salt
2 cups fresh or frozen small lima beans

1½ cups homemade chicken stock (page 612) or low-salt canned chicken broth

Preheat the oven to 425 degrees.

Remove the neck, gizzard, liver, and heart from each duck and set aside. Pat the ducks dry with paper towels. Season the ducks inside and out with the salt and pepper and place them breast side up on a large baking sheet or in a large roasting pan with shallow sides (if the pan sides are too high, the duck will braise rather than roast and will not brown properly). Scatter the necks and gizzards around the ducks (reserve the hearts and livers) and roast for 1 hour.

MEANWHILE, FOR THE VEGETABLES: Cut the turnip into 25 to 30 pieces. Using a paring knife, trim the pieces to make them of approximately equal size and shape. Put the turnip pieces

in a large skillet, add 3 cups water, and bring to a boil over high heat. Boil the turnip pieces for 1 minute, then drain in a sieve and rinse under cold water to stop the cooking.

Return the turnip pieces to the skillet and add the onions (preferably in one layer with the turnips). Add ½ tablespoon of the butter, the oil, 2 teaspoons of the sugar, ½ teaspoon of the salt, and ¾ cup water and bring to a boil over high heat, then cover, reduce the heat to low, and boil gently for about 8 minutes. (The vegetables should still be firm.)

Uncover the skillet, increase the heat to high, and cook until all the water is gone and the turnip and onions have started browning and caramelizing in the pan drippings. Keep cooking and turning them for about 10 minutes, removing them one by one to an ovenproof dish as they are caramelized. Set the turnips and onions aside.

Combine the lima beans and the remaining 1 tablespoon butter, 1 teaspoon sugar, and ½ teaspoon salt in a skillet. Add ¼ cup water if using frozen limas, ½ cup water if using fresh, and bring to a boil. Cover and continue boiling for about 1 minute if using frozen limas, 6 to 8 minutes if using fresh. Remove the lid when the limas are tender and cook them, uncovered, until most of the liquid is gone and the limas are glossy looking. Set aside.

After the ducks have cooked for 1 hour, pour out the fat surrounding them, or use a bulb baster to remove it, and return the ducks to the oven for 45 minutes. (The duck fat can be used to sauté vegetables, especially potatoes.) Then, as a treat for the cook, add the livers and hearts to the pan and cook them along with the ducks for 10 minutes; enjoy them with a glass of wine while you finish preparing the meal.

Transfer the ducks to a platter and pour out all the fat that has accumulated in the pan. Reduce the oven temperature to 160 degrees.

Add the chicken stock to the roasting pan and heat on top of the stove, stirring, until all the solidified juices in the pan have melted. Strain the sauce into a saucepan and set aside.

When the ducks are cool enough to handle, cut each of them into quarters. Cut each breast in half and separate the drumsticks and thighs, so you have 8 pieces from each duck. Place the pieces in an ovenproof dish and keep warm, uncovered, in the oven.

Reheat all the vegetables and the sauce (heat the turnips and onions in the oven or in a microwave).

Divide the vegetables among eight dinner plates and arrange 2 pieces of duck (1 leg piece and 1 breast piece) on top of the vegetables on each plate. Spoon on a little sauce and serve.

Skillet Duck with Red Oak Lettuce Salad
Serves 4

❧ **Easy and delicious, this** duck is cooked in much the same way as Southern fried chicken — fried in its own fat in a covered pot so steam develops, making the meat very moist and tender and the skin crisp. Be sure to use a very large skillet or a lidded saucepan. Some of the rendered fat, a bonus from this recipe, is used in the salad dressing. (You can use the rest for sautéing potatoes.)

  1 duck (about 5 pounds)
  ½ teaspoon salt
  ¼ cup fruity dry white wine

DRESSING
  1 medium garlic clove, crushed and minced (½ teaspoon)
  1 tablespoon chopped shallot
  ¼ teaspoon salt

  ¼ teaspoon freshly ground black pepper
  1 tablespoon white wine vinegar
  3 tablespoons duck fat, peanut or olive oil, or a mixture of the fat and oils
  1 teaspoon light soy sauce

  1 head red oak leaf lettuce, leaves washed and dried (about 6 cups)
  1 bunch arugula, trimmed, washed, and dried (about 2 cups loosely packed)

GARNISH
  2 teaspoons unsalted butter
  2 large eggs, beaten with a fork
     Pinch each of salt and freshly ground black pepper

Reserve the duck neck, gizzard, liver, and heart for another purpose. Using a sharp heavy knife or poultry shears, cut the duck lengthwise in half, slicing through the carcass bones. Then cut each half into 2 pieces: the leg and the breast, with wing attached.

Heat a large skillet or saucepan, either non-stick or heavy aluminum, until hot. Place the duck pieces skin side down in one layer in the pan, sprinkle with the salt, and cook over high heat for 5 minutes. Lift the pieces to dislodge them from the bottom of the skillet and then lay them, still skin side down, back in the skillet. Add the duck neck and gizzard, cover, reduce the heat to medium, and cook for 15 minutes. The duck should be cooking in a deep layer of fat and its skin should be very brown at this point.

Reduce the heat to very low, cover, and cook for 30 more minutes. (The duck pieces should be almost immersed in the fat.) Add the liver and heart, cover, and cook for 5 minutes.

Preheat the oven to 170 degrees.

Remove the duck pieces to a large baking sheet and keep warm in the oven. Pour the fat from the skillet into a bowl and let cool. (Covered and refrigerated, the fat can be used as needed for up to 2 months for sautéing potatoes or other vegetables.) There will be a small residue of glaze, or solidified juices, in the bottom of the skillet. Add the wine to the skillet and stir to melt the solidified juices. Keep warm.

FOR THE DRESSING: Combine all the ingredients in a bowl and stir gently. The dressing should not be homogenized but should look separated.

Toss the salad greens with the dressing and arrange the salad on four serving plates. Place a piece of duck in the center of each and sprinkle the pan drippings on the pieces of duck.

FOR THE GARNISH: Heat a skillet for 1 minute. Add the butter, and when it is hot, add the beaten eggs and stir gently over high heat to scramble. Season with the salt and pepper. The eggs should still be runny.

Arrange spoonfuls of the egg around the duck on each salad. The pieces of duck will be lukewarm to warm, the salad at room temperature, and the eggs warm. Serve.

Roast Duck with Cherries
Serves 4

⅙ **Duck with cherries** is particularly good made with large, dark Bing cherries. The bird can be carved in the kitchen, but it is more impressive to do it in front of guests at the table. Rice or buttered noodles are an excellent accompaniment.

CHERRIES

- 1 pound Bing cherries, pitted
- ½ cup dry Madeira or sherry
- ½ cup cherry brandy

- 1 duck (about 5 pounds)

STOCK

- 1 tablespoon canola oil
- ½ carrot, unpeeled, coarsely sliced (½ cup)
- 1 medium onion, unpeeled, coarsely sliced (¾ cup)
- 1 tomato, coarsely chopped (1 cup)
- 1 garlic clove, crushed but not peeled
- 1 teaspoon black peppercorns, crushed
- 2 bay leaves
- 1 teaspoon fresh thyme leaves or ½ teaspoon dried thyme
- 3 cups homemade chicken stock (page 612) or low-salt canned chicken broth
- 2 teaspoons arrowroot or cornstarch, dissolved in ¼ cup cold water

- ½ teaspoon salt, or to taste
- ½ teaspoon freshly ground black pepper, or to taste

FOR THE CHERRIES: Combine the cherries with the Madeira or sherry and cherry brandy in a bowl and let macerate at room temperature for 2 to 3 hours.

MEANWHILE, FOR THE DUCK: Preheat the oven to 425 degrees.

Remove the neck, gizzard, liver, and heart from the duck. Reserve the liver for another use and cut the neck, gizzard, and heart into 1-inch pieces. Cut off the wing tips from the duck and cut into 1-inch pieces. Set the wing tips, neck, gizzard, and heart aside.

Season the duck inside and out with the salt and pepper. Place in a roasting pan and roast for 1 hour and 45 minutes.

MEANWHILE, FOR THE STOCK: Heat the oil in a large saucepan. Add the wing tips, neck, gizzard, and heart and sauté for 5 minutes. Add the vegetables, garlic, peppercorns, bay leaves, thyme, and stock and bring to a boil. Reduce the heat and simmer for 1 hour.

Strain the stock. You should have 2 cups; if not, adjust the amount with water. Put the strained liquid into a clean saucepan, add the dissolved arrowroot or cornstarch, stirring, and bring to a boil.

Transfer the duck to a platter and keep warm in a low oven or at the back of the stove. Pour off the fat that has accumulated in the roasting pan.

Add the sauce to the roasting pan and boil, stirring, for a few minutes to melt all the solidified juices on the bottom of the pan.

Strain the sauce into a saucepan and add the cherries, with the wine mixture. Cook slowly for about 10 minutes, until the sauce has reduced to about 2½ cups. Season with salt and pepper if needed.

Carve the duck (or cut it up with poultry shears) and serve with the sauce.

FROM ONE DUCK, MANY DISHES

A duck exemplifies how ingredients can be used to their fullest. Here one duck is transformed into four dishes, three of which are main courses. The duck is skinned and boned, and the meat is sautéed and served with a vinegar-flavored sauce (page 293). The skin is turned into my version of Peking duck (page 291). The bones and neck become part of a bean casserole (page 292), and, finally, the liver is made into a pâté (page 290).

Another cook could create four entirely different recipes. For example, the skin could be transformed into cracklings (page 250) for use as a garnish on soup or salad; the bones could be used to create a stock, sauce, or soup; the liver could be cooked briefly and served on toast; and the meat could be sautéed and served with another sauce, such as one made with cognac (page 248).

HOW TO SKIN AND BONE A DUCK: Remove the liver, gizzard, neck, and heart (about 1 pound total) from a 5½-pound duck and set aside.

Remove both wings at the shoulder joints and set them aside with the giblets and neck. Cut a slit through the skin down the backbone and, using a sharp paring knife, carefully separate the skin from the meat and carcass. (Do not worry if you make a few holes in the skin, but try to remove it in 1 or 2 large pieces.) Set the skin aside.

Cut off the 2 legs at the hip joints. Cut into the duck at the shoulder joint on one side and then, holding the duck down with the flat of your knife, pull the breast meat off the bone in one piece. Repeat on the other side.

Lay the legs on the cutting board and, using a small sharp knife, cut along the bone, following down the thigh, around the knee, and down the drumsticks on each side and underneath to separate the meat from the bone. Remove as many sinews as you can from the leg meat. (You will have approximately 1¼ pounds skinless, boneless meat from the 2 legs and the breasts.) Cover the meat with plastic wrap and refrigerate until cooking time. Set the bones and carcass aside with the wings and other parts.

Put the liver and an equal amount of duck fat (the 2 lumps near the rear opening will weigh about the same as the liver) in a small bowl. Cover and set aside.

The duck is now divided into 4 separate groupings: meat; skin; liver and fat; and bones, gizzard, neck, heart, and wings. Each grouping will be used for a different recipe.

DUCK LIVER PÂTÉ Makes 16 toasts

Similar to foie-gras mousse, this simple duck pâté costs only pennies to make. Serve it on toasts.

The pâté will keep, well covered and refrigerated, for 3 to 4 days. If you want to store it longer, cover it with a ½-inch-thick layer of fat reserved from cooking the duck skin (see Mock Peking Duck, page 291) and refrigerate for up to 2 months. When ready to serve, remove the fat; any leftover pâté should be refrigerated again and consumed within 2 days. It also freezes well.

PÂTÉ

3 ounces duck fat (from a 5½-pound duck; see page 289)

1 large shallot, coarsely chopped (2½ tablespoons)

1 duck liver (about 3 ounces; from the same duck), trimmed of any sinew and cut into 4 pieces

¼ teaspoon herbes de Provence

1 garlic clove, crushed and coarsely chopped

¼ teaspoon salt

¼ teaspoon freshly ground black pepper

1 teaspoon cognac

16 ¼-inch-thick baguette slices, toasted

FOR THE PÂTÉ: Cut the fat into ½-inch pieces and cook in a skillet over medium-high heat for 4 to 5 minutes, until most of it has melted and some of it has browned. Add the shallot and cook for about 30 seconds, stirring occasionally. Add the liver, herbes de Provence, and garlic and cook for 1½ to 2 minutes, stirring occasionally. Add the salt and pepper.

Transfer the mixture to a blender, add the cognac, and blend until liquefied. (You should have ½ cup.) Let cool to room temperature, then cover and refrigerate until set.

Stir the pâté with a spoon for a few seconds and chill in the refrigerator. Place a small spoonful of the pâté on each toasted baguette slice and serve.

MOCK PEKING DUCK
Serves 6 (makes 12 pancakes)

My wife and I tasted a Peking duck similar to this one in Beijing several years ago. Although most restaurants use the whole duck for this dish, wrapping pieces of skin and meat in Chinese pancakes, my version uses only the skin.

Skin from a 5½-pound duck
  (see page 289)
¼ teaspoon salt
½ teaspoon sugar, dissolved in
  1 tablespoon water

PANCAKES

1½ cups all-purpose flour
  About ½ cup boiling water
  About 2 teaspoons toasted sesame oil

SAUCE

⅓ cup hoisin sauce
1 tablespoon toasted sesame oil
2 tablespoons water

FILLINGS

4 scallions, trimmed (leaving some
  green) and cut lengthwise into 3
  pieces each
1 small cucumber (about 10 ounces),
  peeled, halved lengthwise, seeded,
  and each half cut lengthwise into
  6 strips
⅓ cup fresh cilantro leaves

Preheat the oven to 375 degrees.

Bring 4 quarts of water to a boil in a pot. Lower the duck skin into the boiling water and cook over high heat, turning it occasionally with tongs, for 2 to 3 minutes; the water should not return to a boil again. Lift the skin from the water and spread it out flesh side down, as flat as possible, on a cookie sheet. Sprinkle it with the salt and moisten it with the sweetened water. Cover with a sheet of parchment paper and another cookie sheet.

Bake for 45 to 55 minutes, until the skin is crispy and brown. Remove from the pan, reserving the fat, if desired. (The fat is good for sautéing potatoes, browning meat prior to roasting, or preserving Duck Liver Pâté, page 290.)

When the skin is cool enough to handle, cut it into 12 long strips. Set aside or put on a tray and keep warm in a 140-degree oven until serving time.

FOR THE PANCAKES: Put the flour in a food processor and, with the motor running, add a scant ½ cup boiling water and process for 15 to 20 seconds, until the mixture forms a ball. (Depending on the amount of moisture in the flour, you may need a little more water.)

Remove the dough from the food processor and knead it for a few seconds, then form it into a cylinder 6 inches long and about 2 inches thick. Cut into 12 slices, each about ½ inch thick. Brush 6 of the rounds with some of the sesame oil and place the remaining 6 rounds on top of the oiled rounds. Press each of the pancake "sandwiches" together, and stretch them to create pancakes 3 to 4 inches in diameter. Using the remainder of the sesame oil, lightly oil your countertop, then roll each pancake on this oiled area into a 7-inch disk.

Heat a large sturdy aluminum skillet until hot. Without adding any oil, cook the pancakes one at a time for 45 seconds to 1 minute on each side, until lightly browned. Transfer to a tray.

Pull the pancake "sandwiches" apart so you have 12 individual pancakes again. (The oil in the middle of the dough rounds makes them separate easily.) Fold each pancake, crusty side in, into quarters. Arrange the pancakes in one slightly overlapping layer on a heatproof plate. (*The pancakes can be made a few hours ahead and kept covered with plastic wrap.*)

At serving time, remove the plastic wrap and set the plate containing the pancakes in a steamer. Steam, covered, over boiling water for 3 to 4 minutes, until the pancakes are hot.

MEANWHILE, FOR THE SAUCE AND FILLINGS: Combine all the ingredients in a small bowl.

To serve, unfold the pancakes. Place a piece of duck skin, a scallion strip, a cucumber strip, a scant tablespoon of the sauce, and a few cilantro leaves in the center of each pancake and roll into a cylinder. Serve.

DUCK AND BEAN CASSEROLE
Serves 6

A quick version of the famous dish from the Southwest of France that is traditionally made with beans, sausages, preserved goose, duck, pork, and lamb, this "poor man's cassoulet" is satisfying, economical, and close enough in taste to the original to make it well worthwhile.

8   ounces (generous 1 cup) dried navy, pea, or Great Northern beans, picked over and rinsed
    Carcass, bones, wings, gizzard, neck, and heart from a 5½-pound duck (see page 289)
1¼ teaspoons salt
½   teaspoon herbes de Provence
1   bay leaf
4   cups cold water
1   leek, trimmed (leaving some green), split, washed, and cut into 1-inch pieces (2 cups)
1   onion (6 ounces), cut into ½-inch pieces (1 cup)
2   carrots (6 ounces), peeled and cut into ½-inch pieces (¾ cup)
1   cup diced (½-inch) tomatoes (fresh or canned)
¼   teaspoon Tabasco sauce

Place the beans in a pot with the duck carcass, bones, wings, gizzard, neck, and heart. Add the salt, herbes de Provence, bay leaf, and water and bring to a boil, then cover, reduce the heat to very low, and cook at a gentle boil for 1 hour. The beans should be almost cooked but still a bit firm. Remove the carcass, bones, wings, neck, gizzard, and heart from the pot and transfer to a platter.

Add the leek, onion, carrots, and tomatoes to the pot and bring back to a boil. Cover, reduce the heat to low, and boil gently for 20 minutes.

When the duck bones are cool enough to handle, pick any meat from the bones and coarsely chop it, along with the gizzard and heart (you should have 1½ to 2 cups). Add to the beans.

After the bean and vegetable mixture has

cooked for 20 minutes, add the Tabasco sauce. The beans should be soft and tender at this point and the mixture should be soupy but not overly liquid in consistency. If it is too watery, boil it gently, uncovered, for 10 to 15 minutes. (If you are making this dish ahead for later serving, keep in mind that it will have a tendency to thicken when reheated.) If the dish is too thick, thin it a little by adding a few tablespoons of water.

Transfer to a serving dish and serve.

VARIATION

For a richer version, divide the bean mixture, which should be very soupy, among six small earthenware tureens (like those you would use for onion soup). Place a 1-inch-thick slice of kielbasa and 1 pork sausage link in each bowl. Top each with 1 tablespoon dried bread crumbs and sprinkle with a bit of duck fat. Arrange the bowls on a cookie sheet and bake in a preheated 350-degree oven for about 30 minutes.

SAUTÉED DUCK IN VINEGAR SAUCE Serves 4

The taste of this classic dish is complex and flavorful, belying the fact that it takes only a few minutes to prepare.

    2 tablespoons unsalted butter
    2 skinless, boneless duck breasts and
         2 skinless, boneless duck legs (from
         a 5½-pound duck; see page 289)
    ¼ teaspoon salt
    ¼ teaspoon freshly ground black pepper
    2 tablespoons chopped onion
    1 teaspoon chopped garlic (2 cloves)

    ⅓ cup dry red wine
    3 tablespoons balsamic vinegar
    2 tablespoons ketchup
    1 teaspoon A1 Steak Sauce
    ¼ cup water
    1 tablespoon minced fresh chives

Preheat the oven to 180 degrees.

Heat the butter in a large skillet. Sprinkle the duck with the salt and pepper. When the butter is hot, add the duck legs to the skillet and cook for about 3 minutes on each side. After the first 2 minutes, add the breasts and cook for 2½ minutes on each side. Transfer the duck to an ovenproof plate and place it in the oven to rest and keep warm while you make the sauce.

Add the onion and garlic to the drippings in the skillet and cook, stirring constantly, for 15 to 20 seconds. Add the wine and vinegar, bring to a boil, stirring to melt the solidified juices, and cook until the liquid is reduced to about ¼ cup.

Add the ketchup, steak sauce, and water, bring to a boil, and cook for 1 minute. Drain off any liquid that has accumulated around the duck and add it to the sauce.

Cut each piece of duck in half and arrange the meat from half a leg and half a breast on each of four plates. Coat with the sauce, sprinkle with the chives, and serve.

Duck Cassoulet
Serves 10 to 12

❧ **Cassoulet, the classic one-dish** meal of the Southwest of France, is a peasant dish — sturdy country fare. How it is made varies according to whoever is preparing it, but it always contains one kind of poultry, some sausage, and one or two kinds of other meat, including pork. In this recipe, I use duck and pork.

It's important to start the beans in cold water so they come to a boil slowly, or they will harden and not cook properly.

BEANS

- 2 pounds dried Great Northern or navy beans, picked over and rinsed
- 1 tablespoon salt
- 1 large leek, trimmed (leaving some green), split, and washed
- 1 large onion, peeled and stuck with 2 whole cloves
- 1 large carrot, peeled and cut in half
- 2 large tomatoes, peeled, halved, seeded, and chopped (3 cups)
- 3 garlic cloves, crushed
- 1 tablespoon tomato paste
- 1 bouquet garni — 2 bay leaves, 2 teaspoons dried thyme, and 4–5 fresh parsley sprigs tied up in a piece of cheesecloth
- 1 1-pound piece pancetta
- 4 cups homemade chicken stock (page 612) or low-salt canned chicken broth
- 6 cups cold water
- 1½ pounds garlic sausage or kielbasa (1 or 2)

MEATS

- 1 duck (about 5 pounds)
- 1 boneless pork shoulder roast (about 3 pounds)

- 2 teaspoons salt
- 2 teaspoons freshly ground black pepper

- 4 slices stale country bread, processed to fine crumbs in a food processor (1½ cups)

FOR THE BEANS: Put the beans in an 8- to 10-quart heavy enameled casserole. Add the salt, leek, onion, carrot, tomatoes, garlic, tomato paste, bouquet garni, pancetta, stock, and cold water and bring slowly to a boil, skimming off the froth. Reduce the heat, cover, and simmer for about 1½ hours.

Prick the sausage with a fork, add to the beans, and cook for about 15 minutes longer.

WHILE THE BEANS ARE COOKING, COOK THE MEATS: Preheat the oven to 375 degrees.

Season the duck and pork with the salt and pepper. Place them side by side in a roasting pan and roast for 1½ hours.

When the beans are cooked (they should be tender but not mushy), turn off the heat. Lift the sausage, pancetta, onion, carrot, leek, and bouquet garni from the casserole onto a baking sheet. Discard the onion, carrot, leek, and the bouquet garni.

When the duck and pork are cooked, pour ¼ cup of the fat from the roasting pan into a measuring cup and set aside. Discard any remaining fat and deglaze the pan by adding ½ cup of the cooking liquid from the beans to the pan and bringing it to a boil, stirring to melt all the solidified cooking juices. Add the liquid to the beans.

Remove the casing from the sausage and cut the sausage into ¾-inch-thick slices. Slice the pancetta into strips ½ inch wide by 3 inches long. Slice the pork roast lengthwise in half and then into 1-inch-thick slices. Cut the duck lengthwise in half with a sharp heavy knife or poultry shears, then cut each half into 5 pieces, bones and all — cut each leg in half and cut the wing and breast pieces into thirds.

(At this point, the cassoulet can be served in individual soup plates with some of the beans and a piece of each kind of meat, poultry, and sausage; this is the way I prefer it. However, for a classic cassoulet, the meat and beans are layered in a large casserole or in individual casserole dishes and baked.)

Preheat the oven to 350 degrees.

Transfer the beans to another container, then layer the various ingredients in the casserole, starting with about one third of the beans, followed by alternating layers of each of the meats and more beans, ending with beans. Moisten the bread crumbs with the reserved fat and spread them over the entire surface of the beans.

Bake for about 20 minutes, until a crust forms on top. Break the crust and push it into the beans with a large spoon, then continue cooking for another 30 minutes. (Pushing the first crust into the dish gives the beans a crunchy, nutty taste.) The top will brown again, leaving a crust intact for serving. At the end of the cooking time, the cassoulet can rest out of the oven for 20 to 30 minutes before serving.

Serve straight from the casserole, giving each person some of the various ingredients.

Seared Duck Livers with Oven-Dried Tomatoes and Peppers

Serves 6 as a first course

❧ **Oven heat evaporates the** moisture of tomatoes and yellow peppers, concentrating their flavor. They make a nice addition to duck liver and are tasty in many other dishes as well.

The tomatoes and the peppers can be prepared ahead and reheated for a few seconds in the oven at serving time so they are lukewarm rather than cold, but the liver must be seared at the last moment.

TOMATOES AND PEPPERS

6 plum tomatoes (about 3 ounces each)
1 large yellow bell pepper (about 12 ounces)
¾ teaspoon salt

SAUCE

1½ teaspoons ketchup
About 10 drops hot chile oil or a pinch of cayenne pepper
1 small garlic clove, finely chopped (¼ teaspoon)
1 tablespoon canola oil
1 teaspoon Worcestershire sauce
2 tablespoons warm water

6 duck livers (about 12 ounces)
1 tablespoon olive oil
¼ teaspoon salt

Preheat the oven to 250 degrees.

FOR THE TOMATOES AND PEPPERS: Cut the tomatoes lengthwise in half and squeeze or scoop out the seeds. Place the tomatoes skin side up on the work surface and flatten gently with the palm of your hand. Core the pepper and cut lengthwise into 8 pieces; remove the seeds. Arrange the tomatoes and pepper skin side up on a large baking sheet and sprinkle with the salt. Bake for 1½ to 2 hours, until the skin has shriveled but the vegetables are still soft and moist inside. Set aside.

Reduce the oven temperature to 160 degrees.

FOR THE SAUCE: Mix together all the ingredients in a small bowl.

Divide each liver in half and remove the sinews in the center. Sprinkle the livers with the olive oil and salt and rub the mixture all over them. Set aside for 5 to 10 minutes to marinate in the oil.

Heat a large heavy skillet until very hot. Add the livers, top side down, and cook for about 1 minute. Turn and cook for another 1 minute for medium-rare. Remove the livers to an ovenproof plate and set in the oven for a few minutes so they can continue cooking in their own residual heat and juices.

Arrange 2 liver halves on each serving plate. Arrange the tomatoes and peppers attractively around the livers. Sprinkle each liver with about 1 teaspoon of the sauce and serve.

Roast Stuffed Goose
Serves 8

⁂ **Roast stuffed goose** is the classic main course for Christmas in France. The stuffing for this one is made with the liver, ground pork, apples, and various seasonings. It's very rich and flavorful, almost like a pâté. Browning the bird first ensures that it is beautifully golden at the end of the cooking time. Serve with roast potatoes.

STUFFING

- 2 tablespoons unsalted butter
- 1½ pounds Pippin or Golden Delicious apples (3 large), peeled, cored, and cut into ½-inch dice
- 3 onions, coarsely chopped (about 2 cups)
- 2 garlic cloves, crushed and finely chopped (about 1 teaspoon)
- 1 pound ground pork
  The reserved goose liver (from below), any sinews removed and very finely chopped
- 1 teaspoon salt
- ½ teaspoon freshly ground black pepper
- ½ teaspoon dried thyme

- ¼ cup Armagnac or cognac
- 1 large egg

- 1 goose (10–12 pounds)
- 2 tablespoons peanut oil
  Salt
- 2 carrots, peeled and coarsely chopped (¾ cup)
- 1 celery stalk, coarsely chopped (½ cup)
- ½ teaspoon dried thyme
- 1 bay leaf
- 2 cups homemade chicken stock (page 612) or low-salt canned chicken broth
- 1 cup dry white wine (such as Chardonnay)

FOR THE STUFFING: Melt the butter in a large skillet. Add the apples and onions, cover, and cook slowly for 10 minutes, stirring occasionally to prevent scorching. Stir in the garlic. Let cool to room temperature.

Combine the apple-onion mixture with the pork, liver, salt, pepper, thyme, Armagnac or cognac, and egg.

FOR THE GOOSE: Preheat the oven to 400 degrees.

Set aside the goose neck, gizzard, and heart. Remove any excess fat from the cavity of the goose. Cut off the 2 wing tips and set aside. Fill the cavity with the stuffing.

Heat the oil in a large roasting pan over medium heat. Sprinkle the bird with the salt, place in the pan, and brown all over for about 20 minutes. Discard the fat in the pan.

Add the carrots, celery, thyme, bay leaf, neck, gizzard, heart, wing tips, stock, and wine to the pan and bring to a boil over medium-high heat. Transfer to the oven and roast for 1 hour.

Reduce the oven temperature to 350 degrees. Roast for another hour or so, basting every 30 minutes with the pan juices, until the goose is nicely browned and the juices have reduced to a rich sauce. The temperature in the middle of the stuffing should be 160 degrees. Transfer the goose to a serving platter, set in a warm spot, and allow to rest for at least 30 minutes. Set aside the neck, gizzard, and heart for another purpose.

Meanwhile, strain the cooking juices through a fine sieve into a bowl, pushing hard with the back of a wooden spoon to extract the liquid from the vegetable pulp. Skim off as much fat as you can from the sauce (approximately 4 cups juice will yield about 2½ cups sauce and 1 cup fat).

Carve the goose and serve with the stuffing and sauce.

Stuffed Quail with Grape Sauce
Serves 4 as a first course

❧ **This is a classic** dish prepared in a modern way. The quail are boned and a stock is quickly made from the bones. Stuffed with a vegetable mixture, the birds are briefly steamed, then roasted and finished under the broiler. A delicious sauce is created from their cooking juices, the stock, a little thickening, and white grapes. Buying semiboneless quail makes the recipe easier; in that case, use chicken bones for the stock.

1 leek (6 ounces), trimmed (leaving some green), split, washed, and cut into 1-inch pieces (2 cups)
2 carrots (4 ounces), peeled and cut into 1-inch pieces (¾ cup)
2 celery stalks (5 ounces), cut into 1-inch pieces (1 cup)
2 tablespoons unsalted butter
2 garlic cloves, crushed and finely chopped (1 teaspoon)
1 teaspoon salt

¼ teaspoon freshly ground black pepper
4 large quail (about 7 ounces each) or semiboneless quail (about 5 ounces each)
1 pound chicken bones if using semiboneless quail
2 teaspoons vegetable oil
4 cups water
1½ tablespoons dark soy sauce
1 teaspoon honey
1 cup seedless white grapes
½ teaspoon cornstarch, dissolved in 1 teaspoon water
1 tablespoon minced fresh parsley or chives

Coarsely chop the leek, carrots, and celery in a food processor. (You should have 3 cups.)

Melt 1 tablespoon of the butter in a large skillet. Add the vegetables, garlic, and ¼ cup water and cook, covered, over medium heat for 10 minutes, or until the vegetables are soft and the water has evaporated. Add the salt and pepper, mix well, and set aside to cool.

TO BONE THE QUAIL: Cut through the shoulder joints of each one and, using your fingers and thumbs, separate the meat from the central carcass. Pull the carcass out, without cutting the skin open. Cut off the ends of the drumsticks and remove the wing tips, leaving the first and second joint of the wings attached to the shoulder. Remove the thighbones. (The bones should weigh about 8 ounces.) The only bones remaining in the quail will be the ones in the drumsticks and attached wings.

Put the quail or chicken bones in a skillet in one layer with the remaining 1 tablespoon butter and the oil and brown over low heat, covered, turning them occasionally, for 20 minutes.

Add the water and 1 tablespoon of the soy sauce to the skillet and bring to a boil. Reduce the heat, cover, and boil gently for 30 minutes. Strain the stock through a fine strainer set over a saucepan and discard the bones.

Boil the stock to reduce it to 1 cup. Set aside in the pan.

Preheat the oven to 425 degrees.

Using a pastry bag without a tip, or a spoon, stuff the quail with the cooled vegetable mixture. Arrange the quail on a heatproof plate, place them in a steamer, and steam, covered, over boiling water for 5 minutes.

Meanwhile, mix the remaining ½ tablespoon soy sauce with the honey in a small bowl.

Transfer the quail to a small ovenproof skillet and brush them with the soy mixture. Roast them for 10 minutes, then baste them with the liquid that has accumulated in the skillet.

Heat the broiler and broil the quail 6 to 8 inches from the heat source for 5 minutes, until nicely browned.

Meanwhile, add the grapes to the reserved stock, bring the mixture to a boil, and boil for 1 minute. Add the dissolved cornstarch and stir until the sauce thickens.

When the quail are cooked, arrange them on a serving platter. Strain the accumulated juices in the skillet into the sauce, then pour the sauce over the quail. Sprinkle with the parsley or chives and serve.

QUAIL

Farmed quail are readily available in specialty markets throughout the country. If you are lucky enough to get wild ones, though, you'll find that they are more flavorful than farm-raised ones. Unlike woodcock or pheasant, quail does not age well and should be eaten fresh. In France we say that the bird is best eaten "at the point of the gun barrel."

Sautéed Quail with Wild Rice and Corn
Serves 6

❧ **These little semiboneless birds** are butterflied and sautéed skin side down to brown the outside, while their flesh remains moist, slightly pink, and tender. The accompanying wild rice, which is good with other poultry and game, as well as meat, is flavored with mushrooms, pine nuts, and chicken livers (replace them with the quail hearts and livers, if you have them). Briefly sautéed corn kernels provide a crunchy, buttery enhancement.

12 semiboneless quail (about 4 ounces each)
2 tablespoons olive oil
½ teaspoon dried thyme

STOCK

2 tablespoons unsalted butter
1 pound chicken bones
½ cup chopped carrots
½ cup chopped onion
1 cup tomato sauce
½ cup chopped celery
½ teaspoon cracked black pepper
6 cups water
   About 2 cups (2 ounces) dried mushrooms
1½ cups lukewarm water

SAUCE

1 tablespoon cider vinegar
1 teaspoon potato starch (see page 318), dissolved in 1 tablespoon water
½ teaspoon salt
⅛ teaspoon freshly ground black pepper

WILD RICE

8 cups cold water

1 cup wild rice

2 tablespoons unsalted butter

⅓ cup pine nuts

1½ cups chopped onions

½ cup raisins

½ cup diced celery

3–4 chicken livers, trimmed of any sinew and cut into ½-inch dice (¾ cup)

¾ teaspoon salt

½ teaspoon freshly ground black pepper

2 tablespoons unsalted butter
Salt and freshly ground black pepper

GARNISH

2 tablespoons unsalted butter

3 cups corn kernels (from about 4 ears)

¼ teaspoon salt

To butterfly the quail, cut them open down the back with a knife or poultry shears (see page 250). Remove the little fillets from the breasts. Rub the quail (including the fillets) with the olive oil and thyme and refrigerate, covered.

FOR THE STOCK: Heat the butter in a medium skillet. When it is hot, add the bones and cook over medium heat for 15 minutes, or until browned.

Add the carrots, onion, tomato sauce, celery, pepper, and the 6 cups water and bring to a boil,

then reduce the heat and simmer gently for 45 minutes.

Meanwhile, soak the mushrooms in the lukewarm water in a bowl for 20 minutes.

Lift the mushrooms from the liquid and cut off and reserve the stems. Coarsely chop the mushrooms and set aside. Slowly pour the soaking liquid into another bowl; discard the sandy part. Add the soaking liquid and mushroom stems to the stock for the last 20 minutes of cooking.

Strain the stock through a fine strainer into a saucepan. (You should have about 2 cups.)

FOR THE SAUCE: Boil the stock to reduce it to 1¼ cups. Add the vinegar and dissolved potato starch, stirring, and bring to a boil. Add the salt and pepper and set aside.

FOR THE WILD RICE: Bring 4 cups of the water to a boil. Put the rice in a saucepan and pour the boiling water over it. Cover and let soak for 45 minutes.

Drain the rice and return it to the saucepan. Add the remaining 4 cups cold water, bring to a boil, and boil gently for 30 minutes, or until the rice is tender; drain.

Meanwhile, preheat the oven to 160 degrees.

Heat 1 tablespoon of the butter in a large skillet until hot. Add the nuts and onions and cook over medium-high heat for 3 to 4 minutes, until the onions are lightly browned. Add the raisins, celery, and reserved chopped mushrooms and cook for 2 to 3 minutes longer. Set aside.

Melt the remaining tablespoon of butter in another skillet. When it is hot, add the liver and sauté over the highest-possible heat for 20 to 30 seconds. Remove from the heat.

Combine the mushroom mixture, rice, and liver in a baking dish and add the salt and pepper. Cover and keep warm in the oven.

FOR THE QUAIL: Heat 1 tablespoon of the butter in each of two large skillets. Sprinkle the quail lightly with salt and pepper. When the butter is hot, add the quail (not the fillets) skin side down and cook over high heat for about 2 to 2½ minutes to brown the skin. Remove from the heat, turn the quail over, add the fillets, cover, and set aside while you prepare the corn. (The heat generated in the covered pan will be just enough to finish cooking the quail.)

FOR THE GARNISH: Heat the butter in a saucepan. When it is hot, add the corn and salt and sauté for 3 to 4 seconds, then cover and cook over medium-high heat for about 2 minutes.

Arrange the wild rice on a platter or individual plates and place the quail skin side up on top.

Transfer the sauce to the skillet used for cooking the quail and bring to a boil, stirring to melt the solidified juices. Spoon over the quail, arrange the corn around the quail, and serve.

Grilled Quail on Quinoa with Sunflower Seeds
Serves 4

❧ **The marinade for these** quail — made with garlic, hot pepper, and sharp, salty fish sauce — gives the birds an exotic flavor. The juices are absorbed by a bed of quinoa flavored with dried currants and sunflower seeds. A grain that dates back to the Incas, quinoa contains more protein than any other grain and is a rich source of vital nutrients. It has a delicate, nutty flavor and becomes almost transparent as it cooks.

MARINADE

- 1 medium shallot
- 1 large garlic clove
- 1 tablespoon nuoc mam (Vietnamese fish sauce)
- ½ teaspoon sugar
- ¼ small jalapeño pepper
- 1 tablespoon water

- 4 semiboneless quail (about 5 ounces each), butterflied see page 250)

QUINOA

- 2 tablespoons peanut oil
- 1 small onion, chopped (½ cup)
- 2 tablespoons hulled sunflower seeds or pumpkin seeds
- 2 tablespoons dried currants
- 1 cup quinoa, rinsed
- 1¾ cups homemade chicken stock (page 612) or low-salt canned chicken broth
- ¾ teaspoon salt, or to taste
- ¼ teaspoon freshly ground black pepper

FOR THE MARINADE: Process the shallot, garlic, nuoc mam, sugar, jalapeño, and water in a mini-chop until liquefied. Arrange the quail side by side in a shallow dish and pour the marinade over them, turning them until they are coated. Cover and refrigerate for at least 1 hour.

FOR THE QUINOA: Heat the oil in a skillet. When it is hot, add the onion and seeds and sauté for 2 minutes. Add the currants and quinoa and mix well. Stir in the stock, salt, and pepper. Bring to a boil, then reduce the heat, cover, and boil gently for about 18 minutes, until the quinoa is fluffy and tender.

Meanwhile, heat a grill until very hot. Preheat the oven to 160 degrees.

Grill the quail for 3 minutes on the skin side, then turn and cook for 1 minute on the other side. Transfer to a heatproof dish and keep warm in the oven. (*The quail can be kept in the oven for up to 45 minutes.*)

Arrange the quinoa in the centers of four individual plates and place the quail on top. Pour any juices that have accumulated in the dish over the quail and serve.

Roast Boned Squab
with Peas in Tomato "Saucers"
Serves 6

✄ **Boning the squab makes** them easier to eat and more elegant, and in this dish, the bones are used to make a sauce. You can use unboned squab as well, substituting chicken bones for the stock. The squab are placed directly on an oven rack, with a pan underneath to catch the fat that drains out, and roasted briefly at a high temperature so they brown all around but the meat remains slightly pink. Brushing them with a mixture of honey and water sweetens the skin and gives it a beautiful dark brown caramel color. (This same technique is used for Peking duck.) The sauce, accented with red wine and flavored with mushrooms, makes a nice accompaniment. The buttered peas, seasoned with lime rind and served in tomato saucers, also go well with other birds, meat, or fish.

The squab can be boned a day or two in advance and the stock made ahead.

- 6 squab (about 1 pound each)
- 3 tomatoes (about 1¼ pounds)

STOCK

- 1 pound chicken bones if not boning the squab
- ½ cup coarsely chopped carrots
- ½ cup coarsely chopped onion
- 5 cups water
- 1 cup dry red wine

SAUCE

- 1 tablespoon unsalted butter
- ⅓ cup chopped onion
- ½ cup diced (¼-inch) white mushrooms
- 1 teaspoon potato starch (see page 318), dissolved in 1 tablespoon red wine
- ½ teaspoon salt
- ¼ teaspoon freshly ground black pepper

- 1 teaspoon honey, mixed with ¼ cup water
- ½ teaspoon salt

PEAS

- 2 tablespoons unsalted butter
- 1 10-ounce package frozen baby peas, thawed
- ¼ teaspoon salt
- ⅛ teaspoon freshly ground black pepper
- ¼ teaspoon sugar
- 1 teaspoon finely grated lime rind

GARNISHES

- 1 bunch watercress, tough stems removed, washed, and dried
- 1 teaspoon chopped fresh garlic chives or regular chives

Bone the squab if you like (see page 302); reserve the bones and gizzards. Pull out the fat from inside the squab and reserve it. Coarsely chop the squab or chicken bones.

FOR THE TOMATO SAUCERS: Drop the tomatoes briefly into a pot of boiling water. Drain and peel, reserving the skin for the stock. Place each tomato stem side down on a cutting board and cut a slice about 1½ inch thick from 2 opposite sides to create 2 "saucers." Using a spoon, scoop out the insides of the tomato saucers. Reserve the seeds and pulp, as well as the remaining tomato centers, for the stock.

FOR THE STOCK: Melt the fat from the squab in a large roasting pan. Add the squab or chicken bones and gizzards and cook over medium-high heat, turning occasionally, for about 15 minutes, until nicely browned all around.

Add the carrot and onion and cook for 5 minutes. Add the water, wine, and tomato seeds and trimmings, bring to a boil, and boil gently for 45 minutes.

Strain the stock into a saucepan, pressing on the solids to extract all the juices; discard the solids. Let the stock rest for about 5 minutes, then skim off as much fat as possible. (You should have about 2 cups stock.)

Boil the stock to reduce it to 1½ cups. Set aside.

FOR THE SAUCE: Heat the butter in a medium skillet. When it is hot, add the onion and sauté for about 1½ minutes. Add the mushrooms and cook for 1 minute. Add the mixture to the stock and stir in the dissolved potato starch, the salt, and pepper. Bring to a boil and set aside.

Bring a pot of water to a boil. Secure the skin of the neck of each squab with a toothpick so it wraps around the neck opening, and submerge each bird in the boiling water for 15 seconds. You will notice the skin will tighten and the boned squab, although smaller, will return to its original shape. Transfer to a tray and brush the squab on all sides with the honey-water-salt mixture.

SQUAB

Squab is a young domesticated pigeon three to five weeks old that has not yet flown and whose flesh is very tender. It occupies a place partway between domesticated poultry and real game such as pheasant and woodcock: it has dark meat, but with a light taste. Roast squab should be served slightly pink.

HOW TO BONE SQUAB AND OTHER SMALL BIRDS: This technique for boning squab can also be used for Cornish hens or smaller birds such as partridge or woodcock.

Lift the skin at the neck of each squab and run your knife along either side of the wishbone. Then use your thumb and index finger to pry out the wishbone.

Cut through the shoulder joint on each side of the wishbone. Insert your index finger and thumb through the opening made by the knife and loosen the meat all around the carcass. The most delicate part of the operation is separating the skin from the back of the bird, as it adheres very tightly there and tends to tear: carefully slide the tip of your index finger between the skin and the carcass to loosen the skin; go slowly to avoid tearing the skin.

After the meat has been separated from the back and shoulders, lift away the breast meat, using the knife to separate it from the top of the breastbone without tearing the skin. The fillets will still be attached to the carcass. When the meat is loosened from the breastbone, turn the flesh inside out (like taking off socks), pulling the meat down and separating it from the carcass; keep pulling down until all the breast meat is separated and most of the carcass — up to the joint of the hip on each side — is visible.

Holding the squab by a thighbone, cut right through the hip joint and pull to separate the leg from the carcass. Repeat on the other side.

With the squab still inside out, scrape the meat from each thighbone with a knife, then cut all around the knee joint and keep scraping to release the meat from the drumstick bone. Break the bone at the foot; leave the knuckle in to hold the skin in place and prevent it from shrinking.

Cut off the wing bones on either side.

Run your thumb along the carcass on each side of the breastbone and remove both fillets, pulling them off.

Turn the squab right side out. It is now completely boned, except for the knuckles.

Preheat the oven to 450 degrees, with the racks in the center and bottom third of the oven.

Sprinkle the squab with the ½ teaspoon salt and place them on the center oven rack; put a large roasting pan on the rack beneath to catch the fat. Roast for about 15 minutes, until nicely browned all around, for medium-rare. Remove the squab to a platter and keep warm.

Skim off as much of the fat as possible from the juices in the roasting pan and strain the juices into the sauce.

Place the tomato saucers on a cookie sheet and heat in the turned-off oven just long enough to warm them.

MEANWHILE, FOR THE PEAS: Heat the butter in a saucepan. When it is hot, add the peas, salt, pepper, and sugar and cook for about 2 minutes. Add the lime rind and toss to mix.

Reheat the sauce if necessary.

Arrange the roast squab on a large platter with the tomato saucers in between them. Fill the saucers with the peas, coat with some of the sauce, and arrange the watercress in the center. Sprinkle the squab with the chives and serve, passing the rest of the sauce at the table.

Roast Woodcock with Cabbage in Bread Cases
Serves 4

✂ **If you hunt or** have a friend who does, you will enjoy this recipe. Woodcock is thought by many gastronomes to be the finest of all the game birds. It is ordinarily cooked with its insides — considered a delicacy — left in the body. Here they are removed (except for the large gizzard, which is discarded) and chopped to make a stuffing, which is placed in bread cases, with the roasted birds on top. The woodcocks are cooked briefly, so their breast meat stays moist and pink.

Woodcock tastes better if it is aged before cooking — certain birds take to aging better than others, and the woodcock is one of them. Leaving it for 3 or 4 days in the refrigerator, ungutted, with the feathers on, will improve its flavor. Pommes Soufflés (page 123) are an ideal side dish.

4 woodcocks (6–8 ounces each), preferably aged (see the headnote)

CABBAGE
½ head savoy cabbage (about 10 ounces)
2 tablespoons unsalted butter
1 tablespoon canola oil
½ cup coarsely chopped prosciutto
½ cup coarsely chopped onion
¼ teaspoon caraway seeds
2–3 garlic cloves, chopped (1 teaspoon)
1 cup water

BREAD CASES
4 slices (about 1½ inches thick) firm white bread, from a 1- to 2-day-old loaf (not dry or soft)
4 teaspoons unsalted butter, softened

STUFFING
1 tablespoon unsalted butter
1½ tablespoons chopped shallots
3 mushrooms, cleaned and coarsely chopped (½ cup)
1 small garlic clove, chopped
⅛ teaspoon salt
⅛ teaspoon freshly ground black pepper
1 teaspoon cognac

1–2 tablespoons unsalted butter
Salt and freshly ground black pepper

SAUCE
1 tablespoon cognac
½ cup Basic Brown Sauce (page 613)
Salt and freshly ground black pepper

Pluck the woodcocks, being very careful not to damage the skin. (It is a tedious and delicate job, but they develop a better flavor if aged with the feathers on.) When the larger feathers have been removed, singe the woodcocks over a gas flame to burn off the very fine feathers. Remove the little pieces embedded in the skin with the point of a knife or tweezers.

Cut the heads off at the neck. Cut the necks off the bodies and discard. Pull out the insides. Remove the gizzards and discard them. You will use the rest of the insides, including the intestines, to make the stuffing. Coarsely chop and set aside.

FOR THE CABBAGE: Cut the cabbage into ½-inch-wide strips (you should have about 6 cups).

Heat the butter and oil in a large saucepan until hot. Add the prosciutto and onion and cook for 1 to 2 minutes. Add the caraway seeds, garlic, water, and cabbage, cover, and cook gently for 20 minutes, or until the water has almost entirely evaporated and the cabbage is just moist. If the cabbage starts browning before it's done, add a little water. Or, if there is still too much moisture when the lid is removed, cook for a few minutes, uncovered, to evaporate the excess. Set aside, covered to keep warm.

FOR THE BREAD CASES: Preheat the oven to 425 degrees.

Remove the crusts from the bread slices. Cut a square in each slice to create a ¾-inch-wide border. Then, ⅜ inch in from the edge, cut a square in each slice, cutting at least ½ inch into the bread, to create a border. Remove the bread in the center by cutting slices of it on the bias, then scraping out the inside to create a case with ¾-inch-thick edges and a bottom of the same thickness.

With the point of a knife or a spatula, butter the bread cases very lightly all over, using 1 teaspoon butter per case. Place on a cookie sheet and bake for 10 to 12 minutes, until nicely browned. Set aside. Turn the oven up to 450 degrees.

FOR THE STUFFING: Melt the butter in a medium skillet. When it is hot, add the shallots and sauté for 1 minute. Add the mushrooms and cook for another 1 to 2 minutes. Add the reserved entrails and cook for about 1 minute, until they change color and become firm. Add the garlic, salt, pepper, and cognac and set aside, covered to keep warm.

TO COOK THE WOODCOCKS: Melt the butter in a large ovenproof skillet. Sprinkle the woodcocks lightly with salt and pepper. When the butter has melted, add the woodcocks, on their sides, and cook for 1 minute over high heat. Turn and cook on the other side for another minute.

Scatter the necks and the heads, if you saved them, around the birds and roast in the oven for about 8 minutes. The woodcocks are cooked sufficiently if when a breast is punctured with a thin sharp knife, the juices run pink (indicating that the meat is pink at the breast). Remove from the oven.

Transfer the woodcocks to a platter. Mix the drippings from the woodcocks into the stuffing. Place the cabbage on a platter and arrange the bread cases in the center. Fill the cases with the stuffing.

FOR THE SAUCE: Add the cognac, brown sauce, and salt and pepper to taste to the skillet. Bring to a boil.

Arrange the woodcocks on top of the stuffing. Spoon a little sauce over each woodcock and serve.

Pheasant Salmis with Red Wine Sauce and Mushrooms

Serves 4

❧ A *salmis* is a stew made with game birds such as pheasant or partridge. Traditionally the whole bird is first roasted briefly, just until very rare, then the meat is removed from the bones and stewed in red wine with aromatics; the dish is often finished with cognac.

In my version, the bird is boned raw. As in the traditional recipe, the sauce is made with the bones and red wine. It can be prepared up to a day ahead, but the meat must be cooked at the last moment.

1	pheasant (about 3 pounds), preferably wild
2	teaspoons olive oil
½	cup coarsely chopped onion
½	cup coarsely chopped carrots
½	cup coarsely chopped celery
½	teaspoon herbes de Provence
1¼	cups fruity dry red wine (such as Syrah or Grenache)
3½	cups water
	Salt
1	tablespoon light soy sauce
12	pearl onions
3	tablespoons unsalted butter
½	teaspoon sugar
16	button mushrooms (about 6 ounces), cleaned
1	teaspoon potato starch (see page 318), dissolved in 1 tablespoon of the red wine
	Freshly ground black pepper

Cut the pheasant into 4 pieces: 2 breasts and 2 legs. Separate the thighs from the drumsticks and remove the skin from the thighs. Remove the breast meat from the carcass and remove the skin. Cover and refrigerate the breasts and thighs.

Coarsely chop the pheasant bones, skin, and drumsticks. Combine with the oil, onion, carrots, celery, and herbes de Provence in a saucepan and cook over medium-high heat, turning frequently, until the bones and vegetables are nicely browned, about 20 minutes. Drain in a colander to eliminate as much of the rendered fat as possible.

Return the bones and vegetables to the saucepan, add 1 cup of the wine, the water, ½ teaspoon salt, and the soy sauce and bring to a boil. Cover, reduce the heat to medium, and cook for 1 hour.

Meanwhile, combine the pearl onions, 1 tablespoon of the butter, the sugar, a pinch of salt, and ½ cup water in a small skillet, bring to a boil, cover, and cook for 5 minutes. Remove the lid and continue cooking over medium heat to evaporate any remaining water, then cook for another 4 to 5 minutes, shaking the skillet occasionally, until the onions are caramelized on all sides. Transfer the onions to an ovenproof bowl and set aside.

Add the mushrooms to the skillet, season with a pinch of salt, and sauté for 5 to 6 minutes, until they are nicely browned. Transfer to an ovenproof bowl and set aside.

Strain the stock through a fine strainer into a saucepan. Bring to a boil and cook over high heat until reduced to 1 cup. Mix in the dissolved potato starch and add salt and pepper to taste. Add 1 tablespoon of butter to the sauce, letting it melt and cover the top of the sauce to prevent a skin from forming. Set aside. (*The sauce can be made up to a day ahead and refrigerated.*)

Preheat the oven to 160 degrees.

Melt the remaining tablespoon of butter in a large skillet, preferably nonstick. Add the pheasant thighs, sprinkle them with salt, and cook over medium heat for about 3 minutes. Add the breasts, sprinkle them with salt, and cook for about 3 minutes on each side, until nicely browned but still pink inside. Continue to cook the thighs, turning them a few times, until they are nicely browned on both sides but still pink inside. Transfer the meat to an ovenproof serving platter, reserving the drippings in the skillet, and place in the oven while you finish the sauce.

Reheat the onions and the mushrooms in the oven.

Add the remaining wine to the skillet and stir to melt the solidified drippings. Add this mixture to the sauce and bring to a boil.

With a sharp, heavy knife, cut each breast and thigh in half. Arrange half a breast and half a thigh on each of four warm dinner plates. Add 3 glazed onions and 4 mushrooms to each plate, coat the meat and vegetables with the sauce, and serve.

Rabbit with Prunes
Serves 6 to 8

✶ **The combination of prunes** and rabbit is common in Belgium and the north of France. A sweet-and-sour sauce offsets the richness of the meat. The dish is even better when made a day ahead.

Serve with boiled potatoes.

    1   young rabbit (about 3 pounds), cleaned
         and skinned, preferably with the liver
         and kidneys
    ½   cup diced (½-inch) pancetta
   20   pearl onions (no larger than an extra-
         large olive), peeled
    2   tablespoons all-purpose flour
    1   cup dry white wine
    1   cup port
    1   cup homemade chicken stock (page 612)
         or low-salt canned chicken broth
    2   teaspoons salt
    1   teaspoon freshly ground black pepper

    2   cups pitted large prunes
    ¼   cup sugar
    3   tablespoons red wine vinegar

Cut the rabbit into 12 pieces: each hind leg split in half; the 2 front legs; 3 pieces from the back; and 3 pieces from the front, ribs, and neck. Chop the liver and kidneys, if you have them, into a paste.

Sauté the pancetta in a large dry pot until crispy and brown.

Pour all the rendered fat into a large skillet (set the pot aside), add the onions in a single layer, and brown on all sides. Add to the pancetta in the pot.

Brown the rabbit on all sides in the remaining fat and add to the pot.

Mix the flour with ½ cup of the white wine and add to the pot, then add the remaining ½ cup wine, the port, stock, salt, pepper, and, if you have it, the chopped liver mixture and bring to a boil. Reduce the heat and simmer for 1 hour and 10 minutes. Add the prunes and simmer for 10 more minutes.

Meanwhile, combine the sugar and vinegar in a saucepan, bring to a boil, stirring to dissolve the sugar, and cook, without stirring, until the mixture turns into a caramel, about 4 minutes.

Pour the caramel into the rabbit stew, mix thoroughly, and simmer for 10 more minutes. Serve.

Braised Rabbit with Morels and Pearl Onions

Serves 4

This stew is made with the rabbit's front and back legs and rib cage. The saddle (the whole back) is roasted, cooking in less time than the stew and staying moist and flavorful. It can be served with the stew or on its own. I use dried morels in the stew (the equivalent of 1 pound of fresh). The dried have more taste than the fresh, and the water obtained from reconstituting them is added to the sauce, giving it a more intense flavor.

- 1 cup (about 1½ ounces) dried morels
- 2 cups hot water
- 1 rabbit (about 3 pounds), cleaned and skinned
- 1 teaspoon herbes de Provence
- ¾ teaspoon salt
- ¼ teaspoon freshly ground black pepper
- 1 tablespoon unsalted butter
- 5 teaspoons olive oil
- 16 pearl onions (about 12 ounces)
- 2 tablespoons chopped shallots
- 1 tablespoon all-purpose flour
- ⅓ cup fruity dry white wine (such as Riesling or Albariño)
- 2 teaspoons chopped garlic (about 3 cloves)
- 1 tablespoon Dijon mustard
- 1 slice firm white bread (¾ ounce)
- 2 teaspoons diced (½-inch) peeled fresh horseradish or 1 tablespoon bottled horseradish

Rinse the morels for a few seconds under running water, then put them in a bowl and pour the hot water over them. Place a small saucepan on top of the morels to push them down into the water and let soak for 30 minutes.

Meanwhile, cut the back legs from the body of the rabbit and halve each of the legs at the joint. Remove the front legs and then the front part of the body (containing the rib cage). Cut this portion in half. You now have 8 pieces plus the saddle, or back.

Mix together the herbes de Provence, ½ teaspoon of the salt, and the pepper in a small bowl. Sprinkle the saddle and the rabbit pieces with the mixture.

Heat the butter and 1 tablespoon of the oil in a Dutch oven or other large heavy pot until hot. Add the rabbit saddle and pearl onions and sauté over medium-high heat, turning occasionally, for 10 minutes, or until the saddle and onions are browned on all sides. Remove the saddle and set it aside. Remove the onions to a bowl and set aside.

Add the rabbit pieces to the drippings in the pot in one layer and brown them on all sides for about 10 minutes.

Meanwhile, lift the morels from the soaking water, pressing on them lightly to release the excess liquid into the bowl. Cut each morel lengthwise in half and rinse off any dirt you see in the hollow centers. Set aside. Slowly pour the soaking liquid into a clean bowl, leaving behind any sandy residue. (You should have 1½ to 1¾ cups.)

When the rabbit pieces have browned for 10 minutes, add the shallots, sprinkle with the flour, and mix gently. Cook for about 1 minute, then add the wine, mushroom liquid, garlic, and the remaining ¼ teaspoon salt and mix well. Bring to a boil, reduce the heat to low, cover, and cook gently for 45 minutes.

MEANWHILE, FOR THE SADDLE: Preheat the oven to 425 degrees.

Place the saddle on a baking sheet lined with aluminum foil and brush the top and sides of it with the mustard. Process the bread and horseradish in a food processor until finely ground. Transfer to a bowl, add the remaining 2 teaspoons olive oil, and mix just enough to combine and moisten the bread. (Do not overmix; the mixture should be light and fluffy.) Pat the mixture lightly over the top and sides of the saddle, so it adheres to the mustard coating.

Roast the saddle for 20 minutes. Remove from the oven and let it rest for at least 10 minutes before serving.

Add the morels and pearl onions to the stew and cook, covered, over low heat for 15 minutes.

To serve, divide the stew among four individual plates. Cut the saddle into 4 pieces. Arrange 1 piece alongside the stew on each plate and serve, or serve the saddle on its own.

Grilled Rabbit
Serves 4

✺ **You'll need a young,** tender rabbit between 2 and 3 months old for grilling, or the meat may be dry. If you prefer, you can broil the rabbit instead, taking care that it is not too close to the heat source, for about 15 minutes on each side.

1	rabbit (about 2½ pounds), cleaned and skinned
1	teaspoon olive oil
½	teaspoon salt
½	teaspoon freshly ground black pepper
⅛	teaspoon cayenne pepper
½	teaspoon chili powder
1	teaspoon herbes de Provence

Heat a grill until hot; make certain that the rack is very clean. Preheat the oven to 160 degrees.

Place the rabbit breast side up on a cutting board. Spread its back legs and cut down the center of the rib cage, splitting it open through the breast. Turn the rabbit breast side down on the board and press on it firmly until it is flattened to a thickness of about 1½ inches, so it will cook uniformly. Rub the rabbit on all sides with the olive oil.

Combine the salt, black pepper, cayenne, chili powder, and herbes de Provence in a small bowl and sprinkle this seasoning mixture on both sides of the rabbit.

Place the rabbit breast side up on the hot grill. If using a gas grill, immediately reduce the heat to medium-low; if using a charcoal grill, move the coals to the sides of the grill so the temperature is lowered. Cover with the lid and cook the rabbit for 15 minutes. Turn it over and cook it for 10 minutes, or until nicely browned on both sides. Transfer the rabbit to an ovenproof platter and let rest in the warm oven for at least 10 minutes. (*The rabbit can be kept warm in the oven for up to 1 hour.*)

At serving time, cut the rabbit into pieces: cut each of the back and front legs into 2 pieces and the body into 4 pieces. Arrange on individual serving plates and serve with the juices that accumulated around the rabbit on the platter.

Saddle of Venison with Red Wine Sauce
Serves 8 to 10

✺ **A saddle, or double back,** also called a short loin, is the choicest part of the deer. Served with a chestnut puree or Celery Root and Potato Puree (page 423), this is a superb dish during hunting season or the holidays. Carving it in the dining room makes it special, but if you do not feel confident enough to do so, carve it in the kitchen and serve on very hot plates.

The recipe may be made with a piece of the leg instead of the saddle.

2 cups hearty dry red wine (such as
Syrah, Grenache, or Merlot)

1 cup red wine vinegar

1½ cups diced leeks

¾ cup diced carrots

¾ cup diced celery

1½ cups diced onions

4 garlic cloves, crushed but not peeled

2 bay leaves

1 teaspoon freshly ground black pepper

1 tablespoon minced fresh thyme or
1 teaspoon dried thyme

1 teaspoon salt

1 bone-in saddle of venison (4–5 pounds;
see the headnote)

SAUCE

2 tablespoons unsalted butter

2 tablespoons all-purpose flour

2 cups Basic Brown Sauce (page 613)

2 tablespoons currant jelly

½ cup heavy cream
Salt and freshly ground black pepper

½ teaspoon salt

½ teaspoon freshly ground black pepper

2 tablespoons unsalted butter, softened

FOR THE MARINADE: Put all the ingredients in a pot and bring to a boil. Boil for 1 minute. Put the saddle in a large baking dish and pour the marinade over it. Let the meat marinate in the refrigerator for at least 4 hours, or up to 8 hours, turning it every hour or so.

Remove the saddle from the marinade and set aside; reserve the marinade.

FOR THE SAUCE: Melt the butter in a heavy saucepan. Sprinkle with the flour and cook, stirring with a wooden spoon, for 1 minute. Add the

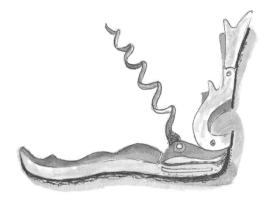

marinade, including the vegetables, and bring to a boil, stirring once in a while. Reduce the heat and cook slowly for 35 minutes, or until 1 cup of the liquid is left.

Add the brown sauce and simmer slowly for another 25 minutes. Strain the sauce through a fine sieve, pressing on the vegetables with a spoon to extract all the juices. Cover and set aside.

Preheat the oven to 425 degrees.

TO COOK THE MEAT: Sprinkle the saddle all over with the salt and pepper. Rub with the butter and place in a roasting pan. Roast for about 35 minutes for medium-rare, basting the saddle every 10 minutes with the pan juices. Transfer the saddle to an ovenproof platter and keep warm in a 160-degree oven to rest for at least 15 minutes. (If you have only one oven, shut it off when the saddle is cooked and open the door until the oven temperature drops to 160 to 180 degrees, then return the venison to the oven.)

Meanwhile, pour the sauce into the roasting pan, add the currant jelly, and bring to a boil, stirring to melt all the solidified juices. Boil for 2 minutes, then strain through a sieve into a saucepan.

Add the cream and salt and pepper to taste (the sauce should be peppery, sour, and sweet at the same time) and bring to a boil.

To serve, pour a few tablespoons of the sauce on top of the saddle and bring to the dining room to carve in front of your guests if you like. Serve the rest of the sauce on the side.

Venison Steaks in Sweet-Sour Sauce

Serves 4

✂ **Venison is traditionally served** with a sweet-sour sauce. This one contains currant jelly or raspberry jam for sweetness and vinegar — cooked with shallots and added at the end — for a contrasting sour taste. Thoroughly trimmed of fat, venison steaks are very lean, quite flavorful, and rich, so 4 to 5 ounces of meat per person is adequate. Serve with Skillet Sweet Potatoes (page 124).

1 venison loin or large tenderloin (about 1½ pounds), trimmed of fat (about 1 pound trimmed) and cut into 4 steaks
1 teaspoon olive oil
1 teaspoon chopped fresh thyme
1 tablespoon ketchup
1 tablespoon currant jelly or seedless raspberry jam
2 teaspoons dark soy sauce
¼ cup cold water
1 tablespoon peanut oil
2 tablespoons unsalted butter
¼ teaspoon salt
¼ teaspoon freshly ground black pepper
1 tablespoon chopped shallot
2 tablespoons red wine vinegar
2 tablespoons hearty red wine

Using a meat pounder, pound the steaks gently until each is about ¾ inch thick. Rub the steaks with the olive oil and sprinkle with the thyme. Arrange the steaks in a single layer on a plate, cover with plastic wrap, and refrigerate for at least 1 hour before cooking. (*The venison can marinate for up to 8 hours.*)

Mix the ketchup, jelly or jam, soy sauce, and water together in a small bowl. Set aside.

When you are ready to cook the steaks, heat the oven to 160 degrees.

Heat the peanut oil and 1 tablespoon of the butter in a large heavy skillet until hot. Sprinkle the steaks with the salt and pepper, place them in the skillet, and sauté over medium-high heat for 2 to 2½ minutes on each side for medium-rare. Transfer the steaks to an ovenproof plate (leaving the drippings in the pan) and keep warm in the oven while you make the sauce.

Add the shallot to the drippings and sauté for about 20 seconds. Add the vinegar and wine and cook until most of the liquid has evaporated, about 1½ minutes. Add the jelly or jam mixture and mix well, then stir in the remaining 1 tablespoon butter. Boil for 10 seconds, then strain through a fine strainer.

Place a steak on each of four plates, coat the steaks with the sauce, and serve.

meat

Meat

Beef

Beef Carpaccio with Pepper Tartlets
Serves 6 to 8 as a first course

✖ **Beef carpaccio is named** after the famous Venetian painter of the fifteenth century Vittore Carpaccio, whose favorite colors were red and white. Traditionally, thin slices of raw beef are arranged on a plate and spread with a mustard-flavored mayonnaise, but I flavor the carpaccio with garlic, oil, onion, and herbs instead.

In restaurants, carpaccio is often prepared with fillet of beef or shell steak (which, in my opinion, is more flavorful than the fillet), and the meat is partially frozen before it is sliced extremely thin, like prosciutto, on a slicing machine. Often, however, the meat releases water as it defrosts on the plate and the carpaccio tends to end up watery and bland. Here the trimmed meat is sliced into small pieces and pounded very thin before being arranged on the plates.

The accompanying little tartlets filled with diced roasted red, green, and yellow peppers are ideal for a buffet to accompany pâté and other cold meats. Highly flavored with garlic and olive oil, the filling will keep for several weeks in the refrigerator and can be used to enhance sandwiches and salads as well. For a simpler recipe, the carpaccio can be served with the peppers only, although the tartlets bring the dish to another level of elegance.

The carpaccio can be prepared several hours ahead and arranged on individual plates; cover with plastic wrap touching the meat to prevent discoloration. It can also be seasoned ahead, but the vinegar should be added at the last moment, or the acid will coagulate the protein, turning the meat whitish.

DOUGH

- 1½ cups all-purpose flour
- 6 tablespoons (¾ stick) unsalted butter, softened
- 2 tablespoons vegetable shortening
- ¼ cup milk
- ⅛ teaspoon salt
- ¼ teaspoon sugar

PEPPERS

- 2 large red bell peppers (1 pound)
- 2 large green bell peppers (1 pound)
- 2 large yellow bell peppers (1 pound)
- 5–6 garlic cloves, chopped (1½ tablespoons)
- ¾ teaspoon salt
- ¾ teaspoon freshly ground black pepper
- 6 tablespoons olive oil

CARPACCIO

- 1¼ pounds thoroughly trimmed shell steak
- 2 garlic cloves, mashed to a paste
- ½ cup oil (half peanut, half olive)
- 2 teaspoons salt
- 1 teaspoon freshly ground black pepper
- ½ cup chopped onion, rinsed under cold water and dried
- 6–8 strips lemon rind, removed with a vegetable peeler, stacked, and sliced into julienne strips
- 2–3 tablespoons drained capers
- 3 tablespoons minced fresh chives
- 1 tablespoon red wine vinegar

FOR THE DOUGH: Combine all the ingredients in a food processor and pulse for 10 to 15 seconds until the dough comes together.

You will need about 30 small tartlet tins, either 1½-inch round ones or small boat-shaped ones. On a floured surface, roll the dough out into a rough rectangle approximately ⅛ inch thick. Arrange the tins side by side in rows to form a rectangle slightly smaller than the piece of dough. Roll the dough up onto the rolling pin and unroll on top of the tins. Use a lump of dough dipped in flour to press the rolled dough into the tins.

Roll the rolling pin over the top of the tins in different directions to cut the dough. Press the dough farther into each tin with your fingers. Put on a cookie sheet and place in the refrigerator or freezer for 1 hour to allow the dough to rest.

Preheat the oven to 425 degrees.

Bake the tartlet shells for 10 to 12 minutes, until nicely browned and well cooked. Cool on a rack.

FOR THE PEPPERS: Preheat the broiler. Arrange the peppers on a broiler tray, place under the broiler 1 to 1½ inches from the heat source, and broil for 12 to 15 minutes, turning the peppers every 3 to 4 minutes, until they blister all around. (The green pepper will tend to char more than the yellow, but the skin on all the peppers should blister.) Put the peppers into a resealable plastic bag and leave for 10 to 15 minutes so the skin softens and steams, making it easy to remove.

Remove the peppers from the bag. They will be limp and soft. Peel off the skin, which should come off very easily. Remove the core, seeds, and stems and cut the flesh into strips about ⅜ inch wide. Then cut each of the strips into ½-inch pieces. (You should have about 1¼ cups of each pepper.) Put the peppers into three separate bowls, one color in each. Top each with 1½ teaspoons of the garlic, ¼ teaspoon each salt and pepper, and 2 tablespoons of the olive oil and mix well. Cover with plastic wrap and refrigerate until ready to use.

FOR THE CARPACCIO: The shell steak should be completely trimmed of sinew and fat. Cut the meat into about 24 slices, each weighing about ¾ ounce. Some pieces will be long and narrow and others will be square. Using a meat pounder, pound each piece between sheets of plastic wrap until very thin and 3 to 5 inches wide.

Arrange 3 or 4 pieces of meat per person on individual plates. As each plate is ready, cover with plastic wrap; then place the next finished plate on top. Refrigerate until serving time.

Mix the garlic with the oil.

Up to 1 hour before serving, sprinkle the carpaccio with the salt, pepper, onion, lemon rind, capers, garlic oil, and chives. Return to the refrigerator.

When ready to serve, fill the tartlet shells with the diced peppers, one color in each.

Sprinkle the wine vinegar on top of the carpaccio and serve immediately, with the pepper tartlets.

PREPARING RAW ONIONS

When onions are chopped, they release a compound of sulfuric acid that darkens them and stings your eyes. To eliminate this problem, rinse the onions under cold water in a sieve, then wrap in a towel and press to remove the extra water. Prepared in this way, the onions will be white and fluffy and will remain so for several days.

Carpaccio with White Truffles
Serves 8 as a first course

✎ **The real white truffle** from Piedmont, *Tuber magnatum,* is in season from around Thanksgiving until January. The most expensive of all truffles, it is a rare and special treat. It makes a wonderful combination with the carpaccio. Grating it extends the truffle, so one truffle is enough to flavor all the meat.

- 1 New York strip steak (about 1 pound), completely trimmed of sinews and fat
- 1 white truffle (1–1½ ounces)
- ¾ teaspoon salt
- ½ teaspoon freshly ground black pepper
  About 3 tablespoons freshly grated Parmesan cheese
  About 3 tablespoons extra-virgin olive oil

CROUTONS

- 1 tablespoon olive oil
- 12 ½-inch-thick slices baguette

- 1 tablespoon extra-virgin olive oil
- 1 tablespoon minced fresh chives

Preheat the oven to 400 degrees.

Cut the steak into 16 thin slices (about 1 ounce each). Wet a meat pounder and cutting board slightly (to keep the meat from tearing) and pound the slices of meat until they are about ⅛ inch thick and 3 to 4 inches across. Alternatively, pound the slices between pieces of plastic wrap. Transfer to a large plate.

Using a cheese grater, grate the truffle.

Sprinkle the pieces of meat with the salt and pepper. Sprinkle each piece with a bit of grated truffle and about ½ teaspoon each of the Parmesan cheese and olive oil. Fold over the long sides of each piece of meat to create straight sides, then roll up into tubes. Refrigerate until serving time, covered with plastic wrap.

FOR THE CROUTONS: Oil a cookie sheet with the olive oil. Lay the slices of baguette on top, pressing them into the oil, then turn them over. Bake for about 8 minutes, until nicely browned. Let cool.

Arrange the carpaccio tubes on a platter, sprinkle with the extra-virgin olive oil and chives, and surround with the croutons. Serve.

Five-Pepper Steak
Serves 6

✎ **Traditionally, coarsely cracked black** peppercorns (*mignonnettes*), rather than ground pepper, are used to coat pepper steak. I use five different types of peppercorns here: black, white (the same berries as black, with the shells removed), green (also the same, but unripe, with a lot of flavor and less hotness), Jamaican (called allspice), and Szechuan (actually the aromatic bud of a flower).

In this recipe, the sauce is finished with shallots, cognac, and brown sauce. As a variation, the sauce can be deglazed with red wine instead of cognac and finished with the brown sauce, or deglazed with cognac and finished with ¾ cup heavy cream instead of brown sauce.

- ¼ cup mixed black, white, green, and Szechuan peppercorns and allspice berries
- 6 New York strip steaks (also called top loin or shell steaks; about 10 ounces each and ¾ to 1 inch thick, trimmed of surface fat; about 8 ounces trimmed)
- 4 tablespoons (½ stick) unsalted butter
- ½ teaspoon salt, or to taste
- ¼ cup chopped shallots
- ¼ cup cognac
- 1 cup Basic Brown Sauce (page 613)

Preheat the oven to 150 degrees.

Roll the bottom edge of a heavy saucepan over the peppercorns and allspice to crush them. Gather them together and roll the bottom of the pan over them again to crush further.

Spread the cracked pepper mixture on the work surface and arrange the steaks on top. Turn the steaks, pressing them gently into the peppers to coat them on all sides.

Melt 1 tablespoon of the butter in each of two skillets. When it is hot, add 3 steaks to each skillet, sprinkle them lightly with the salt, and sauté over high heat for approximately 2½ minutes. Turn and sauté for 1½ minutes on the other side. Remove the steaks to a platter and keep warm in the oven while you finish the sauce.

Add half the chopped shallots to each skillet and sauté for about 30 seconds. Add the cognac and flame (to burn off the alcohol), then stir in the brown sauce. Combine the mixtures in one of the skillets, bring to a boil, and season lightly with salt if needed. Strain through a fine strainer. Finally, whisk the remaining 2 tablespoons butter into the sauce, mixing until well incorporated.

Arrange the steaks on very warm plates, spoon 2 to 3 tablespoons of the sauce over each one, and serve immediately.

ON FLAMBÉING

When you add alcohol to a dish, the alcohol will rise in the form of vapor when the temperature reaches 180 to 190 degrees. At this point, if you ignite the vapor with a match, it will flame. This is the technique of *flambé*. If you do not ignite the vapor, it will still rise and disappear, burning off the alcohol. Flambéing is only important when you want the solid pieces of food, such as crepes or lobster, to be caramelized by the flame.

Wine-Merchant Steak
Serves 4

In this bistro dish, the steak is complemented by a *sauce marchand de vin,* or "wine merchant sauce," made of shallots, mushrooms, garlic, and a good fruity wine, thickened with Dijon mustard, and garnished with chopped chives.

4	New York strip (also called top loin or shell steaks) or sirloin tip steaks (about 9 ounces each and ¾ inch thick; 7 ounces trimmed)
¾	teaspoon salt
½	teaspoon freshly ground black pepper
2	tablespoons olive oil
2	large shallots, finely chopped (¼ cup)
4	large mushrooms, cleaned and cut into julienne strips (1½ cups)
2	large garlic cloves, crushed and finely chopped (1½ teaspoons)
1	cup fruity dry red wine (such as Beaujolais)
1	cup homemade chicken stock (page 612) or low-salt canned chicken broth
1	tablespoon Worcestershire sauce
1	tablespoon Dijon mustard
½	teaspoon potato starch (see page 318), dissolved in 2 teaspoons water
1	tablespoon unsalted butter
1	tablespoon finely chopped fresh chives

Trim the steaks, removing all surface fat and sinews. Sprinkle them with ½ teaspoon of the salt and the pepper.

Heat the oil in a large skillet. When it is hot, add the steaks and sauté for about 2 minutes on each side for medium-rare. Remove the steaks to a platter and set aside in a warm place.

Add the shallots to the drippings in the skillet and sauté for about 10 seconds. Add the mushrooms and garlic and sauté for 1 minute. Stir in the wine and boil until only about 2 tablespoons remain. Add the stock and boil to reduce to about ¾ cup.

Add the Worcestershire sauce, mustard, and the remaining ¼ teaspoon salt and mix well. Stir in the dissolved potato starch and bring to a boil. Swirl in the butter and mix well.

Arrange the steaks on individual plates and spoon some sauce on top of and around each one. Garnish with the chives and serve.

POTATO STARCH

I often use a "pure starch" — generally potato starch or arrowroot — to finish a sauce and give it a bit of viscosity. If nothing else is available, you can substitute cornstarch, but it tends to make a sauce gooey and gelatinous. I prefer potato starch, which is made from steamed potatoes that are dried and ground. Potato starch is gluten-free and sometimes appears in baked goods, particularly Jewish-Passover specialties. Inexpensive and available in 1-pound packages, it can be found in the Kosher section of many supermarkets and in Asian specialty food shops (it is also used in Japanese cooking). Arrowroot, on the other hand, comes in very small containers and is very expensive.

All of these starches are used in the same way: they are diluted with a little cold liquid — water, wine, or stock — and then stirred into a hot sauce. The starch thickens the sauce on contact and then it is usually brought to a boil.

Grilled or Pan-Seared Marinated Flank Steak
Serves 4

❧ **A quick grilling or** pan-searing gives this flank steak a crusty brown exterior and finishing it in a low-temperature oven ensures that the interior will be a rosy pink. The seasonings in the marinade — a mixture of honey, soy sauce, garlic, coriander, and cayenne pepper — can be varied to suit individual tastes. The steak can be marinated for up to a day before it is cooked.

MARINADE

- 1 tablespoon honey
- 2 tablespoons dark soy sauce
- 1 tablespoon finely chopped garlic
- ½ teaspoon ground coriander
- ¼ teaspoon cayenne pepper

- 1 flank steak (about 1¼ pounds and ¾ inch thick), trimmed of all surface fat

FOR THE MARINADE: Mix all the ingredients together in a gratin dish large enough to hold the steak. Place the steak in the dish, turning it to coat all sides with the marinade. Cover with plastic wrap and marinate in the refrigerator for at least 1 hour, or for up to 24 hours.

At cooking time, preheat the oven to 160 degrees. Heat a grill until very hot, or heat a heavy aluminum or cast-iron skillet for at least 5 minutes over high heat, until very hot.

Remove the steak to a plate. Pour the marinade into a saucepan and bring to a boil. Set aside. Place the steak on the hot grill or in the skillet, and cook over high heat for 1½ minutes, then turn and cook for 1½ minutes on the second side to sear the meat and give it a well-browned exterior. Return the meat to the marinade and place it, uncovered, in the warm oven to relax and continue cooking in its own heat for at least 10 minutes. (*The steak can be held in the oven for up to 40 minutes.*)

To serve, cut the steak on the diagonal, against the grain, into very thin (⅛-inch-thick) slices and serve, with the marinade, on very hot plates.

Blade Steak with Herbs
Serves 4

❧ **These small beef steaks** (also called flatiron steaks or chicken steaks) are very lean, with a large sinewy strip running through the center that becomes deliciously gelatinous and chewy when cooked. Cooked quickly — either sautéed, as here, or grilled — they are juicy and flavorful. Braised whole, this same cut of meat makes a delicious pot roast, and it is also great sliced into pieces and cooked in a stew.

4	boneless beef shoulder blade steaks (about 6 ounces each and 1 inch thick)
1½	teaspoons olive oil
¼	teaspoon salt
¼	teaspoon freshly ground black pepper
2	tablespoons chopped shallots
⅓	cup water
1	tablespoon unsalted butter
¼	cup finely chopped fresh herbs, such as tarragon, chives, and parsley

Heat a large cast-iron or heavy aluminum skillet until very hot. Brush the steaks on both sides with the oil, sprinkle with the salt and pepper, and arrange them side by side in the hot skillet. Cook over medium-high heat for 2 to 3 minutes on each side for medium-rare. Remove the steaks from the skillet and place them on a platter. (*The steaks can be kept for 10 to 15 minutes in a 140-degree oven before serving; if doing this, however, wait until serving time to*

add the butter and herbs to the drippings in the skillet.)

Add the shallots to the drippings in the skillet and sauté them for 20 seconds. Add the water, mixing it in well, and cook, stirring, until all the solidified juices in the skillet have melted. Add the butter and herbs and cook for a few seconds, just until the butter melts.

Spoon the butter-herb mixture over the steaks and serve immediately.

Grilled Steak with Lemon-Thyme Butter
Serves 4

❧ **Use good-quality strip steaks** — prime if you can afford it. Grilled so that the grids of the grill rack form a crosshatch design on one side, the steaks are served lattice side up, with a little butter scented with lemon juice and fresh thyme.

LEMON-THYME BUTTER

2	tablespoons unsalted butter
1	tablespoon fresh lemon juice
1	tablespoon dry white wine
¼	teaspoon salt
¼	teaspoon freshly ground black pepper
2	teaspoons fresh thyme leaves

4	well-trimmed New York strip steaks (also called top loin or shell steaks; about 7 ounces each and ¾ inch thick)
1	teaspoon olive oil
½	teaspoon salt
½	teaspoon freshly ground black pepper

FOR THE LEMON-THYME BUTTER: Place all the ingredients in a blender or spice grinder and process to a smooth paste. Set aside.

Heat a grill until very hot.

Rub the steaks with the olive oil and sprinkle

them on both sides with the salt and pepper. Place the steaks on the hot grill and cook for about 1 minute, then turn them over and cook them for 1½ minutes on the other side.

Turn the steaks so they are at a 90-degree angle from their original position to create a crosshatch marking from the grill rack. Cook the steaks for 1 minute longer, for a total of about 3½ minutes for medium-rare (increase or reduce the cooking time if your steaks are thinner or thicker than ¾ inch or if you like your meat less rare.) Let the steaks rest for a couple of minutes.

Arrange the steaks crosshatched side up on plates and top with the lemon-thyme butter.

Beef Tournedos in Mushroom, Mustard, and Red Wine Sauce
Serves 4

Well-trimmed small beef tournedos, cut from the fillet (tenderloin), are sautéed and served on croutons. A light but flavorful sauce, made by incorporating reconstituted shiitake mushrooms, red wine, and mustard into the meat drippings and the mushroom-soaking liquid, lends a modern touch to this old favorite.

1   ounce dried shiitake mushrooms (6–8)
1   cup hot water
1   teaspoon canola oil
4   slices firm white bread (about 4 ounces)
2   tablespoons unsalted butter
4   well-trimmed beef fillet steaks (about 6 ounces each and 1¼ inches thick)
½   teaspoon salt
½   teaspoon freshly ground black pepper
½   cup fruity dry red wine (such as Pinot Noir)
2   tablespoons ketchup
1   tablespoon dry mustard

Preheat the oven to 400 degrees.

Put the mushrooms in a small bowl, cover them with the hot water, and set them aside to soak for at least 1 hour.

Meanwhile, spread the oil lightly over a cookie sheet. Using a round cookie cutter about 3 inches in diameter, cut a round crouton from each of the 4 slices of bread. Press the croutons lightly into the oil on the cookie sheet, then turn them over so they are oiled on both sides. Bake the croutons for about 7 minutes, until they are nicely browned on both sides and crisp. Set the croutons aside.

After the mushrooms have soaked for at least an hour, lift them from the soaking liquid, reserving the liquid. Remove and discard the mushroom stems (or keep them for stock) and cut the mushroom caps into ½-inch pieces. (You should have about ¾ cup.) Slowly pour the soaking liquid into another bowl and discard the sandy residue in the bottom of the original bowl. Set aside.

At cooking time, preheat the oven to 140 degrees.

Heat the butter in a large skillet until hot. Sprinkle the tournedos with ¼ teaspoon each of the salt and pepper and place them in the skillet. Arrange the mushroom pieces around them and sauté the tournedos over medium-high heat for about 2½ minutes on each side for medium-rare. Transfer to a warm platter and let them rest in the oven while you make the sauce.

Add the reserved mushroom liquid to the drippings and mushrooms in the skillet, along with the wine, ketchup, mustard, and the remaining ¼ teaspoon each salt and pepper. Bring to a boil and boil gently for 3 to 4 minutes, until the sauce reduces and thickens slightly. (You should have about 1 cup.)

Place a crouton in the center of each of four warmed dinner plates and place a tournedo on top of each crouton. Coat the meat with sauce, spoon the rest of the sauce around the meat, and serve.

Spicy Rib Roast

Serves 6 to 8

❧ **Although my wife is** normally not an aficionado of roast beef, she loves this recipe. The spicy rub — garlic, ginger, sugar, soy sauce, cayenne, dry mustard, and paprika — is the reason why.

The roast should be from the smaller, less fatty end of the rib section. Cleaned of the layer of fat on top, the meat is roasted in a hot oven, then allowed to rest for at least 20 minutes, and up to 1 hour, in a warm oven before serving so it is totally pink throughout.

RUB

- 3 large garlic cloves
- 1 piece ginger (about the same size as the combined garlic cloves), peeled
- 2 teaspoons sugar
- 2 tablespoons dark soy sauce
- ½ teaspoon cayenne pepper
- 1 teaspoon dry mustard
- 1 teaspoon paprika

- 1 3-rib beef rib roast (about 7 pounds), all visible fat trimmed from top (about 6 pounds trimmed)
- ⅓ cup water
- ⅓ cup sturdy red wine
- ½ cup Basic Brown Sauce (page 613)
- 1 small bunch watercress, trimmed, washed, and dried (optional)

Preheat the oven to 400 degrees.

FOR THE RUB: Blend all the ingredients in a blender until smooth. Rub the mixture over the top and sides of the roast.

Place the roast meat side up in a small roasting pan and roast for 30 minutes. Turn the meat bone side up and roast for another 30 minutes. Remove the roast from the oven and leave the oven door open to cool the oven to about 140 degrees.

Transfer the roast to a platter. Skim off and discard all the fat that accumulated in the roasting pan. Add the water, wine, and brown sauce to the drippings in the pan and stir to melt the solidified juices.

Return the roast bone side up to the roasting pan with the juices and let rest in the warm oven for at least 20 minutes or up to 1 hour before carving.

To serve, carve the roast into thin slices. Arrange on the watercress, if using, on individual plates or a platter, and serve with the juices.

Herb-Rubbed Strip Steak

Serves 4

❧ **Initially seared on top** of the stove, the beef is finished in the oven, producing an exterior crust that intensifies the taste of the meat. A little chicken stock added to the pan at the end melts the natural glaze and creates a simple jus.

- 1 New York strip steak (also called top loin or shell steak; about 1½ pounds and 1¾ inches thick; 1¼ pounds trimmed)
- 1 teaspoon dried thyme
- 1 teaspoon dried oregano
- 1 teaspoon dried rosemary
- ¼ teaspoon freshly ground black pepper
- ¼ teaspoon cayenne pepper
- ¼ teaspoon salt
- 1 tablespoon olive oil
- ½ cup homemade chicken stock (page 612) or low-salt canned chicken broth

Preheat the oven to 450 degrees.

Remove all the surface fat from the steak. (The trimmed steak will weigh about 1¼ pounds.)

Crush the dried herbs between your thumb and finger and mix them together with the black and cayenne peppers. Pat the mixture on both sides of the meat.

When ready to cook, sprinkle the steak with the salt. Heat the oil in a heavy ovenproof skillet. When it is hot, add the meat and cook over medium-high heat for about 3 minutes on each side.

Transfer the steak to the oven and roast for 8 to 10 minutes for medium-rare. Add the chicken stock to the pan and let rest at room temperature for 10 minutes before carving.

Slice the meat and serve with the natural juices.

Braised Stuffed Flank Steak
Serves 4 to 6

✎ **Flank steak is ideal** for stuffing and braising. You can ask the butcher to cut a pocket in the steak for stuffing or do it yourself. If any is left over, serve it cold, sliced, with lettuce and tomatoes.

    1 flank steak (about 2 pounds untrimmed,
          1¾ pounds trimmed of surface fat)

STUFFING

    2 tablespoons olive oil
    1 tablespoon unsalted butter
    3 cups cubes (½-inch) firm white bread
    1 pound ground beef
    1 large egg
    1 onion, chopped (about ¾ cup)
    ½ cup chopped celery
    1 tablespoon chopped fresh parsley
    2 garlic cloves, finely chopped
    1½ teaspoons salt
    ½ teaspoon freshly ground black pepper
    ¼ teaspoon crushed dried thyme or savory

BRAISING

       Salt and freshly ground black pepper
    2 tablespoons unsalted butter
    1 medium carrot, peeled and finely
          chopped (about ¾ cup)
    1 onion, chopped (about ¾ cup)
    1 tomato, coarsely chopped (about 1 cup)
    2 bay leaves
    1 teaspoon fresh thyme leaves
    2 cups homemade chicken stock (page
          612) or low-salt canned chicken broth
    1 cup fruity dry red wine
    1½ tablespoons arrowroot (see page 318),
          dissolved in ¼ cup red wine

If you bought the steak untrimmed, pull off the "skin" and trim off the fat, which will be heavy on one end. If you didn't have the butcher do it, cut a pocket in the steak for stuffing: Place the steak on a cutting board with your palm on the meat. Hold your knife so that the blade is flat, parallel to the board. Cut into the meat lengthwise to make the pocket, taking care not to cut all the way through to the other side or come out at either end.

FOR THE STUFFING: Heat the oil and butter in a large skillet. Add the bread cubes and sauté over medium heat until brown on all sides. Remove from the heat.

Combine the remaining stuffing ingredients in a large bowl and add the bread cubes, mixing them in lightly to avoid making the stuffing mushy.

Stuff the flank steak, then bring the lower lip of the steak up against the stuffing and the top lip down over it, so that you form a nice loaf. Tie with a few pieces of kitchen twine to keep it securely closed.

TO BRAISE THE MEAT: Salt and pepper the loaf all around. Heat the butter in a large deep flameproof casserole until hot. Brown the stuffed flank steak on all sides. Add the carrot, onion, tomato, bay leaves, and thyme and cook over medium heat, uncovered, for 5 minutes.

Add the stock and wine and bring to a boil. Cover and braise over very low heat (or in a 325-degree oven) for 2 hours. Transfer the meat to a serving platter, remove the twine, and keep warm.

Stir the dissolved arrowroot into the sauce in the casserole. Bring to a boil and cook until the sauce has thickened slightly. Stir in salt and pepper to taste. Strain the sauce or leave the vegetables in, according to your taste.

Slice the meat and serve with the sauce.

Beef Daube Arlésienne
Serves 4

✄ **This beef stew, or** daube, comes from Arles, the small town in Provence made famous by Vincent van Gogh. The daube is flavored with pearl onions, baby carrots, white wine, and herbes de Provence. I like to use shoulder blade steaks (sometimes called flatiron steaks or chicken steaks), because they are very lean except for a strip of sinew in the center that becomes gelatinous as the meat cooks and keeps it moist and flavorful.

A mixture of hazelnuts, toasted bread, garlic, and parsley is finely chopped and added to the dish just before it is served. Other last-minute additions are capers, olives, and tomato, ingredients that are typical of Provence.

8	small red potatoes (about 8 ounces), peeled
1½	cups water
8	pearl onions, peeled
12–16	baby carrots (4 ounces), peeled
1	tablespoon olive oil
4	boneless beef shoulder blade steaks (about 8 ounces each trimmed), cut in half

1	cup chopped onion
1	cup dry white wine
1¼	teaspoons salt
1	teaspoon herbes de Provence

ARLÉSIENNE MIXTURE

12–15	hazelnuts (about 2 tablespoons)
1	slice country bread (about 1 ounce), toasted
2	garlic cloves
½	cup loosely packed fresh parsley leaves
2	tablespoons drained capers
¼	cup Niçoise olives
1	tomato (6 ounces), halved, seeded, and cut into 1-inch dice (¾ cup)

Combine the potatoes and water in a saucepan and bring to a boil over high heat. Cover the pan, reduce the heat to low, and boil the potatoes gently for 8 minutes. Add the pearl onions and carrots and bring back to a boil over high heat, then cover, reduce the heat to low, and boil gently for another 8 minutes, or until all the vegetables are tender but still firm when pierced with the point of a sharp knife. Drain the vegetable-cooking liquid into a bowl and reserve. (You should have about 1½ cups.) Set the vegetables aside in the pan.

Heat the oil in a large heavy pot. When it is hot, add the steaks and cook over medium-high heat for 8 to 10 minutes, turning them once midway through, until browned on both sides. Add the chopped onion and cook for 2 minutes, stirring occasionally. Mix in the reserved vegetable-cooking liquid, the white wine, salt, and herbes de Provence and bring to a boil. Cover, reduce the heat to very low, and boil very gently for 1¼ hours. (*The recipe can be prepared to this point a day ahead and refrigerated; bring to a gentle boil before finishing the dish.*)

MEANWHILE, FOR THE ARLÉSIENNE MIXTURE: Preheat the oven to 400 degrees.

Spread the hazelnuts on a small cookie sheet and toast them in the oven for 10 minutes. Combine the hazelnuts, bread, garlic, and parsley in a food processor and process until finely chopped.

TO FINISH THE DISH: At serving time, add the bread and hazelnut mixture, along with the cooked vegetables, to the beef mixture in the pot. Mix well, bring the daube to a boil, and cook gently for 5 minutes to heat it through completely.

Add the capers, olives, and tomato, cook for 1 minute, and serve.

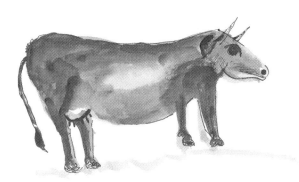

Braised Beef in Red Wine
Serves 6

✶ **An intensely flavored red** wine sauce is the hallmark of this dish. My recipe contains nearly a whole bottle, along with a little soy sauce, vinegar, garlic, onions, and carrots. Bringing the marinade to a boil before pouring it over the beef makes the meat absorb the flavor much faster.

It's important to use beef shoulder or shank. These lean yet gelatinous cuts retain their moistness after cooking — a quality essential to the dish.

I cook the beef in a pressure cooker to save time, but you can make it in a Dutch oven. Brown the meat as directed, add the marinade to the pot, and bring to a boil. Cook, tightly covered, over low heat or in a 275-degree oven, for 3 hours, then fin-ish as described in the recipe. Cooking the meat in a closed pot — either a pressure cooker or a Dutch oven — helps keep it moist.

MARINADE

- 2 onions (about 8 ounces), peeled and quartered
- 2 carrots (about 6 ounces), peeled and cut into 1-inch pieces
- 1 head garlic, separated into cloves (12–15), but not peeled
- 4 bay leaves
- 1 teaspoon dried thyme
- 1 teaspoon dried oregano
- 3 tablespoons red wine vinegar
- ¼ cup balsamic vinegar
- 2 tablespoons dark soy sauce
- 1 tablespoon black peppercorns, crushed
- 3 cups dry red wine, preferably Cabernet Sauvignon or deep, fruity Rhône Valley–style wine

- 1 boneless beef shoulder blade (top blade) roast (about 3 pounds) or boned whole beef shank
- 1 tablespoon olive oil
- ½ teaspoon salt
- 1 tablespoon potato starch (see page 318), dissolved in ¼ cup water

VEGETABLES

About 18 small baby carrots (8–10 ounces), peeled

About 18 small pearl onions (about 8 ounces), peeled

About 18 small potatoes (about 1 pound), peeled

About 18 medium mushrooms (about 12 ounces), cleaned

- 1 tablespoon chopped fresh parsley

FOR THE MARINADE: Combine all the ingredients in a stainless steel saucepan and bring to a boil over high heat.

Meanwhile, place the meat in a heatproof container. When the marinade has come to a boil, pour it over the meat and let cool. When it is cool, cover the container with plastic wrap and refrigerate for at least 6 hours, or as long as 3 days.

When you are ready to cook, remove the beef, reserving the marinade, and pat it dry with paper towels. Heat the oil in a pressure cooker over medium-high heat until hot. Add the beef and sprinkle it with the salt. Cook, uncovered, over medium heat for about 15 minutes, turning occasionally, until the meat has browned on all sides.

Add the marinade and bring to a boil. Cover and bring the cooker to the appropriate pressure, following the manufacturer's guidelines, then reduce the heat to very low and cook for 1 hour.

Depressurize the cooker according to the manufacturer's instructions and remove the meat. Transfer the cooking juices to a saucepan and let them rest for 10 minutes to allow the fat to rise to the top. Return the meat to the cooker.

Skim all the visible fat from the surface of the cooking juices and bring the liquid to a boil. Boil gently for 5 minutes, then stir in the dissolved potato starch to thicken the juices. Strain the sauce through a fine strainer and pour all but 1 cup of it over the meat. Set aside.

FOR THE VEGETABLES: Combine the carrots, onions, and 1 cup water in a saucepan, bring to a boil, cover, and boil gently for 5 minutes. (Most of the liquid should have evaporated.) Set aside.

Meanwhile, put the potatoes in another saucepan and cover with cold water. Bring to a boil and boil gently for about 20 minutes, uncovered, until they are almost cooked but still firm. Drain, add to the carrots and onions, and set aside.

Pour the reserved cup of wine sauce into a medium saucepan. Add the mushrooms, cover, bring to a boil, and boil gently for 5 minutes. If not ready to serve, set aside.

At serving time, reheat the meat in the sauce over low heat until it is heated through. Meanwhile, add the carrots, onions, and potatoes to the mushrooms and heat until hot.

Cut the meat into 1-inch-thick slices and arrange on a large platter. Surround the meat with the vegetables and pour the sauce over and around them. Sprinkle with the parsley and serve.

Pot-au-Feu
Serves 6, with leftovers

✻ **Pot-au-feu, which translates as** "pot on the fire," is the ultimate one-dish meal, with soup, beef, and vegetables. I also add turkey legs, which are readily available and inexpensive. They lend a wonderful complexity to the stock while remaining moist.

If you object to the strong taste of green cabbage or white turnips, you can leave them out or replace them with milder vegetables, like sweet potatoes, parsnips, or napa cabbage.

A very large stockpot (preferably stainless steel or enamel) is essential for pot-au-feu. Mine holds 15 to 20 quarts.

The cornichons traditionally served alongside can be replaced by regular sour pickles. Toasted bread or croutons are often served with the broth, along with grated Swiss or Parmesan cheese, and sometimes the marrow from the bones is spread on toast or croutons and enjoyed with the broth.

1 large beef shank (about 4 pounds)

1½ pounds beef neck bones, as meaty as possible

2 skinned turkey legs, and part of the carcass if available (about 3½ pounds)

9 quarts cool water

3 medium onions (about 14 ounces), 1 left whole, 2 cut into halves

12 whole cloves

4 teaspoons salt

1 teaspoon freshly ground black pepper

4 bay leaves

10–12 carrots (about 1 pound), peeled

8–10 celery stalks (about 1 pound), outside ribs peeled with a vegetable peeler

8–10 red potatoes of about equal size (about 1¼ pounds), peeled

6 small white turnips (about 1½ pounds), peeled

3–5 leeks (about 1½ pounds), trimmed (leaving some green), split, and washed

1 head green cabbage (about 1½ pounds), cut into 8 wedges

FOR SERVING (AS DESIRED)

Croutons or crusty bread

Coarse salt, such as fleur de sel

Cornichons (tiny French gherkins)

Hot mustard

Grated fresh or bottled horseradish

Put the beef shank, neck bones, and turkey in a large stockpot and add the water. (The longer time required to bring cool water to a boil helps draw more impurities from the meat; these will collect on the surface of the water in the form of foam.) Bring to a boil over high heat (this may take as long as 45 minutes).

When the cooking liquid has come to a full boil, use a fine skimmer to remove the foam and discard it. Continue boiling gently for about 20 minutes, removing any additional foam.

Stud the whole onion with the cloves. Add the salt, pepper, bay leaves, and clove-studded onion to the pot (the seasonings are not added to the stock at the outset, because they would get skimmed off along with the foam). Partially cover the pot, leaving about a 1-inch opening for the steam to escape (this keeps the liquid from clouding), and cook gently for about 1½ hours.

Remove the turkey and set aside; continue cooking the beef. When the turkey is cool enough to handle, pick the meat from the bones. Cover the turkey meat to prevent it from drying out and refrigerate it. Return the bones to the pot to continue cooking for 1 hour longer, or until the beef is completely cooked (it should be tender when pierced with a fork).

Remove the pot from the heat. Remove the beef with a large skimmer and place it on a tray. With the skimmer, lift out and discard any particles and pieces of bone from the liquid, to produce as clear a stock as possible. Using a ladle, skim as much fat as you can from the surface of the liquid.

When the beef is cool enough to handle, remove the meat from the bones. Slice it and the reserved turkey into serving pieces. Place in a large gratin dish, add 2 to 3 cups of the stock, cover, and set aside. (*You can prepare the dish up to this point several hours ahead. Refrigerate the remaining stock and the meat separately; bring the meat to room temperature before finishing.*)

About 45 minutes before serving, add all the vegetables, including the remaining 2 onions, to the stock. Bring to a boil (it will take 15 to 20 minutes) and boil gently for about 20 minutes. With the skimmer, transfer all the vegetables to a tray or large platter and cover to keep warm.

Meanwhile, reheat the beef and turkey in the 2 to 3 cups stock on top of the stove or in a microwave.

Serve the stock in large bowls set next to the dinner plates, and bring the meat and vegetables to the table on trays or platters. Serve croutons or crusty bread with the stock, and pass around coarse salt, pickles, mustard, and/or horseradish to eat with the meat and vegetables.

VEGETABLE AND VERMICELLI SOUP Serves 6

Since this recipe is made with leftovers from the pot-au-feu, your proportions may be slightly different. Increase or decrease the amount of pasta you add based on the amount of stock and vegetables. I like vermicelli, a very thin pasta, but you can substitute anything from pastina to alphabet noodles if you prefer.

> 3 quarts stock from Pot-au-Feu (page 325)
> About 4 cups cut-up (1-inch pieces) leftover vegetables from Pot-au-Feu
> 4 ounces (about 2 cups) broken vermicelli
> Bread or toast, for serving
> Freshly grated Parmesan cheese

Combine the stock and vegetables in a pot and bring to a boil. Add the vermicelli, stir, and cook for 8 to 10 minutes, until the pasta is tender. Serve with bread or toast and grated cheese.

BEEF SALAD WITH GARLIC-MUSTARD DRESSING
Serves 6

Beef salad is a classic in France, usually prepared the day after you've made pot-au-feu. Sausage, poultry, or other meats used in the pot-au-feu can be included in this salad, which makes a great main course for lunch. Make sure to warm the meat a bit for a minute or so in the microwave; it greatly improves the taste.

DRESSING

> 2 garlic cloves, crushed and finely chopped (about 1 teaspoon)
> 3 tablespoons hot mustard
> 2 tablespoons red wine vinegar
> ¼ cup peanut oil
> ¼ teaspoon salt
> ½ teaspoon freshly ground black pepper
>
> 3½ cups cut-up (1-inch pieces) leftover meat from Pot-au-Feu (page 325)
> ¾ cup coarsely chopped onion
> 3 scallions, trimmed (leaving some green) and minced (about ⅓ cup)
> ¼ cup coarsely chopped fresh parsley
>
> 12 Boston lettuce leaves, for garnish

Combine all the dressing ingredients in a large serving bowl. Add the meat, onion, scallions, and parsley and toss to mix. Serve on the lettuce leaves.

Corned-Beef Pot-au-Feu
Serves 4

❧ **I use a piece** of corned beef in this pot-au-feu instead of the classic boiled beef. This dish is my interpretation of Irish corned beef and cabbage, conventionally served on St. Patrick's Day. The array of winter vegetables can be varied based on what is available at your market, but make sure you include at least five different vegetables for diversity of taste and color.

    1 piece corned beef (about 2 pounds)
   10 cups cold water
    1 pound red potatoes (about 8), peeled
    1 small savoy cabbage (1 pound), cut into
          6 wedges
    2 medium onions (8 ounces)
    4 white turnips (12 ounces), peeled
    2 medium carrots (6 ounces), peeled
    2 small leeks (8 ounces), trimmed (leaving
          some green), split, and washed
    2 kohlrabi (12 ounces), peeled and halved
    2 bay leaves
   ½ teaspoon dried thyme
      Salt

FOR SERVING

      Coarse salt, such as fleur de sel
      Dijon mustard
      Grated fresh or bottled horseradish

Rinse the corned beef thoroughly under cool water. Place it in a large pot and add the cold water. Bring the water to a gentle boil, then skim off and discard any impurities (in the form of foam) that have collected on the surface. Reduce the heat to low, cover, and cook the meat at a very light boil for 2¼ hours.

Add the vegetables, herbs, and salt (if needed, depending on the saltiness of the meat) to the pot, bring to a boil, and boil very gently for 30 minutes, or until the vegetables are tender.

Remove the meat from the pot and cut it into thin slices.

Place 3 or 4 slices corned beef in each soup plate and spoon in an assortment of the vegetables and some of the cooking liquid. Pass coarse salt, mustard, and horseradish at the table.

Beef Carbonnade Flamande
Serves 8

❧ *Carbonnade,* **beef braised with** onions and beer, is a Belgian specialty that makes a great winter meal. Get chuck (shoulder) beef, which will be moister than round. This dish is usually served with boiled potatoes.

    4 tablespoons (½ stick) unsalted butter
    3 pounds sliced boneless beef chuck (slices
          should be about ¼ inch thick and 3 to
          4 inches in diameter; you can ask the
          butcher to do this)
    1 tablespoon salt
    1 teaspoon freshly ground black pepper
   ½ cup all-purpose flour
    3 cups thickly sliced onions
   ⅓ teaspoon dried thyme
    2 bay leaves
      About three 12-ounce cans beer

Melt the butter in a large skillet. When it sizzles, add half the meat, sprinkle with half the salt and pepper, and brown lightly on both sides. Stir in half the flour and remove to a heavy Dutch oven or cast-iron cocotte. Repeat the process with the remaining meat, seasonings, and flour.

Brown the onions in the meat drippings for about 10 minutes.

Combine the onions and meat and mix well. Put the thyme and bay leaves on top and add the beer; the meat should be barely immersed. Bring to a boil, cover tightly, and simmer for 1½ hours. Serve.

Gratin Parmentier
Serves 6 to 8

❧ *Gratin Parmentier,* **a French** version of shepherd's pie, is two different dishes in one. Beef *mironton,* a stew, is typically made with leftover pot roast or boiled beef. It's topped with mashed potatoes combined with eggs and cheese, which become beautifully golden and look a bit like a soufflé. The potatoes keep the meat moist and the meat, in turn, gives the potatoes flavor. The top becomes browned and crusty in the oven.

BEEF

- 2 tablespoons olive oil
- 1 tablespoon unsalted butter
- 2½ cups very thinly sliced onions
- 2 teaspoons very finely chopped garlic
- 1 tablespoon all-purpose flour
- 2 cups homemade chicken stock (page 612) or low-salt canned chicken broth, or pot roast juices diluted with water to make 2 cups
- 1 teaspoon salt
- ½ teaspoon freshly ground black pepper
- 1¼ pounds leftover pot roast, boiled beef, or roast beef, cut into ⅛-inch-thick slices
- ⅓ cup chopped fresh parsley

POTATOES

- 2 pounds boiling potatoes, peeled and cut into large chunks

- 1 teaspoon salt
- 1⅓ cups half-and-half
  Freshly ground black pepper
- 3 large eggs
- ½ cup grated Gruyère or Emmenthaler cheese

FOR THE BEEF: Heat the oil and butter in a large pot until hot. Add the onions and sauté over high heat for 5 minutes, or until a bit transparent and lightly browned. Add the garlic and flour and mix well. Add the stock, salt, and pepper and bring to a boil, stirring occasionally.

Add the meat and bring to a boil again, then cover, lower the heat, and simmer very slowly for 20 minutes for boiled or braised meat; increase the cooking time if you use meat from a roast that was cooked medium or rare. Stir in the parsley.

The stew could be served alone at this point. For the gratin, put it in a buttered 3-quart flameproof gratin dish and preheat the oven to 400 degrees.

FOR THE POTATOES: Put the potatoes in a saucepan, cover with water, add ½ teaspoon of the salt, and bring to a boil. Boil gently for 30 minutes, or until the potatoes are tender when pierced with the point of a knife. Drain and push through a food mill or ricer into a bowl. (If you don't have a food mill or ricer, use a fork or potato masher; don't use a food processor.)

Add the half-and-half and mix well with a whisk until smooth. Add the remaining ½ teaspoon salt and pepper to taste, then add the eggs one after the other and mix well.

Pour the potato mixture on top of the meat (or put it into a buttered flameproof gratin dish if making it to be served on its own) and spread it gently with a spatula. Sprinkle the cheese on top and bake for 30 minutes.

Place under the broiler for 3 to 4 minutes to brown the top. Serve.

Salisbury Steaks with Vegetable Sauce
Serves 6

❧ In this recipe, a pound and a half of ground beef is extended with chopped vegetables, apples, and fresh bread crumbs. This is basically a meatloaf mixture that can be molded into patties, as here, or formed into a large loaf, which should be cooked in a 400-degree oven for 1 hour. Named for its inventor, James Salisbury, an American physician, it is served with a carrot and onion sauce.

The leftovers are very good cold. Cut the patties, or larger loaf, into thin slices and serve like pâté, or use in sandwiches with hot mustard to set off the mildly sweet taste of the diced apple.

STEAKS

3	tablespoons corn or canola oil
1½	cups chopped onions
1½	cups minced celery
2	apples, such as Rome Beauty or McIntosh (about 1 pound)
1½	pounds ground beef
2	large eggs
2–3	garlic cloves, crushed and finely chopped (about 1 teaspoon)
1	teaspoon salt
½	teaspoon freshly ground black pepper
3	slices firm white bread, processed to crumbs in a food processor (1½ cups)

SAUCE

1	cup peeled, coarsely chopped carrots
1	cup coarsely chopped onion
2	cups water
1	tablespoon dark soy sauce
½	teaspoon salt
¼	teaspoon freshly ground black pepper
2	tablespoons tomato paste
½	teaspoon Tabasco sauce

FOR THE STEAKS: Heat the oil in a large saucepan. When it is hot, add the onions and celery and cook over medium heat for 4 to 5 minutes, until slightly softened.

Meanwhile, core but do not peel the apples. Cut them into ½-inch pieces. (You should have about 2 cups.) Add to the onion and celery mixture and remove from the heat.

Preheat the oven to 400 degrees.

Put the meat in a large bowl, add the onion-celery-apple mixture, eggs, garlic, salt, and pepper, and mix well. Add the bread crumbs and mix well to incorporate. (Fresh bread crumbs are best for this recipe; if substituting dry crumbs, use only ¾ cup.)

Dampen your hands with water and form the mixture into 6 large patties (each weighing approximately 8 ounces). Arrange in a large roasting pan so there is a little space between the steaks and bake for 20 minutes.

MEANWHILE, FOR THE SAUCE: Put the carrots, onion, water, soy sauce, salt, pepper, tomato paste, and Tabasco in a saucepan and bring to a boil, then reduce the heat and boil gently for 5 minutes. Keep warm.

When the steaks have cooked for 20 minutes, remove them from the oven. They will probably stick to the bottom of the pan, so you will easily be able incline the pan and pour off most of the accumulated fat.

Spoon the sauce over and around the steaks and return them to the oven for 15 minutes. Serve.

Fiery Chili with Red Beans
Serves 8 to 10

❧ For this version of chili con carne, I prefer the meat coarsely chopped into ¼-inch pieces, rather than finely chopped or ground. The coarse meat gives the dish texture and chewiness. I also cook the beans separately from the meat and then combine them. By doing so, I have more control over the cooking and can make certain that the beans do not get mushy.

Chili con carne is an ideal dish to make ahead since it actually improves in flavor with reheating. It will keep refrigerated for 4 days to 1 week and also freezes well. Freeze the chili in small containers so that you can thaw it easily on short notice.

2 pounds dried red kidney beans, picked over and rinsed

1 tablespoon salt

2 pounds beef stew meat, cut into 1-inch pieces

8 ounces ham rind pieces or bacon, cut into ½-inch pieces

2 large onions, cut into 1-inch dice (3 cups)

8 garlic cloves, crushed and chopped (about 2 tablespoons)

2 tablespoons chopped jalapeño pepper (or more or less, to taste)

1 28-ounce can whole Italian tomatoes in juice

2 teaspoons coriander seeds

2 teaspoons ground cumin

2 teaspoons dry mustard

1 teaspoon hot pepper flakes

¼ cup chili powder

FOR SERVING

24 corn tortillas or taco shells

2 cups grated cheddar cheese (about 8 ounces)

2 cups chopped onions, rinsed in a sieve (to prevent discoloration and make the flavor milder) and dried

Tabasco sauce

Combine the beans with 3 quarts cold water and 1 teaspoon of the salt in a large pot and bring to a boil. Skim off the foam, cover, reduce the heat, and cook gently for about 1½ hours, until the beans are tender but still firm. Set the beans aside in their liquid.

Coarsely chop the beef by hand or in a food processor.

Cook the pieces of ham rind or bacon in a large saucepan over medium heat for about 10 minutes, until most of the fat has been rendered and the rind or bacon is brown. Add the onions and beef and cook, stirring, for about 5 minutes, until the meat breaks up and loses its red color. Stir in the garlic, jalapeño pepper, and tomatoes.

Using a mini-chop or coffee grinder, process the coriander seeds to a powder. Add to the saucepan, along with the cumin, mustard, hot pepper flakes, chili powder, and the remaining 2 teaspoons salt, and bring the mixture to a boil.

Add the beef mixture to the beans (and their liquid) and bring to a boil, then cover, reduce the heat to low, and simmer for 1 hour; the mixture will be soupy.

Serve in the tortillas or taco shells, with the cheddar cheese, chopped onions, and Tabasco sauce.

Cayettes with Spinach
Serves 6

❧ *Cayettes,* **patties of ground** beef with spinach or Swiss chard, are sold cooked in many markets in France. At home, *cayettes* can be prepared and cooked ahead. Although they can be made without chicken livers, the livers bind the mixture together well and impart a wonderful taste. Serve the *cayettes* hot or cold and pass hot mustard at the table. Excellent with a green salad dressed with a garlicky vinaigrette, they are also wonderful with pasta, beans, mashed or hash brown potatoes, or skillet-roasted potatoes.

The *cayettes* are very good cold — so good, in fact, that instead of eating two of them each for dinner, we usually elect to save one to enjoy cold the following day. To serve them cold, slice them (they will have a nice pink interior) and arrange on a bed of salad greens. Sprinkle with vinegar and olive oil, if you like, and garnish with sliced tomatoes. Pass some Dijon mustard and serve with a good French bread.

10   ounces spinach (or a mixture of spinach, Swiss chard, kale, and salad greens), tough stems removed, washed, and dried (about 10 cups)
2   tablespoons olive oil
1   onion (about 6 ounces), chopped (about 1 cup)
8   scallions, trimmed (leaving some green) and cut into ½-inch pieces (about ¾ cup)
3   large garlic cloves, crushed and chopped (about 1 tablespoon)
5   chicken livers (about 5 ounces total), trimmed of any sinew
1   pound ground beef
½   pound ground pork
1   teaspoon salt

½   teaspoon freshly ground black pepper
¼   teaspoon freshly grated nutmeg
1   tablespoon vegetable oil

Preheat the oven to 375 degrees.

Stack the spinach leaves one on top of another, a few at a time and cut them crosswise into 1-inch-wide strips.

Heat the olive oil in a large skillet. When it is hot, add the onion and scallions and cook for 1 to 1½ minutes, until softened but not browned. Add the garlic and stir well, then add the spinach and sauté, stirring, for about 2 minutes, until the spinach has wilted but is still green. Set aside to cool.

Put the chicken livers in a food processor and process for about 10 seconds, until pureed. Add the ground beef and pork and process for 5 to 10 seconds, just until mixed. Transfer to a bowl.

When the spinach mixture is cool, mix well with the ground meat. Add the salt, pepper, and nutmeg and mix well.

Grease a roasting pan with the vegetable oil. Wet your hands under cold water and form the meat mixture into 12 patties. Arrange the patties close together in the roasting pan and bake for 35 minutes.

Serve hot or cold.

Small Stuffed Cabbages
Serves 8

✀ **An ideal winter dish,** stuffed cabbage can be made ahead and is even better reheated. Although you can substitute regular cabbage, I prefer the leafier savoy cabbage. Braised in a sauce containing vegetables, herbs, and brown sauce, these little stuffed cabbages are moist and tender.

1 savoy cabbage (about 2 pounds)

STUFFING

5 slices bacon, cut into ¼-inch pieces
1 onion, chopped (¾ cup)
   Reserved chopped cabbage heart (from above)
¾ cup water
1½ pounds ground beef (not too lean)
2 large eggs
3–4 garlic cloves
1 teaspoon salt
½ teaspoon freshly ground black pepper

2 medium carrots, peeled and sliced (1½ cups)
1 large onion, sliced (1½–2 cups)
3 large tomatoes, diced (about 2½ cups)
½ teaspoon crushed thyme leaves (fresh is better)
2 bay leaves, broken into small pieces
2 cups Basic Brown Sauce (page 613)
   Salt and freshly ground black pepper if necessary

FOR THE CABBAGE LEAVES: Bring a large pot of water to a boil. Detach the outer leaves from the cabbage, trying not to break any. (You should have about 20 leaves.) Chop the cabbage heart finely and reserve. (You should have about 2 cups.)

Plunge the leaves into the boiling water, bring back to a boil, and cook for 5 minutes. Drain the leaves in a colander and run under cold water until cold; drain well. Lay the leaves flat on the work surface and remove about 2 inches of the stem — the toughest part — from each leaf.

Preheat the oven to 350 degrees.

FOR THE STUFFING: Sauté the bacon in a large skillet until it is browned and has rendered its fat. Add the onion and sauté for 1 minute. Add the chopped cabbage and the water and cook until all the liquid has evaporated and the mixture is sizzling again, about 8 minutes. Transfer to a bowl, add all the remaining stuffing ingredients, and mix thoroughly.

Spoon about 2 ounces (about ⅓ cup) of stuffing onto each leaf and fold the sides over to make a nice neat package. If a leaf is too small, use it to patch bigger leaves, or use several small leaves together to form 1 stuffed cabbage.

TO BRAISE THE CABBAGE: Scatter all the vegetables and herbs in a 10-by-12-by-2-inch-deep roasting pan. Arrange the stuffed leaves side by side, seam side down, on top so they touch one another. Cover tightly with aluminum foil, put in the oven, and cook for 2 hours.

Remove the foil and pour the brown sauce over the cabbages. Return to the oven and bake for 30 minutes, uncovered.

Arrange the cabbages on a serving platter. Taste the sauce, as it may need salt and pepper. Add if necessary, then pour the sauce over the cabbages and serve.

Beef Boulettes
with Financière Sauce
Serves 6

When I have leftovers from a roast or pieces of steak or stew — odds and ends that are not uniform in size or texture, some dry, some fatty — I often make *boulettes* — "small balls" — which are part of every French housewife's repertoire. They're simply meatballs made from cooked meat rather than fresh ground beef.

The classic version of financière sauce is rather esoteric, a tomato-and-Madeira-flavored brown sauce with elaborate garnishes. In French homes, however, the word *financière* is usually associated with a simple tomato sauce with mushrooms and green olives. My sauce, made with fresh tomatoes, is cooked quite fast. Cooking tomatoes for a long time tends to darken them and make them more acidic, robbing them of their sweet fresh taste. In winter, when tomatoes are less flavorful, add a tablespoon of tomato paste for taste and color, or substitute a can of plum tomatoes. The *boulettes* are terrific with mashed potatoes.

BOULETTES

12	ounces leftover beef (boiled beef, pot roast, stew meat, or roast beef)
½	cup finely chopped onion
¼	cup finely chopped celery
1	large garlic clove, crushed and very finely chopped (1 teaspoon)
3	large eggs
¼	teaspoon dried thyme
3	tablespoons all-purpose flour
1	teaspoon salt
¼	teaspoon freshly ground black pepper
1	teaspoon baking powder
¼	cup olive oil

SAUCE

3	tablespoons olive oil
½	teaspoon dried thyme
½	teaspoon dried oregano
½	cup finely chopped onion
3	garlic cloves, crushed (2 teaspoons)
2	pounds tomatoes, cut into 1-inch pieces (about 5 cups)
1	teaspoon salt
¼	teaspoon freshly ground black pepper
2	cups diced (1-inch) mushrooms (about 8 ounces)
⅔	cup slivered green olives

FOR THE BOULETTES: Cut the meat into chunks, then process it in a food processor until it is finely chopped. (You should have 2½ to 3 cups.) Combine it in a bowl with all the other ingredients.

Preheat the oven to 160 degrees.

Heat ¼ cup olive oil in a large skillet. With your hands, make patties with the meat mixture, using about 2 tablespoons for each one. (You should have about 18 patties.) Working in batches, pat the patties gently to flatten them a bit and place them in the hot oil. Cook for approximately 2 minutes on each side, until browned. Transfer to a tray and keep warm in the oven while you make the sauce.

FOR THE SAUCE: Heat the oil in a large saucepan. Add the thyme, oregano, onion, and garlic and cook over medium-high heat for 1 minute. Add the tomatoes, salt, and pepper and bring to a boil. Cover and cook over medium heat for 5 to 6 minutes; at this point, the tomatoes will have liquefied if they were nice and ripe.

Push the mixture through a food mill and return it to the saucepan (if you don't have a food mill, puree the mixture in a food processor and then push it through a sieve). Bring to a boil, add the mushrooms, bring back to a boil, then simmer for 10 minutes. Add the olives and boil for about 1 minute. Serve with the warm *boulettes*.

Veal

Veal Chops en Papillote
Serves 4

✂ A *papillote* is a parchment paper casing. Cooking *en papillote* yields food that is moist and flavorful. Veal chops are at their best when cooked this way, and fish is also excellent prepared in the same manner.

Try to get the best chops, called "the first," from your butcher. Out of the seven or so ribs that you get from a large rack, the three or four chops cut from the side of the loin are the leanest (as opposed to the ones cut from the side of the shoulder, which are called "the second" and are fattier).

2	tablespoons unsalted butter
4	veal loin chops, trimmed of outside fat (about 10 ounces each)
½	teaspoon salt
½	teaspoon freshly ground black pepper
½	cup dry white wine
½	cup heavy cream
20	small baby carrots, peeled
12	small pearl onions, peeled
2	teaspoons chopped fresh parsley

Melt the butter in a large heavy skillet. Sprinkle the chops lightly with half the salt and pepper and sauté over medium-high heat for 1½ minutes on each side; they should be nicely browned. Set aside.

Deglaze the skillet with the white wine, stirring to melt the solidified juices, and boil until most of the liquid evaporates. Add the cream, return to a boil, and season with the remaining salt and pepper.

Meanwhile, put the carrots and onions in a saucepan, cover with cold water, and bring to a boil. Boil for 2 minutes and drain. (The liquid can be retained for stock or soup.)

Preheat the oven to 400 degrees. Cut four rectangles of parchment paper, each about 24 inches by 15 inches. Oil the rectangles lightly on one side; this helps browning in the oven.

Fold each rectangle in half, with the oiled side out, then unfold. Place a chop on one side of one rectangle, along with 5 carrots, 3 onions, and some of the sauce, fold the other side of the paper over the chop to enclose it, and twist the edges of the paper all around to secure the chop inside; be sure to double-fold the edges so the package will not leak during cooking, locking in the moisture to ensure juicy meat. Repeat with the other chops.

Open the paper slightly at one end of each package and, using a straw, blow some air inside to inflate it. (The paper should not touch the top of the meat, or it will dry out while cooking. Inflating the paper creates a "hothouse," allowing condensation to fall back on the meat and vegetables during cooking and, in effect, basting the meat continuously.) Then secure the opened end by twisting it into a "pig's tail."

Place the packages on a cookie sheet and bake for 10 minutes.

Serve immediately, setting the packages, all puffed as they come from the oven, on warm plates. Cut or tear open each package at the table and slide the chop and vegetables onto the plate.

The vegetables should be tender but slightly firm and the chops slightly pink inside and moist. Sprinkle with the parsley and serve.

Grilled Veal Chops with Beans and Shallots

Serves 4

❧ **Veal chops are expensive,** but nothing compares to the taste of milk-fed veal. Combined with shallots and butter, the thin green beans called haricots verts make a splendid accompaniment. Here they are first boiled in water until they are cooked through but remain a bit firm. In many restaurants, they are blanched for only a minute or so and thus do not have much taste.

    1   pound haricots verts or small thin
           green beans, trimmed
    4   veal loin chops (11–12 ounces
           each)
    1   tablespoon peanut oil
    1   teaspoon herbes de Provence
    ½   teaspoon salt
    ½   teaspoon freshly ground black pepper

SHALLOTS

    5   tablespoons unsalted butter
    ¼   cup chopped shallots
    ¼   teaspoon salt
    ⅛   teaspoon freshly ground black pepper
    ½   teaspoon fresh lemon juice

Bring a pot of salted water to a boil. Add the beans and cover the pot so the water comes back to a boil quickly, then uncover and cook over high heat for 5 to 6 minutes, until the beans are al dente — tender but still firm to the bite. Drain and drop in a bowl of ice-cold water to cool. Drain and set aside.

Meanwhile, heat a grill until hot. Preheat the oven to 160 degrees.

Rub the chops with the oil and herbs; allow to marinate for a few minutes.

Sprinkle the chops lightly with the salt and pepper and place on the hot grill. Cook for about 2½ minutes, turning the chops 90 degrees after a minute or so to create a crisscross pattern. Turn and repeat on the other side. At this point, the chops are not completely cooked, but it is best to finish them in the oven to prevent them from drying out.

Arrange the chops on an ovenproof platter and place in the oven for 8 to 10 minutes to continue cooking and to relax the meat.

FOR THE SHALLOTS AND TO FINISH: At serving time, melt the butter in a large skillet. Add the shallots and cook for about 1 minute. Add the beans, salt, and pepper and toss just until heated through. Add the lemon juice and toss again.

To serve, arrange the beans and shallots on individual plates and put a veal chop in the center of each one.

Grilled Veal Chops with Caper and Sage Sauce

Serves 4

❧ **This is a good** summer recipe. I sear the chops briefly on a very hot grill and then transfer them to a warm oven, where they continue to cook slowly in their own residual heat. The sauce, a simple mixture of onion, capers, sage, lemon juice, and olive oil, is made separately and the chops are coated with it before they are served.

Be sure you don't overcook the chops. Although veal is not served rare, as beef is, it should still be slightly pink inside and juicy throughout.

Chicken or even a piece of fish also go well with the caper and sage sauce.

4 veal rib chops, trimmed of excess fat (about 10 ounces each and 1 inch thick)
1 teaspoon canola oil
¼ teaspoon salt
¼ teaspoon freshly ground black pepper

SAUCE

½ cup diced (¼-inch) red onion
2 tablespoons drained capers
1 tablespoon minced fresh sage
2 teaspoons julienned lemon rind
1 tablespoon fresh lemon juice
2 tablespoons olive oil
2 tablespoons chopped fresh parsley
¼ teaspoon freshly ground black pepper
¼ teaspoon salt, or to taste
2 tablespoons homemade chicken stock (page 612) or low-salt canned chicken broth

Heat a grill until it is very hot. Preheat the oven to 160 degrees.

Rub the chops with the oil and sprinkle them with the salt and pepper. Put the chops on the clean grill rack and cook for about 2½ minutes on each side. Transfer them to a heatproof platter, put it in the oven, and let them rest and finish cooking for at least 10 minutes. (*The chops can be kept in the oven for up to 30 minutes.*)

MEANWHILE, FOR THE SAUCE: Mix all the ingredients in a bowl.

At serving time, place a chop on each of four plates and coat with the sauce.

Veal Scaloppini with Cream, Calvados, and Apples
Serves 6

❧ **In this recipe from** Normandy, cream, apple brandy, and apples combine into a sauce for veal. The veal should be lean, cut from one of the muscles of the back leg, like the top round. Cook it in two large skillets.

3 medium sweet apples (Golden Delicious, Pippin, or Granny Smith)
2 tablespoons fresh lemon juice
12 veal scaloppini (⅜ inch thick and about 3½–4 inches in diameter)
1 teaspoon salt, or to taste
1 teaspoon freshly ground black pepper, or to taste
⅓ cup all-purpose flour
4 tablespoons (½ stick) unsalted butter
2 tablespoons vegetable oil
¼ cup Calvados or applejack
1½ cups heavy cream

Peel and core the apples, then cut into ½-inch cubes. Put in a bowl, add the lemon juice, and mix thoroughly so the apples are well coated. Set aside.

Sprinkle the veal with the salt and pepper, dredge in the flour, and shake off any excess.

Preheat the oven to 150 degrees.

Heat the butter and oil in two large heavy skillets until hot. Add the veal, a few pieces at a time, and sauté over high heat until lightly browned on both sides, about 1½ minutes on each side. Transfer the veal to a platter and set in the warm oven.

Combine all the pan drippings and browned bits from the veal in one of the skillets. Stir the apples, with the lemon juice, and Calvados or applejack into the skillet and scrape up all the browned bits in the pan. Cook over medium heat, stirring frequently, for about 2 minutes. Add the cream and cook until the sauce has reduced by about one third and coats the spoon. Taste for seasonings and add additional salt and pepper if needed.

Serve the veal chops on the hot platter or on warm individual plates, spooning the sauce over them.

Veal Scaloppini with Brown Sauce
Serves 4

❧ **The scaloppini in this** recipe are cut from the fillet, or tenderloin, which is the most tender portion. Briefly sautéed in butter, they are finished with a little lemon juice and brown sauce.

  1 piece veal tenderloin (about 1 pound)
  2 tablespoons unsalted butter
  ¼ teaspoon salt
  ⅛ teaspoon freshly ground black pepper
  ½ cup Basic Brown Sauce (page 613)
  1 teaspoon fresh lemon juice
  2 tablespoons chopped fresh chives

Clean the top of the tenderloin of any sinews and cut into 8 pieces, each about ¾ inch thick and weighing 2 ounces. To avoid tearing the meat when pounding it, wet the cutting board and a metal meat pounder, or place the meat between sheets of plastic wrap. Pound the meat slices lightly to flatten the scaloppini to approximately ¼ inch thick. (You will notice that it is easy to pound fillet, as it is a very tender piece of meat.)

Heat the butter in one large or two smaller skillets (if necessary, cook the veal in batches). Sprinkle the scaloppini lightly with the salt and pepper, put them in the foaming (but not too hot)

butter, and sauté over high heat for 1 minute on each side. Remove to a platter and let sit for a few minutes.

Meanwhile, add the brown sauce to the drippings in the skillet(s) and bring to a boil, stirring to melt the solidified juices. Add the lemon juice.

Place 2 scaloppini on each of four warm plates, spoon on the sauce, sprinkle with the chives, and serve.

Veal Vienna-Style
Serves 6

❧ **For veal Vienna, slices** from the top round or top knuckle (muscles from the hind legs) are pounded very thin, breaded, and cooked quickly. The traditional garnishes are a peeled lemon slice with an anchovy fillet–wrapped olive on top of each slice and chopped hard-cooked egg, herbs, and capers surrounding the veal.

  6 large veal scaloppini (each about 6 ounces and ½ inch thick)
  ¼ teaspoon salt
  ⅛ teaspoon freshly ground black pepper
  ⅓ cup all-purpose flour
  2 large eggs
1½ tablespoons water
  1 tablespoon canola oil
3–4 cups fresh bread crumbs (about 8 slices firm white bread, crusts removed)

GARNISHES
  1 lemon
  6 anchovy fillets
  6 green olives, pitted
  2 hard-cooked large eggs (see page 66), yolks and whites finely chopped separately
  ⅓ cup minced fresh chives

> 3 tablespoons unsalted butter
> 3 tablespoons olive oil
> 2 tablespoons drained capers
> ¾ cup Basic Brown Sauce (page 613)
> Salt and freshly ground black pepper

To avoid tearing the meat when pounding it, dampen the work surface and meat pounder with a little water, or pound the meat between sheets of plastic wrap. Pound the meat, driving the pounder straight down and then out — if the pounder does not come down flat on the meat, its edge will tear the piece. The amount of pressure needed to pound down and out depends entirely on the tenderness of the meat; it requires more pressure for the top round, which is tougher, than for tenderloin. The finished pieces should measure 8 to 9 inches long by 6 to 7 inches wide. Sprinkle the meat with the salt and pepper and dust the pieces lightly with the flour, shaking off the excess.

Mix the eggs, water, and oil together in a shallow bowl. Dip the veal gently into the egg mixture, letting the excess drip off, then dip in the bread crumbs. Press lightly on one side, turn, and press lightly again to coat both sides with the bread crumbs. If desired, using the back of a knife, mark the top to create a lattice design. Arrange the pieces of veal on a large cookie sheet, separating the layers with waxed paper so the breaded slices don't stick together.

FOR THE GARNISHES: Peel the lemon completely, removing all the white pith, and cut six ¼-inch-thick slices from it. Roll an anchovy around each of the olives and place in the center of a lemon slice.

Arrange the egg yolks, chives, and egg whites next to each other around the periphery of six individual serving plates.

At serving time, heat the butter and oil in two very large skillets until hot. Place the breaded veal in the skillets and cook over medium heat for approximately 2 minutes, until lightly browned, then turn and cook for 2 minutes on the other side.

Arrange the veal in the middle of the plates, and put a slice of lemon with an anchovy-wrapped olive on top of each slice of veal. Surround with the capers.

Add the brown sauce to the skillet and bring to a boil, stirring to melt the solidified juices. Season with additional salt and pepper if needed. Spoon the sauce around the veal and serve.

Roast Veal with Artichokes
Serves 4

⚶ **Shoulder is the best** choice for this recipe. If you buy the large muscle of the shoulder, you may not have to tie the meat; if, however, the piece separates or is longer and flatter, roll it and tie it with twine. It should be served lightly pink. This roast is good warm, but it is also very good cold with a green salad, tomato salad, or pasta salad.

> 1 boneless veal shoulder roast (about 2½ pounds), trimmed of most surface fat
> ½ teaspoon salt
> ½ teaspoon freshly ground black pepper
> 1 teaspoon dried thyme
> 1 tablespoon unsalted butter
> 1 tablespoon olive oil
> 5 medium artichokes with stems (about 1¾ pounds)
> 12 large pearl onions
> 18 large garlic cloves
> 1 tomato (6 ounces), halved, seeded, and cut into ½-inch pieces (1 cup)
> 1 tablespoon dark soy sauce
> 2 tablespoons water

Preheat the oven to 400 degrees.

Tie the roast with kitchen twine if necessary. Sprinkle it with ¼ teaspoon each of the salt and pepper and with the thyme. Heat the butter and oil in a large ovenproof skillet until hot. Add the meat and brown it on all sides, for a total of about 10 minutes. Remove the roast to a platter and reserve the drippings in the skillet.

With a sharp knife, remove the top third of each artichoke. With scissors, trim off the upper three quarters of the remaining leaves to remove the sharp "prickers" and most of the green leaves. Trim the bottoms of the stems and peel the stems with a paring knife. Cut the artichokes into quarters and remove and discard the chokes.

Add the artichokes, onions, garlic, and the remaining ¼ teaspoon each salt and pepper to the drippings in the skillet and toss the vegetables to coat them with the drippings. Arrange the roast on top of the vegetables, transfer to the oven, and roast for 20 minutes.

Turn the roast over, stirring the vegetables as you do so, and roast for another 20 minutes.

Stir in the tomato, soy sauce, and water and roast for 10 minutes, for a total cooking time of 50 minutes, not including the browning. (My roast was about 8½ inches long by 2½ inches in diameter; if your roast is shorter and thicker, cook it a little longer.) Remove the roast from the oven and allow it to rest for 10 minutes.

Carve the roast and serve with the vegetables, the garlic, and the pan juices.

Veal Blanquette
Serves 4

❧ **This stew is called** a *blanquette*, from the word *blanc*, meaning "white," because the meat is simmered gently in water and wine rather than browned as for a fricassee. It has a milder and more delicate taste than a fricassee. It is conventionally thickened with a roux made of butter and flour and finished with egg yolks and heavy cream. My version is lighter. I use lean veal and break with tradition by thickening the sauce with a mixture of flour and water, finishing the stew with cream and eliminating the yolks.

1½	pounds veal cubes (about 1½ inches each) from the shoulder
¾	cup plus 2 tablespoons water
½	cup fruity dry white wine (such as Chardonnay)
1	teaspoon salt
1	bouquet garni — 1 celery stalk, about 10 parsley stems, 1 large bay leaf, and 2 fresh thyme sprigs, tied together with kitchen twine
12	large pearl onions (about 10 ounces)
16	button mushrooms (about 8 ounces), cleaned
1	tablespoon all-purpose flour
⅓	cup heavy cream
6	cornichons (tiny French gherkins), thinly sliced
¼	teaspoon freshly ground black pepper
2	teaspoons fresh lemon juice

Combine the veal, ¾ cup of the water, the wine, salt, and bouquet garni in a Dutch oven or enameled cast-iron casserole and bring to a boil, uncovered, over high heat. Stir, add the onions, and bring to a boil, then reduce the heat to low and boil gently, covered, for 10 minutes.

Add the mushrooms and cook, covered, for another 5 minutes. Using a slotted spoon, remove the onions and mushrooms to a bowl and set aside.

Continue to cook the meat, covered, over very low heat (it should boil very gently) for 1¼ hours, or until it is soft and tender. Remove and discard the bouquet garni.

Combine the flour and 1 tablespoon of the water in a small bowl and mix well with a whisk or spoon until smooth. Add the remaining tablespoon of water and mix well. Pour the flour mixture into the pot with the veal and mix well. Bring to a boil over high heat, stirring occasionally, and boil gently for 2 minutes. (*At this point, the meat can be set aside in the Dutch oven for a few hours, if desired. Reheat when ready to complete the dish.*)

Add the cream and onions and mushrooms to the pot and bring to a boil over high heat. Stir in the cornichons, pepper, and lemon juice. Serve.

Veal Fricassee with Olives
Serves 6

✂ **For this fricassee, the** veal is first browned, unlike a Veal Blanquette (see opposite), where the meat is boiled in water and white wine. Browning gives the fricassee an assertive taste. (The difference between boiling and browning the meat is somewhat like the difference between a white stock, which involves no browning, and a brown stock.)

Even if you're not serving six, make the full recipe: you can divide it afterward and freeze a portion for later. Be sure to use lean meat from the shoulder, chuck, or shank — it will retain its moistness when stewed and is less expensive than meat from the back leg (top or bottom round), which is good for scaloppini but would be dry prepared in this manner.

Serve the fricassee with pasta or potatoes.

1	tablespoon canola oil
1	tablespoon unsalted butter
2	pounds lean veal from the shoulder, chuck, or shank, cut into 12 large cubes (about 2 inches each)
2½	cups chopped onions
2	tablespoons all-purpose flour
1½	cups water
1	fresh rosemary sprig
¾	teaspoon salt
5	garlic cloves, crushed and coarsely chopped (1½ tablespoons)
8	ounces cremini mushrooms, cleaned and thickly sliced
½	cup sour cream
1	cup pitted green olives

Heat the oil and butter in a Dutch oven or large heavy saucepan until hot. Add the meat and cook over medium-low heat for 15 minutes, turning it often, until browned on all sides.

Add the onions and cook for 5 minutes. Add the flour and cook for 1 minute longer. Stir in the water and add the rosemary, salt, and garlic. Bring to a boil, cover, and boil gently for 1 hour. (*The recipe can be prepared to this point up to 1 day ahead, cooled, and refrigerated. Bring to a gentle boil before completing the dish.*)

Add the mushrooms to the fricassee and boil gently for 5 minutes.

Stir in the sour cream and olives, warm briefly, and serve.

Osso Buco
Serves 4

❧ *Osso buco* **literally means** "bone with a hole" (or "with a mouth") in Italian. The name refers to the veal shank, which is sliced crosswise and composed of about equal parts bone and meat. They're browned in a large sturdy pot, then wine, water, and a multitude of vegetables are added and the dish is simmered slowly until the veal is very tender. At the end, the osso buco is flavored with grated orange and lemon rind and sprinkled with shredded basil leaves.

- 4 slices bone-in veal shank (about 10 ounces each and 1½ inches thick)
- 1 tablespoon unsalted butter
- 1 tablespoon olive oil
- 1 medium onion, finely chopped (1¼ cups)
- 1 small leek, trimmed (leaving some green), split, washed, and coarsely chopped (¾ cup)
- 1 medium carrot, peeled and coarsely chopped (½ cup)
- 6 garlic cloves, crushed and finely chopped (4 teaspoons)
- 2 celery stalks (4 ounces), coarsely chopped (⅔ cup)
- 1 teaspoon herbes de Provence
- ⅔ cup fruity dry white wine
- ½ cup water
- 1 teaspoon salt
- ½ teaspoon freshly ground black pepper
- 2 ripe medium tomatoes, halved, seeded, and cut into ½-inch pieces (1¼ cups)
- 1 tablespoon grated orange rind
- 1 tablespoon grated lemon rind
- 1 teaspoon potato starch (see page 318), dissolved in 3 tablespoons white wine
- ½ cup shredded fresh basil leaves

Pat the veal dry with paper towels. Heat the butter and oil in a Dutch oven or large heavy saucepan until hot. Add the meat in one layer and brown it on all sides over medium-high heat, about 12 minutes.

Add the onion, leek, and carrot, mix well, and cook for 2 minutes. Add the garlic, celery, herbes de Provence, wine, water, salt, and pepper, mix well, and bring to a strong boil. Reduce the heat to low, cover, and cook gently for 1½ hours, or until the meat is tender when pierced with the point of a knife.

Add the tomatoes, orange rind, and lemon rind, mix well, and bring back to a boil. Boil, uncovered, for 2 to 3 minutes. Add the dissolved potato starch and bring to a boil again. Remove the pot from the heat, add the basil, and mix gently. Cover and set aside until ready to serve. (*The dish is more flavorful if allowed to sit for at least 30 minutes before serving. It can be made a day ahead and reheated, with the basil added at the time of reheating.*)

Arrange a slice of shank with bone on each individual serving plate. Pour the sauce over and around the shanks and serve.

Veal Shank Printanière
Serves 6

✂ **Although veal shanks are** most often found sliced crosswise for use in osso buco, the shank meat can also be separated from the bone in one piece and cut lengthwise into pieces. Here these pieces are sautéed, flavored with wine, and finished with an abundance of springtime vegetables, including carrots, onions, sugar snap peas, and green peas.

You may find boneless shank in some markets; if not, buy osso buco and bone it for this recipe.

2¼	pounds boneless veal shank or 3½–4 pounds bone-in veal shank
2	tablespoons unsalted butter
12	medium shallots
18	small carrots, peeled
2	cups water
½	cup chopped onion
2	teaspoons crushed, chopped garlic
1	tablespoon all-purpose flour
1	teaspoon herbes de Provence
½	cup dry white wine
1	teaspoon salt
½	teaspoon freshly ground black pepper
4	ounces sugar snap peas, ends trimmed and any strings removed (1 cup)
1	cup fresh peas (8 ounces unshelled) or frozen baby peas

Cut the shank meat lengthwise into 12 pieces, each about 1½ inches thick. Melt the butter in a large saucepan over medium heat. When it begins to brown, add the meat strips in one layer and cook over medium-high heat for about 15 minutes, turning them occasionally, until nicely browned on all sides.

Meanwhile, put the shallots and carrots in a medium saucepan with the water and bring to a boil, then reduce the heat to low, cover, and boil the vegetables gently for about 8 minutes, until they are tender but still firm. Drain, reserving the cooking liquid. (You should have about 1 cup; add water if necessary to bring it to 1 cup.) Set the shallots and carrots aside in a bowl.

When the veal is nicely browned, transfer it to a plate. Add the onion and garlic to the meat drippings in the pan and cook for 1 minute. Add the flour and herbes de Provence, mix well, and cook for 10 to 20 seconds. Add the reserved cooking liquid from the carrots and shallots to the pan, along with the wine, salt, and pepper, and bring to a boil. Return the meat to the pan and bring back to a boil, then reduce the heat to very low, cover, and cook gently for 1½ hours, or until the meat is tender. (*The recipe can be made to this point a few hours ahead; bring the stew to a gentle boil before finishing the dish.*)

At serving time, add the shallots and carrots to the stew, along with the sugar snaps and peas. Bring the stew back to a boil, reduce the heat to low, cover, and boil gently for 5 minutes. Serve.

Veal Tendrons with Tarragon Sauce
Serves 6

✂ **Tendrons, ribs cut from** a veal breast, are excellent braised. This dish can be made with or without cream; my version contains cream as well as fresh tarragon. Searing the veal creates a crust in the bottom of the pan that lends flavor to the sauce. Brown the meat at a high temperature so that the juices turn into a dark brown glaze. The veal can be prepared ahead and refrigerated or frozen for later use.

If fresh thyme is not available, substitute ½ teaspoon dried thyme and simply add it to the pan with the bay leaves.

1 tablespoon olive oil

1 tablespoon unsalted butter

1 veal breast (about 3½ pounds; about 5 ribs), cut into ribs and each rib cut crosswise in half (you can have the butcher do this)

2 cups coarsely chopped onions

1 tablespoon all-purpose flour

1¼ cups water

4 garlic cloves, crushed and coarsely chopped (about 1 tablespoon)

1 herb bouquet — 2 bay leaves and 5–6 fresh thyme sprigs, tied together with kitchen twine

1 teaspoon salt

½ cup heavy cream

1 tablespoon fresh tarragon leaves or ½ teaspoon dried tarragon

¼ teaspoon freshly ground black pepper

Heat the oil and butter in a large heavy enameled cast-iron, or aluminum pot until hot. Add half the veal ribs in one layer and cook over high heat for about 10 minutes, turning to brown on all sides. Remove the browned ribs to a plate. Repeat with the remaining ribs, placing them on the plate after they are browned.

Drain off all but 1 tablespoon fat from the pot and add the onions. Cook for about 2 minutes, stirring constantly. The onions should be wilted and mixed with the solidified meat juices loosened through stirring. Add the flour and mix well. Add the water and bring to a boil, stirring well.

Return the meat to the pot and add the garlic, herb bouquet, and salt. Bring to a boil, cover, reduce the heat to very low, and cook for 1 hour; by then, the meat should be tender and there should be 1¼ to 1½ cups lightly thickened sauce.

Discard the herb bouquet. Add the cream, bring to a boil, and stir in the tarragon and pepper. Serve.

Veal Breast Cocotte
Serves 6

꙳ **Of all meat juices,** those rendered by veal have the most concentrated taste, especially when the veal is cooked slowly, as it is here, in a cocotte, a type of Dutch oven.

Veal breast is usually relatively inexpensive. It has only a small amount of meat: at least two thirds of the weight is bones and cartilage, both of which add flavor to the sauce. Carrots, onions, and garlic extend and enhance the dish.

1 veal breast (about 3½ pounds; 4–5 meaty ribs)

1 tablespoon herbes de Provence

½ teaspoon salt

1 tablespoon olive oil

1 cup water

1 cup dry white wine

8 ounces baby carrots (about 18), peeled

8 ounces pearl onions (about 18)

1 large head garlic (about 15 cloves), separated into cloves and peeled

Put the veal breast, herbes de Provence, salt, oil, and ½ cup of the water in a large cocotte, Dutch oven, or other heavy pot and bring to a boil over high heat. Reduce the heat to medium and boil, covered, for 15 minutes, or until most of the liquid has evaporated. Continue to cook, uncovered, over medium heat for about 25 minutes, turning the meat often to brown it well on all sides.

Add the remaining ½ cup water and the wine, cover, reduce the heat to low, and simmer slowly for about 1 hour, until the meat is tender when pierced with a fork.

Mix in the carrots, onions, and garlic, cover, and cook over low heat for 30 more minutes.

Divide the meat, carrots, onions, garlic, and sauce among six individual plates and serve.

Lamb

Broiled Herbed Lamb Chops
Serves 4

🥢 **I make this recipe** often in winter when I don't want to start the outside grill. It is easy and fast, and rib lamb chops are always available at my market. I like to use fresh savory, but fresh thyme, sage, or oregano can be substituted.

- 8 lamb rib chops (5 ounces each and about 1½ inches thick), trimmed of excess fat
- ½ teaspoon freshly ground black pepper
- 3 tablespoons chopped fresh savory
- 2 tablespoons olive oil
- ½ teaspoon salt

Sprinkle the chops on both sides with the pepper and savory. Pour the oil onto a plate and dip the chops in it, first one side and then the other. (*You can broil the chops now or arrange them on the plate, cover with plastic wrap, and refrigerate until ready to cook.*)

At cooking time, preheat the broiler.

Sprinkle the chops with the salt and arrange them on a cookie sheet lined with aluminum foil (for easy cleanup). Broil the chops 4 to 5 inches from the heat for about 2½ minutes on each side for medium-rare. Let rest for 5 minutes.

Serve the chops with the natural juices.

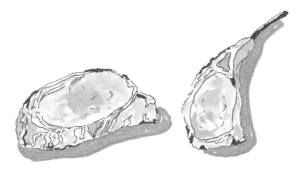

Grilled Lamb Loin Chops Riviera
Serves 4

🥢 **Prepared in the style** of the French Riviera, these chops are served on a base of grilled eggplant, tomatoes, and spinach that has been sautéed with garlic.

- 2 tablespoons olive oil
- 1 small onion, chopped (⅓ cup)
- 3 garlic cloves, crushed and chopped (2 teaspoons)
- 1 pound spinach, tough stems removed, washed, and dried
- 1¼ teaspoons salt
- ½ teaspoon freshly ground black pepper
- 6 plum tomatoes (about 12 ounces), peeled, seeded, and cut into ½-inch pieces (1½ cups)
- 1 eggplant (about 1 pound), ends trimmed and cut crosswise into four 1-inch-thick slices
- 4 lamb loin chops (about 8 ounces each and 1¾ inches thick), trimmed of all surrounding fat (about 6 ounces each trimmed)
- 16 oil-cured black olives

Heat a grill until hot. Preheat the oven to 350 degrees.

Heat 1 tablespoon of the olive oil in a large skillet. When it is hot, add the onion and sauté for 1 minute. Stir in the garlic, then add the spinach, ½ teaspoon of the salt, and ¼ teaspoon of the pepper, cover, and cook over high heat for about 1 minute, just until the spinach wilts. Mix well, bringing the garlic and onions to the top so they don't burn, cover, and cook over medium heat for another 4 minutes. Transfer the spinach mixture to a bowl and set aside in a warm spot.

Add the tomatoes to the skillet, along with ¼ teaspoon of the salt, cover, and cook for about 1 minute over medium heat, just long enough to heat through. Set aside, covered.

Sprinkle the eggplant slices with ¼ teaspoon of the salt and brush them lightly on both sides with about 2½ teaspoons of the oil. Place the slices on the grill rack and cook, turning them once midway through so they are nicely marked by the grill on both sides, for a total of 4 minutes. Transfer the slices to a cookie sheet and place them in the oven for at least 10 minutes to finish cooking.

Meanwhile, sprinkle the lamb chops with the remaining ¼ teaspoon salt and ¼ teaspoon pepper. Brush them on both sides with the remaining oil and place them on the grill rack. Cook, turning them occasionally, for a total of 7 to 8 minutes, until they are nicely browned on both sides. Arrange the chops on a tray and let rest in a warm place for 5 to 10 minutes before serving.

At serving time, spread the spinach on four warmed plates and divide the tomatoes among the plates, sprinkling them on top of the spinach. Arrange a slice of eggplant in the center of each plate and place a lamb chop on top. Put 4 olives on each plate, spoon any juices from the lamb over the chops, and serve.

Braised Lamb Chops and Potatoes
Serves 6

✄ **Shoulder blade chops are** first sautéed, then braised in the oven, smothered with sliced potatoes, herbs, onions, and garlic. Neither stock nor wine is needed, since the lamb has plenty of taste on its own. The braising liquid should be almost completely absorbed by the time the lamb and po-tatoes are ready to serve. This dish is equally good reheated.

1	tablespoon canola or safflower oil
6	lamb shoulder blade chops, as lean as possible (about 7 ounces each)
2	onions (about 8 ounces), sliced (about 2 cups)
2½	cups water
6–7	garlic cloves, thinly sliced (about 2 tablespoons)
1½	teaspoons salt
¾	teaspoon freshly ground black pepper
2	pounds potatoes, peeled, thinly sliced, and put in a bowl of cold water to cover
3	fresh thyme sprigs
2–3	bay leaves
¼	cup coarsely chopped fresh parsley

Preheat the oven to 375 degrees.

Heat the oil in a large skillet. When it is hot, add the lamb chops (3 at a time if necessary to avoid crowding) and cook over high heat for about 4 minutes per side, until nicely browned. Arrange the chops in one layer in a large gratin dish.

Add the onions to the drippings in the pan and sauté, stirring, for about 2 minutes. Add the water, garlic, salt, and pepper and bring to a boil.

Drain the potato slices well and arrange them on top of the lamb chops. Put the thyme and bay leaves in the middle of the dish and press them gently into the potatoes. Pour the onion mixture, with the pan juices, over the dish.

Put the gratin dish on a cookie sheet and bake for about 1¼ hours, until the potatoes are soft, the lamb is tender, and most of the liquid has been absorbed.

Sprinkle with the parsley and allow to sit for a few minutes to develop flavor before serving.

Lamb Steaks with Soy, Vinegar, and Garlic

Serves 4

🐌 **This quick recipe is** ideal for a special dinner. Lamb steaks are sautéed and sauced with a piquant mixture of ketchup, soy sauce, vinegar, and garlic. Fresh noodles or basmati rice make a nice accompaniment, as do sautéed or roasted potatoes or a potato gratin.

- 1 tablespoon unsalted butter
- 1 tablespoon canola oil
- 4 lamb steaks cut from the back leg (about 5 ounces each and 1 inch thick), trimmed of all surface fat
- ¼ teaspoon salt
- ¼ teaspoon freshly ground black pepper
- 3 garlic cloves, crushed and chopped (2 teaspoons)
- ¼ cup balsamic vinegar
- ½ cup water
- 2 tablespoons ketchup
- 1 teaspoon dark soy sauce
- 1 teaspoon Chinese chile sauce with garlic (optional)
- 1 tablespoon shredded fresh mint leaves

Preheat the oven to 150 degrees.

Heat the butter and oil in a skillet large enough to hold the lamb steaks in one layer. Sprinkle the steaks with the salt and pepper and sauté them over high heat for about 2 minutes on each side, or until nicely browned. Remove the steaks to a tray or ovenproof plate and keep warm in the oven while you make the sauce.

Add the garlic to the drippings in the skillet and cook for 10 seconds. Add the vinegar and cook over high heat for 1 minute, until most of the vinegar has evaporated. Add the water, ketchup, soy sauce, and, if desired, chile sauce and boil for

about 30 seconds, stirring to mix in all the melted solidified juices.

Pour the juices that have accumulated around the steaks into the sauce. Arrange a steak on each of four individual plates and coat the steaks with the sauce. Garnish with the mint and serve.

Rack of Lamb Provençal

Serves 3 to 4

🐌 **Since rack of lamb** is expensive, I like to serve it as part of a complete menu, preceded by a first course and followed by a salad, then dessert. The more elaborate the menu, the smaller the portions of meat required.

You can brown the lamb and prepare the herb crust a few hours ahead. Notice that there is butter mixed into the crust mixture, which helps the ingredients hold together and brown nicely.

- 1 (single) rack of lamb (about 1¼ pounds), trimmed of most of the surface fat
- ¼ teaspoon salt
- ¼ teaspoon freshly ground black pepper
- 2 shallots, minced (2 tablespoons)
- 3 tablespoons chopped fresh parsley
- 1 small garlic clove, minced (¼ teaspoon)
- ⅛ teaspoon dried thyme or herbes de Provence
- 1 slice firm white bread (1 ounce), processed to crumbs in a food processor (½ cup)
- 2 tablespoons unsalted butter, melted
- ½ cup Basic Brown Sauce (page 613) Watercress sprigs, for garnish

Preheat the oven to 425 degrees.

Heat a large heavy skillet over high heat. Sprinkle the rack with the salt and pepper and place meat side down in the skillet. There is no need for fat in the skillet, since there is enough remaining on the rack for it to brown in its own fat. Brown the meat and then, holding the rack with tongs, sear it on the bottom. (This does not cook the rack but simply sears it all around.) Place the rack meat side up in a roasting pan; set the skillet aside.

Combine the shallots, parsley, garlic, dried herbs, bread crumbs, and melted butter in a bowl and mix lightly with a fork. Press the bread crumb mixture lightly over the top of the rack. (*The rack can be prepared a few hours ahead and refrigerated; bring to room temperature before proceeding.*)

Roast for 12 to 15 minutes. If the bread crumbs are not browned enough, place under the broiler for about 1 minute to make them a bit darker. Transfer the rack to a plate and let rest, uncovered, on top of the stove or in a warm oven (140 to 150 degrees) for 10 minutes before carving, so the meat will be pink and moist throughout.

Meanwhile, skim the excess fat from the skillet, add the brown sauce, and stir to melt all the solidified juices. Strain the sauce into a little saucepan or a sauceboat.

Carve the rack between the ribs, arrange on individual serving plates, and garnish with the watercress. Serve with the sauce.

Rack of Lamb with Lamb Timbales
Serves 4

✂ **A well-trimmed rack of** lamb is roasted with a coating of flavored bread crumbs and the trimmings are transformed into timbales, which are cooked in molds and served alongside the chops. To get the 6 to 8 ounces of meat for the timbales, you may need to buy a lamb shoulder chop or a few pieces of lamb stewing meat.

TIMBALES

6–8 ounces reserved lamb trimmings (see below; if unavailable, or you have less, substitute meat from a lamb shoulder chop or stewing meat as necessary)

1½ slices firm white bread (1½ ounces), cut into ½-inch dice (1¼ cups)

1 large egg, lightly beaten

¼ cup dry white wine

2 tablespoons chopped shallots

1 tablespoon chopped fresh mint

1 teaspoon chopped fresh thyme

½ teaspoon salt

½ teaspoon freshly ground black pepper

1 (single) rack of lamb (about 3 pounds untrimmed, 1¼ pounds trimmed), fat and skin from trimming discarded but the meat trimmings (6–8 ounces) reserved for the timbales

¼ teaspoon salt

½ teaspoon freshly ground black pepper

2 slices firm white bread (2 ounces)

1 tablespoon fresh mint leaves

1 teaspoon fresh thyme or lemon thyme leaves

1 tablespoon chopped shallot

2 teaspoons olive oil

FOR THE TIMBALES: Cut the meat trimmings (and/or extra meat) into ½-inch pieces and process in a food processor until finely chopped. Add the bread, egg, wine, shallots, mint, thyme, salt, and pepper and process for a few seconds, until well combined.

Divide the timbale mixture among four ½-cup ramekins, spooning about ⅓ cup of the mixture into each. Place the molds in a large saucepan and surround them with 1 cup lukewarm water.

Bring the water in the saucepan to a boil over high heat, then cover with a lid, reduce the heat to low, and cook the timbales gently for 10 to 12 minutes, until they are set and the lamb is cooked through. Set aside. (*The timbales can be cooked up to a few hours ahead and then reheated in the saucepan, surrounded by water, on top of the stove, at serving time.*)

Preheat the oven to 425 degrees.

FOR THE RACK OF LAMB: Heat a large nonstick skillet until hot. Sprinkle the lamb with the salt and ¼ teaspoon of the pepper and lay it in the hot skillet. Cook the rack, turning occasionally, for 4 to 5 minutes, until it is seared on all sides; hold the rack with the tongs to sear it on the bottom. Transfer the lamb to a small roasting pan, placing it meat side up.

Put the bread, the remaining ¼ teaspoon pepper, the mint, and thyme in the food processor and process the mixture until it is chopped but still fluffy. Transfer to a bowl, add the chopped shallots and oil, and mix gently to moisten the bread but not make it pasty or wet.

Lightly press the bread mixture over the top of the rack. (*The rack can be prepared a few hours ahead and refrigerated; bring to room temperature before proceeding.*)

Roast the rack for 15 minutes for medium-rare meat. Let rest in a warm place (a 150-degree oven if possible) for 10 minutes before carving.

Carve the rack and serve with the timbales.

Lamb Saddle with Sage-Mousse Stuffing and Onion-Tomato Sauce
Serves 8 to 10

The whole lamb saddle, also called the double loin or the short back, is the piece that extends the length of the fillet from the first rib of the rack to the pelvic bone of the back leg. In this recipe, a mousse is spread on the loin of the boned saddle.

The mousse, made of lamb trimmings, chicken, and cream, is mild and delicate and complements the meat.

The flanks are folded on top of the mousse to enclose it, creating three layers. If the saddle were simply roasted, the loin would be done much sooner than the mousse. To prevent this, the saddle is first panfried, stuffed side down, to partially cook the mousse, then finished in the oven so that the loin is rare and the stuffing is cooked.

A slightly astringent fresh tomato sauce counters the richness.

1 untrimmed saddle of lamb (about 8 pounds with fat and flanks; if you like, have the butcher trim and bone the saddle as directed in the recipe, reserving 12 ounces of the trimmings)

STUFFING

½ cup sliced (½-inch) leeks
½ cup peeled, very thinly sliced carrots
½ cup water
2 cups spinach, tough stems removed, washed, and dried
12 ounces reserved lamb trimmings (from above)
4 ounces chicken meat
2 large eggs
1 teaspoon salt
½ teaspoon freshly ground black pepper
½ cup heavy cream
6–9 fresh sage leaves

⅛ teaspoon salt
⅛ teaspoon freshly ground black pepper

SAUCE

1 cup chopped onion
1 cup dry white wine
2 cups water
2 cups chopped tomatoes
3–4 garlic cloves, chopped (2 teaspoons)
2 teaspoons potato starch (see page 318), dissolved in 2 tablespoons water

TO PREPARE THE SADDLE: With the saddle upside down and flat, trim about 5 inches off each end of the flanks on either side. For use in this recipe, these pieces should be trimmed of sinews and fat: holding your knife so the blade is flat and parallel to the table, cut into the flank. The meat can be separated into layers. Lift up one layer and cut it off. Set aside.

Turn the saddle over and trim off the reddish skin (called the "fell" or "pell") from the top. Remove most of the fat. The saddle is now completely clean, with just enough of the flank to protect the fillets during cooking.

To bone the saddle, place it on its back and cut off the 2 fillets from the central bone. They should come off easily. Slide your knife flat underneath the bone where the fillets sat and cut, following the contour of the bone, to loosen 1 loin. Repeat on the other side. Finally, lift up the central bone and separate it from the meat: the rim in the center of the bone is against the top skin part of the saddle — be careful not to make holes in the top of the saddle when boning. If you left some meat on the bone while boning, use a spoon to scrape it off, and set it aside for the mousse.

Clean the 2 fillets: notice that each fillet separates into 2 pieces, the fillet and the "chain" of the fillet, which should be scraped with a knife or spoon to separate the meat from the sinews. (Reserve this scraped-off meat for the mousse.) Cut the fillets in half. Keep the thicker part of each fillet to place in the center of the saddle, and keep the "tails" for the mousse.

Arrange the thicker pieces of fillet in the center of the saddle (where there is a space from the removal of the bone) and set the 2 extra pieces of flank on either side of the loins for use as a wrapper for the mousse.

FOR THE STUFFING: Combine the leeks, carrots, and water in a saucepan, bring to a boil, cover, and cook for 3 minutes. Add the spinach and cook for about 1 minute longer. The mixture should be almost dry. Spread on a large platter or cookie sheet to cool quickly and thus preserve the color of the vegetables.

Put the lamb trimmings and chicken meat in a food processor and process for about 5 seconds. Clean the meat from the sides of the bowl with a rubber spatula, add the eggs, and process for 10 seconds longer, or until very smooth. Add the salt and pepper. With the motor running, add the cream and process briefly, just long enough to blend. Transfer to a bowl.

Pile the sage leaves together and shred them into a fine julienne (this is called a *chiffonnade*). Combine the sage with the mousse. Press the cold vegetables with your hands to extract more liquid (too much liquid will make the mousse break down) and mix with the mousse.

Sprinkle the saddle and fillets with the ⅛ teaspoon each salt and pepper and spread the mousse on top. It should be about 1 inch thick. Return the extra pieces of flank to cover the mousse and fold over the flanks from either side to enclose the mousse entirely.

Tie the saddle securely with kitchen twine, without squeezing it too much, so there is room for the stuffing to expand.

Preheat the oven to 400 degrees.

Lift the saddle up by the string and place stuffed side down in a roasting pan on top of the stove. Cook over medium heat for about 25 minutes to partially cook the stuffing and the flank, which take longer than the loin to cook.

Spoon some of the drippings on top of the saddle, transfer to the oven, and roast for 30 to 35 minutes, until nicely browned.

Lift the saddle out of the roasting pan and place on a platter. Let rest in a 150-degree oven or on the side of the stove where it's warm for at least 30 minutes before carving.

MEANWHILE, FOR THE SAUCE: Skim off most of the fat from the roasting pan. Add the onion and sauté for 3 to 4 minutes, until quite brown. Add the white wine, water, tomatoes, and garlic and bring to a boil; boil gently for 8 to 10 minutes. Add the dissolved potato starch. Strain the sauce. (You should have 1¾ to 2 cups.)

Cut the saddle into 8 to 10 slices ½ inch to ¾ inch thick: hold the slices with one hand while

LAMB

The best-tasting lamb is spring lamb, slaughtered when it is six to ten months old. The meat has peak taste and is usually served medium-rare. Older lamb, or mutton, is usually stronger in taste and is often stewed, braised, or roasted until medium or well-done.

Baby lamb, also called "hothouse" or "milk" lamb, comes from an animal approximately four to six weeks old. The uncooked meat will be pinkish white and you should not, therefore, cook it rare. It should be prepared like veal, just medium and slightly pink at the bone.

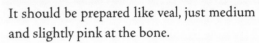

you cut with the other hand; this will help the slices keep their shape.

Arrange the slices of saddle on a large platter or on individual plates, coat the meat with the sauce, and serve.

Roast Leg of Lamb
Serves 8

✂ **A roasted whole unboned** leg of lamb is a great showpiece to carve in the dining room — or in the kitchen, if you are not up to carving in front of your guests. Garlic slivers are customarily inserted into the flesh before cooking, and I also pat flavored bread crumbs on the meat. It is served here medium-rare. Leftovers can be served cold the following day with a salad.

1 small spring leg of lamb (5 pounds with shank and pelvic bone), trimmed of most visible fat and pelvic bone removed (about 4 pounds trimmed)

2 garlic cloves, cut into 6 small slivers each, plus 2 whole peeled cloves

1½ tablespoons olive oil

¼ teaspoon salt

¼ teaspoon freshly ground black pepper

3 small shallots

1½ cups loosely packed fresh parsley leaves

4–5 slices firm white bread (about 4 ounces), processed to crumbs in a food processor (2 cups)

Preheat the oven to 425 degrees.

Make 12 small randomly placed incisions about ½ inch deep on both sides of the leg of lamb, and insert a garlic sliver in each incision. Rub the leg with ½ tablespoon of the oil. Combine the salt and pepper and sprinkle on the lamb.

Place the leg top side down in a roasting pan and roast for 20 minutes.

Meanwhile, process the peeled garlic, shallots, and parsley in a food processor until finely chopped. Put the bread crumbs in a bowl and gently stir in the garlic mixture and the remaining tablespoon of oil, mixing just enough to moisten the crumbs. (Don't overmix; the mixture should be loose, not gooey or lumpy.)

Turn the leg of lamb over and pat the bread crumb mixture on top. Reduce the oven temperature to 400 degrees and cook the lamb for another 30 minutes, or until it reaches an internal temperature of about 130 degrees. Let rest in a warm place (on top of the stove or in a 150-degree oven) for 20 minutes before carving.

Braised Leg of Lamb
Serves 8

Although I usually serve leg of lamb medium-rare, I occasionally enjoy it braised until well-done, as here. Flavored with an anchovy-garlic mixture, the lamb is browned and then cooked slowly on top of the stove in a covered Dutch oven until fork-tender.

1 boneless leg of lamb (about 3½ pounds), as lean as possible

5–6 garlic cloves, crushed and chopped (1 tablespoon)

4 anchovy fillets, coarsely chopped

1 teaspoon herbes de Provence

½ teaspoon salt

1 tablespoon olive oil

2 onions (12 ounces), cut into 1-inch pieces (2 cups)

½ cup water

1 tablespoon chopped fresh chives

If the leg is rolled and tied, cut the string and unroll it; if it is not rolled, lay it as flat as possible. Trim off most of the fat and sinews. (The trimmed weight should be about 3 pounds.)

Combine the garlic, anchovies, and herbes de Provence in a small bowl and spread the mixture on what will be the interior of the lamb after you roll it. Roll it up and tie it securely with kitchen twine. Sprinkle with the salt.

Heat the oil in a cast-iron Dutch oven or similar heavy pot with a tight lid. When the oil is hot, add the lamb and brown it over medium heat, partially covered (to prevent splattering), for about 20 minutes, turning the meat occasionally with tongs so it browns evenly on all sides. Place the lamb on a plate and discard the fat from the pot.

Return the roast to the pot, add the onions

and water, and bring to a boil. Cover the pot, reduce the heat to very low, and cook the lamb for about 3 hours.

Carefully pour the cooking liquid from around the lamb into a measuring cup. (You should have about 2 cups.) Let the liquid stand for a few minutes, then scoop off as much fat as possible from the top (about ⅓ cup). Return the remaining liquid to the pot containing the roast and rewarm to serve as a sauce with the meat.

Cut the meat into slices and arrange on a warm platter. Pour the sauce around and over the meat, sprinkle the chives on top, and serve.

Grilled or Broiled Leg of Lamb
Serves 4

✂ **Boneless split leg of** lamb is usually easy to find at the market and it often comes in a net, ready for the oven. I take it out of the mesh, trim off most of the fat, and marinate it for at least 2 hours, or overnight, before grilling. Split where the bone has been removed, the boneless leg is flat. (It is not butterflied, which would entail cutting into the top round and opening it.) The pungent marinade of sweet, sour, and hot ingredients lends wonderful flavor to the lamb.

If you don't have a grill, you can cook the meat under your oven broiler. After grilling or broiling it, transfer the lamb to a warm oven to finish cooking in its own residual heat.

MARINADE

⅓	cup loosely packed fresh mint leaves
½	small jalapeño pepper, halved and seeds removed
1	piece ginger (about the size of a large olive), peeled
2	garlic cloves

2	tablespoons apricot jam
1	tablespoon dark soy sauce
3	tablespoons water
1	piece boneless lamb from the back leg (about 1½ pounds), trimmed of most visible fat

FOR THE MARINADE: Put all the ingredients in a blender or a mini-chop and process until liquefied. Transfer to a resealable plastic bag.

Place the lamb in the bag with the marinade and seal. Refrigerate for at least 2 hours, or overnight, to allow the meat to marinate in the seasonings, turning the bag occasionally.

When ready to cook, heat a grill until hot or preheat the broiler. Preheat the oven to 170 degrees.

Remove the lamb from the bag (reserve the marinade) and dry it off with paper towels. Grill the lamb over high heat for about 7 minutes on each side. Or place under the broiler (not too close to the heating element — about in the middle of the oven) and broil for 6 to 7 minutes on each side. Transfer the meat to a roasting pan. Bring the reserved marinade to a boil, then pour it around the meat and place it in the oven for at least 15 minutes to finish cooking.

Slice and serve with some of the juices.

Lamb Breast Lyonnaise
Serves 3 to 4

✂ **Lamb breast is a** fatty cut and is always braised until well-done, so the fat melts away. The stuffing mixture here — ground beef, egg, onion, and bread crumbs — is similar to a meat loaf, and an earthy gravy with onions and garlic is a nice counterpoint.

1 untrimmed lamb breast (about 1¾ pounds)

STUFFING

6 ounces ground beef
1 large egg
½ cup chopped onion
2 garlic cloves, crushed and finely chopped (about 1 teaspoon)
¼ cup chopped fresh chives
¼ cup chopped fresh parsley
1 teaspoon dried thyme
½ teaspoon salt
½ teaspoon freshly ground black pepper
2–2½ slices stale baguette (about 2 ounces), processed to crumbs in a food processor (1 cup)

1½ cups water
12 ounces onions (about 4), thinly sliced
About 20 garlic cloves
½ cup dry white wine
½ teaspoon salt

Place the breast flat on the work surface and cut into it with a knife directly between the meat and the ribs to create a pocket.

FOR THE STUFFING: Mix all the ingredients in a bowl. Stuff the breast, pushing the stuffing into the pocket. Don't worry if some of the stuffing is still visible; it will not leak out.

Put the meat fat side down in a large saucepan and brown over medium heat for about 5 minutes. Add ½ cup of the water, cover, reduce the heat to low, and cook slowly for 45 minutes, until the water is evaporated. Discard all the fat that has accumulated in the pan.

Add the onions and garlic to the pan and cook, uncovered, for about 5 minutes over medium heat.

Add the remaining 1 cup water, the wine, and salt, cover, and cook for about 40 minutes over low heat; the meat should be moist and tender.

Slice the meat between the ribs and serve with the natural gravy, onion, and garlic mixture.

Lamb Navarin
Serves 6

A *navarin* is a classic lamb stew, and there are many variations. For a tasty peasant-like dish, I make mine the way my mother used to, with an unboned lamb breast cut into strips. You can make the *navarin* ahead of time up to the point of adding the peas, which should be stirred in at the last moment when the dish is reheated so they don't lose their bright color.

2–3 lamb breasts (about 3 pounds total), most of the fat trimmed off
2 tablespoons all-purpose flour
1 large onion, cut into 1-inch dice (about 1½ cups)
1½ pounds potatoes, peeled and cut into 2-inch chunks
12 ounces carrots, peeled and cut into 2-inch lengths
8 garlic cloves, thinly sliced (about 3 tablespoons)
3 cups water
1½ teaspoons salt
¾ teaspoon freshly ground black pepper
1 teaspoon herbes de Provence or Italian seasoning
1 10-ounce package frozen baby peas
2 tablespoons chopped fresh parsley

Cut the lamb breasts between the rib bones into strips about 1½ inches wide. (You should have about 14 pieces.)

Place the lamb, preferably in one layer, in a large Dutch oven or other heavy pot and cook, partially covered, over medium heat, turning occasionally, for 15 minutes, or until the meat has released most of its fat and is nicely browned on all sides. Remove the lamb to a plate and discard the fat. (There may be up to 1 cup of fat.)

Return the meat to the pot, sprinkle it with the flour, and mix well. Add the onion, potatoes, carrots, garlic, water, salt, pepper, and herbs, mix well, and bring to a boil. Cover, reduce the heat to low, and cook for 45 minutes. (*The navarin can be prepared to this point a few hours ahead. Let cool and refrigerate, then bring to a simmer before finishing the dish.*)

Add the peas and cook, covered, for 5 minutes.

To serve, spoon the *navarin* onto six individual plates and sprinkle with the parsley.

Irish Lamb Stew
Serves 4 to 6

❧ **For this flavorful, hearty** stew, I cook the potatoes, carrots, and celery separately in water and don't add them until the end, so they retain their flavor. The vegetable-flavored water is used to cook the lamb, and the trimmings from the potatoes and celery are added to the stew. Pureed, they become the thickening agent for a gravy made from the natural juices.

1½	pounds potatoes, preferably small Yukon Golds
3	carrots (about 10 ounces)
3–4	celery stalks (about 5 ounces)
3	cups water
1½	pounds boneless leg of lamb, cut into 1½-inch cubes
2	medium onions (about 8 ounces), quartered
3	large garlic cloves
3	fresh thyme sprigs or 1 teaspoon dried thyme
2	bay leaves
1	teaspoon salt
½	teaspoon freshly ground black pepper
2	teaspoons Worcestershire sauce
1	tablespoon chopped fresh parsley
2	hard-cooked eggs (see page 66), quartered

Peel the potatoes and cut them into 18 pieces of about equal size. Round off the cut corners of each potato piece; reserve the trimmings. (You should have about 2 cups trimmings.) Peel the carrots and cut them into sticks 1¾ inches long by ½ inch thick. Trim the celery stalks (reserve the trimmings) and cut them into sticks 2 inches long by ½ inch thick.

Put the potatoes in a saucepan, add the water, and bring to a boil, then reduce the heat and boil gently, covered, for 12 minutes. Add the carrots and celery and bring back to a boil. Boil gently for 5 minutes. Drain, reserving the cooking liquid. (You should have about 2 cups liquid; adjust with water if needed.)

Put the lamb in a Dutch oven or other heavy pot with a tight lid and add the reserved cooking liquid and the potato and celery trimmings. Stir in the onions, garlic, thyme, bay leaves, salt, pepper, and Worcestershire sauce and bring to a boil. Reduce the heat, cover, and boil gently for 1 hour.

Remove the meat. Push the cooking juices and vegetable pieces through a food mill (or puree with a hand or regular blender) and return them to the pot. Add the meat, potatoes, celery, and carrots and bring to a boil. Reduce the heat and simmer for 5 minutes.

Sprinkle the stew with the parsley and serve with the quartered hard-cooked eggs.

Lamb Curry
Serves 6

🌾 **Lamb curry is an** excellent dish, and its heat can be adjusted by cutting down on the curry powder to suit individual preferences. I add apples and banana to this one. The fruit, in concert with curry, cumin, and allspice, makes for a stew that is both spicy and flavorful. It will keep for 5 or 6 days in the refrigerator, or it can be frozen.

Serve the curry with boiled rice, noodles, or potatoes.

1	tablespoon peanut oil
2¾	pounds boneless lamb leg, trimmed of surface fat and cut into 1½- to 2-inch pieces
2	cups water
1	large onion, coarsely chopped (1¼ cups)
2	medium apples, cored but not peeled and cut into ½-inch pieces (2½ cups)
1	banana, sliced
2	bay leaves
¼	cup curry powder, or to taste
1	teaspoon ground cumin
1	teaspoon ground allspice
1½	teaspoons salt
2	tablespoons tomato paste
2	tablespoons chopped fresh parsley

GARNISH

Chutney, ¼ cup raisins, and shredded coconut

Heat the oil in a Dutch oven or other heavy pot (enameled cast-iron is good). When it is hot, add the lamb (it will be in more than one layer) and cook over high heat, stirring occasionally, until the liquid that emerged from the lamb has evaporated and the lamb is sizzling nicely, 10 to 12 minutes.

Add all the remaining ingredients except the parsley (and garnishes) and mix well. Bring to a boil over high heat, then reduce the heat to very low, cover, and cook for 1½ hours, or until the meat is tender, stirring occasionally to prevent the mixture from sticking to the bottom of the pot. Remove and discard the bay leaves.

Sprinkle the curry with the parsley and serve. Pass the chutney, raisins, and shredded coconut.

Lamb Couscous
Serves 4

🌾 **Couscous is an important** dish of the Maghreb, the fertile strip of land in North Africa that includes Morocco, Algeria, and Tunisia. In Algeria, couscous has tomato; in Morocco, it contains saffron; and Tunisian couscous tends to be the spiciest. This is the best-known version, with lamb and vegetables — squash, eggplant, kohlrabi, carrots, tomatoes, and zucchini — and chickpeas.

When prepared with lamb or chicken, couscous is almost always served with the hot sauce called harissa, which is a puree of hot peppers. I make my own here. The recipe is easy and delicious, but harissa can also be purchased at some supermarkets and most specialty food stores. Some of the harissa is mixed with the broth created by the stew, and the remainder is served with the dish itself.

The harissa recipe makes about 1 cup, more than you will need for serving with the couscous. Refrigerate the remainder (it will keep for weeks), and serve it as a seasoning for stews, soups, or vegetable dishes. I always have some on hand.

2 ounces dried ancho chiles (6–8)

5 cups water

8 garlic cloves

2 tablespoons olive oil

1 tablespoon tomato paste

½ teaspoon salt

¼ teaspoon cayenne pepper

STEW

1½ pounds very lean boneless lamb, preferably from the shank or shoulder, cut into 1½-inch chunks

3 cups water

5 garlic cloves

1 piece ginger (about the size of the combined garlic cloves), peeled

2 teaspoons ground cumin

2 teaspoons salt

2 tablespoons tomato paste

2 tablespoons homemade or store-bought harissa, or to taste

1 large onion (8 ounces), sliced

8 ounces kohlrabi or large white turnips (about 2), peeled and cut into 1½-inch chunks

1 small butternut squash (about 12 ounces), halved, peeled, seeded, and cut into 1½-inch chunks

1 small eggplant (about 8 ounces), trimmed and cut into 1½-inch chunks

2 carrots (about 3 ounces), peeled and cut into 1½-inch chunks

1 ripe tomato (about 8 ounces), halved, seeded, and cut into 1-inch dice

1 medium zucchini (about 6 ounces), trimmed and cut into 1½-inch chunks

1 16-ounce can chickpeas

COUSCOUS

1¾ cups water

¼ teaspoon salt

¼ teaspoon freshly ground black pepper

2⅔ tablespoons (⅓ stick) unsalted butter

2 cups instant couscous

4 ounces (about ¾ cup) dried figs, cut into ½-inch pieces

Homemade or store-bought harissa, for serving

FOR THE OPTIONAL HARISSA: Drop the chiles into a bowl with the water. Set a plate on top to hold the chiles underwater and let them soak for at least 3 hours, or overnight.

Remove the chiles from the water; reserve ½ cup of the soaking water. Pull out and discard the stems and seeds and cut the chiles into 1-inch pieces. Place some of the chile pieces in a mini-chop or blender with some of the garlic, some of the oil, and a little of the reserved chile-soaking water and process until pureed. Remove to a bowl. Process (in batches if necessary) the remainder of the peppers with the remainder of the garlic, oil, and soaking liquid and combine with the puree in the bowl. Add the tomato paste, salt, and cayenne, mix well, and put in a jar.

FOR THE STEW: Put the lamb in a large Dutch oven or other heavy pot and add the water.

Puree the garlic cloves and ginger in a mini-chop or food processor (you should have about ¼ cup) and add to the Dutch oven, along with the cumin, salt, tomato paste, and 2 tablespoons harissa. Bring the mixture to a boil and boil gently, covered, for 45 minutes.

Add the onion, kohlrabi or turnips, butternut squash, eggplant, and carrots, return to a boil, and boil gently for 15 minutes. Add the tomato, zucchini, and chickpeas, with their liquid, return to a boil, and boil gently for 15 minutes longer. (*The stew can be made ahead and reheated before serving.*)

MEANWHILE, FOR THE COUSCOUS: Bring the water to a boil in a small saucepan and add the salt and pepper.

Melt the butter in a larger saucepan. Add the couscous and stir until the grains are coated with butter. Stir in the figs, then mix in the seasoned boiling water. Stir well, cover, and set aside for about 10 minutes.

At serving time, reheat the stew if necessary. Pour 1 cup of broth from the hot stew into a serving bowl and add about 3 tablespoons harissa (depending on the hotness you desire). Stir well and place the harissa on the table so guests can add it to the stew at their discretion.

Fluff the couscous and mound it on individual plates. Make a well in the center of each mound and fill with a few pieces of meat and vegetables and some of the juices. Serve.

Lamb Shanks with White Beans
Serves 4

❧ **This earthy stew is** always welcome at my house in colder weather, and I often make enough for more than one meal. If necessary, add a few tablespoons of water to moisten the mixture before reheating it. Lamb shanks are best here; they remain moist while lending wonderful flavor. They are quite lean and milder than other cuts.

8 ounces (about 1½ cups) dried small white or Great Northern beans, picked over and rinsed

5 cups water

4 bone-in lamb shanks (about 14 ounces each)

1 carrot (4 ounces), peeled and cut into ½-inch pieces (¾ cup)

1 large onion, cut into 1-inch pieces (1¼ cups)

5–6 garlic cloves, crushed and coarsely chopped (1½ tablespoons)

3 bay leaves

1 teaspoon dried thyme

1½ teaspoons salt

Tabasco sauce

Put the beans in a bowl and soak in the water while you brown the lamb shanks.

Remove most of the visible fat from the shanks. Put the shanks in one layer in a large heavy pot, preferably cast iron, and brown them, uncovered, over medium-high heat for about 30 minutes, turning occasionally, until browned on all sides. Transfer to a plate and discard any fat rendered by the meat, leaving only a solidified glaze in the pot.

Add the beans and water to the pot, along with the meat and all the remaining ingredients except the Tabasco. Bring to a boil, skim off the foam, then reduce the heat to low, cover, and boil gently for 2 hours. The meat should be moist and tender and there should be just enough liquid remaining in the pot for a moist, thick stew. If there is substantially more liquid than this, boil the stew, uncovered, for a few minutes to reduce it. Conversely, if there is too little liquid remaining, add a few tablespoons of water.

Serve 1 lamb shank per person, with a few generous spoonfuls of stew. Pass the Tabasco sauce.

Pork

Pork Chops with Mustard and Capers
Serves 6

✺ **Sharp Chinese chile sauce**, mustard, and capers are ideal with pork chops. You can make variations in the sauce, perhaps substituting hoisin sauce for the chile sauce. Mashed potatoes are the perfect accompaniment.

- 6 pork loin chops (8–10 ounces each), about 1 inch thick
- ½ teaspoon salt, or to taste
- ½ teaspoon freshly ground black pepper, or to taste
- 2 tablespoons unsalted butter
- 1 onion, finely chopped (about ½ cup)
- 2 teaspoons chopped garlic
- ½ cup dry white wine (such as Soave)
- 1 tablespoon Chinese chile sauce
- 1 tablespoon Dijon mustard
- ½ cup Basic Brown Sauce (page 613)
- 2 tablespoons drained capers
- 2 tablespoons chopped fresh chives

Preheat the oven to 150 degrees.

Sprinkle the chops on both sides with the salt and pepper. Melt the butter in a large skillet. Add the pork chops, arranging them so that they don't overlap. Cook for about 5 minutes over medium heat. Turn the chops, cover, and cook for another 4 to 5 minutes. (Covering the meat at this stage allows it to absorb moisture and become tender.) Transfer the meat to an ovenproof serving platter and keep warm in the oven.

Pour out all but about 2 tablespoons of the fat in the skillet. Add the onion and garlic to the skillet and sauté for 1 to 2 minutes. Add the wine and boil until there are only 2 to 3 tablespoons liquid left. Add the chile sauce, mustard, and brown sauce, bring to a boil, reduce the heat, and simmer for 1 minute. Taste for seasonings (you might have to add salt and pepper). Add the capers.

Pour the sauce over the meat, sprinkle with the chives, and serve.

Grilled Thyme Pork Chops
Serves 6

✺ **These pork chops are** cooked on a grill, but you can also make them on top of the stove. Put the seasoned pork chops in a very hot heavy skillet — cast iron or heavy aluminum is best — and cook for the same time as on the grill.

- 6 pork loin or rib chops (about 8 ounces each and 1 inch thick), as lean as possible
- ½ teaspoon salt
- ½ teaspoon freshly ground black pepper
- 1 teaspoon dried thyme
- 2 tablespoons olive oil

Heat a grill until very hot.

Trim most of the fat from the pork chops. Sprinkle them with the salt, pepper, and thyme and coat with the oil.

Arrange the chops on the hot grill, cover, and cook for about 4 minutes on each side. (If your grill doesn't have a lid, cook the chops for a minute longer on each side.) Let rest in a warm place (like a 150-degree oven) for 5 to 10 minutes, so they continue to cook in their own heat and will be uniformly juicy throughout, then serve.

Pork Loin Tournedos with Cream and Calvados
Serves 6

❧ **In this rich dish,** the pan juices that result from browning boneless pork steaks, or tournedos, are deglazed with apple brandy and the sauce is finished with heavy cream. The tournedos are garnished with prunes.

12	ounces large pitted prunes
1	tablespoon peanut oil
6	boneless pork loin steaks (about 10 ounces each)
1	teaspoon salt, or to taste
1	teaspoon freshly ground black pepper, or to taste
2	tablespoons chopped shallots or scallions
2	tablespoons Calvados or applejack
½	cup homemade chicken stock (page 612) or low-salt canned chicken broth, or as needed
¾	cup heavy cream
1	teaspoon potato starch (see page 318), dissolved in 1 tablespoon water
1	tablespoon grated lemon rind

Put the prunes in a saucepan, cover with cold water, and bring to a boil. Take off the heat, cover, and allow to cool in the cooking liquid.

Preheat the oven to 150 degrees.

Heat the oil in a large heavy skillet. Sprinkle the steaks on both sides with the salt and pepper and cook over medium-high heat for 5 minutes on each side. Place on a platter and keep warm in the oven.

Add the shallots or scallions to the pan and cook for 1 minute. Add the Calvados or applejack and stock and bring to a boil. Add the cream, bring to a boil, and cook for 1 minute. Stir in the dissolved potato starch and bring to a boil. If the sauce seems too thick, add a little more chicken stock to thin it; if it is too thin, reduce it for a few more minutes. Taste for seasoning and add salt and pepper if needed. Stir in the lemon rind and strain the sauce through a fine sieve.

Place a pork steak on each of six plates and top each steak with 2 prunes. Arrange the remaining prunes around the meat, coat generously with the sauce, and serve.

Pork Tenderloin Medallions in Port
Serves 4

❧ **Pork tenderloin is tender** and moist, yet it contains about as little fat and cholesterol as chicken. Here I cut it into small steaks, or filets mignons, briefly sauté them, and serve them with a port wine sauce flavored with sage.

1	large pork tenderloin, trimmed of all visible fat and silver skin (about 1¼ pounds trimmed)
1	tablespoon unsalted butter
1	tablespoon olive oil
¼	teaspoon salt
¼	teaspoon freshly ground black pepper
⅓	cup port
½	cup homemade chicken stock (page 612) or low-salt canned chicken broth
1½	tablespoons ketchup
1	teaspoon chopped fresh sage

Preheat the oven to 150 degrees.

Cut the tenderloin crosswise into 8 small steaks about 1¼ inches thick.

Heat the butter and oil in a large skillet. Meanwhile, sprinkle the steaks with the salt and pepper. When the butter and oil are hot, arrange the steaks in one layer in the pan and cook over high heat for 2½ minutes on each side. Transfer the steaks to a gratin dish and place them in the oven to keep warm while you make the sauce.

Add the port to the drippings in the pan, bring to a boil over high heat, and cook for about 1 minute. Add the chicken stock and ketchup and cook for 2 to 3 minutes. (The sauce should not be too thick.) Add the sage and mix well.

Place 2 small pork steaks on each of four plates, spoon the sauce around them, and serve.

Grilled Marinated Pork Tenderloin
Serves 4

⅗ **Pork tenderloin is marinated** in honey, jalapeño pepper, and *nuoc mam,* or Vietnamese fish sauce, then grilled.

MARINADE

- 1 small piece ginger, peeled and cut into ½-inch pieces (1½ teaspoons)
- 1 garlic clove
- 1 tablespoon honey
- 1 piece jalapeño pepper (size depending on your tolerance for hotness)
- 2 tablespoons *nuoc mam* (Vietnamese fish sauce)
- 3 tablespoons water

- 1 large pork tenderloin (about 1½ pounds), trimmed of all fat and silver skin (about 1 pound 2 ounces trimmed)
- 1 teaspoon canola oil

FOR THE MARINADE: Combine all the ingredients in a food processor and process until pureed. Pour the marinade into a resealable plastic bag, add the pork, and seal the bag. Shake it until the meat is well coated with the marinade. Refrigerate for at least 2 hours, and up to 8 hours.

When you are ready to cook, heat a grill until hot. Preheat the oven to 150 degrees.

Remove the pork from the marinade and pour the marinade into a skillet. Bring to a boil and set aside. Sprinkle the pork with the oil and place it on the hot grill. Cook, covered, for about 6 minutes, then turn the pork over and cook, covered, for 6 minutes on the second side, or until the meat is nicely grilled on all sides.

Return the meat to the marinade and rest it in the oven for at least 10 minutes. (*The meat can be kept in the oven for up to 40 minutes.*)

At serving time, slice the tenderloin and serve it with some of the juices.

Grilled Pork Tenderloin Paillards with Rosemary
Serves 4

⅗ *Paillard* **is the French** name for thin pieces of meat — beef, veal, or pork — that are grilled or sautéed. Lightly seasoned and coated with oil, the *paillards* are seared on a hot grill, then transferred to a warm oven, where they relax and finish cooking in their own heat.

- 1 large pork tenderloin (about 1½ pounds), trimmed of all fat and silver skin (about 1 pound 2 ounces trimmed)
- 3 tablespoons fresh rosemary leaves
- ½ teaspoon salt
- ¼ teaspoon black peppercorns
- 1 tablespoon corn or canola oil

Heat a grill until very hot. Preheat the oven to 150 degrees.

Cut the tenderloin crosswise in half, then split

the halves lengthwise. Pound each piece between sheets of plastic wrap to about ½ inch thick.

Pulverize the rosemary leaves, salt, and peppercorns in a mini-chop or spice grinder. Sprinkle the pork with the seasoning mixture.

Pour the oil onto a plate and dip both sides of the *paillards* in the oil. (*The recipe can be prepared ahead to this point; stack the pieces of pork on the plate, cover with plastic wrap, and refrigerate for up to 8 hours.*)

Place the *paillards* on the grill and cook for about 1½ minutes on each side; the meat should be slightly undercooked at this point. Arrange the pork on an ovenproof serving platter and place it, uncovered, in the warm oven for a few minutes, or until ready to serve.

Serve the pork with the juices that have collected on the platter.

Slow-Cooked Pork Roast
Serves 6

❧ **Some cuts of pork,** such as the loin and tenderloin, are lean and very low in cholesterol and fat. This sirloin roast, from the end of the loin where it attaches to the tenderloin, or fillet, is so lean that it would be dry if cooked in a conventional manner.

MARINADE

2	tablespoons dark soy sauce
1	tablespoon honey
½	teaspoon dry mustard
½	teaspoon ground ginger
1	teaspoon ground cumin
¼	teaspoon cayenne pepper
1	tablespoon canola oil

1	pork sirloin roast (about 2 pounds), trimmed of all surface fat

Preheat the oven to 275 degrees.

FOR THE MARINADE: Mix all the ingredients together in a small bowl.

Place the roast in a roasting pan and rub it on all sides with the marinade. Roast for about 3 hours, turning the meat in the juices every 45 minutes and adding a few tablespoons of water to the pan if a little additional moisture is needed. When the roast reaches an internal temperature of about 150 degrees, remove it to a carving board. Add enough water to the pan to create about ½ cup juices and stir to melt the solidified juices.

Cut the roast into ¼-inch-thick slices and serve about 3 slices per person, with a generous spoonful of the juices.

Braised Pork with Chestnuts
Serves 8 to 10

❧ **My aunt made a** dish similar to this one when I was a child. The chestnuts and rutabagas combine with the richness of the pork shoulder to make it memorable.

When chestnuts are in season, they are available fresh in many markets. They can also be found peeled and bottled (dry) or frozen.

1	shoulder pork roast (about 6 pounds)
1	teaspoon salt, or to taste
½	teaspoon freshly ground black pepper, or to taste
6½	cups water
2	onions, thickly sliced (about 1½ cups)
1	pound peeled (see the sidebar, page 364) chestnuts (about 1½ pounds unpeeled)
3	rutabagas (also called yellow turnips; about 3 pounds)

Sprinkle the meat with the salt and pepper. Place fat side down in a large heavy saucepan, add ½ cup of the water, and bring barely to a boil over medium heat. Cook at a gentle boil, covered, for 15 minutes. Uncover the meat and cook until all the liquid has evaporated and the meat is starting to brown, then brown it all around, about 15 minutes.

Add the onions and 5 cups water, cover, and cook over medium heat for 1 hour. Add the chestnuts and cook, covered, for another hour.

Meanwhile, peel the rutabagas and cut them into 2- to 2½-inch chunks. Trim the pieces with a small knife so that they are equal in size and will cook uniformly. (You should have about 2½ pounds.)

Add the rutabagas and the remaining 1 cup water to the pan and cook, covered, for 45 minutes.

PORK AND POTATO HASH Serves 4

You can use leftover meat from any pork roast recipe to make this hash. If you have less than the amount called for here, add some ham or chicken, or add more potatoes. Hash is traditionally topped with a fried egg.

> 1¾ pounds all-purpose potatoes, peeled, cut into ¼-inch-thick slices, and rinsed in cold water
>
> 1½ cups water
>
> 2 medium onions (about 12 ounces), cut into ½-inch dice
>
> Juices left over from the pork roast (optional)
>
> 3–4 garlic cloves, crushed and chopped (about 1 tablespoon)
>
> ⅓ cup minced scallions (3–4)
>
> 3 tablespoons olive oil
>
> 2 teaspoons Worcestershire sauce
>
> ¼ teaspoon Tabasco sauce
>
> ¾ teaspoon salt
>
> About 1 pound leftover pork roast, cut into ½-inch dice (about 2½ cups)
>
> 4 fried eggs (optional)

Combine the potatoes, water, onions, and any juices left over from the pork roast in a 12-inch nonstick skillet (or two smaller nonstick skillets), bring to a boil, cover, and boil over medium heat for 10 minutes.

Add the garlic, scallions, olive oil, Worcestershire sauce, Tabasco, salt, and pork, mix well, and cook, uncovered, over high heat, stirring, for 5 minutes. Most of the moisture will have evaporated and the mixture should be starting to sizzle. Since the hash will begin to stick at this point, use a flat wooden spatula to scrape up the crusty bits sticking to the bottom of the pan(s) and stir them into the rest of the mixture. Continue to cook over medium heat for about 20 minutes, stirring every 3 to 4 minutes at first; the mixture will brown faster in the last 10 minutes of cooking and should be stirred every 2 to 3 minutes then.

At the end of the cooking time, the moisture will have evaporated and the hash will no longer be sticking to the pan(s). Press down on the hash to make it hold together and then fold the solid mass into an oval omelet shape.

Invert onto a large platter and serve as is, or with the fried eggs on top.

By this time, there should not be much liquid left. Taste for seasonings; it probably will need salt and pepper. Remove the roast to a serving platter. Using a slotted spoon, scoop out the chestnuts and rutabagas and arrange them around the meat.

Tip the pan to one side so that all the juices accumulate in one corner and skim off as much fat as you can. If you have less than 1 cup of juices left, add some water and boil over high heat for 1 to 2 minutes to melt the solidified juices and emulsify the juices. Slice the meat and arrange in a platter.

Pour the sauce over the meat, or into a sauceboat, and serve.

PEELING CHESTNUTS

When buying chestnuts, avoid those with little holes, which indicate worms. With the point of a sharp paring knife, score each chestnut on both sides to help the skin release during cooking. Spread on a cookie sheet and roast in a preheated 400-degree oven for 15 minutes. Remove from the oven and, using a towel to avoid burning your hands, peel the chestnuts. Both the inner and outer skins should come off. Discard any bad ones; you may lose up to one third of the chestnuts.

Braised Pork Loin
Serves 6

✸ **Choose a roast from** the loin on the side of the shoulder. It tends to be a bit fattier, but it becomes moist and tender when cooked. The ginger, jalapeño, and dried tomato make a rich and pungent sauce that goes well with the pork.

> 1 pork loin roast (about 2 pounds), trimmed of most surface fat
> 4 garlic cloves, cut lengthwise in half

> ½ teaspoon salt
> ¼ teaspoon freshly ground black pepper
> 1 tablespoon olive oil
> 1 large or 2 medium onions (8 ounces), quartered
> 3 carrots (8 ounces), peeled and cut into 1-inch pieces
> 1 tablespoon chopped ginger
> 1 tablespoon chopped jalapeño pepper
> ½ cup sun-dried tomatoes, soaked in 1 cup warm water until soft

Make 8 random shallow slits in the pork roast. Push half a garlic clove into each slit. Sprinkle the roast with the salt and pepper.

Heat the oil in a round or oval Dutch oven or a large heavy saucepan. When the oil is hot, add the pork and cook over high heat for 10 minutes, turning the meat to brown it on all sides. Discard the fat in the pot.

Add the onions, carrots, ginger, jalapeño, and tomatoes, including the soaking water, cover, reduce the heat to very low, and cook for about 1½ hours. The meat should be tender when pierced with a fork and there should still be some juices surrounding it.

Slice the roast and serve 2 slices of pork per person, with the vegetables and juices.

Braised Pork Roast with Sweet Potatoes
Serves 6

✸ **This braised pork merges** three cultural influences on my cooking. It is highly seasoned in the manner of Puerto Rico (my wife's heritage), with soy, Tabasco, honey, and cumin. It demonstrates classical French techniques, and it uses sweet potatoes, which I had never tasted before coming to the United States.

The pork shoulder butt is inexpensive, tender, and moister than a center-cut roast.

1 boneless pork shoulder butt (Boston) roast (about 3 pounds)
2 cups water
2 tablespoons dark soy sauce
½ teaspoon Tabasco sauce
2 tablespoons red wine vinegar or cider vinegar
2 tablespoons honey
1 teaspoon ground cumin
2 pounds sweet potatoes (about 4)
1 pound onions (about 2 large)
6 large garlic cloves

Place the pork roast in a Dutch oven or cast-iron or enameled casserole with a lid. Add the water, soy sauce, Tabasco, vinegar, honey, and cumin and bring to a boil, then reduce the heat to very low and boil gently, covered, for 1 hour.

Meanwhile, peel the sweet potatoes and cut into 1½-inch-thick slices. Cut each onion into 4 to 6 wedges, depending on their size.

After the pork has cooked for 1 hour, add the sweet potatoes, onions, and garlic, bring back to a boil, and boil gently, covered, for about 15 minutes.

Preheat the oven to 375 degrees.

Uncover the pot, place it in the center of the oven, and cook for 45 minutes, turning the meat in the juices every 15 minutes. At the end of the cooking period, the juices should be dark and concentrated, the meat tender when pierced with a fork, and the vegetables very soft.

Serve directly from the pot, cutting the meat at the table.

Smoked Pork Roast with Mustard-Honey Glaze
Serves 10

❧ **Smoked pork shoulders, often** called picnic hams, are available at most supermarkets. To enhance the taste of this "fully cooked" cut, simmer it gently in water for an hour or so; the water draws salt from the meat and makes it less salty and substantially more moist and flavorful. Take care that the water doesn't exceed 180 degrees, however, or the ham may split open and lose moisture. This step can and should be done the day before.

Served with Braised Sweet-and-Sour Red Cabbage (page 417) and a simple salad, this glazed pork roast makes a wonderful party menu.

1 bone-in smoked pork picnic shoulder (about 6¼ pounds)

GLAZE

2 tablespoons honey
2 teaspoons dry mustard
½ teaspoon paprika
⅛ teaspoon cayenne pepper

½ cup water
1 tablespoon cider vinegar

Place the pork shoulder in a stockpot and cover it with enough cold water to come ½ inch above the meat. Bring the water to 170 to 180 degrees (this will take about 15 minutes) and simmer gently for 1¼ hours. (Watch the temperature closely; the liquid should not boil.) Let the pork cool in the cooking liquid, then cover and refrigerate overnight.

Preheat the oven to 375 degrees.

FOR THE GLAZE: Mix all ingredients together in a small bowl. Set aside.

Drain the pork and trim it, removing most of

the exterior fat and the rind from around the bones. Also trim the dark and leathery surface of the meat. Score the top every ¾ inch in a crosshatch pattern and spread the glaze over the surface.

Place the pork in a roasting pan and roast for 1 hour; the surface should be nicely browned. Transfer the meat to a serving platter.

Add the water and vinegar to the drippings in the pan. Using a wooden spatula, scrape the bottom of the pan to dissolve the solidified cooking juices.

Strain the juices over the pork shoulder and serve, slicing it at the table.

Ham with Madeira Sauce
Serves 12 to 15

✃ **A fully cooked ham** improves greatly when simmered gently in water for a few hours; this step should be done the day before. It is served with a Madeira sauce and can be carved in the dining room or kitchen. Braised turnips and sautéed fresh peaches are excellent with it.

  1 fully cooked bone-in ham with skin (about 12 pounds)
  2 tablespoons light brown sugar
  1 cup water
  ¾ cup dry Madeira or dry sherry
  2 cups Basic Brown Sauce (page 613)
     Salt and freshly ground black pepper if necessary

Put the ham in a large pot and cover with cold water. Bring to 170 to 180 degrees and cook slowly for about 2½ hours. There is a small bone parallel to the big bone of the shank; when the ham is ready, the bone should come out when pulled. Let the ham cool in the liquid, then cover and refrigerate overnight.

Preheat the oven to 450 degrees.

Remove the ham from the water. Trim the skin and fat, leaving just a thin layer of fat about ¼ inch thick. Trim around the bone near the shank so 2½ to 3 inches of the bone sticks out. Remove the flat hipbone on the bottom side of the ham, opposite the shank.

Place the ham fat side up in a roasting pan. Sprinkle the ham with the brown sugar and pour the 1 cup water around it. Bake for 35 to 45 minutes, until the top is nicely glazed and brown.

Meanwhile, combine the Madeira or sherry and brown sauce in a saucepan, bring to a boil, and boil gently for 10 minutes. Set aside.

Transfer the baked ham to a carving board. Skim off the fat in the roasting pan. Pour the Madeira sauce into the pan and scrape the bottom of the pan with a wooden spatula to melt all the solidified juices. Strain the sauce and add salt and pepper if needed.

Carve the ham and serve 1 or 2 slices per person, with the sauce spooned over and around the meat.

Choucroute Garni
Serves 8 to 10

✃ **Choucroute garnie is the** traditional dish of Alsace, the part of France near the German border. For the "garnishes," an array of sausages are always served with it, as well as what we call in French *petit salé*, spareribs that are cured in brine. Curing the ribs in salt and brown sugar heightens their taste tremendously and is worth the extra effort. Goose, duck, or lamb are also good with the sauerkraut.

Enjoy the choucroute with beer or Alsatian white wine. A simple green salad can be served before or after the meal, and the best dessert is fruit.

1   slab country-style pork spareribs (about 3 pounds; 12–14 ribs, about 15 inches by 7 inches)

½   cup kosher salt or curing salt, preferably Morton Tender Quick

2   tablespoons light brown sugar

6   pounds sauerkraut (three 2-pound packages)

¼   cup duck or goose fat, lard, or peanut oil

2   cups coarsely chopped onions

1½   tablespoons coarsely chopped garlic About 20 juniper berries

3   large bay leaves

½   teaspoon caraway seeds

1   teaspoon salt

1   teaspoon freshly ground black pepper

3   cups homemade chicken stock (page 612) or low-salt canned chicken broth

1½   cups fruity dry white wine (such as Alsace Sylvaner, Riesling, or Pinot Gris)

GARNISHES

2   pounds medium potatoes (about 10), peeled

1   piece thick Polish kielbasa (about 2 pounds and 1½ inches in diameter), cut into ten 2-inch pieces and skinned

10   skinless frankfurters (all beef or mixed pork and beef)

1   piece boiled ham (about 2 pounds and 3 by 4 inches in diameter), trimmed of surface fat and cut into ¼-inch-thick slices (about 1½–2 ounces each)

Assorted mustards: hot Dijon, coarse Pommery, tarragon, and sweet honey mustard

Cutting from the back side, cut the slab of spareribs crosswise in half. Put both halves in a re-

sealable plastic bag with the salt and brown sugar, shake well, and close the bag tightly. Refrigerate for 24 hours.

When ready to continue, remove the ribs from the bag and rinse briefly under cold running water. Discard the brine.

Drain the sauerkraut and put it in a large bowl. Cover with plenty of cold water and stir the sauerkraut in the water to rinse it. Pour into a colander and press handfuls of the sauerkraut between your palms (as though you were making a snowball) to remove excess water.

Preheat the oven to 300 degrees.

Heat the duck or other fat in a large heavy pot (such as a Le Creuset enameled cast-iron pot). Add the onions and garlic and cook gently for 5 minutes, without letting them brown. Add the sauerkraut, juniper berries, bay leaves, caraway seeds, salt, pepper, stock, and wine and bring to a strong boil, stirring occasionally (this will take at least 10 to 12 minutes). Embed the rib pieces in the sauerkraut, cover, and cook for another 3 to 5 minutes, until the mixture is boiling again throughout.

Cover the pot tightly, place in the oven, and cook for 1½ hours. Transfer the slabs of ribs to a carving board, let cool slightly, and cut into individual ribs. Return to the pot. Cool, cover, and refrigerate if desired. (*The recipe can be prepared up to a day ahead to this point.*)

FOR THE GARNISHES: When ready to serve, boil the potatoes in salted water to cover for about 40 minutes, or until tender; drain and keep warm.

Reheat the sauerkraut and ribs, then add the kielbasa pieces and heat for about 5 minutes. Add the frankfurters and cook for 5 minutes, then add the ham slices and cook for 4 to 5 minutes longer, until everything is hot.

Serve the choucroute on very hot plates. Pile some sauerkraut in the center of each plate, push some ribs and kielbasa partially into the sauerkraut, and arrange a frankfurter, some ham, and some potatoes around the sauerkraut. (Alternatively, serve the sauerkraut and garnishes on a large platter and let the guests help themselves.)

Serve with an assortment of mustards.

Puerto Rican Pork and Beans
Serves 4

My wife, Gloria, often prepares this dinner when we have guests. A satisfying one-dish meal, it can be cooked ahead and refrigerated or frozen, and it is even better reheated.

Buy the meatiest, leanest country-style spareribs you can find. The cilantro stems are cooked with the beans to give them an unusual and definitive flavor, and then the leaves are added at the end. If you don't like the taste of cilantro, you can omit it.

Serve with boiled rice and Tabasco.

1 tablespoon canola oil
4 country-style pork loin spareribs (about 1½ pounds)
4 cups cold water
1 medium carrot, peeled and cut into ½-inch cubes (about ½ cup)
2 medium onions (about 10 ounces), cut into ½-inch cubes (2 cups)
6 garlic cloves, crushed and chopped (about 1 tablespoon)
3 bay leaves
1 teaspoon dried oregano
1 16-ounce can whole tomatoes
1 small jalapeño pepper, chopped (about 2 teaspoons), or more if you like
2 teaspoons salt

¾ pound dried red kidney beans, picked over and rinsed
1 bunch cilantro, stems and leaves chopped separately (⅓ cup chopped stems, 3 tablespoons chopped leaves)
Tabasco sauce

Heat the oil in a large heavy saucepan. When it is hot, add the pork in one layer and brown over high heat for about 15 minutes, turning it occasionally, until it is brown on all sides.

Add all the remaining ingredients except the cilantro leaves and Tabasco. Bring to a boil, skim off the foam, then reduce the heat to low, cover, and simmer gently for 2 to 2½ hours, until the meat is tender and the beans are soft.

Divide among four individual plates, sprinkle with the chopped cilantro leaves, and serve with Tabasco.

Sausage and Potato Ragout
Serves 6

A light roux made from the sausage drippings gives smoothness and body to this ragout. Cut the onions into large chunks so they don't disintegrate. At the end of cooking, remove the lid of the pot if necessary to evaporate just enough of the liquid to create a light, creamy sauce. The ragout is delicious with a dollop of spicy mustard and a garlicky salad.

I use hot Italian sausage meat, but you can make your own sausage if you like. Grind 1½ pounds of pork shoulder, or buy ground pork. Season it to your liking with salt, black pepper, cayenne pepper, red wine, and fennel or anise seeds, and form it into 2 dozen plum-sized balls.

1½ pounds bulk hot Italian sausage or
    homemade sausage (see the headnote)
1½ tablespoons all-purpose flour
2 cups water
2½ pounds fingerling potatoes, peeled
4 medium onions, cut into 2-inch pieces
    (3 cups)
5 garlic cloves, thinly sliced
3 bay leaves
1 teaspoon dried thyme
½ jalapeño pepper, chopped, or more to
    taste (optional)
¾ teaspoon salt
¼ teaspoon freshly ground black pepper
2 tablespoons chopped fresh parsley

Form the sausage meat into 24 balls. Arrange them in one layer in a large saucepan, add ½ cup water, and bring to a boil, then cover and cook over medium heat for about 8 minutes. Uncover and cook over high heat for 1 to 2 minutes, until the water has evaporated and the sausages are sizzling in their own fat. Transfer the sausage balls to a plate.

Add the flour to the drippings, stir well, and cook for about 1 minute, until the flour browns lightly in the fat. Add the 2 cups water, stir well, and bring to a boil. Add the sausage balls and the remaining ingredients except the parsley and bring to a boil. Cover, reduce the heat to low, and continue cooking for about 45 minutes. There should be just enough liquid remaining in the pan to moisten the potatoes; if necessary, continue cooking, uncovered, over high heat for 2 to 3 minutes to reduce the liquid and create a creamy sauce.

Sprinkle with the parsley and serve.

Mixed Sausages and Potatoes
Serves 6

✖ **This is one of** those meals that evoke happy memories, because my mother used to make it all the time when I was growing up. I put in kielbasa, knockwurst, and bratwurst, but you can use andouille or Italian sausage as well. The sausages will impart their flavor, whether spicy, anise, or smoky, to the onions and potatoes. An assertive salad, such as Garlicky Romaine with Croutons (page 40), is particularly well suited to this dish.

3 tablespoons olive oil
1 pound kielbasa, cut into 3-inch pieces
1 pound knockwurst (about 6 sausages)
8 ounces bratwurst (about 3 sausages)
6 medium onions (1 pound)
2 pounds small Red Bliss potatoes
    (about 15), peeled
12 garlic cloves
    Salt if necessary

Heat the oil in a large skillet or saucepan until hot. Add all the sausages in one layer and cook, turning them occasionally, for 10 to 12 minutes, until they are brown all over. Remove to a plate and set aside.

Add the onions and potatoes to the fat and brown over medium-low heat, uncovered, for about 20 minutes.

Add the garlic and sausages and cook for another 20 minutes, covered, over very low heat. Taste for seasoning and add salt if necessary. Cut the bratwursts in half.

Serve the potatoes and sausages with a little bit of the natural juices.

Grilled Sausage Patties with Lentils
Serves 6

✎ **Highly seasoned with coriander,** cumin, and hot pepper, these sausage patties are wrapped in blanched savoy cabbage leaves so the meat stays juicy as it cooks. The lentils, which are cooked with seasonings and combined with a little olive oil, Tabasco, and mustard, can be served on their own as a first course or as an accompaniment to other meats.

If you don't have a grill, sauté 6 patties at a time in a nonstick skillet, cooking them in 2 teaspoons canola oil for about 5 minutes on each side.

Be sure to mix the sausage ingredients at least 2 hours and up to 1 day ahead so the seasonings can flavor the meat well.

SAUSAGE PATTIES

- 1¼ pounds ground pork
- 1½ teaspoons salt
- ¼ teaspoon freshly ground black pepper
- ¾ teaspoon fennel seeds
- ½ teaspoon ground coriander
- ½ teaspoon ground cumin
- ⅛ teaspoon cayenne pepper
- ⅛ teaspoon ground allspice
- ½ cup coarsely chopped mushrooms

LENTILS

- 1 pound lentils, picked over and rinsed
- 2 small onions, chopped (1 cup)
- 1½ tablespoons finely chopped garlic
- 2 bay leaves
- 1 teaspoon salt
- ¼ cup olive oil
- ½ teaspoon freshly ground black pepper
- 1 teaspoon Tabasco sauce
- 2 tablespoons Dijon mustard

CABBAGE

- 6 large outer savoy cabbage leaves

- 1 tablespoon canola oil for grilling
- 1 tablespoon chopped fresh parsley or cilantro

FOR THE SAUSAGE PATTIES: Thoroughly mix all the ingredients in a bowl. Refrigerate, covered, for at least 2 hours. (*You can prepare the meat up to a day ahead, but reserve the mushrooms, which might darken and discolor the mixture, then mix them in just before forming the mixture into patties.*)

FOR THE LENTILS: Combine the lentils, 3 cups water, the onions, garlic, bay leaves, and salt in a pot and bring to a boil. Skim off the foam, cover, reduce the heat, and boil gently for about 30 minutes. The lentils should be tender and a little wet; if an excess of liquid remains, drain it off. Add the oil, black pepper, Tabasco, and mustard and mix well. Set aside.

MEANWHILE, FOR THE CABBAGE: Bring 6 cups water to a boil in a large saucepan. Add the cabbage leaves and bring the water back to a boil. Cook the cabbage for 5 minutes, or until soft but still firm. Drain in a colander and cool under cold water.

Cut each leaf in half, cutting on either side of the center stem. Discard the stems (or add them to soup).

TO SHAPE AND GRILL THE PATTIES: Form the sausage mixture into 12 patties, about 1½ to 2 ounces each. Wrap each patty in a cabbage leaf half.

Heat a grill until hot. Brush the patties with the oil, place on the well-cleaned grill, and cook for about 5 minutes on each side.

To serve, divide the lentils among six plates and arrange 2 sausage patties on each plate. Sprinkle with the chopped parsley or cilantro and serve.

Charcuterie
and
Offal

Charcuterie and Offal

Charcuterie

Chicken Liver Mousse

Serves 12 to 14 as an hors d'oeuvre
(makes enough for about 60 toasts)

⚭ With an **extra-smooth, compact** texture, this rich mousse can be quickly prepared, but it does need at least 4 to 6 hours in the refrigerator to set up. Liver and onions are pureed in a food processor, and butter is gradually blended in (the word *mousse* means "foam" in French and refers to anything that is beaten or mixed to produce an emulsion and a light texture).

The optional scallion and tomato decoration and aspic glaze raise a fairly standard preparation to an elegant dish. The aspic sets the decoration, keeping it from curling and wilting, but you can decorate the mousse without glazing it if you serve it soon after it's decorated.

It's important to respect the proportion of fat to liver in this recipe, since excess liver will make the mousse bitter and grainy. If possible, choose pale yellow livers, which tend to have a mellow, rich taste and so are preferable to deep red ones.

Unlike most mousses and pâtés, which become watery and grainy when frozen, this one freezes perfectly. Cover tightly with plastic wrap and then aluminum foil before freezing. Small soufflé dishes are ideal for freezing because they can be defrosted in a couple of hours. If you use a large dish, you'll need to defrost it slowly under refrigeration for 24 hours before serving.

MOUSSE

- 1 pound chicken livers, trimmed of any sinew
- ⅔ cup thinly sliced onion
- 1 garlic clove, crushed
- 2 bay leaves, crushed
- ¼ teaspoon fresh thyme leaves
- 1 cup homemade chicken stock (page 612) or low-salt canned chicken broth
- 2 teaspoons salt
- ¾ pound (3 sticks) unsalted butter, softened
- ¾ teaspoon freshly ground black pepper
- 2 teaspoons cognac or scotch whiskey

DECORATION AND GLAZE (Optional)

- Green from 1 scallion
- A piece of tomato skin
- 1 envelope (about 2 teaspoons) gelatin

- Melba toast, store-bought or homemade (see the sidebar, page 374)

FOR THE MOUSSE: Put the livers, onion, garlic, bay leaves, thyme, stock, and 1 teaspoon of the salt in a saucepan. Bring to a boil, cover, reduce the heat, and cook at a bare simmer for about 3 minutes. Remove from the heat and let the mixture sit for about 10 minutes.

With a slotted spoon, transfer the solids to a food processor. (Strain the liquid through paper towels and reserve to make the aspic; you need about 1 cup.) Process the mixture for 30 seconds, then let it cool for 5 minutes.

With the motor running, add the butter piece by piece, blending well. Add the remaining teaspoon of salt, the pepper, and cognac or whiskey and process for another minute, or until the mixture is very creamy and smooth. Pour into a soufflé dish and refrigerate to set, for 4 to 6 hours, or as long as overnight. (Alternatively, divide the mousse among four or five ½-cup ramekins and freeze for future use.)

FOR THE OPTIONAL DECORATION AND GLAZE: Blanch the scallion green in boiling water for 10 to 15 seconds, until it wilts, then drain in a sieve and cool under cold water. (Blanching makes the green pliable and flattens it, and the cold water sets the color.)

Lay the scallion green on a work surface and pat dry with paper towels. Cut some strips from the green and arrange them around the edges of the mousse to make a "frame" for the flower decoration. Cut some thin, pointed strips to make stems. Use different sizes of leaves and shades of green: fold some of the larger "leaves," make others into long stems, and some into tiny lozenges. Use your imagination; there are no rules for this part. Arrange them on top of the mousse and set them by pressing on them with the tip of your fingers or the point of a knife.

Place a tiny bit of green at the end of each stem to make a calyx for the flower. Cut small pieces of tomato skin with jagged edges for flowers and place them at the ends of the stems. Use smaller trimmings to make wildflowers. Refrigerate the mousse while you prepare the aspic.

Combine the strained liquid from the liver and the gelatin in a saucepan and stir gently over low heat until the mixture almost comes to a boil and the gelatin is completely melted. Place the saucepan in a bowl of ice and stir until the liquid becomes very syrupy. The aspic should be shiny and glistening and about to set; this is the right moment to use it. If it becomes too firm, remelt it and cool again.

Pour and spread 3 or 4 tablespoons of aspic on top of the mousse; the layer of aspic should be approximately ¼ inch thick. The aspic gives the effect of a beautiful stained-glass window. Refrigerate until the aspic is set.

Serve with Melba toast.

Rillettes
Serves 12 as an hors d'oeuvre

✄ **A meat spread, made** most often with pork, rillettes is a favorite hors d'oeuvre in French country cooking. Although rillettes can be made from duck, goose, or rabbit, pork is always added to give it its characteristic smoothness. The spread is packed into small crocks and served very cold. It is excellent with Dijon mustard, crusty French bread, and cold dry white wine.

Like many other dishes, rillettes is good because of its simplicity. I have prepared it using wine, stock, or different seasonings, but it is never as good as in this simple recipe.

- 3 pounds boneless pork chuck or neck (you should have about 75% lean meat to 25% fat), cut into 2- to 3-inch cubes
- 1 tablespoon salt, or to taste
- ½ teaspoon freshly ground black pepper, or to taste

Put the meat in a large heavy saucepan, add the salt, pepper, and enough cold water to cover by 1 inch, and bring to a boil. Cover, reduce the heat, and simmer very slowly for about 5 hours, skimming the foam from the liquid every 20 minutes during the first hour of cooking. (You may have to add water during the cooking process because the fat will melt, and if the water evaporates too soon,

MELBA TOAST

Escoffier invented this thin toast for the famous opera singer Nellie Melba, as he did peach Melba.

Toast thin-sliced bread in the toaster. As soon as it comes out of the toaster, trim off the crusts. Slide your knife through the soft center area and separate the bread into 2 extremely thin slices. It is not necessary to toast the white side. Then cut in half or into quarters.

the fat will get hot and the meat will fry instead of poaching.)

After the poaching, practically all water should have evaporated, and the liquid will start to sizzle. Let it sizzle for about 30 minutes, to give a roasted taste to the meat. Transfer the meat and juices to a bowl and let cool, then refrigerate overnight.

The next day, crush the pieces of meat between your thumbs and fingers to separate the fibers (this is best done by hand, but you can use a stand mixer with a flat beater). Put all the meat and fat in a saucepan and heat over medium-low heat to melt the fat. Taste for seasonings: the mixture will probably need pepper and maybe salt; it should be slightly overseasoned, since the seasonings will be muted when the spread is cold. Let cool.

When the mixture has set, work it with a wooden spatula for a few seconds to make it fluffier. Pack into small crocks, smooth the tops with a spatula, and refrigerate; when cold, cover with plastic wrap. Well sealed, the small crocks will keep for a couple of weeks in the refrigerator; the rillettes can also be frozen.

Pork Liver Pâté
Serves 6 to 8 as a first course

⁊ **This is the standard** meat and liver pâté available in most supermarkets in France, as well as at small restaurants and bistros. A special curing salt gives the pâté its beautiful pink color and great taste. Customarily served cold with French mustard and cornichons, it makes a good first course for an evening meal or a light lunch with a salad and country bread. Serve with a robust red wine.

8 ounces pork liver, sinews removed, diced
2 pounds ground pork (about 70% lean and 30% fat; shoulder or Boston butt is good)
¾ cup dry white wine
2½ teaspoons curing salt, preferably Morton Tender Quick
1½ teaspoons freshly ground black pepper
¼ teaspoon dried thyme
1 garlic clove, crushed and very finely chopped
2 bay leaves

FOR SERVING

Cornichons (tiny French gherkins)
Dijon mustard

Preheat the oven to 325 degrees.

Drop the diced liver into a blender and blend for 35 to 50 seconds, or until smooth. Transfer to a large bowl.

Add the ground pork to the liver, then add the wine, curing salt, pepper, thyme, and garlic and mix thoroughly.

Spoon the meat mixture into a terrine measuring 8 to 10 inches long, 4 to 5 inches wide, and 4 to 6 inches deep. Arrange the bay leaves on top. Cover the terrine with aluminum foil, set it in a baking pan, and pour enough lukewarm water around it to come at least three quarters of the way up the sides of the terrine. Bake for 2½ hours, or until the pâté reaches an internal temperature of about 145 degrees. Remove from the water bath and allow to cool to room temperature, 2 to 3 hours.

Refrigerate the pâté overnight before serving. (*The pâté will keep for up to 1½ weeks refrigerated.*)

Cut into ¼-inch-thick slices and serve with cornichons and mustard.

Fresh Foie Gras with Cognac Aspic

Serves 8 to 10 as a first course

✒ **Foie gras is sometimes** sautéed like calf's liver and served with different garnishes, but I prefer it cold in a strong-flavored aspic, as in this recipe. Truffles and, if possible, a good Sauternes, along with slices of brioche, will bring the foie gras to its pinnacle. The sweet, complex Sauternes complements and balances the richness of the foie gras, making for an exceptional combination.

It is important not to overcook the foie gras, or it will shrink and become dry. This is best served within 48 hours. The leftover fat can be used to sauté potatoes or to make stew.

1 Grade A fresh duck foie gras (about 1 pound 10 ounces)

SEASONING MIXTURE

1½ teaspoons salt, preferably Morton Tender Quick curing salt
1 teaspoon sugar
½ teaspoon freshly ground white pepper
1 envelope (about 2 teaspoons) gelatin

2 tablespoons cognac

ASPIC

1 cup coarsely chopped leek greens
1 cup coarsely chopped celery
½ cup coarsely chopped carrots
½ cup loosely packed fresh chervil sprigs (or, if unavailable, fresh parsley)
2 large fresh tarragon sprigs
1½ teaspoons salt
¾ teaspoon freshly ground black pepper
4 envelopes (about 8 teaspoons) gelatin
2 large egg whites
1 cup dry white wine
4 cups homemade chicken stock (page 612) or low-salt canned chicken broth
3 tablespoons cognac

1 small black truffle, cut into julienne strips (optional)

You will notice that the foie gras has two lobes. Separate them by breaking the liver apart. Remove as much of the sinews, veins, and gristle running through it as possible and discard. (For this recipe, it does not matter if the liver is broken into several pieces, since it will come back together during cooking. If foie gras is to be sliced and sautéed, it is better to slice it before cleaning and then remove the sinews and veins.) Pull gently to remove the visible sinews and bloody veins, using your fingers and the point of a knife to go deeply into the foie gras. To remove even more sinews and veins, split open each lobe and probe with your knife. If any part of the foie gras looks slightly greenish, slice it off and discard (the green probably indicates that the gallbladder broke and ran slightly onto the foie gras; this liquid is extremely bitter).

Put the pieces of foie gras in ice-cold water and refrigerate for at least 3 hours; the object is to drain more blood out of the foie gras to make it whiter. Drain the foie gras and dry with paper towels.

Preheat the oven to 225 degrees.

FOR THE SEASONING MIXTURE: Combine all the ingredients. Sprinkle the foie gras with the mixture and the cognac.

Place some of the large pieces of foie gras on a kitchen towel, arrange the smaller pieces in the center, and cover with the remaining larger pieces. Wrap the towel carefully around the foie gras and gently squeeze to compact it into a tight mass. Tie the ends of the towel tightly with twine and place the foie gras in a terrine that holds it snugly.

Cover the terrine with the lid and then with aluminum foil, securing it tightly around the edges. Place in a roasting pan and add enough tepid tap water to the pan to come at least two thirds of the way up the terrine. Bake for about 1 hour. The inside of the foie gras should reach approximately 125 degrees. Remove the terrine from the water bath.

Cut a piece of wood or heavy cardboard to fit inside the top of the terrine and place it on top of the foie gras. Place a weight of 1 to 1½ pounds (such as a few cans) on top. (The weight will make it more compact.) Let cool, then refrigerate overnight.

The following day, remove the weight, scrape off the surface fat (reserve it), and remove the piece of wood. (The fat can be used to sauté vegetables or added to sauces for flavor.) Run a knife around the towel-encased foie gras to release it. Pull on the towel to unmold. If it doesn't unmold easily, warm slightly to release. Unwrap the foie gras and clean by wiping it with a paper towel. (*The foie gras can be placed back in the clean terrine, with enough fat to cover it completely, and kept in the refrigerator for several weeks.*)

FOR THE ASPIC: Combine the leek greens, celery, carrots, chervil, tarragon, salt, pepper, and gelatin in a saucepan and stir in the egg whites and white wine.

Bring the stock to a boil in a saucepan and add it to the aspic mixture, stirring to combine well. Cook, stirring, until the liquid comes to a strong boil. Remove from the heat and set the mixture aside for about 15 minutes, without stirring — do not disturb the crust, or raft, on top.

Gently strain the aspic through a cloth or paper towel into a saucepan. (You should have about 2 cups.) Let cool for 3 minutes, then add the cognac.

Pour half the aspic into a large fairly shallow glass or crystal bowl and put in the refrigerator

until set. Cut 8 to 10 slices (¾ to 1 inch thick) of foie gras. (Any remaining liver can be kept, refrigerated, for a few days.)

Place the slices on top of the set aspic in a single layer. Sprinkle, if desired, with the julienned truffle. Pour the remaining aspic into a bowl, set it over ice, and stir until the aspic is syrupy and almost ready to set. Spoon on top of the foie gras slices to coat the foie gras (and truffles) completely. Refrigerate for at least 1 hour before serving, or as long as overnight.

The foie gras can be served with a spoon, dishing out a slice per person, with some of the aspic underneath.

FOIE GRAS

The large liver from a force-fed goose or duck is one of the greatest delicacies known to epicureans. The areas in France where the best livers are produced are Alsace, in the northeast, and the Périgord region in the southwest. Foie gras is also produced in Israel, the Czech Republic, Slovakia, Hungary, and the United States and Canada.

The fresh foie gras available in the United States is usually duck liver, and it reaches, at the maximum, 2 pounds. The best quality, Grade A, is pale pink and firm and has a pleasant, mild odor. Inferior foie gras will shrink and melt considerably during cooking.

Buy foie gras at a specialty market or order it online.

Cold Sweetbread Terrine

Serves 10 as a first course

A sweetbread terrine served cold with a glorious Chardonnay makes a very special first course. This one takes several days, so you need to plan ahead. It is well worth the effort.

When buying sweetbreads, insist on the big roundish lobes, which are the pancreas glands.

MEAT MIXTURE

1¼	pounds ground pork (about 75% lean and 25% fat; shoulder or Boston butt is good)
½	cup dry white wine
¼	cup cognac
2½	teaspoons curing salt, preferably Morton Tender Quick
1½	teaspoons freshly ground black pepper
½	teaspoon finely chopped fresh thyme
1	bay leaf, broken into pieces and ground into a powder (¼ teaspoon)
¼	cup peeled pistachios (plunge the shelled pistachios into boiling water for 1 minute; the skins will slide off)
1	large egg yolk
2	black truffles, finely diced (about ⅓ cup; optional)

SWEETBREADS

1¼	pounds pancreas sweetbreads
2	tablespoons unsalted butter
1	teaspoon salt
½	teaspoon freshly ground black pepper
1	small carrot, peeled and diced (¼ cup)
1	small tomato, diced (½ cup)
1	medium onion, diced (½ cup)
3	fresh parsley sprigs, coarsely chopped
2	tablespoons dry sherry
¼	cup Basic Brown Sauce (page 613)

8	strips pork tenderloin, about ¾ inch wide by 8 inches long (about 6 ounces)

Dijon mustard (optional)
Cornichons (tiny French gherkins; optional)

FOR THE MEAT MIXTURE: Combine all the ingredients, mixing carefully. Press into a baking dish, cover with plastic wrap, and macerate for 48 hours in the refrigerator.

MEANWHILE, FOR THE SWEETBREADS: Soak the sweetbreads in cold water for at least 2 to 3 hours to whiten, changing the water once or twice (if they are bloody, soak for as long as overnight in the refrigerator). Drain.

Put the sweetbreads in a saucepan, cover with cold water, bring to a boil, and boil for 1 minute. Drain in a sieve and cool under cold running water. Pull out the sinews.

Lay a kitchen towel on a tray, put the sweetbreads on top, and cover with another towel. Put another tray or a platter on top and press the sweetbreads by putting a weight on the tray (a 3- to 4-pound weight should suffice; canned foods or a pot of water can be used). Refrigerate for at least a few hours, or overnight. (Pressing the sweetbreads extrudes the undesirable pinkish liquid and makes them white and compact.)

TO COOK THE SWEETBREADS: Preheat the oven to 375 degrees.

Melt the butter in a heavy ovenproof saucepan and roll the sweetbreads in it. Add the salt, pepper, carrot, tomato, onion, and parsley and cover with a piece of parchment or waxed paper. Bake for 20 minutes. Remove the paper, add the sherry and brown sauce, and bake, uncovered, for 10 more minutes.

Remove the sweetbreads to a plate and strain the juices, pressing on the solids with a spoon to release all the juices. Pour the juices into a saucepan, bring to a boil, and reduce to ⅓ cup. Let cool, then add the reduced juices to the ground pork mixture and mix well.

TO ASSEMBLE AND BAKE THE TERRINE: Preheat the oven to 325 degrees.

If you have large pieces of sweetbreads, cut them lengthwise in half. Place the tenderloin strips on a large plate. Spread a 1-inch-thick layer of the meat mixture in the bottom of an earthenware terrine or Pyrex loaf pan about 8 inches by 4½ inches by 3 inches deep. Layer the sweetbreads and pork strips alternately with the remaining mixture until all the ingredients are used, finishing with a layer of the meat mixture.

Set the terrine in a deep baking pan and add water to come about two thirds of the way up the terrine. Bake for about 2 hours; the internal temperature should reach about 145 degrees. Remove the terrine from the water and cool to room temperature.

Cover with plastic wrap and refrigerate. Let rest in the refrigerator for at least 1 day before slicing. (*The terrine can be refrigerated for up to 1½ weeks.*)

Serve slices of the terrine with mustard and cornichons, if desired.

Civier Victor with Mustard Sauce

Serves 20 as a first course

❧ Similar to headcheese, *civier* is an inexpensive, rustic, jellied pâté that was a favorite of my father, Victor, who made it when I was a child. The pâté is unmolded, sliced, and served with a mustard-vinegar sauce. Double the sauce recipe if you plan to serve all the civier at one sitting.

2 unsmoked ham hocks (about 2½ pounds)

3 pigs' feet (about 2 pounds), split in half (if you can, buy front legs, which are fleshier than back legs)

1 piece pork rind (about 8 ounces)

1½ teaspoons salt

9 cups cold water

5 carrots (8 ounces), peeled and cut into sticks about 1½ inches long and ½ inch thick

2 cups coarsely chopped onions (8 ounces)

1 cup dry white wine

1 cup coarsely chopped fresh parsley

⅓ cup Dijon mustard

½ cup thinly sliced cornichons (tiny French gherkins)

1 teaspoon freshly ground black pepper, or to taste

SAUCE (see the headnote)

¼ teaspoon salt

¼ teaspoon freshly ground black pepper

2 tablespoons Dijon mustard

1½ tablespoons red wine vinegar

5 tablespoons peanut or olive oil

3 tablespoons chopped shallots

Country bread

Put the ham hocks, pigs' feet, and pork rind in a large pot, add 1 teaspoon of the salt, and cover with the cold water. Bring to a boil and skim off any scum that comes to the top, then boil gently, covered, for 2 hours. Drain the solids, reserving the liquid, and set aside until cool enough to handle.

Pick the meat from the bones. Cut the pork rind and meat into 1-inch pieces.

Put the meat, rind, carrots, and onions in a pot with 5 cups of the reserved cooking liquid and the wine. Bring to a boil, reduce the heat, and cook gently for 30 minutes. Remove from the heat and add the parsley, mustard, cornichons, the remaining ½ teaspoon salt, and the pepper. Adjust the seasoning to taste if necessary.

Ladle the mixture in two 6-cup loaf pans. Refrigerate until the pâté is set, an hour or so, then cover with plastic wrap and refrigerate overnight.

FOR THE SAUCE: Combine the salt, pepper, mustard, and vinegar in a bowl. Whisk in the oil. Add the shallots.

At serving time, run a knife around the edges of the pans and unmold. Cut the *civier* into scant 1-inch-thick slices and serve with the mustard sauce and country bread.

Sausage and Potato Salad Richard
Serves 6

A country dish that my brother, Richard, loved, this rustic sausage and potato salad is ideal with a green salad, fresh bread, and a robust red wine.

SAUSAGE

About 1½ pounds coarsely ground pork (about 25% fat and 75% lean; shoulder or Boston butt is good)

2½ teaspoons curing salt, preferably Morton Tender Quick

1 teaspoon coarsely ground black pepper

1 teaspoon sugar

¼ cup dry red wine

1 garlic clove, crushed and chopped (½ teaspoon)

POTATO SALAD

2½ pounds large red potatoes (about 8), washed

⅓ cup plus 2 tablespoons olive oil

1 leek, trimmed (leaving some green), split, washed, and thinly sliced (1½ cups)

½ cup coarsely chopped fresh parsley

¼ cup coarsely chopped fresh chervil (or a mixture of fresh parsley and fennel sprigs or tarragon)

½ cup chopped onion, rinsed under cold water in a sieve and drained

3 garlic cloves, finely chopped (1½ teaspoons)

3 tablespoons Dijon mustard

3 tablespoons dry white wine

2 tablespoons red wine vinegar

¾ teaspoon salt

½ teaspoon freshly ground black pepper

FOR THE SAUSAGE: Combine the pork, curing salt, pepper, sugar, red wine, and garlic in a bowl and mix well. Using a piece of plastic wrap, shape the mixture into a sausage about 2 inches thick and 10 inches long; press firmly, so there are no air bubbles inside. Place the plastic-wrapped sausage on a piece of aluminum foil and roll up, twisting the ends to enclose the meat. Refrigerate for at least 2 days to cure. (*The sausage can cure for as long as 1 week.*)

At cooking time, place the wrapped sausage in a large saucepan, and cover with cold water. Place a plate or lid on top of the sausage to hold it underwater as it cooks. Bring the water to approximately 150 degrees and poach the sausage at that temperature for 1½ hours. Keep in the hot water until ready to serve.

MEANWHILE, FOR THE POTATO SALAD: Put the potatoes in a saucepan, add cold water to cover by 1 inch, and bring to a boil. Cook for 40 minutes, or until the potatoes are tender when pierced with the point of a knife. Drain and let cool slightly; the moisture in the hot potatoes will evaporate.

When the potatoes are cool enough to handle but still lukewarm, peel or leave unpeeled, and cut into ½-inch-thick slices.

Heat 2 tablespoons of the olive oil in a large

skillet until hot. Add the leek and sauté over high heat for about 1½ minutes. Transfer to a bowl and add the parsley, chervil, onion, garlic, mustard, white wine, vinegar, salt, pepper, and the remaining ⅓ cup olive oil. Mix the ingredients well, then add the potatoes and toss gently, making sure that the potato slices are well coated with the mixture. Let cool to room temperature.

At serving time, arrange the potato salad in a serving dish. Cut the warm sausage into 1-inch-thick slices and arrange on top of the potatoes.

Pistachio Sausage in Brioche with Mushroom Sauce
Serves 6 as a first course

In classic restaurants all over France, pâtés are often cooked in a crust, but cooking sausages in brioche is specific to the Lyon region. Brioche is ideal, because the dough expands during cooking, forming a delicious shell, and the juices of the sausages are sealed in by the dough, keeping the meat moist and flavorful.

This recipe yields 3 sausages. One is cooked in brioche, and the other two can be poached and served with potato salad, or roasted with potatoes, onions, and garlic, as my mother used to do.

Although the sausage can be served without the sauce, it is more special with it.

SAUSAGES

3½ pounds coarsely ground pork (about 25% fat and 75% lean; shoulder or Boston butt is good)
2 tablespoons curing salt, preferably Morton Tender Quick
2 teaspoons coarsely ground black pepper
2 teaspoons sugar
½ cup shelled pistachios, most of the skin removed

¼ cup dry red wine
1 large garlic clove, crushed and chopped (½ teaspoon)

BRIOCHE

1 envelope (2¼ teaspoons) instant yeast
½ cup warm water (about 100 degrees)
1 teaspoon sugar
3 cups all-purpose flour
½ teaspoon salt
4 large eggs
½ pound (2 sticks) unsalted butter, softened

1 large egg
All-purpose flour, for dusting
Unsalted butter, for the foil
1 slice firm white bread, crust removed and processed to crumbs in a food processor (about ½ cup)

SAUCE

2 tablespoons unsalted butter
¼ cup chopped shallots
3 cups diced (¼-inch) mushrooms
½ cup fruity red wine
1 cup Basic Brown Sauce (page 613)
Salt and freshly ground black pepper

FOR THE SAUSAGES: Combine the pork, curing salt, pepper, sugar, pistachios, red wine, and garlic in a bowl and mix well. Divide the mixture into 3 parts and, using plastic wrap, shape them into long sausages: press the meat together thoroughly to make sure there are no air pockets in the center and shape into logs about 10 inches long and 1½ inches thick. Refrigerate for at least 2 days to cure. (*You will be baking 1 sausage in brioche; the remaining sausages can be poached as in Sausage and Potato Salad Richard, opposite. The sausages can be refrigerated for as long as 1 week or frozen.*)

FOR THE BRIOCHE: Mix the yeast, warm

water, and sugar together in the bowl of a stand mixer. Let stand at room temperature for about 10 minutes, until bubbly.

Add the flour, salt, and eggs and mix on medium speed with the flat beater for about 3 minutes. The dough will be very elastic, smooth, and shiny. With the motor running, add the butter, squeezing the butter into the dough with your hands and mixing just long enough to incorporate it. Don't worry if some pieces of butter are still visible.

The dough is easier to handle if it is allowed to rise slowly overnight in the refrigerator. If time allows, wrap the dough in a plastic bag and place in the refrigerator. If you need to use the dough sooner, leave it in the mixer bowl, cover it with a damp towel, and let rise in a warm, draft-free place (70 to 75 degrees) for 3 to 4 hours, until at least doubled in size.

Gently punch down the dough, pressing on it to release the air inside.

TO WRAP THE SAUSAGE IN DOUGH: Crack the egg into a cup and remove and discard half the white (so the proportion of yolk is greater). Beat the egg thoroughly with a fork.

Spread the dough on a lightly floured board. (If the dough is freshly made, it will be softer and more flour will be required in the rolling than if it was made ahead; the freshly made dough also may have to be spread by hand rather than rolled.) Roll it out with a rolling pin or spread it with floured hands into a rectangle large enough to enclose the sausage (approximately 10 inches wide by 13 to 14 inches long). Brush the center with the egg wash and sprinkle with a little flour. Unwrap the sausage and place it on top, brush with the egg wash, and sprinkle with a little flour. (The flour and egg mixture will form a type of glue, which will hold the dough tightly against the sausage.) Fold one side of the dough over the top of the sausage and brush with egg wash. Then fold over the other side of the dough, overlapping it on top. Press out the two ends of the dough to make them thinner, then brush with egg wash and fold them over the top of the package.

Line a large cookie sheet with a nonstick baking mat and place the sausage package seam side down on the sheet. (There is a double layer of dough underneath now, and only one layer on top; by the time the dough has risen, the sausage will have sunk a little and so will be approximately in the center of the dough when it finishes cooking.) Brush the top of the package with egg wash. If you want to make a design on top, score the dough with the back of a small knife. Make 3 holes in the top of the dough; this will permit the steam to be released and prevent the dough from cracking too much during cooking. To prevent the brioche from spreading out too much, wrap a strip of aluminum foil around it: Tear off a sheet of foil long enough to go completely around the sausage and fold it lengthwise into thirds to make it thicker. Butter the strip on one side and wrap it loosely around the sausage, butter side in. Secure it loosely with kitchen twine — don't make it too tight; the brioche needs room to expand. Sprinkle the top with 2 to 3 tablespoons of the bread crumbs to give it a nice finish. Let rise for a good hour in a warm, draft-free place.

Preheat the oven to 375 degrees.

Set the cookie sheet in the center of the oven and bake for about 20 minutes; the brioche will have expanded and set. Remove the string and foil and bake for an additional 30 minutes to finish cooking and brown.

Let the brioche-wrapped sausage cool in a warm place for 20 to 30 minutes before slicing.

MEANWHILE, FOR THE SAUCE: Melt the butter in a large skillet. When it is hot, add the shallots and sauté for about 1 minute, then add the mushrooms and sauté for 2 minutes, or until they have rendered most of their juice. Add the red wine and boil until most of the liquid has evaporated. Add the brown sauce and bring to a boil. Season with salt and pepper to taste.

Using a serrated knife, cut the brioche-wrapped sausage into 1-inch-thick slices. Place 1 slice on each warm plate and surround with 2 to 3 tablespoons sauce. Serve immediately.

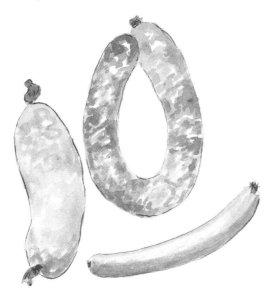

Black Sausage
Makes 16 to 18 sausages

🦚 **Black sausage, also called** blood sausage or black pudding — *boudin* in France — is a common winter country dish. My version is made with leeks. In some parts of France, spinach, chestnuts, and even Swiss chard replace the leeks, and the sausage is often made with heavy cream. Whatever the additions, it is traditionally made with pork blood and fat.

Pork blood is sometimes difficult to get: look for it in Asian markets. It may come frozen; it should be defrosted under refrigeration. Beef blood can be substituted if pork blood is unavailable. The poached *boudins* can be frozen if properly wrapped. They should be defrosted slowly in the refrigerator to keep their moist, smooth texture.

The sausages are cooked twice: they are first poached, which can be done days ahead, and then sautéed at serving time. Although they can be sautéed in the casings, which are edible, it is better to remove them to make the sausages easier to cut and eat at the table.

Thin and delicate, hog casing is approximately 1½ inches in diameter. It comes packed in salt and is easy to use. It is available from butchers or online vendors.

Serve the sausages with Turnip and Potato Puree (page 467) and apples sautéed in butter.

SAUSAGES

	Hog casing (1 small container; about 6–8 feet)
1¼	pounds pork fatback
1	pound onions
3	leeks (10–12 ounces), trimmed (leaving some green), split, and washed
2	tablespoons potato starch (see page 318)
4	cups pork or beef blood
2	teaspoons salt
½	teaspoon freshly ground black pepper
2	tablespoons olive oil

FOR THE SAUSAGES: Soak the casing in tepid water for 5 minutes to remove the salt. Drain.

Open one end of the casing and secure it around the end of the faucet. Run lukewarm water through it to open and thoroughly wash the inside of the casing. Then submerge in cold water.

To tie the end of the casing (it tends to be very slippery and will untie with a conventional knot), tie a piece of kitchen twine (with one knot only) around the casing about 3 inches from one end. Fold the small end of the casing over the knot. Tie the twine around again into a double knot, creating a little loop of casing at the end and securing the casing so it won't slip. Set aside.

Cut the pork fat into ½-inch dice. Put the fat in a large saucepan and heat over medium-high heat for 4 to 5 minutes, until it starts melting.

Meanwhile, thinly slice the onions and leeks.

Add the onions and leeks to the melting fat and cook over medium heat for approximately 20 minutes. Most of the fat will have melted.

Put the onion-leek-fat mixture into a food processor, add the potato starch, and process, pushing the mixture down into the bowl when necessary, until well blended and smooth. Transfer to a bowl, let cool to lukewarm, and stir in the blood. Add the salt and pepper.

Attach the open end of the casing to a funnel and, using a ladle or measuring cup, fill the casing with the sausage mixture. Do not overfill, or the casing will burst. The mixture should flow into the casing; don't force it, or the casing will expand too much during cooking. Tie the casing off about every 5 inches with kitchen twine to create individual sausages. Some of the casing can be left untied to create a long sausage spiral that can be cut into pieces after cooking.

Arrange all the sausages in a large saucepan in one layer. Cover with tepid water, place on a burner, and bring to 160 to 170 degrees. Do not let the temperature go higher; if it boils, the casing is apt to burst. Cook for about 20 minutes; as the sausage tends to rise to the surface during cooking, place a wire rack or plate on it to keep it submerged. To test the sausage, puncture it with a needle; if the juice comes out clear, it is cooked. Pour most of the hot liquid out of the pot and run cold water over the sausage for a few minutes. Then remove the sausage to a plate and let cool. (Discard the cooking liquid.) Refrigerate overnight. (*The sausage can be refrigerated for up to 1 week.*)

Cut through the casing to separate the individual sausages and cut the long piece, if you made it, into sections of 4 to 5 inches.

TO SAUTÉ THE SAUSAGES: Cut through the casing with a knife the length of each sausage and peel it off. The sausage should hold its shape without breaking. Heat the oil in two large skillets (or sauté the sausages in 2 batches in one skillet). When the oil is hot, add the sausages and cook for 3 to 4 minutes over medium-low heat to brown. Turn and cook on the other side for 3 to 4 minutes. Serve.

Walnut Sausage
Serves 4

I am very fond of sausages, especially this delicate one, which I like best served lukewarm with a potato salad, such as Lentil and Potato Salad (page 59). You can also sauté the sausage whole with quartered onions and baby potatoes, as is done with the sausage in the next recipe (opposite). These are made with very lean pork and a little crushed ice, to replace some of the moisture lost with the elimination of most of the fat. I use curing salt, which gives the sausage a beautiful pink color and intensifies its flavor. Refrigerate it to cure for at least 2 days before cooking; it can cure there for up to a week.

- 1 pound boneless lean pork (chops, shoulder, or fillet)
- 3 tablespoons crushed ice
- 2 tablespoons dry red wine
- 2 garlic cloves, crushed and chopped (1½ teaspoons)
- 2 teaspoons curing salt, preferably Morton Tender Quick

½	teaspoon crushed black peppercorns

3	tablespoons walnut pieces

Cut about two thirds of the meat (10 ounces) into ¼-inch pieces and put them in a bowl.

Cut the rest of the meat into 1-inch pieces and process in a food processor with the ice for 20 to 30 seconds, until the mixture is emulsified. Add to the pork pieces in the bowl, along with the remaining ingredients. Mix well.

Using plastic wrap, shape the mixture into a sausage about 10 inches long and 1½ inches thick. Enclose it tightly in the plastic wrap, then roll and seal it as tightly as possible in aluminum foil. Refrigerate for at least 2 days to cure before cooking.

When you are ready to cook the sausage, place it, still wrapped, in a saucepan, cover with cold water, place a wire rack or plate on top of the sausage to submerge it, and bring the water to 150 degrees (this will take about 10 minutes). Cook the sausage at that temperature for 1½ hours. Remove the pan from the heat and let the sausage rest in the hot water for at least 10 minutes and as long as 1 hour.

Unwrap, cut into ¾-inch-thick slices, and serve warm.

Sausage with Potatoes
Serves 4

❧ **This sausage is made** without a casing, so its preparation is very easy. Its taste develops during the curing, which should take place in the refrigerator. I find black trumpet mushrooms, sometimes called "poor man's truffles," in the woods around my house. They can be used fresh or dried. You can substitute dried porcini mushrooms, if they are easier to find.

SAUSAGE

⅓	cup dried black trumpet mushrooms (see the headnote)

1	pound ground pork (about 18–20% fat)

⅓	cup shelled pistachios

2	teaspoons curing salt, preferably Morton Tender Quick

1	teaspoon freshly ground black pepper

1	teaspoon chopped garlic

2	tablespoons dry white wine

2	tablespoons unsalted butter

1	medium onion, quartered

15	small Red Bliss potatoes (about 1½ pounds), peeled and halved

¼	teaspoon salt

¼	teaspoon freshly ground black pepper

FOR THE SAUSAGE: Cover the black trumpet mushrooms with 1 cup water in a saucepan and bring to a boil. Reduce the heat and boil gently for about 10 minutes, until most of the moisture has evaporated. Drain well and coarsely chop.

Mix the mushrooms and all the remaining sausage ingredients together in a bowl. Wrap in plastic wrap to create a log about 10 inches long and 1½ inches thick. Let cure in the refrigerator for at least 48 hours or as long as 1 week.

TO COOK THE SAUSAGE: Melt the butter in a large saucepan. Unroll the sausage from the plastic wrap very carefully, so as not to break it, and place in the saucepan. Brown over low heat on all sides, turning gently, for 6 to 8 minutes.

Add the onion and potatoes, cover, and cook for 30 minutes; turn the sausage and potatoes after 15 minutes so that they brown all around.

Remove the sausage to a cutting board. Sprinkle the potatoes and onion with the salt and pepper and transfer to a warm serving platter. Slice the sausage, arrange next to the potatoes and onion, and serve.

Chitterling Sausages
Makes 15 to 18 sausages

Chitterlings are the fatty small intestines of a pig or calf and sausages made from them are a French charcuterie delicacy. Known as *andouillettes*, they are usually grilled or sautéed with a bit of white wine and are often served with mashed potatoes.

Traditionally, the chitterlings are simply bundled up and stuffed into the casing. In this refined version, however, they are first cooked for 2 hours in lots of water until tender. They are then cut into pieces and flavored with shallots, scallions, garlic, mustard, mushrooms, and wine, placed in the casing, and poached briefly in stock and wine.

This recipe makes 15 to 18 sausages, but I give instructions for sautéing and serving just enough for 6 people. The remaining sausages can be frozen for another meal. Serve the sautéed sausages with Spicy Rice (page 106) and Sautéed Apple Rings (page 412), if desired.

Chitterlings are available at ethnic markets.

SAUSAGES

- 10 pounds chitterlings
- 8 dried shiitake mushrooms, soaked in warm water for 1 hour
- 2 tablespoons unsalted butter
- ½ cup chopped scallions (about 3)
- 1 cup sliced shallots
- 2 teaspoons chopped garlic
- 3 tablespoons chopped fresh parsley
- 1 tablespoon finely chopped fresh tarragon
- ¼ cup Dijon mustard
- 2 teaspoons potato starch (see page 318)
- 1½ cups dry white wine
- 1 tablespoon salt, or to taste
- 2 teaspoons freshly ground black pepper
  Hog casing (1 small container; about 6–8 feet)

- 3 cups homemade chicken stock (page 612) or low-salt canned chicken broth

- 1 tablespoon unsalted butter
- 2 tablespoons dry white wine
  Chopped scallion greens, for garnish

Wash the chitterlings thoroughly, then put in a large pot and cover with tepid water. Bring to a boil, reduce the heat, and simmer gently, covered, for 2 hours. The chitterlings will shrink considerably. Cool, then drain.

Cut the chitterlings into ½-inch pieces and put in a bowl.

Drain the mushrooms and remove the stems (reserve them for stock or a sauce). Coarsely chop the mushroom caps.

Melt the butter in a skillet or a large saucepan. When it is hot, add the scallions and shallots and sauté for 2 to 3 minutes. Add the mushrooms and cook for 1½ minutes. Stir in the garlic, then add the mixture to the chitterlings. Add the parsley, tarragon, mustard, potato starch, ½ cup of the wine, the salt, and pepper and mix well.

Soak the casings in lukewarm water for 4 to 5 minutes. Fit one end of the casing over the end of a faucet and run tepid water gently through the casing to open and rinse it.

Tie the casing at one end as described on page 383. Spoon the chitterling mixture into a pastry bag fitted with a plain 1-inch-wide tip. Fit the casing onto the bottom of a plastic funnel and squeeze the mixture into the funnel, or squeeze it directly from the pastry bag into the casing. As the mixture goes into the casing, push it down by squeezing it gently with your fingers toward the end of the casing. When most of the casing is filled, press with your hand (not too much, or it will burst) to compact the stuffing. Using a trussing needle or other needle, prick it where you see little bubbles of air so the mixture is compact. Tie off with kitchen twine about every 4 to 5 inches to divide the stuffed casing into individual sausages.

TO COOK THE SAUSAGE: Arrange the sausage in a spiral in a large saucepan, in one layer. Pour the chicken stock and the remaining cup of wine on top; there should be just enough to cover. Add a pinch of salt if the stock is not seasoned. Place over medium heat, bring to 160 to 170 degrees, and poach at this temperature for 12 minutes; do not let the mixture boil, or the casing will burst. Let cool in the stock for 2 to 3 hours.

Transfer the sausage to a platter and cut into individual sausages. The filling will be set and will not pop out of the ends of the casing. (The stock can be used to reheat the sausages or for sauces or soups.) Set aside 6 sausages to sauté and serve now and freeze the rest for another time.

TO SAUTÉ THE SAUSAGES: Prick the sausages all over with a fork to prevent them from bursting. Heat the butter in a large skillet. When it is hot, add the sausages and cook over very low heat for 5 minutes. Add the 2 tablespoons wine, cover, and continue cooking for about 1 minute over low heat. (If the heat is too high, the sausages will burst.)

Garnish with the scallion greens and serve.

Hard Country Salami
Makes 7 to 12 salamis
(depending on size of casing)

Hard country salami, called *saucisson* in French, is usually made of cured ground pork that is stuffed into natural casings and air-dried for 8 to 10 weeks. You can also cook these sausages after just 3 or 4 days of drying. Panfry or poach them and serve with potato salad, or bake them in a brioche dough (see page 381) or puff paste. If allowed to dry longer in a well-ventilated area, the sausage will eventually shrink and get hard, becoming what we know as dried sausage, or salami.

Commercial salami is made with special stuffing machines, which fill the casings very tight, eliminating any air bubbles. Air bubbles sometimes remain in hand-stuffed sausages, and the bubbles leave dark areas when the salami is cut, since the meat there has oxidized. This doesn't affect the taste.

Hog casing usually comes packed in salt and can be kept in the refrigerator or frozen until ready to use.

Serve the salami sliced, with bread and butter.

NOTE: **Before attempting this recipe, familiarize yourself with safety considerations (see page 388).**

Hog casing (see the headnote)

6½ pounds boneless pork shoulder
¼ cup curing salt, preferably Morton Tender Quick
4 teaspoons coarsely ground black pepper
2 tablespoons sugar
2 teaspoons finely chopped garlic

Soak the casing in tepid water for 5 minutes to remove the salt. Drain.

Fit the end of the casing over a faucet and run lukewarm water through the casing to rinse and wash the inside. Drain.

Cut approximately 1½ pounds of the leanest meat into ⅜- to ½-inch pieces. Coarsely grind the remainder.

Combine the ground meat, cut meat, curing salt, pepper, sugar, and garlic in a large bowl and mix together thoroughly.

TO STUFF THE CASING: If using the sausage attachment for a KitchenAid mixer, leave the vise inside and remove the knife and screen. Attach the deep funnel under the vise at the end and screw it onto the machine. (If you don't have a sausage attachment, use a hand stuffer or a pastry bag with the largest plain tip you have.)

To tie the end of the casing, first make a knot with kitchen twine about 1 to 1½ inches from the end of the casing. Fold the end of the casing over the knot and tie another double knot on top, leaving a little loop of casing at the end. This way, the knots can't slip. Fit the open end of the casing over the funnel, bunching it up so that most of it is around the funnel. With the machine running at high speed, push the meat down through the feeder while holding the casing with your other hand, so that as the meat comes out, you can regulate its flow and see that the casing fills evenly. Try to pack the casing as tightly as possible without breaking it. When the casing is filled, slip it off the funnel and cut it about 1½ inches above the stuffing.

Tie the open end of the casing as you did above. Press the casing, squeezing to compact the meat, and prick with a fork wherever you see air bubbles. If the casing (more likely with the thinner hog casing) bursts, cut it at the break, remove the meat, and repeat the stuffing procedure.

Tie the sausage at 8- to 10-inch intervals to

Making salami and dry-cured ham was part of my youth. Each farm made its own, with slight differences. Nevertheless, if you are a novice, air-drying meat should not be undertaken lightly: improper curing can result in the creation of toxic compounds. If the meat smells or appears "off," it is best to err on the side of caution and not eat it.

It is important to read my recipes very carefully and follow them exactly, since too much heat or humidity, fluctuations in temperature, and/or lack of ventilation will cause the meat to spoil before it has a chance to dry. Curing salt, which contains sodium nitrite, which prevents bacteria from growing, must be used in the exact proportions specified here.

When making sausage that you plan to air-dry, sanitary conditions are especially important, as is keeping the meat cold while you work. Both salami and ham should be dried in a cool, dry place, preferably a frost-free refrigerator.

make individual sausages, and cut them apart. Make a loop at one end of each with kitchen twine so the salami can be hung. Hang in a cool (40-degree), well-ventilated place, preferably a frost-free refrigerator; see the sidebar. Let dry for 8 to 10 weeks. After a few weeks, the salami should be firm and dry. If dry white spots develop on the surface, it indicates that the salami is drying well.

After 8 to 10 weeks, the salami is ready to eat. Rub the salami with paper towels to clean any dirt from the surface and wrap each one in plastic wrap. They will keep, refrigerated, for 4 to 6 weeks.

Cured Air-Dried Country-Style Ham

One 18-pound ham; serves 50 to 60

Curing meat — whether beef for pastrami or corned beef, or pork for ham or salami — can be done in dry salt or in a brine made of water, salt, sugar, and seasonings. The salt drains the moisture from the meat and, at the same time, deprives bacteria of a necessary living condition, hence preserving the meat.

The great cured and dried hams of France, such as Bayonne, or of Italy, such as Parma, or serrano ham from Spain are not smoked. This recipe produces a ham similar to those. You'll need to allot approximately 1 day of curing per pound of meat.

The addition of herbs and brandy flavors the meat and the canvas or cheesecloth encloses the seasonings and protects the meat from insects. Drying the ham will take 8 months and it is safest to do it in a frost-free refrigerator, which will draw out the moisture — provided that the ham is placed on a wire rack so the air can circulate around it. If you have a well-ventilated area that remains consistently cool, you can hang the ham there, but you should start in the fall so it has a chance to dry before the temperature rises. If it freezes slightly during the drying process (and for freezing to happen, the temperature would have to be very low, because of the salt), that will not hurt the ham.

When ready, the ham can be sliced thinly and eaten with buttered bread. Sliced, it is excellent with fried eggs and ratatouille, in the style of Bayonne. It is often served with fruit, traditionally figs or melon.

After the ham has been cut into, it is best kept hung in a cool, dry place or in the refrigerator. Once you've removed a few slices, cover the remainder with a piece of plastic wrap secured with a rubber band and store until you're ready to slice more.

NOTE: **Be sure to read the sidebar on safety before making this recipe.**

- 1 18-pound fresh ham (leg of pork), preferably organic, with the shank bone in, frozen (see the sidebar) and defrosted slowly under refrigeration (2–3 days)
- 3 pounds (about 9 cups) kosher salt
- 1½ cups packed light brown sugar
- 2 tablespoons Armagnac or other alcohol (such as whiskey, gin, or rum)
- ⅓ cup coarsely ground black pepper
- ⅓ cup herbes de Provence
- 1 bunch fresh thyme

TO CURE THE HAM: Remove the pelvic bone from the ham. Put the ham in a plastic bag (do not seal the bag) and set it on a tray.

Mix the salt and brown sugar together and rub over the ham, especially on the areas where there is no rind. Leave the plastic bag open and put the ham in a cool, dry place (about 40 degrees or lower), preferably a refrigerator; see the sidebar. Let cure for 18 to 20 days, which is about 1 day per pound; check on it every couple of days and press any fallen salt mixture back into place with a spoon.

TO DRY THE HAM: After 18 to 20 days, some of the salt will have dissolved around the ham and the meat should be wet and red from the mixture of still-dry salt and brine. Rinse the ham briefly under cold water and dry it with paper towels. Rub with the Armagnac or other alcohol, then mix the black pepper and herbes de Provence together and rub over the ham so it is well covered all over. Be sure that you press the herb mixture around the bone with your fingers, where there may be little holes, so that you saturate the ham with the seasonings. Pack the fresh thyme all around the ham.

Wrap the ham in a piece of canvas or cheese-cloth, or even an old pillowcase. Secure with twine and hang to dry for a minimum of 8 months. The ham should be in a place that is well ventilated and cool (the temperature can range from freezing to 50 degrees), especially for the first 3 to 4 months. If you have space in a frost-free refrigerator, the ham will dry well there, provided it has good air circulation and the ham is placed on a wire rack so it dries from underneath as well as the top. Alternatively, you can use a garage or another place where you have good air circulation to prevent the ham from spoiling, provided that it maintains a uniformly cool temperature at all times.

AFTER 8 MONTHS: The ham is dried. Remove the wrapping. The rind as well as the fat is very good and can be kept for cooking beans, potatoes, and the like. Trim some of the rind and fat from the top. Trim off the hard surface of the ham to expose the meat. Trim only a few inches down and around the ham, then start slicing. To facilitate the carving of the ham, place it in a large rectangular container; I use a pâté mold to hold it securely, making it steadier and easier to slice. Cut into the thinnest-possible slices with a long, thin knife. Keep slicing until you reach the level at which the ham is untrimmed around. Then trim some more around and continue slicing. Or, if you have access to a slicing machine, slice the ham on it by cutting off a large chunk with a knife and using the slicing machine for ultrathin slices from the chunk.

FOR SAFETY'S SAKE

Because the ham is consumed raw, I recommend freezing it for at least 4 or 5 days at 10 degrees or lower before the curing, to kill any possible trichinae. Be sure to defrost the ham slowly under refrigeration (it will take 2 to 3 days) to prevent loss of moisture.

Mustard Pigs' Feet
Serves 8

❧ **In this country dish** that goes with everything from beans to mashed potatoes, pigs' feet are boiled until they become tender and gelatinous. With the bone in, they are messy to eat and are best for family meals. Here they are boned and the meat is coarsely chopped, combined with ground pork, mushrooms, and seasonings, and formed into elongated patties resembling a pig's foot. Lastly, they are coated with mustard, breaded, and sautéed. They are delicious with the acidic shallot-vinegar sauce, which cuts their richness, but it is optional.

The front feet of pigs are fleshier than the back feet, so buy front ones if possible.

- 4 pigs' feet (4 pounds), split in half
  Salt
- 1 pound lean ground pork
- 1 cup coarsely chopped mushrooms
- ½ teaspoon chopped garlic

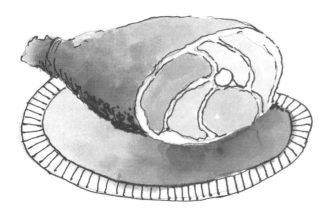

1½ teaspoons freshly ground black pepper

3–4 tablespoons spicy mustard

6 slices firm white bread (about 6 ounces), processed to crumbs in a food processor (3 cups)

2 tablespoons corn oil

OPTIONAL SAUCE

1 tablespoon unsalted butter

⅓ cup chopped shallots

½ cup red wine vinegar

½ teaspoon salt

¾ teaspoon freshly ground black pepper

1 cup Basic Brown Sauce (page 613)

½ teaspoon potato starch (see page 318), dissolved in 1 tablespoon water, if needed to thicken

Put the pigs' feet in a pot, add a good dash of salt, cover generously with cold water, and bring to a boil. Reduce the heat and simmer gently for 2½ to 3 hours, until tender. Cool in the cooking liquid to lukewarm, then drain. (The liquid can be used for soups or for a rich, gelatinous stock.)

The meat should be picked off the bones when still lukewarm, as it hardens when it cools and will be more difficult to remove. Be sure to remove all the tiny pieces of bone, feeling for them with your fingers as you go. (You should have approximately 1½ pounds meat.) Chop into about ¼-inch pieces.

Combine the meat with the ground pork and mushrooms in a bowl. Season with the garlic, 1 teaspoon salt, and ½ teaspoon of the pepper.

Form the mixture into 8 sausage-shaped patties, approximately 6 ounces each and 5 to 6 inches long, wetting your hands first to prevent the mixture from sticking to them and to help you mold the patties. Place on a tray and refrigerate for a couple of hours. After the patties have been refrigerated, they will be quite firm and easier to handle.

Brush the patties generously with the mustard on both sides.

Mix the bread crumbs with the remaining 1 teaspoon pepper on a plate. Place the patties on the crumbs, pressing to make the crumbs adhere all over. (*The patties can be prepared ahead to this point and refrigerated for up to 2 days.*)

TO SAUTÉ THE PATTIES: Heat the oil in one very large or two smaller skillets, preferably nonstick. When it is hot, add the patties and cook over medium-high heat for approximately 6 minutes on each side.

MEANWHILE, FOR THE OPTIONAL SAUCE: Melt the butter in a saucepan. When it is hot, add the shallots and sauté for 2 minutes. Add the vinegar, salt, and pepper and cook over high heat until the vinegar has almost completely evaporated and the shallots just look wet. Add the brown sauce and bring to a boil. If thickening is needed, add the dissolved potato starch and bring to a boil.

Spread the sauce, if you have it, on a large serving platter. Place the patties on top and serve.

Offal

Seared Calf's Liver with Tarragon Lemon Sauce
Serves 4

❧ **Calf's liver is a** delicacy, excellent sautéed in large steaks or thin slices, as in the recipe that follows. I like my liver pink inside — medium-rare — but you can adjust the cooking time to your taste. After the steaks are briefly sautéed in a skillet on top of the stove, they are transferred to a plate and set aside, covered, to finish cooking in their own residual heat while a tarragon-and-lemon-flavored sauce is created from the drippings in the skillet.

Be sure to select calf's liver, not beef liver, for this dish. Much paler in color, it has a milder flavor and is more tender than liver from a mature animal. The best comes from milk-fed veal.

- 2 tablespoons unsalted butter
- 1 tablespoon olive oil
- ½ teaspoon salt
- ½ teaspoon freshly ground black pepper
- 4 calf's liver steaks (slices; about ⅜ inch thick and 5 ounces each), cleaned of skin, membrane, and sinews

SAUCE
- ½ cup coarsely chopped red onion
- 2 scallions, trimmed (leaving some green) and minced (¼ cup)
- 2 tablespoons fresh lemon juice
- ¼ cup homemade chicken stock (page 612) or low-salt canned chicken broth
- 1 tablespoon drained capers
- 2 teaspoons chopped fresh tarragon

Heat the butter and oil in one very large or two smaller skillets until hot. Sprinkle the salt and pepper on both sides of the liver steaks and place them in the skillet(s) in one layer, with no overlap. Sauté over high heat for about 1 minute on each side for medium-rare (adjust the cooking time if your liver is thicker or thinner, or if you like it cooked more or less). Transfer the steaks to a platter and cover them with an overturned plate while you prepare the sauce (they can wait like this for 10 to 15 minutes).

FOR THE SAUCE: Add the onion and scallions to the drippings in the skillet(s). Sauté for about 20 seconds, then add the lemon juice and stir until all the solidified juices have melted. (If you are using two skillets, at this point, combine their contents in one.) Boil the mixture for another 20 seconds, until most of the liquid has evaporated. Add the stock, capers, and tarragon, mix well, and bring to a boil.

Arrange the liver steaks on individual plates, top with the sauce, and serve immediately.

Calf's Liver Slices with Grape and Currant Sauce
Serves 6

❧ **A sweet-sour sauce complements** liver. The sweetness of the grapes and currants in this sauce is balanced by the acidity of the vinegar and works well with the taste and texture of the liver, which should be pink when served. The dish is excellent with fresh noodles.

- 1 whole calf's liver (about 1½ pounds)
- ½ teaspoon salt
- ¼ teaspoon freshly ground black pepper
- 2–3 tablespoons unsalted butter
- 2–3 teaspoons peanut oil

⅔ cup chopped onion

⅓ cup balsamic vinegar

½ cup dry white wine

1¼ cups Basic Brown Sauce (page 613)

2 cups seedless green grapes

¼ cup dried currants

2 tablespoons unsalted butter
Salt and freshly ground black pepper if
necessary

Place the liver upside down on the work surface (the sinewy side on top). With your knife, remove most of the large sinews. Then start peeling off the skin or membrane. When you've removed the skin on the underside, turn the liver over and peel the skin from the top. (Although some cooks do not remove this thin veil of skin, removing it makes the liver much more tender.) Cut the liver into 12 slices, each about 2 ounces.

Sprinkle the liver slices with the salt and pepper. Heat 1 tablespoon of the butter and 1 teaspoon of the peanut oil in each of two skillets until very hot. Add the liver, being careful not to overcrowd the skillets (cook in 3 batches if necessary) and sauté over very high heat for approximately 45 seconds. Turn and cook for 45 seconds on the other side. Remove the liver to a plate and keep warm while you prepare the sauce.

FOR THE SAUCE: Cook the onion in the drippings in the skillets over high heat for 4 to 5 minutes, until dark brown. Add half the vinegar and wine to each skillet and boil over high heat to reduce by half, 3 to 4 minutes. Combine all the onion and liquid in one skillet, add the brown sauce, and bring to a boil.

Put the grapes and currants in a saucepan and strain the sauce on top of them. Bring to a gentle boil, then swirl in the butter and stir until combined with the sauce. Add salt and pepper if needed.

Arrange the liver slices on individual plates, spoon the sauce around them, and serve.

Braised Beef Tongue with Lentils
Serves 8 to 10

✖ **Some supermarkets offer beef** tongue that is raw but cured. If you can find only uncured tongue, you will need to cure it — a simple matter, but note that the curing process will take at least 5 days. Cooked with beans, lentils, or potatoes, tongue makes an excellent winter dish that is easy to prepare ahead and flavorful when reheated. It is also excellent sliced cold for sandwiches.

OPTIONAL CURE

½ cup curing salt, preferably Morton
Tender Quick

¼ cup packed light brown sugar

1 teaspoon herbes de Provence

½ teaspoon hot pepper flakes

1 teaspoon juniper berries

1 beef tongue (3½–4 pounds), cured or
uncured (see the headnote)

8 ounces salt pork, cut into ½-inch dice

12 ounces onions (2–3 medium), cut into
1-inch chunks

10 ounces carrots (about 3 medium), peeled
and cut into 1-inch chunks

2 tablespoons chopped fresh rosemary

1 pound lentils du Puy (French green
lentils), picked over and rinsed

6 cups homemade chicken stock (page
612) or low-salt canned chicken broth
Salt if necessary

IF USING AN UNCURED TONGUE: **Mix** together all the cure ingredients. Place the tongue in a plastic bag and sprinkle the curing mixture on top. Close the bag tightly and refrigerate for at least 5 days, turning the bag over once a day. Remove the meat from the cure.

Put the tongue in a large pot and cover with cold water. Bring to a boil, reduce the heat, and simmer gently for a good 2 hours. Remove from the heat and let cool for about 30 minutes in the cooking liquid, until cool enough to handle; drain.

Peel the tongue and remove the bones toward the throat. (They are the only bones left in the meat.)

Put the pieces of salt pork (lardons) in a saucepan, cover with water, bring to a boil, and boil for about 1 minute. Drain in a sieve, rinse under cold water, and put in a large Dutch oven.

Cook the lardons over medium-high heat for about 10 minutes, until they are nicely browned and most of the fat has been rendered. Add the onions and carrots and cook for about 3 minutes. Add the tongue, rosemary, lentils, and chicken stock, bring to a simmer, and simmer gently for 1 hour, with the pot almost completely covered. Taste the liquid and add salt if needed. Let the tongue sit for at least 30 minutes before carving.

Remove the tongue from the lentils and cut into ½-inch-thick slices. Arrange the tongue on a large serving platter, with the vegetables and lentils, and serve.

If any lentils are left over, they can be pureed with some water in a food processor, and then some of the tongue, or sausage or ham, can be diced and combined with the pureed lentils to make a very flavorful soup.

Grilled Lamb Kidneys with Maître d' Butter
Serves 4

❧ **Kidneys from baby lamb,** as well as spring lamb, are milder than those from older animals. (Often kidneys are damaged by butchers or meat inspectors who slice through the meat to check the condition of the animal. Try to get undamaged kidneys.)

Kidneys are delicious grilled. Don't overcook them — they should remain pink throughout after resting for a few minutes off the heat so the meat relaxes. The kidneys need intense heat so they brown outside and have the proper texture. If the grill isn't hot enough, they will stick.

Traditional with grilled meat or fish, the maître d' butter, which is just softened butter mixed with parsley and lemon juice, can be made a few days ahead and kept refrigerated.

MAÎTRE D' BUTTER

- 2 tablespoons unsalted butter, softened
  Pinch each of salt and freshly ground black pepper
- 1 tablespoon chopped fresh parsley
- 1 teaspoon fresh lemon juice

- 8 lamb kidneys (about 1½ pounds)
- 2 teaspoons peanut oil
  Pinch each of salt and freshly ground black pepper

- 1 small bunch watercress, tough stems removed, washed, and dried

FOR THE MAÎTRE D' BUTTER: Mix together all the ingredients.

If you got the kidneys in their fat, remove them from their casings of fat. Pull and cut off the sinews holding them to the fat.

Put the kidneys flat on the work surface. To butterfly, cut each one open horizontally from the rounded end to within ½ inch of the other side with a sharp knife. Open out the kidneys. Thread the kidneys on skewers, going down on one side of the fatty tissue in the center and coming up on the other side, so the kidneys will lie flat when you grill them. Rub with the oil and sprinkle with the salt and pepper.

Heat a grill until very hot. Preheat the oven to 140 degrees.

Place the kidneys cut side down on the hot grill and grill for 1½ minutes, then turn and cook for another 1½ minutes. Transfer to a plate and let rest, covered, in the oven for 5 minutes. The inside of the kidneys should still be pink.

At serving time, arrange 2 kidneys on each plate. Spoon about a teaspoon of the maître d' butter into each kidney. Garnish with a little watercress, placed in the center, and serve.

Lamb Kidneys in Mustard Sauce
Serves 4

☙ **This is a classic** dish in the bistros of Lyon and Paris. The kidneys should be sautéed in one layer in one or two skillets in very hot butter. The hotter the skillet, the better, as the kidneys should sear on the outside without steaming.

8 lamb kidneys (about 1 pound), cleaned of fat
3 tablespoons unsalted butter
½ teaspoon salt
¼ teaspoon freshly ground black pepper

SAUCE
¼ cup chopped shallots
1 teaspoon chopped garlic
½ cup robust red wine
1 cup Basic Brown Sauce (page 613)
1 tablespoon Dijon mustard
1 tablespoon unsalted butter

A few fresh parsley leaves, for garnish

Split the kidneys lengthwise in half. Cut each half into 3 pieces, removing the piece of fat in the center.

Heat the butter in a very large skillet (or two smaller skillets) until brown and beginning to foam. Add the kidney pieces and sprinkle with the salt and pepper. Sear over the highest-possible heat for 1½ to 2 minutes, using a slotted spoon to stir them occasionally. Transfer the kidneys to a sieve set on a plate. While you prepare the sauce, the kidneys will rest and most of the blood will drain out of them; it is strong, and, if it is eliminated, the kidneys will be milder and less assertive in taste.

MEANWHILE, FOR THE SAUCE: Add the chopped shallots to the drippings in the skillet(s) and sauté for about 1 minute, then add the garlic and red wine and stir. Cook to reduce the liquid until the pan is (pans are) almost dry. If using two pans, combine the ingredients in one skillet. Add the brown sauce, bring to a boil, and boil gently for 1 to 2 minutes. Add the mustard and butter and stir gently to incorporate. (After the mustard has been added, the sauce should not boil again, or it will tend to break down.)

Add the drained kidneys to the mustard sauce (discard the bloody liquid on the plate) and heat gently in the sauce.

Arrange the kidneys on individual plates and spoon the sauce on top of and around them. Sprinkle with the parsley and serve.

Veal Kidney Sauté with Oyster Mushrooms and Port
Serves 4

✴ **Trimmed, cut into slices,** and sautéed, these veal kidneys are served with a port wine, cream, and mushroom sauce.

 2 veal kidneys, cleaned of all fat and sinews (about 10 ounces trimmed), sliced ⅜ inch thick
 ¾ teaspoon salt
 ⅜ teaspoon freshly ground black pepper
 4 tablespoons (½ stick) unsalted butter
 1 tablespoon olive oil
 ½ cup thinly sliced shallots
 ⅓ cup port
 2 cups diced oyster mushrooms or white mushrooms
 ¾ cup heavy cream
 2 tablespoons chopped fresh chives

Sprinkle the kidneys with ½ teaspoon of the salt and ¼ teaspoon of the pepper. Heat the butter and oil in one very large or two smaller skillets. (The kidneys should fit in one layer.) When the butter and oil are very, very hot (almost brown), add the kidneys and sauté quickly (about 1½ minutes total) over high heat, stirring, until they change color, lose any visible red, and become whitish and firm. Sprinkle with the remaining ¼ teaspoon salt and ⅛ teaspoon pepper, remove from the skillet with a slotted spoon, and place in a strainer set over a bowl.

Add the shallots to the drippings in the skillet(s) and cook for about 30 seconds. Add the port and cook until most of the liquid has evaporated. If using two skillets, combine the ingredients in one pan. Add the mushrooms and cook for 1 to 2 minutes. Add the cream, bring to a boil, and boil for about 1 minute. Return the kidneys to the skillet and pour the kidney juices in the bowl back into the skillet, to flavor the sauce. Warm the sauce and kidneys until hot; do not boil, or the kidneys will toughen.

Divide the kidneys and sauce among four plates, sprinkle with the chives, and serve.

Breaded Sweetbreads in Tarragon Sauce
Serves 6

✴ **Moistened with melted butter** and dipped in fresh bread crumbs, these thin slices of sweetbreads brown beautifully, with a crispy exterior and soft, rich inside. The tarragon sauce lends moisture and flavor.

 2½ pounds pancreas sweetbreads
 5 slices firm white bread (about 5 ounces)
 8 tablespoons (1 stick) unsalted butter
 ½ teaspoon salt
 ¼ teaspoon freshly ground black pepper

SAUCE

 1 cup homemade chicken stock (page 612) or low-salt canned chicken broth

½ teaspoon potato starch (see page 318), dissolved in 1 tablespoon water

2 teaspoons fresh lemon juice

4 tablespoons (½ stick) unsalted butter

1 tablespoon chopped fresh tarragon

¼ teaspoon salt

⅛ teaspoon freshly ground black pepper

TO PREPARE THE SWEETBREADS: Soak the sweetbreads in cold water to cover for at least 2 to 3 hours, changing the water frequently (if the sweetbreads are bloody, they may need to soak for as long as 24 hours). Drain.

Put the sweetbreads in a saucepan and cover with cold water. Bring to a boil, reduce the heat, and simmer for 10 minutes. Drain in a colander and rinse the sweetbreads under cold running water until they are completely cold.

Arrange the sweetbreads flat on a cookie sheet lined with paper towels. Place more paper towels and another cookie sheet over them and put a 5-pound weight on top to weight them. Press for at least 2 to 3 hours, or, preferably, overnight, refrigerated.

Pull off any sinews, nerves, or rubbery bits that may still be attached to the sweetbreads. Cut into ⅜- to ½-inch-thick slices.

Trim the crusts from the slices of bread and process the bread to crumbs in a food processor.

Melt 4 tablespoons of the butter in a large saucepan. Sprinkle the sweetbreads lightly on both sides with the salt and pepper. Dip them in the melted butter, running each piece across the edge of the pan to remove the excess (they should just be lightly coated with the butter), and dip in the bread crumbs so they are lightly covered on both sides. Place on a plate and refrigerate until serving time.

FOR THE SAUCE: Pour the stock into a saucepan and boil until reduced to ½ cup. Add the dissolved potato starch and lemon juice and bring

SWEETBREADS

There are two types of sweetbreads. The throat sweetbread, or thymus gland, found in calves, is elongated and knobby and shrinks to nothing as the animal gets older. The second sweetbread, the pancreas gland, called *la noix*, or "the round," by the French, doesn't disappear as the animal ages, but becomes yellow, spongy, and tough. The best sweetbreads are from milk-fed calves and spring lambs. Calf's sweetbreads are readily available, but lamb sweetbreads are difficult to find in markets.

The texture of the thymus is firmer than the more compact, softer pancreas. Some people prefer one, some the other; it is purely a matter of taste: alone, sweetbreads are rather bland in flavor, so they accommodate themselves well to sauces.

Sweetbreads should be soaked in cold water and the water changed periodically, to draw out the blood and make them white. Blanching sweetbreads — boiling them in water — and weighting them presses out their pinkish liquid and makes them white and compact, improving their flavor. The blanching and pressing can be done several days ahead, if desired.

to a boil. Whisk in the butter, piece by piece, until thoroughly incorporated. Bring back to a boil and add the tarragon, salt, and pepper. Set aside.

TO SAUTÉ THE SWEETBREADS: Melt the remaining 4 tablespoons butter in two large skillets. When it is hot, place the breaded sweetbread slices in the skillets and sauté over medium-low heat for approximately 3 minutes. Turn and continue cooking for 3 minutes on the other side.

Spoon the sauce onto warm individual plates. Place the sweetbreads on top and serve.

Calf's Brains Financière
Serves 4

✎ **Calf's brains, available** in butcher shops and some specialized supermarkets, are inexpensive and very good.

Although the brains can be poached as is, it's nicer to remove the membrane from the surface first, since it will darken as it cooks and make the top of the brains tougher. The poached brains can be kept in their cooking liquid in the refrigerator for up to a week.

My wife likes brains — preferably calf's brains — above all other offal. Their soft, creamy texture and mild, rich taste make them her favorite. The financière sauce, made of tomato, green olives, wine, and mushrooms, is slightly acidic and cuts the richness of the dish. The sauce can also be served with dumplings or fish quenelles, as well as sweetbreads or even sautéed chicken breasts.

BRAINS

2	large calf's brains (about 1½ pounds)
3	cups water
¼	cup red or white wine vinegar
1	cup thinly sliced onion
2	large fresh thyme sprigs
3	bay leaves
1	teaspoon salt
½	teaspoon freshly ground black pepper

SAUCE

3	tablespoons unsalted butter
2	tablespoons chopped shallots
1	teaspoon chopped garlic
2	cups button mushrooms, cleaned
¾	cup Basic Brown Sauce (page 613)
½	cup dry white wine
½	cup diced (⅛-inch) boiled ham
½	cup peeled, seeded, and diced tomato

½	cup pitted, coarsely chopped green olives
½	teaspoon salt
½	teaspoon freshly ground black pepper

Chopped fresh parsley, for garnish

TO POACH THE BRAINS: Separate each of the brains into halves. Holding the brains under running water, slide your index finger and thumb through the folds and crevices to remove the thin membrane from the surface, until the brain is completely clean. Rinse again; the brains should be white and clean.

Combine the water, vinegar, onion, thyme, bay leaves, salt, and pepper in a stainless steel saucepan, bring to a boil, and boil for 5 minutes.

Drop the brains into the boiling liquid and bring back to a boil, then lower the heat and poach gently at a bare simmer, for 8 to 10 minutes. Remove from the heat. (*The brains can be blanched ahead and refrigerated in their cooking liquid for up to 1 week.*)

MEANWHILE, FOR THE SAUCE: Melt the butter in a saucepan. Add the shallots and sauté for about 30 seconds. Add the garlic and mushrooms and sauté until the juices start coming out of the mushrooms, 3 to 4 minutes. Add the brown sauce and wine, bring to a boil, and boil gently for 1 minute. Add the ham, tomato, and olives, bring to a boil again, and season with the salt and pepper. Remove from the heat.

To serve, remove the brains from the hot broth and drain. (If they have been refrigerated, reheat in the broth.) Arrange on a platter, coat with the sauce, decorate with parsley, and serve.

Braised Tripe Titine
Serves 10

✂ **This has been a** favorite dish of my daughter, Claudine, nicknamed Titine, since she was a child. The word *tripe* generally refers to the stomachs of oxen or beef. The first and second stomachs are both used. One resembles and is called "honeycomb," while the other is smoother and flatter.

Tripe is rich and flavorful, and its flavor improves with long cooking. If the braised tripe is allowed to cool, it will become hard, like headcheese. It is sometimes sliced and served cold, like headcheese, with a vinegar dressing.

Because tripe takes hours to cook (essential, since it is hard to digest if not cooked for long enough), I often prepare a large amount at a time and freeze the excess for future use. It freezes quite well and should be defrosted slowly under refrigeration.

Steamed potatoes are ideal with tripe. Here boiling potatoes are cut into chunks of approxi-

mately equal size and then rounded with a knife to make uniform pieces. Small red potatoes of equal size can also be used. When steamed, potatoes absorb less water and are creamier and tastier than if boiled.

TRIPE

- 10 pounds tripe (mixture of honeycomb and plain stomach)
- 1 large beef foot (3 pounds), split, or 2 pigs' feet, split
- 1½ pounds carrots, peeled
- 1½ pounds onions
- 4 leeks (12 ounces total), trimmed (leaving some green), split, and washed
- 1 head garlic, separated into cloves and peeled
- 8–10 bay leaves
- 1 tablespoon black peppercorns
- 2 teaspoons fresh thyme
- ½ teaspoon whole cloves
- 2 tablespoons salt
- 1 tablespoon chopped jalapeño pepper
- 1 teaspoon freshly ground black pepper
- 4 cups dry white wine
- 4 cups homemade chicken stock (page 612) or low-salt canned chicken broth
- 1 tablespoon Calvados or applejack

POTATOES

- 3 pounds boiling potatoes
  Chopped fresh chives, preferably garlic chives

FOR THE TRIPE: Leaving it in whole pieces, arrange the tripe in a large pot. Put the beef foot or pigs' feet, carrots, onions, leeks, and garlic on top. With kitchen twine, tie up the bay leaves, peppercorns, thyme, and cloves in a small square of cheesecloth for easy removal after cooking, and place the bouquet garni in the pot. Add the salt, jalapeño, and black pepper and pour in the wine and stock. Bring to a boil, cover, and cook slowly for 3 hours. Remove all the solids to a tray or cookie sheet. Set the pot aside.

When it is cool enough to handle, cut the tripe into 1½- to 2-inch pieces. Remove the bones from the beef foot or pigs' feet and cut the meat into 1-inch pieces. Coarsely chop all the vegetables.

Return the tripe, meat, and vegetables to the pot, bring to a boil, and cook for another hour.

MEANWHILE, FOR THE POTATOES: Peel the potatoes and cut in half, quarters, or thirds, so all the pieces are approximately the same size. (Three pounds of potatoes will yield about 30 pieces, enough for 10 people.) Trim the flat sides to create rounded tops and sides. (If desired, reserve the trimmings in water for use in soup, mashed potatoes, etc.) Continue rounding off the square edges so the potatoes are uniformly round.

Pile the potatoes in a steamer set above boiling water, cover, and cook for about 20 minutes, until tender.

Ladle the tripe into individual soup plates or bowls and sprinkle with the Calvados or applejack. Dip one end of each cooked potato into the chopped chives and arrange (3 or 4 potatoes per serving) around the tripe. Serve.

Vegetables
and
Side Dishes

Vegetables and Side Dishes

Artichokes in Foaming Butter Sauce

Serves 6 as a first course

☙ Artichokes are traditionally served warm with hollandaise, cold with a vinaigrette, or at room temperature with this foaming butter sauce. Removing the spiny choke and the central cone of leaves, and then placing the cone of leaves upside down in the center opening as a decoration, is a classic way of presenting them. Made by emulsifying unsalted butter with water and lemon juice, the sauce is very quick to make and should be prepared at the last minute.

6 good-sized artichokes (about 2¾ pounds), trimmed (see the sidebar, opposite)

6 fresh parsley sprigs

SAUCE

¼ cup water

Pinch of salt

Freshly ground white pepper

Juice of ½ lemon

8 tablespoons (1 stick) unsalted butter, cut into pieces

Stand the artichokes in a large stainless steel pot and add 5 quarts boiling salted water. Bring to a boil again, covering the pot to hasten the process, then place a plate on top of the artichokes to keep them immersed and cook, uncovered, at a rolling boil for about 35 minutes, or until a leaf pulls out easily. Drain in a colander and cool briefly under cold running water to stop the cooking. Drain.

Spread the leaves of each artichoke apart so you can reach the center easily. Pull out the center cone of leaves all at once. This will expose the choke — scrape out the choke with a teaspoon. Turn the cone of leaves upside down and return it to the hollow artichoke center. Place a sprig of parsley on each artichoke. (It is better to serve the artichokes at room temperature; they will lose some flavor if they are cold.)

FOR THE SAUCE: Bring the water, salt, pepper, and lemon juice to a rolling boil in a small saucepan. Add the butter bit by bit, shaking the pan back and forth until all the butter has been absorbed and the mixture starts to foam. At this point, the butter will homogenize with the water and thicken; it is important to stop the cooking right now, because if the butter heats longer, it will break down and thin. Pour into a heated sauceboat and serve immediately with the artichokes.

Artichokes with Ravigote Sauce

Serves 4 as a first course

☙ This versatile *ravigote* sauce — a mixture of red onion, capers, vinegar, oil, and herbs — is also good with poached or grilled fish.

You can cook the artichokes a day ahead, refrigerate them, and then quarter them and remove the chokes shortly before serving. They are best served at room temperature. A quick reheating in a microwave oven, a regular oven, or boiling water will take the chill off them.

4 artichokes (about 2 pounds), trimmed (see the sidebar, opposite)

SAUCE

¼ cup coarsely chopped red onion

1 tablespoon drained capers

¼ teaspoon salt

½ teaspoon freshly ground black pepper

1½ tablespoons red wine vinegar or sherry vinegar

¼ cup olive oil

3 tablespoons chopped mixed fresh herbs, such as parsley, chives, and tarragon

1 tablespoon chopped mixed fresh herbs

Bring 3 quarts water to a boil in a large stainless steel saucepan. Add the artichokes to the boiling water and place a plate on top as a weight to hold them under the water. Bring the water back to a boil and boil the artichokes, uncovered, for about 35 minutes, or until a leaf can be pulled out easily.

Pour the hot water out of the pan and add enough ice-cold water to cover the artichokes and cool them quickly. When they are cool, drain and gently press them between your palms to extract as much water from them as possible without breaking them. Spread the leaves of each one apart and remove the cone of center leaves, pulling them out together (and reserving them) to expose the chokes. Quarter the artichokes lengthwise and scrape out and discard the chokes.

FOR THE SAUCE: Combine the onion, capers, salt, pepper, vinegar, olive oil, and herbs in a small bowl.

To serve, arrange 4 artichoke quarters attractively on each of four plates, with the stems extending outward. Arrange a reserved cone of center artichoke leaves in the middle of each plate and spoon the sauce over the artichokes. Garnish with the herbs and serve.

HOW TO TRIM ARTICHOKES

With a sharp knife, trim 1½ inches from the top of each artichoke. Using scissors, trim off the top thirds of the remaining leaves to remove the sharp "prickers." Trim the artichoke stems and peel the fibrous outer surface from the stems.

Garlic-Bread-Stuffed Artichokes
Serves 8 as a first course, 16 as a side dish

✂ **To prepare artichokes for** stuffing, you must precook them so the cone of center leaves and the choke can be removed. These artichokes can be prepared ahead and braised when needed. Serve a whole or a half artichoke per person, depending on the menu. They can be served alone as a first course or, halved, with any roast meat.

8 medium artichokes (about 3 pounds), trimmed (see the sidebar), stems removed, peeled, and reserved

STUFFING

2 tablespoons unsalted butter
¼ cup peanut or corn oil
4–5 shallots, finely chopped (⅓ cup)
3–5 garlic cloves, finely chopped
4–5 slices firm white bread, processed to crumbs in a food processor (2 cups)
¼ teaspoon salt
¼ teaspoon freshly ground black pepper

2 tablespoons olive oil

Bring 5 quarts water to a boil in a stainless steel stockpot. Add the artichokes, place a plate on top of them to keep them immersed, cover, and bring to a boil again. Boil gently for about 30 minutes. Drain in a colander and rinse under cold water; drain again.

When the artichokes are cool enough to handle, spread the outer leaves of each artichoke apart, grab the center cone of leaves, and pull it out in one clump. Using a sharp spoon, remove the choke. As the artichokes are not completely cooked, it may require some scraping with the spoon to remove the chokes.

FOR THE STUFFING: Heat the butter with the oil in a large skillet until hot. Add the shallots, garlic, and bread crumbs and sauté over medium-high heat, stirring almost constantly, for 4 to 5 minutes, until the crumbs turn a nice brown color. Add the salt and pepper and remove from the heat.

Spoon about 2 tablespoons of the stuffing into each artichoke, placing some in the center cavity and some in between the leaves. Stand the stuffed artichokes side by side in one layer in a large stainless steel saucepan. Sprinkle with the olive oil, add 1 cup water, and put the stems around the artichokes. Cover and bring to a boil, then reduce the heat and cook for about 20 minutes, or until most of the moisture has evaporated and only the olive oil remains with the gently stewing artichokes. If there is still liquid in the pan, remove the lid and boil until it has evaporated.

Arrange the artichokes on a platter, with the stems around them, and serve.

Artichoke Hymn to Spring
Serves 4

✻ **For this stew of** spring vegetables, artichokes are first cooked in water until tender. The leaves are removed and the flesh is scraped from them, and it goes into the pot, along with the stems, a little onion, and sugar. At the last moment, snow peas, asparagus spears, Boston lettuce, and the artichoke hearts are added. The dish makes a great first course as well as an excellent side dish.

4   medium artichokes (about 1½ pounds), trimmed (see page 405), stems removed, peeled, and cut into ½-inch pieces

1   white onion (4 ounces), cut into 1-inch pieces (½ cup)

2   tablespoons olive oil

¾   teaspoon salt

1   teaspoon sugar

1   tablespoon unsalted butter

½   cup water

6   ounces snow peas, ends trimmed and strings removed

6   large asparagus spears, trimmed, peeled, and cut into 1-inch pieces (1¼ cups)

1   small head Boston lettuce (about 6 ounces), washed and cut into 2-inch pieces (2½–3 cups)

Bring 8 cups water to a boil in a large stainless steel saucepan. Carefully drop the artichokes into the boiling water and place a heatproof plate on top of them to hold them under the water. Bring the water back to a boil, partially cover the pot, and boil the artichokes for about 35 minutes, until a leaf can be easily pulled from the base of the artichokes. Drain the artichokes in a colander and cool under cold running water.

Meanwhile, combine the artichoke stem pieces, onion, oil, salt, sugar, butter, and water in a stainless steel saucepan and bring to a boil. Reduce the heat to low, cover, and boil gently for 5 minutes. Remove from the heat and set aside.

Squeeze the artichokes gently to press out the excess water. Remove and reserve the leaves to expose the heart; keep 6 large leaves from each artichoke for decoration. Using a small spoon, scrape the bottoms of the remaining leaves to remove the edible flesh (about ⅓ cup of flesh per artichoke). Add the flesh to the artichoke stem mixture. Remove the chokes from the artichoke hearts and cut each heart into 4 wedges. (*The recipe can be prepared a few hours ahead to this point.*)

About 15 minutes before serving, bring the artichoke stem and onion mixture to a boil. Add the snow peas and asparagus and bring back to a boil over high heat. Boil, covered, for 2 minutes, then add the lettuce and boil, covered, for 2 more minutes. Place the artichoke heart pieces on top of the vegetable stew and heat for 1 to 2 minutes longer.

Spoon the vegetable stew into the center of four plates and arrange the artichoke heart pieces on top. Decorate the edges of each plate with the reserved artichoke leaves and serve.

Baby Artichokes with Anchovies
Serves 6 to 8

❧ **This is one of** my favorite ways of serving small or baby artichokes. They are cooked with wine and garlic, then anchovies are added and they are served lukewarm as a first course or side dish. The smaller the artichokes, the better, because the chokes will not have started forming in the center.

2	pounds baby artichokes (about 20)
2	tablespoons olive oil
¾	teaspoon salt
½	teaspoon freshly ground black pepper
½	teaspoon fennel seeds
3	strips lemon rind, removed with a vegetable peeler
1	onion (6 ounces), coarsely chopped (1½ cups)
5	garlic cloves, thinly sliced (1 tablespoon)
½	cup dry white wine
½	cup water
1	2-ounce can anchovies in oil, coarsely chopped
1	tablespoon chopped fresh chives

Cut off the top half of each artichoke and discard. Cut around each artichoke about ¼ inch deep to remove the tough outside leaves. Cut the artichokes in half.

Combine all the ingredients except the anchovies and chives in a large stainless steel saucepan, bring to a boil, and boil, covered, for about 15 minutes, or until the artichokes are tender and most of the cooking liquid has evaporated.

Mix in the anchovies and bring back to a boil, then remove from the heat.

Serve the artichokes lukewarm, garnished with the chives.

Summer Vegetable Salad in Artichoke Hearts
Serves 6 as a main course, 12 as a side dish

❧ **These artichoke hearts can** also be used to hold poached eggs, vegetable purees, peas, or glazed carrots, as well as cooked fish and shellfish. The dish is excellent as a first course or to complement cold meat. The spicy vegetable salad can be served on its own with cold chicken or cold cuts.

6 artichokes (6–8 ounces each)

½ lemon, plus 2 tablespoons fresh
lemon juice

2 tablespoons olive oil

½ teaspoon salt

VEGETABLE SALAD

3 tablespoons olive oil

1 jalapeño pepper, seeded and chopped
(about 1 tablespoon)

1 pound red bell peppers (about 3), cored,
seeded, and cut into 1-inch-wide strips

1 pound zucchini, trimmed and cut into
1½-inch pieces (2 cups)

2 cups 1-inch pieces mushrooms

1½ tablespoons sliced garlic

1 teaspoon salt

½ teaspoon freshly ground black pepper

1 cup 1-inch pieces sun-dried tomatoes
in oil

1 teaspoon toasted sesame oil

TO PREPARE THE ARTICHOKE HEARTS:

Cut off the stems, peel them, and rub with the
lemon so they don't discolor. Set aside.

Fold the artichoke leaves down on themselves; they will snap and break at the base, leaving the "meat" of the leaves attached to the heart.
Continue until you have snapped all the outer
leaves off in this manner and most of the heart is
exposed. Cut off the center cone of leaves to leave
only the heart.

With a vegetable peeler or a sharp knife, trim
the remaining green from the artichoke heart.
There should be only the tender green flesh remaining and the hearts should be rounded, with
all the "meat" of the leaves left on.

Put the artichoke hearts and stems in a stainless steel saucepan, add 3 cups water, the lemon
juice, oil, and salt, and bring to a boil. Cover,

ARTICHOKE HEARTS — BASIC TECHNIQUE

Artichoke hearts (also known as artichoke
bottoms) are used in countless recipes, cold
or hot, stuffed with ingredients from smoked
salmon to stewed tomatoes to poached beef
marrow. Although it takes some practice to
shape, or "turn," an artichoke properly, it is worth the effort.

With a sharp knife, trim off all
the outer leaves all around each
artichoke heart, as close as you
can without taking the "meat"
out of the heart. Cut off the inner cone of leaves at the point
where they attach to the choke.
Cut off the stem. With a small
knife or vegetable peeler,
trim the remaining greenish
leaves and smooth the bot-
tom as well as you can. There should still be
some light green flesh on the heart. Rub the
heart with lemon and put in a stainless steel
saucepan.

For 6 hearts, add 4 cups water, 2 tablespoons olive oil, 2 tablespoons fresh lemon
juice, and ½ teaspoon salt. Bring to a boil,
reduce the heat, and simmer for 30 to 40
minutes, or until the hearts are tender when
pierced with the point of a small knife. Remove from the heat.

When the hearts are cool enough to handle, remove the chokes with a spoon, then put
the hearts in a container with enough of the
cooking liquid to cover. They can be kept for
at least 1 week in the refrigerator in the broth.
(For an alternative method of preparing artichoke hearts, see Summer Vegetable Salad in
Artichoke Hearts, opposite.)

reduce the heat, and cook gently for 20 to 25 minutes, until the hearts are tender when pierced with the point of a knife. Allow to cool in the liquid.

Drain the artichokes. With a spoon or your thumb, remove the chokes, which should slide off the hearts. To create thin-shelled receptacles, use a measuring spoon (the edges are sharper than a regular spoon) to scoop out ½ inch of the insides of each artichoke heart. Set aside the trimmings for the salad.

FOR THE VEGETABLE SALAD: Heat the olive oil in a large saucepan. Add the jalapeño pepper and sauté for about 30 seconds, then add the red pepper strips and sauté for 2 to 3 minutes. Add the zucchini, mushrooms, garlic, salt, and pepper, cover, and cook over medium-high heat for 4 to 5 minutes. Add the sun-dried tomatoes and cook for 2 minutes. Remove from the heat and add the sesame oil and artichoke heart trimmings, stirring them into the salad. Let cool.

At serving time, put the artichoke hearts on a serving plate, spoon the salad into them, and serve.

Artichoke Hearts with Tarragon and Mushrooms
Serves 6 as a first course

⚘ **I first prepared these** artichokes at the home of my friend and mentor Helen McCully, a cookbook author and the food editor of *House Beautiful* magazine, in the early 1960s. Whipped cream is added to the sauce just before filling the hearts to add richness to the dish and give it a glaze when it is run under the broiler.

- 2 tablespoons unsalted butter
- 2 cups mushrooms cut into ½-inch dice (about 6 ounces)
- 1 tablespoon cognac

- ⅔ cup heavy cream
- ¼ teaspoon salt
- ⅛ teaspoon freshly ground black pepper
- 1 tablespoon chopped mixed fresh tarragon and parsley
- ½ teaspoon potato starch (see page 318), dissolved in 1 tablespoon cold water
- 6 artichoke hearts, prepared according to the directions in the sidebar, chokes removed, and kept warm in the broth
- 1½ tablespoons freshly grated Pecorino Romano cheese

Melt the butter in a large saucepan. Add the mushrooms and cook until the liquid from the mushrooms has evaporated. Add the cognac and cook for 30 seconds. Add ¼ cup of the cream, the salt, pepper, and herbs and bring to a boil. Add the dissolved potato starch, mix well, and boil to thicken. Remove from the heat.

Preheat the broiler. Drain the artichoke hearts.

Whip the remaining cream until stiff. Rapidly fold into the mushroom mixture and immediately fill the artichoke hearts. Sprinkle with the cheese and place under the broiler for 2 to 3 minutes, until nicely browned.

Saffron Artichoke Hearts

Serves 6 as a first course

❧ **Uncooked artichoke hearts are** cut into wedges and the choke is removed from each piece with a knife. The flavor becomes more intense if the artichokes are cooked 24 hours ahead. This is a great summer first course.

6   medium artichokes, trimmed to hearts as described on page 408, cut into 8 wedges each, and chokes removed with a paring knife
1   cup water
½   cup dry white wine
1   tablespoon fresh lemon juice
¾   cup thinly sliced onion
2   tablespoons olive oil
1   teaspoon salt
¼   teaspoon freshly ground black pepper
1   bay leaf
¼   teaspoon saffron threads, crushed

Combine all the ingredients in a stainless steel pot and bring to a boil. Simmer gently for about 20 minutes, until the artichoke hearts are tender.

Transfer the artichokes to a bowl and let cool, then cover with plastic wrap and refrigerate. (*This will keep in the refrigerator for at least 1 week.*) Serve cold.

Asparagus en Fête with Lemon-Mustard Sauce

Serves 4 as a first course

❧ *En fête* means "holiday-style," and this dish has a festive appearance. The cooked asparagus spears are split lengthwise in half up to the tip and the stems spread apart and arranged in a "frame" design on the plates. Colorful olives, capers, and tomatoes are tossed with the trimmed ends of the stalks and piled in the center of the "frames." The dish is served with a lemony mustard sauce.

16   large asparagus spears (about 1¼ pounds), trimmed and peeled

SAUCE

1   tablespoon Dijon mustard
½   teaspoon salt
¼   teaspoon freshly ground black pepper
2   teaspoons fresh lemon juice
¼   cup extra-virgin olive oil

24   oil-cured black olives
2   tablespoons drained capers
1   ripe tomato (5 ounces), halved, seeded, and cut into ½-inch pieces (1 cup)
¼   cup loosely packed fresh parsley leaves

Put the asparagus in no more than two layers in a stainless steel saucepan, add 1 cup boiling water, and bring to a boil over high heat. Cover the pan and boil the asparagus for 3 to 4 minutes, until it is tender but still firm. Remove the asparagus from the pan and spread it out on a platter to speed cooling.

When the asparagus is cool enough to handle, measure about 5 inches down from the tip of each spear and cut off the rest of the stem. Cut the stems into 1-inch pieces and reserve. Split the

HOW TO TRIM ASPARAGUS

Buy large asparagus with firm, not wrinkled, stalks and tightly closed tips. So that the whole spear will be tender, peel the lower half of the stalk using a vegetable peeler: holding the asparagus by the bottom end, peel it from the base of the tip down to your fingers, rotating the stem as you peel. Cut or break off the unpeeled bottom part of the stalk.

spears lengthwise in half, stopping when you get to the tips to leave them attached.

FOR THE SAUCE: Combine all the ingredients in a small bowl.

At serving time, mix the 1-inch pieces of asparagus with the olives, capers, and tomato in a bowl. Arrange 4 asparagus spears on each plate so the tips extend to the edges of the plate and the stalks, spread open where they are cut, connect to create a square "frame." Arrange the tomato-olive mixture in the center of the plates and spoon the sauce over both the spears and the mixture. Sprinkle with the parsley and serve.

Asparagus in Mustard Sauce
Serves 4 as a first course

✎ This is the classic asparagus and mustard vinaigrette of French bistros and family restaurants. As a child, I would place a spoon or fork under my plate when eating it so the pungent vinaigrette collected at the lower edge of the plate. That way, I could dip the tips of the spears and my bread into the sauce before eating them. Not an elegant table maneuver, but effective.

I peel the asparagus stalks for this recipe and boil them in just enough water so that most of it

evaporates by the time the asparagus is cooked. Serve at room temperature.

1¼ pounds large asparagus spears
    (about 16), trimmed and peeled

SAUCE

2 tablespoons Dijon mustard
2 tablespoons canola oil
2 tablespoons walnut oil
2 teaspoons white wine vinegar
½ teaspoon salt
¼ teaspoon freshly ground black pepper

Put the asparagus in a large stainless steel saucepan in one or two layers and add ¾ cup boiling water. Cover, bring to a boil, and boil for 3 minutes, or until the asparagus is just tender but still firm and most of the liquid has evaporated. Drain off any remaining water and put the asparagus on a platter. Let cool.

FOR THE SAUCE: Combine all the ingredients in a small bowl and mix well; do not worry if the mixture is not totally emulsified.

Serve the asparagus with the sauce.

Asparagus Ragout

Serves 4 as a first course

❧ **This asparagus stew can** be ready in about 5 minutes and should be prepared at the last moment, although the spears can be peeled and cut in advance and refrigerated. Most of the small amount of water used to cook the asparagus evaporates, and the little bit remaining emulsifies with butter to create a smooth, creamy, flavorful sauce. The dish makes an ideal first course.

- ½ cup water
- 1 tablespoon olive oil
- 16 large asparagus spears (about 1½ pounds), trimmed, peeled, and cut into 1½-inch pieces (about 4 cups)
- 2 tablespoons unsalted butter
- ¼ teaspoon salt

Bring the water and olive oil to a boil in a large stainless steel saucepan. Add the asparagus and bring the water back to a boil. Cover and boil for 2½ minutes over high heat. There should be 2 to 3 tablespoons of water left; if necessary, add water or boil to reduce to bring it to this amount.

Add the butter and salt, bring to a strong boil, and boil for about 1 minute, stirring well once or twice. Serve immediately.

Sautéed Apple Rings

Serves 6 to 8

❧ **These apple rings complement** fish and sautéed meat or game and are good with Chitterling Sausages (page 386) or other sausages.

- 3 Golden Delicious apples
- 1 tablespoon unsalted butter
- ¼ teaspoon salt
- ¼ teaspoon freshly ground white pepper
- 1 teaspoon sugar

Leaving the skin on, cut the apples crosswise into slices approximately 1 inch thick. Using a small round cookie cutter or the large end of a pastry tip, remove the apple cores to create rings.

Heat the butter in a large skillet. When it is hot, add the apple slices in one layer. Sprinkle with the salt, white pepper, and sugar and sauté for about 5 minutes. Turn and cook for 5 minutes on the other side, or until nicely browned and tender. Transfer the slices to a plate and serve.

Sautéed Haricots Verts and Shallots

Serves 4

❧ **This harmonious combination of** green beans, shallots, and butter is a winner. Try to get authentic haricots verts, thin very young green beans — available in specialty food stores or at farmers' markets — or choose the smallest, firmest regular string beans you can find. Make sure to cook them fully; they should be tender, not crunchy. Too often beans are just blanched, and their taste is not what it should be.

- 1 pound haricots verts or very small string beans, tips removed
- 1 tablespoon unsalted butter
- 1 tablespoon peanut oil
- 2 tablespoons finely chopped shallots
- ¼ teaspoon salt
- ¼ teaspoon freshly ground black pepper

Bring 1½ cups water to a boil in a large saucepan. Add the beans and cook, covered, over high heat for 7 to 8 minutes, until they are tender but still firm to the bite. Drain the beans and spread them on a large platter to cool.

At serving time, heat the butter and oil in a large skillet. When they are hot, add the shallots and sauté for about 10 seconds. Add the beans, salt, and pepper and sauté for about 2 minutes, until the beans are heated through. Serve.

Beans and Broccoli Rabe

Serves 4

Broccoli rabe has a slightly bitter taste that complements white beans well. Any type of little white bean — navy, Great Northern, pea, or Boston — will work well. Serve warm, sprinkled with a little olive oil, if you like.

- 8 ounces dried white beans, such as navy or Great Northern, picked over and rinsed
- ¾ teaspoon salt
- 2 fresh thyme sprigs or ½ teaspoon dried thyme
- ⅓ cup diced (½-inch) ham
- 1 large onion, cut into ¾-inch dice (1¼ cups)
- 8 ounces broccoli rabe or Chinese broccoli
- 2 tablespoons olive oil, plus (optional) olive oil for serving
- 2 garlic cloves, crushed and finely chopped (1 teaspoon)
- ¼ teaspoon hot pepper flakes

Combine the beans, 4 cups cold water, the salt, thyme, ham, and onion in a large saucepan and bring to a boil. Skim off the foam, cover, reduce the heat to low, and cook at a gentle boil for 1½ to 2 hours, until the beans are tender and most of the water has been absorbed; just enough water should remain to make the beans look moist.

Meanwhile, wash the broccoli rabe or Chinese broccoli. If necessary, peel the fibrous end of the stems. Cut the stems into 2-inch pieces (you should have about 3 cups).

Heat the oil in a skillet until hot. Add the garlic and pepper flakes and sauté for about 10 seconds. Add the broccoli (still wet from washing) and sauté for about 1 minute. Cover and cook over medium heat for 5 to 6 minutes, until the broccoli softens, becomes tender, and renders some of its juices. Remove from the heat.

At serving time, combine the beans and broccoli, rewarming them if necessary. If desired, sprinkle a little olive oil on each serving.

Stewed Navy Beans

Serves 8 to 10

Flavored with bacon, onion, tomato, and thyme, these stewed beans are ideal with lamb. They can also be transformed into a cassoulet by adding sausages and poultry.

- 1 pound dried navy or pea beans, picked over and rinsed
- 1 teaspoon salt
- 6 ounces bacon, cut into ¼-inch-wide strips
- 2 onions, coarsely chopped (1¾ cups)
- 2 medium or 4 small tomatoes, quartered and seeded (1½ cups)
- ½ teaspoon dried thyme

Combine the beans with 8 cups cold water and the salt in a pot and bring to a boil. Skim off the foam, reduce the heat, and simmer gently, uncovered, for 1½ hours, or until tender but a bit firm.

Meanwhile, cook the bacon in a heavy saucepan over medium-high heat for 8 to 10 minutes, until nicely browned. Add the onions and cook for 2 minutes longer.

Drain the beans, reserving 2 cups of the cooking liquid. Add the tomatoes, thyme, beans, and reserved liquid to the onions and bring to a boil, then reduce the heat and simmer gently for 45 minutes, or until the beans are very tender.

Transfer approximately 1 cup of the bean mixture to a food processor and process until pureed. (This will serve as a thickening agent to make the beans the right consistency.) Return the puree to the saucepan. Alternatively, blend the mixture with a hand blender for a few seconds to get the same result. If the beans are still too liquid, cook them, uncovered, over high heat for a few more minutes to reduce the liquid further. If, on the other hand, the bean mixture is too thick, add a little water to thin it. Serve.

Flageolets with Diced Vegetables
Serves 4

⚘ **Flageolets are a variety** of French bean. Although I occasionally find them fresh, they are more usually available dried in specialty food stores. Long, narrow, and light green in color because they are picked when only half ripe, they look somewhat like small dried lima beans. Dried white beans, such as navy or pea beans, can be substituted.

I prepare the beans with a mixture of finely diced vegetables, called *mirepoix*. A traditional accompaniment to lamb, flageolets go very well with Braised Leg of Lamb (page 352).

The beans can be cooked ahead and reheated before serving.

8 ounces dried flageolets, picked over and rinsed
1 small onion, chopped (½ cup)
1 carrot (2 ounces), peeled and cut into ¼-inch dice (⅓ cup)
1 small celery stalk, peeled and cut into ¼-inch dice (⅓ cup)
1 2-ounce piece leek (white and green parts), thinly sliced and washed (½ cup)
½ teaspoon herbes de Provence
1½ cups homemade chicken stock (page 612) or low-salt canned chicken broth
1½ cups cold water
1 teaspoon salt, or to taste
1 tomato, halved, seeded, and cut into ½-inch dice (¾ cup)
1 tablespoon olive oil

Combine the flageolets, onion, carrot, celery, leek, herbes de Provence, stock, water, and salt in a small pot and bring to a boil. Skim off the foam, cover, reduce the heat to low, and simmer gently for about 1½ hours, until the beans are tender and most of the liquid has evaporated.

Using a hand blender, puree the bean mixture for 10 seconds. Or remove a cup of the beans, puree in a food processor or mini-chop, and return the puree to the pot. Stir the puree into the rest of the beans to thicken the whole mixture slightly.

Stir in the tomato and oil and serve.

Braised Red Beans

Serves 8

❧ **Slightly larger than dried** white beans, kidney beans are reddish and heavier in texture. Here they are first simmered in water with seasonings, which can be done up to a day ahead, and finished with garlic, parsley, tomatoes, and butter. Serve with roast lamb or pork.

1	pound dried kidney beans, picked over and rinsed
2	teaspoons salt
1	very large onion (8–10 ounces), cut into eighths
4	cloves
1	fresh rosemary sprig
2	bay leaves
2	medium carrots, peeled and cut into 1-inch pieces (2 cups)
5	tablespoons unsalted butter
3	medium tomatoes, coarsely chopped (about 2 cups)
1	teaspoon crushed and finely chopped garlic (2–3 cloves)
½	teaspoon freshly ground black pepper
¼	cup chopped fresh parsley

Put the beans in a large heavy saucepan, add 8 cups cold water, 1½ teaspoons of the salt, the onion stuck with the 4 cloves, the rosemary, bay leaves, and carrots and bring to a boil. Skim off the foam, cover, reduce the heat, and simmer slowly for 1 hour and 45 minutes, or until the beans are tender and most of the liquid has cooked away. (*The beans can be prepared to this point up to a day ahead and refrigerated; bring to a simmer before finishing the dish.*)

Meanwhile, melt 3 tablespoons of the butter in a saucepan. Add the tomatoes and cook over medium heat for 2 minutes. Add the garlic, the remaining ½ teaspoon salt, and the pepper, mix well, and set aside.

When the beans are cooked, combine the parsley with the tomato mixture and add to the beans. Add the remaining 2 tablespoons butter and simmer over medium heat for 5 minutes. Serve.

Dried Lima Bean Puree

Serves 4

❧ **Dried lima beans cook** quickly and are very good pureed. I cook them in chicken stock flavored with a little salt and herbes de Provence. You can substitute water for the stock if you want a vegetarian dish. When tender, the beans are transformed into a smooth puree in a food processor. The puree can be prepared ahead. Reheat it in a double boiler or microwave oven (it tends to scorch if warmed in a saucepan on top of the stove).

4	ounces dried large lima beans, picked over and rinsed
1½	cups homemade chicken stock (page 612), low-salt canned chicken broth, or water
⅓	teaspoon salt, or to taste
¼	teaspoon herbes de Provence
2	tablespoons olive oil

Combine the beans, stock or water, salt, and herbes de Provence in a saucepan and bring to a boil over high heat. Skim off the foam, cover, reduce the heat to low, and cook the beans gently for about 35 minutes, until they are soft. There should be only a little liquid remaining in the pan.

Transfer the beans and liquid to a food processor and process for 15 to 20 seconds. Add the oil and process for a few seconds, until incorporated. Serve.

Black-Eyed Pea
and Kale Ragout
Serves 6 to 8

This inspired combination of ham, kale, and beans makes a great lunch with a green salad.

1 pound dried black-eyed peas, picked over and rinsed

1 teaspoon salt

1 jalapeño pepper, seeded and coarsely chopped (1 tablespoon; optional)

8 ounces rind and trimmings from Virginia ham, or pancetta or bacon, cut into ½-inch pieces

2 onions (about 8 ounces), cut into 1-inch pieces

4 garlic cloves, sliced (about 2 tablespoons)

1½ pounds kale, collard greens, or turnip greens, leaves cut into 2-inch pieces, stems cut into ½-inch pieces

Tabasco sauce (optional)

Put the peas in a small pot, add 6 cups cold water, the salt, and jalapeño pepper, if using, and bring to a boil. Skim off the foam, reduce the heat to very low, cover, and cook for 45 minutes, or until the peas are tender. Most of the liquid will have been absorbed by the peas. (*You can cook the dried peas ahead, but they tend to dry out if left to stand for a few hours or longer. Before adding the kale mixture, add some water to the peas if needed — they should be soupy — and bring to a boil.*)

Meanwhile, cook the ham or bacon in a large saucepan over medium-low heat until the fat is rendered and the ham or bacon is browned, about 10 minutes. Add the onions and garlic and sauté for about 1 minute.

Wash the greens under cool water and add, still wet from washing, to the saucepan, pressing down on the greens so they fit in the pan. Cover and cook until wilted and soft, about 10 minutes for kale, less for collard greens or turnip greens. Remove from the heat.

At serving time, add the greens mixture to the peas, stir, and bring to a boil. Reduce the heat and simmer for 8 to 10 minutes.

Serve the peas and greens with Tabasco sauce, if desired.

Piquant Steamed Broccoli
with Lemon Sauce
Serves 4

Steamed briefly so that it keeps its texture and deep green color, the broccoli is tossed with a simple sauce made of lemon juice, olive oil, and Tabasco. This dish can be served as a first course or a side.

SAUCE

1½ tablespoons fresh lemon juice

¼ cup extra-virgin olive oil

¼ teaspoon Tabasco sauce

¼ teaspoon salt

1½ pounds broccoli

FOR THE SAUCE: Combine the lemon juice, olive oil, Tabasco, and salt in a bowl. Mix well and set aside.

Cut the broccoli florets from the stems and separate into 2-inch-wide florets. Peel the stems and cut them into strips about ½ inch thick by 2 inches long.

Arrange the broccoli florets and stems on a heatproof plate, place in a steamer, and steam, covered, over boiling water for 11 to 12 minutes, until tender.

Toss gently with the sauce and serve.

Broccoli Velvet Puree

Serves 4

❧ **This is a delicious** way to serve broccoli. First I cook it with some garlic and jalapeño pepper until it is tender. Then I emulsify the mixture with a little butter and olive oil in a blender to create a smooth, creamy puree.

 1½ pounds broccoli
 1½ cups water
 ¾ teaspoon salt
 1 garlic clove
 1 teaspoon coarsely chopped jalapeño pepper
 2 tablespoons unsalted butter
 1 tablespoon extra-virgin olive oil

Cut the broccoli heads from the stalks and separate the florets. Peel the stalks and cut them into 2-inch-long pieces.

Bring the water to a boil in a medium saucepan. Add the broccoli, salt, garlic, and jalapeño pepper and bring back to a boil over high heat. Cover the pan and cook for 10 minutes, or until the broccoli is very tender.

Transfer the broccoli and ⅔ cup of the cooking liquid to a blender. Add the butter and oil and blend for about 1 minute, until the mixture is very smooth. Serve.

Broccoli with Butter

Serves 4

❧ **I love broccoli** in everything from salads to soups, and this simple preparation is one of my favorites. Choose bunches with heads that are very tight and deep green. Peel the tough outer layer of the stems so people can enjoy the entire stalk, which I think is the best part.

 1 pound broccoli, separated into florets about 2 inches wide, stems peeled
 1½ tablespoons unsalted butter
 ¼ teaspoon salt

Put the broccoli and 1 cup water in a large saucepan, bring to a boil, cover, and cook over medium heat for 5 minutes, or until tender. (Most of the liquid will have evaporated.)

Add the butter and salt, mix thoroughly, and serve.

Braised Sweet-and-Sour Red Cabbage

Serves 4

❧ **The combination of apple** cider and cider vinegar creates a sweet-and-sour effect. The cabbage complements pork especially well and also goes with goose or duck.

 1 pound red cabbage, halved, cored, and cut into 1-inch-wide slices
 1 large onion, thinly sliced (1½ cups)
 ¾ cup raisins
 1 apple, peeled, cored, and cut into cubes (about 1½ cups)
 1 cup apple cider
 3 tablespoons cider vinegar
 ¾ teaspoon salt
 ¼ teaspoon freshly ground black pepper
 1½ teaspoons canola oil

Combine the cabbage, onion, raisins, apple, cider, vinegar, salt, pepper, and oil in a large stainless steel saucepan and bring to a boil. Cover, reduce the heat to medium, and boil for 45 minutes.

Most of the liquid should have evaporated, but the cabbage should still be moist; cook for a bit longer if excess moisture remains in the bottom of the pan. The cooking juices should be caramelized and the cabbage a little crunchy. Serve.

Little Braised Cabbages
Serves 6

❧ **A large cabbage** is separated into individual leaves and blanched, and the larger leaves are stuffed with the smaller ones and formed into small "cabbages." They are braised with bacon, onions, and tomato to create a flavorful sauce. These are very good reheated.

1	large savoy cabbage (about 2 pounds)
10	slices bacon (8 ounces), coarsely chopped
1	medium tomato, cubed (1 cup)
2	medium onions, thinly sliced (1¾ cups)
5	garlic cloves, crushed and coarsely chopped (1 good tablespoon)
5	carrots, peeled and thinly sliced (1½ cups)
¼	teaspoon freshly ground black pepper
½	teaspoon dried thyme
2	bay leaves, broken into pieces
1	teaspoon salt
2	cups homemade chicken stock (page 612) or low-salt canned chicken broth
1	tablespoon cider vinegar
1	teaspoon arrowroot or cornstarch

Remove and discard any torn or bruised leaves from the cabbage. Cut out the core and separate the leaves. Try not to damage the large leaves; you will use them later as wrappers.

Drop all the cabbage leaves into a large pot of boiling salted water. Push the leaves down into the water and bring to a boil again. It will take at least 5 minutes for it to start boiling once more; when it does, cover and continue to boil for 12 minutes. Set the whole pot of cabbage under cold running water and let the water run until the leaves are thoroughly cold. Drain in a colander.

Select 10 of the largest leaves to use as wrappers. Cut away the triangular rib sections, which are tough.

Gently press a large leaf into the cup of an 8-ounce ladle or a small bowl of the same size, so that it hangs over the sides. Fill the center of it with smaller cabbage leaves, pushing on them to make them compact. Fold the overhanging edges of the large leaf over the center, press them together, and unmold. You will have a nice round little "cabbage." Press on it gently to draw out some of the excess water. Repeat until you have made 10 miniature cabbages.

Preheat the oven to 400 degrees.

Put the bacon in a large flameproof baking dish. Top with the tomato, half of the onions, the garlic, and half of the carrots and sprinkle with the pepper. Arrange the little cabbages on top. Sprinkle the remaining onions and carrots, the thyme, bay leaves, and salt over them and pour the chicken stock over the assembled dish.

Bring the stock and cabbages to a boil on top of the stove. Cover the baking dish tightly with aluminum foil, place on a cookie sheet, and bake for 1 hour.

Reduce the oven heat to 350 degrees and bake for 30 minutes longer. Take off the aluminum foil and arrange the little cabbages on a platter; garnish by sprinkling all of the cooked vegetables on top of them.

You should have about 1½ cups of juices left in the baking dish. Mix the vinegar with the arrowroot until smooth, add it to the juices, and, stirring constantly, bring to a boil. Let boil for a few seconds, then pour over the cabbages and serve.

Sautéed Napa Cabbage

Serves 6

❧ **Napa cabbage, a tight,** white, tender oblong variety, is also excellent in salad or soup, or stir-fried Chinese-style. This simple, unadorned recipe pairs well with a rich piece of meat or grilled fish.

- 1 large or 2 small heads napa cabbage (about 2 pounds total), cut into 1½-inch chunks (about 14 cups loosely packed)
- 3 tablespoons safflower or canola oil
- 2 tablespoons unsalted butter
- ½ teaspoon salt
- ½ teaspoon freshly ground black pepper

Wash the cabbage well in cold water and drain it in a colander.

Heat the oil in a large saucepan until hot. Add the butter and, as soon as it melts, add the still-wet cabbage. Cover and cook over medium-high heat, stirring occasionally, for 4 to 5 minutes, until the cabbage is wilted and tender but still slightly firm. The cabbage will sizzle initially but then stew as the moisture emerges from it. Cook over high heat, uncovered, for 2 to 3 minutes to evaporate the moisture left in the cabbage. Stir in the salt and pepper and serve.

Glazed Carrots with Olives

Serves 4

❧ **Combined with salt, a** bit of sugar, butter, and water, baby carrots are cooked until the moisture evaporates and they begin to glaze. They are finished with olives and capers.

- 1 pound baby carrots, peeled
- 1 teaspoon sugar
- ¼ teaspoon salt
- 1 tablespoon unsalted butter
- ½ cup oil-cured black olives, pitted
- 2 tablespoons drained capers
- 2 teaspoons minced fresh chives

Combine the carrots, sugar, salt, butter, and ⅔ cup water in a heavy saucepan, cover, and cook over high heat for about 8 minutes, until all the water is gone and the carrots are tender and starting to glaze. (If some moisture remains in the pan when the carrots are tender, cook them, uncovered, for 2 to 3 minutes to evaporate the water so they glaze lightly on all sides.)

Add the olives and capers and cook for 1 minute, just long enough to heat the olives through. Sprinkle with the chives and serve.

Carrots with Orange and Dill

Serves 4

❧ **Orange juice sweetens the** carrots and they are sprinkled with fresh dill. This dish can be made up to a day ahead, but don't add the dill until the last moment, since it tends to lose its flavor and darken if put in too soon.

- 1 pound carrots, peeled and cut into 1-inch pieces (3 cups)
- 1¼ cups fresh orange juice
- 1 tablespoon unsalted butter
- ½ teaspoon salt
- ½ teaspoon freshly ground black pepper
- ¼ cup loosely packed fresh dill leaves

Combine the carrots, orange juice, butter, salt, and pepper in a stainless steel saucepan, bring to a boil, and boil, covered, over medium-high heat for 10 minutes, or until the carrots are tender.

Uncover and cook over high heat until all the liquid has evaporated and the carrots are beginning to glaze in the butter. Sprinkle on the dill and serve.

Butter-Glazed Carrots
Serves 6

✍ **The water, sugar, and** butter blend together to glaze the carrots in this easy, refined dish. It's especially good made with very fresh, sweet carrots, in which case, cut the amount of sugar in half. The carrots must be sliced as thin as possible. If you are not proficient with a knife, use a vegetable slicer.

2	pounds carrots (about 16), peeled and very thinly sliced (about 8 cups)
4	tablespoons (½ stick) unsalted butter
2	teaspoons sugar
1	teaspoon salt
½	cup water
1	tablespoon finely chopped fresh parsley
2	garlic cloves, crushed and finely chopped

Combine the carrots, butter, sugar, salt, and water in a pot, bring to a boil, and boil, covered, for 10 minutes.

Uncover and boil for another 5 minutes, or until all the liquid has evaporated and the carrots are just moist. Sprinkle with the parsley and garlic and serve.

Carrot Crepes
Serves 6 (makes about 12 crepes)

✍ **Carrots give these crepes** a slightly sweet taste and a beautiful color. Delicate and delicious, they can be served as a side dish alongside meat or fish or as a first course. Although the crepes are best when just out of the skillet, they can be made up to an hour ahead, laid out in one layer on a cookie sheet or tray, and then reheated in a 200-degree oven until warmed through.

3	large carrots (12 ounces), peeled and cut into 2-inch pieces
1½	cups water
3	tablespoons all-purpose flour
1	tablespoon cornstarch
½	teaspoon salt
¼	teaspoon freshly ground black pepper
¼	teaspoon sugar
¼	cup milk
2	large eggs
2	tablespoons finely minced scallion greens
3–4	tablespoons canola oil

Drop the carrot pieces into a saucepan, add the water, and bring to a boil over high heat. Cover, reduce the heat to low, and boil gently for 18 to 20 minutes, until the carrots are fork-tender and all but about 2 tablespoons of the cooking liquid has evaporated.

Transfer the carrots and cooking liquid to a food processor and process for 10 to 15 seconds. Add the flour, cornstarch, salt, pepper, sugar, and milk and process for a few seconds. Add the eggs and process until very smooth. Pour into a bowl and stir in the scallions.

Preheat the oven to 200 degrees.

TO COOK THE CREPES: Heat 1 tablespoon of the oil in a 10-inch nonstick skillet. When it is hot, add about 2 tablespoons of the carrot mixture per crepe, making 3 or 4 crepes, each about 3 inches wide, and cook over medium heat for 2 minutes. Using a spatula, gently turn the crepes over and cook for 2 minutes on the other side. Transfer to a platter and keep warm in the oven while you cook the remaining crepes in batches, adding more oil to the pan as needed.

Serve warm.

Steamed Cauliflower with Chives
Serves 4

✻ **Especially flavorful if prepared** at the last moment, these steamed cauliflower florets are tossed with a little butter, peanut oil, chives, salt, and pepper. When choosing cauliflower, make sure the heads are very white and firm, with compact florets and no black spots.

1	firm white cauliflower (about 1½ pounds)
¼	teaspoon salt
¼	teaspoon freshly ground black pepper
1	tablespoon unsalted butter
1	tablespoon peanut oil
¼	cup minced fresh chives

Remove the green leaves from the cauliflower, cut out the core, and divide it into 12 to 16 florets of approximately equal size.

Put the cauliflower florets in a steamer basket, set over boiling water, cover, and cook over medium-high heat for about 10 minutes, until the florets are tender but still firm.

Transfer the cauliflower to a bowl, add the salt, pepper, butter, peanut oil, and chives, and toss briefly to mix. Serve.

Sautéed Cauliflower with Bread Crumbs and Eggs
Serves 6

✻ **Sautéed cauliflower florets can** simply be tossed with butter, toasted bread crumbs, and chopped egg, but reassembling the florets into a head of cauliflower and garnishing it is nice for an elegant dinner party. The classic egg and bread crumb garnish is called *polonaise*.

1	large or 2 small firm white cauliflower (about 3½ pounds total)
8	tablespoons (1 stick) unsalted butter
1	tablespoon olive oil
1	teaspoon salt
¼	teaspoon freshly ground white pepper
1	large hard-cooked egg (see page 66), finely chopped
2	tablespoons chopped fresh parsley
1	large slice firm white bread, processed to crumbs in a food processor (¾ cup)

Bring a large pot of salted water to a boil. Meanwhile, cut the leaves from the cauliflower and separate the florets by cutting around the core(s) with a knife.

Place the florets in the boiling water and bring the water to a boil again; reduce the heat and boil gently for 6 to 8 minutes, until the stems are tender when pierced with the point of a knife. Drain.

Melt half of the butter in a very large heavy skillet. (If you don't have an extra-large skillet, use two.) Add the oil. When the mixture is hot, carefully place the florets head down in it, sprinkle with the salt and white pepper, and cook over medium-low heat for 5 to 7 minutes, until the florets are golden brown.

If you'd like to present the florets as a reassembled head of cauliflower (or 2 heads), arrange in the following way: Make a circle of florets — about 5 or 6 inches in diameter — on a dinner plate (or on each of two plates), with the stems pointing toward the center. Continue building up by placing florets, stems always pointed down, in smaller and smaller circles until the construction resembles a head of cauliflower. Mix the chopped egg and parsley together and sprinkle on the cauliflower.

Melt the remaining butter in a skillet. Add the bread crumbs and cook, shaking the skillet constantly, until the crumbs are golden brown. Pour over the cauliflower and serve.

Alternatively, toss the sautéed florets with the chopped egg and parsley, sprinkle with the toasted bread crumbs, and serve.

Cauliflower Gribiche
Serves 4

✶ *Gribiche* is a simple oil-and-vinegar dressing that is conventionally garnished with hard-cooked eggs, gherkins, and herbs; I add anchovy fillets. It is terrific for dressing vegetables, as here, and it is also good with poached fish and cold meat. I enjoy this dish with a chunk of bread for lunch or for an appetizer or salad course.

The cauliflower should be served at room temperature. If you make it ahead and refrigerate it, take the chill off by heating it momentarily in a microwave oven.

- 1 firm white cauliflower (1¼–1½ pounds)
- ¼ cup coarsely chopped sour pickles
- ⅓ cup diced (¼-inch) red onion
- ⅓ cup coarsely chopped fresh parsley
- 1 2-ounce can anchovy fillets in oil, drained (reserve the oil) and cut into ¼-inch pieces
- 1 tablespoon red wine vinegar
- 2 tablespoons olive oil
- ½ teaspoon salt
- ½ teaspoon freshly ground black pepper
- 1 large hard-cooked egg (see page 66), cut into ¼-inch pieces (use an egg cutter if you have one — slice the egg, then turn the slices 90 degrees in the cutter and cut again to dice)

Remove the leaves from the cauliflower, cut out the core, and separate into florets. Cut each floret into smaller florets about 1 inch across. (You should have about 6 cups.)

Drop the cauliflower into a large saucepan, add 1 cup water, and bring the water to a strong boil. Cover and cook over high heat for 3 to 4 minutes, until the water has evaporated. Transfer the cauliflower to a bowl and let cool to room temperature.

Add the pickles, onion, parsley, anchovies, with the reserved oil, vinegar, olive oil, salt, and pepper to the cauliflower and mix well. Transfer to a serving platter, sprinkle the egg on top, and serve.

Cauliflower with Toasted Crumbs
Serves 4 to 6

✶ **These toasted bread crumbs** add a wonderful crunch to cauliflower. Make your own crumbs in a food processor using day-old bread.

- 1 firm white cauliflower (about 1½ pounds)
- 2 slices firm white bread, processed to coarse crumbs in a food processor
- ¼ teaspoon salt
- ¼ teaspoon freshly ground black pepper
- 2 tablespoons olive oil
- 2 tablespoons unsalted butter

3–4 scallions, trimmed (leaving some green) and minced (about ½ cup)

2 teaspoons finely chopped ginger

Remove the leaves from the cauliflower and cut out the core; reserve the core. Separate the head into 14 to 16 florets. Peel off the thick outer layer from the core and split the core into 2 or 3 pieces.

Arrange the florets and core in one layer in a large saucepan and add 1½ cups water. Bring to a boil over high heat, cover, and boil for 6 to 8 minutes, until the cauliflower is tender but still slightly firm. Drain the cauliflower, spread it out in one layer in a serving platter, and set aside.

Spread the crumbs evenly on a small cookie sheet and brown in a toaster oven or under the broiler. Set aside.

At serving time, reheat the cauliflower in a microwave oven, or in a saucepan with 4 to 5 tablespoons water — boil for 2 to 3 minutes, until heated through. Arrange the cauliflower core and florets, stem side down, on the platter and sprinkle with the salt and pepper.

Heat the olive oil and butter in a skillet until hot. Add the scallions, ginger, and bread crumbs and cook for 30 seconds. Sprinkle on top of the cauliflower and serve.

Cauliflower au Gratin
Serves 6

❧ **Made with a béchamel** sauce and finished with cheese, this cauliflower dish is one I remember well from my childhood.

1 firm white cauliflower (about 1½ pounds)

3 tablespoons unsalted butter

3 tablespoons all-purpose flour

1½ cups milk

¾ cup heavy cream

½ teaspoon salt

¼ teaspoon freshly ground white pepper

⅛ teaspoon freshly grated nutmeg

½ cup grated Gruyère or Emmenthaler cheese

2 tablespoons freshly grated Parmesan cheese

Preheat the oven to 400 degrees.

Remove the green leaves from the cauliflower, cut out the core, and separate the cauliflower into florets. Drop the florets into a large stainless steel saucepan of boiling salted water, bring back to a boil, and cook, uncovered, for about 5 minutes; they will be crunchy. Drain and set aside.

Melt the butter in a medium saucepan. Add the flour and cook over low heat for about 1 minute, stirring with a whisk; do not let the mixture brown. Add the milk and bring to a boil over medium heat, stirring constantly to prevent scorching, then simmer over low heat for 1 minute. Add the cream, salt, white pepper, and nutmeg and bring to a boil. Remove from the heat.

Generously butter a gratin dish. Put the florets in the dish stem side down and coat with the béchamel. Sprinkle with the cheeses. Place on a cookie sheet and bake for about 30 minutes, or until golden brown. Serve.

Celery Root and Potato Puree
Serves 4

❧ **Although of the same** family as stalk celery, celery root, or celeriac, is a different vegetable entirely, with an intense flavor that is more nutty and rich and less sharp than that of celery. Here I combine it with potatoes and puree the two together. The result is delightful, especially with game. Celeriac is available in winter in most markets.

1 large celery root (celeriac; 1¼ pounds),
    peeled and cut into 2-inch chunks
1¼ pounds potatoes, peeled and cut into
    2-inch chunks
1¼ cups water
¾ teaspoon salt
2 tablespoons unsalted butter
¾ cup milk, warmed

Combine the celery root, potatoes, water, and ¼ teaspoon of the salt in a saucepan and bring to a boil, then reduce the heat, cover, and boil the vegetables gently until tender, about 30 minutes. Most of the liquid should be gone.

Push the vegetables and their cooking liquid through a food mill or a ricer set over a saucepan. Whisk in the butter, then add the remaining ½ teaspoon salt and the milk and whisk into the puree. Reheat gently and serve.

Spicy Celery with Garlic

Serves 4

꙳ **Celery is not served** often enough as a cooked vegetable. I peel the outer stalks first, then cut the celery into pieces and braise gently in a little chicken stock flavored with salsa.

1 bunch celery (1½ pounds), with inner
    stalks as white as possible
3–4 garlic cloves, thinly sliced
    (1½ tablespoons)
1½ cups homemade chicken stock (page 612)
    or low-salt canned chicken broth
¼ cup hot red salsa
3 tablespoons olive oil
¼ teaspoon salt

Using a vegetable peeler, peel the outer celery stalks to remove the tough, fibrous strings (leave the bunch of celery intact). Trim the celery and cut it crosswise into 2-inch pieces. (You should have 6 to 7 cups.)

Put in a large bowl, cover with cold water, and wash thoroughly.

Lift the celery from the water and put it, still wet, in a large stainless steel saucepan. Add the garlic, stock, salsa, olive oil, and salt and bring to a boil, then reduce the heat, cover, and cook gently for about 25 minutes, until most of the liquid is gone and the celery pieces are tender. If necessary, cook, uncovered, to reduce the liquid. Serve.

Braised Celery

Serves 4

꙳ **A combination of butter** and brown sauce coats the celery, making it rich and mellow, a good accompaniment to most roasts. Use only the tender lower part of the heart, about 6 inches up from the base; reserve the top of the ribs and leaves for stock or soup.

2 celery hearts, with inner stalks as
    white as possible
½ teaspoon salt, or to taste
2 tablespoons unsalted butter
½ cup Basic Brown Sauce (page 613)

Trim the tops of the celery hearts so they are about 6 inches long. Using a vegetable peeler or small knife, remove most of the fiber from the outer celery stalks and trim the bases. Put the celery in a saucepan, cover with cold water, add the salt, and bring to a boil. Cover and simmer gently for 30 minutes. Drain and cool. (The cooking liquid can be used in stock or soup.)

Cut each bunch of celery lengthwise into 6 pieces.

Melt the butter in a large skillet. When it is

hot, add the pieces of celery and sauté for about 2 minutes on each side. Add the brown sauce, cover, and simmer for 7 to 8 minutes, until the sauce is reduced and beginning to coat the celery. Uncover and cook for 3 to 4 minutes to further reduce the sauce and coat the celery, rolling and turning it in the sauce. Add salt to taste and serve.

Chestnut Puree

Serves 6

Chestnut puree is excellent with venison or roast goose or turkey. When buying chestnuts, watch out for little holes, which indicate that they are wormy. In some markets, peeled frozen or peeled vacuum-packed chestnuts are available. Although they are expensive, they are easy to use. Chestnuts can also be found dried, and these have to be reconstituted in water.

- 2 pounds fresh chestnuts (about 1 pound 5 ounces after peeling)
- ⅓ celery stalk
- 2½ cups homemade chicken stock (page 612) or low-salt canned chicken broth
- 4 tablespoons (½ stick) unsalted butter
- ½ cup heavy cream
- ¼ teaspoon salt, or to taste
- 1 teaspoon freshly ground white pepper

Preheat the oven to 400 degrees.

With the point of a paring knife, score each chestnut on both sides. The incisions will help the skin to break open during roasting. Spread the chestnuts on a cookie sheet and roast in batches for 12 minutes, until the skin pulls away. Remove from the oven.

Peel the chestnuts while they are still warm, holding them with a towel to avoid burning your hands. Both the inner and outer skin must come off. Discard any bad chestnuts. Repeat with the remaining chestnuts. (An alternative way to peel them is to score the chestnuts and microwave them for 2½ minutes. Let cool for a couple minutes and, using a knife, remove the outside and inside skins.)

Put the chestnuts in a large heavy saucepan, add the celery and chicken stock, and bring to a boil. Cover, reduce the heat, and simmer slowly for 45 minutes. There will be very little stock left in the pan.

Put the entire mixture through a food mill into a saucepan. Add the butter and stir vigorously with a wooden spatula until well blended. Add the cream, salt, and white pepper and stir over medium heat until the mixture comes to a boil. Serve.

Corn off the Cob

Serves 6

Cooked briefly in this way, the corn kernels remain crunchy. Because the sugar in corn begins to turn to starch as soon as it is picked, corn is best fresh from the garden.

- 6 large ears corn, husked and kernels cut off (about 6 cups)
- 1 tablespoon peanut oil
- 2 tablespoons unsalted butter
- ½ teaspoon salt
- ¼ teaspoon freshly ground black pepper

Combine the corn, 2 tablespoons water, the oil, butter, salt, and pepper in a saucepan and bring to a boil over high heat, stirring. Cover and boil for 1 to 2 minutes. Serve.

Corn and Pepper Sauté
Serves 4

❧ **This is one of** my favorite ways to prepare corn and red bell peppers. Fresh corn kernels are quickly sautéed with red pepper in a skillet, so both stay firm and sweet.

I first peel the red pepper with a vegetable peeler, instead of broiling it and peeling off the blistered skin as is done conventionally. This keeps its fresh flavor and sweetness. Use a good vegetable peeler and take off as much of the skin from the pepper as possible before cutting it into segments and removing any remaining skin.

- 1 large red bell pepper
- 2 tablespoons unsalted butter
- 3 large ears corn, husked and kernels cut off (about 3 cups)
- ¼ teaspoon salt
- ¼ teaspoon freshly ground black pepper

Using a vegetable peeler, remove as much of the skin as you can from the red pepper. (The firmer the pepper, the easier it is to peel.) Cut the pepper into sections at the recesses. Remove the seeds from each section and peel off the remaining skin. Cut the pepper into ¼-inch pieces. (You should have about 1 cup.)

Heat the butter in a large skillet until hot. Add the corn and pepper pieces and sauté over high heat for about 2 minutes. Stir in the salt and pepper and serve.

Little Corn Fritters
Serves 4 as a first course

❧ **These little fritters are** a treat served with an aperitif or drinks before a meal or as an accompaniment for soup. You can prepare them a few

hours ahead and reheat them on a wire rack set over a cookie sheet in a 375-degree oven for a few minutes.

- ⅓ cup all-purpose flour
- 2 tablespoons cornstarch
- ½ teaspoon baking powder
- ¼ teaspoon salt
- 1 large egg
- ⅓ cup ice-cold water
- 2 large ears corn, husked and kernels cut off (2 cups)
- 6 tablespoons canola oil

Mix the flour, cornstarch, baking powder, and half the salt together in a bowl. Add the egg and ¼ cup of the water and mix with a whisk until smooth. Add the remainder of the water and mix until smooth. Mix in the corn kernels.

Heat 3 tablespoons of the oil in a large skillet until hot. Drop 1 tablespoon of batter into the skillet for each fritter, making about 10 fritters, and cook over medium-high heat for 3 to 4 minutes on each side, until golden brown. Transfer to a wire rack (this will keep them from becoming soggy) and repeat with the remaining batter and oil. Sprinkle them with the remaining salt and serve immediately.

Crispy Corn Pancakes
Serves 6
(makes about sixteen 3-inch pancakes)

❧ **Serve these pancakes as** an hors d'oeuvre or a first course or as an accompaniment to pork. It's important to use a nonstick pan and very hot oil for cooking them; canola oil can withstand high temperatures without burning, but for best results, the pan should be cleaned between each batch of pancakes.

When you prepare the batter, you add only half of the club soda at first to the flour and egg mixture, to create a thick batter that you make very smooth with a whisk before adding the remainder of the club soda. If you put it in all at once, the flour would form into little lumps and the batter would have to be strained.

Although the pancakes are best when made at the last moment, they can be made ahead and reheated in a hot oven or under the broiler.

⅔ cup all-purpose flour
¾ teaspoon baking powder
1 large egg
2 large ears corn, husked and kernels cut off (about 2 cups)
1 cup chilled club soda
¼ teaspoon salt
¼ teaspoon freshly ground black pepper
½ cup canola oil

Combine the flour, baking powder, egg, corn kernels, and half of the club soda in a food processor and process for 10 seconds. Add the remaining club soda, the salt, and pepper and process for a few seconds, until well combined. Transfer to a bowl.

At cooking time, heat 2 tablespoons of the oil in a large nonstick skillet. When it is hot, spoon 3 tablespoons of batter per pancake into the skillet, making 4 pancakes. (To make the pancakes faster, use two skillets.) Use a splatter-guard if you have one and cook the pancakes over high heat for 3 minutes, then turn them and cook for 2 minutes on the other side, or until crispy at the edges and brown. Transfer the pancakes to a wire rack (the rack allows air to circulate under them, so they won't become soggy). Wipe out the skillet and repeat with the remaining oil and batter in batches. Serve.

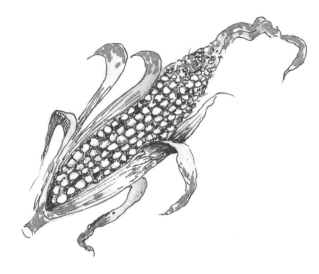

Corn Crepes
Serves 6 (makes about 20 crepes)

✻ My wife, who is a corn lover, suggested this recipe, which is easy to make and light in texture. Serve as a first course or as an accompaniment to meat or fish.

5 medium ears corn
⅓ cup all-purpose flour
4 large eggs
1 teaspoon salt
¼ teaspoon freshly ground black pepper
⅓ cup milk
3 tablespoons unsalted butter, melted

Husk the corn. With a sharp knife, cut straight down the middle of each row of kernels, slitting the kernels open. Then stand each ear on end and, with a spoon, scrape the pulp out of the kernels, scraping down the full length of the ear and then all around the ear, to extract all of the pulp. (You should have about 1¼ cups pulp.)

Put the pulp in a large bowl, add the flour, and mix well with a whisk. Add the eggs, salt, and pepper and mix well. Add the milk and melted butter and mix well.

Preheat the oven to 180 degrees.

Put a nonstick crepe pan over medium heat. When it is hot, pour 2 tablespoons of the batter into the pan and tilt the skillet to spread the batter into a very thin crepe 4 inches in diameter. Cook for 1 minute on one side, then flip over or turn with a large spatula and cook for 1 minute on the other side. Keep the cooked crepes hot on a wire rack on a cookie sheet in the oven while you make the others. Serve.

Fresh Corn Soufflés
Serves 6

✼ **There's nothing like a** soufflé to start a fine meal, and individual soufflés like these are quicker to cook than larger ones. I like the flavor of chervil with corn, but chives work well too. Serve as a first course or as an accompaniment to poultry or meat.

4	tablespoons (½ stick) unsalted butter
6	tablespoons dried bread crumbs
2	tablespoons chopped onion
¼	cup all-purpose flour
¾	teaspoon salt
⅛	teaspoon freshly ground black pepper
1	cup milk
2	cups fresh corn kernels
5	large eggs, separated
2	tablespoons chopped fresh chervil or chives
2	tablespoons freshly grated Parmesan cheese

Using 1 tablespoon of the butter, butter six 1-cup soufflé dishes. Coat the dishes with the bread crumbs. Refrigerate.

Preheat the oven to 375 degrees.

Melt the remaining 3 tablespoons butter in a saucepan. Add the onion and sauté over medium heat for about 2 minutes, until the onion is softened and transparent. Stir in the flour, salt, and pepper and cook, stirring constantly, for 30 seconds. Add the milk, stirring constantly with a whisk, and cook, stirring constantly, until the sauce comes to a boil and thickens. Stir in the corn and remove from the heat. Add the egg yolks and mix in well with a whisk, then mix in the herbs.

Beat the egg whites in a large bowl until stiff but not dry. Vigorously whip about one third of the whites into the sauce, then fold in the remainder.

Pour into the prepared dishes and sprinkle with the cheese. Bake for 15 to 20 minutes, until puffed and golden brown. Serve immediately.

Cucumbers with Tarragon
Serves 4

✼ **Although cucumbers are usually** eaten raw, when they are cooked, they make an absolutely delightful light side dish, particularly for fish. I use a seedless cucumber and cut it so that most of the few seeds that are present are trimmed away. Chopped tarragon gives a special accent.

1	seedless cucumber (about 1 pound)
1	tablespoon unsalted butter
¼	teaspoon salt
¼	teaspoon freshly ground black pepper
1	tablespoon chopped fresh tarragon

Trim off the ends of the cucumber and cut it into 1½-inch chunks. (You should have about 7 chunks.) Cut each chunk lengthwise into 6 wedges and, using a paring knife, round the sharp edges and trim the wedges into football-shaped ovals, eliminating most of the seeds and skin as you do so.

Bring 3 cups water to a boil in a saucepan. Add the cucumber ovals and bring the water back to a strong boil. Immediately drain the cucumber. (*The cucumber can be blanched ahead.*)

At serving time, melt the butter in a large skillet. Add the cucumber, salt, and pepper and toss to mix. Cook for 1 to 2 minutes, just until the ovals are hot throughout. Add the tarragon and toss with the cucumber. Serve.

Cucumbers in Cream
Serves 6 to 8

❧ **These are great with** poached fish, such as salmon.

    4   cucumbers (about 3½ pounds)
    1   tablespoon unsalted butter
    ½   teaspoon salt
    ¼   teaspoon freshly ground white pepper
    ⅓   cup heavy cream
    2   tablespoons chopped fresh chives

Peel the cucumbers, cut into 1½- to 2-inch chunks, and cut each chunk lengthwise into quarters. Remove and discard the seeds.

Melt the butter in a large skillet. Add the cucumbers, salt, and white pepper and sauté over medium heat for 1 minute. Add the cream and boil over medium-high heat until it is reduced and thick enough to coat the cucumbers, 3 to 4 minutes. Sprinkle with the chives and serve.

Cucumber and Tomato Stew
Serves 4

❧ **I first encountered this** recipe in the French Caribbean. Cucumbers are stewed with tomatoes, onion, and garlic and finished with cilantro. The taste of this dish is so fresh that it may persuade you to cook cucumbers more often.

    2   tablespoons olive oil
    1   onion (4 ounces), chopped (¾ cup)
    4   scallions, trimmed (leaving some green) and minced (½ cup)
    3   garlic cloves, sliced (1 tablespoon)
    2   seedless cucumbers (about 1¾ pounds), peeled and cut into 1-inch-thick rounds
    5   plum tomatoes (1 pound), cut into 1-inch pieces (2½ cups)
    1   teaspoon salt
    ½   teaspoon freshly ground black pepper
    ¼   cup coarsely chopped fresh cilantro

Heat the oil in a large stainless steel saucepan until hot. Add the onion, scallions, and garlic and sauté for 1 minute over high heat. Add the cucumbers, tomatoes, salt, and pepper and cook for about 1 minute, then stir, cover, reduce the heat to medium, and cook for 20 minutes.

Add the cilantro, mix well, and serve.

Eggplant Cushions
Serves 4

❧ **Thick slices of eggplant** are lightly coated with oil on both sides, then baked in one layer on a baking sheet until soft. Cooked this way, the slices absorb only about a quarter of the oil they would if fried in a skillet. Then cubes of leftover bread are processed with garlic, herbs, and olive oil in a food processor, the crumbled mixture is piled atop the eggplant slices, and they are broiled until the eggplant is hot and the topping nicely browned. The slices can be baked ahead but should be finished under the broiler at the last minute. This dish makes a good first course or a pleasing accompaniment to meat or fish.

2 eggplants, about 3–4 inches in diameter (about 1¾ pounds)
1½ tablespoons canola oil
¾ teaspoon salt
1 cup 1-inch pieces leftover bread, preferably from a baguette
¼ cup chopped mixed fresh chives and parsley
1 garlic clove, crushed
2 teaspoons olive oil

Preheat the oven to 400 degrees.

Trim the eggplants, peel them, and cut them crosswise into thick slices, about 1¼ inches thick. (You should have about 8 slices total.)

Line a large baking sheet with a nonstick baking mat or parchment paper and coat with the oil. Press the eggplant slices into the oil and sprinkle them with half the salt. Turn the slices over, arranging them in one layer, and sprinkle with the remaining salt. Bake for 30 minutes, or until the eggplant flesh is very soft.

Meanwhile, put the bread cubes, herbs, and garlic in a food processor and process for about

15 seconds, until the bread is coarsely crumbled. Transfer the mixture to a bowl and toss lightly with the olive oil.

When the eggplant slices are cooked, spoon the crumbs on top of them. (*The eggplant can be prepared to this point several hours in advance.*)

Preheat the broiler. Position the pan of eggplant so that the crumb mixture is 6 to 8 inches from the heat and broil for 5 to 6 minutes, until the topping is nicely browned. Serve.

Sautéed Eggplant Rolls
Serves 4

✂ **In this great party** dish, perfect for a buffet table, sautéed slices of eggplant are rolled up around a mushroom stuffing and served with tomatoes in vinaigrette. You can sauté and stuff the eggplant ahead of time, and you can change the filling mixture at will to accommodate leftover meat or fish. The tomatoes are also good with poached fish or mixed into a green salad.

¼ cup canola oil
2 eggplants (2 pounds total), each cut lengthwise into 8 ⅜-inch-thick slices
Salt and freshly ground black pepper

FILLING

3 tablespoons olive oil
1 small onion, finely chopped (about ½ cup)
3 ounces mushrooms, cleaned and coarsely chopped (about 1¼ cups)
2–3 large garlic cloves, crushed and finely chopped (1½ teaspoons)
4 ounces Monterey Jack or other soft cheese, coarsely chopped or grated
3 tablespoons golden raisins
1 tablespoon Worcestershire sauce

½ teaspoon salt
½ teaspoon freshly ground black pepper
3 tablespoons chopped fresh chives

TOMATOES VINAIGRETTE

2 large ripe tomatoes (1 pound), halved, seeded, and cut into ¼-inch pieces
1 small onion, chopped (about ½ cup)
2 teaspoons red wine vinegar
2 tablespoons extra-virgin olive oil
½ teaspoon salt
¼ teaspoon freshly ground black pepper

1 tablespoon chopped fresh chives
Extra-virgin olive oil, for drizzling

Heat 2 tablespoons of the canola oil in a large nonstick skillet. When it is hot, add enough eggplant slices to fill the pan, sprinkle lightly with salt and pepper, and cook over medium heat for 3 minutes on each side. Remove to a plate and repeat with the remaining oil, salt and pepper, and eggplant. Set aside.

FOR THE FILLING: Heat 2 tablespoons of the olive oil in a large skillet until hot. Add the onion and sauté for 1 minute. Add the mushrooms and sauté for another minute. Stir in the garlic, remove from the heat, and let cool.

Combine the cheese with the onion-mushroom mixture in a bowl. Mix in the raisins, Worcestershire sauce, salt, pepper, chives, and the remaining tablespoon of olive oil. Divide the mixture among the slices of eggplant, mounding it in the center.

FOR THE TOMATOES: Combine the tomatoes, onion, vinegar, oil, salt, and pepper in a bowl. Spread the tomato mixture on a large serving plate. Roll each eggplant slice up around the onion-mushroom filling and arrange the rolls seam side down on top of the tomato mixture. Sprinkle with the chives and olive oil and serve.

Eggplant and Tomato Gratin
Serves 4

❧ **Lightly oiling slices of** eggplant, spreading them out on a baking sheet, and baking them is easier than cooking them in batches in a skillet and requires much less oil. The slices are then layered with tomatoes in a gratin dish, topped with flavored bread crumbs, and finished in the oven.

2 long, narrow Japanese or Chinese eggplants (1 pound)
2 tablespoons corn oil
½ teaspoon salt
1 large slice firm white bread, processed to crumbs in a food processor (⅔ cup)
⅓ cup freshly grated Parmesan cheese
1 teaspoon chopped fresh thyme
1 tablespoon olive oil
4 medium ripe tomatoes (about 1 pound), cut into ⅜-inch-thick slices

Preheat the oven to 400 degrees.

Trim the ends of the eggplants (do not peel) and cut them lengthwise into ½-inch-thick slices. (You should have 8 slices.)

Line a baking sheet with a nonstick baking mat and coat the mat with the corn oil. Lay the eggplant slices in a single layer in the oil and turn them over in the pan so they are lightly oiled on both sides. Sprinkle the slices with the salt. Bake for 25 minutes. Let the eggplant cool to lukewarm. (Leave the oven on.)

Meanwhile, mix the bread crumbs, Parmesan cheese, thyme, and olive oil in a small bowl.

Arrange alternating slices of eggplant and tomato in a 4- to 6-cup gratin dish, overlapping the slices as necessary to fit them all into the dish. Sprinkle the bread crumb mixture evenly on top. (*At this point, the dish can be covered and refrigerated overnight.*)

Bake the gratin for 20 to 25 minutes, until the vegetables are soft and heated through and the crumb topping is nicely browned. Serve.

Tempura-Fried Eggplant
Serves 6

❧ **Fried vegetables are always** welcome at our table, and my wife and I consider fried eggplant, soup, salad, and cheese to be a fine dinner.

Here eggplant is dipped into a tempura-style batter made of flour, egg yolk, and ice-cold water. I often shred a mixture of vegetables — carrots, zucchini, broccoli, cauliflower, scallions, and the like — and stir them into the same batter, then fry large spoonfuls in oil.

This batter produces a very crisp, thin coating. Make sure the water is ice cold. If it's not cold, the coating never seems to get as crisp as it could.

6	thin Japanese or Chinese eggplants (about 1½ inches in diameter)
1⅓	cups all-purpose flour
2	large egg yolks
1⅓	cups ice-cold water
	Canola oil, for frying
	Salt

Slice the eggplants lengthwise into ¼-inch-thick slices, leaving the slices attached at the stem end. (Small eggplant can be sliced whole; larger eggplant should be cut crosswise in half vertically and then sliced lengthwise.) Press down on the eggplant to fan out the slices. This fan shape not only looks beautiful on the plate, but it also exposes the maximum surface area to the oil; consequently, it won't take very long to cook.

Combine the flour, egg yolks, and half the water in a bowl and mix with a whisk until the mixture is smooth. Whisk in the rest of the water.

Heat about ½ inch of oil in a large skillet until very hot. (If your skillet is not large enough to accommodate all the eggplant fans, cook them in batches or use two skillets.) Dip the eggplant fans in the batter. (The batter is quite runny and not too much will adhere to the eggplant.) Lay the fans flat in the hot oil and cook over medium-high heat for 4 to 5 minutes. Turn and cook for another 3 minutes, or until nicely browned and cooked through. Remove to a wire rack to drain, sprinkle with salt, and serve.

Eggplant Fritters
Serves 6 (makes about 15 fritters)

❧ **These fritters are best** when they have just come out of the fryer. Corn (fresh kernels sliced from the cob), artichoke hearts, or cauliflower can be substituted for the eggplant.

1	large eggplant (about 1 pound)
1½	cups all-purpose flour
1	tablespoon baking powder
1½	cups chilled club soda
½	cup peanut or corn oil
	Salt

Trim the eggplant and peel it. Cut it lengthwise into ⅛-inch-thick slices, then stack the slices and cut crosswise into julienne strips about ⅜ inch thick. (You should have about 3½ cups.)

Mix the flour, baking powder, and 1 cup of the club soda in a bowl, stirring with a whisk until smooth. Add the remaining ½ cup club soda and mix again until smooth. (If you added all the club soda at once, the batter might get lumpy.) Mix in the eggplant with a spoon.

Heat the oil in a large skillet. When it is hot, drop about 2 tablespoons of the eggplant batter into the oil for each fritter and spread it into a round 3 to 4 inches in diameter. Make 3 or 4 fritters at a time, and cook for 3 minutes over medium heat on the first side and about 2 minutes on the other side, until golden brown. Drain on a wire rack and sprinkle lightly with salt. Serve.

Asian-Style Grilled Eggplant
Serves 6

✄ **Serve this as a** salad course or with broiled or grilled fish or meat. It can be made ahead and will keep, refrigerated, for several days, although it should be brought to room temperature or reheated briefly in a microwave oven before serving.

If a grill is not available, you can cook the eggplant in a covered stainless steel or cast-iron skillet over very high heat for 5 minutes a side, or until soft.

6 small, thin Japanese or Chinese eggplants (about 1½ inches in diameter; about 1¼ pounds)
2 tablespoons canola or safflower oil
¼ teaspoon salt

DRESSING

2 tablespoons dark soy sauce
2 teaspoons rice vinegar
½ teaspoon sugar
2 tablespoons vegetable oil

1 tablespoon minced fresh chives

Heat a grill until very hot.

Cut the (unpeeled) eggplants lengthwise in half. Score the cut sides with the point of a knife, cutting through the flesh to a depth of about ¼ inch every inch or so, to make a crosshatch pattern. (This lets the seasoning penetrate the flesh and makes the eggplant cook more evenly and quickly.) Sprinkle with the oil, being especially generous on the cut sides, and the salt.

Place the eggplant cut side down on the clean grill rack, cover with the lid, and cook for 5 minutes. Turn the eggplant halves over, cover again, and cook for 5 minutes longer, or until soft. Arrange the eggplant on a platter, cut side up.

FOR THE DRESSING: Mix all the ingredients together.

Spoon the dressing over the eggplant and sprinkle with the chives. (*This is best done 1 to 2 hours ahead of serving so the flavors have time to blend.*)

Serve at room temperature.

Eggplant and Red Pepper Terrine
Serves 8 as a first course

✄ **Ideal for a summer** party, this beautiful terrine is made by layering cooked eggplant slices, red pepper, cheese, and herbs. I like to use long, narrow Japanese eggplants so I can make nice layers with lengthwise strips. If you can't get them, just select regular eggplants that are thin and somewhat elongated.

The eggplant slices have a smoky flavor because they are grilled rather than fried. If you don't have a grill, you can also get a low-fat result by baking the slices. Slice the eggplant and oil and salt the slices as indicated in the recipe, then arrange in one layer on a baking sheet lined with a nonstick baking mat or parchment paper and bake in a preheated 400-degree oven for about 30 minutes, until soft.

The peppers and eggplants can be cooked and the dish assembled a day ahead, but don't unmold the terrine until just before serving.

The raw tomato sauce can be served on its own as a cold tomato gazpacho.

3 large red bell peppers (about 1½ pounds)
2 long (11-inch), firm eggplants (about 2½ pounds)
2 tablespoons peanut oil
¾ teaspoon salt
1½ cups loosely packed fresh parsley leaves
8 ounces firm Brie
½ teaspoon freshly ground black pepper

TOMATO SAUCE

3 garlic cloves
2–3 ripe tomatoes (1¼ pounds), cut into 6–8 pieces each
⅓ cup water
¼ cup olive oil
2 tablespoons red wine vinegar
½ teaspoon salt
¼ teaspoon freshly ground black pepper
¼ teaspoon Tabasco sauce

Preheat the broiler. Arrange the red peppers on a cookie sheet and place them under the broiler so that their upper surfaces are about ½ to 1 inch from the heat. Broil for about 12 minutes, turning occasionally, until the peppers are blistered and black on all sides. Immediately transfer the peppers to a large plastic bag and seal the bag. Let the peppers steam in their residual heat for 10 minutes.

Peel the peppers (the skin will slide off), split them open, and remove the seeds under cool running water. Dry with paper towels. Cut lengthwise into 2-inch-wide strips.

Heat a grill until very hot.

Cut the eggplants lengthwise into ½-inch-thick slices. (You should have 10 to 12.) Brush the slices on both sides with the peanut oil and sprinkle with half the salt. Lay the eggplant slices on the grill, cover with the lid, and cook for about 4 minutes on each side, or until nicely browned and soft.

Meanwhile, soften the parsley by blanching it in boiling water for 5 to 10 seconds. Drain in a strainer, cool under cold water, and drain again.

Scrape off a little of the rind from the top and bottom of the Brie and cut the cheese into ⅛-inch-thick slices. (You should have about 14 slices.)

Line a 6- to 8-cup terrine mold or loaf pan with plastic wrap, leaving an overhang. Arrange a layer of eggplant in the bottom of the mold and top it with about a third each of the red pepper pieces, parsley, the remaining salt, the pepper, and cheese. Repeat until all the ingredients are used, ending with a layer of eggplant. Cover with plastic wrap and press on the wrap to compact the ingredients. Refrigerate until cold. (*The terrine can be assembled up to 1 day ahead.*)

FOR THE TOMATO SAUCE: Process the garlic in a food processor for 10 seconds. Add the tomatoes and process until pureed. Push the mixture through a food mill fitted with a fine screen into a bowl. Add the water, olive oil, vinegar, salt, pepper, and Tabasco and mix well.

To serve, pour some of the sauce onto a large platter and unmold the terrine in the center. Cut it into slices and serve with the remainder of the sauce.

Endive with Olives
Serves 4

❧ **Ready in a few** minutes, this dish — bitter endive with garlic, olives, and soy sauce — is an attractive and light first course. It also goes well with grilled meat or grilled or broiled fish.

    3   large Belgian endives (about 12 ounces
            total), quartered lengthwise
    2   garlic cloves, crushed and chopped
            (1 teaspoon)
    ½   cup water
    1½ tablespoons olive oil
    1   tablespoon red wine vinegar
    ¼   teaspoon salt
    ¼   teaspoon freshly ground black pepper
    2   tablespoons coarsely chopped oil-cured
            pitted black olives
    1   teaspoon light soy sauce
    1   tablespoon chopped fresh chives

Combine the endives, garlic, water, oil, vinegar, salt, and pepper in a stainless steel saucepan and bring to a boil, then cover, reduce the heat to low, and boil gently for 10 minutes.

Stir in the olives and soy sauce and divide among four plates, allowing 3 pieces of endive per plate. Sprinkle with the chives and serve.

Endive with Tarragon Oil
Serves 4

❧ **In this simple, flavorful** dish, endive is cut into wedges, cooked with a little sugar, salt, lemon juice, and water, and served drizzled with tarragon oil (or extra-virgin olive oil).

    4   Belgian endives with tight heads
            (about 1¼ pounds)
    ¼   teaspoon salt
    ¼   teaspoon sugar
    1   teaspoon fresh lemon juice
    1   tablespoon extra-virgin olive oil
    ¼   cup water

    ¼   cup Tarragon Oil (recipe follows)
            or extra-virgin olive oil

Halve the endives lengthwise. Taking care to keep the leaves attached at the root end, cut each half lengthwise into 4 wedges.

Combine the endive, salt, sugar, lemon juice, olive oil, and water in a large stainless steel saucepan and bring to a boil over high heat, then cover, reduce the heat to medium, and cook for 8 to 10 minutes, until no liquid remains and the endive wedges are beginning to brown.

Divide the endive wedges among four plates, drizzle with the oil, and serve.

Tarragon Oil Makes 1 cup

❧ **Blanching the leaves before** pureeing them in a blender (which works much better than a food processor) locks in the vibrant bright green color of the tarragon.

    1   cup loosely packed fresh tarragon
            leaves
    ¼   teaspoon salt
    1   cup canola oil

Bring 1 cup water to a boil in a small saucepan. Add the tarragon leaves, stir well, return the water to a boil, and boil for 10 seconds. Drain the leaves in a sieve, spraying cold water on them as you do so to cool them quickly.

Place the leaves in a blender with the salt and ½ cup of the oil and blend for 30 seconds, then scrape down the sides of the blender. Add the remaining ½ cup oil and blend for another 30 seconds. Transfer the oil to a glass jar with a tight-fitting lid. The oil can be stored in the refrigerator for up to 2 weeks. If any is left at that point, pour the oil into another jar (the tarragon leaves will have settled to the bottom of the jar by then and be starting to discolor; discard them). Cover the jar and refrigerate for up to several weeks.

Braised Endive
Serves 8

❧ **Braised endive is a** delicious accompaniment to stews or roast meats. Wrapping it in slices of ham, covering it with a light cream sauce and cheese, and glazing it under the broiler transforms it into endive Flemish-style.

- 2 pounds Belgian endives (8 medium), trimmed of any damaged leaves
  Rind of 1 lemon, removed with a vegetable peeler
- 1 tablespoon fresh lemon juice
- 4 tablespoons (½ stick) unsalted butter
- 2 teaspoons sugar
- 1 teaspoon salt
- ¾ cup water

Arrange the endives in a large stainless steel or enameled cast-iron pot that holds them tightly. Add the lemon rind, lemon juice, 2 tablespoons of the butter, the sugar, salt, and water. Cover with a round of parchment paper cut to fit, so that the steam that rises during cooking will just touch the paper and fall back on the endives (this makes for a moister dish and prevents the endives from discoloring). Place a plate that fits inside the pot upside down on top to keep the endives submerged in their juices, cover with a lid, and bring to a boil. Turn the heat to low and boil gently for 15 to 20 minutes, until the endives

are tender. (*The endives can be cooked ahead and set aside in a warm spot.*)

Remove the endives from the liquid, drain, and arrange on a platter. Melt the remaining 2 tablespoons butter, pour over the endives, and serve.

Sautéed Fennel
Serves 4

❧ **With its anise flavor,** fennel makes a good accompaniment to any grilled meat or fish.

- 2 large fennel bulbs (1½ pounds each), stalks trimmed, any bruised or damaged layers discarded, and cut lengthwise in half
- 2 tablespoons unsalted butter
- ¼ teaspoon salt

Put the fennel in a saucepan, cover with cold water, and bring to a boil. Reduce the heat and boil gently for 10 minutes. Drain.

Melt the butter in a 12-inch skillet. While it is heating, cut the fennel lengthwise into ½-inch-thick slices. Arrange in the skillet in one layer and sauté over medium-high heat for about 1 minute on each side to brown lightly. Sprinkle with the salt and serve.

Stewed Crinkled Kale
Serves 6

❧ **Almost any green can** be stewed for a very fast and appealing vegetable dish. Escarole and spinach are also excellent made this way; spinach cooks in 1 minute, escarole in 2 to 3 minutes. Sometimes I cook broccoli rabe this way and serve it cold, sprinkled with olive oil and pimientos.

About 12 cups lightly packed kale leaves

⅓ cup canola or olive oil

2 garlic cloves, crushed and finely chopped (1 teaspoon)

¼ teaspoon hot pepper flakes

1 teaspoon salt

Remove and discard the center rib of the kale leaves if they are tough; leave them in if the kale is tender and young.

Combine the oil, garlic, and pepper flakes in a large saucepan and cook for 1 minute over medium heat, or until the garlic sizzles and starts to brown. Add the kale, salt, and 1½ cups water, cover, bring to a boil, and cook over medium-high heat for 8 to 10 minutes. The water should be practically gone. If the water evaporates too fast during cooking, add some so the kale stays moist; or, if there is too much water left after 10 minutes, boil uncovered until it evaporates.

Serve hot or at room temperature.

Leeks with Tomatoes and Olive Oil
Serves 4 as a first course

✄ **Cooked until just tender,** these leeks are served with a tangy sauce flavored with diced tomatoes, olive oil, and Dijon mustard. Serve them at room temperature.

Keep the water that you boil the leeks in for use in soups; it has a wonderfully intense flavor.

4 medium to large leeks (about 1¼ pounds), trimmed (leaving most of the green), split, and washed

1 ripe tomato (about 7 ounces), peeled, halved, seeded, and cut into ¼-inch pieces

3 tablespoons olive oil

1 tablespoon red wine vinegar

1 tablespoon Dijon mustard

1 teaspoon Worcestershire sauce

½ teaspoon salt

¼ teaspoon freshly ground black pepper

Bring 2 cups water to a boil in a large saucepan. Add the leeks and bring back to a boil, then reduce the heat and boil gently, covered, for 15 minutes, or until tender. Drain (reserve the liquid for soup, if you like).

When they are cool enough to handle, squeeze the leeks to extract most of the remaining liquid (reserve it with the rest of the liquid). Cut the leeks into 2-inch pieces and arrange them in a gratin dish, mixing the white and green parts.

Mix together the tomato, oil, vinegar, mustard, Worcestershire, salt, and pepper. Spoon over the leeks. Serve at room temperature.

Leek Gratin
Serves 4

✄ **For this simple, flavorful** gratin, leeks are cooked in just enough water that by the time they are tender, the water has evaporated. Arranged in a gratin dish and topped with a mixture of bread crumbs, cheese, a bit of garlic, and olive oil, they are finished in a hot oven or under a hot broiler.

4 large leeks (about 1¾ pounds), trimmed (leaving some green), split, and washed

3 slices firm white bread (about 4 ounces)

3 large garlic cloves

1 4-ounce piece Gruyère or Emmenthaler cheese

½ teaspoon salt

½ teaspoon freshly ground black pepper

1½ teaspoons olive oil

2 tablespoons unsalted butter

Bring 1 cup water to a boil in a large skillet. Place the leeks in one layer in the skillet and bring the water to a boil again over high heat, then cover, reduce the heat to medium-high, and cook for about 20 minutes, until the leeks are tender and most of the moisture has evaporated. If there is any water remaining in the skillet, boil the leeks, uncovered, for a minute or so longer to eliminate it. Remove the leeks from the skillet and place them on a cutting board.

Preheat the oven to 475 degrees or preheat the broiler. Butter a 4- to 5-cup gratin dish.

When they are cool enough to handle, cut the leeks into 3-inch lengths. Arrange the pieces, alternating white and green pieces, in one layer in the gratin dish.

Process the bread, garlic, cheese, salt, and pepper in a food processor until the mixture is finely chopped. Transfer to a bowl, add the oil, and mix gently with your hands to lightly coat the bread mixture with the oil. (Don't overmix, or it will become pasty.)

Spread the mixture on top of the leeks. Cut the butter into small pieces and dot the top of the gratin with the butter.

Place the gratin in the oven, or place it under the broiler, 9 to 10 inches from the heat, and cook for 7 to 8 minutes, until heated through and nicely browned on top. Serve.

Leeks in Béchamel Gratin
Serves 6

❧ **This rich gratin made** with bacon and a cream sauce is ideal to serve with a veal roast, roast beef, or pot roast for a special occasion.

5–6 large leeks (about 1¾ pounds), trimmed (leaving some green)

8 slices bacon, cut into 1-inch-wide pieces

¼ teaspoon freshly ground white pepper

⅛ teaspoon dried thyme

2½ tablespoons unsalted butter

2½ tablespoons all-purpose flour

1½ cups milk

½ cup heavy cream

¼ teaspoon salt, or to taste

1 tablespoon freshly grated Parmesan cheese

Quarter the leeks lengthwise and cut into 2-inch pieces. (You should have about 8 cups.) Wash thoroughly in a good amount of water and lift them from the water by hand (if you drain them, they may retain some of the sand).

Sauté the bacon in a large saucepan until golden brown. Add the leeks, 1 cup water, the white pepper, and thyme, cover tightly, and cook over medium heat for about 20 minutes; the leeks should be tender and the water cooked away. Remove from the heat.

Preheat the oven to 375 degrees. Butter a 6- to 8-cup gratin dish or shallow baking dish with ½ tablespoon of the butter.

Melt the remaining 2 tablespoons butter in a saucepan. Add the flour, mixing well with a whisk, then add the milk and bring to a boil, whisking constantly to prevent scorching. Add the cream and salt and bring to a boil, stirring to prevent scorching. Remove from the heat.

Put the leeks in the buttered dish and pour

the sauce over, making sure all the leeks are coated. Sprinkle with the cheese, place the dish on a cookie sheet, and bake for 30 minutes, or until golden brown. Let rest for at least 10 minutes before serving.

Sautéed Lettuce Packages
Serves 4

✄ **People don't often think** of cooking lettuce, but I'm very fond of it sautéed with garlic, mixed into soufflés, or combined with peas or carrots in a stew. Here I poach whole heads of Boston lettuce, then halve them, fold them into triangle-shaped packages, and sauté them in a little butter and oil. They make a great accompaniment for almost any roast meat.

The sautéed lettuce packages can be kept warm in a gratin dish in a 160-degree oven for up to 30 minutes before serving.

4 firm heads Boston lettuce (2 pounds), washed (left whole)
1 tablespoon unsalted butter
1 tablespoon peanut oil
¼ teaspoon salt
⅛ teaspoon freshly ground black pepper

Bring 3 quarts of water to a boil in a large pot. Add the heads of lettuce to the boiling water and cover them with an inverted plate that fits inside the pot to keep them submerged. Bring the water back to a boil, then reduce the heat to medium and boil gently for 20 minutes. Remove the plate, drain off the water, and add enough cold water and ice to the pot to cover the lettuce and cool it quickly.

When the lettuce is cold, remove it from the pot and, holding it gently to preserve the original shape, press each head between your palms to re- move as much liquid as possible. Cut the heads lengthwise in half, then fold each half head into a triangular package so the ends of the leaves are underneath. (*The lettuce can be prepared to this point up to a day ahead, covered, and refrigerated.*)

At serving time, heat the butter and oil in a large skillet until hot. Add the lettuce packages, folded side up, and sprinkle with half the salt and pepper. Cook over medium-high heat for 3 to 4 minutes. Turn the packages over, sprinkle with the remaining salt and pepper, and cook for 3 to 4 minutes longer, until lightly browned.

Arrange the lettuce packages on a serving platter and serve.

Wild Mushroom Toasts
Serves 4

✄ **I often go mushrooming** in the woods with my wife and daughter, my friends, or sometimes just my dog. For this dish, one of my favorite summer first courses, I use a mixture of domestic and wild mushrooms and spoon them over toast. The mushrooms are also good on the side with steak or grilled veal or lamb chops.

If you don't know wild mushrooms, do not pick them on your own, since some are toxic. Mycological societies throughout the country or- ganize tours, however. If this activity appeals to you, contact the society nearest to you, and go on a hunt with people who are knowledgeable. It's great fun, and the wild mushrooms you find your- self are free!

2 tablespoons unsalted butter

1 tablespoon olive oil

1 pound mixed cultivated and wild
  mushrooms (such as cèpes/
  porcini, chanterelles, and oyster
  mushrooms), cleaned and cut into
  2-inch pieces or left whole, depending
  on size

4 shallots, thinly sliced (½ cup)

½ cup chopped mixed fresh oregano,
  chives, and parsley

½ teaspoon salt

½ teaspoon freshly ground black pepper

4 slices firm country bread, each
  about 4 inches in diameter and
  ½ inch thick

  Extra-virgin olive oil, for garnish
  (optional)

Heat the butter and olive oil in a large skillet until very hot and hazelnut in color. Add the mushrooms and sauté over high heat for 10 seconds. Cover and continue cooking for 3 minutes. Uncover and cook for 2 to 3 minutes, until the liquid the mushrooms released has evaporated. Add the shallots, herbs, salt, and pepper and cook for 1 minute longer.

Meanwhile, toast the slices of bread and arrange them on a plate.

Spoon the mushroom mixture on top of the toasts, sprinkle a little extra-virgin olive oil on top, if desired, and serve.

Stuffed Mushrooms
Serves 6 as an hors d'oeuvre

✂ **Stuffed mushrooms are especially** good with grilled meat — from lamb chops to pork chops to steak. Or serve them as an hors d'oeuvre with drinks.

25 firm white mushrooms (about 2 inches
  in diameter; about 1½ pounds), cleaned

1 teaspoon salt

5 tablespoons unsalted butter

1 medium onion, very finely chopped
  (¾ cup)

1 celery stalk, peeled and finely chopped
  (⅓ cup)

½ teaspoon freshly ground black pepper

1 garlic clove, crushed and very finely
  chopped (½ teaspoon)

3 slices firm white bread (about 3 ounces),
  crusts trimmed and processed to
  fine crumbs in a food processor (about
  1¼ cups)

Preheat the oven to 400 degrees.

Select 20 of the nicest mushrooms and break off the stems inside the caps, so that each cap becomes a receptacle; reserve the stems.

Arrange the caps hollow side up in a baking pan. Sprinkle with ½ teaspoon of the salt and place in the oven for 10 minutes. Remove from the oven, turn the caps over to drain, and let cool for 5 minutes; drain off any liquid in the pan. Raise the oven heat to 450 degrees.

FOR THE STUFFING: Using a food processor, chop the remaining 5 mushrooms and all of the stems very fine. (You should have about 2¾ cups.)

Melt 2 tablespoons of the butter in a large heavy saucepan over medium heat. Add the onion and cook for 2 minutes. Add the celery and cook for another 2 minutes, stirring to prevent scorching. Add the chopped mushrooms, the remaining ½ teaspoon salt, and the pepper and cook for about 5 minutes. The mushrooms will release liquid; continue cooking until it has evaporated. Add the garlic and cook for about 20 seconds, then set the stuffing mixture aside to cool to lukewarm.

Melt the remaining 3 tablespoons butter in a

large skillet. Add the bread crumbs and cook, stirring constantly, until the crumbs are loose again and beginning to brown. Transfer the crumbs to a plate.

Fill each mushroom cap with stuffing, shaping it into a nice rounded dome. Dip the mushrooms stuffed side down into the bread crumbs, or press the bread crumbs evenly over each dome, heavily enough so that the whole top is coated. Arrange in a baking dish.

Bake for 8 to 10 minutes. Serve.

Caramelized Mushrooms with Shallots
Serves 4

⚜ **I prefer medium to** large mushrooms in this recipe, choosing older, somewhat darker specimens with visible gills, because they are more flavorful. To achieve the concentrated taste I want, I cook the mushrooms for a long time — it takes a while for the moisture to emerge from them and evaporate, and for them to brown. When they are done, they are almost meaty in texture.

1½ tablespoons olive oil
1 pound mushrooms, preferably older specimens with opened and darkened gills, cleaned
3–4 shallots, thinly sliced (1 cup)
1 tablespoon unsalted butter
⅓ cup chopped fresh parsley
½ teaspoon salt
½ teaspoon freshly ground black pepper

Heat the oil in a large skillet. When it is hot, add the mushrooms and cook, covered, over medium heat for 20 to 25 minutes, until all the liquid that emerges from them has evaporated and they are nicely browned.

Add the shallots and sauté, uncovered, for 2 to 3 minutes, until soft and brown. Add the butter, parsley, salt, and pepper and sauté for 10 seconds longer. Serve.

Marinated Mushrooms
Serves 8 as an hors d'oeuvre

⚜ **This dish will keep** for a couple of weeks in a jar in the refrigerator. In fact, the flavor improves after a few days.

1½ pounds cultivated or wild mushrooms, cleaned
3 medium onions (about 12 ounces), quartered andlayers separated
3 bay leaves
½ teaspoon crushed thyme leaves (fresh is better)
1 teaspoon salt
2 teaspoons black peppercorns
½ teaspoon coriander seeds, crushed
1 cup dry white wine
⅓ cup olive oil
3 tablespoons fresh lemon juice

Quarter the large mushrooms and cut the medium mushrooms in half. Combine with all the remaining ingredients in a stainless steel saucepan, bring to a boil over high heat, and boil, covered, for 6 to 8 minutes. Transfer to an earthenware or other container and let cool to room temperature.

Cover and refrigerate until ready to serve.

Mushroom Pâtés
with Tomatillo Sauce or
Tomato Dressing
Serves 4 as a first course

✎ **I like to make** this dish in summer with wild mushrooms that I pick in the woods, but it can be prepared with any type, wild or cultivated. The mushrooms are cooked for a fair amount of time, then the reduced liquid surrounding them is lightly thickened with gelatin. The mixture is molded into small containers, similar to individual pâtés. Because of the gelatin, the pâtés hold their shape when unmolded, and they are served with one of two sauces. The first, made with tomatillos, is acidic; the other is a traditional tomato dressing. Both are emulsified, which gives them a beautiful color and a smooth consistency.

You can make the pâtés ahead.

1	pound mushrooms (white, cremini, portobello, shiitake, and/or oyster), cleaned and cut into ½-inch pieces (6½ cups)
1	envelope (about 2 teaspoons) gelatin
2	tablespoons olive oil
3	large shallots, finely chopped (⅓ cup)
4	scallions, trimmed (leaving some green) and minced (⅓ cup)
1	large garlic clove, crushed and finely chopped (1 teaspoon)
¾	teaspoon salt
½	teaspoon freshly ground black pepper
¼	teaspoon Tabasco sauce
	Tomatillo Sauce or Tomato Dressing (recipes follow)

Put the mushrooms in a saucepan, cover, and cook over high heat for 1 minute. Reduce the heat to low and continue to cook, covered, for 15 minutes. Drain, reserving the liquid. You should have about ½ cup liquid. If you have more, reduce by boiling the liquid; if you have less, add water to bring the liquid to ½ cup.

Sprinkle the gelatin over the hot liquid and let stand for 5 minutes.

Stir the gelatin into the liquid and pour into a food processor. Add ½ cup of the mushrooms and process until pureed. Transfer the puree to a bowl and stir in the remainder of the mushrooms.

Heat the olive oil in a skillet. Add the shallots, scallions, and garlic and cook over medium heat for 2 to 3 minutes. Add to the mushroom mixture and mix well, then stir in the salt, pepper, and Tabasco.

Fill four ½-cup ramekins or soufflé dishes with the mushroom mixture, packing it tightly. Cover and refrigerate for at least 2 hours. (*The pâtés can be refrigerated overnight.*)

At serving time, spoon about ¼ cup of the tomatillo sauce onto each of four plates, unmold the pâtés, and place a pâté in the center of the sauce on each plate; pass the remaining tomatillo sauce. Alternatively, unmold a pâté onto each of four plates and spoon 2 to 3 tablespoons of the tomato dressing around each one.

Tomatillo Sauce Makes 1¾ cups

4	tomatillos (10 ounces), husks removed, rinsed, and cut into 1-inch pieces (2 cups)
1	small Anaheim chile (also called California pepper), seeds and ribs removed, flesh cut into 1-inch pieces
½	cup chopped (1-inch pieces) onion
2	garlic cloves
2	tablespoons extra-virgin olive oil
½	teaspoon salt
½	teaspoon sugar
2	tablespoons water
1	tablespoon finely chopped fresh cilantro

Put all the ingredients except the cilantro in a food processor and process for 20 to 30 seconds. Transfer the sauce to a bowl. (For a smoother-textured sauce, emulsify the mixture with a hand blender.) Add the cilantro and mix well.

Tomato Dressing Makes about 1 cup

- 1 medium tomato, cut into 1-inch pieces (¾ cup)
- 2 teaspoons Dijon mustard
- ¼ teaspoon salt
- ¼ teaspoon freshly ground black pepper
- ¼ cup olive oil

Put all the ingredients in a food processor and process until smooth. Strain, if desired.

Wild Mushroom Soufflé
Serves 4 to 6 as a first course

✄ **This refined soufflé can** be made with regular cultivated mushrooms if wild ones are unavailable or too expensive.

- 2½ tablespoons unsalted butter
- 3 tablespoons fresh bread crumbs
- 8 ounces wild mushrooms (cèpes/porcini, oyster, or chanterelles), cleaned and minced

BÉCHAMEL SAUCE

- 3 tablespoons unsalted butter
- 3 tablespoons all-purpose flour
- 1 cup milk
- ½ teaspoon salt
- ½ teaspoon freshly ground black pepper
- ¼ teaspoon freshly grated nutmeg

- 5 large eggs, separated

Butter a 4-cup soufflé dish with ½ tablespoon of the butter and coat it with the bread crumbs. Refrigerate.

Preheat the oven to 375 degrees.

Melt the remaining 2 tablespoons butter in a saucepan. Add the mushrooms and sauté for about 3 minutes. Transfer to a food processor and puree.

FOR THE BÉCHAMEL: Melt the butter in a saucepan. Add the flour, mix well, and cook, stirring, for 30 seconds. Add the milk, salt, pepper, and nutmeg, stirring constantly with a whisk, then bring to a boil, stirring. Boil for 30 seconds, then add the mushroom puree and mix well with the whisk. Mix in the egg yolks. (*The soufflé mixture can be prepared to this point a few hours ahead and set aside, covered with plastic wrap.*)

When ready to bake the soufflé, whip the egg whites until stiff but not dry. Vigorously whisk about one third of the whites into the béchamel mixture, then fold in the remaining whites.

Pour into the prepared soufflé dish and bake for 30 to 35 minutes, until puffed and golden brown. Serve immediately.

Mushrooms en Papillote
Serves 6

✄ **When food is** prepared *en papillote*, the French term for "in paper," it is generally baked inside a wrapping of parchment paper. I get the same effect with aluminum foil: whole mushrooms cook and steam inside their package, retaining all their flavor and moisture. The recipe couldn't be simpler or tastier.

1 pound medium cultivated or wild
  mushrooms, cleaned
½ teaspoon salt
½ teaspoon freshly ground black pepper
6 garlic cloves, thinly sliced
  (2 tablespoons)
1 tablespoon unsalted butter
1 tablespoon olive oil
1 tablespoon chopped fresh parsley

Preheat the oven to 400 degrees.

Arrange a 16- to 18-inch square of aluminum foil on a work surface. Pile the mushrooms in the center of the foil. Sprinkle with the salt, pepper, and garlic. Dot with the butter and sprinkle with the oil. Gather up the edges of the foil and fold them together securely to encase the mushrooms in a square package, making sure there is air space above the mushrooms so they can steam during cooking.

Place the foil package seam side up on a cookie sheet and bake for 45 minutes.

Open the package and serve the mushrooms in their own juices, with a sprinkling of the parsley on top.

Mushrooms in Puff Pastry
Serves 6 to 8 as a first course

✤ **A puff pastry of** mushrooms, called a *feuilleté*, makes a showy and delicious first course. You can use wild or cultivated mushrooms. When the puff pastry is sliced, the mushroom filling may run a bit, but this is fine.

FILLING

12 ounces cultivated or wild mushrooms,
  cleaned and sliced
2 tablespoons peanut oil
3½ tablespoons all-purpose flour

1 cup milk
½ cup heavy cream
1 teaspoon salt
½ teaspoon freshly ground black pepper
1 tablespoon chopped fresh tarragon

1 pound Puff Pastry (page 597), Fast
  Puff Pastry (page 598), or store-
  bought puff pastry, preferably all-
  butter
1 large egg, beaten

FOR THE FILLING: Cook the mushrooms in a nonstick skillet over medium heat until all their liquid comes out and boils away, 3 to 4 minutes. Set aside.

Pour the oil into a saucepan, whisk in the flour, and cook over medium heat for 1 minute. Add the milk and cream, whisking, and bring to a boil, whisking constantly. Whisk in the salt and pepper, then add the mushrooms and any juices and the tarragon and bring to a boil. Pour into a bowl, cover, and refrigerate until cold.

FOR THE PASTRY: Roll the pastry out on a lightly floured board into a strip 16 inches long and 10 to 12 inches wide. Cut lengthwise in half. Spoon the cold mushroom mixture down the center of one strip, leaving an edge all around. Dampen the edges of the pastry around the mushrooms with water, place the second strip on top, and press the edges together tightly. With a sharp knife, trim the edges all around. Brush the pastry with the beaten egg, then score the top, making a design, and make 3 small holes, equidistant, to allow steam to escape. Let the pastry rest in the refrigerator for 30 minutes.

Preheat the oven to 375 degrees.

Bake the *feuilleté* for 20 minutes. Reduce the heat to 350 degrees and bake for another 20 minutes. Allow to rest for a few minutes before serving, then cut into slices and serve warm.

Grilled
Portobello Mushrooms
Serves 4

❧ **Meaty, big-capped portobello mushrooms** are ideal for grilling. They make a striking, flavorful side dish for fish, poultry, or meat. I grill only the caps here, but the stems can be cooked alongside them or reserved and frozen for later use — chopped, since they are tougher than the caps — in soups or stuffings.

    4 large portobello mushrooms (about
          1 pound), stems removed (reserved for
          soup or stuffing, if desired)
  1½ tablespoons olive oil
    ¼ teaspoon salt

Heat a grill until very hot.

Rub the tops of the mushroom caps with the oil, which will be absorbed quickly, and sprinkle them with the salt. Arrange the caps top side down on the hot grill and cook for 3 minutes. Turn them over and cook for 3 minutes on the other side.

Serve, or, if serving the mushrooms within 30 minutes, keep them warm in a 160-degree oven until serving time. Otherwise, allow the mushrooms to cool, then reheat them in a 400-degree oven or in a skillet on top of the stove just before serving.

Port-Glazed Onions
Serves 6

❧ **These thick glazed onion** slices are ideal with game and lamb. Use large Bermuda onions.

    2 tablespoons olive oil
    2 tablespoons unsalted butter
    4 large onions (2 pounds), sliced
          1 inch thick
    1 teaspoon salt
    ½ teaspoon freshly ground black pepper
    ½ cup homemade chicken stock
          (page 612) or low-salt canned
          chicken broth
    ¼ cup port

Heat the oil and butter in one large or two smaller nonstick skillets. Add the onion in one layer and sear over high heat for 2 minutes. Season with the salt and pepper, add the stock, cover, and simmer for 10 minutes, or until just tender.

Add the port and let it cook down for a couple of minutes, until the onions are glazed and all the liquid is gone. Serve.

Onions and
Carrots Greek-Style
Serves 6 to 8 as a first course

❧ **In classic French cooking,** *à la grecque* refers to different types of vegetables cooked with lemon or vinegar, oil, and coriander seeds and served cold. The vegetables are cooked for just a short time so they retain some crunchiness. Because there are always vegetables in season that are excellent prepared *à la grecque*, this dish can be made at any time of the year. Mushrooms, artichoke hearts, cauliflower, and even zucchini are also very good prepared in this manner.

The marinated vegetables improve in flavor in the refrigerator, and they will keep for at least 1 week refrigerated. They are ideal for buffets or to serve as a first course or mix with a green salad.

1 pound carrots (6–7), peeled
1 pound medium onions (4–5)
½ cup dry white wine
½ cup water
¼ cup red wine vinegar
¼ cup olive oil
1 teaspoon coriander seeds
½ teaspoon black peppercorns
½ teaspoon dried thyme
½ teaspoon fennel seeds
3 bay leaves
1½ teaspoons salt
¼ teaspoon freshly ground black pepper
2 tablespoons extra-virgin olive oil

Crunchy French bread, for serving

Cut the carrots into 2-inch segments, then cut each segment into sticks about ⅜ inch thick. Cut the onions into sixths and separate each section into layers. (You should have approximately 3 cups carrots and 4 cups onions.)

Combine the carrots, wine, water, vinegar, the ¼ cup olive oil, the coriander, peppercorns, thyme, fennel seeds, bay leaves, salt, and pepper in a large stainless steel saucepan and bring to a boil. Cover and boil for about 6 minutes. Add the onions, bring to a boil, reduce the heat, and simmer for 3 to 4 minutes. The carrots should be a bit soft but

still crunchy and the onions still firm. Pour the vegetables and broth into a bowl and let cool.

Stir in the extra-virgin oil. Serve at room temperature or cool, with crunchy French bread.

Stuffed Onions
Serves 4

✂ **Large onions are hollowed** out and stuffed with a mixture of Swiss chard and sausage and sprinkled with Parmesan. The onions are first baked for about 45 minutes, until they are soft enough that the centers can be removed with a sharp-edged measuring spoon.

4 large onions (about 10 ounces each), stem and root ends removed
2 tablespoons olive oil
8 ounces Swiss chard, cut into 1-inch pieces, washed, and drained well (4 cups)
3 garlic cloves, crushed and chopped (2 teaspoons)
¾ teaspoon salt
½ teaspoon freshly ground black pepper
8 ounces sweet Italian sausage, removed from casings if necessary and crumbled
2 tablespoons freshly grated Parmesan cheese

Preheat the oven to 425 degrees.

Arrange the onions in one layer on a large piece of aluminum foil, then fold the foil up around the onions to enclose them. Leave enough air space above the onions so they will steam. Place the foil package on a cookie sheet and bake for 45 minutes. The onions should be almost cooked at this point. Let cool slightly.

Cut a ½-inch-thick slice from the top (stem

end) of each onion. Scoop out (and reserve) the inside, to create a receptacle with walls about ½ inch thick. Coarsely chop the onion tops and insides. (You should have about 3½ cups.)

Heat the oil in a large skillet until very hot but not smoking. Add the chopped onions and cook for 3 minutes over medium-high heat. Add the Swiss chard, garlic, salt, and pepper and mix well. Cover and cook over medium heat for 10 minutes, or until the mixture is just slightly moist and lightly browned. Let cool to lukewarm, then mix in the sausage.

Turn the oven down to 400 degrees.

Stuff the onions with the chard mixture, dividing it evenly among them and mounding it so that all the stuffing is used. Arrange the stuffed onions in a gratin dish and sprinkle them with the Parmesan.

Pour ½ cup water around the onions and bake for 30 minutes, or until brown on top and very soft throughout. Serve.

Onion Puree
Serves 6

❧ **These onions are cooked** gently with a little water and oil until very tender. Then they are thickened with cornmeal, blended to a puree, and enriched with cream. The puree goes well not only with fish, but also with sautéed chicken or roast veal.

2 pounds mild yellow or white onions, thinly sliced (about 7 cups)
1 teaspoon herbes de Provence
2 tablespoons peanut oil
1½ teaspoons salt
½ teaspoon freshly ground black pepper
¼ cup yellow cornmeal
¼ cup heavy cream

Combine the onions, herbes de Provence, oil, salt, pepper, and 1 cup water in a stainless steel saucepan, bring to a boil over high heat, and stir well. Reduce the heat to low, cover, and cook gently for 30 to 35 minutes, until the onions are very tender.

Sprinkle the cornmeal over the onion mixture, stirring it in as you add it. Cover the pan and continue cooking for 5 minutes, stirring occasionally to prevent scorching.

Using a hand blender, process the mixture into a coarse puree. (Or puree in a regular blender and return to the pan.) Stir in the cream and bring to a boil, then immediately remove from the heat. Serve.

Scallion Gratin
Serves 4

❧ **The scallions can be** cooked ahead and covered with the half-and-half and bread crumbs, then reheated at the last minute. If you do this and allow them to cool, increase the baking time by 5 minutes.

4 bunches scallions (about 6 scallions to the bunch)
½ cup half-and-half
½ slice firm white baguette (½ ounce), processed to crumbs in a food processor (¼ cup)
2 tablespoons freshly grated Parmesan cheese
¼ teaspoon salt
¼ teaspoon freshly ground black pepper

Preheat the oven to 450 degrees.

Remove and discard the top 2 inches and any damaged or wilted leaves from the scallions; rinse them thoroughly. Put the scallions and 1 cup water in a stainless steel saucepan and bring to a boil, then cover and cook over high heat for 5 minutes, or until the scallions are tender.

Arrange the scallions in a gratin dish and pour the half-and-half over them.

Mix the bread crumbs, cheese, salt, and pepper in a small bowl and sprinkle over the scallions.

Bake for 10 minutes. Serve.

Peas à la Française
Serves 4

✂ **In this classic dish,** Boston lettuce and tiny pearl onions are cooked with a dash of oil and water, then peas are added and cooked for a little longer. If fresh peas are not available, frozen baby peas work well. Boston lettuce is the best for this recipe. It remains slightly crunchy, with a hint of bitterness that goes well with the onions and peas.

    8   ounces small pearl onions (about 24), peeled
    ½   teaspoon herbes de Provence
    1   tablespoon sugar
    1   teaspoon salt
    ¼   teaspoon freshly ground black pepper
    2   tablespoons olive oil
    1   cup water
    1   small head Boston lettuce (8 ounces), washed and cut into 2-inch pieces

    1½ pounds fresh peas, shelled (about 2½ cups), or 2½ cups (1¼ 10-ounce packages) frozen baby peas
    1   teaspoon potato starch (see page 318), dissolved in 1 tablespoon water
    1   tablespoon unsalted butter

Combine the onions, herbes de Provence, sugar, salt, pepper, oil, and water in a saucepan and bring to a boil, then reduce the heat, cover, and cook for 5 minutes. Add the lettuce, and cook, covered, for 3 to 4 minutes longer, until the lettuce has wilted. (*The dish can be made ahead to this point. Reheat before proceeding.*)

Add the peas to the lettuce mixture and bring to a boil. Boil for about 5 minutes if using fresh peas (adjusting the timing as required based on the size of the peas) or 2 minutes if using frozen peas.

Mix in the dissolved potato starch and bring back to a boil to thicken the juices. Mix in the butter and serve.

Braised Green Peas with Egg Yolks
Serves 6

✂ **In this refined recipe,** peas are cooked in a broth of butter and water, to which egg yolks and cream are added just before serving. Add the yolks very gradually on low heat; they may curdle if the pea mixture is brought to a boil.

    3   cups small fresh peas or 1½ 10-ounce packages frozen baby peas
    3   tablespoons unsalted butter
    ½   cup water
    2   teaspoons sugar
    2   tablespoons minced fresh parsley
    ½   teaspoon salt

½   teaspoon freshly ground black pepper

2   large egg yolks, well beaten

3   tablespoons heavy cream

Combine the peas, butter, water, sugar, parsley, salt, and pepper in a stainless steel saucepan and bring to a boil. Reduce the heat and boil gently for 3 to 4 minutes if using fresh peas or about 2 minutes if using frozen peas, until the peas are tender to the bite.

Mix the yolks and cream together. Gradually stir the mixture into the peas and cook over low heat, stirring constantly, for a few seconds, until the sauce has thickened; do not allow it to boil. Serve.

If you use fresh peas in any of these recipes, reserve the pods for Pea Pod Soup (page 6).

Stew of Peas and Ham
Serves 4

❧ **This is the type** of cooking my aunt used to do when I was a child. She would add a little flour to sautéed onions to make a roux, as I do here, and then use it as a base for a fricassee or stew like this one.

While the stew is a fine side dish for meat, poultry, or fish, it also makes a good first course for dinner or a light lunch.

When fresh peas are in season, I use them, but frozen baby peas can be substituted.

1½   teaspoons unsalted butter

1   tablespoon corn or canola oil

1   onion (4 ounces), chopped (¾ cup)

2   scallions, trimmed (leaving some green) and minced (⅓ cup)

1½   teaspoons all-purpose flour

1½   cups water

3   carrots (6 ounces), peeled and cut into ½-inch pieces

½   teaspoon salt

¼   teaspoon freshly ground black pepper

¼   teaspoon herbes de Provence

1½   pounds fresh peas, shelled (about 2½ cups), or 2½ cups (1¼ 10-ounce packages) frozen baby peas

⅔   cup diced (½-inch) ham

Heat the butter and oil in a saucepan. When they are hot, add the onion and scallions and sauté over medium-high heat for 2 minutes. Add the flour and mix well. Gradually stir in the water, then add the carrots, salt, pepper, and herbes de Provence and bring to a boil. Cover and boil for 2 minutes.

Add the peas and bring to a boil again. Cover, reduce the heat to low, and boil gently for about 4 minutes if using fresh peas, 2 minutes if using frozen, or until the peas are as tender as you like. Add the ham, mix well, and bring to a boil. Serve.

Marinated Peppers
Serves 6

❧ **This is a very** useful concoction to have on hand, and it keeps for a couple of weeks, refrigerated. I make it often, since it's a favorite of my wife, who has it for lunch on a slice of toasted French bread, maybe with a few anchovy fillets on top. It is also good as an antipasto or as a garnish, and it adds color and flavor to green salad, bean salad, or potato salad.

Fleshy green, red, or yellow bell peppers are all excellent for this dish. Avoid soft, wilted, or wrinkled peppers; look for shiny, plump ones with thick flesh. The long, tapered, pale green peppers called Italian frying peppers are also good in this recipe, and here I use a mixture of the two.

Roasting the peppers to release the skin partially cooks them and makes them more tender and sweet. The peeled peppers can also be stuffed with a mixture of rice and meat, baked, and served hot or cold.

3 thick-fleshed roundish green, red, or yellow bell peppers (12–14 ounces)
3 long Italian frying peppers (7–8 ounces)
1 ripe tomato, peeled, halved, seeded, and cut into ½-inch dice (1 cup)
3–4 garlic cloves, crushed and very finely chopped (1 tablespoon)
⅓ cup olive or vegetable oil
1 teaspoon salt
½ teaspoon freshly ground black pepper

Crunchy French bread, for serving

Preheat the broiler. Broil the peppers about 1 inch from the heat, for about 12 minutes, turning them every few minutes or so, until they are black, charred, and blistered all over. Immediately enclose them in a plastic bag and let them steam for 10 minutes. (The steam releases the skin, making it very easy to slide the skin off.)

Pull the skin off. Split the peppers in half, remove the stems, and scrape out the seeds. Cut into ½-inch-wide strips and put in a bowl. (You should have approximately 2½ cups.)

Mix the diced tomato with the peppers. Add the garlic, oil, salt, and pepper and mix well. (*The mixture will keep, refrigerated, for 1 to 2 weeks.*)

Serve with crunchy French bread.

Vegetable-Stuffed Peppers
Serves 8

✽ **Poblano peppers are sometimes** mild and sometimes quite hot, so if you prefer a mild pepper, use Italian frying peppers instead. The vegetable stuffing is delicate and lean, ideal to serve with a rich dish like Chicken Breasts with Chervil Mousse (page 257).

8 poblano peppers (about 3 ounces each)

STUFFING
1 tablespoon unsalted butter
1 tablespoon corn oil
1 cup diced (¼-inch) onion
1 cup diced (¼-inch) carrots
2 cups cauliflower florets (½- to 1-inch pieces)
1 cup diced (½-inch) zucchini
½ teaspoon finely chopped garlic
¼ teaspoon salt
¼ teaspoon freshly ground black pepper
2 tablespoons olive oil

Preheat the broiler.

Arrange the peppers on the broiler pan, place them no more than 1 inch from the heat source, and broil, turning, for 12 to 15 minutes, until they are charred and blistered all over. Immediately transfer the peppers to a large plastic bag, close the bag, and set aside for 10 minutes. (Steaming in their own heat in the plastic bag will help the peppers release their skin.)

Remove the peppers from the bag and peel off the skin; it will come off easily. Carefully tear the peppers open, scoop out the seeds, and scrape off the membranes on the inside. If possible, leave the stems of the peppers in place, as they look more attractive this way for serving.

FOR THE STUFFING: Heat the butter and corn oil in a large skillet until hot. Add the diced onion and carrots and sauté for about 1 minute. Add 1 cup water, cover, bring to a boil, and cook for 3 minutes. Add the cauliflower and zucchini, cover, and cook for another 3 minutes, until most of the water has evaporated. Add the garlic, salt, and pepper and cook, uncovered, until most of the water has evaporated and the mixture is sizzling. Let cool to lukewarm.

Preheat the oven to 400 degrees.

Carefully stuff each of the peppers with 2 to 3 tablespoons of the stuffing; don't worry if the peppers split a little. Fold the peppers over the stuffing to reconstruct them and arrange them in a gratin dish or casserole.

Sprinkle with the olive oil, cover with a piece of parchment paper, and bake for 15 minutes.

Remove the peppers from the oven, brush them with the oil from the gratin dish, and arrange them in a serving dish. Serve.

Pumpkin au Gratin
Serves 6

✶ **In the part of** France that I come from, Bourg-en-Bresse, pumpkin is served not as a dessert but as a vegetable and is cooked au gratin. In a bind, you can use canned unseasoned puree of pumpkin (one 15-ounce can) to make this a fast dish. It's very good with broiled steak, lamb chops, or chicken.

1	small to medium pumpkin, halved, peeled, seeded, and cut into 3-inch chunks (approximately 3 pounds pulp)
1½	teaspoons salt
3	large eggs
1	cup heavy cream
½	teaspoon freshly ground black pepper

½ cup grated Gruyère or Emmenthaler cheese

Combine the pumpkin chunks and 1 teaspoon of the salt in a large saucepan, cover with cold water, and bring to a boil. Cover, reduce the heat, and simmer slowly for 20 to 25 minutes, until the pumpkin is tender when pierced with the tip of a knife. Drain thoroughly.

Preheat the oven to 425 degrees. Butter a 6-cup gratin dish.

Put the pumpkin through a food mill to puree it (or use a food processor; see below).

With a fork, beat the eggs in a bowl until well combined. Mix in the cream until blended. Add the pumpkin puree, the remaining ½ teaspoon salt, and the pepper and pour into the gratin dish. Alternatively, you can puree the cooked pumpkin with the eggs, cream, salt, and pepper in a food processor.

Place the dish on a cookie sheet, sprinkle the gratin with the cheese, and bake for 35 to 45 minutes, until golden brown. Remove from the oven and let rest for 10 minutes before serving.

Skillet Spinach with Nutmeg
Serves 4

✶ **The combination of nutmeg** and spinach is classic in French cooking. Here, cleaned spinach, still wet from washing, is briefly cooked in a little butter and oil, then seasoned with salt, pepper, and nutmeg and cooked a few minutes longer to boil away any excess liquid.

2 tablespoons unsalted butter
1 pound spinach, tough stems removed, washed, and drained
1 tablespoon olive oil
¼ teaspoon salt
¼ teaspoon freshly ground black pepper
¼ teaspoon freshly grated nutmeg

Heat the butter in a large skillet until very hot and lightly browned. Add half the spinach, still wet from washing, and stir well, then add the olive oil. When the spinach begins to wilt, add the remainder of the spinach to the skillet, cover, and cook for 1 minute over high heat. Remove the lid; the spinach will be wilted and liquid will have emerged from it. Add the salt, pepper, and nutmeg, mix well, and continue cooking, uncovered, for 3 to 4 minutes, stirring occasionally, until most of the liquid has boiled away. Serve.

Spinach with Pine Nuts and Croutons
Serves 4

❧ **Here sautéed spinach** is combined with croutons and nuts for a special touch and topped with a sprinkling of chopped hard-cooked egg.

3 tablespoons olive oil
2 ounces day-old baguette, cut into ¾-inch pieces (1¼ cups)

2 tablespoons pine nuts
4–5 large garlic cloves, thinly sliced (3 tablespoons)
1¼ pounds spinach, tough stems removed, washed, and drained
¼ teaspoon salt
¼ teaspoon freshly ground black pepper
1 hard-cooked egg (see page 66), coarsely chopped (use an egg cutter if you have one — slice the egg, then turn the slices 90 degrees in the cutter and cut again to dice)

Heat 1½ tablespoons of the olive oil in a large skillet. Add the bread pieces and cook, stirring, for 2 minutes. Add the nuts and garlic and cook, stirring, for 1 minute, or until the bread, nuts, and garlic are nicely browned. Transfer to a bowl.

Add the spinach, still wet from washing, to the skillet, then add the salt, pepper, and the remaining 1½ tablespoons oil. Cover and cook for about 4 minutes, until the spinach is wilted and soft.

Transfer the spinach to a serving bowl, add the crouton mixture, and combine well. Sprinkle the chopped egg over and serve.

Spinach Custards with Cream Sauce
Serves 6 as a first course

❧ **Ideal for a formal** dinner or as a luncheon dish, these small spinach timbales can be cooked ahead and reheated in hot water when needed. You can serve them without the sauce, if you prefer.

TIMBALES

3 tablespoons unsalted butter
6 slices firm white bread, cut into rounds about 2½ inches in diameter
2 tablespoons peanut oil

1 pound spinach, tough stems removed, washed, and drained
½ teaspoon salt
½ teaspoon freshly ground black pepper
⅛ teaspoon freshly grated nutmeg
2 tablespoons all-purpose flour
¾ cup milk
½ cup heavy cream
3 large eggs

SAUCE

2 teaspoons unsalted butter
2 teaspoons all-purpose flour
¼ cup milk
¼ cup heavy cream
1 large hard-cooked egg (see page 66), coarsely chopped
1 tablespoon minced fresh chives

FOR THE TIMBALES: Preheat the oven to 375 degrees. Using ½ tablespoon of the butter, grease six small metal or porcelain dariole or baba molds or ½-cup ramekins or custard cups. Set aside.

Brush the bread rounds on both sides with the oil. Place on a cookie sheet and toast in the oven for about 8 minutes. Set aside.

Drop the spinach into 2 cups of boiling salted water and boil, uncovered, over high heat for 2 minutes. Drain in a colander and cool under cold running water. Press the spinach to rid it of excess water.

Coarsely chop the spinach. (You should have about 1 cup.) Toss with the salt, pepper, and nutmeg.

Melt the remaining 2½ tablespoons butter in a heavy saucepan over high heat and cook until it is brown. (Brown butter gives a nutty taste to the spinach.) Add the spinach and mix well, separating the spinach with a fork. Sprinkle with the flour and mix well. Add the milk and cream

and mix well, then reduce the heat to medium and bring to a boil, stirring constantly; the mixture will thicken. Remove from the heat and let cool to lukewarm.

Beat the eggs with a fork to combine well and stir them into the spinach mixture. Fill the buttered molds with the spinach mixture and place them in a baking pan. Fill the pan with enough water to reach about two thirds of the way up the molds.

Bake for 25 to 30 minutes, or until set. The tip of a knife inserted in a timbale should come out clean. Remove from the oven.

MEANWHILE, FOR THE SAUCE: Melt the butter in a saucepan. Add the flour and mix well with a whisk. Add the milk and cream and bring to a boil, stirring constantly, then simmer for 2 minutes over very low heat. Remove from the heat and set aside.

To serve, run a knife around the inside of the molds to loosen the timbales. Unmold each timbale and place it on a toasted round of bread. Arrange on a platter or on individual plates. Spoon 2 tablespoons of the sauce over each timbale, sprinkle with the chopped egg and chives, and serve.

NOTE: Instead of six individual molds, this recipe can be made in a 4-cup charlotte mold or soufflé dish. It will need 5 to 10 minutes longer in the oven.

Red Swiss Chard

Serves 4

✂ **Green Swiss chard or** spinach can be substituted for the colorful chard here.

- 1 pound young, tender red Swiss chard, washed and drained
- 2 tablespoons unsalted butter
- ½ teaspoon salt

Cut the Swiss chard so all the pieces will cook in the same amount of time: since the leaves will cook faster than the stems, which are tougher, cut the leaves into large pieces and the stems into thin slices 2 to 2½ inches long.

Bring about ½ inch of water to a boil in a large saucepan. Add the Swiss chard, return to a boil, cover, and cook for about 3 minutes. Drain in a colander and rinse briefly under cold water to stop the cooking and retain the vegetable's beautiful color. Squeeze it lightly between your palms to extract the excess water.

At serving time, heat the butter in a skillet. Notice that when the foam subsides, the butter turns a light brown. Add the Swiss chard, toss the chard in the butter with the salt, and cook just long enough to heat through. Serve.

Baked Swiss Chard

Serves 6

✂ **Cooked chard is mixed** with cheese and baked just before serving.

- 1½ pounds young Swiss chard, cut into 2-inch pieces, washed, and drained
- 1 cup grated Gruyère or Emmenthaler cheese
- ½ teaspoon salt

- ¼ teaspoon freshly ground black pepper
- 3 tablespoons olive oil

Preheat the oven to 375 degrees.

Bring ½ inch of water to a boil in a large saucepan. Add the Swiss chard, cover, bring back to a boil, and boil for 5 to 6 minutes, until tender. (Or divide the chard between two plastic bags and cook each bag in a microwave oven for 4 to 6 minutes. Drain.)

Put the Swiss chard in a gratin dish and mix in the cheese, salt, pepper, and olive oil. (*The recipe can be prepared to this point a few hours ahead.*)

Bake the chard for 15 minutes. Serve.

Swiss Chard au Gratin

Serves 6

✂ **Only the wide central** stalks of the chard are used in this gratin, which is commonly served in the Lyon area of France. Mature chard should be peeled to remove the tough surface fibers of the ribs. Serve with any roast.

- 4 tablespoons (½ stick) unsalted butter
- 3 pounds Swiss chard
- 3 tablespoons all-purpose flour
- 2½ cups half-and-half
- ½ teaspoon salt
- ¼ teaspoon freshly ground black pepper
- 2 tablespoons freshly grated Parmesan cheese

Preheat the oven to 400 degrees. Butter a gratin dish (I use a 12-by-5-inch oval dish) with a little of the butter.

Cut the green leafy pieces from both sides of the chard ribs and keep them for a soup or puree. If necessary, using a vegetable peeler, remove the tough fibers from the tops of the ribs. Cut or break the ribs crosswise in half and pull off any additional tough fibers. Wash the ribs and cut into 2-inch pieces. (You should have about 3½ cups.)

Drop the rib pieces into boiling salted water to cover, bring back to a boil, and cook, uncovered, for 6 to 8 minutes, or until tender. Drain in a colander.

Melt the remaining butter in a heavy saucepan over medium heat. Add the flour and mix well. Add the half-and-half and, stirring constantly with a whisk, bring to a boil so it thickens. When the mixture begins to boil, reduce the heat and simmer for 1 minute. Add the salt and pepper; mix well. Remove from the heat.

Arrange the Swiss chard ribs in the buttered gratin dish and pour the cream sauce over them. Be sure that all the pieces are coated with the sauce. Sprinkle with the cheese, place on a cookie sheet, and bake for 30 to 35 minutes, until golden brown. Serve.

Stuffed Butternut Squash
Serves 4

❧ **The stuffing for this** squash is made primarily of the flesh of the squash itself, with garlic, a bit of ginger, and minced scallions added for flavor. (If you are not fond of ginger, use less of it or eliminate it altogether.) Bread crumbs tossed with a little oil and sprinkled on top of the filling become brown and crisp in the oven, and their crunchiness contrasts nicely with the filling.

  1 butternut squash (about 2¼ pounds)
3½ tablespoons canola oil

7–8 scallions, trimmed (leaving some green) and minced (1 cup)
  3 garlic cloves, crushed and finely chopped (2 teaspoons)
1½ teaspoons chopped fresh peeled ginger
  ½ teaspoon salt
  ¼ teaspoon freshly ground black pepper
  2 slices firm white bread (about 2 ounces), processed to crumbs in a food processor (1 cup)

Preheat the oven to 400 degrees.

Split the squash lengthwise in half and remove the seeds. Score the flesh of the squash, making ½-inch-deep cuts through it one way and then the other in a crosshatch pattern. Arrange the squash halves cut side up on a cookie sheet and bake for about 1 hour, until the flesh is tender when pierced with a fork. Remove from the oven.

Meanwhile, heat 2 tablespoons of the canola oil in a large skillet. When it is hot, add the scallions and sauté for 1½ minutes. Mix in the garlic and ginger and set the pan aside.

When the squash is cool enough to handle, use a spoon to gently scoop the flesh from the shells, leaving walls about ¼ inch thick, and add it to the scallions, along with the salt and pepper. Mix well, stirring until the squash flesh and scallions are combined but the mixture is still chunky. Fill the squash shells with the mixture.

Lightly mix the bread crumbs with the remaining 1½ tablespoons oil in a small bowl and sprinkle over the stuffed squash.

Arrange the squash halves on a cookie sheet and bake for about 20 minutes (a little longer if the stuffing was cool). The crumb mixture should be nicely browned; if it is not, place the squash under a hot broiler for a few minutes.

Cut each of the squash halves in half again and serve. (The skin of the squash is edible.)

Butternut Squash Gratin
Serves 6

✄ **This rich butternut squash** gratin is a perfect companion to a roast leg of lamb or a grilled steak.

- 1 large butternut squash (3¾ pounds)
- 1 teaspoon salt
- ¼ teaspoon freshly ground black pepper
- 1 cup heavy cream
- ½ cup grated Jarlsberg or other Swiss-type cheese

Preheat the oven to 400 degrees.

Cut off the stem of the butternut squash and split it in two at the bottom of the neck; this will make it easier to peel. Peel the neck lengthwise with a sharp knife or vegetable peeler, removing enough skin so the orange flesh appears (there is a layer of green under the first layer of skin). For the body of the squash, remove the skin with a knife by going around it in a spiral fashion (it is easier to peel a round object in this manner); then cut lengthwise in half and, using a sharp spoon, remove the seeds. With the slicing blade of a food processor or a knife, cut the squash into ⅛- to ¼-inch-thick slices.

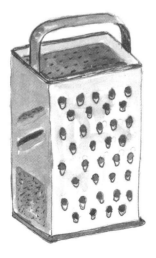

Put the squash in a saucepan, cover with water, and bring to a boil. Boil over high heat for 1½ to 2 minutes, then drain in a colander; the pieces will break a little.

Transfer the squash to a gratin dish and add the salt, pepper, and cream, mixing with a fork to distribute the ingredients. Cover with the cheese.

Bake for 30 to 40 minutes, until nicely browned. Serve.

Butternut Squash Puree
Serves 4

✄ **This simple, delicious puree** goes well with roast poultry or sautéed veal. It can be made ahead and reheated in the microwave at serving time.

- 1 butternut squash (about 2 pounds)
- 1 garlic clove
- ¾ teaspoon salt
- ¾ cup water
- ⅓ cup light cream
- 1 tablespoon unsalted butter
- ⅛ teaspoon freshly ground black pepper

Cut off the stem and cut the squash crosswise at the base of the neck, dividing it into 2 pieces. Peel both pieces with a sharp knife or a vegetable peeler, removing a thick-enough layer of skin so there is no green visible on the squash. Halve the body of the squash and remove the seeds with a sharp spoon. Cut the squash into 2-inch pieces.

Combine the squash pieces, garlic, salt, and water in a saucepan and bring to a boil over high heat. Cover, reduce the heat to medium, and cook for 20 to 25 minutes, until the squash is tender and there are only 2 to 3 tablespoons of liquid remaining in the pan.

Transfer the squash and liquid to a food processor, add the cream, butter, and pepper, and process for 45 seconds to 1 minute, until the mixture is very smooth. Serve.

Spaghetti Squash in Fresh Tomato Sauce
Serves 4

❧ **We often enjoy spaghetti** squash at our house and occasionally serve it as a substitute for pasta, since its fresh flavor and crisp texture are complemented by pasta sauces. Roasting the squash, as I do here, is especially easy.

For this tomato sauce, two heads of garlic are halved crosswise, wrapped in foil, and roasted alongside the squash. When the cloves are soft and nicely browned on their cut edges, their flesh is squeezed out and added to a sauce composed of onion, fresh tomatoes, and seasonings. Mild and tender, the roasted garlic can also be served on its own or with other dishes.

1	large spaghetti squash (2½–3 pounds)
2	teaspoons canola oil
2	heads garlic (about 6 ounces)
3	tablespoons olive oil
1	onion (about 4 ounces), chopped (¾ cup)
1	pound ripe tomatoes (3–4), cut into 2-inch pieces
1	teaspoon herbes de Provence
1½	teaspoons salt
¾	teaspoon freshly ground black pepper
⅓	cup water
1	tablespoon chopped fresh chives
2–3	tablespoons freshly grated Pecorino Romano cheese (optional)

Preheat the oven to 400 degrees.

Cut the squash crosswise in half and scoop out the seeds with a spoon. Brush the cut sides of the squash halves with 1 teaspoon of the canola oil and place them cut side down on a cookie sheet or in a roasting pan.

Cut a rectangle of aluminum foil about 6 by 12 inches and spread the remaining teaspoon of canola oil over half its surface. Cut the heads of garlic horizontally in half and place them cut side down next to one another on the oiled side of the foil. Fold the unoiled side over the garlic and fold the edges of the foil together tightly.

Put the foil package next to the squash halves and bake for 40 to 45 minutes. The squash should be tender when pierced with a knife and its cut sides nicely browned; the garlic cloves should be soft throughout and their cut surfaces nicely browned. Remove from the oven.

Heat 2 tablespoons of the olive oil in a medium stainless steel saucepan until very hot but not smoking. Add the onion and sauté for 2 to 3 minutes. Add the tomatoes, herbes de Provence, 1 teaspoon of the salt, and the pepper. Squeeze the soft garlic cloves out of their skins and add them to the saucepan. Mix well, add the water, and bring to a strong boil. Cover and boil over high heat for 10 minutes. Push the mixture through a food mill set over a saucepan. Set aside.

Using a fork, loosen and release the "spaghetti" strands from the squash halves and transfer them to a bowl. Mix gently but thoroughly with the remaining ½ teaspoon salt and 1 tablespoon olive oil.

At serving time, reheat the "spaghetti" in a microwave oven for 1½ to 2 minutes or in a 400-degree oven for 10 to 12 minutes. Reheat the sauce until it is hot.

Ladle a large spoonful of sauce onto each of four dinner plates. Divide the "spaghetti" among the plates and drizzle about 1 tablespoon of the remaining sauce on top of each serving. Sprinkle with the chives and serve, with the cheese, if desired.

Herbed Sautéed Zucchini
Serves 6

❧ **When you buy zucchini**, choose long, firm, and shiny specimens. They should break if twisted or bent. Long narrow ones have fewer seeds. If the center is very soft and cottony, halve the squash and remove it.

> 3 zucchini (1½ pounds)
> ¼ cup vegetable oil
> 1 tablespoon minced fresh chives
> ½ teaspoon salt
> ¼ teaspoon freshly ground black pepper
> 1 tablespoon unsalted butter
> 1 tomato, cut into ½-inch pieces (1 cup)

Cut the zucchini lengthwise into ¼-inch-thick slices. Stack the slices and cut them into ¼-inch-wide julienne strips about 2½ inches long. (You should have approximately 7 cups.)

Heat the oil in one large or two small skillets. When it is hot, add the zucchini; it shouldn't be layered more than ½ inch thick, or it will steam and soften without browning. Sauté over high heat for 4½ to 5 minutes, until soft and a bit transparent but not soggy. Add the chives, salt, pepper, and butter and mix well.

Add the tomato, toss, and transfer to a serving dish. Serve.

Zucchini and Tomato Fans
Serves 4

Make this beautiful dish in summer, when small firm zucchini are plentiful. To make the "fans," the zucchini are cut lengthwise into slices that are left attached at the stem end, then fanned out in a roasting pan. Long, narrow slices of plum tomatoes and thin slices of garlic are inserted between the zucchini and the dish is baked. Leftovers are good served cold with a little vinaigrette on top.

> 4 small firm zucchini (about 1½ inches in diameter and 6 inches long; 1¼ pounds)
> 4 long narrow plum tomatoes (about 12 ounces), cut lengthwise into 4 slices each
> 4 large garlic cloves, cut lengthwise into 8 slices each
> 2 tablespoons olive oil
> ½ teaspoon herbes de Provence
> ¼ teaspoon salt
> ¼ teaspoon freshly ground black pepper

Preheat the oven to 400 degrees.

Trim off the stem end of each zucchini. Starting at the flower end, cut each zucchini lengthwise into about ¼-inch-thick slices, leaving the slices attached at the stem end; each zucchini should have 4 slits. Arrange the zucchini side by side in a roasting pan or large gratin dish with enough space between that each one can be fanned out. Press down firmly on the zucchini to fan them out, then slide a slice of tomato into each slit. Slide the garlic slices into the fans alongside the tomato slices. Brush the entire surface of the fans with the oil and sprinkle the herbes de Provence, salt, and pepper on top.

Bake for 30 minutes, or until the vegetables are soft and the fans are nicely browned on top. Using a large spatula, transfer the fans to four plates and serve.

Zucchini Boats
with Red Pepper Sauce
Serves 4

✎ **Stuffed eggplant and zucchini** are traditional in both southern French and Middle Eastern cooking. This stuffing includes not only onion, garlic, and bread, but also the insides of the squash. The boats are served with a colorful sauce of red bell pepper and tomato. Serve this main dish either hot or, in the summer, lukewarm.

ZUCCHINI

- 6–8 dried shiitake mushroom caps (1 ounce)
- 2 cups hot water
- 4 small firm zucchini (about 2 inches in diameter and 5 inches long; 1¼ pounds)
- 2 tablespoons olive oil
- 1 large onion, finely chopped (2 cups)
- 5–6 garlic cloves, crushed and coarsely chopped (1 tablespoon)
- 2 ounces stale bread, preferably from a baguette, processed to coarse crumbs in a food processor (1¼ cups)
- ½ cup grated mozzarella cheese
- 2 tablespoons chopped fresh parsley
- 2 tablespoons chopped fresh chives
- ¾ teaspoon salt
- ½ teaspoon freshly ground black pepper

SAUCE

- 1 ripe tomato (about 8 ounces), cut into 1-inch chunks
- 1 red bell pepper (about 8 ounces), cored, seeded, and cut into 1-inch chunks
- ¼ cup water
- 2 tablespoons olive oil
- ¼ teaspoon salt
- ¼ teaspoon freshly ground black pepper

FOR THE ZUCCHINI: Put the mushroom caps in a bowl, cover them with the water, and let soak for at least 30 minutes.

Trim the zucchini and split lengthwise in half. Using a melon baller or a metal measuring teaspoon, remove (and reserve) the seeds and most of the flesh, leaving 8 "boats" of zucchini with bases and sides about ¼ inch thick. (You should have about 2½ cups flesh and seeds.) Coarsely chop the flesh and seeds and set aside.

Remove the mushroom caps from the soaking liquid (reserving the liquid), press them lightly to remove excess liquid, and coarsely chop them. (You should have about ½ cup.)

Heat the oil in a large skillet. When it is hot, add the onion and mushrooms. Slowly pour in the reserved mushroom soaking liquid, leaving behind any sandy residue in the bottom of the bowl. Bring the mixture to a boil, cover, and boil for 6 to 8 minutes, or until all the liquid has evaporated. Uncover and cook for another 2 to 3 minutes to brown the onion and mushrooms lightly.

Add the reserved zucchini flesh and the garlic and cook, covered, for 3 to 4 minutes, until soft. Transfer the mixture to a bowl and let cool to room temperature.

Preheat the oven to 350 degrees.

Add the bread crumbs, cheese, parsley, chives, ½ teaspoon of the salt, and the pepper to the zucchini mixture and toss gently but thoroughly.

Sprinkle the remaining ¼ teaspoon of salt over the zucchini boats. Stuff them with the mushroom mixture, dividing it evenly and packing it lightly in place.

Arrange the boats on a cookie sheet and bake for 30 minutes. Then place under a hot broiler for 2 to 3 minutes to brown the tops lightly.

MEANWHILE, FOR THE SAUCE: Drop the tomato chunks into a food processor. Add the red pepper, along with the water, oil, salt, and pepper, and process until the mixture is liquefied. Transfer to a small saucepan. (You should have 2 cups.)

Bring the sauce to a boil, reduce the heat to low, and simmer gently for 5 minutes. Use as is or, for a smoother sauce, puree the mixture with a hand blender (or in a regular blender).

Place 2 zucchini boats on each plate, surround with the sauce, and serve.

Zucchini-Tomato Gratin

Serves 6

✻ **You can prepare this** colorful gratin up to 1 day ahead. Fresh oregano will add the most flavor, but dried can be used if fresh is not available.

    4 zucchini (about 6 inches long; 1½–
         1¾ pounds)
    3 large ripe tomatoes (about 1½ pounds),
         cut into 12 slices each
    ¼ cup olive oil

TOPPING

    3 tablespoons freshly grated Parmesan
         cheese
    1 slice firm whole wheat bread, cubed
         (½ cup)
       Leaves from 3 fresh oregano sprigs
         (about 30) or ½ teaspoon dried
         oregano

    ½ teaspoon salt
    ½ teaspoon freshly ground black pepper
    1 tablespoon extra-virgin olive oil

Preheat the oven to 400 degrees.

Trim the zucchini and cut it crosswise in half. Cut each half lengthwise into 4 slices.

Arrange alternating slices of the zucchini and tomato in a 12-by-9-by-2-inch gratin dish, and pour the olive oil on top. (*The gratin can be prepared to this point up to a day ahead, covered, and refrigerated.*)

FOR THE TOPPING: Combine the cheese, bread, oregano, salt, and pepper in a mini-chop and process to crumbs. Transfer the mixture to a bowl and stir in the oil.

At serving time, sprinkle the vegetables with the topping. Bake for 35 minutes, or until the gratin is tender and moist and the top is nicely brown. Serve.

Rice-Stuffed Zucchini

Serves 6

✻ **For this summer dish**, which is best served at room temperature, firm medium zucchini are split lengthwise, hollowed out, and stuffed with rice, onions, and seasonings, then finished with cheese and baked. The zucchini can be prepared ahead and will keep for several days in the refrigerator.

    ½   cup long-grain white rice
           (Carolina is a good choice)
    1½   cups water
    6   medium zucchini (about
           2½ pounds)
    2   teaspoons salt
    3   tablespoons olive oil
    1   medium onion, finely chopped
           (about ¾ cup)

1 cup coarsely chopped tomatoes
3 large garlic cloves, crushed and
    chopped (2 teaspoons)
½ teaspoon freshly ground black pepper
1½ teaspoons seeded and finely chopped
    jalapeño pepper
1 cup grated mozzarella cheese
2 slices firm white bread (2 ounces),
    processed to crumbs in a food
    processor (1 cup)
1 teaspoon paprika
⅓ cup vegetable oil

Combine the rice and water in a small heavy saucepan and bring to a boil over medium heat. Cover and simmer very gently for 20 minutes, or until all the water is absorbed and the rice is cooked. Set aside.

Meanwhile, trim the zucchini and cut lengthwise in half. With a sharp teaspoon, remove the seeds and some of the pulp (reserve) from each half to create shells about ¼ inch thick; be careful not to break through the zucchini shells. Coarsely chop the seeds and pulp. (You should have about 4 cups.) Arrange the shells next to each other in a large glass baking dish and sprinkle with 1 teaspoon of the salt. Set aside.

Heat the olive oil in a large stainless steel saucepan. Add the onion and sauté for 2 to 3 minutes. Add the zucchini pulp, tomatoes, garlic, the remaining 1 teaspoon salt, the black pepper, and jalapeño pepper and cook over medium heat for 10 minutes to evaporate most of the liquid, stirring once in a while to prevent scorching. Combine with the cooked rice and let cool slightly, about 15 minutes.

Preheat the oven to 400 degrees.

Empty each zucchini shell of any accumulated liquid. Fill with the stuffing so that it slightly overlaps the rims of the shells. Combine the grated cheese, bread crumbs, and paprika, mixing well,

and top the stuffing generously with the mixture. Sprinkle the vegetable oil on top of the crumb mixture.

Bake for 45 minutes, or until the topping is golden brown. Allow to rest for at least 10 minutes before serving.

Quick Ratatouille
Serves 6

✎ **The cooking time for** this ratatouille is shorter than that for more traditional versions. The tomatoes and garlic are added only in the last few minutes so the taste stays fresh.

¼ cup olive oil, plus extra for garnish
3 onions (about 1 pound), cut into 1-inch
    pieces (about 3 cups)
1 large green bell pepper, cored, seeded,
    and cut into ½-inch pieces (about
    1½ cups)
1 eggplant (about 1 pound), trimmed but
    not peeled and cut into 1-inch pieces
    (about 6 cups)
4 small zucchini (about 1¼ pounds),
    trimmed and cut into 1-inch pieces
    (about 4 cups)
¼ teaspoon hot pepper flakes
1½ teaspoons salt
6–8 garlic cloves, sliced (about 3 tablespoons)
4 tomatoes (about 1½ pounds), cut into
    1-inch cubes (about 4 cups)
1 cup shredded fresh basil leaves
    Freshly ground black pepper

Heat the oil in a large saucepan. When it is hot, add the onions, green pepper, eggplant, zucchini, hot pepper flakes, and salt and cook over high heat for 5 minutes. Reduce the heat to medium, cover, and cook for 25 minutes, stirring occasionally to prevent the mixture from sticking.

Add the garlic and tomatoes and continue cooking, covered, for 5 minutes. Transfer to a serving bowl and let cool to room temperature.

Just before serving, stir half the basil into the ratatouille. Sprinkle the remaining basil on top and garnish with a few tablespoonfuls of olive oil and a few grindings of black pepper.

LEFTOVER RATATOUILLE

Leftover ratatouille can be chopped fine into a "caviar," seasoned with hot pepper flakes or cayenne pepper, and served as a dip with potato chips, corn chips, or crackers. It makes a great stuffing for ravioli too, and the ravioli can be served with tomato sauce for a light lunch (see Ratatouille Ravioli, page 97).

Classic Ratatouille
Serves 6

Ratatouille is the epitome of Provençal vegetable stews. The vegetables are sautéed individually in oil before being stewed so they keep their shape and texture. If you prefer, though, you can put all the cubed vegetables into a casserole and top with the seasonings and water. Ratatouille is excellent reheated and it is superb cold as an hors d'oeuvre, topped with small black olives and olive oil.

About ½ cup olive oil
1   eggplant (1¼ pounds), trimmed but not peeled and cut into 1-inch cubes (about 4 cups)
3   medium zucchini (about 1¼ pounds), trimmed and cut into 1-inch cubes (about 3 cups)
12 ounces onions (2–3), cut into 1-inch cubes

1   pound green bell peppers (2–3), cored, seeded, and cut into 1-inch squares (about 3 cups)
4–5 ripe tomatoes, peeled, halved, seeded, and coarsely cubed (about 4 cups)
5–6 garlic cloves, crushed and very finely chopped (about 1 tablespoon)
½   cup water
2   teaspoons salt
½   teaspoon freshly ground black pepper

Heat ¼ cup of the oil in one or, better, two large skillets. First sauté the eggplant cubes until browned, about 8 minutes; remove with a slotted spoon and transfer to a large heavy flameproof casserole. (The eggplant will absorb more oil while cooking than the other vegetables.) Then sauté the zucchini cubes until browned, about 8 minutes. Transfer to the casserole. Add about ¼ cup more oil to the pan and sauté the onions and peppers together for about 6 minutes. Add them to the casserole.

Add the tomatoes, garlic, water, salt, and pepper to the casserole and bring to a boil over medium heat. Reduce the heat to low, cover, and cook for 1 hour.

Remove the cover, increase the heat to medium, and cook for another 20 minutes to reduce

PEELING AND SEEDING TOMATOES

Dip the tomatoes briefly in boiling water or hold them over the flame of a gas stove, then peel them with a knife; the skin should slide off easily. Alternatively, peel the tomatoes with a sharp vegetable peeler. To seed the tomatoes, cut them crosswise in half and squeeze the seeds out. The seeds, juice, and skin can be frozen for use in stock.

the liquid; stir once in a while to prevent scorching. Let the ratatouille rest for at least 30 minutes before serving.

Olive and Tomato Toasts
Serves 4 as a first course or hors d'oeuvre

These "toasts"—baked and served hot from the oven or baked ahead and served at room temperature — are great to pass around at a large party. The fresh tomatoes, cut into little cubes, have a sweet taste that goes well with the concentrated flavor of the oil-cured black olives.

¼ cup olive oil
16 ½-inch-thick slices baguette
2 tomatoes, halved, seeded, and cut into ¼-inch dice (1⅓ cups)
½ cup oil-cured black olives, pitted and cut into ¼-inch pieces
¼ cup minced fresh cilantro
¼ teaspoon salt
½ teaspoon freshly ground black pepper
3 tablespoons grated mozzarella cheese
1½ tablespoons freshly grated Pecorino Romano cheese

Preheat the oven to 400 degrees.

Spread 2 tablespoons of the oil on a cookie sheet and dip both sides of the bread slices in the oil. Arrange on the sheet and bake for 6 to 8 minutes, until lightly browned. Remove from the oven. (Leave the oven on.)

Meanwhile, combine the tomatoes, olives, the remaining 2 tablespoons oil, the cilantro, salt, and pepper in a bowl.

Divide the tomato mixture and spread evenly on top of the toasts. Mix the cheeses together and sprinkle on generously. Return to the oven for 6 to 8 minutes. Serve warm or at room temperature.

Tomatoes Provençal
Serves 6

This is one of my favorite ways to cook tomatoes from the garden when they are ripe and plentiful. Any leftovers can be chopped and added to a tomato sauce. Use a cast-iron or aluminum skillet, not a nonstick one.

6 large very ripe tomatoes (about 2½ pounds)
1 cup lightly packed fresh parsley leaves
4 large garlic cloves, crushed
¼ cup olive oil
½ teaspoon salt
½ teaspoon freshly ground black pepper

Preheat the oven to 350 degrees.

Core the tomatoes and cut them crosswise in half. Chop the parsley and garlic together to make a *persillade*. (You should have ½ cup.)

Heat about 1 tablespoon of the oil in each of two heavy skillets until very, very hot. Arrange the tomatoes cut side down in the skillets and cook, partially covered to avoid splattering, over high heat for about 4 minutes, until they soften and are lightly browned on the cut side. Arrange the tomatoes cut side up in a gratin dish and sprinkle with the salt and pepper.

Add the remaining 2 tablespoons oil and the *persillade* to the drippings in one of the pans and stir over the heat for 10 to 15 seconds to cook

slightly, then divide the mixture equally among the tomatoes, spreading it over the tops.

Bake the tomatoes for 5 minutes. Serve.

Stuffed Tomatoes Maison
Serves 4

❧ **My mother used to** make dishes like this when she had a little stale bread on hand and some leftover meat from a roast or stew. Most any meat — beef, veal, pork, or ham as well as chicken — will work, adding a little richness to the stuffing and transforming leftovers into a fresh new dish. The tomato insides make a delicious sauce for the stuffed tomatoes, which can be served as a first course or as a main, preceded by a soup.

      4 ounces leftover country-style bread,
           cut into ½-inch pieces (2 cups)
      ¾ cup room-temperature water
      6 ounces leftover meat from a roast (pork,
           veal, or beef) or cold cuts, coarsely
           chopped (2 cups)
      ¼ cup chopped onion
      4 scallions, trimmed (leaving some green)
           and coarsely chopped (½ cup)
      2 mushrooms (about 3 ounces), cleaned
           and coarsely chopped (1 cup)
      3 garlic cloves, crushed and chopped
           (2 teaspoons)
      1 teaspoon salt
      ½ teaspoon freshly ground black pepper
      1 large egg
      4 large tomatoes (about 2 pounds)

Preheat the oven to 400 degrees.

Drop the bread pieces into a bowl and sprinkle with the water. Squeeze the bread gently until it absorbs the water and becomes soft. Add

the meat, onion, scallions, mushrooms, garlic, ½ teaspoon of the salt, ¼ teaspoon of the pepper, and the egg. Mix well. The mixture should hold together but not be pasty.

Using a sharp knife, remove the top ½ inch from the stem end of each tomato; reserve these "caps." Scoop out the insides of each tomato with a metal measuring spoon or other sharp spoon, leaving only the fleshy shell of the tomato.

Coarsely chop the tomato insides. (You should have about 2 cups.) Sprinkle with the remaining ½ teaspoon salt and ¼ teaspoon pepper.

Stand the tomato shells upright in a gratin dish and fill them with the stuffing. Place the reserved tomato caps on top and pour the chopped tomato mixture around the tomatoes.

Bake for 50 to 60 minutes, until the tomatoes are nicely browned and the stuffing mixture is cooked and hot throughout. Serve with the surrounding juices.

Tomatoes Stuffed with Yellow Grits
Serves 4

❧ **This combination of grits,** scallions, and mushrooms is perfect for a meatless lunch or dinner. The grits mixture can be served on its own as a side dish or under a piece of poached or grilled fish or sautéed meat.

      2½ cups water
      1¼ teaspoons salt
      ½ cup quick-cooking yellow grits or
           yellow cornmeal
      4 large firm but ripe tomatoes (about
           2 pounds)
      3 tablespoons olive oil
      6 scallions, trimmed (leaving some green)
           and cut into ½-inch pieces (1 cup)

1 medium onion, chopped (1 cup)
2 garlic cloves, chopped (1½ teaspoons)
6 ounces mushrooms, cleaned and coarsely chopped (2 cups)

Preheat the oven to 375 degrees.

Bring the water to a boil in a saucepan. Stir in ½ teaspoon of the salt and the grits or cornmeal, return to a boil, and boil, covered, removing the lid and stirring with a whisk occasionally, for 5 minutes, or until most of the water has been absorbed and the grits are tender. Spread them on a plate and let cool to lukewarm.

Meanwhile, cut a ½-inch-thick slice from the stem end of each tomato. Reserve these "caps." Using a metal measuring tablespoon or other sharp spoon, remove the interior of each tomato, leaving a shell ½ inch thick. Chop the tomato insides in a food processor. Add ¼ teaspoon of the salt and 1 tablespoon of the oil and process briefly to mix. (You should have 1½ to 2 cups.) Set aside.

Heat the remaining 2 tablespoons oil in a large skillet. Add the scallions and onion and sauté over medium-high heat for 2 minutes. Stir in the garlic, mushrooms, and the remaining ½ teaspoon salt and cook for about 4 minutes, until most of the juices have evaporated. Transfer to a bowl and stir in the grits.

Fill the tomato shells with the grits mixture and top each with a "cap." Arrange the stuffed tomatoes in a gratin dish and pour the processed tomato sauce around them.

Bake for 40 minutes. Let cool to lukewarm before serving.

Corn-and-Ham-Topped Tomatoes
Serves 4

✎ **For this side dish,** first course, or luncheon main, large tomatoes are halved, seeded, and cooked cut side down in hot oil until their flesh begins to caramelize. Then they are turned over and topped with a mixture of sautéed corn, ham, and chives.

2 tablespoons olive oil
2 large tomatoes (about 8 ounces each)
1¾ cups corn kernels (from about 2 ears)
2 slices ham (2 ounces), cut into julienne strips (½ cup)
¼ cup ½-inch pieces fresh chives
½ teaspoon salt
¼ teaspoon freshly ground black pepper

Heat 1 tablespoon of the oil in a large heavy skillet (not nonstick) until very hot. Meanwhile, cut the tomatoes crosswise in half and, holding them cut side down, squeeze them gently over a bowl to remove the seeds. (The seeds and juice can be reserved for use in a stock.)

Put the tomatoes cut side down in the hot oil in the skillet and cook over high heat for 5 to 6 minutes, until they begin to caramelize on the cut side. Transfer the tomatoes to a gratin dish, arranging them cut side up.

Add the remaining tablespoon of oil to the skillet, then add the corn kernels and sauté over high heat for about 3 minutes, stirring and scraping the bottom of the pan occasionally. Add the ham, chives, salt, and pepper and cook for 1 minute.

Spoon some of the corn and ham mixture into the tomato halves and the remainder around them. Serve.

Tomato "Petals" with Tarragon
Serves 4

❧ **Looking like the petals** of a large flower, tomato segments are cooked in the oven until they dry out a little and their taste becomes concentrated. Moistened with a little olive oil and seasoned with tarragon, they are served at room temperature.

    4   large firm but ripe tomatoes (about
        2 pounds)
    ¼   teaspoon salt
    2   tablespoons extra-virgin olive oil
    ¼   teaspoon freshly ground black pepper
    1   tablespoon chopped fresh tarragon

Preheat the oven to 400 degrees.

Bring 3 cups water to a boil in a medium saucepan. Submerge the tomatoes in the boiling water for 30 seconds. Drain and peel the tomatoes.

Cut each tomato from top to bottom into 4 segments. Remove the juice, seeds, and some of the ribs from the segments with your fingers. (The skin, juice, flesh, and seeds can be reserved for soup or stock.)

Arrange the tomato petals rib side down in a nonstick baking pan and sprinkle with the salt. Press down on them gently to flatten them. Bake for 30 minutes.

Arrange the petals on a platter, sprinkle with the olive oil, pepper, and tarragon, and serve at room temperature.

Tomato and Bread Gratin
Serves 4

❧ **This combination**—tomatoes, bread, garlic, olive oil, parsley, and Parmesan cheese — is everybody's favorite. For variety, I sometimes substitute yellow cherry tomatoes for the red.

    1¼ pounds cherry or grape tomatoes (about
        3½ cups), any stems removed
    3   ounces day-old bread, preferably from a
        country or whole wheat loaf, cut into
        1-inch cubes (about 3½ cups)
    6   garlic cloves, sliced (2 tablespoons)
    ½   cup coarsely chopped fresh parsley
    ½   teaspoon salt
    ½   teaspoon freshly ground black pepper
    3   tablespoons olive oil
    ¼   cup freshly grated Parmesan or Pecorino
        Romano cheese

Preheat the oven to 375 degrees.

Put the tomatoes in a bowl and toss with the bread, garlic, parsley, salt, pepper, oil, and cheese. Transfer to a 6-cup gratin dish.

Bake for 40 minutes. Serve.

Sautéed Turnip Greens
Serves 4

❧ **A number of different** greens — from kale to mustard greens — can be prepared in the same manner as these turnip greens. I use a little bacon and its rendered fat to enrich the greens.

    4   slices bacon, cut into ¼-inch pieces
    1½ pounds turnip greens, tough stems
        and damaged leaves removed,
        remainder cut into 2-inch pieces
        (about 1¼ pounds trimmed)

2 teaspoons sugar
¼ teaspoon salt, or to taste
½ teaspoon freshly ground black pepper

Spread the bacon in one layer in a large saucepan and cook over medium heat until all the pieces are well browned, about 6 minutes.

Meanwhile, wash the turnip greens in cool water (several times if necessary to clean) and drain them in a colander.

Add the greens, still wet from washing, to the saucepan and sprinkle on the sugar, salt, and pepper. Cook the greens, covered, over high heat for 3 to 5 minutes, until they wilt. Then reduce the heat to low and continue cooking, covered, for 15 to 20 minutes, until all the moisture is gone and the greens are glazed with the sugar and bacon fat. (If there is still moisture remaining in the pan after 20 minutes, cook, uncovered, for a few minutes to evaporate it.) The greens should be tender but not mushy.

Add salt to taste if needed, depending on the saltiness of the bacon, and serve.

Turnip and Potato Puree
Serves 8

✎ **A puree made only** with potatoes and a few cloves of garlic is a favorite of my family and the addition of white turnips is a delightful variation. At certain times of the year, the flavor of turnips is stronger, and the proportion of turnips to potatoes can increase or decrease accordingly. The mixture should never be more than half turnips, though, because the potatoes give body to the puree. Serve with roasted or grilled meat.

2 pounds boiling potatoes, peeled
1 pound white turnips, peeled
4 large garlic cloves

1¾ teaspoons salt
4 tablespoons (½ stick) unsalted butter
¼ teaspoon freshly ground black pepper
2 tablespoons milk (optional)

Put the potatoes, turnips, and garlic cloves in a saucepan, cover with tepid water, and add 1 teaspoon of the salt. Bring to a boil and cook for about 45 minutes, until the vegetables are very tender.

Drain and push the mixture through a food mill, using the fine screen, or a ricer into another saucepan. Mix in the butter, the remaining ¾ teaspoon salt, and the pepper and serve. Or cover the top with 2 tablespoons milk (so it doesn't form a skin) and set aside until serving time; to serve, stir in the milk and reheat briefly.

Vegetable Tempura
Serves 8 to 10

✎ **For these delicious pancakes,** vegetable slices are stirred into a tempura batter and fried. They are best cooked at the last minute, but the vegetables can be prepared a few hours ahead. Serve alongside any roast meat or poultry, cutting the pancakes in half, if desired. The tempura can be served as an hors d'oeuvre by cutting the vegetables into smaller pieces and making smaller pancakes. Pass them as soon as they are fried.

Don't limit yourself to the vegetables used here. Other vegetables, from cabbage and eggplant to turnips, can also be used.

BATTER

- 2 cups all-purpose flour
- 1 teaspoon baking powder
- 2 large egg yolks
- ¼ teaspoon salt
- 2½ cups ice-cold water

VEGETABLES

- 1 medium carrot, peeled
- ½ medium onion
- 1 small zucchini, trimmed
- ½ cup mushrooms
- ½ cup corn kernels
- 1½ cups loosely packed stemmed spinach
- 1 cup loosely packed fresh parsley leaves

Corn oil, for cooking the tempura
Salt

FOR THE BATTER: Mix together the flour, baking powder, egg yolks, salt, and 1 cup of the ice water in a bowl with a whisk. The batter will be very thick at this point; work with the whisk until smooth. (If a batter is thick enough, the wires of the whisk going through it will break up any lumps of flour and produce a thick but smooth batter.) Add the remaining 1½ cups ice water and mix to combine. The mixture should be about the thickness of a crepe batter.

FOR THE VEGETABLES: Slice all the vegetables except the corn, spinach, and parsley very thin by hand or in a food processor fitted with the 1-millimeter slicing blade.

At serving time, stir all the vegetables and the parsley into the batter. Heat 1 tablespoon corn oil in each of two 7-inch (measured across the bottom) nonstick skillets. When it is hot, add approximately ½ cup of the vegetable mixture to each skillet and spread the mixture with a spoon so the pancakes are very thin, about 5½ inches in diameter. Cook on the first side over high heat for 3 minutes, or until nicely browned. Turn the pancakes and cook on the other side for 3 minutes. Sprinkle lightly with salt and serve immediately, or place on a cookie sheet and keep warm in a hot oven or under the broiler for a few minutes while you cook the remainder of the pancakes.

fruit

Desserts

Fruit Desserts

"Good Lady" Apples
(Apples Bonne Femme)
Serves 6

❧ **For these baked apples,** ubiquitous in home cooking as well as in country inns and restaurants, only a few ingredients are needed. Inexpensive and quickly prepared, the dish can be made year round. Use an apple that will keep its shape during cooking, such as Golden or Red Delicious, russet, Granny Smith, or Pippin.

The apples look best when they have just emerged from the oven, puffed from the heat and glossy with rich color. But it's best to serve them barely lukewarm, even though they will shrivel a bit as they cool. If you have leftovers, the apples can be reheated the next day (baste them with the juice). These are delicious served with a slice of pound cake or with sour cream.

The mixture of apricot jam, maple syrup, and butter makes a flavorful sauce. If you don't have maple syrup, substitute granulated sugar. You could also add lemon juice and cinnamon, mace, nutmeg, or any other spice that you like.

> 6 large apples (2 pounds)
> ⅓ cup apricot jam
> ⅓ cup light maple syrup
> 3 tablespoons unsalted butter, cut into 6 pieces

Preheat the oven to 375 degrees.

Using a corer or a knife, core the apples. Be sure to plunge the corer or knife straight down so that it doesn't miss the core (if this happens, remove any remaining seeds).

With the point of a knife, make an incision in the skin about a third of the way down each apple and cut through the skin ⅛ to ¼ inch deep all around. As the apple cooks, the flesh expands, and the part of the apple above this cut will lift up like a lid. Without scoring, the apple could burst.

Arrange the apples in a gratin dish or other baking dish that is attractive enough to be brought to the table. Coat the apples with the apricot jam and maple syrup and dot with the butter. Bake for 30 minutes.

Baste the apples with the juice and cook for another 30 minutes. The apples should be cooked throughout — plump, brown, and soft to the touch. Let cool to lukewarm before serving.

Cheese, Apples, and Pecans
with Black Pepper
Serves 4

❧ **The combination of flavors** here — blue cheese, nuts, and apples that have been rolled in lemon juice and sprinkled with black pepper — is delicious.

To coarsely crush whole peppercorns (creating what the French call a *mignonnette*), spread them on a flat work surface and press on them with the base of a saucepan until they crack open. Pepper prepared this way is much less hot than ground pepper. If you must use a pepper mill, set it to grind the pepper as coarsely as possible.

> 2 large apples, such as russet, Red Delicious, or Rome Beauty
> 2 tablespoons fresh lemon juice
> ½ teaspoon black peppercorns, coarsely crushed
> ⅔ cup pecans
> 5 ounces blue cheese (Gorgonzola, Stilton, or Roquefort), cut into 4 pieces
> Leaves from 4 fresh basil sprigs or a handful of arugula leaves (about 5 ounces)
>
> Crusty French bread, for serving

Preheat the oven to 375 degrees.

Cut the unpeeled apples into quarters, remove the cores, and roll the quarters in the lemon juice. Sprinkle with the pepper.

Spread the pecans on a cookie sheet and bake for 8 minutes, or until lightly toasted.

To serve, arrange 2 pieces of apple, a piece of cheese, and a few pecans on each of four plates. Arrange a few basil or arugula leaves around the apples. Serve with crusty French bread.

Apple Compote with Calvados

Serves 6

✂ **Pureed apples capped with** sweetened whipped cream is a classic home dessert. Choose a soft-fleshed apple. Serve with thin slices of pound cake or cookies.

COMPOTE

7–8 large apples, such as McIntosh or Rome Beauty (about 3 pounds), peeled, quartered, and cored
½ cup sugar
½ cup water
Grated rind and juice of 1 lemon
2 tablespoons unsalted butter
2 tablespoons Calvados or applejack

GARNISH

1 cup heavy cream
1 tablespoon confectioners' sugar
2 tablespoons Calvados or applejack

FOR THE COMPOTE: Combine all the ingredients except the Calvados or applejack in a heavy casserole. Bring to a boil, reduce the heat to low, and simmer, covered, for 30 minutes.

Uncover the pot and push the apple pieces down into the juices. Cook, uncovered, over very low heat for 30 more minutes. By this time, practically all the liquid should have evaporated.

Stir the mixture with a whisk to break the apple pieces into a very coarse puree. Cover with plastic wrap and refrigerate. When the compote is cold, add the Calvados or applejack.

FOR THE GARNISH: Whip the cream. Whip in the sugar and Calvados or applejack.

Transfer the cold apple puree to a serving bowl. Put the whipped cream into a pastry bag fitted with a star tip and decorate the top of the compote with the cream, or just spoon the cream onto the compote. Serve.

Caramelized Apple Timbales

Serves 4

✂ **Arranging the cooked caramelized** apples for these timbales in plastic-lined soufflé dishes or ramekins makes them easy to unmold. The apples are not peeled; the skin gives some chewiness and texture to the dish. The timbales can be made up to a day ahead.

4 large Golden Delicious or Pippin apples (about 1½ pounds)
2 tablespoons fresh lemon juice
¼ cup sugar
⅓ cup plus 3 tablespoons water
2 teaspoons julienned lemon rind
1 tablespoon unsalted butter
¼ cup sour cream or plain yogurt

Using a paring knife, remove the apple stems with a little of the adjoining skin and flesh and toss them in a bowl with the lemon juice, for use as a decoration. Cover and refrigerate.

Cut the apples lengthwise in half and core them. Cut each half crosswise into ¼-inch-thick slices. (You should have about 6 loosely packed cups.)

Combine the sugar and the 3 tablespoons water in a large skillet and cook over medium-high heat until the mixture turns into a dark brown caramel, 3 to 4 minutes. Add the apple slices, lemon rind, the remaining ⅓ cup water, and the butter, mix well, reduce the heat, and cook at a gentle boil, covered, for about 7 minutes. The apples should be tender and most of the moisture gone.

Remove the lid and cook over high heat, stirring the apples in the liquid, for about 5 minutes, until the juices have turned into caramel again and the apple pieces are browned. Let cool to lukewarm.

Meanwhile, line four small soufflé dishes or ramekins (½- to ¾-cup capacity) with plastic wrap.

Pack the lukewarm apple mixture into the soufflé dishes, cover with plastic wrap, and refrigerate until cold. (*The timbales can be refrigerated for up to 24 hours.*)

At serving time, unmold the timbales onto serving plates and decorate with the reserved apple stems. Top each with a tablespoon of sour cream or yogurt.

Caramelized Apple Loaf with Apple Ice Cream

Serves 8

For this autumn or winter dessert, apples are caramelized, then a portion is poured into a loaf pan, where it sets. (Only part of the apples' skin is removed; it lends texture to the mixture.) The remaining portion is pureed with cream, sour cream, milk, and Calvados. Part is made into a sauce, and the rest is frozen into an apple ice cream to be served with the dish.

The loaf should be made at least 1 day ahead so it has time to set in the refrigerator.

- 5 pounds Golden Delicious apples (about 12)
- 8 tablespoons (1 stick) unsalted butter
- Grated rind and juice of 1 large lime (1 tablespoon rind plus 3 tablespoons juice)
- ½ cup sugar

SAUCE AND ICE CREAM

- Reserved caramelized apples (from above)
- 1½ cups milk
- 1 cup heavy cream
- 1 cup sour cream
- ¼ cup sugar
- 2 tablespoons Calvados or applejack

DECORATIONS

- 8 strips lime rind, removed with a vegetable peeler and cut into leaf shapes (optional)
- 1–2 teaspoons grated lime rind

With a vegetable peeler, remove 1 wide strip of peel from around the middle of each apple. Cut the apples lengthwise in half and remove the cores and seeds. Cut each apple half into thirds.

Melt half the butter in each of two saucepans, preferably nonstick. When the butter is hot, add half the apples to each pan and sprinkle each with half the lime rind, juice, and sugar. Cover and cook over medium-high heat for 20 to 30 minutes, until the apples are soft and caramelized and there is basically no liquid left in the saucepans. Remove from the heat.

Line the bottom and ends of a narrow 6-cup loaf pan or terrine mold (preferably porcelain or enamel) with a strip of parchment paper to make unmolding easy later.

Reserve one third of the apple mixture for the sauce and ice cream. Pack the remaining apples into the mold, pressing them well with a spoon so they are tight. Cover with plastic wrap, pressing the wrap lightly on the surface of the apples, and refrigerate overnight.

MEANWHILE, FOR THE SAUCE AND ICE CREAM: Put the reserved apples in a food processor, add the milk, heavy cream, sour cream, and sugar, and process until pureed. (You should have 4½ to 5 cups.) Transfer 2 cups of this mixture to a bowl for the sauce and add the Calvados or applejack to it. Refrigerate.

Spoon the remaining mixture into an ice cream freezer and freeze according to the manufacturer's instructions. Transfer the ice cream to a freezer container and freeze until hard.

Using an ice cream scoop, make 8 ice cream balls. Arrange the balls on a tray, cover with plastic wrap, and put in the freezer.

At serving time, unmold the apple loaf onto a serving platter and remove the paper. Pour some of the sauce around the loaf. Place the ice cream balls on top of the sauce and, if desired, decorate them and the cake with the lime rind cut to resemble leaves. Sprinkle the grated lime rind on the sauce (for color as well as taste) and serve with the remaining sauce on the side.

Apple Fritters
Serves 4 to 6 (makes about 12 fritters)

✂ **Apple fritters sprinkled with** confectioners' sugar and eaten piping hot are simplicity itself. The fruit can be cut into sticks or slices or fan shapes and dipped into the batter and fried, or it can be coarsely chopped or cut into julienne.

If you are making the fritters ahead, be sure to cook them until they are crisp and well browned. Then reheat and recrisp them in a toaster oven or under the broiler just before serving them heavily dusted with sugar.

1 cup all-purpose flour
1 large egg
1 cup ice-cold water
1 pound apples (any variety; about 3)
1 cup canola oil
½ cup confectioners' sugar

Vigorously mix the flour, egg, and ⅓ cup of the water in a bowl with a whisk. The mixture will be fairly thick. When it is smooth, add the remaining ⅔ cup water and mix again until the water is incorporated and the batter is thin and smooth.

One at a time, stand the unpeeled apples upright on a cutting board and cut each one vertically into ½-inch-thick slices, stopping when you reach the core; pivot the apple and cut again, and repeat until only the core remains. Stack the apple slices and cut them into ½-inch-thick sticks. (You should have 4 cups.) Stir the apple sticks into the batter.

Heat the oil in a large heavy skillet. When it is hot, pour about ⅓ cup of the batter into the pan for each fritter, making 4 or 5 at a time. Using two forks, spread the batter out so the fritters are no more than ½ inch thick. Cook for about 4 minutes on one side, until brown and crisp, then turn and cook for about 3 minutes on the other side. Drain the fritters on a wire rack. Repeat with the rest of the batter.

Sprinkle the fritters liberally with the sugar and serve.

VEGETABLE FRITTERS

Instead of adding apples to the fritter batter, stir in some thinly sliced vegetables — anything from carrots, onions, and zucchini to whole parsley leaves. Drop large spoonfuls of the mixture into the hot oil and cook for 3 to 4 minutes on each side. Serve 1 large pancake per person as a vegetable side dish with a roast or stew.

Spiced Apple Charlotte
Serves 6 to 8

For this charlotte, apple slices are cooked on top of the stove in a flavorful mixture of sugar, honey, and spices. Then, when most of the moisture has evaporated and the apple slices are brown, they are baked between layers of bread in a cake pan. The charlotte is unmolded and sauced with peach jam, sliced, and served, warm or at room temperature, with sour cream or yogurt, if desired.

I like to use russet apples, which are available in my market in the fall. They are firm, juicy, and tasty, with a hint of quince flavor. If they are unavailable, use another variety that holds its shape such as Pippin, Golden Delicious, or Granny Smith.

2 tablespoons unsalted butter
1½ tablespoons corn or safflower oil
2 pounds russet apples (see the headnote; about 5), peeled, cored, and cut into ¼-inch-thick slices

¼ cup sugar
¼ cup honey
1 teaspoon ground cinnamon
¼ teaspoon ground allspice
⅛ teaspoon ground cloves
11 thin slices fine-textured white bread (6½ ounces)
3 tablespoons strained peach jam
1½ teaspoons Calvados or applejack (optional)
Sour cream or plain yogurt, for serving (optional)

Preheat the oven to 375 degrees.

Heat the butter and 1 tablespoon of the oil in a large saucepan until hot. Add the apples and sauté for 1 minute. Add the sugar, honey, cinnamon, allspice, and cloves, mix gently, cover, and cook over medium heat for 10 minutes. Most of the moisture from the apples should be gone at this point. Remove the lid and cook the apples, uncovered, for 5 to 6 minutes, until nicely browned. Remove from the heat.

Using the remaining ½ tablespoon oil, oil an 8-inch round cake pan.

Cut 7 slices of the bread into triangles: first cut the slices in half diagonally, then trim the crusts to create smaller triangles; reserve the trimmings. Lay the triangles side by side to cover the bottom of the prepared pan. Trim the remaining 4 slices bread, cut each of them in half to make rectangles, and arrange them around the sides of the pan.

Spoon the apple mixture on top of the bread and spread it evenly into the corners of the pan. Smooth the surface and arrange the bread trimmings on top of the apples so most of them are covered.

Bake the charlotte for 20 to 25 minutes. Let the charlotte cool on a rack for 10 minutes, then invert it onto a plate and remove the mold.

Meanwhile, combine the peach jam with the

Calvados or applejack, if using, in a small bowl.

No more than 30 minutes before serving, coat the surface of the charlotte with the peach jam mixture (if it is applied earlier, the coating will be absorbed by the dessert).

Slice the charlotte and serve with dollops of sour cream or yogurt, if desired.

Poached Apricots with Sour Cream and Raspberry Sauce
Serves 8

🍴 **Large, firm, ripe apricots,** usually available in the market only in full summer, are best for this recipe. Ripe apricots will cook very fast — in 1 to 2 minutes — and should be allowed to cool in the cooking syrup. The skin will not slip off after cooking, so there is no need to peel them. They can be poached several days ahead and kept, refrigerated, in their syrup in a sealed container.

The apricots can be served with pound cake, brioche, or your favorite cookie — or with only the reduced syrup, without the raspberry sauce.

APRICOTS

    8   large firm but ripe apricots (about
          1½ pounds)
        Rind of 1 lemon, removed in strips
          with a vegetable peeler
   ½   cup sugar
    2   cups water

SAUCE

    1   12-ounce package frozen unsweetened
          raspberries, defrosted
   ¾   cup seedless raspberry preserves

    1   cup sour cream
    2   tablespoons water
    1   tablespoon sugar
        Rind of 1 lime, removed with a vegetable
          peeler and cut into ovals to resemble
          leaves (optional)

Arrange the apricots in a stainless steel saucepan that holds them snugly in one layer. Add the lemon rind, sugar, and water, cover, and bring to a boil. Reduce the heat and cook gently for 2 to 5 minutes, or until the fruit feels tender when pierced with the point of a knife. Set the apricots aside in the cooking liquid to cool to lukewarm.

Transfer the lukewarm apricots to a bowl and boil the liquid to reduce it to ½ cup. Pour the reduced liquid over the fruit. (*At this point, the apricots can be stored, covered, in the refrigerator, for several days.*)

FOR THE RASPBERRY SAUCE: Push the defrosted berries and the preserves through a food mill; if you feel there are still too many seeds, strain through a sieve.

At serving time, mix the sour cream with the water and sugar.

Spoon enough raspberry sauce onto a serving platter to cover the bottom. Spoon the sour cream mixture into a pastry bag fitted with a tip with the smallest-possible opening (no bigger than a pencil lead), or spoon into a paper cornet (see page 565) and cut the tip off it, and pipe a swirled design around the edges of the platter to create a decorative border; alternatively, use a spoon to make a ribbon design of cream in the sauce around the fruit. Remove the apricots from their liquid and arrange them in the center of the platter. Drizzle a little raspberry sauce over the apricots and decorate, if you like, with the lime "leaves." Serve with the remaining raspberry sauce on the side.

Baked Apricots with Walnuts
Serves 6

❧ **Be sure to choose** very ripe, full-flavored fruit, preferably from an organic farm, for this dish. I make the dessert with heavy cream, but you can use half-and-half.

- 1 pound ripe apricots (6–7), halved and pitted
- 3 tablespoons orange marmalade
- ¼ cup heavy cream
- 2 tablespoons walnut pieces
- 1 tablespoon sugar

Preheat the oven to 350 degrees.

Arrange the apricot halves cut side down in a gratin dish. Spoon the marmalade over the fruit and pour the cream around it. Sprinkle the walnut pieces and sugar on top.

Bake for 30 to 35 minutes, until the apricots are tender. Serve warm or at room temperature.

Apricot Compote
Serves 4

❧ **Fresh apricots, processed with** orange juice into a puree, are mixed with dried apricot slices and cooked with a little honey and some pine nuts. Serve at room temperature, topped with sour cream or yogurt.

- 12 ounces ripe apricots (about 5), halved and pitted
- 1 cup orange juice
- 5 ounces dried apricots, cut into ½-inch-wide slices (1¼ cups)
- ¼ cup pine nuts
- 2 tablespoons honey
- ½ cup sour cream or plain yogurt

Combine the fresh apricots with the orange juice in a food processor and process until pureed. Transfer to a stainless steel saucepan, add the dried apricots, nuts, and honey, and bring to a boil over high heat. Reduce the heat to low, cover, and cook for 10 minutes, scraping the bottom of the pan with a wooden spoon a few times to ensure that the mixture is not sticking. Remove from the heat and let cool to room temperature.

To serve, divide the compote among four dessert bowls and top each serving with a spoonful of sour cream or yogurt.

Broiled Bananas
with Lemon and Vermouth
Serves 4

❧ **The best choice for** this dish are bananas with black-speckled skin, indicating that the fruit is very ripe. Bananas are often moved to the quick-sale rack when they reach this stage, so look for them there at greatly reduced prices.

- 4 very ripe bananas
- ¼ cup fresh lemon juice
- ¼ cup packed brown sugar
- 2 tablespoons golden raisins
- ¼ cup sweet red vermouth

Preheat the broiler. Peel the bananas and arrange them in one layer in a gratin dish. Pour the lemon juice over the bananas and roll them in the juice to prevent them from discoloring. Sprinkle the brown sugar evenly over the bananas.

Place the bananas about 4 inches from the heat and broil until they are brown on top, about 4 minutes. Turn the bananas over and broil for 3 to 4 minutes, until brown on top. They should be soft when pierced with a fork. Add the raisins and let cool until lukewarm.

Sprinkle the bananas with the vermouth, shake the dish to mix it in, and serve.

Flambéed Bananas
Serves 6

❧ **Though flambéing is a** way of making the evaporation of alcohol visible, it is more than a theatrical device. It serves a purpose: it caramelizes the sugar in desserts like this one and it browns and crisps certain foods, like crepes.

This banana dish comes together quickly. Lemon, sugar, and butter make a syrup in which the bananas are baked. When everything is hot, the rum is added and ignited and the platter brought to the table. Rum goes especially well with bananas, but bourbon is a good choice too.

    4 tablespoons (½ stick) unsalted butter, softened
    ¾ cup packed dark brown sugar
    6 very ripe bananas
    1 lemon
    ⅓ cup dark rum

Preheat the oven to 450 degrees.

Butter the bottom of a large stainless steel platter or other ovenproof platter with half the butter and sprinkle with one third of the brown sugar. Peel the bananas, split them lengthwise in half, and arrange them flat side down on the buttered platter.

Grate the lemon rind with a Microplane or box grater. Sprinkle the grated rind over the bananas and squeeze the juice from the lemon over them. Dot bananas with butter, sprinkle with sugar, and bake for 10 minutes.

See to it that everyone is seated at the table before you proceed. Remove the hot platter from the oven. Pour the rum on top (it needn't be heated) and carefully ignite with a long match. Using pot holders, bring the platter of flaming bananas into the dining room. Incline the platter slightly so that the juice runs to one side and spoon the flaming juice back on top of the bananas. Keep basting the bananas with the flaming liquid until the flame dies, then serve.

Banana Fritters
Serves 4 (makes about 12 fritters)

❧ **The nearer to serving** time you cook these fritters, the better; they emerge from the oil crunchy, thanks to the addition of ice-cold water, which makes the batter similar to a tempura. If you must cook the fritters ahead, drain them on a rack, as here, when you remove them from the hot oil, then serve them at room temperature or place them under a hot broiler or in a toaster oven for a few minutes to rewarm and recrisp them. Dust them with sugar just before serving.

    ¾ cup all-purpose flour
    1 large egg, lightly beaten
    1 cup ice-cold water
       About 1 cup canola oil
    2 ripe bananas
       About ⅓ cup granulated or confectioners' sugar

Put the flour, egg, and about half the water in a bowl and mix with a whisk for a few seconds, until the mixture is smooth. Whisk in the remainder of the water. (*If not completing the recipe immedi-*

ately, refrigerate the batter until you are ready to cook the fritters; whisk gently before proceeding.)

Heat ¼ cup of the oil to about 400 degrees in a large nonstick skillet. Meanwhile, peel the bananas and, holding them over the bowl containing the batter, cut them into ¼-inch-thick slices, letting the slices fall into the batter.

Make 3 or 4 fritters at a time, using about ¼ cup of the batter with a few banana slices for each. Pour it into the hot oil and spread the batter lightly as it hits the pan to create fritters about 3 inches in diameter. Cook for 2 to 3 minutes, turn, and cook for 2 to 3 minutes on the other side, until nicely browned. Remove the fritters with a slotted spoon and place them on a wire rack to drain. Continue to make fritters, adding more oil as needed, until all the batter has been used.

Sprinkle the drained fritters generously with the sugar and serve.

Lemon Bananas in Crisp Shells
Serves 4

✂ **For this quick, simple dessert,** packaged wonton wrappers are blanched in boiling water, lightly oiled, and baked until brown and crisp. Then banana slices flavored with lemon juice and rind, bourbon, and peach preserves are sandwiched between them.

8	wonton wrappers (about 3 inches square)
2	teaspoons canola oil
1½	tablespoons confectioners' sugar, plus 1 teaspoon for decoration
2	teaspoons grated lemon rind
2	tablespoons fresh lemon juice
¼	cup peach preserves
2	tablespoons bourbon
2	large ripe bananas

Preheat the oven to 375 degrees.

Bring 8 cups water to a boil in a saucepan. Drop in the wonton wrappers one at a time and bring the water back to a boil. Boil the wrappers for 1½ minutes, then drain them carefully in a colander and return them to the pan. Fill the pan with cold water to stop the wrappers from cooking further and cool them.

Brush a large cookie sheet with the oil. Using both hands, carefully lift the wrappers from the cold water, shaking off as much of the water as you can, and arrange them side by side on the oiled sheet. Spoon the 1½ tablespoons confectioners' sugar into a sieve and sprinkle it on top of the wet wonton wrappers.

Bake the wrappers for 16 to 18 minutes, until they are nicely browned, crisp, and glazed on the surface. Using a metal spatula, remove the hot wrappers from the cookie sheet and place them on a rack to cool completely.

Mix the lemon rind, lemon juice, peach preserves, and bourbon in a bowl large enough to hold the sliced bananas. Peel the bananas. Cut them crosswise in half, then cut into thin (⅓-inch-thick) lengthwise slices. Add them to the bowl and mix gently to coat them with the sauce.

At serving time, arrange a wonton crisp on each of four dessert plates. Divide the banana mixture among the plates, spooning it on top of the crisps. Place the remaining wonton crisps on

top of the bananas, sprinkle the remaining tea-spoon of confectioners' sugar on top, and serve.

Berries Rafraîchis
Serves 4

❧ *Rafraîchis* **means "refreshing,"** which is what this beautiful summer berry dish is. The berries are cooked with red wine, jam, and sugar and fla-vored with mint. This dessert is even better when made a few hours ahead. I make double the quan-tity of berries needed to have enough for the Berry Jam (recipe follows).

1	cup fruity red wine (such as Beaujolais)
¼	cup sugar
1	cup jam or preserves (such as cherry, strawberry, raspberry, or apricot, or a mixture of these)
2	fresh mint sprigs, tied together with kitchen twine
1	pound strawberries, washed, hulled, and halved (4 cups)
12	ounces (2 cups) blueberries
6	ounces (1 cup) raspberries

GARNISHES (Optional)

Slices of pound cake
Sour cream
Fresh mint sprigs

Combine the wine, sugar, jam, and mint in a large stainless steel saucepan and bring to a boil. Mix well. Add the strawberries, blueberries, and raspberries and bring back to a boil over high heat, stirring and shaking the pan occasionally to mix the liquid with the fruit. When the whole mixture is boiling (this will take about 5 minutes), cover the pan, remove it from the heat, and let steep for 5 minutes.

Transfer the berry mixture to a bowl and let cool to room temperature. (You should have about 5 cups.)

To serve, spoon about ⅔ cup of the berry mix-ture onto each of four dessert plates. Serve, if de-sired, with cake, garnished with sour cream and mint.

The remaining berries (about 2½ cups) can be refrigerated for serving the following day, cool or at room temperature, or used to make Berry Jam.

Berry Jam Makes 1¾ cups
This jam is as good spooned over ice cream as it is spread on toast or pancakes. It will keep for sev-eral weeks in the refrigerator.

2½ cups leftover berry mixture from Berries Rafraîchis

Preheat the oven to 200 degrees.

Pour the berry mixture into a glass baking dish or stainless steel pan large enough that the mixture is about 1 inch deep in the pan. Bake for about 5 hours to evaporate the moisture and con-centrate the flavor of the fruit. The juices will have

reduced by three fourths and will be thick and syrupy.

Pour the jam into a jar and let cool, then cover and refrigerate. Use within 1 month.

Blackberries in Creamy Honey Sauce
Serves 4

✳ **Ripe blackberries are tossed** in a little sugar and mounded on plates coated with a sauce composed of honey, orange juice, thick Greek yogurt, and mint. Other berries — strawberries, raspberries, boysenberries — can be substituted. For maximum sweetness, choose very ripe berries.

  1 pint (2 cups) blackberries
  1 tablespoon sugar
  3 tablespoons honey
  ¼ cup orange juice
  1 cup plain yogurt, preferably Greek
  1 tablespoon shredded fresh mint leaves

Gently toss the blackberries with the sugar in a small bowl. Cover and refrigerate for at least 30 minutes.

Mix the honey and orange juice in another small bowl. When the mixture is smooth, add the yogurt and mint and mix just until smooth. Cover and refrigerate until serving time.

To serve, divide the yogurt sauce among four dessert plates. Mound the berries in the center, dividing them equally among the plates, and serve.

Blueberries with Brown Sugar
Serves 4

✳ **This is a simple,** terrific combination. Look over the blueberries carefully and remove and discard any damaged ones. If you wash them, be sure to dry them with paper towels so the water doesn't dilute the yogurt.

  1 pint blueberries
  ½ cup plain yogurt, preferably Greek
  ¼ cup packed dark brown sugar
     Fresh mint leaves, for garnish

Divide the blueberries among four plates. Make a well in the center of the berries on each plate and spoon in the yogurt. Sprinkle the berries and yogurt with the brown sugar, decorate with a few mint leaves, and serve.

VARIATION
Substitute 1 pint strawberries, washed and hulled, for the blueberries, and 2 cups sour cream for the yogurt, and use ¼ cup packed light brown sugar.

Blueberry Crumble
Serves 4

✳ **I especially like this** crumble made with blueberries, but blackberries, boysenberries, or raspberries are good too. The berries are flavored with fruit preserves, moistened with a little apple juice, and topped before baking with cake or croissant crumbs. The crumble can be served on its own or with sour cream or whipped cream.

2   cups (about 10 ounces) fresh
       or frozen blueberries
¼   cup apricot preserves
2   tablespoons apple juice
1½   cups crumbled pound cake,
       sponge cake, or leftover
       croissants
       Sour cream or whipped cream,
       for serving (optional)

Preheat the oven to 375 degrees.

Mix the blueberries, preserves, and apple juice together in a bowl. Transfer the mixture to a 3-cup gratin dish. Sprinkle the crumbs on top, covering the blueberries entirely.

Bake for 30 minutes. Let cool to lukewarm.

To serve, spoon the crumble into bowls. If desired, top each serving with sour cream or whipped cream.

Cream of Raspberries and Yogurt
Serves 4

✂ **In this dessert, which** looks much richer than it is, berries are blended with yogurt to create a smooth but relatively low-calorie cream.

2   pints (4 cups) raspberries
¾   cup plain yogurt, preferably Greek
¼   cup sugar
4   fresh mint sprigs

Put about one third of the berries, including any that are less than perfect (damaged, wilted, or soft) in a food processor, add the yogurt and sugar, and process until very smooth. There will be small seeds in the mixture; push the puree through a fine sieve or a food mill fitted with a fine screen into a bowl.

Stir in the remaining berries gently. Refrigerate until chilled, or for up to 6 hours.

Divide the cream among four dessert dishes, garnish with the mint sprigs, and serve.

VARIATION

Do not combine the berries and yogurt sauce. Instead, at serving time, divide the sauce among four dessert plates and mound the berries in the center. Top each serving with a mint sprig and serve.

Raspberry Trifle with Nectarine Sauce
Serves 4

✂ **Fresh raspberries are the** centerpiece of these individual trifles, which also include pound cake moistened and flavored with a little coffee extract. Drained yogurt used in place of the traditional fresh cream makes the dessert lighter.

1   pint yogurt, preferably Greek
4   ounces pound cake
¼   cup coffee "extract" (the first ¼ cup
       from a pot of drip coffee)
8   ounces (about 1⅓ cups) raspberries

SAUCE

⅓   cup peach preserves
3   tablespoons nectarine juice
1   nectarine, peeled, pitted and cut
       into ¼-inch pieces (1 cup)
1   tablespoon cognac

4   small fresh mint sprigs

Set a strainer lined with paper towels over a bowl. Add the yogurt, cover with plastic wrap, and drain in the refrigerator for at least 12 hours, or as long as 24. There will be about 1 cup of liquid whey in the bowl, which can be drunk or discarded, and about 1 cup (8 ounces) yogurt cheese in the strainer.

Cut the pound cake into 8 slices, about ½ inch thick. With a cookie cutter, cut the slices into rounds 2½ to 2¾ inches in diameter. Reserve the cake trimmings. Place a cake round in the bottom of each of four ½-cup soufflé dishes, about 2¾ inches in diameter.

Using a brush or teaspoon, moisten each round of cake with about 1 teaspoon of the coffee. Place a good tablespoon of yogurt cheese on top of each round and press about 8 raspberries into the cheese. Coarsely crumble some of the reserved cake trimmings on top of the cheese and moisten the trimmings with about 1 teaspoon of the remaining coffee. Add another good tablespoon of cheese and press another 8 raspberries into the cheese. Top each dessert with another cake round, moisten the rounds with the remaining coffee, and press them into place. Cover tightly with plastic wrap and refrigerate until chilled. (*The trifles can be prepared to this point up to 8 hours ahead.*)

FOR THE SAUCE: Combine the preserves, nectarine juice, nectarine pieces, and cognac in a bowl. Mix well, cover, and refrigerate until chilled.

At serving time, run a knife around the edges of the soufflé dishes and unmold the trifles onto dessert plates. Coat with the nectarine sauce and decorate each serving with a sprig of mint.

Red Wine and Cassis Strawberries
Serves 4

✎ **In wine-growing regions of** France, berries — particularly strawberries — are typically combined with the wine from that area, and sometimes a liqueur. Here I mix strawberries with a fruity red wine and black currant or blackberry liqueur and serve them in the classic way, spooned into wine goblets. Top the desserts with a little whipped cream and serve them with cookies.

3 cups ripe strawberries, washed, hulled, and quartered
3 tablespoons sugar
3 tablespoons crème de cassis or crème de mûres (blackberry liqueur)
¾ cup fruity dry red wine (such as Merlot)
1 tablespoon shredded fresh mint leaves
½ cup heavy cream, whipped to soft peaks

Mix the berries, sugar, liqueur, wine, and mint in a bowl. Serve, or refrigerate for up to 8 hours before serving.

To serve, spoon the berries and liquid into wine goblets and top each with a dollop of whipped cream.

Glazed Strawberries
Serves 4

✎ **These berries are dipped** in warm currant jelly, which hardens around them as it cools. If they will stand for a long time, you might want to add a little unflavored gelatin to the jelly to make it even more binding and resistant to melting.

Choose large, ripe, full-flavored berries with stems.

12 large strawberries with stems
1 10-ounce jar currant jelly
A few fresh basil or other herb sprigs or edible flowers, for garnish (optional)

Chill a plate in the refrigerator. Wash the berries and dry them thoroughly with paper towels. Chill in the refrigerator.

Warm the currant jelly in a saucepan over low heat until it has melted and is smooth. (Strain to make it smooth if necessary.)

Holding the berries by their stems, dip them one at a time into the currant jelly, turning until thoroughly coated, then lift out and remove any excess jelly by scraping the berries gently against the rim of the pan. Place the glazed berries on the very cold plate. Refrigerate until serving time.

At serving time, arrange 3 berries on each plate and decorate with the herbs or flowers, if desired.

Strawberries in the Sun
Serves 6 to 8

⁊ **Whole strawberries are almost** candied in a sugar syrup, which contains half as much sugar as for a conventional berry jam. The syrup is neither stirred nor cooked for very long, so the berries remain whole. Then the mixture is placed in a roasting pan, covered with a screen to keep out insects, and placed in the sun. The heat gradually evaporates the liquid and the berries swell in the syrup. It takes about 2 to 3 consecutive sunny days to "cook" the berries. (Bring them inside at night.)

You can also cook the berries in a low oven, which will take up to 20 hours, depending on how much liquid you want around the berries and how thick you want the syrup to be; it will thicken substantially as it cools. If you plan to serve the berries as a sauce or topping, you will want syrup of a slightly thinner consistency than if you want to eat the berries as a jam on bread.

3 cups sugar (more if the berries are not ripe)
1½ cups water
3 pounds (about 1½ quarts) small ripe strawberries, washed and hulled
Toast or cookies, for serving (optional)

Combine the sugar and water in a large stainless steel saucepan, bring to a boil, and boil for 4 to 5 minutes. Add the berries, cover, and cook until the syrup comes back to a strong boil. Shake the pan gently, rather than stirring, and set the pan aside, covered, for about 10 minutes. At this point, the berries will have rendered their liquid and be very limp.

Transfer the mixture to a roasting pan, preferably stainless steel. (The berry mixture should be about 1 inch thick in the pan.) Cover the pan with a window screen, place it in direct sun, and let stand for 2 to 3 days, until the syrup is reduced to the thickness of maple syrup. Or, if sunlight is not available, bake the berries in a 175- to 180-degree oven for 15 to 20 hours, until the syrup is of the thickness of honey.

Pour the mixture into jars and refrigerate until ready to use. (They will keep for a couple of weeks.)

To serve, spoon 3 to 4 tablespoons of the preserves into each small dessert dish. Serve as is or with toast or cookies.

Strawberries with Raspberry Sauce
Serves 6

⁊ **This dessert is as** simple as it is superb. Serve it in a plain crystal bowl or in individual glasses.

Thin slices of génoise or pound cake go well with it.

1 pint raspberries
1 quart strawberries, washed and hulled
½–¾ cup sugar, depending on the sweetness of the fruit
2 tablespoons raspberry brandy

Put the raspberries in a blender. If you have any imperfect strawberries, trim them and add them to the blender. Add the sugar and brandy and blend for 30 seconds. Strain through a sieve to remove the seeds.

Put the (remaining) strawberries in a bowl, pour the raspberry sauce over them, and cover with plastic wrap. Refrigerate and allow the strawberries to macerate in the sauce for about 2 hours; toss the berries from time to time.

Serve cold in cocktail glasses.

Strawberry and Orange Coupe
Serves 6

⟩ **With different fruits substituted** for the strawberries, this fruit dessert can be served year-round. The berry mixture can be prepared a few hours ahead, but no longer, or the fruit will get soft and mushy.

1 quart strawberries, washed and hulled
3–4 medium oranges
1 cup strawberry jam
2 tablespoons dark rum
Fresh mint sprigs, for garnish

Cut larger berries into 3 or 4 pieces and smaller ones in half. Set aside in a serving bowl.

With a vegetable peeler, cut 3 or 4 strips of rind from 1 of the oranges. Stack the strips to-gether and slice them into fine julienne strips. (You should have 2 to 3 tablespoons.) Add to the strawberries. Squeeze the juice from the oranges and strain it. (You should have 1 cup.)

With a whisk, mix the orange juice, strawberry jam, and rum in a small bowl. Add this mixture to the strawberries and stir. Refrigerate until serving time, or for up to 3 hours.

Serve cool (but not ice-cold) in cocktail or wineglasses, garnishing each with a sprig of mint.

Strawberry Buttermilk Shortcakes
Serves 4

⟩ **Homemade strawberry shortcake** is a hit with everyone, and this very easy version is no exception. Be sure to mix the ingredients for the short-cakes lightly and quickly, combining them just enough so they hold together, so the biscuits will be light and flaky.

1 pint strawberries, washed and hulled
½ cup strawberry jam

SHORTCAKES
½ cup all-purpose flour
½ cup cake flour
1 teaspoon baking powder
½ teaspoon baking soda
1½ tablespoons sugar
½ teaspoon salt
3 tablespoons unsalted butter, softened
⅓ cup buttermilk

½ cup sour cream
4 fresh mint sprigs

Cut off about ¼ inch from the stem end of each strawberry. (This part of the berry tends to be less sweet, especially if the berries are not completely ripe.) Reserve the trimmings for the sauce. (You should have about 1½ cups.) Cut the berries into wedges and place them in a bowl.

Combine the trimmings and jam in a food processor and process until smooth. Pour the sauce over the berries, toss well, and refrigerate for at least 1 hour.

Preheat the oven to 450 degrees.

FOR THE SHORTCAKES: Combine the flours, baking powder, soda, sugar, and salt in a bowl. Add the butter, mixing gently with a spoon for 30 seconds at most. (The mixture should not be completely smooth.) Add the buttermilk and mix just enough to combine the ingredients into a soft dough.

Invert the dough onto a nonstick or parchment-lined cookie sheet and cover it with a piece of plastic wrap. Press on the dough until you have extended it to a 5-inch square about ⅜ inch thick. Cut it into four 2½-inch squares (no need to separate them). Bake for 10 to 12 minutes, or until golden brown. Remove to a rack to cool.

At serving time, separate the shortcakes and cut them horizontally in half. Arrange the bottoms in four dessert dishes and spoon the berry mixture on top. Cover with the shortcake tops and garnish each with a dollop of sour cream and a sprig of mint. Serve.

Cherry Compote
Serves 4

✖ When the large Bing cherries of summer come into the market, I make this dessert. I pit the cherries and then, to concentrate their flavor, I cook them along with the cracked pits in a sturdy white wine flavored with cherry jam. The pits give the fruit a slightly bitter, almond-like taste that is particularly appealing.

1¼ pounds large Bing cherries, stems removed
¾ cup mellow white wine (such as Sémillon or Chenin Blanc)
3 tablespoons light corn syrup
⅓ cup cherry jam
1 teaspoon cornstarch, dissolved in 1 tablespoon water
1 tablespoon kirsch (optional)
¼ cup sour cream

Pit the cherries; reserve the pits. Place the cherries, wine, corn syrup, and jam in a stainless steel saucepan.

Arrange the reserved cherry pits on a piece of plastic wrap on a cutting board and cover them with another piece of plastic wrap. Using a meat pounder or the base of a small heavy saucepan, pound the pits to crack them. Place the cracked pits on a piece of cheesecloth and tie them into a compact package with kitchen twine. Add the package to the cherry mixture.

Bring the mixture to a boil, cover, reduce the heat to low, and boil gently for 5 minutes. Discard the pits. Add the dissolved cornstarch and mix well. Let cool, then stir in the kirsch, if desired.

Serve the compote in goblets with 1 tablespoon of sour cream on top of each serving.

Cherry Summer Pudding with Port
Serves 4

✖ For this popular English summer dessert, sour cherries are cooked in wine and sugar, then layered with cake crumbs in a bowl lined with pound cake. After a few hours, the juices from the cherries seep into the cake and it takes on the shape of the bowl. Unmolded at serving time, it is presented here with a sauce of mango, honey, and port.

1½ pounds sour cherries, pitted
½ cup fruity dry red wine (such as
      Beaujolais)
¼ cup sugar
1 10¾-ounce pound cake

SAUCE

1 large ripe mango (about 1 pound)
2 tablespoons honey
¼ cup tawny port
⅓ cup water

½ cup champagne grapes, or ½ cup seedless
      grapes cut into ¼-inch dice

Put the cherries in a stainless steel saucepan with the wine and sugar, bring to a boil over medium heat, and cook for 5 minutes to reduce the juices. (You should have 2¼ cups.) Let cool.

Trim off the brown surface of the pound cake, reserving the trimmings. Cut the trimmed cake lengthwise into 5 slices, about ½ inch thick.

Place a strip of parchment paper in a 4- to 6-cup bowl so that the paper covers the bottom and comes up two opposite sides of the bowl. (This will help in the unmolding.) Arrange 3 slices of the cake in the bowl so the cake covers the bottom and sides.

Spoon half the cherry mixture on top of the cake and crumble half the reserved cake trimmings over the cherries. Spoon the remaining cherry mixture on top and crumble the remaining cake trimmings over it. Finish with the remaining 2 slices of cake, arranging them so that all the cherries are covered.

Cover the bowl with plastic wrap, pressing it against the cake. Place a weight of about 1 pound on top of the dessert so it will compact the layers of cake and cherries. Refrigerate. (*The recipe can be prepared to this point up to 2 days ahead.*)

FOR THE SAUCE: Peel the mango and cut the flesh from the pit. Put the flesh in a food processor or blender, add the honey, port, and water, and process until smooth. Refrigerate until ready to serve. (*The sauce can be made up to 1 day ahead.*)

When ready to serve, unmold the cake onto a serving plate, pour the mango sauce around it, and sprinkle with the grapes. Spoon onto dessert dishes at the table.

Cranberry Kissel
Serves 4

↪ **A traditional Russian kissel** is a puree of acidic berries. Cranberries are classic, but any tart berries can be used. Sometimes the berries are combined with sugar and thickened with a little cornstarch. I serve my kissel with sour cream and a garnish of pomegranate seeds and mint sprigs.

1 12-ounce package cranberries
¾ cup fresh cranberry juice
¼ cup packed light brown sugar
1 teaspoon cornstarch
¼ cup sour cream
2 tablespoons pomegranate seeds
    A few fresh mint sprigs

Put the cranberries, cranberry juice, brown sugar, and cornstarch in a stainless steel saucepan and bring to a boil over high heat, stirring occasionally. Cover, reduce the heat, and cook gently for approximately 10 minutes. The berries will pop and the mixture will be thick and bright red. (You should have about 2 cups.) Set aside to cool. (*The kissel can be made up to 1 day ahead and refrigerated; serve cool.*)

Divide the kissel among four goblets. Garnish with sour cream, a sprinkling of pomegranate seeds, and mint and serve.

Pecan-and-Armagnac-Stuffed Dates

Serves 4

꙳ **These dates are an** appealing dessert or a welcome snack at any hour of the day. I use the very large Medjool dates when they are available, but regular dates are fine. The stuffing mixture is mostly cookies and any type you have on hand will work.

3 ounces cookies (I use gingersnaps, but chocolate chips, tuiles, or even graham crackers can be substituted), coarsely crushed (1¼ cups)
1½ tablespoons fresh lemon juice
1½ tablespoons Armagnac or Scotch (for a nonalcoholic version, substitute orange juice)
⅓ cup coarsely chopped pecans
1 tablespoon minced fresh mint, plus 12 or 20 small mint leaves for garnish
20 medium pitted dates or 12 very large pitted Medjool dates

Put the crushed cookies in a small bowl and lightly mix in the lemon juice and Armagnac or Scotch (or orange juice). Add the pecans and minced mint and mix until well combined.

Using a sharp knife, split the dates, stopping before cutting them entirely in half, and open each one like a book. Spoon 1 to 2 teaspoons of the cookie mixture onto each date, then gently fold the date to partially close it around the stuffing.

Decorate the dates by inserting the stem of a small mint leaf in the center of the stuffed edge. Arrange the dates on a platter and refrigerate until serving time. Serve cool.

Figs Vilamoura

Serves 4 to 6
(makes about 24 pieces)

꙳ **In Vilamoura, a town** in southern Portugal, dried figs are prepared this way in the market. The figs are partially split and spread out and pairs of them are "sandwiched" together with almonds inserted in the corners. They are then dried in the oven to concentrate their taste and brown the almonds. To make the shaping easier, get the largest dried figs that you can find.

Serve with a glass of sweet port, some Gorgonzola cheese, and a chunk of crusty bread.

1 pound dried Black Mission figs (about 24)
   About 48 unblanched whole almonds

Preheat the oven to 350 degrees.

Split the figs in half, starting at the base, but leave them attached at the stem end. Split each half in half again in the same way, turn the figs skin side up, and gently press them open. (They should look like flowers or four-leaf clovers, with each "petal" or "leaf" still attached at the stem.)

When all the figs have been split and pressed, make a sandwich with 2 figs, pressing them together, flesh against flesh. Then push 4 almonds, rounded ends first, about one third of the way into the figs where the "petals" connect near the stem, and press to ensure that the almonds are held securely. Repeat with the remaining figs and almonds.

Arrange the fig "flowers" on a cookie sheet and bake for 20 minutes to brown the almonds and dry the figs, concentrating their flavor. Let cool.

Store in a tightly covered container until ready to serve. The figs will keep for up to 2 weeks.

Calimyrna Figs in Spicy Port Sauce

Serves 6

❧ **Port wine complements the** intense sweet flavor of dried figs. The wine's sweetness is curbed by bitter Campari, whose flavor is enhanced by cayenne pepper. The poaching liquid is thickened and the figs are served with this sauce and some yogurt.

Calimyrna is the name coined for a variety of fig grown in California that is native to Smyrna, Turkey. When dried, they are pale yellow or beige and have a thicker wall than the jet-black Mission figs.

  1 pound dried Calimyrna figs (about 20)
1½ cups water
  1 cup port
  ¼ cup Campari
    Pinch of cayenne pepper
  1 teaspoon cornstarch, dissolved in
      1 tablespoon water
  1 cup plain yogurt, preferably Greek

Stand the figs in a large stainless steel saucepan and add the water. Cover and bring to a boil over high heat, then reduce the heat and boil gently for 5 minutes. Add the port, Campari, and cayenne, bring back to a boil, cover, and boil for another 5 minutes.

Stir in the dissolved cornstarch, mix well, and return to a boil. Remove from the heat and cool the figs in the cooking liquid.

To serve, spread the yogurt onto six serving plates. Arrange the figs on top of the yogurt, 3 or 4 to each plate, spoon some cooking liquid over them, and serve.

Grapefruit in Nectar

Serves 4

❧ **Wedges of grapefruit flesh** are removed from their surrounding membranes and served in a sauce of caramel, grapefruit juice, and — for added flavor — grenadine and Cointreau. For best results, use large, flavorful pink grapefruit.

  2 large pink grapefruit
  ¼ cup sugar
  2 tablespoons water
  1 tablespoon grenadine
  1 tablespoon Cointreau (or other
      liqueur to your liking)

Using a vegetable peeler, remove 6 strips of grapefruit rind from the areas where the skin color is brightest. Stack the strips together and cut them lengthwise into thin julienne strips. (You should have about ¼ cup.)

Place the julienned rind in a small high-sided saucepan, cover with 1½ cups water, and bring to a boil. Boil for 15 to 20 seconds, then drain in a sieve and rinse the rind under cold running water. Drain well and set aside in a small bowl.

Using a sharp knife, peel the grapefruit, removing all the remaining skin and cottony pith so the flesh of the fruit is totally exposed. Then cut between the membranes on either side of each grapefruit segment to remove it. (You should have 10 to 12 segments per grapefruit.) Put the segments in a bowl and sprinkle the blanched rind on top. Squeeze the juice from the membranes through a sieve set over a bowl, pressing on them to remove as much juice as possible. (You should have ⅓ to ½ cup.)

Combine the sugar and water in a small saucepan, bring to a full boil, and boil over high heat for about 3 minutes, until the mixture becomes a dark blond caramel. Remove the pan from the heat and carefully add 1 to 2 tablespoons of the reserved grapefruit juice, taking care to avoid splatters from the hot caramel. Shake the pan to mix in the juice. Add the rest of the juice and mix well with a whisk until it is incorporated.

Pour the caramel sauce over the grapefruit segments in the bowl and mix well. Add the grenadine and Cointreau and mix again. Cover and refrigerate until serving time. (*The recipe can be prepared up to 8 hours ahead.*)

To serve, lift the grapefruit segments from the bowl with a slotted spoon and divide them among four dessert plates. Pour the sauce over and around them and serve.

Broiled Grapefruit Suprêmes
Serves 4

❧ **You can prepare this** easy dessert ahead up to the broiling step. Broil the fruit at the last moment so that the sections are warm, soft, and slightly caramelized on top.

2 large grapefruit, preferably pink
3 tablespoons light brown sugar
1 tablespoon unsalted butter
1 tablespoon gin (optional)

Using a sharp knife, remove the skin and underlying cottony pith from each grapefruit, leaving the fruit totally exposed. Then cut between the membranes on either side of each grapefruit segment to remove it. (You should have about 24 sections of grapefruit in all.) Squeeze the membranes over a bowl to extract the juice and drink this at your leisure. Arrange the grapefruit sections in one layer in a gratin dish.

When ready to serve, preheat the broiler.

Sprinkle the grapefruit with the sugar and dot with the butter. Place about 4 inches under the broiler and broil for 8 to 10 minutes, or until the edges of the segments are lightly browned. If desired, sprinkle with the gin. Serve.

Grapes in Red Wine Sauce
Serves 4

❧ **Red grapes are cooked** with wine and currant jelly and flavored with a little cinnamon. Serve this refreshing summer dessert in stemmed glasses topped with sour cream, whose acidity contrasts nicely with the sweetness of the grapes and accompanying wine sauce.

Be sure to use Red Flame grapes, which won't fall apart the way many other grapes do when cooked.

1 cup sturdy fruity red wine
1½ pounds Red Flame grapes, removed from the stems (4 cups)
¼ cup currant jelly
¼ teaspoon ground cinnamon
2 teaspoons potato starch (see page 318)
1 cup sour cream

Reserve 1 tablespoon of the wine. Place the grapes in a stainless steel saucepan with the rest of the wine, the jelly, and cinnamon. Bring to a boil, cover, reduce the heat, and boil gently for 4 to 5 minutes, just until the grapes begin to crack open. Remove from the heat.

Dissolve the potato starch in the reserved tablespoon of wine and stir into the grape mixture. Let cool to room temperature.

Serve the grapes and sauce in stemmed glasses, topped with generous spoonfuls of sour cream.

Cooked Grapes with Cream

Serves 6

Cooked in water with a little vinegar, these grapes are flavored with honey, mint, and cognac and served with sour cream. The dish, which takes only a few minutes to prepare, is a great way to use firm red or white grapes that have begun to discolor and shrivel. After 5 minutes of cooking, their skins will just be beginning to blister and break. (Avoid softer grape varieties, which will turn into mush after barely a minute of cooking.)

- 1½ pounds white Muscat, Thompson, or California seedless grapes, removed from the stems (about 4 cups)
- 1 tablespoon red wine vinegar
- ½ cup water
- 2 teaspoons grated lemon rind
- 1½ tablespoons fresh lemon juice
- ¼ cup honey
- 1 tablespoon shredded fresh mint leaves
- 1 tablespoon cognac or Armagnac
- ½ cup sour cream

Combine the grapes, vinegar, and water in a stainless steel saucepan and bring to a boil over high heat. Reduce the heat to low, cover, and cook gently for about 5 minutes. The skins of the grapes will begin to crack open.

Meanwhile, combine the lemon rind, lemon juice, honey, and mint in a bowl.

When the grapes are cooked, add them to the mixture in the bowl, stir well, and let cool.

Add the cognac or Armagnac to the grapes and serve in wineglasses, garnished with spoonfuls of the sour cream.

Crystallized Grapes and Oranges

Serves 6 to 8

Grapes and sections of oranges are lightly coated in beaten egg white, then in granulated sugar. The sugar crystallizes around the fruit in less than 1 hour. The crystallized fruit will keep for several days in a cool, dry place. Different fruits can be used, as long as they are dry. Uncut whole fruits, from cherries to strawberries to blueberries, are good.

An excellent variation is to freeze the crystallized fruits. With their hard sugar coating, they resemble sherbet or frozen fruit jellies.

- 1 large egg white
- 2 cups sugar
- 3 cups seedless grapes, preferably 1 cup each Thompson grapes, Red Flame grapes, and black grapes
- 2 oranges or tangerines, peeled and separated into segments (be sure not to break the membranes; the segments should be dry)
- 6–8 small fresh mint sprigs

Put the egg white in a bowl and beat it lightly with a fork just until slightly frothy. Spread the sugar out in a cake pan or on a rimmed cookie sheet.

One piece at a time, dip the fruit into the egg white, then lift it up using a fork or your fingers. Don't take too much egg white; the fruit should be just barely wet. (The egg white could also be

brushed on the fruit with a pastry brush.) Put the dipped fruit into the sugar and shake the pan so that the fruit rolls around and gets coated with the sugar (turn the citrus segments in the sugar if necessary to coat). Transfer the coated fruit to a cookie sheet and let it dry, either at room temperature or in the refrigerator. (Sieve the used sugar to rid it of lumps and return it to the sugar canister.)

Serve with sprigs of mint for decoration.

Mangoes with Rum
Serves 4

✂ **This simple mango dessert** is a winner, provided it is made with ripe mangoes. They are available most of the year now but are usually of better quality at summer's end.

2 ripe mangoes
3 tablespoons sugar
2 tablespoons dark rum
3 tablespoons fresh lime juice
1 tablespoon grated lime rind

Peel the mangoes, cutting deeply enough into the fruit so that any green-colored flesh is removed. Then, cutting inward toward the pit, slice each mango into slivers about ½ inch thick. Discard the pits.

Combine the mango slivers, sugar, rum, and

lime juice in a bowl. Serve immediately or, for added flavor, chill for at least 2 hours, stirring occasionally, before serving.

Serve in chilled glasses, sprinkled with the grated lime rind.

> If you have any fruit left over, puree it in a food processor and spread it on toast for breakfast the following morning.

Mango Symphony
Serves 4

✂ **After marinating in a** honey-rum sauce, pieces of red plums are spooned into the center of plates ringed with mango slices and the remaining sauce is drizzled over both fruits. The result is a wonderfully complementary blend of flavors. If Santa Rosa or Black Friar plums are not available, use Italian plums or another red plum variety.

1 large ripe mango
2 Santa Rosa or Black Friar plums
3 tablespoons honey
2 tablespoons dark rum

Peel the mango and slice it thin, cutting all around the central pit; discard the pit. Place the slices in a bowl, cover, and refrigerate until cold.

Meanwhile, halve the plums, discard the pits, and cut the flesh into ½-inch pieces. (You should have about 2 cups.)

Mix the honey and rum in a bowl large enough to hold the plums. Add the plum pieces, mix well, cover, and refrigerate until cold.

At serving time, arrange the slices of mango around the periphery of four dessert plates. Spoon the plums into the center of the plates and drizzle the remaining liquid from the plums over all the fruit. Serve.

Mangoes and Kiwi with Pastry Cream

Serves 4

❊ **For this attractive dessert** — essentially a fruit tart without the dough — cold pastry cream is covered with sliced fruits and glazed with apricot preserves.

Although vanilla extract can be substituted for the vanilla bean, I like to use the bean, which I grind into a powder and add to the pastry cream. I generally use older (and so somewhat dry) vanilla beans. They create a finer-textured powder than soft fresh ones.

Serve with pound cake or cookies.

PASTRY CREAM

1	vanilla bean (see the headnote)
3	tablespoons sugar
1	cup milk
2	large egg yolks
1½	tablespoons cornstarch

1	ripe mango
1	kiwi
½	cup apricot preserves
2	tablespoons Grand Marnier
1	tablespoon unsalted pistachio nuts

FOR THE PASTRY CREAM: Break the vanilla bean into pieces. Place it with the sugar in a spice grinder or mini-chop and process until the mixture is reduced to a powder.

Bring the milk to a boil in a saucepan. Meanwhile, combine the vanilla sugar with the egg yolks in a bowl and stir well with a whisk for about 1 minute. Add the cornstarch and stir well.

Pour the boiling milk on top of the sugar-yolk mixture, incorporating it with the whisk, then return the mixture to the saucepan. Bring to a boil, stirring constantly with the whisk, and boil for 10 seconds. Pour into a bowl, cover with plastic wrap, and let cool, then refrigerate.

MEANWHILE, PREPARE THE FRUIT: Peel the mango and cut it into slices; discard the pit. Peel the kiwi and cut it into slices.

Mix the preserves with the Grand Marnier in a small bowl.

At serving time, spread the pastry cream in a layer about 1 inch deep in a nice gratin dish or other attractive serving dish. Arrange the fruit slices on top in a decorative layer. Using a spoon, coat the fruit with the preserves mixture. Sprinkle the nuts on top.

Spoon the fruit and pastry cream onto individual dessert plates at the table and serve.

Honeyed Rum Melon

Serves 6

❊ **You must have a** ripe melon for this dessert. If you can't find one, use ripe peaches or plums instead. For best results, prepare the dessert ahead and let the fruit macerate in the sauce for a few hours in the refrigerator.

1	large ripe cantaloupe or honeydew melon (about 3 pounds)
¼	cup honey
½	cup fresh orange juice
3	tablespoons dark rum

Cut the melon in half and, using a spoon, remove the seeds. Cut the rind off the melon. Place the flesh halves flat side down on the work surface and cut them into slices as thin as you can.

Combine the honey, orange juice, and rum in a bowl. Add the melon slices and mix gently but thoroughly. Cover with plastic wrap and refrigerate for several hours, or until serving time.

Serve the melon in soup plates with some of the juices.

Melon in Port Wine
Serves 4

In France this dish is often served as a first course, but I like it for dessert as well. The melon of choice in France is the small flavorful Cavaillon — named for the town in the South of France where it was first grown. I substitute a ripe cantaloupe in my rendition. After first scooping as many balls from the fruit as possible, I scrape out the remaining flesh and puree it into a sauce. The melon balls are macerated in the sauce and some port and served with an optional sprinkling of pepper.

    1 ripe cantaloupe (2¾–3 pounds)
    ¼ cup tawny or vintage port
    2 fresh sage sprigs
       Freshly ground black pepper (optional)

Cut the cantaloupe crosswise in half. Spoon out and discard the seeds. Using a melon baller, scoop out a layer of balls from the flesh of one of the halves and drop them into a bowl. Then, still using the melon baller, scrape out the flesh trimmings from between the holes and set them aside in another bowl. Repeat this procedure, working layer by layer, until all the flesh has been removed from both melon halves. (You should have about 2½ cups melon balls and 1 cup trimmings.) Reserve the empty melon shells.

Add the port to the melon balls and mix thoroughly.

Process the melon trimmings in a food processor or blender until liquefied. Add to the melon balls and mix well. Cover and refrigerate for at least 1 to 2 hours.

Meanwhile, using a sharp paring knife, cut the edge of each reserved melon shell into decorative pointed "teeth."

At serving time, fill the shells with the melon balls and sauce and decorate each with a sprig of sage. At the table, spoon the melon balls and some sauce onto individual dessert plates and serve, with pepper sprinkled on top, if desired.

Melon in Madeira
Serves 6

You can make this fast dessert with any kind of melon, though a mixture (honeydew and cantaloupe here) provides contrast in color as well as texture. Choose heavy melons and rely on your nose to find one with a sweet, ripe taste.

    4 cups balls, slices, or pieces of a mixture
       of honeydew and cantaloupe (or
       other melon)
    1 large lemon
    ¼ cup honey
    ¼ cup dry Madeira

Put the melon in a bowl.

Remove the rind from the lemon with a vegetable peeler. Stack the strips of rind together and slice into fine julienne strips. Add them to the melon.

Juice the lemon. (You should have approximately ⅓ cup.) Add the lemon juice, honey, and Madeira to the melon. Stir the mixture and macerate at room temperature for 1 hour if time allows.

Serve in small deep dishes.

Oranges in Blackberry Sauce
Serves 6

✎ **Segments of orange are** arranged over a blackberry sauce and served with cookies or brioche. The sauce can be prepared several days ahead or even frozen, then thawed before serving.

6 large navel oranges

SAUCE

12 ounces frozen blackberries, defrosted
¾ cup blackberry preserves, preferably seedless

6 fresh mint sprigs
Warmed brioche slices or cookies, for serving

With a vegetable peeler, peel the rind from 1 of the oranges. Pile up the strips of rind and cut them into fine julienne strips. Set aside. With a sharp knife, peel all the oranges, cutting closely all around so that the cottony white pith as well as the rind is removed and the flesh is completely exposed. Cut between the membranes on either side of each orange segment to remove it and put the segments on a plate.

FOR THE SAUCE: Push the berries and preserves through a food mill fitted with the finest screen. If there are still too many seeds, strain the mixture through a sieve. Alternatively, puree the berries in a food processor or blender and then strain.

To serve, spoon about ¼ cup of the blackberry sauce onto each of six plates. Arrange the orange segments in a flower design in the center of the sauce and place some julienned orange rind around the edges of the sauce to form a border. Garnish the center with the mint sprigs and serve with slices of lukewarm brioche or cookies.

Orange Cubes in Orange "Baskets"
Serves 4

✎ **This is a classic** way of serving oranges in some Chinese restaurants. Since it's the simplest of fresh fruit desserts, be sure to use good-quality seedless oranges.

2 large seedless oranges
4 fresh mint sprigs

Cut a ½-inch-thick slice from both ends of each orange; set these slices aside.

Cut each orange in half crosswise. Using a paring knife, cut all around the flesh in each orange half to release it, then remove it in one piece from the surrounding cottony pith. You will have 4 disks of orange flesh and 4 hollow orange halves, which will be used as "baskets."

Gently press a reserved end slice, flesh side up, into each orange basket to create a bottom. Quarter each of the orange flesh disks and arrange the orange pieces in an orange basket in their original form, to simulate the appearance of an uncut orange half.

Decorate each orange basket with a mint sprig and serve with toothpicks for easy removal of the orange cubes.

Poached Oranges
Serves 6

✄ **Generally pears or dried** fruits such as apricots or prunes come to mind when people think about poaching fruit. Oranges, however, are excellent poached. The poaching intensifies their flavor and the syrup keeps them fresh and glossy. Orange slices can also be poached, in which case you should reduce the cooking time to 1 minute.

- 6 large navel oranges
- ⅓ cup sugar
- ⅓ cup water
- 1–2 tablespoons Grand Marnier or Cointreau

Using a sharp knife, remove the peel and the cottony white pith from each orange so that the flesh is completely exposed.

Put the whole oranges in a saucepan, add the sugar and water, cover, and bring to a boil. Reduce the heat and simmer gently for 5 minutes. Remove the oranges to a bowl or serving dish.

Boil the syrup to reduce it to approximately ⅓ cup, then pour the syrup over the oranges. Let cool.

At serving time, sprinkle the oranges with the orange liqueur and serve 1 per person, with some sauce.

Orange and Grapefruit Suprêmes
Serves 4

✄ **To make a sauce** for orange and grapefruit suprêmes, which are simply segments that have been removed from their membranes, I mix the juice squeezed from the membranes with a little maple syrup. Garnished with mint and dried cherries, this makes a delightful dinner dessert with a slice of sponge cake or with cookies. It's very pretty, especially if you use blood oranges, which contrast nicely with the grapefruit.

- 2 navel or blood oranges
- 2 Ruby Red grapefruit
- 2 tablespoons maple syrup
- 2 tablespoons dried cherries
  Fresh mint leaves, for garnish

Using a Microplane or box grater, grate the rind from 1 of the oranges. (You should have about 1 tablespoon.) Using a sharp knife, cut all the rind and cottony white pith from both the oranges and the grapefruit so the flesh is completely exposed. Cut between the membranes on either side of each orange and grapefruit segment to release the segments and put them on a plate. Refrigerate.

Meanwhile, squeeze the juice from the membranes into a bowl. (You should have about 1 cup combined juices.) Whisk the maple syrup and grated rind into the juices until combined. Refrigerate to cool.

Arrange alternating segments of orange and grapefruit in four dishes and pour the sweetened juice over them. Garnish with the dried cherries and mint leaves and serve.

Citrus and Raisin Compote
Serves 6

✄ **This bittersweet compote is** superior served ice-cold with a slice of pound cake, or with rice or vanilla pudding, as well as with ice cream. It can also be used as a filling between cake layers if you reduce the liquid completely, until the fruits are just moist. Slice the unpeeled fruit thin, by hand or in a food processor.

The compote can be made ahead; it improves when left to macerate in the refrigerator for a few days. Choose firm, thick-skinned citrus fruits — grapefruit, oranges, and limes. Unless you can find seedless varieties, be sure to remove the seeds, which impart bitterness when cooked.

½ medium grapefruit, cut into ¼-inch-thick slices and seeds removed (about 1 cup)
2 medium oranges, cut in half, sliced into ¼-inch-thick slices, and seeds removed (about 2½ cups)
1 large lime, cut in half, sliced into ¼-inch-thick slices, and seeds removed (about ¾ cup)
4 cups water
¾ cup sugar
½ cup raisins
1 tablespoon dark rum, cognac, or other spirits (optional)
6 fresh mint sprigs

Drop the fruit into a stainless steel saucepan, cover generously with water, bring to a boil, and boil for 10 to 15 seconds. (Blanching the fruit eliminates some of its tartness.) Drain in a colander and rinse under cold water.

Return the fruit to the saucepan, add the water and sugar, and bring to a boil. Boil gently, uncovered, for 50 minutes. Skim off any scum that comes to the surface, especially during the first half hour of cooking.

Add the raisins and cook for another 10 minutes. There should be just enough liquid left to baste and wet the fruit. Let cool to room temperature, then cover and refrigerate until ready to serve.

At serving time, add the rum, cognac, or other spirits to the fruit, if using. Serve in small deep dishes, decorated with sprigs of mint.

Peaches in Red Wine
Serves 4

❧ In full summer, when peaches are ripe, soft, and juicy, I make this dessert often. I prepare it here with a little black currant liqueur and red wine, but it can also be made with white wine and a little honey or with Champagne and a dash of framboise (raspberry brandy). When fresh peaches are not available, substitute unsweetened individually quick frozen (IQF) peaches, defrosting them slowly in the refrigerator overnight.

4 ripe yellow peaches (about 1½ pounds)
3 tablespoons sugar
3 tablespoons crème de cassis
½ cup fruity red wine (such as Beaujolais or Zinfandel)
4 fresh mint sprigs

Using a vegetable peeler, peel the peaches. Cut each of them into 6 wedges, discarding the pits. (You should have about 3 cups peach wedges.)

Put the peaches in a bowl with the sugar, cassis, and wine. Mix well and refrigerate until serving time, or up to 8 hours.

To serve, divide the peaches and surrounding juice among four wine goblets. Top each dessert with a mint sprig.

Poached White Peaches with Almond "Leaves"

Serves 8 to 10

✁ **Locally grown white peaches**, available in late summer, are very delicate, with a velvety skin and a pale white, juicy flesh. There are several varieties of white peaches, both freestone and clingstone. They bruise easily and can spoil faster than yellow peaches, but they have an intense flavor and juiciness.

The skin, left on the fruit during cooking, transfers its color to the flesh. (If the color of the skin is red-purple, it turns the whole peach a luscious pastel color.) After the peaches have been cooled in the poaching syrup, they can be peeled and stored with their syrup in the refrigerator for at least a week. For a sophisticated garnish, almond paste, available in most markets, is fashioned into leaves.

1½	cups sugar
	Grated rind and juice of 1 lemon
5	cups water
8–10	ripe white peaches (3½–4 pounds), at room temperature

ALMOND PASTE LEAVES

8	ounces almond paste
	Confectioners' sugar
½	teaspoon egg white if needed
	Green food coloring

Combine the sugar, lemon rind and juice, and water in a stainless steel saucepan and bring to a boil. Add the peaches, cover, and boil gently until the fruit is tender, 5 to 12 minutes, depending on the ripeness of the peaches; the flesh should resist only slightly when pricked. Let the peaches cool in the syrup until they reach room temperature.

Peel the peaches; the skin should slide off, or use a sharp paring knife.

Reduce the peach cooking liquid to 1 cup heavy syrup by boiling it down.

Arrange the peaches in a gratin dish and strain the syrup over them. Cover tightly with plastic wrap and refrigerate until chilled.

FOR THE ALMOND PASTE LEAVES: If the almond paste is a bit soft, add a few spoonfuls of confectioners' sugar and knead to tighten the paste. If, on the other hand, it is too stiff, soften it with the egg white, kneading until malleable. Add a few drops of green food coloring to the paste and mix thoroughly to color it evenly.

Sprinkle confectioners' sugar on a cutting board and roll out the almond paste to a thickness of about ¼ inch. With a knife, cut long, narrow ovals to simulate the leaves of peaches. With a knife, mark the "veins" of the leaves on each side and place the leaves, slightly twisted, on a plate so they will dry in that position.

Roll out little strings of almond paste and cut them to resemble stems. If possible, let the almond paste leaves and stems dry for a couple of hours at room temperature so they harden and hold their shape.

At serving time, arrange the peaches in an attractive, preferably glass, serving dish and spoon some syrup on top. Pierce the top of each peach with a knife and stick the almond stems and leaves into the incisions. Serve the peaches with the remaining syrup.

Cold Peach Soup

Serves 6 to 8

✁ **I used to make** this summer soup at my restaurant, La Potagerie, in New York City in the 1970s. It will surprise and delight your guests. It can be poured over slices of pound cake and decorated with whipped cream, and it can be made with frozen peaches.

1½ cups water
4 whole cloves
¾ cup sugar
1 cinnamon stick, broken into small pieces
2 tablespoons cornstarch, dissolved in ¼ cup cold water
1½ cups mellow dry white wine (such as Sémillon or Chenin Blanc)
3½ pounds very ripe yellow peaches (about 12)
1 cup heavy cream
1 cup blueberries

Combine the water, cloves, sugar, and cinnamon in a small saucepan and bring to a boil. Reduce the heat and simmer for 10 minutes, then add the dissolved cornstarch and stir with a whisk to blend the starch with the syrup. Bring the syrup to a boil again, remove from the heat, and let cool.

When the syrup is cool, strain into a large bowl, add the wine, and refrigerate.

To peel the peaches, remove the skin with a sharp paring knife or dip the peaches in boiling water for 30 seconds, then peel them by hand. (You can also make the soup without peeling the peaches.) Split the peaches lengthwise and remove the pits.

Cut enough of the peaches into ¾-inch dice to make 2 cups, and set aside. Puree the remaining peaches in a blender.

Combine the peach puree with the syrup and top with the reserved diced peaches. Refrigerate overnight, or for at least a few hours, before serving. Softly whip the cream and refrigerate.

At serving time, divide the soup among individual bowls, sprinkle the blueberries on the soup, and top each with a few generous tablespoons of whipped cream.

Peach Gratin
Serves 6

✖ **Sliced peaches are arranged** in a flower pattern in a shallow baking dish, sweetened with brown sugar, coated with a custard of egg and cream, sprinkled with sliced almonds, and baked. The recipe can be made with bananas, plums, pineapple, apples, or just about any soft and juicy fruit — including berries, although they will leak a bit and bleed into the custard. Harder fruits such as pears need to be partially cooked before baking unless they are very ripe.

If prepared in a pastry shell, this becomes a classical fruit tart. The shell should be baked for about 20 minutes before the peaches and the custard are added, because the crust takes longer to cook than the custard.

3 ripe peaches (about 1 pound)
⅓ cup packed light brown sugar
1 large egg, lightly beaten
½ cup heavy cream
2 tablespoons sliced almonds
1 tablespoon confectioners' sugar

Preheat the oven to 375 degrees.

Slice the unpeeled peaches into ¾-inch-thick wedges, discarding the pits, and arrange in a circular pattern in a shallow round baking dish about 1 inch deep. Place a few peach segments in the center in a decorative pattern to simulate the center of a flower. Sprinkle the peaches with the brown sugar.

Mix the beaten egg with the cream and pour the mixture on top of the fruit. Sprinkle with the sliced almonds and bake for about 40 minutes. The peaches should be browned and lightly caramelized.

Sprinkle with the confectioners' sugar and let cool to lukewarm before serving.

Croûte of Fruit

Serves 8

✄ **Make these super-easy fruit** toasts when you have very little notice and nothing much on hand. They take just minutes to prepare and you can use any fruit. They're very good made with pound cake, brioche, or sponge cake but they are also fine on slices of white bread. Serve them for dessert or breakfast or brunch, with sour cream or plain.

- 4 tablespoons (½ stick) unsalted butter, softened
- 8 slices white bread or cake
- ⅓ –½ cup sugar
- 2 medium ripe peaches, pitted and cut into ¾-inch-thick slices
- 2 large apricots, pitted and cut into ¾-inch-thick slices
- 1 banana, sliced
  Sour cream, for serving (optional)

Preheat the broiler. Spread about ½ teaspoon of the butter on one side of each slice of bread or cake. Sprinkle about ½ teaspoon of sugar on top of the butter on each slice of bread — not on the cake.

Put the bread or cake slices on a cookie sheet. Arrange the peach and apricot slices on top, working from the outside toward the center of each to imitate an open flower. Use the banana slices as the center of the "flowers." It is important to cover all the bread or cake, or the uncovered bread or cake will burn under the broiler.

Sprinkle 1 teaspoon sugar over the fruit on each slice and add 1 teaspoon butter cut into little dots to each one. Broil in the middle of the oven (so the croûtes don't cook too fast) for about 10 minutes. The bread or cake will be moist and sweet underneath and the fruit barely cooked and a bit caramelized on top.

Serve right out of the oven, with or without sour cream.

Fresh Fruit with Minted Apricot Fondue

Serves 4

✄ **Colorful and multitextured, this** fruit fondue makes an excellent party dessert. Each guest dips pieces of fresh and dried fruit in a sauce made of apricot preserves, minced mint leaves, and bourbon. You can flavor the sauce with rum, cognac, or whiskey, if you prefer, or eliminate the alcohol altogether.

APRICOT FONDUE

- 1 cup apricot preserves
- 2 tablespoons bourbon
- 1 tablespoon minced fresh mint
- 1 tablespoon water

- 1 ripe Anjou or Bartlett pear
- 8 ounces strawberries (8 large), washed, hulled, and halved
- 2 teaspoons fresh lemon juice
- 1 large navel orange, peeled
- 12 dried Calimyrna figs
- ⅓ cup raisins
- 8–10 fresh mint leaves

FOR THE FONDUE: Mix together all the ingredients in a small glass serving bowl. Set aside.

Peel the pear and cut it into quarters. Remove and discard the core.

Gently toss the pear, strawberries, and lemon juice in a bowl.

Halve the orange lengthwise and cut each half into ⅜-inch-thick slices.

At serving time, arrange the bowl of dipping sauce in the center of a platter and surround it with the fresh and dried fruits. Sprinkle with the mint leaves and serve with fondue forks or toothpicks.

Pears in Red Wine
Serves 6

✎ **Cooking the pears in** red wine tints their flesh a deep mahogany color. Use your judgment on how long to cook the fruit: if the pears are tender and falling apart after 5 minutes, remove them from the liquid, reduce the syrup by itself, and add it to the fruit. On the other hand, if the pears are still hard after 25 minutes, keep on cooking them until they are tender when pierced with a fork. Bartlett, Comice, and Williams pears cook faster than Seckel or Bosc varieties. When you buy pears, be sure that they are all equally ripe or unripe, so that they will cook in the same amount of time.

4 large Bartlett, Comice, or Williams pears, peeled, quartered, and cored
1½ cups dry red wine (such as Beaujolais, Côtes du Rhône, Gamay, or Zinfandel)
⅓ cup sugar
Grated rind and juice of 1 large lemon
6 slices pound cake or sponge cake

Combine the pears, wine, sugar, and lemon rind and juice in a large stainless steel saucepan and bring to a boil. Cover, reduce the heat, and boil gently for about 25 minutes — less if the pears are very ripe, more if they are hard.

You should have approximately ⅔ cup syrup; if the pears have rendered a lot of liquid, you may have more. Transfer the pears to a bowl. If necessary, reduce the syrup to ⅔ cup, then combine it with the pears. Let cool. The liquid will get syrupy.

Serve in small deep dishes with some of the syrup and the slices of cake.

Pears in Grenadine
Serves 6

✎ **I use firm Bosc** pears here, peeling and coring them before cooking. Other varieties can be substituted: well-ripened Anjou, Comice, or Bartlett pears are ready in as little as 2 or 3 minutes, while Seckels can take as long as 1 hour. Folded paper towels placed on top of the pears in the pan absorb some of the liquid as they cook and keep the tops moist, thus preventing them from discoloring.

6 medium Bosc pears (about 2 pounds)
⅓ cup fresh lime juice
⅓ cup sugar
⅓ cup grenadine
1 cup dry white vermouth
1 cup water

Peel the pears, leaving the stems attached and a little of the skin around the stems for decoration, and core them from the bottom. Stand the pears upright in a stainless steel saucepan that will hold them snugly and add the lime juice, sugar, grenadine, vermouth, and water. (The liquid should barely cover the pears.) Fold a length of paper towel in half and then in half again and place it over the pears to cover their tops completely. Bring the liquid to a boil over medium-high heat, then reduce the heat to low, cover, and boil the pears gently for about 30 minutes, or until they are very tender when pierced with the point of a sharp knife. Remove the pears from the heat and let them cool in the pan for about 15 minutes.

Lift the pears from the pan and stand them upright in a serving dish. Return the pan to the stove and boil the cooking liquid over high heat until it is reduced to a syrup. (You should have 1 cup.)

Pour the syrup over the pears, cover, and refrigerate until cold.

Serve the pears with some of the surrounding syrup.

Pears in Espresso
Serves 4

✎ **The combination of espresso,** brown sugar, and lemon rind creates a savory liquid that is ideal for poaching pears. I like to use espresso, but any leftover brewed coffee will do. Bosc pears lend themselves especially well to this preparation, but you can use another variety instead. Tiny Seckel pears are also very good.

    4 Bosc pears (about 1½ pounds)
    2 cups brewed espresso
       About 2 cups water
   ⅓ cup packed light brown sugar
    1 teaspoon grated lemon rind
    2 tablespoons Kahlúa or other coffee-flavored liqueur

Peel the pears, leaving the stems attached and a little of the skin around the stems for decoration, and core them from the bottom. Stand the pears upright in a stainless steel saucepan that will hold them snugly. Add the espresso and enough water to cover the pears completely, then add the brown sugar. Bring to a boil, cover, reduce the heat to low, and boil gently until the pears are tender, 30 to 35 minutes.

Remove the pears from the liquid and arrange them in a serving bowl. Boil the liquid until it is reduced to 1 cup. Stir in the lemon rind and pour the mixture over the pears.

Let cool, then add the Kahlúa to the cooled pears and refrigerate until cold. Serve cold.

Pears in Chocolate
Serves 4

✎ **These pears are cooked** simply with sugar, water, and vanilla. When they are tender, cocoa powder and bittersweet chocolate are added to the cooking liquid to create a sauce.

    4 ripe Anjou pears (about 2 pounds), peeled, quartered, and cored
   ¼ cup sugar
   ¾ cup water
   ½ teaspoon pure vanilla extract
    2 ounces bittersweet chocolate, chopped
    1 tablespoon unsweetened cocoa powder
    4 fresh mint sprigs

Combine the pears, sugar, water, and vanilla in a stainless steel saucepan and bring to a boil over high heat, then reduce the heat to low, cover, and cook the pears for 10 to 12 minutes, or until they are very tender when pierced with the tip of a sharp knife.

Using a slotted spoon, transfer the pears to a bowl. You should have about ½ cup cooking liquid. If you have more, boil it until reduced to ½ cup; if you have less, add water to bring it to ½ cup. Add the chocolate and cocoa powder to the liquid in the pan and mix with a whisk over low heat until the chocolate has melted and the mixture is smooth. Transfer the chocolate sauce to a bowl and let cool to room temperature. It will thicken to a syrup-like consistency.

Divide the sauce among four dessert plates and arrange the pear quarters on top of the sauce. Decorate each serving with a sprig of mint and serve.

Pear Brown Betty with Pear Sauce
Serves 12

🥄 **Rich, moist, and satisfying,** this mixture of brioche, cubed pears, butter, and cinnamon can be baked in individual molds and unmolded onto dessert plates or cooked in a large gratin dish, then scooped onto the plates and served with the pear sauce. You can assemble and cook the Betty a couple of hours before serving. It can be served plain or with whipped cream instead of the sauce.

The brioche can also be enjoyed fresh by itself. For this recipe, you'll need to make it at least a day or even several days ahead, because it is best slightly stale; keep it in a plastic bag so it doesn't dry out too much. Leftover brioche, croissants, or pound cake can be substituted.

BRIOCHE DOUGH

- 1 envelope (2¼ teaspoons) active dry yeast
- ¼ cup warm water
- 1 teaspoon sugar
- 1½ cups all-purpose flour
- 2 large eggs
- 3 tablespoons unsalted butter
- ¼ teaspoon salt

PEARS

- 9 large ripe Bartlett, Anjou, or Comice pears (about 3 pounds)
- ¾ cup sugar
- ⅓ cup apple or pear juice
- 1½ tablespoons ground cinnamon

- 8 tablespoons (1 stick) unsalted butter, melted
- ½ cup raisins

SAUCE

- 1 pound ripe Bartlett, Anjou, or Comice pears (about 3)
- ¼ cup sugar
- 3 tablespoons apple or pear juice
- ½ cup heavy cream
- 1 tablespoon pear brandy

Julienned lemon rind, for garnish

This pear sauce can also be served with crepes or other desserts.

AT LEAST A DAY AHEAD, MAKE THE BREAD: Combine the yeast with the warm water and sugar in the bowl of an electric mixer and let stand for about 5 minutes, until bubbly.

Add the flour, eggs, butter, and salt and beat with the flat beater for about 15 seconds on low speed, just enough to mix the ingredients. Increase the speed to medium and mix for about 3 minutes. Cover the bowl with plastic wrap and let rise in a warm, draft-free place for 1 hour, or until doubled.

With wet hands, so the dough doesn't stick to them, spread the dough on a baking sheet into a rectangle approximately 12 inches by 10 inches and ¼ inch thick. Let rise for about 30 minutes.

Preheat the oven to 375 degrees.

Bake the bread for about 20 minutes, until nicely browned. Transfer to a rack to cool. (*Once cool, the bread can be stored in a plastic bag at room temperature for 2 to 3 days.*)

Preheat the oven to 400 degrees. Butter twelve ¾-cup baba molds or ramekins or an 8- to 10-cup gratin dish.

Cut the bread into 1- to 2-inch pieces. (You should have 5 to 6 cups.) Set aside.

FOR THE PEARS: Peel the pears, cut them in half, and remove the cores. Reserve 2 of the pears and cut the remainder into 1-inch pieces.

Cut the 2 reserved pears into chunks. Process them in a food processor with the sugar and apple or pear juice until smooth and well pureed. Combine the puree with the bread, diced pears, cinnamon, melted butter, and raisins in a bowl. Press into the buttered baba molds or gratin dish.

Place the mold(s) on a cookie sheet and bake for about 45 minutes for baba molds, 1 hour for the larger mold. The mixture will have risen in the oven; press down lightly to make it level with the top of the mold(s). Let cool slightly and then, if using baba molds or ramekins, unmold.

MEANWHILE, FOR THE SAUCE: Peel, core, and quarter the pears. Process them in the food processor with the sugar and apple or pear juice until smoothly pureed. Add the cream and process.

Transfer to a saucepan and cook over medium heat, stirring with a whisk, until the mixture comes to a strong boil. Let cool, then add the pear brandy.

Pour a few spoonfuls of the sauce onto each individual plate, center a lukewarm brown Betty on top, garnish with the lemon rind, and serve with the extra sauce on the side. Or scoop the Betty from the gratin dish onto the plates, garnish, and serve with the sauce on the side.

Braised Pears in Caramel Sauce

Serves 6

✻ **Sprinkling pears with sugar** helps draw out their juices and makes a natural caramel. Depending on the ripeness of the pears, you may need to modify the cooking time as indicated so they are tender at the same time as the juice and sugar are caramelized.

- 6 medium Anjou or Bartlett pears (not too ripe)
- ¼ cup sugar
- 1 cup heavy cream
- 2 tablespoons crushed pistachios

Preheat the oven to 425 degrees.

Peel the pears, split them lengthwise, and remove the cores. Arrange flat side down in one layer in a large gratin dish. Sprinkle the sugar on top.

Bake for about 35 minutes. By this time, the sugar should have dissolved in the pear juices and cooked into a caramel and the pears should be tender when pierced with the point of a knife. If the pears are still hard, cook for another 5 or 10 minutes; if the sugar is caramelized but the pears are not cooked, add ½ cup water to prevent the caramel from burning during this extra cooking period. On the other hand, if the pears are cooked through before the syrup is caramelized, remove the fruit to a plate and reduce the juice on top of the stove until it caramelizes, then return the pears to the dish.

Add the cream to the dish and bake for 10 to 15 minutes longer, basting the pears every 5 minutes. The sauce should have reduced and thickened and be a nice ivory color. (Cooking the caramel with the cream will form a rich and delicious sauce.) Let cool. The sauce will thicken.

Serve the pears at room temperature, with the sauce on top, sprinkled with the pistachios.

Caramelized Roast Pears
Serves 4

❧ **Comice pears are roasted** at a high temperature for about an hour, until their juices caramelize and turn a rich mahogany color. The juices are then diluted with a little Madeira and the pears are served at room temperature.

- 4 Comice pears with stems (about 2 pounds)
- 2 teaspoons unsalted butter
- 1 tablespoon fresh lemon juice
- ¼ cup sugar
- 3 tablespoons sweet Madeira
  Fresh mint leaves, for garnish

Preheat the oven to 425 degrees.

Peel the pears, leaving the stems intact. Then, using a melon baller, grapefruit spoon, or ½-teaspoon measuring spoon, remove the core and seeds from each pear by digging them out from the base.

Melt the butter in a small gratin dish over low heat. Stir the lemon juice into the butter, roll the pears in this mixture, and sprinkle them with the sugar.

Stand the pears upright in the gratin dish and roast for 45 to 60 minutes, basting them with their cooking juices every 15 or 20 minutes, until they are nicely browned and tender when pierced with the point of a knife. The juices should be caramelized and a rich brown color; if they should begin to burn during cooking, immediately add 3 to 4 tablespoons water to the gratin dish.

When the pears are tender, remove them from the oven, add the Madeira to the dish, and stir well to combine it with the juices. Let the pears cool to room temperature.

Serve the pears with the juices spooned over and around them. Garnish with mint leaves.

Pears au Gratin
Serves 4

❧ **This is a nice** way to use leftover French bread. Cookies or leftover cake can be substituted, in which case you should eliminate the butter and sugar.

Be sure to use well-ripened pears, even if you have to buy fruit that is slightly damaged or has darkened skin. Any remaining spots on the flesh will be concealed under the crumbs of the topping. Sour cream or whipped cream makes a nice addition, but the dish is very good without it.

- 4 very ripe Bartlett or Comice pears (about 1½ pounds), peeled, halved lengthwise, cored, and cut lengthwise into ¼-inch-thick slices
- 3 ounces day-old French bread
- 2 tablespoons unsalted butter
- ¼ cup sugar
- ½ cup pecan halves
- 1 teaspoon ground cinnamon
  Sour cream or whipped cream, for serving (optional)

Preheat the oven to 375 degrees.

Arrange the pears in one slightly overlapping layer in a 6-cup gratin dish.

Break the bread into a food processor and process to coarse crumbs. (You should have about 1¾ cups.) Add the butter, sugar, pecans, and cinnamon and process until the mixture is mealy. Sprinkle the bread crumb mixture evenly over the pears.

Bake for 30 minutes, or until the topping is nicely browned. Allow to cool slightly.

Serve the pears lukewarm, with a little sour cream or whipped cream, if desired.

Pineapple in Peach Sauce
Serves 4 to 6

❧ **The bottom half of** a pineapple is sliced horizontally for this dessert, and the slices are arranged on a platter around the uncut top half, which is decorated with a collar of strawberries. Served with a peach sauce, this dessert couldn't be more refreshing.

Be sure to buy a well-ripened pineapple.

1 large very ripe pineapple (about 4 pounds)
6 strawberries

SAUCE

1 cup peach preserves
2 tablespoons fresh lime juice
2 tablespoons kirsch
2 tablespoons shredded fresh mint leaves

Using a sharp knife, remove a thin layer of skin from the surface of the pineapple to expose the flesh. (The eyes will still be visible.) Then, using the sharp knife, cut V-shaped diagonal furrows to remove the eyes and, at the same time, create a diagonal line design all around the fruit. Pull or cut off all the lower leaves from the stem of the pineapple, leaving only a few leaves at the top of the stem for decoration.

Starting at the bottom, cut about half the pineapple crosswise into thin slices. Using a small round cookie cutter or a knife, remove the core from the center of these slices. Place the top half of the pineapple on a large attractive platter, and arrange the pineapple slices around it.

Using round toothpicks, attach the strawberries to the uncut pineapple to create a decorative collar.

FOR THE SAUCE: Mix all the ingredients together in a small bowl until smooth.

Serve 2 slices of pineapple per person, with a little sauce spooned over them. If additional pineapple slices are needed, slice them from the remaining pineapple.

Diced Pineapple with Crème de Cassis
Serves 6

❧ **Diced ripe pineapple is** seasoned with crème de cassis, cognac, and brown sugar. Raisins add a chewy texture that is just right with the crisp pineapple. Ripeness is important here. If you are fortunate enough to find a particularly sweet pineapple, reduce the sugar.

1 ripe pineapple (3 pounds)
¼ cup crème de cassis
2 tablespoons cognac or whiskey
3 tablespoons light brown sugar
1 tablespoon raisins

Trim the pineapple at both ends and cut it lengthwise into quarters. Cut out the core. Cut each quarter lengthwise in half and remove the wedges of fruit from the skin. Cut each wedge into 8 pieces.

Combine the pineapple with the crème de cassis, cognac or whiskey, and brown sugar in a bowl. Refrigerate until chilled, or until serving time.

Spoon the pineapple into six dessert bowls. Serve very cold, garnished with the raisins.

Pineapple Finale
Serves 4

❧ **The center of the** pineapple is removed from the rind for this dessert, flavored with honey, grapefruit juice, and brandy, and then returned to the empty shell. For a simpler effect, though, you can just peel, slice, and core the pineapple and serve the slices with the sauce.

Select fruit that is slightly soft to the touch and has a pleasant, fruity smell. If the pineapple isn't ripe, this dessert isn't worth making.

    1   large ripe pineapple (about 4 pounds)
    ½   cup grapefruit juice
    2   tablespoons honey
    2   tablespoons pear brandy

Make a crosswise cut about 1 inch below the top of the body of the pineapple, removing the leaves and top of the fruit. Reserve the pineapple top and leaves. Cut a ½-inch-thick slice from the bottom of the pineapple.

Place the pineapple on its side, push the sharp blade of a long, thin, sturdy knife into the flesh of the pineapple as close as possible to where the flesh meets the shell, and cut all around the flesh until you can remove intact a cylinder of pure pineapple flesh. Reserve the hollowed-out pineapple shell.

Cut the pineapple flesh crosswise into 8 slices of about equal thickness. Using a small round cookie cutter or sharp knife, remove the tough center (about 1¼ inches in diameter) from each slice.

Stack the slices in the order in which they were cut and place them back in the shell. Set the reassembled pineapple in a glass serving bowl.

Mix the grapefruit juice, honey, and brandy together in a small bowl and pour it over the pineapple slices. Refrigerate, covered, until chilled. (*The pineapple can be refrigerated for up to 8 hours.*)

At serving time, place the reserved pineapple top with leaves on top of the re-formed pineapple and bring the dessert to the table. Serve 2 slices of pineapple per person, with some of the surrounding juice.

Grilled Pineapple with Maple, Rum, and Mint Sauce
Serves 4

Grilled to intensify their taste, slices of pineapple are served with a sauce of maple syrup, dark rum, lemon juice, and mint that complements them perfectly.

SAUCE

    1   tablespoon maple syrup
    1   tablespoon fresh lemon juice
    1½ tablespoons dark rum
    2   tablespoons finely shredded fresh
        mint leaves

    4   ½-inch-thick slices fresh pineapple, skin
        and core removed

Heat a grill until hot.

FOR THE SAUCE: Mix all the ingredients together in a small bowl. Set aside.

Place the pineapple slices on the grill and grill for 1 to 2 minutes on each side, just enough to mark the slices and give them a grilled flavor. Remove to a serving platter, pour the sauce over the pineapple slices, and serve.

Potted Plums with Phyllo Dough
Serves 4

Plum pieces are sautéed in butter with pistachios and plum preserves to create a stew of sorts, which is topped with "hats" of phyllo. For each hat, a sheet of the tissue-like pastry is gathered into a loosely formed ball and perched atop an individual serving — the "potted" plums are arranged in small ramekins. Then the dish is baked until the hats are brown and crisp.

Any fruit can be stewed in this way and finished with the dough on top. Phyllo dough is available in the frozen food section of most supermarkets.

1 pound Santa Rosa plums (about 10)
2½ tablespoons unsalted butter
3 tablespoons skinned pistachio nuts
⅓ cup plum preserves
1 tablespoon water
1⅓–2⅓ tablespoons sugar
4 sheets phyllo (14 by 18 inches each), kept wrapped until ready to use
Sour cream or whipped cream, for serving

Preheat the oven to 350 degrees.

Pit the plums and cut each into 4 wedges.

Heat 1½ teaspoons of the butter in a saucepan. When it is hot, add the plums, pistachios, preserves, and water and cook, covered, over high heat for 5 minutes, or until the plums are soft. Remove the lid and cook for 2 to 3 minutes longer to eliminate any moisture remaining in the pan. (The mixture should be thick, not watery.) Add 1 tablespoon of sugar to the plums if they are too tart and transfer them to a bowl.

Melt the remaining 2 tablespoons butter. Unwrap the phyllo sheets, lay them out on a work surface, and, working quickly so the paper-thin pastry doesn't dry out, brush the top of each sheet of phyllo with the butter and sprinkle with 1⅓ tablespoons sugar.

Spoon ½ to ⅔ cup of the plum mixture into each of four 1-cup ramekins. Fold each sheet of phyllo in half, butter side out, and gather it gently into a loose tissue-like ball, taking care not to squeeze it. Place a ball of the phyllo on top of each ramekin and arrange the ramekins on a cookie sheet.

Bake for 25 to 30 minutes, until the phyllo is browned and crisp.

Serve lukewarm, with sour cream or whipped cream.

Prune Plums au Sucre
Serves 4

⁂ **Wedges of plum are** macerated in lemon juice, corn syrup, and brandy and served with a topping of crème fraîche. You can make the plums a few hours ahead. Serve them cool but not cold.

1 pound prune plums (also called Italian plums), 6–8
2 tablespoons fresh lemon juice
¼ cup light corn syrup
1 tablespoon plum brandy (mirabelle or quetsche) or other fruit brandy, such as pear or kirsch (optional)
⅓ cup crème fraîche

Cut the plums in half. Discard the pits and cut each half plum into thirds. Put the plum pieces in a bowl.

Add the lemon juice, corn syrup, and brandy, if desired, to the plums and mix well. Cover with plastic wrap and refrigerate for at least 1 hour, and as long as 6 hours.

Spoon the plums and surrounding juice into wineglasses or onto dessert plates and serve with a dollop of crème fraîche.

Stew of Red Summer Fruits
Serves 8 to 10

⁂ **Basil lends a delightful** fragrance and a slightly licorice taste to this stew. A tasty hodgepodge of red summer fruits, it can be made in winter with fruits such as bananas, apples, and oranges. The dessert even improves after one day in the refrigerator, when the juices thicken slightly and the flavor of the fruit becomes more intense. It will keep for several days refrigerated.

Serve with warm slices of brioche or pound cake and ice cream or crème fraîche.

STEWED FRUIT

- 1 tablespoon grated orange rind
- ⅓ cup pomegranate juice
- 1 cup mellow dry white wine (such as Chenin Blanc or Gewürztraminer)
- 1 cup crème de cassis
- ¼ cup strawberry jam
- 1 pound firm red Santa Rosa plums (about 10), pitted and cut into wedges
- 1 pound Bing cherries, pitted
- 4 large fresh basil sprigs, tied in a bundle with kitchen twine
- 1 pound seedless grapes
- 1 pound blueberries
- 1 pound strawberries, washed, hulled, and cut into wedges

SAUCE

- 1 pint sour cream
- 2 tablespoons sugar
- ¼ cup water

Fresh mint leaves, preferably with flowers, for garnish

FOR THE FRUIT: Combine the orange rind, pomegranate juice, white wine, cassis, and strawberry jam in a stainless steel saucepan and bring to a boil. Boil for about 1 minute. Add the plums, cherries, and basil, bring to a strong boil, and boil for about 1 minute (1½ minutes for less ripe fruit).

With a slotted spoon or a skimmer, remove the fruit from the boiling liquid and put it in a bowl. Add the grapes to the cooking liquid, return

to a boil, and cook for 30 seconds. Transfer the grapes to the bowl and add the blueberries and strawberries to the saucepan and return the mixture barely to a boil. Remove the fruit and add it to the bowl.

Drain as much juice from the fruit as you can and return to the saucepan. (You should have approximately 3 cups.) Boil the juice to reduce it to 2 cups and pour it on top of the fruit, with the basil. Let cool, then remove and discard the basil. (*The fruit can be made ahead and refrigerated for several days; serve cool, not cold.*)

FOR THE SAUCE: At serving time, combine the sour cream and sugar with the water in a bowl and mix until just slightly liquid.

Spoon about 3 tablespoons of the juices from the fruit onto each plate. Swirl about 1 tablespoon of the sauce in a design in the juice, using a spoon or the point of a knife. Spoon the fruit into the center of the plates, arranging it attractively. Decorate with mint flowers, if you have them, and leaves, and serve.

Prunes and Grapefruit in Red Wine Sauce
Serves 4

✎ **A welcome ending to** a rich meal, this combination of cooked prunes and raw grapefruit in a red wine sauce is tart and pleasing to the eye.

- 8 ounces large pitted dried prunes (about 24)
- 2 tablespoons light brown sugar
- ¾ cup fruity dry red wine (such as Beaujolais)
- 1 vanilla bean, split
- ¼ teaspoon black peppercorns
- 4–6 whole cloves
- 2 small Ruby Red grapefruit

Combine the prunes, brown sugar, wine, and vanilla bean in a stainless steel saucepan. Put the peppercorns and cloves in a small square of cheesecloth and tie them up together into a package with kitchen twine (for easier removal after cooking). Add the package to the saucepan and bring to a boil. Cover, reduce the heat to low, and cook gently for 10 minutes.

Meanwhile, peel the grapefruit with a sharp knife, removing all the peel and cottony white pith. Cut between the membranes on either side of each grapefruit segment to release it; set aside. Squeeze the membranes over a bowl to release the juice.

Add about ⅓ cup of the juice to the prunes and let cool.

At serving time, remove and discard the cheesecloth package and divide the prunes among four plates. Arrange about 4 grapefruit segments alongside the prunes on each plate. Pour the cooking juices over the fruit and serve.

Rhubarb Compote
with Mascarpone
Serves 6

✻ Leftover preserves, jellies, or jams can be used in this quick compote. Orange, apricot, and currant are all compatible flavors.

    2   pounds rhubarb
    ½   cup apple cider
    1½ cups jam, jelly, or preserves
    1   cup mascarpone
        Pound cake or brioche, for serving

Wash the rhubarb and trim off and discard any leaves or imperfections. Cut the ribs into pieces 2 to 3 inches long, splitting the larger ones in half before cutting them into pieces.

Put the rhubarb in a stainless steel saucepan with the cider and jam, cover, and bring to a boil over high heat. Reduce the heat and boil gently for about 5 minutes. Remove the cover and continue boiling for about 10 minutes, until the rhubarb shreds into pieces. Transfer to a serving bowl and let cool.

At serving time, divide the compote among six dessert bowls. Serve with a dollop of mascarpone and a slice of pound cake or brioche.

Rhubarb and Strawberry Coulis
Serves 4

✻ Rhubarb and strawberries are especially good when cooked together into a coulis, or thick soup. Sweetened with a little sugar and some jam, the coulis is tasty and beautiful served in deep plates, with a spoonful of cream on top and cookies or sliced pound cake on the side.

    1½ pounds rhubarb, washed, trimmed of any leaves and imperfections, and cut into pieces 1 inch across by 3 inches long (4 cups)
    1   cup strawberries, washed, hulled, and halved or quartered, depending on size
    ¾   cup jam (any type of berry)
    ¼   cup sugar
    ¼   cup water
    ½   cup sour cream
    ¼   cup heavy cream, whipped to soft peaks
        Cookies or pound cake, for serving

Combine the rhubarb, strawberries, jam, sugar, and water in a large stainless steel saucepan and bring to a boil over high heat. Reduce the heat to medium, cover, and cook for 10 minutes, or until the fruit is well cooked. Cool to room temperature, then refrigerate until serving time.

Fold the sour cream and heavy cream together.

Ladle the coulis into soup plates and garnish each with a few tablespoonfuls of the cream mixture. Serve a few cookies or a slice of pound cake alongside.

Rhubarb and Blueberry Nectar with Mint
Serves 4 to 6

✖ **This is one of** my favorite desserts in full summer, when rhubarb is available and mint abounds in my garden. I like a deep, berry-flavored red wine, like a Cabernet Sauvignon here, and I add cranberry juice along with the wine. Take this opportunity to use all the little dabs of leftover jams taking up space in your refrigerator.

½ bunch fresh mint (to yield about 1 cup loosely packed leaves)

1 pound rhubarb, washed, leaves and any imperfections removed, and cut into 2-inch pieces

⅓ cup dry red wine (such as Cabernet Sauvignon)

½ cup cranberry juice

¾ cup strawberry or other jam

2 tablespoons sugar

6 ounces (1 cup) blueberries

½ cup crème fraîche or mascarpone

4–6 slices brioche or pound cake

Remove the stem tips, with a few leaves attached, from 4 to 6 of the mint sprigs and set aside for use as a decoration. Gather the remaining sprigs of mint into a bundle and tie them together with kitchen twine. Drop into a stainless steel saucepan, add the rhubarb, wine, cranberry juice, jam, and sugar, and bring to a boil. Cover,

reduce the heat to low, and cook for about 8 minutes. Add the blueberries, bring back to a boil, and cook, covered, for 2 minutes. The mixture should be somewhat soupy. Let cool, then cover and refrigerate until chilled.

At serving time, spoon the fruit mixture into deep plates. Place a rounded tablespoon of crème fraîche or mascarpone in the middle of each and top with a reserved mint sprig tip. Serve with slices of brioche or pound cake.

Jam "Sandwiches"
Serves 4

✖ **Jam sandwiches are fun** to make for a party. Thin slices of firm-textured pound cake are spread with different-flavored jams and served in traditional sandwich fashion, or open-faced, with the colorful jam spread on the surface of each slice. To add diversity to your dessert tray, select several jam flavors and cut the sandwiches into unusual shapes. I begin with a piece of pound cake 6 inches long by 5 inches wide.

Serve the sandwiches on their own or with sherbet or ice cream.

6 ounces pound cake

1½ tablespoons raspberry jam

1½ tablespoons apricot jam

1½ tablespoons blackberry jam

Trim away the outside of the pound cake and cut the cake into 6 slices, each ¼ inch thick.

Spread the raspberry jam on 1 slice, the apricot jam on another slice, and the blackberry jam on a third slice. Top with the remaining pound cake slices, to create 3 sandwiches. Cut each into different shapes: one into 4 squares, one into 4 triangles, and one into 4 rectangles.

Arrange on a plate and serve.

Puddings, Sweet Soufflés, and Crepes

Puddings, Sweet Soufflés, and Crepes

Chocolate Pudding with Almond Topping

Serves 4

❧ **Quick to make and** not too rich, this pudding is prepared like a chocolate pastry cream and can be used as such. It will keep in the refrigerator for a week or so. Be certain to cover it well with plastic wrap, so the pudding doesn't absorb other flavors.

1½ cups milk
1 tablespoon espresso powder or instant coffee granules
1 large egg
1 large egg yolk
3 tablespoons sugar
1½ tablespoons all-purpose flour
6 ounces bittersweet chocolate, broken into pieces
1 tablespoon sliced almonds

Preheat the oven to 400 degrees.

Bring the milk and espresso powder or coffee granules to a boil in a saucepan.

Meanwhile, mix the egg, egg yolk, and sugar in a medium bowl. Add the flour and mix it in well.

Whisk about 1 cup of the hot milk and coffee into the egg mixture and combine well. Pour the contents of the bowl back into the saucepan and bring to a boil, stirring constantly with the whisk. Transfer the hot mixture to a bowl, add the chocolate pieces, and let stand for about 2 minutes.

Whisk until the chocolate is melted and mixed in well. Cool, then refrigerate until serving time.

Before serving, spread the almonds on a small cookie sheet and bake them for 6 to 8 minutes, until they are nicely browned.

Divide the pudding among four dessert bowls or cups, sprinkle with the sliced almonds, and serve.

Mocha and Chocolate Cream

Serves 6 to 8

❧ **You can serve this** mousse on its own, or put it between cake layers in place of buttercream or use it to fill profiteroles, puffs, éclairs, or other pastries. You can make it a day or two ahead, but cover it tightly with plastic wrap before refrigerating it.

3 tablespoons strong brewed coffee (from the first ½ cup that comes out of the coffeemaker) or instant coffee granules
1 envelope (about 2 teaspoons) gelatin
¼ cup boiling water
2 cups heavy cream
2 tablespoons sugar
1 ounce semisweet chocolate, chopped
½ ounce unsweetened chocolate, chopped

Combine the hot coffee with the gelatin in a bowl, add the boiling water, and stir gently until the gelatin is completely dissolved (if using coffee granules, combine in a saucepan and stir over low heat until dissolved). Let cool to lukewarm.

Beat the heavy cream and sugar in a bowl until the cream is fluffy and holds a soft peak. Be careful not to overbeat the cream, or the mousse will be grainy.

Pour the coffee-gelatin mixture into the whipped cream all at once and whisk rapidly for 10 to 20 seconds, until the mixture begins to set. Let firm for 1 hour in the refrigerator.

Melt the semisweet and unsweetened chocolates together. Spoon the coffee cream into individual dishes or a large bowl and drizzle the chocolate over the top in a design. Refrigerate for at least 30 minutes before serving.

Chocolate Mousse
Serves 6

❧ **Made with a warm** emulsion of egg yolks and sugar and finished with cream, this is the most classic of chocolate mousses. Cognac works well with chocolate, but it can be replaced by dark rum or Grand Marnier for a different flavor.

⅓ cup sugar
4 large egg yolks
2 cups heavy cream
10 ounces bittersweet or semisweet
    chocolate, melted
2 teaspoons cognac

Reserve 2 tablespoons of the sugar and combine the rest of the sugar with the egg yolks in a stainless steel bowl. Place the bowl in a skillet of hot tap water (or use a double boiler) and whisk the mixture for 3 minutes, or until it is fluffy, smooth, and at least doubled in volume.

Beat the reserved sugar with the cream in a large chilled bowl for a few minutes, or until soft peaks form; do not overwhip. Transfer about ¾ cup of the whipped cream to another bowl to use as a decoration and refrigerate.

Using a rubber spatula, combine the melted chocolate and cognac with the yolk mixture. If the mixture starts to seize or break down, immediately stir in 1 to 2 tablespoons of the whipped cream to smooth out the mixture. Gently fold in the (remaining) whipped cream until incorporated. Transfer the mousse to a decorative bowl, cover, and refrigerate until set, at least 2 hours.

At serving time, whip the reserved ¾ cup whipped cream until stiff peaks form. Spoon the cream into a pastry bag fitted with a star tip and decorate the top of the mousse with the cream, or spoon dollops of the cream onto the top of the mousse. Serve.

MELTING CHOCOLATE

Chocolate should be cut into small pieces of about equal size before melting it; the smaller the pieces, the faster they will melt.

To melt chocolate in a microwave oven, put it in a bowl, cover it and microwave it for 1-minute periods, leaving 2- to 3-minute intervals between the microwaving periods, so it does not scorch.

To melt chocolate conventionally, put the chocolate pieces in a stainless steel bowl set over a saucepan of hot water and stir occasionally until the chocolate melts.

Meringue Chocolate Mousse
Serves 4

❧ **In this lightened mousse,** the standard ingredients — chocolate, whipped cream, egg yolks, and butter — are replaced with cocoa powder (which is low in fat), espresso, a little gelatin, and a boiled, or Italian, meringue.

MERINGUE

3 large egg whites
½ cup sugar
3 tablespoons water

CHOCOLATE MIXTURE

⅓ cup unsweetened cocoa powder
½ cup strong espresso or scant
    2 tablespoons espresso powder
    dissolved in ½ cup hot water
1 envelope (about 2 teaspoons)
    gelatin

1 teaspoon grated tangerine
    or orange rind

FOR THE MERINGUE: Put the egg whites in the bowl of a mixer fitted with the whisk attachment.

Place the sugar and water in a small stainless steel saucepan and mix just enough to combine them. Bring to a boil over medium-high heat without stirring, then cover the pan and cook the sugar mixture for 1 minute to melt any crystals of sugar that have collected around the sides of the saucepan.

Meanwhile, start beating the egg whites at medium-high speed.

Remove the pan lid, insert a candy thermometer, and cook the sugar syrup for 3 to 3½ minutes, or until it registers 240 degrees (soft-ball stage) on the thermometer.

At this point, the egg whites should be firm and glossy but not grainy. While continuing to beat the whites, pour the syrup from the pan in a steady thin stream into the bowl, avoiding the whisk. Continue beating the whites for about 2 minutes longer at medium-high speed. The mixture should be glossy and elastic. Set aside to cool to room temperature.

FOR THE CHOCOLATE MIXTURE: Combine the cocoa powder, espresso, and gelatin in a medium saucepan and heat over medium-high heat, stirring constantly, until the gelatin is melted. Alternatively, heat the mixture in the microwave for about 1 minute. Set aside until cooled to room temperature, about 5 minutes.

Add the cooled chocolate mixture to the meringue and fold it in gently but thoroughly with a whisk. Pour the mousse into a serving bowl. Cover the bowl with plastic wrap and refrigerate for at least 3 hours, or as long as overnight.

To serve the mousse, scoop it into individual bowls and sprinkle each with a little grated tangerine or orange rind.

Custard with Blueberry Sauce
Serves 4

With its sauce of fresh blueberries, orange or tangerine preserves, and cognac, this easy custard makes a beautiful dessert. Remove the soufflé dishes from the oven as soon as the custard is lightly set yet still somewhat jelly-like if shaken. It will continue to firm as it cools.

CUSTARD

2	large eggs
¼	cup sugar
1	teaspoon pure vanilla extract
1¾	cups half-and-half

SAUCE

¼	cup orange or tangerine preserves
2	tablespoons cognac
1	tablespoon water if necessary
1	cup blueberries

Preheat the oven to 350 degrees.

FOR THE CUSTARD: Beat the eggs in a bowl with a fork until they are well combined and there is no visible sign of egg white. Add the sugar, vanilla, and half-and-half and mix well to dissolve the sugar.

Arrange four ¾-cup soufflé dishes or ramekins in a roasting pan and strain the custard mixture into the molds. Add enough lukewarm tap water to the pan to come about three quarters of the way up the sides of the dishes.

Bake for about 35 minutes, until the custard is lightly set. Remove the custards from the water bath and let cool, then refrigerate for at least 3 hours.

MEANWHILE, FOR THE SAUCE: Mix the preserves and cognac together in a small bowl, adding the water if needed to thin to the consistency of a sauce. Stir in the blueberries. Refrigerate until serving time.

To serve, unmold the custards onto individual plates. Spoon the blueberry sauce over and around them and serve.

COOKING CUSTARDS IN A WATER BATH

It's important that flans, crème brûlées, pots de crème, and other similar custards be cooked slowly in a water bath in the oven. Use lukewarm water from the tap. The water should never come to a boil; if it does, add some ice cubes to lower the water temperature quickly. If the custard cooks too fast, little holes will form all around the sides; it should be very smooth and silky in texture.

Vanilla Flan with Caramel-Cognac Sauce
Serves 6

❧ This rich custard, cooked in a soufflé dish, unmolded, and topped with caramel, is a sure crowd-pleaser. The delicate part is the cooking; the flan is cooked in a water bath, which should not boil. Rum or Grand Marnier can be substituted for the cognac in the sauce, or the alcohol can be omitted entirely.

CARAMEL AND SAUCE

¾ cup sugar
⅓ cup plus ¼ cup water
2 tablespoons cognac or Armagnac
1 tablespoon fresh lemon juice

FLAN

4 large eggs
1 large egg yolk
1½ teaspoons pure vanilla extract
⅓ cup sugar
2 cups milk
1 cup light cream

FOR THE CARAMEL AND SAUCE: Mix the sugar and the ¼ cup water together in a heavy saucepan, bring to a boil over medium-high heat, and boil, uncovered, for 6 to 7 minutes, until the mixture becomes a dark blond caramel. Pour about ¼ cup of the caramel into a 4- to 5-cup soufflé dish and tilt the dish so the caramel coats the bottom. (There should be just enough caramel to cover the bottom of the dish.)

Slowly add the ⅓ cup water to the caramel remaining in the pan, to prevent splattering. When all the water has been added, bring back to a boil and mix well with a wooden spoon. All the caramel should have melted, with no thick layer underneath stuck to the bottom of the pan. If necessary, keep stirring until this layer is dissolved. Transfer the caramel sauce to a bowl and let cool; it will thicken to the consistency of a heavy syrup.

When the caramel is cool, add the cognac or Armagnac and lemon juice and stir well. Set aside. (*The sauce can be made ahead and refrigerated in a jar with a tight-fitting lid for several months; bring to room temperature before serving.*)

Preheat the oven to 350 degrees.

FOR THE FLAN: Mix the eggs, egg yolk, vanilla, and sugar in a bowl with a whisk. Add the milk and cream and mix until incorporated.

Strain the mixture into the caramel-lined soufflé dish and place the dish in a large baking pan. Add enough water to the baking pan so that it comes about halfway up the sides of the soufflé dish.

Bake for about 55 minutes, until the custard is set in the center. To check, insert the tip of a paring knife into the center of the custard; if the blade comes out clean, the custard is set, although it may still look and feel soft in the center.

Remove the dish from the water and let cool, then refrigerate for at least 5 hours, or preferably overnight.

To unmold the flan, run a sharp knife around the edges of the dish, making sure that the knife does not cut into the flan. Place a platter on top of the flan and invert it, moving the dish gently to dislodge the custard. Some liquid will come out of the dish as the flan dislodges; discard this thin caramel and pour some of the thick caramel-cognac sauce over the custard.

Serve the flan with the remaining caramel-cognac sauce.

Crème Brûlée with Verbena
Serves 6

✂ **Crème brûlée is a** rich custard and, for this reason, I cook it in small molds, approximately ½ cup each. It can be made even more luxurious by using only heavy cream, but I prefer milk and cream in equal proportions. Because crème brûlée is made mostly with egg yolks, it cannot be unmolded, since there is not enough albumin (found in egg whites) to hold the cream.

I flavor the crème brûlée with verbena, one of my favorite herbs, and accent it with lemon rind. It can also be flavored with vanilla, rum, chocolate, or almond, according to your preference. Light brown sugar is used for the topping; dark brown is too strong in taste.

The custards can be made 2 or 3 days ahead and kept covered in the refrigerator, but the brown sugar crust should not be made more than an hour before serving, or it will melt.

1	cup milk
½	cup loosely packed verbena leaves (fresh or dried) or 2 verbena tea bags
2	teaspoons grated lemon rind
1	large egg
4	large egg yolks
¼	cup granulated sugar
1	cup heavy cream

TOPPING

6	tablespoons light brown sugar

Preheat the oven to 350 degrees.

Combine the milk, verbena leaves or tea bags, and lemon rind in a saucepan and bring to a boil. Cover, remove from the heat, and let steep for 5 minutes.

Beat the egg and egg yolks with the sugar in a bowl and add the cream. Add the steeped milk mixture, stirring well to mix thoroughly. Strain through a fine strainer.

Arrange six ½-cup soufflé dishes or ramekins in a roasting pan and fill them with the crème brûlée mixture. Add enough lukewarm water to the pan to come halfway up the sides of the dishes. Bake for 25 to 30 minutes, until the crème is set. (The water around the dishes should not boil; if it begins to boil, add some ice to lower the temperature and stop the boiling.) Remove the custards from the water bath and let cool.

When the custards are cool, cover and refrigerate until cold. (*The custards can be made up to 3 days ahead.*)

FOR THE TOPPING: At serving time, or no more than 1 hour beforehand, preheat the broiler. (This can also be done with a propane torch.) Spread 2 teaspoons of the brown sugar evenly over the top of each custard. Place the custards under the broiler and broil, moving them around and watching them closely, until the sugar bubbles and turns uniformly brown, approximately 3 minutes. Let cool for at least 10 minutes, until the sugar surface hardens, before serving.

Vanilla Pots de Crème
Serves 8

⚹ **Served right in the** little pots in which they are cooked, these custards are similar to crème brûlée but lack the crackling sugar topping. Classic petit pot molds hold about ½ cup each and look like old-style Boston baked beans earthenware casseroles, but you can use ramekins.

- ½ cup sugar
- 6 large egg yolks
- 1½ teaspoons pure vanilla extract
- 2 cups milk
- ½ cup heavy cream
- ¼ teaspoon arrowroot

Preheat the oven to 400 degrees.

Using a wire whisk, whip the sugar, yolks, and vanilla in a large bowl for about 20 seconds.

Mix the milk, cream, and arrowroot together and bring to a boil in a saucepan. Gradually add to the yolk mixture in a thin stream, whipping constantly.

Pour the mixture into eight petit pot molds or ½-cup ramekins. Set them in a large baking

pan and add enough lukewarm water to the pan to come about halfway up the sides of the molds. Bake for 30 minutes, or until just set. (Do not allow the water in the pan to boil, or the custard will become grainy. Should it boil, add enough ice cubes or cold water to stop the boiling.)

Remove from the oven and let cool, then cover and refrigerate until thoroughly chilled. (*The pots de crème can be refrigerated for up to 2 days.*)

Serve in their little pots or ramekins.

Bread-and-Butter Pudding
Serves 4 to 6

⚹ **One of my favorite** desserts, especially during the Christmas holidays, this British pudding is flavored with candied lemon rind. Buttered browned baguette slices are covered with a rich custard, topped with almonds, and baked in a gratin dish. The pudding is best served cool (but not ice-cold) or at room temperature.

Serve with whipped cream or crème anglaise for a richer effect.

- 8 strips lemon rind, removed with a vegetable peeler
- ⅓ cup granulated sugar
- ½ cup water
- 2 cups milk
- 10 thin (⅜-inch-thick) slices baguette, preferably 1 or 2 days old
- 2 tablespoons unsalted butter
- ⅓ cup golden raisins
- 2 large eggs
- 2 large egg yolks

1 teaspoon pure vanilla extract

⅓ cup heavy cream

3 tablespoons sliced almonds

1 teaspoon confectioners' sugar

 Whipped cream for serving (optional)

Preheat the oven to 375 degrees.

Stack the lemon rind strips and cut them into thin julienne strips. (You should have about ¼ cup.) Put the strips in a saucepan with 2 cups water and bring to a boil. Boil for 10 seconds, drain in a strainer, and rinse the saucepan and the julienne strips under cool running water.

Return the julienne strips to the saucepan, add the sugar and the ½ cup water, and bring to a boil. Boil for 7 to 8 minutes, until the sugar cooks down to a syrup. Remove the pan from the heat and add 1 cup of the milk. Mix well to dilute the syrup and set aside.

Arrange the bread slices in one layer on a cookie sheet and bake for 8 to 10 minutes, until nicely browned. Remove from the oven and let cool to lukewarm. (Do not turn the oven off.)

Spread the butter generously on one side of each slice of bread. Arrange the slices buttered side down in one layer in a 5-cup gratin dish. Sprinkle the raisins on top.

Beat the eggs and egg yolks in a bowl with a fork or whisk until well mixed and smooth. Add the vanilla, cream, the remaining cup of milk, and the milk–lemon rind mixture, stir well, and pour over the bread.

Place the gratin dish on a cookie sheet and sprinkle the almonds on top. Bake for 35 minutes, or until set. Place under a hot broiler for 2 minutes to brown the top if necessary. Let cool to room temperature, then sprinkle with the confectioners' sugar.

Serve the pudding plain, or garnish it with whipped cream or crème anglaise.

Banana Bread Pudding
Serves 6

❧ **An excellent way to** use up extra bananas, this frugal pudding is a simple mixture of whole eggs and milk. It can be assembled and baked ahead, and it is best served at room temperature. Serve it alone or with a dollop of sour cream or a scoop of vanilla ice cream.

3 large eggs

3 cups milk

¾ cup honey

3 ripe bananas, cut into ½-inch-thick slices

12 thin (¼-inch-thick) slices baguette

2 tablespoons confectioners' sugar

Preheat the oven to 375 degrees.

Beat the eggs gently with a whisk in a bowl, then add the milk and honey and mix thoroughly.

Arrange the banana slices in one layer in a 6-cup gratin dish and arrange the bread slices over them, completely covering the bananas. Pour the egg mixture evenly over the bread.

Put the gratin dish on a cookie sheet and bake for about 25 minutes, until set and slightly puffed. If desired, brown under a hot broiler for a few seconds. Remove from the oven and let cool to room temperature.

Just before serving, sprinkle the pudding with the confectioners' sugar.

Cherry Bread Pudding
Serves 6

✄ **This is a great** dessert to make when Bing cherries are in full season. You can also use berries or pieces of plums instead of the cherries.

        3   slices pound cake (3 ounces), toasted and cut into ½-inch pieces
        1   cup milk
        1   pound ripe cherries, preferably Bing, pitted
        ½   cup sliced almonds, toasted
        ½   cup cherry preserves
        4   teaspoons granulated sugar
        1   teaspoon unsalted butter
            Scant 1 teaspoon confectioners' sugar
        1   cup crème fraîche or plain yogurt (optional)

Preheat the oven to 350 degrees.

Combine the pound cake and milk in a bowl, mixing well, then add the cherries, 6 tablespoons of the almonds, and the cherry preserves.

Mix the remaining 2 tablespoons almonds with 2 teaspoons of the granulated sugar in a small bowl.

Grease a 6-cup gratin dish with the butter and sprinkle with the remaining 2 teaspoons granulated sugar. Pour the cherry mixture into the dish and top with the almond-sugar mixture.

Bake for 35 to 40 minutes, until set and nicely browned. Let cool to lukewarm.

To serve, sprinkle the bread pudding with the confectioners' sugar and serve with the crème fraîche or yogurt, if desired.

Strawberry Summer Pudding
Serves 6

✄ **Although there is no** cooking involved for this pudding, and only a few minutes are needed to assemble the ingredients, the pudding tastes best if it sits overnight. White bread holds the berry puree together. The bread can be replaced by a like amount of sponge or pound cake, and you can, of course, use other types of berries. Make your selection based on what the season and/or your garden has to offer.

        1½   pints (1¼ pounds) strawberries, washed and hulled
        ½   cup sugar
        4   slices firm white bread (4 ounces)
        ¾   cup strawberry jam
        1   cup sour cream (optional)

Cut 12 of the strawberries into thin slices. (You should have about 1¼ cups.) Mix them with 2 tablespoons of the sugar in a bowl and refrigerate.

Process the bread in a food processor to coarse crumbs. (You should have 2 cups.) Transfer to a bowl and set aside.

Add the whole berries, the jam, and the remaining 6 tablespoons sugar to the processor and process until smooth. Transfer to a bowl and lightly fold in the bread crumbs.

Divide the pudding among six 1-cup ramekins or other containers. Cover and refrigerate for at least 2 to 3 hours or, preferably, overnight before serving.

To serve, spoon the reserved berry slices onto six dessert dishes. Unmold the puddings on top and serve with the sour cream, if desired.

English Christmas Pudding
Serves 8 to 10

❧ **Make this dense, intense** pudding weeks ahead and keep it, tightly wrapped, in the refrigerator; as it ages, it will develop more flavor. This recipe has many ingredients, but it's easy to put together. It makes one steamed cake, but the recipe can be tripled to make several puddings to give as gifts and serve to friends during the holiday season, as is done in England before Christmas.

PUDDING

- 2 ounces beef suet (white fat from steak can be used), cut into ½-inch pieces
- 2 slices firm white bread (2 ounces)
- ¾ cup all-purpose flour
- 2 large eggs
- ½ cup dark rum
- 1 tablespoon grated lemon rind
- 1 tablespoon grated orange rind
- 2 tablespoons fresh lemon juice
- 2 tablespoons fresh orange juice
- ½ teaspoon ground allspice
- ¼ teaspoon ground cinnamon
- ⅛ teaspoon ground cloves
- 2 teaspoons pure vanilla extract
- ¼ cup packed light brown sugar
- ½ cup dark raisins
- ½ cup golden raisins
- ⅓ cup diced (¼-inch) dried apricots
- ½ cup diced (¼-inch) dried apples
- ⅓ cup diced (¼-inch) prunes
- ⅓ cup diced (¼-inch) dried pears
- ⅓ cup diced (¼-inch) dried peaches
- ½ cup walnut pieces (¼-inch)

SOAKING SYRUP

- 2 tablespoons confectioners' sugar
- 2 tablespoons cognac
- 1 tablespoon fresh lemon juice

HARD SAUCE

- 12 tablespoons (1½ sticks) unsalted butter, softened
- ½ cup confectioners' sugar
- ¼ cup Scotch

FOR THE PUDDING: Put the suet, bread, and flour into a food processor and process until the fat is well ground and the mixture is smooth. Add the eggs, rum, lemon and orange rind and juice, allspice, cinnamon, cloves, vanilla, and brown sugar and process until well homogenized.

Transfer the mixture to a 4- to 6-cup round-bottomed, high-sided, heatproof bowl. Add the fruit and walnuts and stir to mix well. Cover with a piece of plastic wrap and refrigerate for at least a few hours, or overnight, so the mixture develops flavor.

Using a piece of plastic wrap, press down on the pudding to pack it tightly into the bowl and to eliminate any air bubbles. Leaving the plastic wrap in place, wrap the bowl completely in aluminum foil to seal it and place it in a large pot that is deep enough to contain it completely. Pour enough lukewarm water around the bowl to come approximately three quarters of the way up the sides of the bowl.

Place the pot over high heat and bring the water to a boil, then reduce the heat to very low, cover the pot, and steam the pudding for about 5 hours. The water should not boil; it should be maintained at a heat of 160 to 180 degrees. Replenish the water occasionally as necessary to keep it at the appropriate level. (Alternatively, place the covered pot in a 180-degree oven for 5 hours.)

When the pudding is cooked, carefully remove it from the pot. Remove the foil and plastic wrap. The internal temperature of the pudding should be about 180 degrees. Unmold the pudding onto a large piece of plastic wrap; it should slide out of the bowl easily. Let cool, then wrap tightly in plastic wrap and refrigerate (it will keep for several weeks) or freeze.

At serving time, return the cake to the bowl in which it was cooked, cover with plastic wrap and aluminum foil, and steam it again in the same manner for about 1 hour, until warm in the center.

MEANWHILE, FOR THE SOAKING SYRUP: Mix the confectioners' sugar, cognac, and lemon juice in a bowl, stirring until smooth.

FOR THE HARD SAUCE: Process the butter, confectioners' sugar, and Scotch in a food processor until smooth and spoon into a serving dish.

To serve, unmold the pudding and brush it with the syrup to flavor it. Place the pudding on an attractive serving platter and serve each slice with a dollop of hard sauce on top. Pass the extra hard sauce.

CHRISTMAS CAKE CUBES
Makes 12 cubes

Leftover English Christmas Pudding can be cut into small squares and soaked with a dark rum syrup for an after-dinner treat. These are excellent served with Mocha and Chocolate Cream (page 515) and can replace cookies as an accompaniment to many desserts.

RUM SYRUP

- 1 tablespoon dark rum
- 2 teaspoons water
- 2 teaspoons sugar
- 2 slices (about 1 inch thick) leftover English Christmas Pudding (page 523), cut into 1-inch cubes

FOR THE SYRUP: Mix together the rum, water, and sugar in a small bowl until the sugar is dissolved. Brush the syrup on the cake cubes until they are well soaked. Pass any extra syrup at the table.

Old-Fashioned Rice Pudding with Dried Fruit
Serves 4

✒ **The proportion of liquid** to rice is quite high here, producing a creamy, almost soupy, mixture that is not at all like the tight, pasty rice pudding you may have encountered as a child. I add raisins, apricots, apples, and figs, but you can choose the dried fruits that are most to your liking.

- 4 cups milk, or as needed
- ⅓ cup sugar
- 1½ teaspoons pure vanilla extract
- ½ cup long-grain white rice
- 1 teaspoon grated lemon rind
- ¾ cup diced (½-inch) dried fruits (apricots, figs, apples, etc.) and raisins
- ¾ cup mascarpone or crème fraîche

Bring the 4 cups milk, the sugar, and vanilla to a boil in a saucepan. Add the rice, mix well, and bring back to a boil. Cover, reduce the heat to very low, and simmer, covered, for 45 to 50 minutes, until the rice is very soft. The mixture should still be soupy at this point; if it is not, add enough additional milk to make it soupy.

Add the lemon rind and dried fruits to the pudding, mix, and let cool to room temperature.

To serve, spoon into four dessert dishes and serve with a couple of tablespoons of mascarpone or crème fraîche on top.

Semolina-Cream Pudding
with Apricot Sauce
Serves 6 to 8

❧ **I love desserts made** with semolina cooked in milk; they represent a taste of my youth. I flavor this custardy dessert with vanilla and grated orange and lemon rind, adding a bit of gelatin so the pudding is firm enough to be unmolded. Served with apricot preserves flavored with lemon juice and bourbon, this is an ideal party dessert.

PUDDING

  2½ cups milk
  1 tablespoon grated orange rind
  1 tablespoon grated lemon rind
  1 teaspoon pure vanilla extract
  ¼ cup fine semolina
  1 envelope (about 2 teaspoons) gelatin
  ⅓ cup sugar
  ½ cup heavy cream

APRICOT SAUCE

  ¾ cup (about 8 ounces) apricot preserves
  2 tablespoons fresh lemon juice
  2 tablespoons bourbon
  2 teaspoons julienned lemon rind

FOR THE PUDDING: Combine the milk, orange rind, lemon rind, and vanilla in a large saucepan and bring to a boil over medium-high heat.

Meanwhile, mix together the semolina, gelatin, and sugar in a small bowl. When the milk comes to a boil, stir in the semolina mixture and bring back to a boil. Reduce the heat to low and boil gently, stirring occasionally, for 4 to 5 minutes, until the semolina is cooked and the mixture is creamy and thick. Remove from the heat and set aside to cool to lukewarm.

Pour the cream into a small bowl and beat it until firm. Add the cream to the lukewarm semolina mixture and fold it in gently but thoroughly.

Oil an 8-inch round cake pan and line the bottom with a circle of parchment paper to make unmolding the pudding easier. (If you like, you can also lay a 1-inch strip of parchment paper across the bottom of the pan with the ends extending about 1 inch beyond the edges of the pan; pulling gently on these ends will help lift the pudding and release it from the pan.) Pour the semolina mixture into the pan, smooth the top, and cover with plastic wrap. Refrigerate for at least 2 hours, or as long as 48 hours.

FOR THE APRICOT SAUCE: Mix the preserves, lemon juice, bourbon, and julienned rind together in a small bowl. For a thinner sauce, add up to 2 tablespoons water.

To serve, unmold the pudding onto a serving plate, so it is upside down; remove the parchment. Cut into wedges and serve on dessert plates, spooning about 2 tablespoons of the sauce over each serving.

Baked Alaska
Serves 8

❧ **Made of ice cream** surrounded by pound cake, covered with a meringue, and baked briefly just before serving, baked Alaska is always impressive, and the contrast of cold ice cream and hot meringue is sensational. This classic dessert can be assembled ahead and kept in the freezer until ready to bake.

1 pound cake (about 12 ounces)
2 tablespoons espresso or strong coffee
2 tablespoons maple syrup
1 quart vanilla ice cream, slightly softened
6 large egg whites
1 cup granulated sugar
  Confectioners' sugar, for sprinkling

Cut the cake into ½-inch-thick slices. Cover the bottom of a stainless steel platter or other ovenproof platter with some of the slices.

Mix the coffee and maple syrup and pour half of it over the cake slices to moisten them.

Using plastic wrap, press the ice cream into a brick shape. Place the ice cream on the cake, then cover the sides and top of the ice cream with the remaining cake slices. Moisten with the remaining coffee mixture. Place in the freezer until frozen. (*The cake can be frozen for a couple of days.*)

When the cake is frozen, whip the egg whites in a large bowl until stiff. Add the granulated sugar in a steady stream, then beat at high speed for 30 seconds.

Cover the frozen cake with half of the meringue, smoothing the meringue with a spatula and making sure the ice cream is completely covered. Spoon the remaining meringue into a pastry bag fitted with a star tip and decorate the top and sides of the cake. Place back in the freezer until you are ready to bake.

When you are ready to serve, preheat the oven to 425 degrees.

Bake for 10 minutes, or until the meringue is tinged with gold. Sprinkle the baked Alaska with confectioners' sugar. Serve immediately, spooning or cutting the dessert into bowls, or slicing it and arranging in bowls.

Pistachio Floating Island with Strawberry– Black Currant Sauce
Serves 6

✂ **Essentially a baked meringue**, this dessert is light and delicate, the perfect finish after a heavy meal. It must be made ahead so it can chill and set before being unmolded. I make it in a loaf pan, but it can be made in a round cake pan too.

½ teaspoon unsalted butter
5 large egg whites
½ cup sugar
⅓ cup coarsely chopped pistachios
2 large strawberries, washed, hulled, and cut into ¼-inch dice (⅓ cup)

SAUCE
1½ cups strawberries, washed and hulled
½ cup black currant preserves
2 tablespoons crème de cassis

2 tablespoons chopped pistachios

Preheat the oven to 350 degrees. Grease an 8½-by-4½-inch loaf pan (preferably ovenproof glass) with the butter.

Beat the egg whites in a large bowl until stiff. Add the sugar all at once and beat for 20 to 30 seconds. Fold in the pistachios and diced berries and transfer the mixture to the loaf pan.

Set the pan in a small roasting pan and add enough lukewarm water to come halfway up the sides of the loaf pan. Bake for 30 minutes, or until set and lightly browned. Remove the pan from the water bath and allow the dessert to cool on a rack; it will deflate slightly. (*The recipe can be prepared to this point up to 1 day ahead, covered with plastic wrap, and refrigerated.*)

FOR THE SAUCE: Slice 2 or 3 strawberries to use for garnish and set aside. Put the remaining strawberries and the preserves in a food processor and process until pureed. Add the crème de cassis and blend well. (*The sauce can be made up to 1 day ahead and refrigerated.*)

At serving time, unmold the dessert onto a rectangular platter. Sponge up any surrounding liquid with paper towels. Sprinkle the dessert with a little sauce and decorate with the reserved sliced berries and the chopped pistachios. Divide the remaining sauce among six dessert plates, top each with a slice of the cold floating island, and serve.

Iced Grand Marnier Soufflé
Serves 6 to 8

✄ **Iced soufflés are not** real soufflés that cook and inflate in the oven, but look-alike frozen desserts. A 3- to 4-inch-high collar of aluminum foil or parchment paper is attached to the soufflé dish, so the mixture can be molded higher than the sides. When the collar is removed, the dessert looks like a baked soufflé that has just emerged from the oven. It's perfect for a party, and it must

be made ahead. After the soufflé is prepared and frozen hard, wrap it tightly in plastic wrap and then aluminum foil so it doesn't pick up flavors from the freezer.

1	cup sugar
⅓	cup water
1	tablespoon grated orange rind
6	large egg yolks
½	cup Grand Marnier, Cointreau, or homemade orange liqueur (see the sidebar)
2½	cups heavy cream
6–8	ladyfingers, homemade (page 546) or store-bought, or the equivalent amount of sliced génoise or pound cake
1	tablespoon unsweetened cocoa powder

Combine the sugar, water, and orange rind in a saucepan, bring to a boil, and boil for 3 to 4 minutes, until the mixture turns into a light syrup.

Meanwhile, put the yolks in the bowl of an electric mixer.

While beating at high speed, pour the hot syrup in a steady stream over the yolks, then continue beating for 12 to 15 minutes. The mixture should be thick, smooth, and pale yellow. Add ¼ cup of the Grand Marnier or Cointreau and beat for another 30 seconds on high speed.

Whip the cream in a large bowl to a soft peak. With a rubber spatula, fold the whipped cream into the soufflé mixture. Cover the bottom of a 1-quart soufflé dish with a thick layer of the mixture (about 2 inches thick). Arrange the ladyfingers or cake slices on top. Sprinkle with the remaining ¼ cup liqueur. Fill the dish right to the top with more of the cream mixture; refrigerate the remainder.

Using a doubled long sheet of aluminum foil or parchment paper, make a collar around the dish, so it extends 2 to 3 inches above the rim, and tie securely with kitchen twine. Place the dish in the freezer for 1 hour, or until it is firm.

When the frozen soufflé mixture is firm, add the remainder of the mixture, which should bring the soufflé to at least 2 inches above the rim of the dish. Return to the freezer until frozen.

About 30 minutes before serving, transfer the soufflé to the refrigerator.

Just before serving, sprinkle the top of the soufflé with the cocoa. Remove the collar and serve.

HOMEMADE ORANGE LIQUEUR

Grand Marnier, a liqueur made of cognac and a distillate of oranges, is expensive. Here's an alternative.

Remove the rind from 7 or 8 oranges with a vegetable peeler. Drop the rind into a bottle and cover it with 3 cups good brandy or Armagnac. Add 2 tablespoons sugar. Shake the bottle a few times to dissolve the sugar. Let stand for 3 weeks to 1 month.

Cold Caramel Lime Soufflé with Lime Sauce
Serves 8 to 10

✶ **Delicate and light, this** caramel lime soufflé can be served hot or cold. To serve cold, make it ahead, at least 5 hours before serving, but preferably the day before, then unmold and serve it cold with a lime sauce.

The soufflé dish is coated with caramel and the soufflé is baked in a water bath. Soufflés cooked in this manner rise evenly without cracking and will hold their height for 15 to 20 minutes after they come out of the oven.

CARAMEL

- 2 cups sugar
- ½ cup water

SAUCE

- ⅓ cup fresh lime juice
- 1 tablespoon water
  Half the caramel (from above)
- 2 tablespoons pear brandy or Grand Marnier

SOUFFLÉ

- 5 large eggs, separated, plus 1 large egg white
- ¼ cup sugar
- 2 tablespoons cornstarch
- 1 teaspoon pure vanilla extract
  Grated rind of 1 lime
- 1¼ cups milk

FOR THE CARAMEL: Combine the sugar and water in a saucepan and stir gently, just enough to moisten the sugar. Bring to a boil and cook over high heat, without stirring, until the mixture turns a golden caramel color, 10 to 12 minutes.

Immediately pour half the caramel into a 6-cup soufflé dish. Incline the dish on its side, holding it over a cookie sheet to catch any drippings, and, using a bristle brush (not nylon), turn the dish and brush the caramel over the inside as it flows, until the sides of the dish are completely coated. Work quickly, to finish coating the dish before the caramel hardens. Set aside.

FOR THE SAUCE: Add the lime juice and water to the remaining caramel and bring to a boil, stirring until the mixture is liquid. Remove from the heat and let cool, then refrigerate.

FOR THE SOUFFLÉ: Preheat the oven to 350 degrees.

Combine the egg yolks, sugar, cornstarch, vanilla, and grated lime rind in a bowl and mix well with a whisk.

Bring the milk to a boil in a medium saucepan and gradually whisk it into the egg yolk mixture. Pour back into the saucepan and bring to a boil, stirring with the whisk, especially around the bottom edges of the saucepan, to prevent the mixture from scorching. As soon as it comes to a boil (it should be thick and smooth), remove from the heat.

Beat the 6 egg whites in a large bowl until firm. Add one quarter to one third of them to the egg yolk mixture, mixing them in well with the whisk to lighten the mixture. Then add the soufflé base to the rest of the beaten egg whites and fold in with a spatula. Work quickly to prevent the mixture from getting grainy; it should not take more than 20 to 30 seconds.

Pour the mixture into the caramel-lined soufflé dish. Place the dish in a baking pan and surround it with enough lukewarm water to come halfway up its sides. Bake for about 1 hour and 10 minutes. The soufflé should have risen at least a couple of inches above the dish and be brown on top. (The soufflé will hold its shape for 15 to 20 minutes and can be served hot, if desired, with the lime sauce.)

To serve the soufflé cold, allow it to cool, then refrigerate for at least 5 to 6 hours, or overnight, covered (so the edges of the soufflé dish don't dry out and get sticky from the sugar, thus causing the soufflé to stick to the sides; also, if covered, the soufflé will develop moisture and the outside will stay moist). The soufflé will sink down, but not much below its original volume before baking.

At serving time, stir the pear brandy or Grand Marnier into the lime sauce.

With the tips of your fingers, pull the edges of the soufflé gently toward the center to loosen it all around. Unmold the soufflé onto a serving

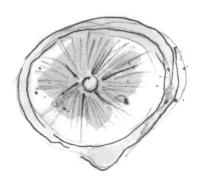

platter; it will slide out easily. Coat with some of the sauce. Cut the soufflé into wedges and serve with the remaining sauce.

Warm Chocolate Fondue Soufflés
Serves 4

✖ In **both texture and** taste, these individual desserts have elements of soufflé, cake, and pudding. They remain slightly runny in the center. To make them ahead, bake them for about 5 minutes only, then cool, cover, and refrigerate for up to 24 hours. When you're ready to serve, heat them in a preheated 350-degree oven for 5 minutes, or until warm inside and still slightly runny.

3   tablespoons unsalted butter
3   ounces bittersweet chocolate, coarsely chopped
1½ tablespoons sugar
2   large eggs, separated
1   teaspoon pure vanilla extract
¼   cup sour cream (optional)

Preheat the oven to 350 degrees.

Heat about 2 cups water in a small saucepan. Reserve ½ teaspoon of the butter for the bowls and combine the chocolate, the remaining butter, and 1 tablespoon of the sugar in a heatproof bowl. Place the bowl over the hot water and stir occasionally until the chocolate and butter are melted. (Alternatively, melt the chocolate, butter, and sugar in a preheated 180-degree oven or in a microwave.)

Beat the egg whites in a bowl until they hold a soft peak, then add the remaining ½ tablespoon sugar and beat for another 5 seconds. (The whites should not be too stiff.)

Add the yolks and vanilla to the melted chocolate mixture and mix them in well. The mixture will thicken. Add the beaten whites and mix them in with a rubber spatula until well combined.

Arrange four ¾- to 1-cup ovenproof bowls, ramekins, or aluminum foil cupcake molds on a cookie sheet and butter them with the reserved ½ teaspoon butter. Divide the batter among the bowls. Bake for 10 minutes; the soufflés still should be soft and runny in the center. Let them rest for 5 to 10 minutes.

Unmold the soufflés onto four individual dessert plates and serve each dessert with 1 tablespoon of the sour cream on top, if desired.

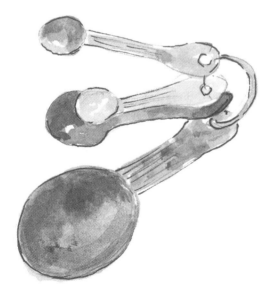

Apricot and Pistachio Soufflé
Serves 6

❧ **Made from a puree** of dried apricots, egg whites, and crushed pistachios, this intensely flavored soufflé is sweetened by the corn syrup in the apricot puree, which also helps the soufflé hold together during cooking and prevents it from cracking.

The soufflé mixture can be made a couple of hours ahead and placed in the prepared dish. Although the soufflé is served hot here, it can be cooled, unmolded, sliced into wedges, and served with the whipped cream.

    8   ounces dried apricots
    1   teaspoon unsalted butter
    2   tablespoons granulated sugar
    ⅓   cup light corn syrup
    5   large egg whites
    ½   cup pistachios, skinned and crushed

WHIPPED CREAM

    1   cup heavy cream
    2   tablespoons confectioners' sugar
    1   teaspoon pure vanilla extract

    Confectioners' sugar, for dusting

Mix the dried apricots with 2 cups water in a saucepan and bring to a boil, then reduce the heat and simmer gently for 25 minutes. Most of the moisture should be gone.

Meanwhile, preheat the oven to 375 degrees. Coat a 6-cup soufflé dish with the butter and sprinkle the granulated sugar over the entire surface.

Drain the apricots in a sieve and discard the liquid. Put the apricots in a food processor with the corn syrup and process until pureed. Transfer to a large bowl.

Beat the egg whites in a large bowl until stiff. Using a whisk, mix approximately one third of the beaten whites into the apricot mixture. Then add the rest of the beaten egg whites, with ⅓ cup of the crushed pistachios, and fold in gently and quickly with a rubber spatula; this should not take more than 20 to 25 seconds. Reserve the extra pistachios for use as a garnish.

Spoon the mixture into the prepared soufflé dish. Smooth the top with a spatula and then, holding the spatula on edge, press it gently into the top of the soufflé to form lines and create a crisscross pattern. Run your finger all around the dish to clean the edges and recess the soufflé slightly.

Place on a cookie sheet and bake for 25 to 30 minutes. The soufflé should be well set in the center and nicely browned.

MEANWHILE, MAKE THE WHIPPED CREAM: Combine the cream with the confectioners' sugar and vanilla in a bowl and whip just until it holds a shape. Refrigerate until ready to serve.

To serve, spoon 1 or 2 spoonfuls of the cream onto each individual plate, spread it out on the plate, and sprinkle with some of the reserved pistachios. Dust the soufflé with confectioners' sugar as soon as it has emerged from the oven and spoon onto the plates. Serve immediately.

Mango Soufflé with Mango Sauce
Serves 4

The flesh of two ripe mangoes is pureed, then half the puree is strained to make the sauce and the remainder is combined with beaten egg whites for the soufflé. (Be sure to use ripe mangoes.) Because there are no egg yolks in the base — it consists solely of the puree, egg whites, and a little sugar — it will keep, refrigerated, for a few hours before baking, provided the egg whites are well beaten and stiff. In fact, the unbaked soufflé can even be frozen for up to 2 weeks.

1	teaspoon unsalted butter
¼	cup granulated sugar
2	very large ripe mangoes (about 1 pound each)
2	tablespoons grenadine
2	tablespoons raspberry brandy or Grand Marnier
2	tablespoons water
3	large egg whites
1	teaspoon confectioners' sugar
2	kiwis, peeled and cut into ½-inch dice (⅔ cup)

Preheat the oven to 375 degrees. Using the butter and 1 tablespoon of the sugar, butter and sugar a 4-cup soufflé dish.

Peel and pit the mangoes. Puree the flesh in a food processor. (You should have 2 cups.) Set 1 cup of the puree aside in a bowl large enough to hold the finished soufflé mixture.

Strain the remaining puree through a fine strainer into a small bowl. (You should have about ¾ cup.) Add the grenadine, raspberry brandy or Grand Marnier, and water to the puree. Cover the sauce and refrigerate.

Beat the egg whites in a bowl until stiff. Add the remaining 3 tablespoons sugar and beat for a

few more seconds. Add about half of the beaten whites to the reserved mango puree and mix with a whisk. Then, working as quickly as you can, gently but thoroughly fold in the rest of the egg whites with a rubber spatula.

Fill the prepared dish with the soufflé mixture. Smooth the top, then decorate it with ridges or lines, if desired, using a knife or metal spatula. (*At this point, you can refrigerate the soufflé, uncovered, for a couple of hours, or freeze it; see the Note.*)

Place the soufflé in the oven and bake for about 25 minutes, until puffed and golden on top.

Sprinkle the hot soufflé with the confection-ers' sugar. Divide the sauce among four dessert plates and sprinkle the diced kiwi on top. Bring the soufflé to the table and serve large spoonfuls of it on top of the sauce.

NOTE: To freeze the unbaked soufflé, freeze it, uncovered, until solid, at least 12 hours, then cover it with plastic wrap — which won't stick to the frozen soufflé — and freeze for up to 2 weeks. Remove the soufflé from the freezer 1 hour before baking, peel off the plastic wrap, and let sit in the refrigerator to partially defrost. Preheat the oven to 375 degrees and bake for 35 to 40 minutes, until it is puffed, golden, and set.

BEATING EGG WHITES

When beating egg whites, use eggs right from the refrigerator. Cold contracts, so if your whites are cold, they'll beat into very small, tight bubbles that hold well. Lukewarm egg whites give greater volume but may become too airy and break down. (If possible, use fresh organic eggs from a farm, which are higher in albumin and can be beaten cold or at room temperature without breaking down.)

Eggs beaten in a copper bowl (cleaned well with vinegar and salt or copper polish) have a nice spongy texture that's perfect for a soufflé. A chemical reaction between the copper and the egg whites lowers the pH, or acidifies the whites, giving them the proper texture. If you are not using a copper bowl, add a few drops of lemon juice or vinegar or a bit of cream of tartar to acidify the egg whites.

I prefer to beat small quantities of egg whites by hand, because in a stand electric mixer, the whisk follows a path without any deviation, so a portion of the whites won't get mixed in, and that can make the whites grainy. However, for 10 or more whites, the electric mixer is my choice.

If you do beat the egg whites by machine, finish them by hand. Use a large flexible balloon whisk and beat them for a few seconds in a 12- to 14-inch bowl.

Cranberry Soufflés with Cranberry–Red Wine Sauce
Serves 4

❀ **Fresh cranberries are cooked** with a little sugar and preserves, then some of the mixture is pureed and folded into egg whites for the soufflés; the rest is combined with wine for a sauce. Small disposable aluminum foil molds can be used, or the soufflés can be baked in ceramic, glass, or metal molds.

The soufflés can be refrigerated for a few hours, or even frozen, before cooking.

    1   12-ounce package cranberries
    ⅓   cup granulated sugar
    ½   cup cherry or seedless blackberry
          preserves
    ¼   cup water
    1   tablespoon unsalted butter
    ¾   cup fruity dry red wine (such as
          Cabernet Sauvignon or Merlot)
    3   large egg whites
        Confectioners' sugar, for sprinkling

Combine the cranberries, sugar, preserves, and water in a large stainless steel saucepan and bring to a boil over medium-high heat. Cover, reduce the heat to very low, and cook gently for 20 minutes. (You will have about 1¾ cups.) Transfer to a medium bowl and let cool.

Preheat the oven to 375 degrees. Butter four ¾-cup aluminum foil, ovenproof glass, or ceramic molds or ramekins with the 1 tablespoon butter. Set aside.

Transfer ¾ cup of the cranberry mixture to a food processor and process until smooth. Add the red wine and process briefly, then strain the mixture through a fine strainer into a bowl. Set the sauce aside until serving time.

Beat the egg whites in a bowl until they are firm. Working as quickly as you can, fold them into the remaining cooked cranberries. Fill the prepared molds with the mixture.

Arrange the molds on a cookie sheet and bake for 13 to 15 minutes, until they are puffy on top and set in the center. If the soufflés begin to darken on top after 10 to 12 minutes, place a sheet of aluminum foil loosely on top of them for the remainder of the cooking period.

To serve, sprinkle the hot soufflés with the confectioners' sugar. Divide the sauce among four plates. Using a large spoon, scoop the soufflés from the molds and place one in the center of each plate. Serve immediately.

NOTE: The assembled soufflés can be refrigerated for a couple of hours before baking and then baked as directed; they can also be frozen. Freeze them uncovered until firm, then cover and freeze for up to 2 weeks. Place the frozen soufflés on a cookie sheet and bake, directly from the freezer, in a preheated 375-degree oven for about 20 minutes.

Crepes Suzette
Serves 4 (makes 12 to 15 crepes)

❀ **In French restaurants, crepes** Suzette are often made at the table. First, lumps of sugar are rubbed over oranges so they absorb the essential oil in the skins and are cooked with butter and orange juice almost to a caramel. The crepes are then dipped in the mixture to coat them on each side, sprinkled with cognac and Grand Marnier, and flamed. Since only 3 or 4 crepes can be flambéed at a time, this method is less than ideal for serving groups at home. In my recipe, the crepes are made ahead, placed on an ovenproof platter, broiled, and then flamed at the table.

The orange butter is also excellent spread on cake layers as an orange buttercream.

As you make crepes, stack them one on top of the other to prevent them from drying out.

CREPES

- ¾ cup all-purpose flour
- 2 large eggs
- ½ cup milk
- ⅛ teaspoon salt
- ½ teaspoon sugar
- ⅓ cup cold water
- 2 tablespoons canola oil
  About 1 tablespoon unsalted butter, for the pan

ORANGE BUTTER

- 6 tablespoons (¾ stick) unsalted butter, softened
- ¼ cup sugar
- 1 tablespoon grated orange rind
  Juice of 1 orange (⅓ cup)

- 1 tablespoon unsalted butter, softened
- 3½ tablespoons sugar
- ½ cup cognac or bourbon
- ¼ cup Grand Marnier, Cointreau, or homemade orange liqueur (see page 528)

FOR THE CREPES: Combine the flour, eggs, ¼ cup of the milk, the melted butter, salt, and sugar in a bowl and mix well with a whisk. (The mixture will be thick and smooth.) Add the remaining milk, the cold water, and oil. Stir well.

Heat a 6-inch crepe pan or skillet, preferably nonstick, and butter it lightly (butter it only for the first crepe). Pour about 3 tablespoonfuls of the batter into one side of the skillet and immediately tilt the skillet, shaking it at the same time, to make the batter run all over the bottom. (The speed at which the batter spreads determines the thickness of the crepe; if you do not move the skil-

let fast enough, the batter will set before it has a chance to spread, and the crepe will be thicker than desired.) Cook over medium-high heat for about 1 minute, until browned. To flip, bang the skillet on a pot holder on the corner of the stove to loosen the crepe, then flip it over. Or, lift up an edge of the crepe with your fingers or a fork, grab the crepe between your thumb and forefinger, and turn it over. Cook for about 30 seconds on the other side and transfer to a plate. Notice that the side of the crepe that browned first has the nicer color; be sure to serve the crepes so that this is the side that is visible. Repeat with the remaining batter, stacking the crepes (you should have 12 to 15 crepes).

FOR THE ORANGE BUTTER: Put the butter, sugar, and grated orange rind in a food processor and process until the mixture is a uniform orange color. With the machine running, add the juice slowly, so that the butter absorbs it.

Spread approximately 1 tablespoon of the orange butter on each crepe. Fold the crepes into quarters. Butter a large ovenproof platter about 17 inches by 10 inches with the softened butter and sprinkle it with 1½ tablespoons of the sugar. Arrange the stuffed crepes on it, overlapping them slightly and leaving a space at the end of the platter where the sauce can accumulate.

Preheat the broiler. Sprinkle the crepes with the remaining 2 tablespoons sugar and place them under the broiler (approximately in the middle of the oven, so they won't burn) for 2 to 3 minutes, until the surface of the crepes caramelizes.

Pour the cognac or bourbon and orange liqueur on the very hot crepes and carefully ignite with a long match. Bring the platter to the table and incline it slightly so that the flaming juices gather in the space you left. Spoon up the liquid and pour it back, still flaming, onto the crepes. When the flame subsides, serve the crepes, 2 or 3 per person, with some of the sauce.

When making crepes, the quantity of liquid in the batter can be changed to make the crepes thicker or thinner. Milk or a mixture of milk and water is usually used, but some recipes use cream or even beer. The number of eggs varies from recipe to recipe as well. Cream or extra egg yolks make a crepe that is tender and soft but difficult to turn. The more water and less fat, the more the batter is like a bread dough, making a crepe that's stronger and more elastic.

Crepe batter does not have to rest before it can be used. When it rests, it tends to thicken slightly, but this is barely noticeable in the final product.

There are special steel crepe pans that have very short sides, which makes it easy to flip crepes. However, any pan that has a non-stick surface is fine. I usually use a pan that is 6 inches in diameter.

Crepes can be made ahead and stacked, especially if they are to be stuffed or used in Crepes Suzette (page 533), then reheated as necessary. If you cover them with plastic wrap so that they don't dry out and absorb other flavors, they will keep well for a couple of days in the refrigerator. They can also be frozen.

Crepes with Jam

Serves 4 (makes about 12 crepes)

✃ **As children, my brother** and I would sit and watch my mother prepare crepes. We ate them as quickly as they came out of the pan — usually with homemade jam, but sometimes with just a lump of butter and a sprinkling of sugar or a little grated chocolate. Now I duplicate this treat and make large crepes for my daughter and grand-daughter for breakfast.

The crepes are best made and filled just before eating.

- ¾ cup all-purpose flour
- 2 large eggs
- ½ teaspoon sugar
- ¾ cup milk
- 3 tablespoons unsalted butter, melted
- 1½ teaspoons canola oil

FILLINGS

Jam or preserves (strawberry, apricot, quince, blackberry, plum, or the like), sugar, or grated chocolate

Combine the flour, eggs, sugar, and ¼ cup of the milk in a bowl and mix with a whisk until smooth. (The mixture will be fairly thick.) Add the remaining ½ cup milk and the butter and mix until smooth.

Lightly grease the bottom of an 8- or 9-inch nonstick skillet with the canola oil and heat the pan over medium-high heat. When it is hot, add about ¼ cup of the crepe batter and quickly tilt and move the skillet so the batter coats the entire bottom of the pan. (Work fast, or the batter will set before the bottom of the skillet is coated, and the crepe will be thicker than desired.) Cook for about 1 minute on the first side, then flip the crepe over using a fork, your fingers, or a spatula, and cook for about 30 seconds on the other side. Transfer the crepe to a plate, with the side that browned first down, so that when the crepes are filled and folded, this nicer side will be visible. Repeat with the remaining batter (there is no need to grease the skillet again), stacking the crepes.

To fill, spread each crepe with about 2 teaspoons jam or sprinkle with 1 teaspoon sugar or 2 teaspoons grated chocolate. Fold in half, enclosing the filling, and then in half again. Eat immediately, while still warm.

Frangipane Crepes with Tangerine Sauce
Serves 4 to 6 (makes 12 filled crêpes)

This complex dish has several subrecipes: crepes; frangipane, a pastry-cream filling flavored with ground almonds; and a tangerine custard sauce made with mandarin orange brandy or Cointreau. Serve the crepes lukewarm.

CREPES

- ¾ cup all-purpose flour
- ½ teaspoon sugar
- ⅛ teaspoon salt
- 2 large eggs
- ¾ cup milk
- 2 tablespoons unsalted butter, melted
- 2 tablespoons dark rum
- 1 teaspoon canola oil

SAUCE

- 1 large egg
- 2 large egg yolks
- ⅓ cup sugar
- ½ cup tangerine juice
- 1 tablespoon fresh lemon juice
- 2 teaspoons cornstarch
- ⅔ cup water

- ¾ cup heavy cream
- 1 tablespoon mandarin orange brandy or Cointreau
- 2 teaspoons grated (preferably with a Microplane) tangerine rind

FRANGIPANE CREAM

- ½ cup slivered almonds
- 1 cup milk
- 2 large egg yolks
- ¼ cup sugar
- 1½ tablespoons cornstarch
- 2 tablespoons unsalted butter, softened
- 1 tablespoon dark rum

GARNISHES

Reserved toasted almonds
Strip of tangerine rind, removed with a vegetable peeler

FOR THE CREPES: Whisk together the flour, sugar, salt, eggs, and ¼ cup of the milk in a bowl. You will notice that the batter is thick and lumpy; work the batter with a whisk without adding more liquid. (Because the mixture is thick, the wires of the whisk will break down any lumps in the flour and make the batter smooth.) When it is smooth, add the remaining ½ cup milk and mix in thoroughly, then add the melted butter and rum and whisk until smooth. The batter should have the consistency of heavy cream; if it is too thick, add up to 2 tablespoons water.

Heat the oil in a 6-inch crepe pan, preferably nonstick. When it is hot, spoon about 3 tablespoons of the batter into the near side of the inclined pan and immediately shake and tilt the pan so the batter spreads over the entire surface of the bottom of the pan. (The thinness of the crepe is determined by the speed with which the batter is spread — as soon as the batter touches the hot pan surface, it will set, and if it is not spread quickly, the crepe will be too thick.) If there are holes in the crepe, they can be filled in with a few drops of batter. (If the batter was liquid enough and was spread quickly, the edges of the crepe will look lacy; this is called a *crêpe dentelle* — the word means "lace" in French. Cook the crepe on the first side for approximately 1 minute. Flip the crepe, or lift up an edge of the crepe with your fingers or a fork, grab the crepe between your thumb and forefinger, and turn it over. Cook for approximately 30 seconds on the other side. Then remove the crepe to a plate, with the side browned first underneath; when the crepe is stuffed and rolled, you want to have this side show, because it looks best. Repeat with the remaining batter, stacking the crepes (there is no need to grease the pan again). Cover with plastic wrap and set aside. (The crepes will stay very moist and pliable and will separate easily when needed.)

Preheat the oven to 400 degrees.

FOR THE SAUCE: Combine the egg, egg yolks, sugar, tangerine juice, lemon juice, cornstarch, and water in a saucepan, whisking until smooth. Bring it barely to a boil over high heat, whisking, and immediately strain through a very fine strainer into a bowl.

Add the cream, brandy or Cointreau, and tangerine rind and mix to blend. Set aside.

FOR THE FRANGIPANE CREAM: Spread the almonds on a cookie sheet and bake for 6 to 8 minutes, until nicely browned. Let cool.

Transfer ½ cup of the almonds to a food processor and process until powdered. (Reserve the remaining almonds for garnish.)

Bring the milk to a boil in a small saucepan.

Meanwhile, beat the egg yolks with the sugar and cornstarch in a bowl. Add the boiling milk to the egg yolk mixture, whisking constantly, then return it to the saucepan and bring to a boil to thicken, mixing with the whisk to keep it from

scorching in the corners of the pan. The cream should be smooth and thick. Strain through a fine-mesh sieve and let cool to lukewarm, then mix in the powdered almonds, butter, and rum.

Spread 1 tablespoon of the frangipane cream on each crepe. Roll up each crepe to make a little cylinder.

To serve, arrange the lukewarm crepes (if necessary, they can be reheated in the oven) on a platter. Coat with some of the sauce and spoon the rest of the sauce around them. Sprinkle the reserved almond slivers on top and decorate with the tangerine rind. Serve.

Orange Soufflé Crepes
Serves 6

✂ **These crepes are folded** over a soufflé mixture, then baked in the oven, where they puff, becoming very light and pretty.

Any soufflé mixture can be used: here I use a cross between an orange soufflé base and a meringue mixture.

1	tablespoon unsalted butter
¾	cup granulated sugar
	Grated (preferably with a Microplane) rind of 1 large orange (about 2 tablespoons)
5	large egg whites
6	crepes (from the recipe Crepes with Jam, page 535)
1	tablespoon confectioners' sugar, plus more for dusting

Preheat the oven to 350 degrees. Use the butter to coat a large stainless steel or other oven-proof platter with a center at least 10 inches by 8 inches and sprinkle it with enough of the sugar to coat the butter.

Mix the remaining ⅔ cup sugar together with the grated orange rind.

Beat the egg whites in a large bowl until firm. Add the sugar mixture fairly quickly and beat for another 30 seconds, or until the mixture is fluffy and shiny.

Arrange the crepes on the platter so that half of each one hangs over the edges. Spoon ½ to ¾ cup of the beaten egg whites on the inner half of each crepe and fold the other half over.

Sprinkle the crepes with 1 tablespoon confectioners' sugar. Bake for about 12 minutes, until puffed. Sprinkle with a bit more confectioners' sugar and serve right away.

Cakes,
Cookies,
and
Candies

Cakes, Cookies, and Candies

Cakes

Chocolate Soufflé Cake with Raspberry-Rum Sauce
Serves 6 to 8

✳ **Fluffy and delicate, this** light cake contains fewer egg yolks and less butter than is customary. Serve warm, with or without the sauce.

CAKE

- 2 tablespoons almond or canola oil
- 6 ounces bittersweet chocolate, coarsely chopped
- 4 tablespoons (½ stick) unsalted butter
- ¼ cup granulated sugar
- 2 tablespoons potato starch (see page 318)
- 2 large eggs, separated
- 4 large egg whites
- ½ teaspoon confectioners' sugar

SAUCE

- ½ cup raspberry preserves, preferably seedless
- 1 tablespoon dark rum
- 1 tablespoon water

Preheat the oven to 325 degrees, with a rack in the center.

FOR THE CAKE: Grease a 3-inch-deep 9-inch round cake pan or springform pan with 1 teaspoon of the oil.

Combine the chocolate, butter, the remaining 5 teaspoons oil, and the sugar in the top of a double boiler (or in a microwave-safe bowl) and heat over boiling water (or in the microwave) until the chocolate and butter have melted. Stir to combine. Add the potato starch and mix it in with a whisk.

Remove from the heat and whisk in the egg yolks; the mixture will thicken.

Whip the egg whites in a large bowl until firm. Fold them lightly and as quickly as possible into the chocolate mixture.

Pour the batter into the pan and bake for about 20 to 25 minutes. The cake should still be soft in the center. Let cool to lukewarm.

Invert the cake onto a plate, then invert again onto a serving platter so it's top side up; or remove the sides of the springform pan and transfer the cake to the platter. Sprinkle with the confectioners' sugar.

FOR THE SAUCE: If not using seedless preserves, strain them. Combine the preserves with the rum and water.

To serve, arrange a slice of cake on each of six to eight dessert dishes and spoon some sauce alongside.

Quick Almond and Plum Cake
Serves 6 to 8

✳ **It takes just a** few seconds to mix the flour, sugar, and almonds for this fast food-processor cake, and then you blend in the remaining ingredients. You can bake the cake in a springform pan or in a loaf pan, like a pound cake.

Made without the plum topping, the cake freezes well. (Do not freeze the cake with the fruit, since it becomes mushy when defrosted.) For best results, wrap the cake carefully in plastic wrap and aluminum foil before freezing it, and defrost it in the refrigerator while still wrapped.

4 tablespoons (½ stick) unsalted butter, softened

1 cup all-purpose flour

1 cup unblanched whole almonds

⅔ cup sugar

1 teaspoon baking powder

1 teaspoon pure vanilla extract

2 tablespoons canola oil

2 large eggs

⅓ cup milk

TOPPING

4–6 ripe plums, preferably Black Friar or Santa Rosa (1¼ pounds)

3 tablespoons sugar

½ cup plum jam

1 tablespoon plum brandy or Calvados

Preheat the oven to 350 degrees, with a rack in the center. Butter a 9-inch springform pan with ½ teaspoon of the butter.

FOR THE CAKE: Process the flour, almonds, sugar, and baking powder in a food processor until the mixture is a coarse powder. Add the vanilla, the remaining butter, the oil, and eggs and process for a few seconds, just until incorporated. Add the milk and process for a few seconds, until the mixture is smooth. Pour the batter into the prepared pan.

FOR THE TOPPING: Using the point of a sharp knife, remove the pit through the stem end of each plum. (If the plums are not fully ripened and feel hard, prick them all over with the point of a sharp knife to soften them.) Rinse the whole plums well under cold water. While they are still wet, roll them in the sugar. Arrange the plums on top of the cake, spacing them evenly, and push them down into the batter until the bottom half of each is immersed.

Place the cake on a cookie sheet and bake

for 50 to 60 minutes, or until puffy and nicely browned on top. Cool on a rack to lukewarm.

Mix the plum jam and brandy together in a small bowl and brush the top of the lukewarm cake with the mixture. Remove the sides of the pan.

To serve, cut the cake into 6 to 8 wedges, so that each serving contains at least half a plum. Serve warm or at room temperature.

Angel Food Cake

Serves 8 to 10

Angel cake is one of the delightful cakes I discovered in America. I like it plain or with berries. My friend and mentor Helen McCully made the best one, and this recipe was inspired by hers.

1 cup sifted confectioners' sugar

1 cup sifted cake flour

¼ teaspoon salt

10 large egg whites

1 teaspoon pure almond extract

½ teaspoon cream of tartar

1¼ cups granulated sugar

Fresh berries, for serving (optional)

Preheat the oven to 350 degrees, with a rack in the center.

Sift together the confectioners' sugar, cake flour, and salt. Set aside.

Combine the egg whites, almond extract, and cream of tartar in the bowl of a stand mixer or a very large stainless steel bowl and beat at high speed until the whites stand in peaks when you lift up the beater. Gradually add the granulated sugar and keep beating for 30 seconds. Carefully sift in the flour mixture and mix with a rubber spatula, folding only until the batter is well combined.

Pour into an ungreased 10-inch tube pan. Bake for 35 minutes, or until the cake springs back when touched lightly. Invert the pan onto a cake rack and let cool; the cake will usually unmold itself.

If the cake clings to the pan, run a sharp thin-bladed knife around the sides of the pan with one long, steady stroke. Invert the cake onto a serving plate, shaking the pan to loosen it. Serve in slices, with berries, if desired.

Custard Cream-of-Wheat Cake with Peaches

Serves 10 to 12

✶ **Light and tender in** texture, this custard wheat cake is similar to a Bavarian cream, with the custard bound by gelatin rather than being baked. It's stunning when surrounded by poached fruit.

You can use semolina, tapioca, or farina instead of Cream of Wheat (only a small quantity is needed). The cake can be made several days ahead, but be sure to use a soufflé dish in that case; the cake will discolor if it sits in a metal savarin mold. After the cake is made and has set, it can be placed upside down on a serving plate, still in the mold, and stored this way until ready to unmold (which will make the unmolding easier).

The poached peaches can also be served on their own.

CAKE

2	teaspoons grated lime rind
3	large egg yolks
½	cup granulated sugar
1	envelope (about 2 teaspoons) gelatin
1	teaspoon pure vanilla extract
1½	cups milk
3	tablespoons instant Cream of Wheat

1½	cups heavy cream
	Safflower or corn oil

PEACHES

1½	cups granulated sugar
5	cups water
1	tablespoon grated lemon rind
3	tablespoons fresh lemon juice
8	peaches (about 2½ pounds)

PEACH SAUCE

1½	cups peach jam or preserves, strained
2	tablespoons pear brandy or cognac

WHIPPED CREAM

1	cup heavy cream
1	tablespoon confectioners' sugar
1	candied violet (optional)

FOR THE CAKE: Mix together the lime rind, egg yolks, sugar, gelatin, and vanilla in a bowl with a whisk.

Bring the milk to a boil in a medium saucepan. Add the Cream of Wheat, return the mixture to a boil, stirring constantly, and cook, stirring, until it thickens into a creamy texture, 2 to 3 minutes. Add to the egg yolk mixture, whisking to incorporate, then return the mixture to the saucepan, place back on the stove, and bring to a boil, stirring. The mixture will thicken slightly. Transfer to a bowl and let cool slightly until tepid. (If the mixture is allowed to set for too long, it will become firm, and folding in the cream will be difficult. If this should occur, reheat it to soften. On the other hand, if the whipped cream is added to the mixture while it is still hot, the cream will melt.)

Whip the heavy cream until it holds a soft peak. Fold it into the Cream of Wheat mixture.

Lightly oil a 6- to 8-cup savarin mold or soufflé dish or a 9-inch round cake pan. Pour the cake mixture into the mold and smooth the top. Cover with plastic wrap. (Refrigerate if not serving within a couple hours.)

FOR THE PEACHES: Combine the sugar, water, and lemon rind and juice in a stainless steel saucepan and bring to a boil. Add the peaches, cover, and return to a boil, then reduce the heat and cook, covered, over low heat until the peaches are tender, 6 to 10 minutes, depending on the ripeness of the peaches. Let the peaches cool in the syrup until lukewarm.

Remove the peaches from the syrup and reduce the syrup to approximately 2 cups by boiling it. Transfer to a bowl.

The skin of the peaches can be removed now or later. If the skin is left on and the peaches are very ripe and stored in the syrup, the skin color will tend to seep into the flesh of the peaches, giving them a nice color. If the skin of the peaches does not slide off easily, peel with a sharp knife or vegetable peeler.

Add the peaches to the syrup. (*The peaches can be prepared up to a day ahead and refrigerated.*)

FOR THE SAUCE: Combine the peach jam, pear brandy or cognac, and a few tablespoons of the syrup from the peaches, enough to make the mixture of spreading consistency. (The remaining syrup can be reserved for poaching other fruits.)

At serving time, turn the mold (or pan) over onto a serving platter and unmold the cake. (You may have to shake the mold or cover it with a towel dipped in warm water to get the cake to unmold.)

Peel the peaches if you have not already done so.

FOR THE GARNISH: Whip the cream with the confectioners' sugar until firm. Spoon into a pastry bag fitted with a star tip and decorate the center of the cake with the whipped cream, or use a spoon to decorate the cake (or spoon a dollop of cream onto each serving). Place the candied violet on top, if desired. Arrange the peaches around the cake and coat them with the peach sauce. Serve.

Vanilla-Bourbon Génoise with Bourbon Buttercream
Serves 10 to 12

A génoise is a basic sponge cake. Its lightness and even crumb is achieved by beating room-temperature eggs with sugar at high speed: the eggs, rather than baking powder, give the cake its lift. The addition of melted butter improves the flavor but tends to deflate the batter. To prevent this, I beat the egg mixture longer than usual so that when everything is incorporated, the texture is correct.

This génoise is sprinkled with a light bourbon syrup and spread with a bourbon buttercream, then decorated with a drizzle of chocolate and a ribbon of buttercream — your own fancy may suggest other designs. The buttercream, made with custard cream and soft butter, is the most classic type.

GÉNOISE

- 4 large eggs
- 1 large egg yolk
- ⅓ cup sugar
- 1½ teaspoons pure vanilla extract
- ¾ cup pastry flour
- 3 tablespoons unsalted butter, melted

BOURBON SYRUP

- 3 tablespoons warm water
- 1 teaspoon pure vanilla extract
- 2 tablespoons sugar
- 3 tablespoons bourbon

BUTTERCREAM

- ¼ cup heavy cream
- 1 cup milk
- 3 large egg yolks
- ⅓ cup sugar
- 2 teaspoons pure vanilla extract

2 tablespoons bourbon

10 ounces (2½ sticks) unsalted butter, softened

OPTIONAL DECORATION

1 ounce bittersweet chocolate, melted (about 1 tablespoon)
  Canola oil

Preheat the oven to 350 degrees, with a rack in the center. Butter and flour a 2-inch-deep 10-inch round cake pan.

FOR THE GÉNOISE: Beat the eggs, yolk, sugar, and vanilla in the bowl of an electric mixer or another large stainless steel bowl, passing the bowl over a flame a few times, until it is about body temperature; or mix over hot water. (When you dip your finger in, you should not feel any change in temperature.) Then beat on medium speed for 8 to 10 minutes, or until the mixture quadruples in volume.

Sift the flour directly on top of the mixture, folding it in gently until well combined. (You can secure the bowl by placing it in a heavy saucepan to keep it steady while folding.) Add the melted butter by sprinkling it on top of the batter and gently folding it in. If poured in too quickly, the butter will sink to the bottom of the bowl; also, the butter will tend to break down the batter, so be gentle and do not overfold.

Pour into the prepared cake pan, place on a cookie sheet, and bake for 25 to 30 minutes, until the cake is nicely browned and the sides have shrunk slightly from the edges of the pan. Remove from the oven and keep in a warm place for 15 to 20 minutes before unmolding.

MEANWHILE, FOR THE SYRUP: Mix the warm water, vanilla, sugar, and bourbon together in a bowl until the sugar dissolves. Set aside.

Unmold the cake onto a wire rack. When cool, place in a plastic bag and refrigerate.

FOR THE BUTTERCREAM: Pour the cream into a medium bowl and have a fine sieve handy; the custard mixture will be strained through the sieve into the cold cream, which will stop further cooking and prevent curdling. (The delicate part of making a custard cream is to keep the eggs from scrambling.)

Pour the milk into a saucepan and bring to a boil.

Meanwhile, put the egg yolks and sugar in a bowl and beat with a whisk for about 30 seconds, until fluffy and pale yellow. Add the boiling milk to the yolk-sugar mixture, whisking constantly, then pour the custard back into the saucepan and cook over medium heat, stirring constantly, until it thickens and reaches about 180 degrees. (It should not take more than 1 minute.) Strain immediately through the sieve into the cold cream and mix well. Add the vanilla and let cool to tepid.

Add the bourbon to the custard; it should be thick enough to coat a spoon.

Meanwhile, beat the softened butter in a large bowl with a whisk until fluffy and soft. Add the custard cream ¼ cup at a time, beating after each addition until smooth and fluffy. Set aside at room temperature.

TO BUILD THE CAKE: Cut a piece of cardboard the size of the bottom of the cake pan. Using a long serrated knife, slice the cake into 3 horizontal layers. As you slice, keep the blade level and rotate the cake; the blade should not be removed from the cake until each cut is complete. (If you find the cutting technique difficult to master, use guides such as spatulas with handles ⅜ to ½ inch thick. Place the spatulas on opposite sides of the cake. The blade of the knife should be long enough to go through the cake and rest on both guides.)

Place the first layer, from the top of the cake, upside down on the cardboard. Brush with bourbon syrup. Spread a thin layer of buttercream on top. Add the second layer. Brush with syrup and coat with buttercream. Place the third layer on top, brush with the remaining syrup, and coat the top with buttercream, spreading it as smoothly as you can with a long thin metal spatula.

Holding the cake up (it will be secure on the cardboard), spread more buttercream as smoothly as possible all around the sides.

FOR THE OPTIONAL DECORATION: Melt the chocolate and add a few drops of oil to it. Make a cornet (see page 565) and pour the chocolate into it. Cut off the tip and draw a design to your liking on top of the cake.

Fill a pastry bag fitted with a star tip with the remaining buttercream and pipe a pattern all around the top edge of the cake. Transfer to a serving platter and refrigerate until serving time. (*If the cake is to be kept for several hours, cover it with plastic wrap after the buttercream has set to prevent it from absorbing the flavor of other foods in the refrigerator.*)

Cut into wedges and serve.

Ladyfingers
Makes 12 to 14 ladyfingers

⚬ **Ladyfingers are often incorporated** into desserts like frozen soufflés (see page 527). In France, they are often served with Champagne. You can buy ready-made ladyfingers at many supermar-

GÉNOISE

Texture is the key to a good génoise. If the egg mixture is underbeaten, the cake will not be moist enough. Overbeating, on the other hand, makes the batter too fluffy, producing a cake that is dry and crumbly. And if the flour is not properly folded in, the cake will be gooey and heavy. Nonetheless, the process is straightforward.

A génoise is unusually versatile, lending itself to an enormous variety of pairings with creams, custards, fruits, and syrups.

kets, but the quality of the homemade is vastly superior. They are crisp on top and moist inside.

> About 1 tablespoon unsalted butter
> ⅓ cup plus 3 tablespoons all-purpose flour
> 2 large eggs, separated
> 1 large egg white
> ½ teaspoon pure vanilla extract
> ⅓ cup confectioners' sugar, plus 2–3 tablespoons for dusting the ladyfingers

Preheat the oven to 325 degrees, with the racks in the center and upper third of the oven. Grease two large baking sheets (about 12 by 18 inches) with the butter. Sprinkle the 3 tablespoons flour on one sheet and shake the sheet to coat it evenly with the flour. Dump the excess flour onto the second sheet and repeat the operation. Bang each sheet upside down over the sink to get rid of excess flour.

Mix the egg yolks, vanilla, and ⅓ cup confectioners' sugar in a bowl with a whisk for 1 minute, until the mixture is pale yellow. Add the remaining ⅓ cup flour and stir gently with the whisk until smooth.

Beat the egg whites until they hold a firm peak. Add half of the whites to the egg yolk mixture and mix with the whisk. (It is important that the whites be incorporated into the mixture very quickly with the whisk; the remaining whites will start to "grain" as soon as they are not being whipped, so you cannot let them sit too long.) Add the remaining whites and fold in with a spatula; do not overwork the mixture.

Scoop some of the batter into a pastry bag fitted with a large plain tip (with an opening of at least ¾ inch) and squeeze out "fingers," approximately 4 inches long and 1½ inches wide, a good inch apart, on one of the prepared baking sheets. Continue until all the batter has been used. Sift confectioners' sugar generously over the ladyfingers. Let sit for 20 to 30 seconds, then sift more sugar onto the ladyfingers.

Bake for 15 to 18 minutes, or until the ladyfingers are a pale beige with a slight crust. After a few minutes out of the oven, lift the ladyfingers from the baking sheets and cool on a rack.

Chocolate Roll
Serves 8

❧ **Light, delicate, and tender,** this chocolate roulade is made without flour and bakes very quickly. It is a bit fragile to roll, but the result is delectable. If it is overcooked, it will break when you roll it; in that case, simply cut the roulade into 4 strips and stack them up with whipped cream in between the layers.

CAKE

½ cup granulated sugar
¼ cup water
6 large eggs, separated
6 ounces semisweet chocolate, melted
2 tablespoons very strong coffee

FILLING

1½ cups heavy cream
2 tablespoons confectioners' sugar
½ teaspoon pure vanilla extract
2 teaspoons kirsch

1 tablespoon unsweetened cocoa powder

Preheat the oven to 375 degrees, with a rack in the center.

FOR THE CAKE: Mix the sugar and water in a saucepan, bring to a boil, and cook over medium heat for 2 minutes to make a light syrup. Set aside.

Put the egg yolks in the bowl of an electric mixer or another large bowl. Slowly pour the hot sugar syrup over the yolks, mixing vigorously with the whisk. Continue whipping the mixture for about 5 minutes, until fluffy, smooth, and pale yellow in color. Add the melted chocolate and coffee and mix well.

Whip the egg whites in a large bowl until they hold firm peaks. Add about one third of the whites to the chocolate mixture and mix vigorously with the whisk. Add the remaining whites and fold in with a rubber spatula, mixing just enough to combine the ingredients; do not overmix.

Cut a piece of parchment paper large enough to line a 11-by-16-inch baking sheet. Butter the paper and coat with flour, shaking off any excess.

Spread the batter in the pan; it will be about ½ inch thick. Bake for about 12 minutes, until set and puffy. Cool to room temperature, then cover with plastic wrap. (Rolling the cake is a delicate operation, but the parchment paper aids in the removal and rolling of the cake. The plastic wrap keeps the cake moist, making it possible to be rolled.)

FOR THE FILLING: Whip the cream until

it holds a soft peak. Add the confectioners' sugar, vanilla, and kirsch and continue beating until the cream is firm.

TO ROLL THE CAKE: Remove the plastic wrap and slide a knife all around the sides to loosen the cake. Spread the whipped cream on the cake. Starting from a long side, roll up the cake, still in the pan, peeling the paper off a little at a time. Avoid pressing down on the cake as you roll, so the whipped cream is not squeezed out. Continue rolling and removing the paper and finish with the seam underneath so the cake is smooth on top. Use two large spatulas to slide the cake onto a serving platter. Put the cocoa powder in a sieve and shake it over the cake to coat the top. Refrigerate until ready to serve.

Cut into slices and serve.

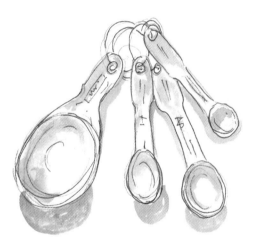

COFFEE AS AN INGREDIENT

Many recipes call for very strong coffee to flavor cakes, creams, or syrup. You can use instant espresso powder mixed with boiling water, or the first few tablespoons of espresso from the machine, or even the initial stream of coffee from a regular coffeemaker, which is stronger than the full portion from the pot.

Bûche de Noël (Christmas Yule Log)
Serves 8

❧ **Years ago it was** the custom in France to burn a Christmas log of great size, which, once lighted, would last through Christmas Eve supper. Apparently this was the inspiration for *bûche de Noël*, one of the most charming traditional French holiday cakes. Usually the *bûche* is a rolled cake that is filled with buttercream, pastry cream, or even currant jelly as it is here and coated with buttercream that is then scored with a fork to imitate tree bark.

CAKE

- 4 large eggs, separated
- ½ cup sugar
- ⅓ cup plus 1 tablespoon all-purpose flour
- 2 tablespoons cornstarch
- 1 tablespoon unsalted butter, melted

BUTTERCREAM

- ⅓ cup sugar
- 2 tablespoons water
- 3 large egg yolks
- ½ pound (2 sticks) unsalted butter, softened
- 2 ounces bittersweet chocolate, melted

- 1 10-ounce jar currant jelly
- 2 tablespoons kirsch

Preheat the oven to 400 degrees, with a rack in the center. Line an 11-by-16-inch baking sheet with parchment paper or a nonstick baking mat.

FOR THE CAKE: Combine the egg yolks and sugar in a large bowl and beat with an electric mixer for about 2 minutes, until the mixture is very light and makes "ribbons" when the beater is lifted. Mix in the flour and cornstarch.

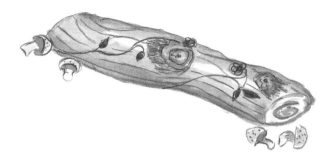

Beat the whites in a large bowl until they hold firm peaks. With a whisk, vigorously beat about one third of the whites into the batter. Then, using a rubber spatula, fold in the remainder. (Go as fast as you can when adding the whites, or they will be grainy.) Finally, fold in the melted butter. Pour into the prepared pan, smoothing the batter evenly so that it touches all sides.

Bake for 12 minutes, or until the cake begins to shrink from the sides of the pan. Let cool for 30 minutes, then cover lightly with plastic wrap and refrigerate until ready to use.

FOR THE BUTTERCREAM: Combine the sugar and water in a small saucepan, bring to a boil, and boil for 3 to 4 minutes over medium heat.

Put the egg yolks in the bowl of an electric mixer fitted with a whisk and add the hot syrup very gradually, beating constantly. Beat for at least 5 minutes to gain the proper texture and consistency. Add the butter bit by bit, beating in each addition thoroughly. (If the buttercream curdles during the addition of the butter, heat it slightly over hot water so the edges start melting and work with a whisk to combine again.) When all the butter has been added, the buttercream should be firm enough to hold a shape. Mix in the melted chocolate. (*If not using immediately, cover and refrigerate for up to 1 day; bring to room temperature before using.*)

TO ASSEMBLE THE BÛCHE DE NOËL: Spoon the currant jelly into a bowl and beat with a fork.

Sprinkle the kirsch all over the surface of the cake. Spread the jelly over the entire surface. Then, starting from a long side, roll up tightly, and transfer to a platter, seam side down. Spread the buttercream thickly over the top and sides, but not the ends. Draw the tines of a fork down the full length of the roll, sides and top, to simulate bark. Refrigerate until ready to serve.

Cut into slices to serve.

Christmas Fruitcake
Makes 1 large cake

✀ **Even without the mixture** of dried and candied fruit, this is a very rich pound cake, but the fruit changes the cake and makes it festive.

The candied citrus peels are homemade — an easy, inexpensive procedure that gives you better-quality candied peels than you can buy. The mixture of peels and dried fruits will keep almost indefinitely covered with rum or cognac and stored in a jar in the refrigerator. They can be added to soufflés as well as to other cakes or fruit salads.

The cake is cooked slowly for a long time, until completely set inside. When cool, it should be wrapped well and refrigerated; it can also be frozen.

You can cut the cake into tiny pieces and use them for petits fours (see page 551).

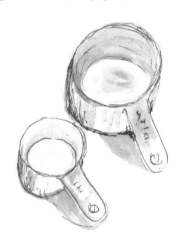

CANDIED PEELS

1	grapefruit
1	tangerine
1	lime
1	lemon
¾	cup sugar
1½	cups water

DRIED FRUIT

½	cup diced (¼-inch) dried apricots
⅓	cup diced (¼-inch) dried pears
⅓	cup diced (¼-inch) dried peaches
⅓	cup raisins
⅓	cup dark rum or cognac

CAKE

10	ounces (2½ sticks) unsalted butter, softened
1	cup sugar
5	large eggs
3	tablespoons orange juice
¼	teaspoon salt
2	cups all-purpose flour
½	cup cake flour, sifted

FOR THE CANDIED PEELS: The candied peels include both the colored part of the skin and the white pith. Score the skin of each fruit into wedges and pull the skin away from the fruit. Cut the peels into ½-inch dice. (The fruit can be used for juice or in salads.)

Add the diced peel to 4 cups cold water in a saucepan, bring to a boil, and cook over high heat for about 1 minute. Drain in a colander and rinse for a few seconds under cold water. (This blanching process removes the bitterness.) Rinse the saucepan with cold water, return the diced peel to the pan, and add another 4 cups water. Repeat the boiling, draining, and rinsing procedure and rinse the saucepan again. Put the diced peel back in the pan, add the sugar and 1½ cups water, and cook

for about 15 minutes, until the liquid is reduced to a very thick syrup and the pieces of skin are shiny and almost transparent. Transfer to a bowl.

FOR THE DRIED FRUIT: Mix the dried apricots, pears, and peaches with the raisins and combine with the candied peels and syrup. Mix in the rum or cognac. (*The mixture can be stored in a jar and kept, refrigerated, almost indefinitely.*)

FOR THE CAKE: Preheat the oven to 350 degrees, with a rack in the center. Cut a strip of parchment paper long enough to run the length of a 9-by-5-inch loaf pan and extend 1½ inches beyond it at either end. (This makes it easy to un-mold the cake after baking.) Butter the pan, bottom and sides, and paper, and position the paper in the pan, pressing to make it adhere to the bottom and ends.

Beat the butter and sugar in the bowl of an electric mixer or another large bowl until light and creamy, about 40 seconds. Add the eggs, orange juice, salt, all-purpose flour, and cake flour and beat with the flat beater or a handheld mixer just enough to incorporate. Add the candied peel and dried fruit and fold in gently with a spatula.

Pour the batter into the prepared pan and smooth the top with a spatula. Place the loaf pan on a cookie sheet and bake for 45 minutes.

Reduce the heat to 325 degrees and bake for another 60 to 70 minutes, until the cake is completely set inside; a skewer inserted in the center should come out clean. Allow the cake to cool in the pan.

When the cake is cool, unmold it and wrap in plastic wrap and/or aluminum foil, and keep in the refrigerator, or freeze.

At serving time, cut the cake into ½-inch-thick slices and serve.

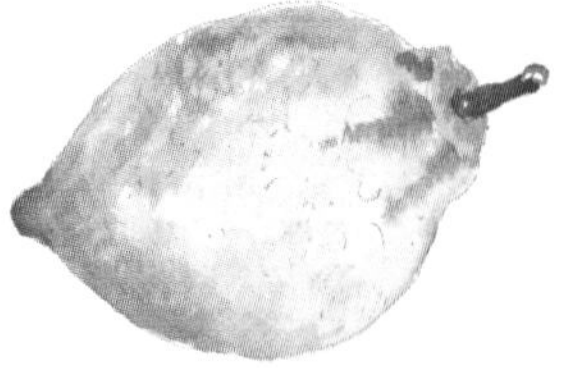

FRUITCAKE FINGERS

Makes 12 fingers

These colorful petits fours are made by cutting leftover fruitcake into little strips and soaking them with cognac syrup.

   2   1-inch-thick slices leftover Christmas
        Fruitcake (page 549)

(page 549)

SYRUP

   1   tablespoon cognac
   1½   teaspoons water
   2   teaspoons sugar

Trim the slices of cake and cut them into strips about 2 inches long by ½ inch wide.

Mix the cognac, water, and sugar in a small bowl until the sugar is dissolved. Using a brush, saturate the cake fingers with the syrup. Arrange on a plate and serve as after-dinner petits fours.

Cheesecake with Apricot-Blueberry Sauce

Serves 8 to 10

✄ **This cheesecake recipe remains** my wife's favorite and was also a favorite of my brother, who discovered it on his first trip to America. It's dense and rich, yet delicate. I like it served cool, but not ice-cold. The apricot-blueberry sauce not only is delectable, but also looks stunning.

Don't use frozen blueberries, which would bleed through the sauce.

CHEESECAKE

   2   tablespoons unsalted butter, softened
   ½   cup graham cracker crumbs

   4   8-ounce packages cream cheese,
        at room temperature
   1   cup sugar
   1   tablespoon grated lemon rind
   2   tablespoons fresh lemon juice
   1   teaspoon pure vanilla extract
   4   large eggs

SAUCE

   1   12-ounce jar apricot preserves
   2   tablespoons water
   3   tablespoons apricot brandy or
        plum brandy (slivovitz)
   1   cup fresh blueberries

Preheat the oven to 350 degrees, with a rack in the center.

FOR THE CHEESECAKE: Butter a 3- to 4-inch-deep 8-inch round cake pan or an 8-inch soufflé dish with the butter. Add the crumbs and shake the pan (best done over the sink), tipping it back and forth, to coat the sides and bottom of the pan with the crumbs.

Process the cheese, sugar, lemon rind and juice, and vanilla extract in a food processor for 20 seconds. Add the eggs and process for another 30 seconds, or until smooth. Pour the batter into the prepared cake pan.

Place the cake pan in a roasting pan and add enough lukewarm water to reach at least two thirds of the way up the cake pan. Bake for 1 hour. (The water should not boil around the pan; if it does, add a few ice cubes to lower the temperature.) Turn off the oven and allow the cake to remain in the oven until lukewarm, about 1 hour.

Remove the cake from the oven and allow it to stand for a couple of hours before unmolding. (*The cake can be refrigerated, covered, for several days.*)

To unmold, place a serving platter upside down on top of the pan and invert. If the cake is hard to unmold, the butter in the pan may have set, especially if the cake has been refrigerated. Dip the pan in hot water for a few seconds before inverting. Or, wrap the pan in a hot towel and wait for approximately 1 minute before lifting it off the cake.

FOR THE SAUCE: Combine the preserves, water, and brandy in a bowl, mixing until smooth. Add the blueberries.

Serve each slice of cheesecake with 2 to 3 tablespoons sauce.

Strawberry Fondant Valentines with Glazed Berries

Makes 8 to 10 hearts

✄ **These pretty cakes baked** in individual heart-shaped molds are ideal for Valentine's Day, but the batter can also be baked as a large cake (see Variations, page 554). It takes only a couple of minutes to make the fondant, but it should be used within an hour or so of preparation. Keep it covered with plastic wrap so it doesn't get hard on top. Be sure to choose ripe strawberries with stems, so you can hold them easily as you dip them into the extremely hot sugar syrup. The berries should be dry, so they won't splatter. (The strawberries can also be dipped in fondant, but I prefer cooked sugar.)

If the berries are ripe and the sugar syrup is used while it is very hot, the shells of sugar around the berries will be thin, and the sugar will partially cook the ripe berries. Within 15 to 20 minutes, they will release some juice, which will begin to melt the sugar shells, so don't glaze the berries more than 1 hour before serving.

Serve when the sugar shells are partially melted and close to breaking open and the berries are lukewarm, juicy, and a bit soft inside when you bite into them. The glazed berries can be served with after-dinner drinks as well as used to decorate cakes or cold soufflés.

CAKE

3 large eggs, separated
¾ cup granulated sugar
1 teaspoon pure vanilla extract
¼ cup canola oil
½ cup cake flour
½ cup all-purpose flour
1 teaspoon baking powder
½ cup milk

FONDANT

2 tablespoons warm water
1 tablespoon light corn syrup
3–4 drops red food coloring
2 cups confectioners' sugar, or as needed

FILLING

½ cup strawberry jam or preserves
2 cups sliced strawberries
1 cup heavy cream
2 tablespoons granulated sugar

GLAZED STRAWBERRIES

1½ cups granulated sugar
½ cup cool water
6–8 drops fresh lemon juice (optional)
12 very large ripe strawberries with stems, washed and patted thoroughly dry

STRAWBERRY SAUCE

2 cups strawberries, washed, hulled, and cut into pieces
½ cup strawberry jam
1 tablespoon raspberry brandy or cognac

Small pansies or other edible flowers, for decoration (optional)

Preheat the oven to 325 degrees, with a rack in the center. Butter and flour eight ¾-cup or ten ½-cup heart-shaped molds or tartlet tins.

FOR THE CAKE: Mix the egg yolks, sugar, and vanilla together with a whisk in a bowl. Add the oil, whisking to incorporate. Mix together the cake flour, all-purpose flour, and baking powder and add to the bowl, mixing well with the whisk. Add the milk and mix with the whisk for a few seconds so that the mixture is smooth and light.

Beat the egg whites in a large bowl until stiff but not dry. Mix one third of the whites into the batter with a whisk to lighten it and then, using a rubber spatula, fold in the remainder of the whites until well incorporated.

Pour about ⅓ cup of the batter into each mold, filling them three-quarters full. Bake for 25 to 30 minutes, until puffed and lightly browned. Let cool for 10 to 15 minutes, then unmold and let cool completely on a rack. (*The cakes can be made ahead, placed in airtight containers, and kept for a few days at room temperature or frozen.*)

FOR THE FONDANT: Mix together the warm water, corn syrup, and food coloring in a cup. Put the confectioners' sugar in a bowl, add the corn syrup mixture, and stir with a whisk until well mixed, then beat with the whisk for 20 to 30 seconds, until very smooth. Depending on the moisture in the sugar, you may need slightly more water (approximately ½ teaspoon); or, if the fondant is too thin, add a little more sugar.

If the heart batter ran over slightly and the cakes are irregular in shape, trim them to make them neat. Split each one horizontally in half to make 2 layers. Arrange the top halves of the hearts right side up on a wire rack and spread a good tablespoon of the fondant on each one so a little of it runs down the sides. (*This can be done a few hours ahead, so the fondant dries slightly but remains shiny.*)

FOR THE FILLING: Spread about 1 tablespoon of the jam on the bottom half of each heart. Arrange 3 to 4 tablespoons of the sliced berries on top of each, pressing them into the jam.

Whip the cream with the sugar until stiff. Spoon into a pastry bag fitted with a plain ½-inch tip and pipe on top of the cut berries; or spoon it over the berries. Place a fondant-covered cake top on top of each bottom.

TO GLAZE THE BERRIES: Put the sugar and water in a small heavy saucepan (unlined copper if you have one) and stir just enough to wet the sugar and create a syrup. Then insert a candy thermometer and cook over medium-high heat until the syrup reaches between 310 and 320 degrees (hard-crack); this will take approximately 15 minutes after the mixture comes to a boil. (An unlined copper sugar pan helps prevent the sugar from crystallizing; if unavailable, add the lemon juice to the syrup when it is almost cooked to prevent crystallization.)

Meanwhile, very lightly oil a tray.

Put the pan of sugar syrup on a pot holder. Holding a berry by the stem, dip it into the hot syrup, making sure it is completely coated all around; lift the berry out of the syrup and drag it lightly over the lip of the pan to remove excess syrup, then set on the oiled tray. Repeat with the remaining berries. Set aside until serving time. The sugar will harden around the berries.

FOR THE SAUCE: Put the strawberries in a food processor, add the strawberry jam and raspberry brandy or cognac, and puree until smooth.

At serving time, spoon the sauce onto a serving platter. Arrange the heart cakes on top and the glazed strawberries decoratively around them. Decorate with small pansies or other edible flowers, if using, and serve.

VARIATIONS

The batter can also be made into a large cake (in a 9-inch round or heart-shaped pan) and the inside filled with strawberry jam and cream. In winter, fill the cake with orange marmalade and orange sections and serve it with an orange sauce. You can use any kind of fruit, according to the season.

Mont Blanc with Chestnut-Chocolate Cream
Serves 10 to 12

✂ **All the components of** this dessert can be transformed into other desserts or served on their own. The meringues can be used for other cakes; the chestnut-chocolate cream can be molded in a loaf pan, chilled, sliced, and served cold with a vanilla sauce; and the glazed chestnuts can be stored in a jar, perhaps with whisky or rum, and used to top cakes or flavor pastry cream.

The meringues can be made days ahead and kept in an airtight container, so moisture doesn't soften them. The chestnut-chocolate cream can also be prepared ahead and refrigerated, but it will need resoftening to make it pliable enough to squeeze through a pastry bag. The cake can be assembled ahead and refrigerated for several hours.

If you prefer, you can substitute a commercial chestnut cream (*crème de marrons*) for the chestnut-chocolate cream. Available in cans, jars, and even tubes at specialty stores or online, it is chestnut puree flavored with vanilla and sugar. Simply add the chocolate and rum to about 1 pound chestnut cream for this recipe.

2 pounds large fresh chestnuts or about 1½ pounds plain bottled chestnuts

GLAZED CHESTNUTS

1 cup cooked chestnut pieces (from above; use the larger pieces)
½ cup granulated sugar
1 teaspoon pure vanilla extract
½ cup water

CHESTNUT-CHOCOLATE CREAM

Remaining cooked chestnuts (from above)
8 tablespoons (1 stick) unsalted butter, softened
⅓ cup granulated sugar
2 tablespoons dark rum
8 ounces bittersweet chocolate, melted

MERINGUE

5 large egg whites
1¼ cups granulated sugar

WHIPPED CREAM

1½ cups heavy cream
2 tablespoons confectioners' sugar
2 tablespoons dark rum

Crystallized violets, for decoration (optional)

Preheat the oven to 400 degrees.

IF USING FRESH CHESTNUTS: To peel the chestnuts, score them with a knife by cutting right through the skin the entire length of each side (both outer shell and inside membrane); this will make them easier to peel. Roast the chestnuts in two batches, not one — the peels will come off more easily if removed while the chestnuts are quite warm. Arrange half the chestnuts on a baking sheet and roast for 10 to 12 minutes; the nuts will start to burst at the slits, indicating that they are ready to be peeled. Let cool slightly, then peel by pulling them apart, removing the outer skin and inner membrane at the same time. (Use a towel for this if the nuts are too hot.) Roast and peel the remainder of the chestnuts. (Alternatively, the chestnuts can be scored and placed, a few at a time, in the microwave for 1 to 1½ minutes, until the skin begins to separate from the flesh.)

Put the peeled chestnuts in a saucepan with 6 cups cold water and bring to a boil, then cook over medium heat for about 45 minutes, until tender. Remove from the heat and let steep in the hot water for about 30 minutes, then drain.

IF USING BOTTLED CHESTNUTS: Cover with water and boil for about 2 minutes, just to soften them.

FOR THE GLAZED CHESTNUTS: Put the 1 cup chestnut pieces in a saucepan with the sugar, vanilla, and water. Bring to a boil, reduce the heat, and simmer for 12 to 15 minutes; stir as little as possible to avoid breaking the chestnuts further. The chestnuts are ready when they are glazed and most of the liquid has evaporated, leaving only some heavy syrup. Remove from the heat.

FOR THE CHESTNUT-CHOCOLATE CREAM: Push the remainder of the chestnuts through a food mill fitted with a fine screen. (You should have about 1 pound chestnut puree.)

Transfer the chestnut puree to a food processor, add the butter, sugar, and rum, and process for 30 to 45 seconds, until smooth and light. Add the melted chocolate and process just to mix lightly. Pour into a bowl and stir with a spatula to finish the mixing. Set aside.

Preheat the oven to 225 degrees, with a rack in the center.

FOR THE MERINGUE: Beat the egg whites in a large bowl with an electric mixer until stiff. Add the sugar in a stream, beating on high speed until it is incorporated. (This should not take more than 10 to 15 seconds; the sugar should not be completely melted into the egg whites.)

Butter a piece of parchment paper cut to fit a cookie sheet. Place it buttered side down on the sheet, then turn it over and press to make it adhere to the sheet; the residue of butter on the sheet will hold the paper firmly in place and it will lie flat. Flour the paper lightly. To create 2 different circles, mark the paper with a 10- to 10½-inch flan ring (or use a lid as a guide) and a 6-inch ring (or lid).

Place the meringue in a large pastry bag fitted with a large (about ¾-inch) plain tip and pipe out a large circle of meringue, following the markings. Fill the circle with meringue and smooth the surface with a spatula. Repeat to make the smaller meringue disk.

Bake the meringue disks for about 3 hours. They should lift easily from the paper.

Trim each circle to make it uniformly round.

TO ASSEMBLE THE CAKE: Put the chestnut-chocolate cream into a pastry bag fitted with a star tip. Pipe some of the cream into the center of the larger meringue disk to form a circle about the size of the smaller meringue round. Spread it to a thickness of ¼ to ½ inch.

Place the smaller meringue on top of the cream. Pipe mounds of the cream around the edge of the larger meringue, leaving about 1 inch space between them.

FOR THE WHIPPED CREAM: Whip the cream with the confectioners' sugar and rum until stiff. Spoon into a pastry bag fitted with a star tip and pipe mounds of whipped cream between the mounds of chestnut-chocolate cream.

Finish decorating the cake by piping additional mounds of the chestnut-chocolate cream and whipped cream on the top of the cake. Arrange the glazed chestnuts and crystallized violets, if using, on the cake to complete the dessert. (*The cake can be refrigerated for several hours before serving; cover lightly with plastic wrap to prevent it from picking up tastes from other refrigerated foods.*)

To serve, cut into wedges and arrange on individual dessert plates.

Coffee and Hazelnut Dacquoise
Serves 8

❧ **A dacquoise is a** type of meringue made with ground nuts as well as sugar and whipped egg whites. Spread into disks, the cake layers are baked at a higher temperature than a regular meringue so they become crisp. *Dacquoise* cakes are usually filled with whipped cream or buttercream, as here. If you do not have the rings for baking the meringues that are called for in this recipe, spread the mixture directly onto the buttered and floured cookie sheet to make a large rectangle and bake it. After it has cooled, cut the rectangle into halves and fill with the buttercream.

CAKE

- ½ cup unblanched hazelnuts
- ½ cup unblanched whole almonds
- ¾ cup granulated sugar
- 1½ tablespoons cornstarch
- 6 large egg whites

BUTTERCREAM

- ½ cup granulated sugar
- ¼ cup water
- 3 large egg yolks
- ½ pound (2 sticks) unsalted butter, softened
- ⅓ cup very strong coffee or 1½ tablespoons instant espresso powder, dissolved in ⅓ cup hot water

GARNISH

- 3 tablespoons coarsely chopped almonds or hazelnuts
- 1 tablespoon confectioners' sugar

Preheat the oven to 400 degrees, with a rack in the center.

FOR THE CAKE: Spread the hazelnuts and almonds on a cookie sheet and toast in the oven for about 8 minutes. Remove from the oven and reduce the oven temperature to 350 degrees. Some skin will separate from the hazelnuts and some will still stick to the nuts, which is fine.

Butter and flour a cookie sheet (or use a non-stick baking mat) and two 1-inch-high 9-inch tart rings. Place the rings on the cookie sheet.

Put the sugar, cornstarch, almonds, and hazelnuts in a food processor and process to a coarse powder.

Whip the egg whites in a large bowl until they hold a nice peak. Immediately fold in the nut mixture.

Pour the mixture into the two prepared rings and spread until smooth. Bake for 20 to 25 minutes, or until nicely browned. Let cool.

FOR THE BUTTERCREAM: Mix the sugar and water in a saucepan. Insert a candy thermometer and cook over medium heat for about 3 minutes, until the syrup reaches about 230 degrees (the thread stage).

Meanwhile, beat the yolks in the bowl of an electric mixer with the whisk attachment on medium speed. Slowly pour the syrup into the yolks, beating constantly, and continue beating for about 6 minutes. The mixture should be as thick as a light mayonnaise and very pale yellow. Add 1 stick of the butter, bit by bit. Add the coffee and mix well. Add the remaining stick of butter, bit by bit. (If the buttercream starts to break down, the butter is probably too cold. Place the bowl in hot water for a few seconds or pass it over a gas flame and let it start to melt around the edges, then beat again until it smooths out.)

Remove the rings from the disks of meringue. (The sides that touched the cookie sheet will be very flat.) Place 1 layer flat side down on a serving platter. Spread all but ¼ cup of the buttercream on top. Place the other layer flat side up on top of the cream. Using a spatula, smooth the remaining buttercream around the cake. Press the chopped nuts into the cream all around the cake.

Put the confectioners' sugar in a sieve and sprinkle over the cake so that the top is covered with a white blanket. Refrigerate until chilled.

Serve cold, cut into small wedges.

Cookies

Chocolate, Walnut, and Cherry Cookies
Makes about 20 cookies

✂ **An oversized version of** the chocolate chip cookie, this one also includes nuts and dried cherries. Raisins or dried cranberries can be substituted for the cherries — either will lend acidity, which counterpoints the sweetness of the choco-

late. The dough is made in the food processor in just seconds, with the chocolate chips, nuts, and dried fruit mixed in right before it is dropped in large spoonfuls onto a cookie sheet and baked.

⅔	stick (5⅓ tablespoons) unsalted butter, softened
3	tablespoons canola or peanut oil
⅔	cup packed light brown sugar
2	large eggs
2	teaspoons pure vanilla extract
1⅓	cups all-purpose flour
1	teaspoon baking powder
⅔	cup walnut pieces
⅓	cup diced (¼-inch) dried cherries
⅔	cup semisweet chocolate chips

Preheat the oven to 375 degrees, with a rack in the center.

Put the butter, oil, brown sugar, eggs, and vanilla in a food processor and process for a few seconds, just until smooth. Add the flour and baking powder and process until they are incorporated and the dough is smooth, about 5 seconds.

Transfer the dough to a bowl and stir in the nuts, cherries, and chocolate chips. For each cookie, drop about 2 tablespoons of dough onto an ungreased cookie sheet, leaving about 2½ inches between the mounds.

Bake for 8 to 10 minutes, until nicely browned. Cool on racks and store in an airtight container.

Chocolate Oatmeal Cookies

Makes about 18 cookies

❧ **Coat these oatmeal cookies** with the chocolate or leave them plain. Either way, they are delicious. They will remain crisp if stored in an airtight container.

8 tablespoons (1 stick) unsalted butter, softened

¼ cup sugar

1 teaspoon baking powder

⅔ cup all-purpose flour

1 cup old-fashioned oatmeal (not quick-cooking)

⅓ cup dried currants

4 ounces bittersweet or semisweet chocolate, chopped

Preheat the oven to 400 degrees, with a rack in the center.

Process the butter, sugar, baking powder, and flour in a food processor for 5 to 10 seconds, until the mixture forms a ball. Transfer to a board and add the oatmeal and currants, mixing by hand to combine.

With your fingers, roll about 1 tablespoon of the dough at a time into a log and place 1 inch or so apart on an ungreased heavy cookie sheet.

Press down slightly on each log with your fingers to flatten it into an oval shape. Bake for 18 to 20 minutes, until nicely browned. Cool on a rack.

Melt the chocolate in the top of a double boiler or in a microwave oven. Using a little spatula or knife, spread some chocolate (approximately 1 teaspoon) on the flat underside of each cookie. Place the cookies chocolate side down on a cookie sheet lined with parchment or waxed paper and press on them firmly so the chocolate becomes very flat and smooth. Refrigerate the cookies or place them in the freezer for a few minutes, so the chocolate hardens. Peel the paper from the cookies — it will come off easily.

VARIATION

Coat the flat side of one cookie with chocolate and press it against the flat side of another cookie to create a sandwich. Repeat with the remaining cookies. Store the cookies in an airtight container so they don't get soggy. Makes 9 sandwiches.

Macaroons

Makes 15 to 18 cookies

❧ **Macaroons are always welcome** at my house. They can be sandwiched together with 1 teaspoon of apricot jam in the middle.

Commercial almond paste can be used instead of the almonds. Combine one 8-ounce can almond paste with just 3 tablespoons sugar, then continue as directed, adding the egg whites and vanilla.

¾ cup unblanched whole almonds

1 cup sugar, plus extra for sprinkling

2 large egg whites
Dash of pure vanilla extract

Preheat the oven to 325 degrees, with a rack in the center. Grease a baking sheet and coat with flour, dumping off any excess, or line with a nonstick baking mat.

Combine the almonds and sugar in a food processor and process to a powder. Mix in the egg whites one at a time, then the vanilla. The dough will be soft.

Spoon the dough into a pastry bag fitted with a large plain tip and pipe it into mounds on the prepared pan, using about 2 tablespoons for each macaroon and leaving about 1½ inches space between them; or spoon the dough into mounds. Moisten the tops with a finger dipped into water and sprinkle the tops with sugar.

Bake for 20 minutes, or until light brown. Lift off the pan and cool the macaroons on a wire rack. Store in an airtight container.

Meringue Shells with Chantilly Cream
Serves 8 to 10

✂ **My wife likes her** meringues with sweetened whipped cream, and this is how I ate them as a child — with *crème chantilly* sandwiched between two shells. Once the meringues are cooled to room temperature, they can be kept for weeks in a tightly closed container; there is no need to refrigerate them.

- 4   large egg whites
- 1   cup granulated sugar
- ⅓   cup plus 3 tablespoons sifted confectioners' sugar
- 2   cups heavy cream
  - About 1 teaspoon pure vanilla extract
  - About 1 tablespoon unsweetened cocoa powder

Preheat the oven to 225 degrees, with racks in the center and upper third. Line two cookie sheets with parchment paper or nonstick baking mats.

Put the egg whites in the bowl of an electric mixer or another large bowl and beat with the whisk or a handheld mixer until they begin to hold a peak. Sprinkle half of the granulated sugar over the whites and beat at high speed for about 10 seconds. Reduce the speed to low, add the remaining granulated sugar, and mix for just 10 seconds. (This will give you a tender, crunchy meringue.) The meringue should be very shiny and stiff enough to stand in peaks when you hold up the beater.

Spoon the meringue into a pastry bag fitted with a ¾-inch plain tip and pipe out oval shells, 1½ inches wide and 4 inches long, on the prepared cookie sheets, or use a spoon to create meringues of about the same size. (You should have 18 to 20 shells.) Sprinkle the meringues with the 3 tablespoons confectioners' sugar.

Bake for 2½ to 3 hours. The baked shells should be pale beige, my favorite color for meringues, instead of pure white, as they are classically done. Let cool for 15 minutes, then lift with a spatula from the sheets and cool on wire racks.

At serving time, whip the cream in a large bowl until it begins to hold a shape. Add the remaining ⅓ cup confectioners' sugar and the vanilla and continue to whip until the cream is stiff. (Take care not to overwhip, or the cream will become grainy and turn to butter.) Spoon the cream into a pastry bag, if desired.

To serve, pipe or spoon about 3 tablespoons of the cream onto the flat side of a meringue shell and press another shell into the cream to make a sandwich. Repeat with the remaining meringues and cream. Using a sieve, sprinkle the tops with a little shower of cocoa powder and serve.

Lily's Lace Cookies
Makes 45 to 50 cookies

✂ **One of the best** and easiest cookies to make, this recipe from a friend is one of my favorites. Because of the amount of butter and sugar they contain, the cookies spread and develop tiny holes so they resemble lace.

½ cup almonds or a mixture of
    almonds and other nuts
2 tablespoons all-purpose flour
6 tablespoons (¾ stick) unsalted
    butter, melted
½ cup sugar
1 tablespoon milk

Preheat the oven to 350 degrees, with racks in the center and upper third. Butter and flour several cookie sheets or line them with nonstick baking mats.

Process the nuts and flour in a food processor for 20 to 30 seconds, until the consistency of a coarse powder.

Mix the butter and sugar together in a bowl. Stir in the almond powder until smooth. Mix in the milk.

Spoon 1 teaspoon of the dough for each cookie onto the prepared sheets; the cookies spread quite a bit during baking, so leave a lot of space between them — make about 4 to 6 cookies per sheet. Bake for 8 to 10 minutes, until browned. Remove the sheets from the oven and allow the cookies to rest for 1 minute. With a spatula, transfer the cookies to a rack to cool and harden. Store in an airtight container.

Almond Shortbread Cookies
Makes about 4 dozen 1- to 1½-inch cookies

❧ **These traditional Christmas cookies** disappear rapidly at my house. Crunchy and sandy in texture, they are great dipped in coffee. Although I roll the dough out here and cut it into shapes, you can also form it into small balls, the size of olives, and press them into flat rounds.

12 tablespoons (1½ sticks) unsalted butter,
    softened
½ cup sugar
2 cups all-purpose flour
½ cup blanched almonds, ground to a
    fine powder in a food processor
¼ teaspoon salt
1½ teaspoons pure almond extract
1 large egg yolk
1–2 tablespoons heavy cream if needed
    About ¼ cup blanched whole almonds

Mix the butter and sugar together in a bowl until smooth and creamy. Combine the flour, ground almonds, and salt, add to the butter mixture, and mix well. Add the almond extract and egg yolk and knead until well combined. If the dough seems dry and doesn't come together well, mix in enough cream to enable you to form it into a ball. Refrigerate the dough for at least 1 hour.

Preheat the oven to 375 degrees, with racks in the center and upper third.

Roll out the dough on a lightly floured surface until it is about ⅓ inch thick. Cut into desired shapes and arrange on ungreased cookie sheets. (Alternatively, make small balls about the size of large olives and press each gently to about ⅓ inch thick on the cookie sheets.) Press a whole almond into the center of each of the cookies.

Bake for 14 to 18 minutes, until golden. Cool on a rack and store in an airtight container.

Orange Tuiles
Makes about 20 cookies

✎ *Tuile* means "tile," and these cookies are shaped like curved roof tiles. Although tuiles are not usually flavored with orange rind, this is a nice variation.

½ cup sugar
¼ teaspoon pure vanilla extract
2 large egg whites
⅓ cup all-purpose flour
4 tablespoons (½ stick) unsalted butter, melted
½ cup sliced almonds
2 teaspoons grated orange rind

Preheat the oven to 400 degrees, with a rack in the center. Line a baking sheet with a nonstick baking mat.

Combine the sugar, vanilla, and egg whites in a bowl and beat with a whisk for a few seconds, until foaming. Add the flour, butter, almonds, and orange rind, mixing them in well. (The batter will be runny.)

Drop about 1½ tablespoons of batter for each cookie onto the prepared pan, leaving at least 4 inches between them to allow for spreading. Bake for 10 to 12 minutes, until lightly browned.

Let the cookies "settle" for a few minutes and then, while they are still hot, lift them off the baking sheet and bend each cookie over a rolling pin or place it in a baguette mold so it takes on the shape of a curved roof tile. Allow to cool long enough so they will maintain their shape, then remove and cool completely. Store in an airtight tin.

Cats' Tongues
Makes about 45 cookies

✎ **Easy, elegant, and addictive,** these small buttery cookies are long and narrow, like a cat's tongue. They're perfect with fruits or chocolate. They spread out as they cook, becoming very thin and crunchy. You can also shape them with a teaspoon instead of using a pastry bag.

8 tablespoons (1 stick) unsalted butter, softened
½ cup sugar
    Dash of pure vanilla extract
2 large egg whites
⅓ cup all-purpose flour

Preheat the oven to 400 degrees, with racks in the center and upper third. Thoroughly grease two cookie sheets or line with nonstick baking mats.

Process the butter, sugar, and vanilla in a food processor until smooth. Add the egg whites and process for a few seconds. Add the flour and process for a few more seconds.

Fill a pastry bag fitted with a large plain tip with the batter. Pipe the batter out onto the prepared pans in strips about as thick as a cigarette and 3 inches long, leaving about 1 inch between them to allow for spreading. Before placing it in the oven, give each sheet a good bang on your worktable to flatten the cookies.

Bake for 12 minutes, or until light brown. After a minute or so, transfer the cookies from the cookie sheets to wire racks and allow to cool. Store in a tightly covered tin in a cool place.

VARIATION
LEMON CATS' TONGUES
In place of the vanilla, add 1 teaspoon grated lemon rind and 1 tablespoon fresh lemon juice.

Cigarettes

Makes about 2 dozen cookies

❧ **Harkening back to an** earlier era, these cookies bake into thin disks and then, while still warm and pliable, are rolled into little tubes or cigarettes. If you prefer, you can skip the rolling and keep them as rounds.

- 2 large egg whites
- 3 tablespoons all-purpose flour
- ¾ cup sugar
- 4 tablespoons (½ stick) unsalted butter, melted
  Dash of pure vanilla extract

Preheat the oven to 375 degrees, with racks in the center and upper third. Grease two baking sheets and coat with flour, knocking off any excess, or line with nonstick baking mats.

Beat the egg whites in a large bowl until they stand in soft peaks when you hold up the beater or whisk. Add the sugar and mix for a few seconds. Fold in the 3 tablespoons flour thoroughly but gently, then stir in the melted butter and vanilla.

Spoon the batter by the tablespoon onto the prepared pan, leaving about 5 inches between the cookies to allow for spreading. Give the pan a good bang on a flat surface to flatten the cookies before putting it in the oven. Bake for 12 to 15 minutes, or until golden brown. Remove from the oven.

After a few minutes, while the cookies are still warm, roll each one around a pencil or a wooden spoon handle to give it the shape of a cigarette. Since the cookies cool very fast once they are out of the oven, you must work quickly; if cool, they will break when you try to roll them. Allow them to cool on the pencil or spoon handle long enough to maintain their shape, then remove and let cool completely.

Store in an airtight container.

Apricot and Hazelnut Biscotti

Makes 2 dozen cookies

❧ **Dried apricots lend tang** and chewiness to these biscotti. The dough is mixed for just a few seconds in a food processor, shaped into a log, and baked for half an hour, then sliced and baked again to dry the cookies.

- 2 cups all-purpose flour
- ¾ cup sugar
- ¼ teaspoon salt
- 1 teaspoon baking powder
- 1 large egg
- 3 tablespoons milk
- 2 tablespoons canola oil
- 1½ teaspoons pure vanilla extract
- ¾ cup hazelnuts or cashews
- 4 ounces dried apricots, cut into
  ¼-inch-thick slices (⅔ cup)

Preheat the oven to 375 degrees, with a rack in the center. Line a cookie sheet with parchment paper or a nonstick baking mat.

Put the flour, sugar, salt, and baking powder in a food processor and process for 5 seconds. Add the egg, milk, oil, and vanilla and process for 10 seconds, or just until the mixture begins to hold together.

Transfer to a bowl, add the nuts and apricots, and mix by hand until the mixture is thoroughly combined.

Place the dough in a mound on a piece of plastic wrap about 18 inches long and press on it to form it into a log about 12 inches long by 3 inches wide by 1 inch high. Invert the dough log onto the lined cookie sheet and peel off the plastic wrap.

Bake for 30 minutes, or until lightly browned on all sides and cracked on top. Remove and cool for about 10 minutes. Reduce the oven heat to 350 degrees.

Using a serrated knife, cut the log crosswise into ½-inch-thick slices. Arrange the slices on the prepared cookie sheet and bake for 20 minutes, or until nicely browned on both sides. (There is no need to turn the biscotti over; they brown nicely on both sides without turning.)

Cool the biscotti thoroughly on a wire rack. Store in an airtight tin (or wrap well and freeze).

Zimfours
Makes 16 to 20 cookies

❧ **Essentially thin tartlets made** of cookie dough covered with orange strips, raisins, and almonds and garnished with chocolate, these petits fours are cut into squares for serving. They are named for my friend Gloria Zimmerman. They freeze well and will keep, covered, in the refrigerator or in a cool place for several days. Instead of being cut into squares, the dough rectangle can be served as an open-faced tart and cut into wedges with, perhaps, some whipped cream on top.

Pieces of dried figs or apricots can be substituted for the raisins in the filling and the decorative lines of chocolate can be made with white chocolate or a mixture of bittersweet and white.

DOUGH

  1 cup all-purpose flour
  4 tablespoons (½ stick) unsalted butter
1½ tablespoons sugar
  1 large egg yolk
  1 teaspoon pure vanilla extract
1½ tablespoons cold milk

FILLING

  2 oranges
  ½ cup water

  ⅓ cup sugar
  ⅓ stick (2⅔ tablespoons) unsalted butter
  ⅓ cup golden raisins
  ½ cup sliced almonds
  2 tablespoons heavy cream

GARNISH

About 1½ ounces bittersweet chocolate, melted (2 tablespoons)

Preheat the oven to 400 degrees, with a rack in the center.

FOR THE DOUGH: Process the flour, butter, and sugar in a food processor for about 10 seconds. Mix the egg yolk with the vanilla and milk, add to the processor, and process for another 8 to 10 seconds, until the mixture forms a ball. (*The dough can be made ahead, wrapped in plastic wrap, and refrigerated until ready to roll out.*)

Roll out the dough between two sheets of plastic wrap into a very thin rectangle about 9 by 12 inches. Remove the sheet of plastic wrap from the top of the dough and invert the dough, with its plastic wrap liner, onto a cookie sheet. (The dough is rich enough that it won't stick to the cookie sheet.)

Remove the second sheet of plastic wrap. If need be, the dough can be pressed with your fingers to extend it on the cookie sheet to make it a little thinner. Make a border all around the edges by rolling some of the dough back onto itself and pinching it to make it pointed on top.

Bake for about 20 minutes, until the dough is set and just beginning to brown slightly.

MEANWHILE, FOR THE FILLING: Remove the rind from the oranges with a vegetable peeler; you should get about 12 strips of rind total. (Save the fruit itself for another use.)

Pile up the strips one on top of the other and cut into fine julienne strips. (You should have about ½ cup.) Put the julienned rind in a saucepan with 2 cups cold water and bring to a boil. Boil for about 10 seconds, then drain in a sieve and rinse under cold water. Rinse the pan and return the orange rind to it, along with the ½ cup water and sugar. Bring to a boil and cook for about 6 minutes. The liquid should be reduced to a fairly heavy syrup and the julienne should be soft and translucent.

Add the butter, raisins, sliced almonds, and cream to the orange rind mixture and stir to mix well.

Spread the mixture over the precooked dough rectangle and bake for another 10 to 12 minutes, until the dough is well cooked and the filling is brown on top. Transfer to a rack and let cool.

FOR THE GARNISH: Pour the melted chocolate into a cornet (see the sidebar), fold down the top of the cornet, and cut off the tip. Drizzle the chocolate over the zimfours to form a chocolate lattice. Let set for at least 30 minutes.

Cut the zimfours into 16 to 20 squares.

Summer Fruit Cornets
Serves 12

The almond dough for these summery fruit-filled horns of plenty will stay crisp even after being filled. Before filling, the cornets can be brushed on the inside with chocolate or with melted jam, or they can be left plain. They can be transformed into a winter or fall dessert by using different fruits such as sliced pears, apples, bananas, oranges, or pineapple. The fruits can be used plain, as they are here, or rolled in jam and lemon juice.

You can also use this recipe to make single-portion cups that can accommodate ice cream as well as fruit. Press the hot cookies (top side out) around ½-cup molds (little Pyrex custard cups are ideal), pushing gently all around so they conform to the shape of the molds. Allow to harden before removing.

DOUGH

¾ cup blanched whole almonds
2 tablespoons all-purpose flour
⅔ stick (5⅓ tablespoons) unsalted butter, cut into pieces
1 tablespoon milk
¾ cup granulated sugar

FILLING

4 ounces bittersweet or semisweet chocolate, melted, or ¼ cup berry or fruit jam (optional)
1 cup heavy cream
2 tablespoons granulated sugar

FRUITS

About 6 cups mixed fruits: cherries, red currants, raspberries, loganberries, strawberries, wineberries (bilberries), and/or blueberries

GARNISH

Fresh mint leaves
Confectioners' sugar, for dusting (optional)

Preheat the oven to 350 degrees, with a rack in the center. Line a cookie sheet with a piece of parchment paper oiled very lightly on both sides,

MAKING A PAPER CORNET

Cut a right triangle of parchment paper measuring about 12 inches on the long side. Grab the 2 opposite ends of the triangle, each with the thumb and forefinger of one hand, and twist the paper onto itself to make a cone. Don't worry if the cone isn't very pointed at this time. Holding the cone with both hands, your thumbs inside and your forefingers on the outside, move your thumbs down and your fingers up to make the paper slide up between them, and tighten the cone in this way to make the cornet needle-sharp at the tip. Fold the top edge of the paper inside the cone to secure it and prevent the cone from uncoiling.

To use, fill the cornet, fold the top over, and cut off the tip to make a very small opening.

then cut the paper into quarters and press flat against the sheet.

FOR THE DOUGH: Grind the almonds with the flour in a food processor until fine. (The flour will absorb any oil released by the almonds and will produce a finer mixture.) Add the butter, milk, and sugar and process for 8 to 10 seconds, just long enough for the mixture to form into a ball.

Place about 1½ tablespoons of the dough on each of the four pieces of paper on the cookie sheet. Wet your fingers or a spoon and press the dough into disks about 2½ inches across, making them as round as possible.

Bake for approximately 12 minutes, or until the dough has spread and is nicely browned all around. Lift up each piece of paper, turn it over, and peel the paper from the cookie. Reserve the paper (it does not have to be oiled again) for the

next cookies. The top of the cookie (side exposed during baking) will be the outside of the cornet, since it looks a little nicer than the underside. Let the cookies sit for 1 to 2 minutes before rolling them up. (If rolled immediately, they will break. If cooled too much, however, they will become brittle and can't be rolled. If this happens, return them to the oven and reheat them slightly until they become soft and pliable enough to roll.)

Roll each cookie around a metal cornet or coated-paper cone-shaped cup and let cool until set. Or simply roll them free-form into cornet shapes (the shape may not be as perfect as with a mold) and, as soon as the cornet is rolled, slide a small ball of aluminum foil inside to prevent the cornet from collapsing while it cools. Repeat with the remaining dough to make more cornets.

FOR THE FILLING: When the cornets are completely cool, brush them inside with the melted chocolate or jam, if using.

Whip the cream with the sugar until stiff. Spoon the cream into a pastry bag fitted with a star tip and partially fill the cornets, or spoon the cream into the cornets.

Arrange the cornets on individual serving plates. Add a little more cream to each cornet, so it appears to be flowing out of the opening, and pipe a few small mounds of cream around the plate. Arrange the fruit on the plates. Stick a few leaves of mint into the cream mounds for color. For a different look, dust the fruit, cookies, and rims of the plates with confectioners' sugar. Serve.

Almond Sandwich Cookies with Raspberry Sauce

Serves 8 (makes 16 cookies)

This recipe uses the same dough as the Summer Fruit Cornets (page 564), but here it's made into cookies that are served with whipped cream, berries, and a sweet raspberry sauce. You should assemble the dessert at the last minute, but the cookies can be made ahead and stored in an airtight container.

Dough from Summer Fruit Cornets (page 564)

SAUCE

- 1½ cups frozen unsweetened raspberries, defrosted
- ½ cup seedless raspberry preserves

- 1 cup heavy cream
- 1 tablespoon confectioners' sugar, plus additional for dusting
- About 1½ cups blackberries or loganberries
- About 1½ cups raspberries
- A few fresh mint leaves, for decoration (optional)

FOR THE COOKIES: Preheat the oven to 350 degrees, with a rack in the center. Line a cookie sheet with parchment paper.

Using about 2 teaspoons of the dough for each cookie, roll the dough into uniformly round balls and press them down flat, about ⅓ inch thick, onto the parchment-lined sheet, leaving space between them. Bake for 12 minutes, or until nicely browned. Cool on a rack.

FOR THE SAUCE: Push the berries and preserves through a food mill fitted with the finest screen or a fine-mesh strainer. Spoon 2 to 3 tablespoons of the raspberry sauce onto each of eight dessert plates.

Whip the cream with the confectioners' sugar until stiff and spoon it into a pastry bag fitted with a star tip (or simply spoon the whipped cream onto the plates and cookies). Drop a dot of the whipped cream into the center of the sauce on each plate and press a cookie onto it. (This will make the cookies sit above the sauce and hold them securely on the plates without sliding.) Pipe whipped cream into the centers of the cookies and arrange the blackberries and all but 8 of the raspberries on the cookies. Place another cookie on top of each one to create a sandwich. Pipe a mound of whipped cream in the center of each cookie and decorate with a raspberry and, if desired, a few mint leaves. Dust lightly with confectioners' sugar and serve.

Candies

Dulcet Chocolate Squares

Makes 12 to 15 squares

You can vary these little squares of white chocolate with fresh fruit, dried fruit, and nuts by using colorful combinations of different fruits, or you can use milk chocolate. Instead of making just one layer of the fruit-nut mixture over the chocolate base, you can build one or two more layers, drizzling melted chocolate over them to act as a glue, with a final layer of fruit and nuts on top.

The chocolate must be cut into squares when it has just set — before it gets too hard. It can also be cut into rounds with a cookie cutter or into little strips.

    6 ounces white or semisweet chocolate, chopped
   12 dark raisins
   12 golden raisins
  1–2 strawberries, washed, hulled, and halved
 8–10 pecans, preferably toasted, broken into halves
 8–10 unblanched whole almonds, preferably toasted, cut into pieces
  1–2 dried apricots, sliced

Melt the chocolate in a double boiler over hot water or in a microwave oven. Pour 2 lines (about 16 inches long) of chocolate onto a sheet of parchment paper. With a spatula, spread the chocolate out so each strip is about 2 inches wide and no more than ⅛ inch thick.

Before the chocolate hardens, embed a combination of the dried fruit, fresh fruit, and nuts the length of the strips, leaving space between each cluster.

Refrigerate until set but not too hard, so the strips can be cut.

If the chocolate is too hard and brittle to cut, let stand at room temperature to soften somewhat. Trim the edges and cut the strips into squares. Refrigerate until serving time or freeze.

At serving time, arrange on a tray and serve.

Chocolate and Fruit-Nut Cups
Makes 12 chocolate cups

❧ **These candies are especially** fun to make with children, who love to select their own assortment of fruits and nuts and press them into the soft chocolate. They're a perfect after-dinner treat.

    4 ounces bittersweet chocolate, melted
    1 tablespoon pistachios
    1 tablespoon walnut pieces
    1 tablespoon pumpkin seeds
    1 tablespoon dried cranberries
    1 tablespoon golden raisins
    2 tablespoons dried cherries
    3 fresh mint leaves, cut into pieces

Divide the melted chocolate among twelve small foil or paper candy cups (1½ inches by 1 inch deep), filling the base of each with about ¼ inch of chocolate. While the chocolate is still soft, arrange the nuts, pumpkin seeds, cranberries, raisins, cherries, and mint leaves on top and press on them lightly to partially embed them in the chocolate. Refrigerate for at least 1 hour, until hardened.

To serve, remove the cups from their foil or paper casings and arrange them on a plate.

Chocolate Mint Trufflettes
Makes 20 small truffles

❧ **These truffles are especially** nice to box and give to friends over the holiday season. They keep well in the refrigerator and can also be frozen.

    4 ounces bittersweet chocolate, chopped
    4 ounces milk chocolate, chopped
    3 tablespoons heavy cream
    1 large egg yolk
    2 teaspoons finely minced fresh mint
    2 teaspoons unsweetened cocoa powder

Heat the chocolates and cream in a double boiler over hot water or in a microwave oven until the chocolate has melted. Stir to combine. Add the egg yolk and mint and mix well; the mixture will thicken.

Line a cookie sheet with parchment and spoon the chocolate onto the sheet, making 20 small mounds. Refrigerate for 20 to 30 minutes.

Press each piece of chocolate into a roundish ball; the balls should be uneven so they look like real truffles. Put the balls on a plate, sprinkle the cocoa over them, and shake the plate so the trufflettes roll around and become coated.

Transfer the trufflettes to a clean plate and refrigerate until serving time.

Candied Citrus Peels

Makes 4 dozen pieces

✻ **Candied peels of oranges** and other citrus fruits — grapefruit, limes, and lemons — are delicious by themselves and are also used in pastries and innumerable other desserts. Cut into julienne strips, they can be sprinkled over buttercream frosting on a cake or a cold or hot orange soufflé or poached fruit. Packed into little jars, candied peels make a great gift for friends. They keep for at least a month in a jar in the refrigerator.

Traditionally the peel is removed with a vegetable peeler so only the thin part of the skin is candied, but in this recipe, I candy the whole peel, first blanching it twice in water to remove most of the bitterness. And I give two variations: chocolate-dipped peels and candied peels mixed with dried apricots and macerated in spirits.

- 3 large navel oranges with thick, shiny skin
- 1 grapefruit, preferably pink
- 2 large limes
- 2 lemons
- 8 cups water
- 1½ cups sugar, plus extra to roll the peels in

With a knife, cut through the skin of each orange to make 8 sections and through the grapefruit to make 10 sections. Cut through each lime and lemon to make 6 sections. Separate the skin from the fruit. (The fruits can be reserved for juice.)

Drop the peels into a stainless steel pot and cover generously with cold water. Bring to a strong boil and boil for about 30 seconds. Drain in a colander, rinse under cold water, and rinse out the pot. Return the peels to the pot, add water to cover, and repeat the blanching process. Return the drained peels to the clean pot and add the 8 cups water and the sugar. Bring to a boil and boil

---

MACERATED CANDIED FRUITS Makes about 2½ cups

These diced candied fruits are of higher quality than store-bought ones, have no artificial coloring or preservatives, and are very inexpensive. They are ideal for fruitcakes, soufflés, or charlottes or as a flavoring for pastry cream.

- ½ cup dried apricots, cut into ¼-inch dice
- 1½ cups mixed Candied Citrus Peels, cut into ¼-inch dice
- ½ cup golden raisins
- ½ cup cognac, Scotch, rum, or orange liqueur

Combine the apricots, candied peels, raisins, and liquor in a bowl, mixing well. Pour into a small jar, cover tightly, and store in the refrigerator for up to 6 months.

gently, uncovered, for about 1 hour, or until the peels are tender. They should be almost transparent and there should be just enough thick syrup to coat them.

Cover a cookie sheet with a layer of granulated sugar. Using a fork, lift the peels and place on the cookie sheet. Turn and press them in the sugar. Arrange them on a wire rack and let them cool, dry, and harden for at least 1 hour. (Strain the sugar and return it to the sugar bin.)

CHOCOLATE-COVERED CANDIED CITRUS PEELS
Makes 12 pieces

Chocolate-dipped candied peels make a delicious ending to a meal. Serve them with after-dinner brandy or liqueur. You can also use them to decorate a cake, or chop them to flavor pastry cream for crepes or a cake.

- 2 ounces semisweet chocolate, chopped
- 1 ounce unsweetened chocolate, chopped
- ½ teaspoon canola or peanut oil
- 12 Candied Orange Peels

Melt both kinds of chocolate together in a small bowl over hot water or in a microwave oven. Stir in the oil.

Line a small tray with parchment paper. Dip about half of an orange peel into the chocolate, then lift it up, let the excess chocolate drip off for a few seconds, and place on the lined tray. Repeat with all the peels. Let set in the refrigerator for at least 30 minutes.

Lift the pieces from the tray and arrange them on a platter or place them in a jar for storage in the refrigerator for up to 1 month.

Glazed Fruits
Makes 24 pieces

✌ **Dried fruits, such as** apricots, figs, dates, and prunes, can be filled with tinted marzipan and dipped into sugar cooked to about 310 degrees, the hard-crack stage. The fruits should be coated while the sugar is very hot so the syrup is not too thick and so does not form too heavy a layer around the fruit.

Since the dried fruits don't release any juices, they keep better than glazed fresh berries or other fresh fruit; you can make them several hours or more in advance. You can use them to decorate Croquembouche (page 588) or other pastries.

- 2 ounces marzipan
- 3–4 drops red food coloring
- 3–4 drops green food coloring
- 12 small Black Mission figs
- 12 dried apricots

GLAZE

- 1 cup sugar
- 3 tablespoons water
  Pinch of cream of tartar or a few drops of fresh lemon juice (optional)

Mix half the marzipan with the red food coloring and the other half with the green food coloring. Cut the figs and apricots almost in half, so you can open them like a book, and stuff with little pieces of the tinted marzipan. Re-form the fruit around the stuffing so it holds well. Secure each fruit on a toothpick so that it is easier to dip into the sugar.

FOR THE GLAZE: Oil a baking sheet.

Stir together the sugar and water in a heavy saucepan (an unlined copper sugar pan, if you have one) just enough to wet the sugar. A copper pan tends to acidify the sugar, and acid helps pre-

vent crystallization; if you don't have a sugar pan, add the cream of tartar or lemon juice to achieve the same result. Bring the mixture to a boil, cover, and continue cooking for about 30 seconds to melt any sugar crystals that have collected around the sides of the pan. (The steam created by covering the pan will melt them.) Remove the cover, insert a candy thermometer, and cook, without stirring, to about 310 degrees, the hard-crack stage; the sugar should not take on any color. Remove the pan from the heat.

Holding each piece of fruit by the toothpick, dip it into the syrup, then lift and drag it along the side of the pan to eliminate the excess syrup and place on the oiled baking sheet. When the sugar is set, remove the toothpicks by twisting and pulling.

At serving time, arrange the stuffed fruit attractively on a platter and serve.

Crystallized Mint Leaves or Rose Petals
Makes 12 pieces

✎ **Many desserts can be** enhanced by crystallized mint leaves or rose petals. Basil or sage leaves can be treated in the same manner. The leaves or petals are dipped first in lightly beaten egg whites, then in granulated sugar. When the sugar dries, it hardens, forming a coating on the leaves and petals. Easy to make, they can be kept for at least a week in a tightly closed container. They provide a special decorative touch for cakes, ice cream, or custard.

- 1 large egg white
- ⅓ cup sugar
- 12 large fresh mint leaves, washed and thoroughly dried, or 12 pink or red rose petals, preferably from organic flowers

Beat the egg white lightly with a fork in a bowl to loosen and liquefy it. Spread the sugar on a small cookie sheet. Line another cookie sheet with plastic wrap.

One at a time, dip the mint leaves or petals in the egg white, then run your finger lightly over both sides to remove most of the white (the leaves or petals should be wet but not heavily coated), lay the leaf or petal flat in the sugar, and sprinkle some of the surrounding sugar on top. Press firmly with your fingers so the sugar completely covers the surface and adheres. Transfer to the cookie sheet lined with plastic. Set the coated leaves or petals aside to dry at room temperature. (Discard any leftover egg white and sugar.)

Store the crystallized leaves or petals at room temperature in a container with a tight lid. They will keep for up to a week.

Tarts, Pies, and Pastries

Tarts, Pies, and Pastries

Mémé's Apple Tart
Serves 6

❀ **This is my mother's** famous apple tart that she made almost every day in her small Lyon restaurant, Le Pélican. Her dough, unlike any other, achieved its tender, crumbly, airy texture from a combination of vegetable shortening or lard, baking powder, and warm milk. Since the dough is too soft to roll, it is pressed into the pan by hand.

DOUGH

- 1¼ cups all-purpose flour
- 1 teaspoon sugar
- ½ teaspoon baking powder
- ¼ teaspoon salt
- 6 tablespoons vegetable shortening or lard, at room temperature
- ¼ cup milk, heated to lukewarm

FILLING

- 2 pounds Golden Delicious or McIntosh apples (6 medium)
- 3 tablespoons sugar
- 2 tablespoons unsalted butter

Preheat the oven to 400 degrees, with a rack in the center.

FOR THE DOUGH: Combine the flour, sugar, baking powder, and salt in a bowl. Add the shortening or lard and mix with a spoon or your hands until the mixture feels and looks sandy. Add the warm milk and stir rapidly for a few seconds, until the dough is well mixed.

Using a sheet of plastic wrap to help you, fit the dough into a 9-inch quiche pan or tart pan with a removable bottom. With your fingers, press the dough evenly into the bottom and up the sides of the pan. Set aside.

FOR THE FILLING: Peel the apples, quarter them, and remove the cores. Arrange the apple

quarters, cut side up, in circles on top of the dough and sprinkle the sugar evenly over them. Cut the butter into small pieces and dot the apples with the butter.

Place the tart pan on a cookie sheet and bake for 1 hour, or until the apples are browned and crusty.

Let cool to lukewarm, then cut into wedges and serve.

Country Apple Galette
Serves 8

❀ **I often make this** galette, a thin, crusty tart, and especially like it for buffet-style entertaining. It is important to use only the amount of apples called for here. A thin layer will yield a better galette. You can brush the top with lukewarm peach jam to make it a bit fancier.

The dough, a *pâte brisée*, should be rolled to a very thin rectangle. The tart can be made in a conventional pie plate or tart ring, but I prefer it free-form, so that no trimming is necessary and all the dough is used. Be sure to cook the tart for long enough — the pastry should be dark brown and crusty and the apples tender. The finished tart has a wonderfully rustic look.

1½ cups all-purpose flour

1½ teaspoons sugar

¼ teaspoon salt

10 tablespoons (1¼ sticks) cold unsalted butter, cut into ½-inch pieces

⅓ cup ice-cold water

TOPPING

4 Golden Delicious apples (1¾ pounds)

2 tablespoons honey

2 tablespoons sugar

½ teaspoon ground cinnamon

1 tablespoon unsalted butter

FOR THE DOUGH: Put the flour, sugar, salt, and butter in a food processor and process for about 5 seconds. Add the water and process for another 10 seconds, until the dough just begins to come together. Remove the dough from the processor and press it into a disk (there should still be visible pieces of butter). Wrap in plastic wrap and refrigerate while you prepare the apples.

Preheat the oven to 400 degrees, with a rack in the center.

FOR THE TOPPING: Peel, halve, and core the apples. Place them cut side down on the cutting board and cut crosswise into ¼-inch-thick slices. Set aside the larger center slices and coarsely chop the end slices and any broken slices. (About half the slices should be sliced, half chopped.)

On a lightly floured work surface, roll the dough into a 12-by-14-inch rectangle. Transfer to a cookie sheet.

Arrange the chopped apples on the dough, spreading them out to within 1 inch of the edges. Sprinkle the honey over the chopped apples. Arrange the apple slices in one slightly overlapping layer on top of the chopped apples, positioning them to imitate the petals of a flower.

Mix together the sugar and cinnamon in a small bowl. Sprinkle on top of the sliced apples and dot them with the butter. Fold the edges of the pastry over the apples to create a 1-inch border.

Bake for 1 hour, or until the pastry is brown and crisp and the apples tender. Serve the tart lukewarm or at room temperature.

MAKING PÂTE BRISÉE

Pâte brisée can be made by hand, but a food processor does the job well and easily. In the summer, it is a good idea to keep the flour in the freezer and the butter refrigerated until ready to use, since it is important to mix all the ingredients together quickly to keep the gluten from developing too much. The butter should remain visible in the dough, not blend into it. The slivers of butter will melt during the baking and give the dough some of the flakiness you find in puff pastry.

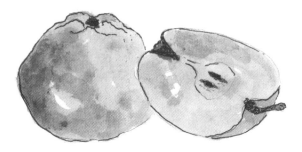

Apple Tart with Almond Filling
Serves 8

⚘ In this tasty apple tart, a layer of frangipane, or almond paste, is spread on the dough and covered with apple slices. The almond mixture rises around the apples as a soft, fragrant dough, and the tart is coated with an apricot glaze. It is best enjoyed at room temperature.

Dough from Country Apple Galette
(opposite)

FRANGIPANE

¾ cup unblanched whole almonds

¼ cup sugar

1 large egg

1 teaspoon pure vanilla extract

2 tablespoons unsalted butter, melted

APPLES

4–5 Granny Smith or Red Delicious apples

3 tablespoons sugar

2 tablespoons unsalted butter

GLAZE

6 tablespoons apricot jam

1 tablespoon Calvados or applejack

1 tablespoon water

On a floured board, roll the dough out to about a 13-inch circle. Roll the dough up on the rolling pin and unroll over a 9- to 10-inch pie pan or pizza pan, then carefully fit it into the pan. Roll and press the excess dough in on itself to create a thicker border all around.

FOR THE FRANGIPANE: Grind the almonds and sugar to a coarse powder in a food processor. Add the egg, vanilla, and melted butter and blend for a few seconds to make a smooth paste.

Spread the frangipane evenly over the dough. Refrigerate.

Preheat the oven to 400 degrees, with a rack in the center.

FOR THE APPLES: Peel, halve, and core the apples. Slice the halves crosswise about ¼ inch thick. Arrange the slices, overlapping, in concentric circles on top of the frangipane. Sprinkle with the sugar and dot the top with the butter, cut into small pieces.

Bake for 1¼ hours, or until the apples are tender and the pastry has browned. Let cool to room temperature.

FOR THE GLAZE: Combine the apricot jam, liquor, and water in a bowl. Spoon the glaze over the apples and spread it evenly with the back of the spoon so that the whole tart top is glazed.

Cut the tart into wedges and serve.

Tarte Tatin
Serves 8 to 10

✂ *Tarte Tatin,* **the famous** upside-down caramelized apple tart created many years ago by the two Tatin sisters, is an example of a dish that originated in a home kitchen and eventually made its way into most of the great restaurants.

I cook the apples with the skins on to give a chewier texture. Dried currants (raisins can be substituted), slivered almonds, and dried apricots fill the gaps between the apple chunks and additional apples on top create a flat surface for the pastry to sit on, which gives the tart a nicer shape when it is unmolded.

The tart should be served at room temperature or slightly warm. If you make it ahead, keep it in the skillet. The caramel may stick to the bottom, but the dough on top will stay dry. Then, at serving time, put the tart on the stove over medium heat for a couple of minutes, shaking the pan to melt the caramel, so the tart will unmold easily.

DOUGH

- 1 cup all-purpose flour
- 6 tablespoons (¾ stick) very cold unsalted butter, cut into ¼-inch-thick slivers
- ½ teaspoon sugar
- ⅛ teaspoon salt
- 3 tablespoons ice-cold water

FILLING

- 3 pounds russet, Pippin, or Golden Delicious apples (6–8)
- ¼ cup sugar
- ½ cup plus 2 tablespoons water
- 1 tablespoon fresh lemon juice
- ¼ cup slivered almonds
- 3 tablespoons unsalted butter, cut into bits
- ½ cup sliced dried apricots
- ⅓ cup dried currants

- 2 teaspoons sugar

GARNISH

- 1 cup heavy cream

FOR THE DOUGH: Put the flour in a food processor, add the butter, sugar, and salt, and process for 5 to 10 seconds. Pieces of butter should still be visible in the dough. Add the cold water and process for another 10 seconds, just until the mixture starts gathering together. Turn the dough out onto a large piece of plastic wrap, press it into a disk, wrap in the plastic, and refrigerate.

FOR THE FILLING: Remove the core from each apple at the stem end and at the opposite end, using your thumb as a pivot and rotating the tip of a sharp paring knife as you cut into the apple. Quarter the apples and remove the rest of the cores.

Combine the sugar, 2 tablespoons of the water, and the lemon juice in a 12-inch ovenproof non-stick skillet and cook until the mixture becomes a caramel, about 4 minutes. Add the almonds and cook for 10 seconds. Remove from the heat and let cool for 5 minutes, so the caramel hardens.

Arrange the apple quarters on top of the set caramel, placing them side by side and skin side down in one layer, making two concentric circles, with a piece of apple in the center. Sprinkle the butter, apricots, and currants on top.

Slice the remainder of the apples thin. (You should have about 3 cups.) Arrange on top of the circles of apples to fill the skillet completely.

Add the remaining ½ cup water, bring to a boil, cover, and boil gently for 10 minutes. The object here is to soften the apples so they sink down and form a flat surface. Remove the lid and continue cooking over medium heat for 7 to 8 minutes, until there is no liquid visible when you incline the pan slightly. This indicates that most of the water and juices have boiled away and what remains is the sugar and butter, which are beginning to caramelize again. Set aside. (*The apples can be made several hours ahead.*)

Preheat the oven to 400 degrees, with a rack in the center.

Remove the dough from the plastic wrap and place it on a board. Sprinkle with a little flour and roll out to a very thin circle (no more than ⅛ inch thick). Trim the edges and then fold the dough in on itself to form an edge that is a little thicker all around.

Place the circle of dough on top of the apples. Press it down with your hands so it lies completely flat. Pierce all over with a fork and sprinkle with the 2 teaspoons sugar, which will caramelize and glaze the dough during cooking.

Bake for 35 to 40 minutes, or until nicely

browned. Let cool until warm or at room temperature.

At serving time, if the tart has cooled beyond lukewarm, place the skillet back on medium heat and cook, shaking the pan lightly, until the caramel melts. To unmold the tart, place a flat serving dish on top of the skillet and turn the tart out onto the plate.

Beat the heavy cream until firm but not too stiff (no sugar is needed, since the apples are sweet).

Cut the tart into wedges and serve with a good spoonful of whipped cream per serving.

Pear Tatin
Serves 6

✄ **Pears replace apples in** this variation of tarte Tatin.

CARAMEL

- ¼ cup sugar
- 3 tablespoons pear or apple cider

FILLING

- 3 large Bosc pears (about 1½ pounds)
- 2 tablespoons unsalted butter
- ½ cup pear or apple cider

DOUGH

- ½ cup all-purpose flour
- 2 tablespoons unsalted butter
- 2 teaspoons confectioners' sugar
- 1½ tablespoons milk

TOPPING

- ½ cup crème fraîche
- 1 tablespoon confectioners' sugar
- 1 tablespoon pear brandy

FOR THE CARAMEL: Combine the sugar and cider in a 10-inch ovenproof skillet and cook over medium-high heat for about 5 minutes, until the mixture becomes a light caramel. Remove from the heat and swirl the caramel in the skillet to cool and harden it. (If the caramel starts to darken too much as it continues to cook in the pan's residual heat, plunge the base of the skillet in cool water to stop the cooking.)

FOR THE FILLING: Peel the pears, cut them lengthwise in half, and core them. Arrange the pear halves cut side up in the caramel-lined pan so the stem ends of the pears meet in the center.

Add the butter and cider and bring to a boil (the caramel will melt). Cover the skillet, reduce the heat to low, and cook gently for 10 minutes. Remove the lid and keep cooking, checking occasionally, until all the water has evaporated and the mixture in the pan has caramelized again, about 10 minutes longer, and the pears are tender.

MEANWHILE, FOR THE DOUGH: Process the flour, butter, and confectioners' sugar in a food processor for about 10 seconds. Add the milk and process for another 10 seconds.

Transfer the mixture to a sheet of plastic wrap and form it into a ball. Place another piece of plastic wrap on top of the dough and roll it between the plastic into a 10-inch circle. Refrigerate the dough (still encased in plastic) to firm it slightly.

Preheat the oven to 400 degrees, with a rack in the center.

After the pears have cooked for about 20 minutes, remove the dough from the refrigerator, peel off the top sheet of plastic wrap, and invert the dough onto the pears. Peel off the remaining plastic. Place the skillet in the oven and bake for about 30 minutes. The dough should be nicely browned on top and, when you tilt the pan, there should be a rich layer of caramel in the bottom. Let cool to lukewarm or room temperature.

At serving time, if the Pear Tatin has cooled beyond lukewarm, rewarm it over medium heat until the caramel dissolves (the pear mixture will move in the pan when you shake it). To unmold the tart, invert a serving plate on top of the dough and turn the tart out onto the plate.

FOR THE TOPPING: Mix the crème fraîche, sugar, and brandy together.

Slice the tart into portions, half a pear per person, and serve with the topping.

Raspberry Cookie-Dough Galette
Serves 6 to 8

The *pâte sucrée* (or cookie-dough crust) for this galette is buttery and keeps well, so it can sit for hours without softening. Berries combined with raspberry preserves are spread over the cooked shell and more berries are arranged on top.

DOUGH

1¾	cups all-purpose flour
12	tablespoons (1¼ sticks) unsalted butter, softened
3	tablespoons confectioners' sugar
1	large egg yolk
1–2	tablespoons cold water

FILLING AND GLAZE

4	cups raspberries
1	cup seedless raspberry preserves
1	tablespoon raspberry brandy

Preheat the oven to 375 degrees, with a rack in the center.

FOR THE DOUGH: Put the flour, butter, and sugar in a bowl and mix with a spoon or your hands until they are roughly combined.

Mix the egg yolk and water together in a small bowl and stir into the flour mixture.

Gather the dough together and, using the technique known as *fraisage*, with the heel of your hand, smear about 3 tablespoons of the dough at a time forward on the board or countertop, continuing until the ingredients are blended and the dough is completely smooth and the same color throughout. Repeat the procedure a second time to make sure the ingredients are well combined.

Place the dough in the center of a piece of plastic wrap about 14 inches square and cover it with another square of plastic wrap. Roll the dough between the pieces of plastic wrap into a circle about 14 inches in diameter. Peel off the top sheet of plastic wrap and invert the dough onto a large cookie sheet or pizza pan. Pull off the remaining sheet of plastic wrap.

Roll the edges of the dough inward to create a border about ½ inch thick all around. Press on the border so that it is tapered at the top and then, using your thumb and index finger, pinch it all around to create a decorative border.

Bake for about 30 minutes, until the crust is nicely browned and cooked through. Let cool. (*The crust can be baked up to 12 hours ahead.*)

FOR THE FILLING: No more than 2 hours ahead of serving, mix about 1½ cups of the berries, using any damaged or soft berries, with ¼ cup of the preserves in a bowl. Spread the mixture over the baked crust. Arrange the remaining berries on top so that they cover the surface of the galette.

FOR THE GLAZE: Mix the remaining ¾ cup preserves and the brandy together in a small bowl. Using a spoon or brush, coat the top of the berries with the mixture.

To serve, cut the galette into wedges with a bread knife (the crust has a tendency to break when cut).

Banana Tart with Guava Glaze
Serves 8

❧ **Made with a banana** filling combined with pastry cream, this banana tart is best at room temperature, when it is still soft and the flavors are more pronounced.

The bananas, sautéed with butter and lime juice, can be eaten by themselves or flambéed with dark rum and served with ice cream or crepes.

DOUGH

- 1¼ cups all-purpose flour
- 8 tablespoons (1 stick) unsalted butter, softened
- 1 tablespoon sugar
- ⅛ teaspoon salt
- 2 tablespoons ice-cold water

BANANAS

- 2 tablespoons unsalted butter
- ⅓ cup sugar
- ⅓ cup fresh lime juice
- 1½ pounds bananas (about 4), cut into slices (about 2½ cups)

PASTRY CREAM

- 1 cup half-and-half
- 1 large egg
- 1 large egg yolk
- 4 teaspoons cornstarch
- ¼ cup sugar
- ½ teaspoon pure vanilla extract

GLAZE

- ½ cup guava jelly

Preheat the oven to 400 degrees, with a rack in the center. Set a 10-inch tart pan or flan ring on a cookie sheet.

FOR THE DOUGH: Combine the flour, butter, sugar, salt, and ice water in a bowl and work the mixture with your fingers until crumbly.

Place the dough on the work surface and, using the technique called *fraisage*, smear about ¼ cup of the dough forward on the surface with the palm of your hand to blend it thoroughly. Repeat until the whole mixture has been blended. One additional *fraisage* of the dough should be sufficient for the ingredients to be completely combined.

On a lightly floured board, roll the dough (rolling from the center out in every direction) into a circle approximately ⅛ inch thick and 14 inches in diameter. Brush any excess flour from the top of the dough, then roll it up on the rolling pin. Unroll the dough over the tart pan or flan ring and brush any excess flour from the top. (Note that the top of the dough at this point was table side down in the previous step, so by rolling the dough up over the rolling pin and then unrolling it, you are able to remove the excess flour from both sides.) Lift up the dough hanging over the sides of the pan and ease it gently into the pan; it is important not to stretch it, or it will shrink during baking. Push the excess dough in on itself all around into the rim to create a thicker edge.

Roll the rolling pin over the edges of the pan, pressing down and rolling in one direction and then the other to cut off the excess dough. (If desired, reserve the excess dough, refrigerated or frozen, for future use.) With your thumb and index finger, press on the dough all around the edges to create a border. Then, with your thumb, roll a small amount of the dough over the rim of the pan all around, pressing it gently to anchor the shell and hold it in place so it won't collapse on itself during cooking. (This technique makes it unnecessary to line the shell with paper or foil and weight it.) Prick the bottom of the dough all over with a fork. Freeze the dough for 10 minutes.

Bake for about 20 minutes, until lightly browned. Set on a rack. (Leave the oven on.)

MEANWHILE, FOR THE BANANAS: Combine the butter, sugar, and lime juice in a skillet and cook until the mixture forms a pale blond caramel, 8 to 10 minutes. Add the sliced bananas and sauté gently in the caramel for 2 to 3 minutes. Remove from the heat.

FOR THE PASTRY CREAM: Heat the half-and-half in a saucepan until it comes to a boil.

Meanwhile, combine the egg, egg yolk, cornstarch, sugar, and vanilla in a bowl, mixing with a whisk until smooth. Whisk in the boiling half-and-half, mixing well, then return to the saucepan and cook over medium-high heat, stirring constantly with the whisk so it doesn't scorch, until the pastry cream comes to a boil and thickens. Cool for about 10 minutes.

Pour the pastry cream into the pastry shell and spread it evenly all around. Pour the caramelized bananas on top and stir gently to mix the bananas with the pastry cream. Smooth the top.

Bake for 30 minutes, or until lightly browned. Remove from the oven and let the tart cool for 15 to 20 minutes, then scrape off any overhang of dough holding the tart to the pan or ring. Remove the sides of the tart pan or the ring.

FOR THE GLAZE: Melt the guava jelly if it is not soft. Brush the top of the tart with the jelly.

At serving time, slide the tart onto a serving platter and cut it into wedges.

White Peach and Walnut Tart
Serves 6

White peaches are one of my favorite fruits. To absorb some of the peach juices and give added flavor, both the tart shell and the peaches are sprinkled with a mixture of walnuts, flour, sugar, and dough trimmings ground together into a powder. While still warm, the tart is glazed with peach preserves. It is served at room temperature.

DOUGH
- ⅔ cup all-purpose flour
- 3 tablespoons unsalted butter
- 1 tablespoon corn oil
- ½ teaspoon sugar
- ⅛ teaspoon salt
- 1 tablespoon ice-cold water

WALNUT MIXTURE
- ¼ cup walnut pieces
- 1 tablespoon all-purpose flour
- 1 tablespoon sugar

- 4 ripe white peaches (about 1¼ pounds), pitted and cut into quarters
- ¼ cup peach preserves, warmed

Preheat the oven to 400 degrees, with a rack in the center.

FOR THE DOUGH: Combine the flour, butter, oil, sugar, and salt in a food processor and process for about 15 seconds, just until the mixture looks sandy. Add the water and process for another 5 seconds, or just until the mixture begins to gather together. Transfer the mixture to a piece of plastic wrap and, using the wrap, gather it into a ball.

Roll the dough out between two sheets of plastic wrap to a circle about 10 inches in diameter; it will be very thin. Place an 8-inch flan ring or tart pan with a removable bottom on a cookie sheet and fit the dough inside the ring or pan, pressing it into place. Trim the edges to remove the excess dough; reserve the trimmings.

FOR THE WALNUT MIXTURE: Put the walnuts, flour, and sugar in a food processor, add the dough trimmings, and process until well combined.

Spread half of the walnut mixture in the bottom of the tart shell. Arrange the peach quarters in one layer, skin side down, around the circumference of the shell; reserve 2 peach quarters. Cut the 2 peach quarters in half and arrange them, skin side down, in the middle of the tart to create a different look. Sprinkle the rest of the walnut mixture evenly on top.

Bake for 1 hour, or until nicely browned. Cool to lukewarm on a cooling rack.

Using a spoon, spread the peach preserves carefully over the top of the tart. Remove the ring from the tart (the dough will have shrunk enough in cooking to allow easy removal). Using two large spatulas, transfer the tart to a serving platter, then let cool to room temperature before serving, cut into wedges.

Mixed Fruit Tartlets
Serves 4

✎ **Thin disks of dough** are baked with a topping of lightly sugared apricot and plum wedges until the pastry is crisp and the fruit soft.

DOUGH

- ⅔ cup all-purpose flour
- 3 tablespoons cold unsalted butter, cut into 3 pieces
- 1 tablespoon canola oil
- ½ teaspoon sugar
- ⅛ teaspoon salt
- 1 tablespoon ice-cold water if needed

- 4 small ripe apricots (8–10 ounces), pitted and cut into 8–10 thin wedges each
- 4 small ripe dark plums (8–10 ounces), pitted and cut into 8–10 thin wedges each
- 2 tablespoons sugar

Preheat the oven to 400 degrees, with a rack in the center.

FOR THE DOUGH: Put the flour, butter, oil, sugar, and salt in a food processor and process for about 10 seconds. Feel the dough; if it is soft enough to gather together into a ball, remove it from the bowl and form it into a ball. If it is still dry to the touch, add the tablespoon of ice water and process for another 5 or 6 seconds, then remove from the bowl and form into a ball. (*The dough can be made ahead and refrigerated.*)

Lightly flour a work surface and roll the ball of dough into a very thin square, no more than ⅛ inch thick. Using a round cutter with a 5-inch diameter, cut out 4 disks, or use a lid as a guide and cut out with a knife (gather up and reroll the trimmings if required). Carefully transfer the disks to a large cookie sheet lined with a nonstick baking mat, leaving a few inches of space between the disks.

Arrange the apricots and plums, alternating them, in a spiral on top of each dough disk. Sprinkle the fruit with the sugar. Bake for 30 to 35 minutes, until the fruit is soft and the dough nicely browned.

Some of the juice from the fruit will have leaked out onto the cookie sheet. Before it hardens and makes the disks stick to the sheet, lift the tarts with a broad spatula and transfer them to a cooling rack or platter. Serve lukewarm or at room temperature.

Lime and Orange Tartlets
Serves 12

❧ **Individual tartlets filled with** a delicate mixture of lime and orange juices, rind, and egg yolks are served with a mousse-like cognac sauce.

Instead of tartlets, you can make one large tart.

DOUGH

- 2 cups all-purpose flour
- ½ pound (2 sticks) unsalted butter, softened
- ¼ cup confectioners' sugar
- 1 tablespoon heavy cream

FILLING

- 2 large eggs
- 4 large egg yolks
- 1 teaspoon cornstarch
- ⅓ cup granulated sugar
- 1 tablespoon grated orange rind
- 1½ teaspoons grated lime rind
- ¼ cup orange juice
- ¼ cup fresh lime juice

COGNAC SAUCE

- 1 large egg yolk
- ⅓ cup confectioners' sugar
- 1 tablespoon fresh lime juice
- 3 tablespoons cognac
- 1 cup heavy cream

Grated orange rind, for garnish

Preheat the oven to 375 degrees, with a rack in the center. Arrange twelve 3-inch fluted round tartlet tins side by side in 3 rows of 4 each on the work surface.

FOR THE DOUGH: Combine the flour, butter, and confectioners' sugar in a food processor and process for about 20 seconds. Add the cream and process for another 5 to 10 seconds, until the mixture comes together. Turn the dough out and shape it into a disk.

Roll the dough out between sheets of plastic wrap (to avoid using too much flour) to a large rectangle; the dough should be approximately ¼ inch thick. Remove the piece of plastic wrap from the top of the dough and invert the dough (supporting it with the other piece of plastic wrap) on top of the tartlet tins. Peel off the remaining piece of plastic wrap and use it to press the dough lightly into the tins. Using a rolling pin, roll over the top of the tins so the excess dough is cut away around the top edges of the tins; remove and reserve the extra dough. Sprinkle your fingers with flour so they won't stick and press the dough firmly into each pan so it adheres well to the bottom and sides. The dough will be quite thin.

To prevent the dough from collapsing while cooking, line each tartlet tin with waxed paper or aluminum foil and fill with weights (rice, pie weights, or dried beans). Or, if you have enough extra tins, place one directly on top of each pastry-lined tin and press it down to hold the dough in position. Arrange on a cookie sheet and bake for 10 minutes; by then, the dough will be set. Remove the paper or foil weights and the empty tins and bake for about 5 minutes longer, until the dough is almost cooked through. Patch any cracks in the tartlet shells with little pieces of raw dough, smearing it into place with your thumb to seal the pastry.

MEANWHILE, FOR THE FILLING: Combine the eggs, egg yolks, cornstarch, sugar, orange and lime rind, orange juice, and lime juice in a food processor and process until well mixed. Pour into a bowl.

Using a spoon, fill the tartlet shells with the filling (about 3 tablespoons per shell). Bake for 15 minutes, or until nicely browned. Remove the tartlets from the oven and let cool slightly before unmolding. Unmold and let cool to room temperature.

MEANWHILE, FOR THE SAUCE: Combine the egg yolk, confectioners' sugar, and lime juice in a bowl and whisk for about 1 minute to lighten the mixture. Add the cognac.

Whip the cream in a medium bowl until it holds a firm peak. Add the cognac mixture and mix well.

At serving time, spoon some of the sauce onto each serving plate. Sprinkle a little orange rind on top of the sauce, for flavor as well as color, place a tartlet in the center of each plate, and serve.

Brioche Galette with Port-Poached Prunes
Serves 8

❧ **A specialty of a** small town named Pérouges, located between Lyon and Bourg-en-Bresse, where I was born, this thin, crusty, buttery tart of prunes poached in port wine is served with a mixture of whipped cream and sour cream, similar to crème fraîche. Poached apricots can be substituted for the prunes.

The galette is best when served still slightly warm, soon after it comes out of the oven. If allowed to cool, it should be reheated slightly in the oven before serving. The prunes (which traditionally are not pitted) should be cool but not cold.

DOUGH

1   envelope (2¼ teaspoons) active
      dry yeast or 1 cake (0.6 ounce)
      fresh yeast, crumbled
¼   cup milk, warmed to about 100 degrees
½   teaspoon sugar
2   cups all-purpose flour
¼   teaspoon salt

3   large eggs
10 tablespoons (1¼ sticks) unsalted
      butter, softened

PRUNES

1   pound unpitted or pitted prunes
      (choose the largest you can find)
1   cup boiling water
1½ cups port
1   teaspoon potato starch (see page 318),
      dissolved in 1 tablespoon prune juice
      (from the soaked prunes)

TOPPING

3   tablespoons unsalted butter,
      melted
¼   cup sugar

SAUCE

1   cup heavy cream
1   cup sour cream

FOR THE DOUGH: Combine the yeast, milk, and sugar in the bowl of a stand mixer and let stand for about 5 minutes, until bubbly.

Add the flour, salt, and eggs and beat with the flat beater on medium speed for about 3 minutes. Add the softened butter and mix for approximately 30 seconds, just long enough for the butter to be incorporated. Cover with plastic wrap and let rise in a warm, draft-free place (70 to 75 degrees) for 1½ to 2 hours, until doubled in bulk.

MEANWHILE, FOR THE PRUNES: Put the prunes in a bowl and pour the boiling water and 1 cup of the port on top of them. Cover with plastic wrap and let soak for a couple of hours.

Drain off the juice (approximately 1 cup) from the prunes, pour into a saucepan, and bring to a boil. Add the dissolved potato starch and return to a boil. Add the prunes to the pan and bring to a boil. Remove from the heat and let cool to lukewarm, then add the remaining ½ cup port.

Break down the dough gently by kneading it briefly to release the air inside. Butter a cookie sheet and place the dough on it. Wet your hands (to prevent sticking) and spread the dough into a rectangle about 12 by 15 inches and ¼ to ⅜ inch thick.

FOR THE TOPPING: Brush the top of the dough rectangle with the melted butter and sprinkle it with the sugar. Some of the sugar will be absorbed by the melted butter and some will form a crust on top. Let rise at room temperature for 20 to 25 minutes.

Preheat the oven to 425 degrees, with a rack in the center.

Bake the galette for about 20 minutes, or until nicely puffed and browned. Let cool to lukewarm.

MEANWHILE, FOR THE SAUCE: Whip the heavy cream until soft peaks form. Fold in the sour cream. (There is no sweetener added to the cream, because the prunes and galette are sweet enough.)

CRÈME FRAÎCHE

Many desserts in this book are served with a creamy topping: whipped cream, sour cream, or yogurt. You can substitute crème fraîche, commercial or homemade, for any of these toppings.

Crème fraîche is a thick natural cream with a butterfat content of at least 45 percent. You can make your own version by mixing a little yogurt with heavy cream; after a few hours at room temperature, the mixture will thicken into a reasonable facsimile of crème fraîche. You can also combine whipped heavy cream with an equal amount of sour cream, as in the recipe above.

Serve a crunchy wedge of the pastry per person, with some prunes and cream.

Phyllo Tart with Fruit
Serves 4

✶ **Phyllo dough, available frozen** in most supermarkets, is rolled, cut into strips, tossed with butter, oil, and sugar, patted into a tart shell, and baked. The fruit, a mixture of plums and blueberries thickened with preserves, can be varied based on what you have on hand. The fruit can be prepared several hours before serving, as can the tart shell.

FRUIT

- ⅓ cup boysenberry or plum preserves
- 1½ tablespoons fresh lemon juice
- 12 ounces large damson or Burbank plums (about 3), peeled if the skin is tough, pitted, and cut into ½-inch dice
- 1 cup blueberries

PHYLLO

- 4 sheets (14 by 18 inches) phyllo dough, thawed (keep covered until ready to use)
- 2 tablespoons unsalted butter, melted
- 1 tablespoon canola oil
- 2 tablespoons sugar

- 4 small fresh mint sprigs or strips of lemon rind, for garnish

FOR THE FRUIT: Mix the preserves and lemon juice together in a bowl large enough to accommodate all the fruit. Add the plums and blueberries and mix well. Cover and put in a cool place until serving time.

Preheat the oven to 350 degrees, with a rack in the center.

FOR THE PHYLLO: Roll the sheets of phyllo together into a scroll and cut them crosswise into about ½-inch-wide strips. (You should have about 3 cups.)

Put the shredded phyllo on a nonstick cookie sheet. Add the butter, oil, and sugar and mix gently until all the strands of dough are coated with the fat and sugar. Gather up the phyllo strips and press them gently into an 8-inch tart pan (or flan ring) set in the center of the cookie sheet.

Bake the phyllo shell for 15 to 18 minutes, until nicely browned and crisp. Cool the crust in the pan on a rack, then transfer it to a serving platter.

At serving time, spoon the fruit onto the phyllo crust. Decorate with the mint sprigs or lemon rind, cut into wedges at the table, and serve.

Top-Crust Cherry Pie

Serves 6

Here's an easy way of making cherry pie: the cherries are baked in a gratin dish with only a top crust. Serve the pie by cutting pieces of the crisp crust, inverting them onto dessert plates, and piling the cherries on top or alongside. If fresh cherries are not available, substitute unsweetened IQF (individually quick frozen) cherries.

- 2 pounds large Bing cherries or a mixture of Bing, Rainier, and/or Montmorency cherries, pitted (about 5½ cups)
- ⅔ cup sugar
- 2 tablespoons potato starch (see page 318)
- 1 teaspoon pure vanilla extract
- ½ teaspoon pure almond extract

DOUGH

- ¾ cup all-purpose flour
- 2 tablespoons unsalted butter
- 1½ tablespoons sugar
- Pinch of salt
- 6 tablespoons cottage cheese

Ice cream, sour cream, or plain yogurt, for serving (optional)

Preheat the oven to 375 degrees, with a rack in the center.

Put the cherries, sugar, starch, vanilla, and almond extract in a bowl and mix well. Transfer the mixture to a round or oval gratin dish with a capacity of about 5 cups.

FOR THE DOUGH: Combine the flour, butter, sugar, salt, and cottage cheese in a food processor and process for 15 to 20 seconds, until the mixture begins to come together.

Transfer the dough to a piece of plastic wrap 3 to 4 inches larger than the gratin dish and form it into a ball in the center of the wrap. Place another piece of plastic wrap (about the same size as the first piece) on top, then roll the dough out to a circle or an oval about 3 inches larger than the dish. Peel the top piece of plastic wrap from the surface of the dough and, holding the edges of the plastic wrap, invert the dough over the gratin dish. Peel off the plastic wrap.

Carefully lift the dough overhang with your fingers and roll it onto itself to create a thicker layer all around the edges of the dish. Using your thumb and fingers, press on the thick dough edge to seal it to the dish and create a decorative border. Prick the dough in the center a few times with a sharp knife, to enable steam to escape.

Place the gratin dish on a cookie sheet and bake for 50 to 60 minutes, until browned, covering the dish with aluminum foil for the last 10 minutes if necessary to prevent the dough from becoming too brown. Cool to room temperature on a rack.

To serve, break through the crust with a

spoon and arrange a section of crust with a portion of the filling on top of or alongside it on each of six plates. Serve, if desired, with ice cream, sour cream, or yogurt.

Individual Chocolate Nut Pies

Serves 4

❧ **The rich filling for** these little pies is a mixture of bittersweet chocolate, corn syrup, egg, and mixed nuts. Baked in a classic graham cracker crust in individual ramekins, they are both easy and delicious. The pies can be made up to a day ahead and refrigerated, but they should be rewarmed in a low oven to bring them back to room temperature before serving.

CRUST

5	graham crackers (3½ ounces)
1½	tablespoons unsalted butter, softened
1	tablespoon canola oil
2	tablespoons sugar

FILLING

½	cup pecans
¼	cup unblanched whole almonds
¼	cup pine nuts
3½	ounces bittersweet chocolate, coarsely chopped
2	teaspoons unsalted butter
1	teaspoon cornstarch
⅓	cup light corn syrup
1	large egg, lightly beaten
1	teaspoon pure vanilla extract

Preheat the oven to 350 degrees, with a rack in the center.

FOR THE CRUST: Process the graham crackers, butter, canola oil, and sugar in a food processor for 1 minute, or until the mixture is mealy and starting to come together.

Divide the mixture among four 1-cup ramekins or aluminum foil muffin cups and press it evenly over the bottom and up the sides of each one.

FOR THE FILLING: Process the pecans and almonds in the food processor for a few seconds to coarsely chop them. Mix with the pine nuts and divide among the ramekins or cups lined with the crust.

Melt the chocolate with the butter in a bowl in a microwave oven or in a double boiler. Add the cornstarch and mix well, then add the corn syrup and mix well. Add the egg and vanilla and mix well.

Divide the mixture among the ramekins. Arrange the ramekins on a cookie sheet and bake for about 20 minutes, until the filling is set but still somewhat soft in the middle. Let cool to lukewarm or room temperature on a rack.

At serving time, invert each of the pies onto a dessert plate. Carefully turn the pies right side up and serve.

Cream Puffs with Chocolate Sauce

Serves 6

❧ **Similar to ones my** mother used to prepare, these cream puffs are filled with blackberry preserves and whipped cream and served on a simple but particularly flavorful chocolate sauce made of melted chocolate and milk.

A common mistake is to let the cream puffs dry in the oven for too long. They should not be like dry bread; rather, they should hold their shape but remain soft and moist inside.

You can, of course, make smaller puffs, cooking them a proportionately shorter time, and serve several per person. Small puffs, called profiteroles, are often stuffed with ice cream and served with hot chocolate sauce.

DOUGH

- ¾ cup milk
- 3 tablespoons unsalted butter
- ⅛ teaspoon salt
- ¾ cup all-purpose flour
- 3 large eggs

FILLING

- 1½ cups heavy cream
- ¼ cup confectioners' sugar
- 2 teaspoons pure vanilla extract
- ¼ cup blackberry preserves

- 1 teaspoon confectioners' sugar

CHOCOLATE SAUCE

- 8 ounces bittersweet or semisweet chocolate, coarsely chopped
- 1¼ cups milk

Preheat the oven to 350 degrees, with a rack in the center.

FOR THE DOUGH: Combine the milk, butter, and salt in a saucepan and bring to a boil over high heat. Immediately remove from the heat, add the flour all at once, and mix it in with a wooden spatula. Return the pan to the stove and stir over medium-high heat until the mixture comes away from the sides of the pan and collects into one soft lump about the consistency of modeling clay. Cook for about 20 to 30 seconds, still stirring, to dry the mixture further, then transfer to a food processor and process for 4 to 5 seconds to cool the mixture slightly.

Beat the eggs in a bowl with a fork until well mixed. Reserve 1 tablespoon of the beaten eggs to brush on the puffs and add the remaining eggs to the dough mixture. Process for 20 to 30 seconds, until very smooth.

Lightly butter a cookie sheet. Spoon 6 rounds of dough, each about the size of a Ping-Pong ball (approximately 3 tablespoons), onto the sheet, spacing them evenly to allow for expansion. Brush with the beaten egg to smooth the tops and coat the surface of the balls.

Bake for about 40 minutes, until the puffs are nicely developed, browned, and cooked through. They should hold their shape but still be soft. Open the oven door halfway and let the puffs dry for 10 minutes in the oven. Set aside in a draft-free area to cool.

FOR THE FILLING: Whip the cream with the confectioners' sugar and vanilla in a bowl until firm. Refrigerate.

Remove the top of each puff, cutting around the puff about a quarter of the way down and lifting off the resulting cap; reserve the tops. Spoon 2 teaspoons of the blackberry preserves into the base of each puff. Spoon the cream mixture into a pastry bag fitted with a star tip and pipe it into the puffs, piping in enough whipped cream to come up about 1½ inches above the cut edges. Replace the caps and sprinkle with the confectioners'

sugar. Cover and refrigerate. (*The puffs can be assembled a few hours before serving.*)

FOR THE SAUCE: Heat the chocolate and milk in a saucepan over medium-low heat, stirring occasionally, just until the chocolate melts. Mix well with a whisk, transfer to a bowl, and refrigerate, stirring occasionally, until cold.

Place a puff on each of six individual dessert plates and serve with the chocolate sauce.

Croquembouche
Serves 8 to 10

✂ From *croque* ("to crunch") and *bouche* ("mouth"), croquembouche is a tower of cream puffs held together with caramel. In this scaled-down version, which is narrow and not too tall, the tops of light, unstuffed pastry puffs are glazed with caramel and built into a small pyramid. The inside of the pyramid is brushed with cherry jam and filled with sweetened whipped cream.

DOUGH

1 cup milk
4 tablespoons (½ stick) unsalted butter
¼ teaspoon granulated sugar
⅛ teaspoon salt
1 cup all-purpose flour
4 large eggs

CARAMEL

1 cup granulated sugar
3 tablespoons water

DECORATIONS

Small silver balls, crystallized violets, or other decorations
A flower to decorate the top (optional)

3 tablespoons cherry jam, warmed

FILLING

2 cups heavy cream
2 tablespoons confectioners' sugar
1 teaspoon pure vanilla extract
1 tablespoon kirsch

Preheat the oven to 375 degrees, with a rack in the center. Line a cookie sheet with a nonstick baking mat.

FOR THE DOUGH: Combine the milk, butter, sugar, and salt in a saucepan and bring to a boil. Remove from the heat, add the flour in one stroke, and mix with a wooden spatula. Place back over low heat and cook, stirring, for about 30 seconds, until the dough comes away from the sides of the pan. Transfer to a food processor and let cool for 10 minutes.

Add the eggs to the dough and process for 30 seconds, until smooth. Spoon the dough into a pastry bag fitted with a 1-inch plain tip. Pipe the dough into 2-inch mounds about 1½ inches apart on the lined cookie sheet. (You should have about 20 puffs.) Smooth the tops of the choux with a moist finger.

Bake for 30 minutes. Turn off the oven, prop open the oven door a little, and let the choux remain in the oven for 10 to 20 minutes, to allow the moisture trapped inside to escape. Remove.

FOR THE CARAMEL: Mix the sugar and water together in a saucepan and cook over medium heat until the mixture turns a light amber color. Remove from the heat and place on a pot holder. Holding each choux at the base, dip the top into the caramel, then scrape the pastry against the edge of the pan to remove any excess and set on a tray, caramel side up. Immediately, before the caramel hardens, sprinkle a few silver balls, crystallized violets, or other decorations onto the top of each choux.

When all the choux have been glazed, halve 2 or 3 of them, drizzle a bit of caramel along the sides of each piece, and arrange cut side down in a circle to form a "crown" for the base of the cake. Stick the point of a knife into the caramel and drizzle a little caramel between each choux half, then hold them together firmly for a few seconds, until the caramel hardens and the choux adhere.

Start building the croquembouche by dipping one side of each of the remaining choux into the caramel and placing it caramel side down onto the choux crown to hold it in place. With the point of the knife, paint a little caramel between the choux as needed to make them stick together. Hold each layer in place for a few seconds, until the caramel hardens and the choux hold firmly, before moving to the next layer. Place the last choux on top and drizzle on additional caramel as needed, using only the minimum amount required to hold the structure together. If the caramel hardens too much during the building, return it to the top of the stove to melt, or microwave it. Wait for about 5 minutes; the croquembouche will hold together.

Stand the croquembouche upside down in a tall narrow pot, a flower vase, or a carafe so that it is held securely in place. Using a long brush, coat the inside with the cherry jam.

FOR THE FILLING: Beat the cream with the confectioners' sugar, vanilla, and kirsch until firm. Place in a pastry bag fitted with a large star tip and fill the inside of the croquembouche with most of the cream.

Carefully turn the croquembouche right side up onto a serving plate. Pipe the remainder of the whipped cream around the base as a decoration. If desired, add the flower to decorate the top.

The croquembouche is traditionally cut starting at the top. The first layer is cut with scissors or a knife to separate it from the rest of the structure. Then individual choux can be broken off and served with a spoonful of the whipped cream from inside.

Cream Puff Fritters
Serves 6 to 8

✄ **An ideal winter dessert,** these fritters are light and delicious as well as easy. The *pâte à choux* dough can be flavored with vanilla, lemon, almond extract, coffee, or even chocolate — this one contains vanilla and sugar. In France it is often made with orange-blossom water. The dough can be made a day or more ahead and kept in the refrigerator, but the puffs should be made at the last moment.

The balls of dough should not be too big — about 2 teaspoons — and they should be cooked long enough so they brown and expand, with a beautiful crust forming all around.

DOUGH

1	cup milk
3	tablespoons unsalted butter
2	teaspoons granulated sugar
1	teaspoon pure vanilla extract
1	cup all-purpose flour
3	medium eggs

4–5 cups canola oil, for deep-frying
Confectioners' sugar, for sprinkling

FOR THE DOUGH: Combine the milk, butter, sugar, and vanilla in a saucepan and bring to a boil. As soon as the mixture boils, remove the pan from the heat, add the flour all at once, and combine well and fast with a wooden spatula; stir the mixture until it forms a ball and comes away from the sides of the pan — this will take only a few seconds. Return the pan to the heat and cook and stir the mixture for 30 seconds to a minute to dry it further. Transfer the dough to a food processor and let cool for 10 minutes.

Add the eggs and process until they are incorporated. Transfer the dough to a bowl, cover with an oiled piece of plastic wrap, and refrigerate until ready to use; it should be cool when used.

Heat 3 inches of oil to 325 to 350 degrees in a deep pot. Working in batches, scoop up about 2 teaspoons of dough for each fritter, push the mixture to the edge of the spoon with your index finger, and into the hot oil; work quickly, making about a dozen fritters at a time. Let the fritters cook for 7 to 8 minutes at the same temperature. The balls will float to the top and turn over by themselves as they brown and expand; they should become almost hollow inside, very light and very delicate. Remove the puffs from the oil and drain on a wire rack.

Arrange the fritters on a serving dish, sprinkle generously with confectioners' sugar, and serve.

Chocolate Paris-Brest
Serves 8 to 10

✂ **Resembling a wheel, this** French pastry is thought to have been created by a Parisian pastry chef to celebrate the famous bicycle race from Paris to Brest, in Brittany. The traditional version consists of an almond-topped ring of cream puff pastry that is split and filled with a praline-flavored buttercream. My rendition has a chocolate cream filling and is topped with sweetened whipped cream flavored with a little rum.

DOUGH

¾	cup milk
3	tablespoons unsalted butter
¼	teaspoon granulated sugar
⅛	teaspoon salt
¾	cup all-purpose flour
3	large eggs
2	tablespoons sliced almonds

CHOCOLATE CREAM

¾	cup milk
2	large egg yolks
2	tablespoons granulated sugar
1½	tablespoons all-purpose flour
4	ounces bittersweet chocolate, finely chopped

GARNISH

1	cup heavy cream
1	tablespoon dark rum
1½	tablespoons granulated sugar
1	teaspoon confectioners' sugar

Preheat the oven to 375 degrees, with a rack in the center.

FOR THE DOUGH: Combine the milk, butter, sugar, and salt in a saucepan and bring to a boil over medium-high heat. Remove from the heat, add the flour in one stroke, and mix well with a wooden spoon. Then place back over the heat and cook, stirring constantly, for 15 to 20 seconds, until the mixture comes away from the sides of the pan. Transfer the dough to a food processor and let cool for 10 minutes.

Crack the eggs into a small bowl and mix them well with a fork. Set aside 1 tablespoon of the beaten egg for use as a glaze. Pour the remaining eggs into the processor and process for 20 to 30 seconds, until the eggs are well incorporated and the dough is smooth.

Line a cookie sheet with a nonstick baking mat or use a nonstick cookie sheet. Spoon the dough into a pastry bag fitted with a ¾-inch plain tip. Pipe a ring with an outside circumference of 8 to 8½ inches on the cookie sheet. Pipe another circle of dough inside and another on top of the rings, using all the dough, so you have a circle that is 1½ to 1¾ inches high with a hole in the center that measures about 5 inches across. Do not start and end the dough circles in the same spot, since this could cause the pastry to open at the seam during baking.

Brush the dough with the reserved tablespoon of egg. Using a fork, mark the top and sides of the dough, running the tines of the fork gently around the circle to create a crosshatch effect. Sprinkle with the sliced almonds.

Bake for 20 minutes. Reduce the heat to 350 degrees and bake for an additional 35 minutes, or until browned. (If the pastry begins to brown excessively, cover it loosely with a piece of aluminum foil.) Turn the oven off and let the pastry remain in the oven for 30 minutes with the door partially open to evaporate some of the moisture.

Remove from the oven and let cool to room temperature before removing from the cookie sheet.

FOR THE CHOCOLATE CREAM: Bring the milk to a boil in a medium saucepan.

Meanwhile, combine the yolks and sugar in a bowl, mixing them with a whisk for about 30 seconds. Add the flour and mix it in with the whisk. Pour the boiling milk in on top of the egg yolk mixture and mix it in well with the whisk. Return the mixture to the saucepan and bring to a boil, mixing constantly with the whisk. Boil for about 10 seconds, then remove from the heat and add the chocolate. Stir occasionally until the chocolate has melted and is completely incorporated into the pastry cream.

Transfer to a bowl, cover, and let cool, then refrigerate until chilled.

FOR THE GARNISH: Whip the cream, rum, and sugar in a bowl until stiff. Refrigerate until ready to use.

TO FINISH THE PASTRY: Use a sharp knife to remove a ½-inch-thick horizontal slice, or "lid," from the top; set it aside. Using a spoon, spread the chocolate cream in the bottom of the pastry round, pushing it gently into the cavities of the pastry. Transfer the whipped cream to a pastry bag fitted with a ½-inch star tip and pipe the cream on top of the chocolate cream. It should come at least 1 inch above the rim of the cake.

Cut the pastry lid into 8 to 10 equal pieces and reassemble them in order on top of the pastry to make it easy to cut into portions. Sprinkle with the confectioners' sugar. (*The pastry can be assembled a few hours ahead and refrigerated.*)

At serving time, using the separations on the lid as guides, cut through the bottom half of the pastry and arrange on individual dessert plates.

Cherry-Raspberry Pillow
Serves 8 to 10

✂ **For this large free-form** pie, cherries and raspberries are thickened with a little cornstarch and sweetened with preserves. The uncooked mixture is folded into a pastry rectangle and baked.

If you plan to make the dessert more than 1 hour ahead, you might want to use the *pâte brisée* from the Country Apple Galette, since this dough will keep its crunchiness longer than puff pastry. Coarse sugar gives the pastry a nice crispy finish.

1	pound Puff Pastry (page 597), Fast Puff Pastry (page 598), or store-bought puff pastry, preferably all-butter; or dough from Country Apple Galette (page 573)
1	pound cherries, pitted (see the sidebar, page 592)
⅔	cup seedless raspberry preserves
1½	tablespoons cornstarch
8	ounces raspberries
2	tablespoons unsalted butter, cut into bits
	Egg wash made with 1 large egg, half the white removed, beaten
1	tablespoon coarse sugar
	Confectioners' sugar, for dusting

A cherry pitter is the easiest way to pit cherries. If you don't have one, hold each cherry between the thumb and forefinger of one hand so the hole from the stem shows. With the other hand, insert the tip of a small pointed knife into the hole until you feel the pit. Squeeze the cherry to soften the flesh and loosen the pit while simultaneously bringing the pit up through the hole with the point of the knife. After a bit of practice, you'll be able to pit cherries quite quickly.

Preheat the oven to 400 degrees, with a rack in the center.

Roll the dough out into a large very thin rectangle, about 14 by 22 inches and 1/16 inch thick. Roll the dough up on the rolling pin and unroll it across a cookie sheet (the width of the dough will be almost the length of the cookie sheet), so that almost half of it extends beyond one side of the cookie sheet (it will be folded over the filling later).

Combine the cherries with the preserves and cornstarch. Spread the cherry mixture on top of the dough covering the cookie sheet, leaving a 1½-inch border around the fruit. Scatter the raspberries and butter on top. Brush the edges of the pastry with water and fold the pastry extending beyond the cookie sheet over the fruit to encase it. Press to seal the dough around the edges and trim the corners to round them slightly. Press gently on the top of the "pillow" to distribute the fruit

evenly inside. Brush with the egg wash and press down on the edges of the pastry with the tines of a fork about 1½ inches all around to create a border.

Sprinkle the coarse sugar on top and mark a crisscross pattern on top of the pastry with a knife. (It's all right if you cut through the dough at certain points, because that will allow the steam to escape during cooking.) Bake for 45 minutes, or until golden brown. The filling may leak slightly, so be sure to move the pillow a little on the cookie sheet as it comes out of the oven, before the hot juices have a chance to harden and stick to the pan. Let cool, then sprinkle with confectioners' sugar.

At serving time, cut the dessert into slices on a board and arrange on a serving platter. Serve.

Puff Pastry Tartlets with Oranges and Cream
Serves 8

✻ **Caramelized puff pastry rounds** are covered with pastry cream and orange segments and finished with a glaze. The components can be prepared ahead, but the tartlets are at their best when assembled at the last moment.

PASTRY CREAM

- 1 cup milk
- 2 large egg yolks
- 3 tablespoons sugar
- 1½ tablespoons cornstarch
- 1 teaspoon pure vanilla extract
- 4 tablespoons (½ stick) unsalted butter, softened

  About 1½ pounds Puff Pastry (page 597), Fast Puff Pastry (page 598), or store-bought puff pastry, preferably all-butter
- 6 tablespoons sugar

Egg wash made with 1 large egg, half the white removed, beaten

6–8 large navel oranges

GLAZE

½ cup peach preserves

½ cup orange marmalade

Fresh mint sprigs, for garnish

FOR THE PASTRY CREAM: Bring the milk to a boil in a medium saucepan.

Meanwhile, beat the egg yolks, sugar, cornstarch, and vanilla together in a bowl for about 30 seconds, until well mixed. Pour the milk into the egg yolk mixture while beating with a whisk, then return the mixture to the pan. Bring to a strong boil, stirring — especially around the edges of the pan — so the mixture doesn't scorch as it thickens. Boil for 5 to 10 seconds. Pour into a bowl, cover with plastic wrap, and refrigerate until lukewarm.

Whisk the soft butter into the lukewarm pastry cream. Cover with plastic wrap pressed against the surface of the cream and refrigerate until cold. (*The pastry cream can be made up to a day ahead.*)

Preheat the oven to 400 degrees, with a rack in the center.

Roll the pastry out to a large rectangle, about 13 by 27 inches and ⅛ inch thick. Let it rest for a few minutes so it won't shrink too much when cut. Using a lid or plate approximately 6 inches across, mark 8 rounds, then cut out the rounds.

Line two cookie sheets with nonstick baking mats or parchment paper and sprinkle each with 1 tablespoon of the sugar. Place 4 rounds on each sheet. Brush the pastry rounds with the egg wash and sprinkle 2 tablespoons of the remaining sugar on the 4 rounds on each tray. With the point of a knife, mark a circle inside each round approximately ¾ inch from the edges.

Bake for 15 to 20 minutes, until well cooked and crispy. If the rounds do not get brown enough, place under the broiler (not too close) for a few seconds. Cool on a rack.

Peel all the oranges with a sharp knife, moving the knife in a jigsaw motion so all the white pith is removed and each orange is completely nude. Working over a bowl, cut between the membranes on either side of each orange segment to remove the segments, letting them drop into the bowl. When all the flesh has been removed, squeeze the membranes over the bowl to release the remaining juice. Set the orange segments and juice aside.

At serving time, cut around the scored circle in each pastry round and push the crystallized top down into the pastry to create a crisp, brown base. Spread 2 tablespoons of the pastry cream in the bottom of each pastry receptacle. Drain the orange segments and arrange on top of the pastry cream.

FOR THE GLAZE: Melt the peach preserves and orange marmalade together, then strain.

Coat the top of each pastry with 1½ to 2 tablespoons of the glaze. Place on individual plates, decorate with sprigs of mint, and serve.

Sugared Puff Pastry Sticks
Makes 70 to 80 sticks

Rolled in sugar and cut into little strips, puff pastry dough becomes crispy and caramelized. This is a faster, simpler version of what are called *palmiers* (palm trees) in France and "elephant ears" in the U.S. You can use puff pastry trimmings to make these.

½ cup sugar
8 ounces Puff Pastry (page 597),
   Fast Puff Pastry (page 598),
   or store-bought puff pastry,
   preferably all-butter

Preheat the oven to 400 degrees, with a rack in the center. Line a cookie sheet with parchment paper.

Sprinkle about ¼ cup of the sugar on a board and roll out the puff pastry to a rectangle about 9 by 15 inches. Sprinkle 3 tablespoons of the remaining sugar on top of the pastry. Turn it over and roll it out again so both sides are well coated with sugar. The finished pastry rectangle should measure about 10 by 16 inches.

Cut the rectangle lengthwise into 2 strips and stack one on top of the other. (The sugar coating will prevent them from sticking.) Cut the pastry into thin strips or sticks approximately 5 inches long and ⅜ inch wide.

Separate the strips and arrange them on the cookie sheet; they can be fairly close together, as they tend to shrink a little during cooking. Sprinkle with the reserved 1 tablespoon sugar.

Bake for 10 to 12 minutes, or until crisp and brown. Cool on a rack and store in an airtight container.

Pear-Almond Puff Pastry Squares
Serves 8

❧ **These delicate pastries consist** of a crisp layer of puff pastry covered with almond cream and topped with poached pears. Wait until the last moment to put them together: if all the components are ready, you won't need more than a few seconds to assemble them.

The cooking time for poached pears can vary greatly. They need just 1 to 2 minutes in a boiling syrup if they are very ripe; hard pears, such as Seckel or Bosc, can take 45 minutes to an hour. Other poached fruit, such as apricots or peaches, or even uncooked fruit, such as sliced bananas or berries, can be used instead of the pears.

8 small Bartlett pears (2½–3 pounds)
1 large lemon
4 cups water
⅔ cup sugar
1 teaspoon pure vanilla extract

PASTRY CREAM
½ cup unblanched whole almonds
1 cup half-and-half
3 large egg yolks
3 tablespoons sugar
1½ tablespoons cornstarch
1 teaspoon pure vanilla extract

About 1½ pounds Puff Pastry (page 597), Fast Puff Pastry (page 598), or store-bought puff pastry, preferably all-butter
Egg wash made with 1 large egg, half the white removed, beaten
3 tablespoons sugar

½ cup heavy cream

GLAZE
1½ cups apricot preserves
1 tablespoon pear brandy (optional)

Fresh mint sprigs, for garnish

Peel the pears with a vegetable peeler: peel the round base of each pear in a circular motion. Where the pear narrows at the neck, peel upward toward the stem, again following the shape of the pear. Using a melon baller, remove the core and seeds from the bottom (you will probably need to remove 2 or 3 balls of pear to get all the seeds), or use a paring knife to remove the core. Leave the stems attached for decoration.

TO POACH THE PEARS: Remove the lemon rind with a vegetable peeler and juice the lemon.

Mix together the water, sugar, lemon rind, juice, and vanilla in a stainless steel saucepan deep enough so the pears will be submerged in the syrup, then add the pears. The pears will float to the top, but anything above the level of the syrup will discolor during cooking, so place a folded paper towel and an inverted plate on top of the pears to keep them submerged. Bring to a boil, cover with a lid, and boil gently until the pears are tender but still slightly firm when pierced with the point of a knife; timing will depend on the ripeness of the pears. Let the pears cool in the syrup. (They will continue to cook as they cool.)

When the pears are cool, remove the plate and paper towel. Notice that the pears are beautifully white and are now sinking into the syrup; as they cool, the specific gravity of the pears changes, so they absorb some of the syrup and sink into the syrup and they will not discolor. Set aside.

FOR THE PASTRY CREAM: Preheat the oven to 400 degrees.

Spread the almonds on a cookie sheet and bake for 10 to 12 minutes. Let cool, then grind in a food processor; set aside.

Bring the half-and-half to a boil in a medium saucepan.

Meanwhile, beat the egg yolks, sugar, cornstarch, and vanilla in a bowl with a whisk, mixing well. Add the hot half-and-half in a stream while whisking constantly. Return the mixture to the saucepan and bring to a boil, mixing constantly with the whisk — especially around the edges of the base of the pan — so the mixture doesn't scorch as it thickens. Boil for 5 seconds. Pour into

a bowl and add the ground almonds. Cover with plastic wrap pressed against the surface of the cream and refrigerate until cold.

FOR THE PASTRY: Preheat the oven to 400 degrees, with a rack in the center.

On a lightly floured surface, roll the dough out into a ¼-inch-thick rectangle about 16 by 8 inches. Trim the sides of the rectangle, then cut it lengthwise in half and across into eight 4-inch squares. Let it rest, preferably refrigerated, for a few minutes. Brush with the egg wash.

Sprinkle 2 tablespoons of the sugar on a cookie sheet lined with a nonstick baking mat or parchment paper. Place the 8 squares of pastry on top. With the point of a knife, mark a square about ½ inch from the edges of each square. Sprinkle with the remaining tablespoon of sugar.

Bake for about 20 minutes, until golden brown. Let the dough squares cool for 10 to 15 minutes, then cut into each pastry with the point of a knife, following the lines you marked before baking, and ease the knife under to remove this top section. After you have released the top, press it down into the pastry shell to create a golden brown, crisp base.

Beat the heavy cream until firm. Add the whipped cream to the cold pastry cream and mix with a whisk.

Drain the pears and dry on paper towels. (The syrup can be poured into a jar and kept in the refrigerator almost forever, for use in poaching other fruits.)

At serving time, spoon about 2 tablespoons of the pastry cream into each pastry receptacle.

FOR THE GLAZE: Strain the apricot preserves through a food mill (a food processor would whip the preserves and make them whitish and full of air bubbles) into a bowl. Or melt the preserves and press through a fine-mesh sieve; let cool. If the preserves are quite thick, dilute with the pear brandy or 1 to 2 tablespoons of the syrup from the pears.

Put a little ring of the glaze on each plate and place a pastry receptacle on top. Dip the pears into the glaze, rolling them so they are completely coated, lift them out, and place one on top of each filled pastry receptacle. Decorate with sprigs of mint, pushed right into the pears so they stand firmly, and serve immediately.

Almond Pithiviers
Serves 10

❧ **Named after the small** town of Pithiviers, between Paris and Orléans, this dessert consists of an almond filling sandwiched between rounds of puff pastry. It's etched with a spiral design on top and finished with confectioners' sugar that becomes glazed and shiny when baked.

The pastry is best eaten lukewarm. If there are pieces left over, they should be reheated slightly in the oven before serving. The pastry is also excellent with ice cream.

FILLING
- ¾ cup unblanched whole almonds
- ½ cup confectioners' sugar
- ½ teaspoon cornstarch
- 4 tablespoons (½ stick) unsalted butter, softened
- 1 large egg
- 1 tablespoon dark rum
- ½ teaspoon pure vanilla extract

- 2½ pounds Puff Pastry (page 597), Fast Puff Pastry (page 598), or store-bought puff pastry, preferably all-butter
  Egg wash made with 1 large egg, half the white removed, beaten
- 2 tablespoons light corn syrup, for glazing the top

Preheat the oven to 400 degrees, with a rack in the center.

FOR THE FILLING: Spread the almonds on a cookie sheet and bake for about 8 minutes, until lightly browned. Set aside to cool.

Process the toasted almonds, confectioners' sugar, and cornstarch in a food processor until the mixture is finely ground. Add the butter, egg, rum,

coat the top of the pastry with the corn syrup. Bake for 15 to 20 minutes more. By that time, the syrup should have created a beautiful glaze. If not, place under the broiler (not too close) for a few minutes to finish glazing. Let cool for 20 to 30 minutes.

Cut into wedges and serve lukewarm.

Puff Pastry
Makes 2½ to 3 pounds

✂ **Puff pastry is one** of the most difficult doughs to make; even for professionals, it has its pitfalls. It is always made with flour and butter in close to equal proportions, and the object is to keep the layers of butter enclosed between the dough layers, so as to achieve the proper flaky texture. The butter and the dough must be at the same temperature to roll uniformly. Soft butter will "squish" and run between the layers, destroying them; if the dough is too soft, it will do the same. The flour used to roll out the dough must be dusted off the surface of the dough before folding it, or the dough may become tough and dry. It is important to work quickly, but if the dough gets elastic, do not fight it; let it rest refrigerated for 30 minutes or so before continuing.

and vanilla and process for about 20 seconds until smooth. Transfer to a bowl. (*The almond filling can be made up to 2 hours ahead and refrigerated; it tends to thicken as it cools.*)

Roll the puff pastry into a large rectangle approximately ¼ inch thick. Using a 10-inch flan ring or pot lid as a guide, mark 2 circles in the dough. With a sharp knife, cut out the circles. (Don't use the flan ring to cut the dough, as it would crush it, preventing it from rising properly.)

Place one of the circles on a cookie sheet lined with parchment paper. Place the almond filling on top and spread it with a spatula to within 1 inch of the edges of the circle.

Moisten the exposed edges of the dough with water and place the remaining circle of dough on top. Press around the edges to seal the 2 rounds together. Place the pastry in the freezer for 5 to 10 minutes, so the dough hardens a little.

Press on the edges of the pastry with your thumb while notching the dough with your index finger to create a design all around; press firmly with your thumb to make firm indentations. Brush the top of the pastry with the egg wash. Using a knife, mark concentric lines from the outer edge to the center of the pastry. Make a small steam hole in the center of the dough with the point of the knife.

Bake for about 35 minutes.

Reduce the heat to 375 degrees. Using a brush,

1	pound (about 3 cups) cold all-purpose flour
½	teaspoon salt
1–1¼	cups ice-cold water
1	pound very cold unsalted butter

Put the flour, salt, and 1 cup ice water in a food processor and process for about 10 seconds. If the dough is not holding together in a smooth paste, add up to ¼ cup more water and process again for a few seconds, just until it gathers together.

Cut each stick of butter lengthwise into 3 slices. On a lightly floured surface, roll the dough into a rectangle about 20 by 9 inches. Turn the dough so a short end faces you. Starting at the top of the dough, arrange the butter slices touching each other in a single layer so they cover about two thirds of the dough, keeping the slices about 1 inch from the edges all around. Bring the lower third of the dough (not covered with butter) over half of the buttered dough. Fold the remaining third of buttered dough down over the top, creating a "sandwich" with 5 alternating layers of dough and butter. Press all along the sides to secure the butter inside.

Flour the work surface and gently roll the dough out, adding flour as needed, into a rectangle about 20 by 10 inches. Brush a little extra flour on the dough and bring each short end of the rectangle over so they join in the center. Press gently to seal, then fold the dough in half again, creating a 4-layer package; this is known as a double turn. Let rest, refrigerated, for 20 minutes or so.

Roll the dough again into a 20-by-10-inch rectangle and give it another double turn. Give the dough 2 more double turns (for a total of 4 double turns), letting it rest in the refrigerator between rolling if it gets too elastic.

Wrap the dough in plastic wrap and refrigerate. After it has rested for 1 hour, it is ready to be used.

The dough can be kept in the refrigerator for a few days or in the freezer for a couple of months. (If kept in the refrigerator too long, it has a tendency to become rubbery and difficult to roll out.) If you freeze it, be sure to defrost it under refrigeration before using. (If using only a piece of the dough, cut off the piece you need crosswise.)

> All-butter puff pastry is available in many specialty markets. Traditional (above), fast (opposite), or store-bought puff pastry can be used interchangeably in any of my recipes.

Fast Puff Pastry
Makes about 2½ pounds

✂ **Faster and easier than** traditional puff pastry (page 597), this version is very good, though not quite as tender and flaky as the classic one. I often use it for wrapping fish or pâtés or as the crust for a tart. Instant flour makes the dough roll out easily. Be certain that the flour, butter, and water are all very cold.

1	pound (about 3 cups) all-purpose flour or instant flour, such as Wondra
14	ounces (3½ sticks) very cold unsalted butter, cut into 1-inch pieces
½	teaspoon salt
1	cup ice-cold water, or a bit more as needed

Put the flour, butter, salt, and ice water in a large bowl and mix together with your hands for a few seconds, just enough to gather all ingredients into a ball. The butter should still be in large pieces. Alternatively, put the ingredients in a food processor and pulse a few times, just enough so the ingredients start to hold together. If need be, add up to a couple more tablespoons of ice water. Gather the dough into a ball. (Chunks of butter will still be visible throughout the dough.)

Sprinkle a board with flour. Press and roll the dough into a rectangle about 18 by 8 inches. Work as quickly as possible and be sure to have enough flour on the board so that the dough can slide and expand during the rolling. Sprinkle the dough with flour to coat all the visible pieces of butter, then brush the excess flour from the surface of the dough and give it a double turn (see the instructions for Puff Pastry, page 597), then give it another double turn.

Allow the dough to rest, refrigerated, for 20 to 30 minutes, and then give one more double turn (a total of 3 double turns). Allow the dough to rest refrigerated for about 30 minutes before using.

Follow the same storing (and cutting) procedures as for the conventional puff pastry.

Bourbon Babas
Makes 10 to 12 babas

❧ **Babas are spongy, yeasty** individual cakes, somewhat like brioche, but with much less butter. Because they have a dry, airy texture, they are soaked in a syrup, often flavored with rum, before serving. I use bourbon instead. They can be made ahead and kept in an airtight container for several days.

DOUGH

  1⅛ teaspoons active dry yeast
   ½ cup milk, heated to 100 degrees
   1 teaspoon granulated sugar
   2 cups all-purpose flour
   3 large eggs
   ½ teaspoon salt
   ¼ cup raisins
   ¾ stick (6 tablespoons) butter, softened

      Egg wash made with 1 large egg,
        half the white removed, beaten

SYRUP

   ¾ cup granulated sugar
  1½ cups warm water
   ½ teaspoon pure vanilla extract
   3 tablespoons bourbon

GLAZE

   1 tablespoon bourbon
   ½ cup confectioners' sugar

GARNISH

   1 cup heavy cream, whipped with
      1 tablespoon confectioners' sugar
      to soft peaks
     Candied violets (optional)

FOR THE DOUGH: Combine the yeast, warm milk, and sugar in the bowl of a stand mixer. Let stand for about 5 minutes, until bubbly.

Add the flour, eggs, and salt and beat with the flat beater on medium speed for approximately 3 minutes. The dough should be very elastic. Add the raisins and butter and beat for approximately 1 minute more to combine; don't worry if some pieces of butter are still visible. Cover the dough with a towel or plastic wrap and let rise in a warm, draft-free place (70 to 75 degrees) for about 1 hour, until doubled.

Stir the dough to push out the air. Butter twelve ½-cup or ten ¾-cup baba molds and fill each one half full with dough. Let rise at room temperature for 30 to 40 minutes, until doubled.

Preheat the oven to 375 degrees, with a rack in the center.

Brush the tops of the risen babas with the egg wash. Arrange them on a cookie sheet and bake for 20 to 25 minutes, until puffed and golden brown. Let cool for 15 to 20 minutes, then remove them from the molds and let cool completely. (*The cooled babas can be wrapped airtight and frozen for up to 2 months.*)

FOR THE SYRUP: Mix the sugar, warm water, vanilla, and bourbon together in a bowl until the sugar is completely dissolved.

Arrange the babas in a gratin dish so they are fairly snug, one against the other, and pour the syrup over them. Let the babas soak for 20 minutes or so, turning them occasionally so they absorb as much syrup as they can. The syrup may not be completely absorbed after this amount of time: if you push a knife through a baba and the center is soft, you can assume that the syrup has penetrated into the middle of the babas; if it is still firm, soak longer.

Cut the babas lengthwise in half.

FOR THE GLAZE: Combine the bourbon and confectioners' sugar in a bowl and mix until smooth. With a spoon or brush, coat the outside of each half baba with the glaze.

To serve, place 2 baba halves cut side down on each serving plate. Mound some of the whipped cream in the center, decorate with a candied violet, if desired, and serve.

Frozen Desserts

Frozen Desserts

Raspberry Velvet
Serves 4

✻ **Raspberries are pureed and** strained, then the mixture is partially frozen and the slush is served in sugar-rimmed glasses. If you prepare the dessert ahead and freeze the mixture until hard, defrost it in the refrigerator for an hour or so before serving, to achieve the desired silky consistency.

Individually quick frozen (IQF) berries, available year-round at most supermarkets, are generally of high quality and have been picked at the peak of ripeness and frozen without sugar. If fresh raspberries are in season, of course, you can use them.

- 1 12-ounce package frozen unsweetened raspberries, defrosted, or 12 ounces fresh raspberries
- ⅓ cup seedless black raspberry preserves
- ¼ cup water
- 2 teaspoons fresh lime juice
- 1 tablespoon sugar
- 4 fresh mint sprigs

Push the raspberries and preserves through a food mill, then strain through a fine-mesh strainer set over a stainless steel bowl to eliminate any remaining seeds. Or puree the berries with the preserves in a food processor, then strain through a fine-mesh strainer into the bowl. Add the water and mix well. (You should have about 2 cups.)

Place the bowl in the freezer and freeze, stirring every hour or so, until the mixture is half frozen and velvety.

Meanwhile, pour the lime juice into one small saucer and put the sugar in another. Dip the rims of four stemmed glasses (preferably tulip champagne glasses) into the lime juice and then into the sugar. Place the glasses in the freezer or refrigerator until serving time.

At serving time, divide the Raspberry Velvet among the prepared glasses and decorate each with a sprig of mint. Serve immediately.

Frozen Watermelon Slush
Serves 8

✻ **This is the perfect** dessert for a hot day. Watermelon is pureed and frozen until solid. A few hours before it is to be served, the mixture is softened in the refrigerator, then it's broken into flakes or shavings and spooned into glass goblets or bowls.

- 1 medium watermelon (about 12 pounds)
- ¾ cup fresh lime or lemon juice
- ¾ cup sugar

Halve the watermelon lengthwise, halve again, and cut into 2-inch pieces. Remove and discard the rind, black seeds, and as many of the softer white seeds as possible. Cut the flesh into 1-inch chunks. Place in a food processor, in batches if necessary, and process until liquefied; some small chunks may remain. (You should have about 10 cups.) Add the lime or lemon juice and sugar and process just until incorporated.

Transfer the watermelon mixture to a stainless steel bowl, cover, and freeze until solid, 8 to 10 hours.

About 2 to 3 hours before serving, move the bowl to the refrigerator to soften the mixture. In the hour before serving, use a fork to break the softened mixture into shavings.

Serve in chilled glass goblets or bowls.

Blood Orange Sorbet
Makes 1 scant quart

❦ When blood oranges are out of season, you can use other oranges, but the sorbet will not have the same rich color unless you add 1 to 2 tablespoons grenadine. This sorbet is best eaten the day it is made. If it has been in the freezer for several hours, you may want to soften it a bit in the refrigerator before serving.

> Finely grated rind of 1 small blood orange
> 3 cups strained fresh blood orange juice (from about 3 pounds oranges)
> ⅓ cup honey, or to taste
> ¾ cup seedless raspberry preserves, or to taste

Combine the rind and juice in a bowl. Add the honey and raspberry preserves and stir to dissolve them. Taste and add more honey or preserves to sweeten as desired.

Pour into an ice cream machine and freeze according to the manufacturer's instructions. Serve, or transfer to a container, cover tightly, and keep in the freezer until serving time.

Black Velvet
Serves 4

❦ Kahlúa, figs, and chocolate-coated coffee beans make this almost-instant dessert elegant. Served in crystal goblets, it is a terrific finish for a meal.

> 1 pint vanilla ice cream or frozen yogurt
> ¼ cup Kahlúa or other coffee-flavored liqueur
> 4 dried figs, cut into about 6 wedges each
> 12 chocolate-covered coffee beans

Divide the ice cream or frozen yogurt among four dishes. Pour 1 tablespoon of the Kahlúa over each serving. Arrange the fig wedges on top of and around the ice cream, sprinkle on the coffee beans, and serve.

Hazelnut Parfait
Serves 6

❦ Because it can be made well ahead of serving, this hazelnut parfait is an ideal party dish. It can be frozen for several weeks.

> ¼ teaspoon canola oil
> 1 cup hazelnuts
> 1¼ cups heavy cream
> 3 tablespoons confectioners' sugar
> ½ teaspoon pure vanilla extract
> 3 crystallized violets or other candied or crystallized flowers (optional)

Preheat the oven to 400 degrees.

Grease a 3-cup soufflé dish with the oil. Cut two long narrow strips of parchment paper and position them in the dish so they form a cross in the bottom and extend up over the sides. Place a round of parchment paper in the bottom of the dish. (The paper strips and round will facilitate unmolding.)

Spread the nuts on a cookie sheet and toast them in the oven until lightly browned, about 8 minutes. Transfer the hot nuts to a dish towel and rub them in the towel to remove as much skin as possible. (Don't worry if half the skin remains.)

Drop the nuts into a food processor and process until coarsely chopped.

Whip the cream with the confectioners' sugar and vanilla until semifirm, then fold in the nuts. Transfer the mixture to the greased dish. Bang the mold firmly on the table to tighten the mixture and eliminate air bubbles. Cover with plastic wrap, pressing on it to flatten the top of the parfait. Place in the freezer for at least 5 hours. (*The parfait can be kept frozen for several weeks.*)

At serving time, unmold the frozen parfait onto a serving plate by pulling gently on the paper strips to release it from the dish; remove the parchment round. If desired, crumble the crystallized or candied flowers on top. Cut into wedges and serve immediately.

French Vanilla Ice Cream
Serves 4

✂ **Real French vanilla ice** cream is a frozen custard that is made mostly of milk and egg yolks. The mixture is frozen in an ice cream maker, which lightens it. Along with vanilla extract, the vanilla bean lends flavor and color, producing the black flecks characteristic of French vanilla ice cream.

    1 vanilla bean, cut into ½-inch pieces
    ⅓ cup sugar
    ⅓ cup heavy cream
    6 large egg yolks
    1 tablespoon pure vanilla extract
    2 cups milk

Grind the vanilla pieces and 3 tablespoons of the sugar in a mini-chop or spice grinder until the vanilla appears as small black dots in the mixture. Transfer the vanilla sugar to a large bowl.

Bring the cream to a boil in a small saucepan and add it to the vanilla sugar. Let steep and cool to room temperature.

Whisk together the egg yolks, the rest of the sugar, and the vanilla extract in a bowl.

Bring the milk to a boil in a saucepan. Add the milk to the yolk mixture, stirring constantly until all the milk is incorporated. Return the mixture to the saucepan and cook over medium heat, stirring with a wooden spatula, until the mixture reaches 170 to 175 degrees. (Stir constantly as the mixture thickens, or it will curdle.) Immediately pour it through a fine strainer into the cream mixture. Mix well to combine the ingredients and lower the temperature of the yolk mixture. Let cool to room temperature.

Transfer the mixture to an ice cream maker and freeze according to the manufacturer's instructions. Serve, or transfer to a container and store it in the freezer. (Transfer ice cream that has been stored for 12 hours or more in the freezer to the refrigerator to soften for at least 45 minutes before serving.)

To serve, divide the ice cream among four goblets or decorative dishes and serve immediately.

Banana-Mint Ice Cream with Rum-Raisin Sauce
Serves 4

❧ **When you have overripe** bananas languishing in your fruit bowl, make this. All you need to do is slice them, freeze them on a tray, and puree them in a food processor with some honey, mint, and sour cream. Freeze for several hours before serving with the delicious sauce made of peach preserves, orange juice, rum, and raisins.

ICE CREAM

3	ripe bananas, cut into ½-inch-thick slices
¼	cup honey
6–8	fresh mint leaves
¾	cup sour cream

SAUCE

¼	cup peach preserves
¼	cup orange juice
1	tablespoon dark rum
¼	cup golden raisins

4	fresh mint sprigs (optional)

FOR THE ICE CREAM: Arrange the bananas in a single layer on a cookie sheet. Place in the freezer for at least 2 hours.

Remove the bananas from the freezer and allow them to soften for a few minutes. They should still be partially frozen.

Put the bananas in a food processor, add the honey, mint, and sour cream, and process for at least 1 minute, until the mixture is smooth and creamy. Transfer to a bowl, cover, and place in the freezer for several hours, until solidly frozen.

FOR THE SAUCE: Mix the preserves, orange juice, and rum together in a small bowl until smooth. Stir in the raisins.

At serving time, spoon the ice cream into bowls and coat with the sauce. Decorate each serving with a mint sprig, if you like, and serve.

Chocolate Goblets with Espresso Ice Cream
Serves 6

❧ **These showy chocolate goblets** are made by molding melted chocolate around small balloons. The goblets can be filled with espresso ice cream or with a mixture of strawberries and Cointreau; see the variation (page 608). Other filling possibilities include whipped cream, fruit salad, custard, or other kinds of ice cream served alone or with a sauce.

The chocolate that accumulates at the bottom of the shells forms a stable base as the shells harden on a tray lined with parchment paper. You can create a marbled effect by piping white chocolate either onto the surface of the goblets or directly onto the balloons before dipping them in the chocolate. The goblets are not too large — the balloons are blown up to a circumference of only 4 to 4½ inches — but a larger balloon can be used for a single large bowl serving 6 to 8 people.

The espresso ice cream can be served as a separate dessert by itself, and, likewise, the strawberries can be served alone or with whipped cream or cake.

ICE CREAM

1¼	cups milk
⅓	cup finely ground French-roast espresso beans

2 cups heavy cream
5 large egg yolks
½ cup sugar

GOBLETS

12 ounces bittersweet or semisweet
    chocolate, chopped
2 ounces white chocolate, chopped
    (optional)
    Corn oil if necessary

6 small balloons

6 chocolate-covered coffee beans,
    for garnish

FOR THE ICE CREAM: Bring the milk to a strong boil in a saucepan. Add the coffee and stir, then cover and let steep off the heat for about 5 minutes.

Strain the milk through a paper towel lined sieve into a large saucepan. (You should have about 1 cup.) Add 1 cup of the cream and bring to a boil.

Meanwhile, mix the egg yolks and sugar together in a bowl with a whisk until thick. Add the boiling coffee cream, whisking, then return the mixture to the saucepan and cook, stirring, until it reaches 170 to 175 degrees; be careful not to overcook, or it will curdle.

Meanwhile, pour the remaining cup of cream into a clean bowl. Strain the hot cream mixture

FOR BEST RESULTS

Some balloons release better from the chocolate than others. Silicone-rubber balloons work best. Be certain that the chocolate is only tepid or at room temperature when you make the goblets so the balloons don't burst and splatter chocolate all over the kitchen.

through a very fine strainer into the cold cream; this will lower the temperature of the coffee-cream mixture and stop any further cooking. Let cool.

Pour the cream mixture into an ice cream maker and freeze according to the manufacturer's instructions. Transfer the ice cream to a bowl, packing it firmly, cover with plastic wrap, and place in the freezer until serving time.

TO MAKE THE CHOCOLATE GOBLETS: Melt the two chocolates separately in double boilers or in a microwave oven, making certain that no water gets into the chocolate, as this would cause it to seize and lose its shine. If the melted chocolate is too thick, add a little corn oil. Transfer the dark chocolate to a bowl and cool the chocolates to tepid (about 100 degrees).

Line two baking sheets with parchment paper. Blow up the balloons until they are 4 to 4¼ inches wide, then tie them closed. If desired, to decorate the inside of the goblets, using a paper cornet (see page 565), pipe lines of white chocolate directly on the outside of some of the balloons; it will run slightly into the dark chocolate when the balloons are dipped and create a marbled effect.

Dip each balloon into the melted bittersweet chocolate, inclining it slightly to form a roundish shape on one side, like a large petal. Turn the balloon and dip it in the chocolate again to create another large petal shape, then turn it and dip it again — 3 or 4 times in all; the chocolate shell should look like a large tulip. Stand the dipped balloons on the parchment-lined baking sheets. Some of the chocolate will run down the balloon and accumulate at the base to form a thicker and more stable pedestal. If you like, pipe lines of white chocolate over the still-soft chocolate on the dipped balloons. Refrigerate until set.

When the chocolate is hard, prick the balloons so they burst and release the air inside. The balloons should separate easily from the chocolate. Carefully pry up the balloons at the base with your fingers. Transfer to a container and refrigerate until serving time. (*The goblets can also be carefully wrapped in plastic wrap and frozen.*)

To serve, put a scoop of the espresso ice cream in each chocolate goblet. Top with a chocolate-covered coffee bean and serve immediately.

VARIATION

Instead of the ice cream, fill the chocolate goblets with strawberries macerated in Cointreau. Just before serving, combine 2 cups strawberries, washed, hulled, and quartered, with ¼ cup strawberry jam and 1 tablespoon Cointreau, tossing gently. Spoon into the chocolate goblets.

Caramel Cups with Coffee Ice Cream

Serves 4

For this showstopper, caramel is drizzled over inverted small Pyrex ramekins that have been lightly oiled. The hardened caramel cups are then removed and used to hold the ice cream.

When making the cups, it's important to stop the caramel from cooking as soon as it reaches a rich brown color. The best way to do this — and to help the caramel mixture thicken to the right consistency — is to dip the base of the pan into a bowl of cool water for a few seconds.

- ¼ teaspoon canola oil
- ⅓ cup sugar
- 2 tablespoons water
- 1 pint coffee ice cream
- Crystallized mint leaves or rose petals (optional)

Lightly oil the outside of four 6-ounce ovenproof Pyrex bowls and place them upside down 3 to 4 inches apart on a cookie sheet lined with parchment paper.

Combine the sugar and water in a small to medium heavy saucepan, bring to a boil over medium heat, and continue boiling until the syrup turns a deep caramel color, 5 to 6 minutes. Immediately dip the base of the saucepan into a bowl of cool water and hold it there for 4 to 5 seconds to stop the cooking.

Stir the caramel with a metal spoon; it should have thickened. When it is the consistency of a thick syrup, spoon out about a teaspoon and drizzle it around the sides and across the bottom of one of the inverted bowls, creating a net or grid pattern. Repeat with the remaining caramel, drizzling it over and around the remaining bowls.

Let the bowls sit for about 5 minutes, until the caramel hardens, then lift the caramel cups off the bowls by pushing up with the tip of your thumb at the edge of the caramel lines. The cups can sit at room temperature for a few hours before serving. (*Sealed in a plastic container, the cups will keep for up to a week if the weather is not humid; in humid weather, they will keep for only a few hours before becoming sticky.*)

To serve, place a caramel cup on each of four dessert plates. Fill the cups with the ice cream and decorate the plates, if desired, with a few crystallized mint leaves or rose petals.

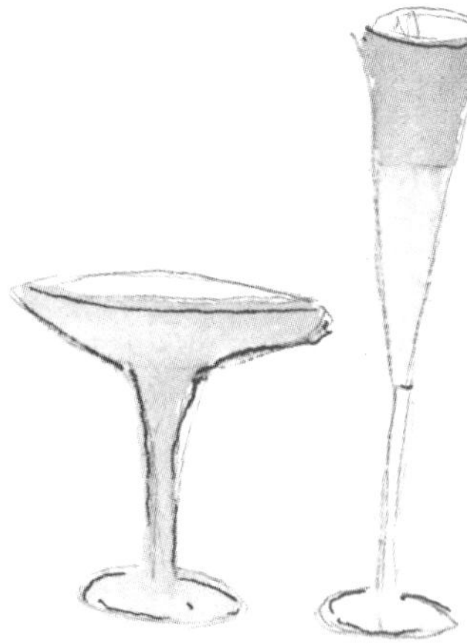

Basics

Basics

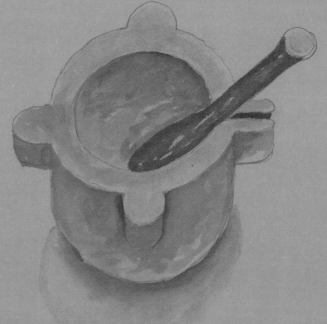

Seasonings

Bouquet Garni

A **bouquet garni is** a mixture of aromatic fresh herbs used as a flavoring for stocks, stews, and casseroles. Traditionally the herbs are tied together in a small bunch with kitchen twine and submerged in the cooking vessel. When they have imparted sufficient flavor to the dish, they are easily removed and discarded.

A classic bouquet garni is made of parsley stems (the leaves are chopped for other uses), thyme sprigs, and bay leaves. Often, however, leek greens, a celery stalk, a carrot, and sprigs of other herbs, such as tarragon, rosemary, and savory, are added.

15–20	fresh parsley stems
6	fresh thyme sprigs
2–3	bay leaves

OPTIONAL HERBS AND VEGETABLES

	A few tarragon, rosemary, and/or savory sprigs
	Greens from 1 leek
2	celery stalks
1	carrot

Bundle the herbs and vegetables, if using, together and tie them securely with kitchen twine. Or, if you are using thyme leaves or pieces of bay leaves too small to secure with twine, wrap the mixture in a cheesecloth package and tie it.

Herbes de Provence

A **blend of dried** herbs frequently used in the cooking of southern France, herbes de Provence always contains thyme, savory, marjoram, and oregano in equal proportions; often lavender flowers are added. Lesser amounts of other herbs can also be included. Herbes de Provence can be purchased in specialty food stores and many supermarkets. The homemade version is prepared with fresh herbs that you dry yourself. A microwave is ideal for drying small amounts of herbs in a few minutes.

If fresh herbs aren't available, or if only some of the ones listed here are available, you can use store-bought dried herbs in the proportions indicated below and omit the drying.

Fresh thyme leaves
Fresh savory leaves
Fresh marjoram leaves
Fresh oregano leaves

OPTIONAL HERBS AND SPICES

Fresh sage leaves
Fresh rosemary leaves
Lavender flowers, preferably organic
Fennel seeds

You can use a microwave oven to dry smaller quantities of herbs. Use a conventional oven if you are drying large amounts of herbs. You can also air-dry herbs outdoors in the summer shade.

FOR MICROWAVE-DRYING: Arrange the thyme, savory, marjoram, and oregano (one variety at a time) in one layer on a paper towel. Cook on high in the microwave, checking the herbs every minute, for 2 to 4 minutes, depending on the herbs, until dry but still somewhat pliable.

FOR OVEN-DRYING: Preheat the oven to 180 degrees. Arrange the herbs (one variety at a time) in one layer on one or more cookie sheets and heat them in the oven until dry, 2 hours or more, depending on the herbs.

Mix together equal amounts of the dried herbs.

FOR THE OPTIONAL HERBS: Dry the sage and rosemary leaves and the lavender flowers as indicated above. Mix together equal proportions of these herbs with a like amount of fennel seeds.

Then mix 2 portions of the basic herb mixture with 1 portion of the optional herb mixture.

Store in jars or plastic bags, tightly sealed to preserve the freshness of the herbs, preferably in the freezer, removing some as needed.

Stocks

Chicken Stock
Makes 3 quarts

❧ **It takes very little** work to make your own stock; mostly it is a matter of being at home for the several hours it takes to cook. A flavorful money saver that is practically fat- and salt-free, homemade stock can be frozen in small quantities and used as needed.

Chicken backs and necks are available at most supermarkets. If you don't see them, ask the butcher to set aside some for you. I also make stock from the bones of roasted chicken or turkey.

4 pounds chicken bones (necks, backs, wings, etc.), skinless or with as little skin as possible
6 quarts cold water

1 large onion (about 8 ounces), quartered
1 tablespoon herbes de Provence
12 whole cloves
4 bay leaves
1 tablespoon dark soy sauce (optional)

Combine the bones and water in a large stockpot and bring to a boil over high heat. Reduce the heat and boil gently for 30 minutes. Most of the fat and impurities will rise to the surface; skim off as much of them as you can and discard them.

Add the onion, herbes de Provence, cloves, bay leaves, and soy sauce, if using, return to a boil, and boil gently for 2½ hours. Strain the stock through a fine strainer or a colander lined with dampened paper towels. Allow to cool.

Remove the surface fat and refrigerate the stock for up to 5 days, or pour into containers and freeze.

Beef Stock
Makes about 4 quarts

❧ **I use chicken stock** more often than beef stock, which has a more assertive taste, but some soups are better with beef stock, so when I find beef bones at my market, I make stock and freeze it. For a stock with a nice brown color and appealing taste, burn the onion halves. When I have leftover veal, pork, and even turkey bones, I add them to the beef bones to supplement them.

5 pounds beef bones (shins, marrow, ribs, knuckles, and/or necks), plus (optional) leftover veal, pork, or turkey bones
8 quarts cold water
1 large onion, unpeeled, cut crosswise in half

1 head garlic, unpeeled, cut
    horizontally in half
2 celery stalks
1 leek, trimmed (leaving most of the
    green), split, and washed
3 fresh thyme sprigs
4 bay leaves

Put the bones and water in a large stockpot and bring to a boil.

Meanwhile, place the onion halves cut side down in a stainless steel or cast-iron skillet (there's no need to grease the pan) and cook over medium heat for 20 minutes, or until the cut sides are burned and black. Remove from the heat.

Skim the stock when it has come to a boil, removing and discarding the surface foam, and continue to skim it occasionally for the next 20 minutes.

Add the onion, garlic, celery, leek, thyme, and bay leaves and bring back to a boil. Reduce the heat, so the stock barely boils, and cook for about 4 hours.

Strain the stock through a fine strainer or a colander lined with dampened paper towels (reserve the bones if making Meat Glaze, page 614). You should have about 4 quarts; add water if necessary, or boil to reduce to 4 quarts. Let cool.

Remove and discard the surface fat and refrigerate the stock for up to 5 days, or pour into containers and freeze.

Basic Brown Sauce
Makes about 2 quarts

✼ A basic and essential ingredient for the cook, brown sauce is added to other sauces or used to create a sauce for meat or poultry. Mine is slightly thickened with flour, which loses its raw taste through the long cooking process. The sauce can be made with all chicken bones or with turkey bones.

4 pounds veal or beef bones (shins, necks, tails, etc.), cut into 3-inch pieces (you can have the butcher do this)
1 pound chicken bones (necks, wings, backs, etc.)
2 cups diced onions
1 cup diced carrots
1 cup diced celery
6 garlic cloves, crushed but not peeled
⅓ cup all-purpose flour, dissolved in 1½ cups water
¼ cup tomato paste
8 quarts cold water
1 cup dry white wine
2 tablespoons dark soy sauce
1 teaspoon black peppercorns
3 bay leaves
1 teaspoon crushed dried thyme

Put the bones in a large stockpot and cook over high heat, stirring occasionally, for 15 minutes. Reduce the heat to medium and cook for another 15 minutes, until they are browned and have rendered some fat. (There should be enough fat on the bones and in the skin to brown the bones.)

Add the onions, carrots, celery, and garlic and cook for another 15 minutes or so, stirring, until the bones and vegetables are lightly browned.

Drain the bones and vegetables in a colander to eliminate the fat and return them to the pot.

Add the flour mixture, tomato paste, water, wine, soy sauce, peppercorns, bay leaves, and thyme to the pot and bring to a boil, then reduce the heat and simmer slowly, uncovered, for about 3 hours, until reduced to about 8 cups. Skim off and discard the foam that comes to the top after 30 minutes. Strain the sauce through a fine strainer.

The sauce can be kept covered in the refrigerator for up to 1 week, or it can be divided among small plastic containers and frozen.

VARIATION

ALTERNATE METHOD: Heat the oven to 400 degrees. Arrange the bones in one layer in a large roasting pan or on a baking sheet and roast for 1 hour, stirring the bones to brown on all sides. Sprinkle the onions, carrots, celery, and garlic on top and roast for another 30 minutes.

Drain the bones and vegetables in a colander and discard the fat. Add the bones to a stockpot. Deglaze the roasting pan or cookie sheet with 2 to 3 cups water and heat to melt the solidified glaze. Add to the stockpot.

Continue with the recipe, adding the flour, tomato paste, the water, and the other ingredients.

Meat Glaze (Glace de Viande)
Makes about 1 cup

⚶ **Usually made with bones** that have already been used for stock, *glace de viande* can enhance sauces, soups, and stews.

Reserved bones from Beef Stock
(page 612)
7 quarts water

Put the bones and water in a large stockpot and bring to a boil. Reduce the heat and boil very gently for 5 hours, adding water as necessary to keep the bones covered.

Strain the stock through a fine strainer or a colander lined with dampened paper towels. Bring to a boil and reduce over high heat. As the liquid reduces, transfer to smaller pans as necessary and reduce the heat so it does not burn. The reduced mixture should be almost the color of caramel, with large bubbles on top, and the texture thick,

like jam. (You should have about 1 cup.) Let cool; the glaze will get firm and rubbery.

Cut the glaze into 1-inch pieces and freeze in a freezer bag until ready to use. The glaze can be used directly from the freezer.

Sauces, Butters, and Oils

Mayonnaise
Makes about 2 cups

⚶ **One of the best** of all sauces and perhaps the most useful, mayonnaise is a smooth emulsion of raw egg yolks and oil that lends itself to an infinite number of variations. It's good with many cold foods — eggs; cooked vegetables such as asparagus, broccoli and artichokes; fresh tomatoes and vegetable salads; poached fish and shellfish; and chicken. I like it made with mustard, because it is a powerful binder and, with the yolks, holds the emulsion together. Mayonnaise can be made by hand or in a food processor or blender. The oil should be at room temperature; if it's cold, the mayonnaise will separate. While, like most people, I rely on store-bought mayonnaise for everyday use, for a special party, I always make my own.

Whether you use store-bought, handmade, or machine-made mayonnaise, the variations that follow will expand your culinary repertoire.

3 large egg yolks
1 tablespoon Dijon mustard
2 teaspoons tarragon vinegar or white
wine vinegar

½ teaspoon salt

½ teaspoon freshly ground white pepper

1 tablespoon cold water (if using a food processor or blender)

2 cups oil (peanut or olive oil, or half and half)

TO MAKE THE MAYONNAISE BY HAND: Put the yolks, mustard, vinegar, salt, and white pepper in a large bowl. Beat for a few seconds with a whisk. Then add the oil slowly, especially at first, whipping vigorously and constantly until all the oil is incorporated.

TO MAKE THE MAYONNAISE IN A FOOD PROCESSOR OR BLENDER: Put all the ingredients except the oil in a food processor or blender. Add the 1 tablespoon cold water and process or blend for a few seconds. With the motor running, add the oil in a slow, steady stream. It should not take more than a few seconds to get a smooth, creamy mayonnaise.

VARIATIONS

SAUCE VERTE (GREEN SAUCE)

If all the following greens are not available, increase the others in proportion. *Sauce verte* is sometimes referred to as *sauce Vincent*. Serve with poached fish, such as salmon or trout.

Pick the leaves from 10 watercress sprigs and 4 fresh tarragon, 4 parsley, and 4 chervil sprigs. Drop into a pot of boiling water along with 10 spinach leaves and blanch for a few seconds, then drain in a sieve and cool under cold water. Chop into a fine puree. Stir into 2 cups mayonnaise, along with 1 tablespoon chopped fresh chives.

ANDALOUSE SAUCE

Serve with cold chicken or hard-cooked eggs.

Combine ¼ cup very thick smooth tomato sauce with 2 cups mayonnaise. Add 2 tablespoons seeded and finely chopped red bell pepper, along

TO SALVAGE BROKEN (CURDLED) MAYONNAISE

Spoon 2 tablespoons boiling water into a bowl. Add 1 to 2 tablespoons of the broken mayonnaise and whisk until smooth. Add another tablespoon or two of the broken mayonnaise and whisk again until the mixture is creamy and smooth. Keep adding the mayonnaise and whisking — you can go faster at the end — until the mayonnaise is back together.

with 1 tablespoon or so chopped fresh basil or chives, or a mixture of the two.

GRIBICHE SAUCE

This sauce is especially good with fried fish or mixed with cold shelled mussels and served as a first course.

Add to 2 cups mayonnaise: 1 coarsely chopped hard-cooked egg (see page 66); 1 tablespoon chopped gherkins or cornichons (tiny French gherkins); 1 tablespoon drained, chopped capers; 1 tablespoon chopped shallots or scallions; the minced leaves from about 3 fresh parsley sprigs; 4 or 5 fresh tarragon leaves, chopped; and 1½ teaspoons chopped fresh chives. Taste for seasoning and add salt and freshly ground black pepper if needed.

MAYONNAISE WITH APPLESAUCE AND HORSERADISH

Serve with cold pork or roast goose.

Add to 2 cups mayonnaise: ¾ cup thick applesauce and 1 tablespoon grated fresh horseradish.

RÉMOULADE SAUCE

Serve with sliced hard-cooked eggs, shellfish, or cold meats such as tongue or chicken.

Add to 2 cups mayonnaise: 1 tablespoon Dijon mustard; 2 tablespoons each chopped gherkins or cornichons (tiny French gherkins), capers, and fresh parsley; 1 tablespoon chopped fresh basil or chervil; and 1 teaspoon anchovy paste. Allow to mellow for a couple of hours in the refrigerator before serving.

GLOUCESTER SAUCE

Serve with cold meats.

Add to 2 cups mayonnaise: about ¾ cup sour cream, 1 tablespoon fresh lemon juice, 1 teaspoon chopped fresh fennel leaves, and 1 teaspoon Worcestershire sauce.

CHANTILLY OR MOUSSELINE SAUCE

Serve with cold fish, green salads, or cold hard-cooked eggs.

Fold ¾ cup whipped heavy cream into 2 cups mayonnaise. Add salt and freshly ground black pepper to taste.

AÏOLI

A combination of egg yolks, garlic, oil, and, sometimes, the pulp of a baked potato, aïoli is known in Provence as *la pommade* — or the butter of Provence. Sometimes aïoli is made with a mortar and pestle, and sometimes ground almonds are added to it.

Add to 2 cups mayonnaise: 1 small boiled red potato, pushed through a ricer; 2 tablespoons finely chopped or pureed garlic; 1 tablespoon fresh lemon juice; and salt and freshly ground black pepper to taste.

Hollandaise
Makes about 2 cups

Made with egg yolks and butter, hollandaise is the classic hot emulsion sauce. It is the counterpart of mayonnaise, the classic cold emulsion sauce made with egg yolks and oil. An aristocrat among sauces, hollandaise can adorn everything from vegetables to fish to meat to poultry.

Although most professional chefs cook the yolks and water (called a *sabayon*) directly over heat, it is a bit safer to cook them initially in a double boiler to avoid scrambling the eggs.

Hollandaise also can be made with soft rather than clarified unsalted butter for a thinner but still delicious sauce or with brown butter.

¾ pound (3 sticks) unsalted butter
4 large egg yolks
2 tablespoons water
¼ teaspoon salt
⅛ teaspoon cayenne pepper
1½ teaspoons fresh lemon juice

TO CLARIFY THE BUTTER: Cut the butter into pieces and heat in a saucepan over medium heat. When it has melted and foamed, take it off the heat and let it rest so the clear liquid can rise to the top. Then slowly and carefully pour the clarified butter into a small saucepan; discard the milky residue in the bottom. Keep warm.

Combine the egg yolks and water in the top of a stainless steel double boiler or a bowl that can be set over a saucepan of simmering water. With a whisk, mix well, then place over the simmering water and, whipping vigorously with the whisk, beat for 8 to 10 minutes, or until the mixture is thick and creamy. The mixture should be cooked enough to absorb the clarified butter — when it is perfectly combined, you will be able to see the bottom of the pan between strokes — but take care not to curdle the eggs.

Take the pan off the heat and place on a damp cloth to keep it from sliding around. Add the clarified butter slowly, in dribbles at first, whipping constantly. Season with the salt and cayenne. Stir in the lemon juice. If not serving the hollandaise immediately, keep it warm by setting the saucepan or bowl in a pan of warm water — not boiling, or the hollandaise will curdle. Hollandaise is always served lukewarm.

If the hollandaise is too thick, with a whisk, beat in 1 tablespoon hot water to bring it to the right consistency.

VARIATIONS

Although I've made serving suggestions for these sauces, most of them can be used interchangeably.

BÉARNAISE SAUCE

Serve with broiled steaks or chicken and broiled or fried fish.

Combine 2 tablespoons dry white wine, 2 tablespoons tarragon vinegar, and ⅓ cup finely chopped shallots in a small saucepan and cook over medium heat until all but about a tablespoon of the liquid has evaporated. Let cool, then stir into the hollandaise, along with 1 tablespoon each finely chopped fresh tarragon and parsley.

TOMATO-FLAVORED BÉARNAISE

Serve with steaks, fish, chicken, or poached eggs.

Peel and seed 1 large ripe tomato, then coarsely chop it. Melt 2 or 3 tablespoons unsalted butter

TO SALVAGE CURDLED HOLLANDAISE

Heat the broken hollandaise slowly until it is almost hot and is more curdled, then allow to stand, without disturbing it, for at least 10 minutes. The clarified butter will separate from the solids and rise to the top.

With a spoon or ladle, scoop up as much clear butter as you can and set it aside. You now have your hollandaise in two parts — a thick curdled part and a liquid part. Spoon 1 tablespoon boiling water into a stainless steel bowl. Add 1 tablespoon of the curdled mixture to the water and beat with a whisk until it is homogeneous (this will take only a few seconds). Continue adding the thick sauce tablespoon by tablespoon at first; you can add a greater amount once the sauce binds together and thickens. Then add the liquid part you set aside as if you were making the hollandaise for the first time.

in a small skillet. Add the tomato and sauté for 5 minutes over medium heat. Stir in 1 tablespoon tomato paste and bring to a boil. Mash well and let cool, then mix into Béarnaise Sauce.

FOYOT SAUCE

Serve this sauce, named for a famous nineteenth-century chef, with broiled or deep-fried fish or grilled or breaded chicken breasts.

Add 1 tablespoon melted Meat Glaze (page 614) to Béarnaise Sauce.

MALTAISE SAUCE

This is especially good with asparagus or broccoli.

Stir the grated rind of 1 orange and 2 tablespoons juice into the hollandaise.

Garlic and Herb Butter ("Snail Butter")

Makes about 5 cups

✎ This compound butter is good for seasoning mushrooms, vegetables, potatoes, shellfish, or even soup. It can be divided into ½-cup portions and frozen for a month or two, to have ready as needed.

  1 pound unsalted butter, softened
  ½ cup chopped fresh parsley
  2 tablespoons finely chopped shallots
     or fresh chives
 1½ tablespoons crushed and finely
     chopped garlic
  1 tablespoon Pernod, Ricard, or
     other anise liqueur (optional)
 1½ teaspoons salt
  1 scant teaspoon freshly ground black
     pepper
  1 slice firm white bread (about 1 ounce)
     processed to crumbs in a food
     processor (½ cup)
  2 tablespoons dry white wine

Combine the butter, parsley, shallots or chives, garlic, liqueur, salt, and pepper in a bowl and mix well. Add the bread crumbs and wine and mix just enough to incorporate. The butter will keep for up to 2 weeks, covered, in the refrigerator.

Blender Hollandaise

Makes about 1½ cups

✎ **Blender hollandaise is a** cinch to make (20 to 30 seconds from start to finish) and is very good, although not as delicate and light as classic hollandaise (page 616); it has a firmer, tighter texture. The butter must be hot enough to cook the yolks. If you cook the butter until brown, the hollandaise sauce becomes a hazelnut sauce, so-called for its nutty taste.

  ¾ pound (3 sticks) unsalted butter
  4 large egg yolks
  2 tablespoons water
  ¼ teaspoon salt
  ¼ teaspoon freshly ground white pepper
  ⅛ teaspoon cayenne pepper
 1½ teaspoons fresh lemon juice

Melt the butter in a small saucepan over low heat and heat until bubbling but not brown.

Put the yolks, water, salt, white pepper, cayenne to taste, lemon juice, and water in a blender, cover, and turn the blender to high. Immediately, with the blender running, add the hot butter in a steady stream. Serve warm.

In the following dishes, be careful not to burn the butter, or the garlic will taste bitter and the dish will be ruined.

ESCARGOTS

Snails are sold in cans and the shells are packaged separately. Make certain to buy real snails, not achat, which are mud snails from Taiwan.

Preheat the oven to 375 degrees. Push ½ teaspoon of the butter into each snail shell and place a snail on top. Add another full teaspoon of butter to the top of the snail. Arrange the shells on a tray and bake for 10 to 12 minutes, or until the butter bubbles and clarifies.

SHRIMP PROVENÇAL

Preheat the oven to 375 degrees. Arrange peeled shrimp in one layer in a gratin dish. Sprinkle with fresh lemon juice and cover with dots of the butter. Bake in a 375-degree oven as you would snails (opposite).

TOMATOES PROVENÇAL

Split tomatoes in half and fry cut side down in a skillet in very hot olive oil, seasoned with salt and pepper, for 4 to 5 minutes. Arrange the fried tomatoes on a tray, cut side up, and add some of the butter to each one. Bake in a 450-degree oven for about 5 minutes and serve.

POTATOES OR VEGETABLE SOUP

Toss sautéed potatoes with a little of the butter just before serving them. Or add a little "nut" of the butter to each bowl before you pour in a vegetable soup.

Tarragon Oil
Makes ½ cup

🐝 **Herb-flavored oils add another** dimension to salads and stews, and they are delicious brushed on grilled meat, fish, or poultry. So that the tarragon leaves retain their bright green color, blanch them first, which will lock in their color.

- ½   cup loosely packed fresh tarragon leaves
- ¼   teaspoon salt
- ½   cup corn, canola, or peanut oil

Bring 1 cup water to a boil in a saucepan. Add the tarragon leaves, stir, and blanch for about 30 seconds, or just until the water returns to a boil. Drain the leaves in a strainer and rinse them under cool water.

Coarsely chop the tarragon with a sharp knife, then process in a mini-chop or blender with the salt and ¼ cup of the oil until thoroughly blended. Transfer to a bowl and stir in the remaining oil. The oil can be refrigerated for a few days.

Basil Oil
Makes 2½ cups

🐝 **Drizzle this flavored oil** over soup, pasta, poached fish, mashed potatoes, or grilled steak. For the first week, you can use the basil paste that sinks to the bottom of the oil as well as the oil itself. But after 8 to 10 days, it's best to strain the oil and discard the solids, which will have begun to discolor and lose their flavor. The strained oil will keep for several months in the refrigerator.

4 cups loosely packed fresh basil leaves (4 ounces)

1 teaspoon salt

2½ cups canola or olive oil, or a mixture

Bring 6 cups water to a boil in a large saucepan. Drop in the basil leaves, stir, and blanch for 45 seconds, or just until the water returns to a boil. Drain the leaves in a colander and rinse them under cold water until cool. Drain again, then press the leaves gently between your palms to remove excess water.

Put the leaves in a blender (it gives a better result than a food processor) with the salt and ½ cup of the oil and process for 1 minute, stopping the machine a few times and pushing any of the mixture collected on the sides of the blender bowl down into the mixture, or until you have a smooth puree. Add the remaining 2 cups oil and process for 5 seconds. Transfer the basil oil to a jar or bottle, cover, and refrigerate.

After 2 days, you will notice that the solids have sunk to the bottom and the green oil has risen to the top. Use as needed over the next 6 to 8 days, shaking the jar first to recombine the mixture. Alternatively, after at least 2 days (but no more than 10 days), strain the mixture through a kitchen towel, pressing on it to extrude as much of the oil as possible. Discard the solids, put the oil in a clean jar or bottle, cover, and refrigerate.

Cilantro Oil

Makes about ½ cup (strained)

✎ **This oil is excellent** drizzled on poached fish or grilled chicken. Shaken well before each use, the flavored oil can be used as is, or you can strain out and discard the herbs and then remove and reserve the oil that rises to the top of the remaining liquid. Combined with vinegar and seasonings,

the unstrained oil makes a great vinaigrette; it can also be used to make an herb mayonnaise.

1 bunch (4 ounces) fresh cilantro with stems, roots trimmed

⅓ cup water

¼ teaspoon salt

½ cup olive or peanut oil

Process the cilantro with the water and salt in a mini-chop or blender until pureed. Transfer the puree to a saucepan and bring it to a boil, then immediately remove from the heat.

When the puree has cooled, pour it into a jar with a tight-fitting lid. Add the oil, cover, and shake well. Refrigerate for at least 2 hours to develop the flavor.

Use the oil within a few days, refrigerating it between uses. Or, for a more refined variation, after the 2-hour macerating period, pour the mixture into a bowl lined with a clean kitchen towel and press it through the towel into the bowl. Set the liquid aside for 30 to 45 minutes, then skim off the green oily residue from the top of the mixture and discard it. Pour out and reserve the green oil in the middle; discard the liquid in the bottom of the bowl. Refrigerate and use within a few days.

Curry Oil

Makes ½ cup

✎ **Adding color and flavor** to vinaigrettes, soups, stews, and sauces, this curry-flavored oil is also good for sautéing fish.

½ cup corn oil

1 teaspoon curry powder

Pour the oil into a jar with a tight-fitting lid, add the curry powder, screw on the lid, and shake well. Refrigerate for 12 hours, shaking the jar a few times.

Pour the clear oil into another jar and discard the curry powder mixture that remains in the bottom of the jar. Refrigerate the oil and use within a few days.

Relishes and Pickles

Grapefruit and Peach Relish
Serves 4 (makes about 1½ cups)

✼ **A fresh-tasting blend of** peach and grapefruit, with a little mint and jalapeño pepper added, this relish is an ideal accompaniment to everything from game to pâtés to cold cuts to roasts. It also goes well with Venison Steaks in Sweet-Sour Sauce (page 310). It can be refrigerated for up to a week.

¼ red bell pepper, peeled and
      coarsely chopped (¼ cup)
1 ripe yellow peach, peeled, pitted,
      and coarsely chopped (1 cup)
1 small grapefruit, peeled, segments
      separated from membranes and
      coarsely chopped (about 1 cup)
¼ cup loosely packed fresh mint leaves,
      minced
1 small jalapeño pepper, seeded
      and finely chopped (about
      2 teaspoons)
2 teaspoons cider vinegar
¼ teaspoon ground cumin

½ teaspoon salt
1 tablespoon sugar

Mix all the ingredients in a bowl. Cover and refrigerate for up to 1 week.

Cucumber-Yogurt Relish
Makes 4½ cups

✼ **Often served as an** accompaniment to hot dishes in Indian cooking, this palate cleanser goes particularly well with almost any highly seasoned food, such as Spicy Chicken Breasts (page 256). The relish will keep, refrigerated, for a couple of days.

2 cucumbers (1½ pounds), peeled, halved
      lengthwise, seeded, and cut into
      ½-inch dice (3½ cups)
1 cup plain yogurt, preferably Greek
¼ cup thinly slivered fresh mint leaves
1 teaspoon salt
1 teaspoon sugar
¾ teaspoon Tabasco sauce
1 tablespoon cider vinegar
1 small garlic clove, crushed and finely
      chopped (½ teaspoon)
¼ teaspoon curry powder

Mix all the ingredients together in a bowl. Let macerate for at least 1 hour at room temperature, or cover and refrigerate overnight before using.

Braised Onion
and Raisin Chutney
Serves 8 to 10

❧ **A flavorful and spicy** accompaniment to any roast, these braised onions with raisins can also be served with meat pâtés or cold meats, or as part of the hors d'oeuvres on a buffet.

1½	pounds small pearl onions (about 50, the size of a giant olive)
5	tablespoons tomato paste
2	tablespoons sugar
3	tablespoons olive oil
2	bay leaves
1½	teaspoons salt
1	teaspoon freshly ground black pepper
¾	cup raisins
2	tablespoons white vinegar
2½	cups water
1	teaspoon coriander seeds

Combine all the ingredients in a stainless steel saucepan and bring to a boil over medium-high heat. Reduce the heat, cover, and simmer for 15 minutes.

Remove the cover and boil for about 5 minutes to reduce the liquid to a thick sauce-like consistency. Transfer to a bowl and refrigerate until serving time. The chutney will keep, refrigerated, for a few weeks.

Pickled Vegetables
Serves 6

❧ **These pickled vegetables make** a good partner with meats and sandwiches. They are ready after just a couple of days and will keep for weeks in the refrigerator.

Tarragon or other fresh herbs can replace the dill or oregano. If you don't have store-bought pickling spices, you can substitute dried thyme, black peppercorns, pieces of bay leaves, and coriander seeds. You can use any combination of the vegetables below, depending on what you have.

1	cup white vinegar
1½	cups water
1½	tablespoons salt
1	tablespoon sugar
1	teaspoon pickling spices (see the headnote)
2	dried ancho chile peppers
2	fresh dill or oregano sprigs
3	garlic cloves

VEGETABLES (enough in combination to fill a 1-quart jar)

4–5	green tomatoes, halved
2	cups 2-inch sticks peeled carrots
2	cups 2-inch chunks small zucchini
2	cups broccoli or cauliflower florets
1	large onion (8 ounces), peeled and cut into 8 wedges

Combine the vinegar, water, salt, sugar, pickling spices, chile peppers, dill or oregano, and garlic in a stainless steel saucepan and bring to a boil.

Meanwhile, layer the vegetables in a 1-quart canning jar. Pour the boiling liquid over the vegetables. Seal the jar and refrigerate for a few days before serving. This will keep, refrigerated, for several weeks.

Pickled Hen-of-the-Woods
Makes about 5 cups

❧ **The amazing hen-of-the-woods mushroom** is one of the treasures of summer. Called *Grifola frondosa*, or maitake, it was considered a miracle mushroom by the American Indians and a cure of various illnesses. A single mushroom can range from 8 ounces to 10 pounds and I'm often lucky enough to gather several pounds of them close to my house. Crunchy, flavorful, and mild, they are great as a side dish with fish or meat. When I have a few pounds of them, I make this pickle recipe, which keeps in the refrigerator for several weeks and is great with cold cuts and roasts; or serve it as an hors d'oeuvre.

Do not pick wild mushrooms unless you can recognize safe varieties with certainty.

About 2 pounds hen-of-the-woods
    mushrooms
5 cups water
2 cups white vinegar
4 teaspoons salt, or to taste
2 medium onions, cut into 6 wedges
    each and separated into layers
½ cup pitted oil-cured kalamata or
    other black olives
2 cups extra-virgin olive oil, or as needed
1 teaspoon freshly ground black pepper
2 bay leaves
3 fresh thyme sprigs

Remove any debris or dirt from the mushrooms. Cut off and discard the stems if they are tough. Cut the mushrooms into 1- to 2-inch pieces. Wash thoroughly in tepid water and drain.

Bring the water and vinegar to a boil in a medium stainless steel saucepan. Add 1 tablespoon of the salt and the onions, bring back to a strong boil, and boil for 10 seconds. Remove the onions with a slotted spoon or skimmer and drain them on a cookie sheet lined with paper towels.

Add the mushroom pieces to the hot liquid in the pan and bring to a boil. Boil for 5 minutes, then drain and spread out on the cookie sheet to drain further for 10 to 15 minutes.

Combine the mushrooms, onions, olives, oil, and pepper in a bowl and mix well. Add the remaining teaspoon of salt and taste; the dish should be well seasoned.

Spoon into a couple of glass jars and divide the bay leaves and thyme sprigs between the jars. The mixture should be well packed and covered with oil. Cover tightly and refrigerate. This mixture will keep for 2 to 3 weeks in the refrigerator.

Cornichons (Sour French Gherkins in Vinegar)
Makes 4 cups

❧ **I grow my own** cornichons, little pickling cucumbers. I pick a few each morning when they are still very small and then prepare them in the French style, in vinegar with tarragon, pearl onions, and peppercorns. The cucumbers should be no more than 1½ to 2 inches long, and they often have their small flowers still attached. They will keep in the vinegar for as long as a year.

1 pound tiny gherkins or pickling cucumbers (60–70)
3 tablespoons kosher salt
2–3 fresh tarragon sprigs
20 tiny pearl onions (the size of regular olives)
1½ teaspoons black peppercorns
1 small hot chile pepper, if hotness is desired
About 1½ cups white vinegar (4- to 5-percent-acid strength)

Rub the cornichons with a damp paper towel or other towel to rub off the prickles or bumps and flowers. Toss and roll the cornichons in the salt in a bowl. Set aside for at least 3 hours, or preferably overnight, to cure.

Dry each cornichon individually with a paper towel and arrange them in a 1-quart canning jar, interspersing them with the tarragon sprigs, pearl onions, peppercorns, and hot pepper, if using. Tap the bottom of the jar with the palm of your hand to move the cornichons and make them fit more tightly, then fill the jar with the vinegar.

Cover tightly with the lid and set aside in a cool place or the refrigerator for at least 2 weeks before using.

Cherries in Vinegar

Makes 4 cups

Like cornichons, pickled sweet cherries are delicious with pâtés or cold cuts.

1½ pounds sweet red cherries (such as Bing), with stems
1 teaspoon salt
¼ cup sugar
1 cup white vinegar (4- to 5-percent-acid strength)
½ cup water
⅛ teaspoon cayenne pepper

Trim the cherry stems, leaving about ½ inch of stem on each so the cherries stay firm. (If the skin pulls away from the cherries, the pickling liquid will seep in and soften them.) Pack the cherries into a 1-quart canning jar, tapping the jar on the bottom to make the cherries fit snugly.

Mix together the salt, sugar, vinegar, water, and cayenne pepper in a bowl. Pour the pickling solution over the cherries; it should barely cover them. Cover the jar tightly with the lid and set aside in a cool place or the refrigerator for at least 2 weeks before using.

Drinks

Cozy Cider

Serves 6

I call this delicious drink my New England cold remedy; it's my prescription for getting rid of a stuffy nose or sore throat.

6 cups unfiltered apple cider
12 allspice berries
12 whole cloves
2 cinnamon sticks, broken into pieces
¾ cup bourbon

Combine the cider, allspice, cloves, and cinnamon sticks in a saucepan and heat over medium heat until the mixture is just below a boil. Cover, remove from the heat, and let steep for 5 minutes.

The allspice and cloves will have floated to the top; remove and discard them. Pour 2 tablespoons of the bourbon into each of six mugs and pour some of the cider mixture over it. Spoon a few cinnamon stick pieces into each mug and serve.

Sun Mint Tea
Makes 12 to 16 glasses

✿ **Here's a wonderful use** for fresh mint from your garden. Although sun intensifies the flavor of the tea, don't rule out this recipe if 2 consecutive days of sunshine are not a certainty where you live. You'll get a satisfactory result by setting the jar aside in a warm place indoors for the same amount of time. I get good water from my well, but if you don't, use filtered or bottled water.

 3 tea bags, preferably of Chinese black tea
4–6 cups loosely packed fresh mint leaves
 About 4 quarts room-temperature water
⅔ cup honey, or to taste
⅓ cup fresh lemon juice, or to taste
 Lemon slices, for garnish

Drop the tea bags and mint into a gallon jar and fill the jar with the water. Cover the jar and set it in the sun for 2 days.

Strain the tea and season it with the honey and lemon juice. Serve over ice, with slices of lemon as a garnish.

Plum and Cherry Cordials
Makes 4 cups

✿ **In France, it's customary** to serve fruit in alcohol with some of the juices in a brandy snifter as an after-dinner drink. For these cordials, it is best to use grain alcohol, which is almost pure alcohol (190 proof), and dilute it with water. The fruit juices dilute the alcohol further, and after the fruit is macerated in it, the alcohol content will be 60 to 70 proof at most, depending on the juiciness of the fruit.

In states where grain alcohol is not sold, plain vodka can be substituted, although it is not as strong as grain alcohol. Prunes can be done in the same manner as the plums and cherries, covering them first with hot water to make them rehydrate a bit and then using the water to dilute the alcohol.

PLUMS

1¼ pounds small to medium firm white Reine Claude or red Santa Rosa plums, or a mixture (18–24)
¾ cup light corn syrup
¼ cup water, boiled and cooled (if using grain alcohol)
 1 cup 190-proof grain alcohol (or 1½ cups highest-proof vodka; see page 626)

CHERRIES

1¼–1½ pounds sweet cherries, with stems
½ cup water, boiled and cooled (if using grain alcohol)
 1 cup 190-proof grain alcohol (or 1½ cups highest-proof vodka; see page 626)
 7 tablespoons sugar

FOR THE PLUMS: The plums will be more flavorful if you prick them all over with a needle.

Combine the corn syrup, water, and alcohol in a bowl. (If grain alcohol is not available, omit it and the water and replace it with the vodka.)

Pack the plums into a glass jar with a lid, tapping the jar on the bottom with the palm of your hand to make the plums fit more tightly in the jar. Add the alcohol mixture; the liquid should just about cover the plums. Cover tightly and set aside in a cool place for at least 2 months before using.

FOR THE CHERRIES: Trim the stems of the cherries, leaving about ½ inch of stem on each so the cherries stay firm. There is no need to prick the cherries. Make sure the cherries are dry and pack them into a glass jar.

Mix together the water, grain alcohol, and sugar in a bowl, stirring until the sugar is dissolved. (If grain alcohol is not available, omit the water and combine the sugar with 1½ cups vodka.)

Pour the mixture over the cherries. Cover tightly and set aside in a cool place for at least 4 weeks before using.

Serve the cordials in brandy snifters as an after-dinner drink.

Mulled Wine
Serves 6

✶ **On cold winter nights,** this is the drink of choice for farmers in the Beaujolais area of Burgundy, where I come from.

6 cups (about 2 bottles) robust, fruity wine (Beaujolais, Cabernet Sauvignon, Merlot, or Zinfandel)
½ cup sugar
1 large lemon, cut into 6 wedges

Pour the wine into a stainless steel saucepan and stir in the sugar. Heat slowly until just below a boil.

Meanwhile, squeeze the juice from a lemon wedge into each of six mugs, then drop the wedges into the mugs.

Divide the wine among the mugs and serve.

Producer's Acknowledgments

✂ **Working with Jacques over** the years has been a gift — one that I value dearly. When I spend time with him, I invariably discover something new and exciting, and I never fail to enjoy his company, whether I'm standing in the kitchen after a long day drinking a little wine from a measuring cup or joining him in a relaxed conversation with the rest of the team. His wisdom, sincerity, lack of pretension, genuine enjoyment of good food and wine, and sense of family and fun warm all of our hearts.

It takes a dedicated and loyal group of people to make a television series, and working closely with more than twenty other individuals involves learning, wonder, hard work, frustration, joy, organization, and chaos. I love every moment of it. None of it would be possible without our funders.

Thank you to KitchenAid, for wonderful appliances and the best equipment; C. Donatiello Winery, for delicious Russian River Pinot Noir and Chardonnay; and to OXO Good Grips, for equipment that we did hold on to.

KITCHENAID
www.kitchenaid.com

FOR THE WAY IT'S MADE.®

C. DONATIELLO WINERY
www.cdonatiello.com

OXO
INTERNATIONAL INC.
www.oxo.com

Thank you to our director, Bruce Franchini, for wholeheartedly embracing the series. Thank you to associate producers June Mesina Ouellette and Ariana Reguzzoni, who worked tirelessly throughout the project and far beyond, and to Elizabeth Pepin (no relation to Jacques), who procured the wine so that Jacques was able to pair every dish with the appropriate bottle. Culinary producers Christine Swett and David Shalleck were extraordinary at ensuring that every ingredient and piece of equipment was in the right place at the right time. David, along with his assistant, Cara, tweaked each dish to make it more beautiful for the website photographs, which were taken by the very talented Wendy Goodfriend, who is also our web producer.

Thanks to Marcus Guillard and Chrisray Collins of Scene 2; they constructed the studio set in record time. Andrea Pannes arrived in the driver's seat of a huge van full of props to transform the stark space into Jacques's "home." Alongside these preparations in the studio, the back kitchen team, including Robert Villegas, made over the loading dock and scene turnaround into a workable kitchen, complete with stove and refrigerators. Caroline Faye and Richard Ju joined devoted volunteer Michael Pleiss and Jacques's long-time friend Jean-Claude Szurdak to work marvels in the back kitchen. They were supported by intern Ron McClary and our diligent helper Hubert Garcia. Together they peeled, cut, kneaded, and stirred in preparation for each show. Interns Samantha Alvarez and Lydia Bell learned quickly that television is definitely not all glamour, as they unpacked boxes of equipment; washed dishes, pots, and pans; and removed three years' worth of storage dust and grime from the stove. Michael Maldonado and Kenrick Mercado took over to assist with postproduction. And for the first time in ten seasons, our kitchen was equipped with a fully functioning sink with running water and a real drain. A huge thank-you to Michael Welch!

It takes an enormous amount of props and equipment to transform a blank studio into a living kitchen. We thank all of the generous vendors for supplying stylish props and the very best equipment to make Jacques's kitchen so beautiful, comfortable, and efficient:

ANGRAY FANTASTICO
www.fantasticosf.com

ANTIQUE & ART EXCHANGE
www.antiqueandartexchange.com

CHEF'S WAREHOUSE, BIA OUTLET
www.biaoutlet.com

CHICAGO METALLIC BAKEWARE
www.chicagometallicbakeware.com

COUNTY RESTAURANT SUPPLY
www.crscatalog.com

DOVER METALS COMPANY
www.dovermetals.com

DURALEX
www.duralexusa.com

EMILE HENRY USA
www.emilehenryusa.com

LE CREUSET
www.lecreuset.com

MAUVIEL
www.mauvielusa.com

MICROPLANE
www.microplane.com

RSVP INTERNATIONAL, INC.
www.rsvp-intl.com

SHUN CUTLERY
www.shuncutlery.com

SOULÉ STUDIO
www.soulestudio.com

THE BUTLER & THE CHEF
www.thebutlerandthechef.com

TOTALLY BAMBOO
www.totallybamboo.com

TRIMARK ECONOMY
RESTAURANT FIXTURES
www.trimarkeconomy.com

TRUE MANUFACTURING
www.truemfg.com

WÜSTHOF
www.wusthof.com

Once the setup was complete, the crew got to work. Thank you to Greg King for lighting the set, and to Harry Betancourt, Mike Elwell, James Greenfield, and Greg King, behind the HD cameras. Stage managers Randy Brase and Jean Tuckerman choreographed the dance between the food, the equipment, and the set. In the control room, Rick Santangelo, Jose Valenzuela, Eric Shackelford, and Helen Silvani conversed with director Bruce Franchini, while John Andreini kept the tape rolling, all painstakingly following Jacques's every move.

Behind the studio action, Frank Carfi, Kim McCalla, Simon Hui, Ernie Neumann, and a whole host of others kept the wheels oiled, the paperwork up to date, and everyone in their place. Others who worked hard to make the series include David Rhodes, Fred Tetzner, and Rick Warren.

Jacques slept well thanks to the generosity of THE PRESCOTT HOTEL (www.prescotthotel.com); he calls it his home away from home. Back on set, Jenny Zielon kept him looking neat and beautiful in the right shirt and apron. Jacques's clothing arrived thanks to a generous gift from MACY'S (www.macys.com).

Working with Jacques is all about the food, and it took a lot of food to complete the series! We're grateful to the generous contributions of produce and supplies from some of the best places here in California.

Thank you to:

ACME BREAD
www.acmebread.com

BIRITE FOODSERVICE DISTRIBUTORS
www.birite.com

CALIFORNIA CAVIAR COMPANY
www.californiacaviar.com

C. J. OLSON CHERRIES
www.cjolsoncherries.com

CLOVER STORNETTA FARMS
www.cloverstornetta.com

CORTO OLIVE
www.corto-olive.com

DIAMOND FOODS, INC.
www.diamondnuts.com

DRAKES BAY OYSTERS
www.drakesbayoyster.com

OAKVILLE PRODUCE PARTNERS LLC DBA
GREENLEAF
www.greenleafsf.com

MARKET HALL FOODS & THE PASTA SHOP
www.markethallfoods.com

MORTON SALT, INC.
www.mortonsalt.com

MODESTO FOOD DISTRIBUTORS, INC.
www.modestofood.com

MONTEREY FISH MARKET
www.montereyfish.com

MORTON & BASSETT
www.worldpantry.com/morton/home.html

NIMAN RANCH
www.nimanranch.com

PACIFIC GOURMET
www.pacgourmet.com

PEET'S COFFEE & TEA
www.peets.com

RANCHO GORDO
www.ranchogordo.com

SMART & FINAL
www.smartandfinal.com

STRAUS FAMILY CREAMERY
www.strausfamilycreamery.com

SWANSON BROTH
www.swansonbroth.com

This season coincided with Jacques's seventy-fifth birthday, and three restaurants in San Francisco combined with the KQED community to help him celebrate in style with parties, dinners, and other gatherings. Special thanks to the generosity of Roland Passot of LA FOLIE and LEFT BANK BRASSERIE (www.leftbank.com) and to Mark Franz at FARALLON RESTAURANT (www.farallonrestaurant.com) and WATERBAR (www.waterbarsf.com).

Wine and beverages of all kinds play an important role in Jacques's life. As he says, "A day without wine is like a day without sunshine." For helping make every day on the set a day of sunshine for Jacques, we are very grateful to:

ANCHOR BREWING COMPANY
www.anchorbrewing.com

BROADBENT SELECTIONS, INC.
www.broadbent.com

BROC CELLARS
www.broccellars.com

BUTY WINERY
www.butywinery.com

CHAMPAGNE PERRIER-JOUËT
www.perrier-jouet.com

DANTE ROBINO
www.bodegadanterobino.com

DEPT. C WINES
www.deptcwines.com

JAMES FAMILY CELLARS
www.jamesfamilycellars.com

JUDD'S HILL WINERY
www.juddshill.com

K&L WINE MERCHANTS
www.klwines.com

KERMIT LYNCH WINE MERCHANT
www.kermitlynch.com

KQED WINE CLUB
www.kqedwineclub.org

KUNIN WINES
www.kuninwines.com

MAISONS MARQUES & DOMAINES
www.mmdusa.net

MARTINE'S WINES, INC.
www.martineswines.com

PEPIN VINEYARD
www.pepinvineyard.com

STAG'S LEAP WINE CELLARS
www.cask23.com

YORK CREEK VINEYARDS
www.yorkcreek.com

Twenty-six shows make up this series, and once they were taped and we'd waved good-bye to Jacques and Jean-Claude, another team stepped in. Aaron Drury is the editor and my right hand; with the able help of Peter Borg, who created each step-by-step recipe, Aaron built each show and transformed it into what you see in your living room. Both these editors spent hours in a dark room listening to every word and checking every shot from all four cameras. Robert O'Geen then completed the online finessing. They are all remarkable and phenomenal to work with.

Jon Herbst wrote and produced the music, while Zaldy Serrano and Christina Zee created the graphics. And, finally, the individuals who strive to accommodate and spread the word about Jacques: we thank Janet Lim Young, Jacqueline Murray, Scott Walton, Yoonhyung Lee, Robin Smith, Suzanne Romaine, Lisa Landi, and Meredith Gandy. Thank you to Sandy Schonning and her watchful eye that kept us all in line, and last but by no means least, *merci* to our intrepid leader Michael Isip for his guidance.

This production was a labor of love for us all, and we're indebted to Jacques for making each series the wonderful experience that it becomes — every time.

—Tina Salter, Series Producer,
Essential Pépin, KQED

Index

B

babas, bourbon, 599–600

bacon:

   and bean salad, warm, 61

   dandelion salad with croutons and, 48–49

   lardons, 48

   leeks in béchamel gratin, 439–40

   little braised cabbages, 418

   quiche with, 79–80

baguettes, 132–33

   bread-and-butter pudding, 520–21

   pissaladière, 140–41

baked Alaska, 525–26

baker's wife potatoes, 119

ballottine, chicken, stuffed with red rice or spinach, cheese, and bread, 253–55

banana(s), 478–81

   black bean soup with, 20–21

   bread pudding, 521

   broiled, with lemon and vermouth, 478–79

   croûte of fruit, 501

   flambéed, 479

   fritters, 479–80

   lemon, in crisp shells, 480–81

   mint ice cream with rum-raisin sauce, 606

   tart with guava glaze, 579–80

barley:

   lamb soup, 32

   and lentil soup, 33

basil:

   oil, 619–20

   pesto, spicy, spaghetti with, 91–92

   pistou, 18, 19

   sauce, salmon fillets in, 194

   sautéed capon with peaches and, 278–80

   tomato, and cheese soufflés, 83

   tomato, mozzarella, and cucumber salad, 57

   tomato salad with red onion and, 55–56

basting, 249

bean(s), 412–16

   black, soup with bananas, 20–21

   black-eyed pea and kale ragout, 416

   cranberry, and tuna salad, 60–61

   dried, cooking, 61

   flageolets with diced vegetables, 414

   and mussel soup, cold, 160

   see also haricots verts; lentil; lima bean(s); red beans; string beans; white bean(s)

James Beard's onion sandwiches, 142

béarnaise sauce, 617

   tomato-flavored, 617

béchamel sauce, 443

beef, 312, 314–35

   blade steak with herbs, 319

   blood, in black sausage, 383–84

   boulettes with financière sauce, 334–35

   braised, in red wine, 324–25

   carbonnade Flamande, 328–29

   carpaccio with pepper tartlets, 314–15

   carpaccio with white truffles, 316

   cayettes with spinach, 332

   chili with red beans, fiery, 330–31

   consommé, 29–30

   corned-, pot-au-feu, 328

   daube Arlésienne, 323–24

   flank steak, braised stuffed, 322–23

   flank steak, grilled or pan-seared marinated, 318–19

   gratin Parmentier, 329

   Hanoi soup, 30–31

   mironton, 329

   petite marmite, 25–27

   pot-au-feu, 325–27

   rib roast, spicy, 321

   salad with garlic-mustard dressing, 327

   Salisbury steaks with vegetable sauce, 330

   small stuffed cabbages, 333

   steak, five-pepper, 316–17

   steak, grilled, with lemon-thyme butter, 319–20

C

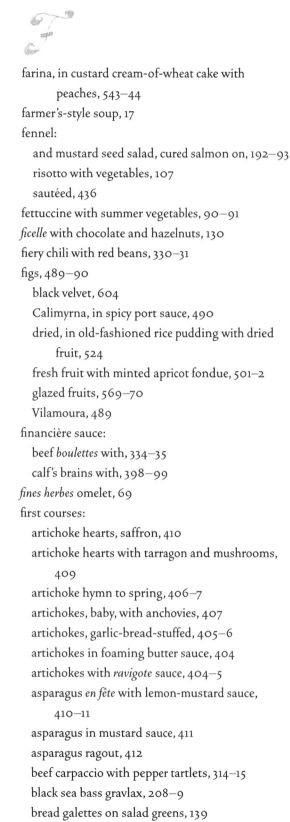

G